D1598434

DERBY DIARIES

A SELECTION FROM

THE DIARIES
OF
EDWARD HENRY STANLEY, 15th
EARL OF DERBY
(1826–93)

BETWEEN SEPTEMBER
1869 AND MARCH 1878

edited by
JOHN VINCENT

CAMDEN FIFTH SERIES
VOLUME 4 (1994)

LONDON
OFFICES OF THE ROYAL HISTORICAL SOCIETY
UNIVERSITY COLLEGE LONDON
GOWER STREET WC1
1994

British Library Cataloguing in Publication Data

Diaries of Edward Henry Stanley, 15th Earl of Derby (1826–93); Selections
(Camden fifth series; v.3)
1.   History – Periodicals
I.   Royal Historical Society II Series

ISBN 0–86193–137–9

Printed and bound in Great Britain by
Butler & Tanner Ltd., Frome and London

To Kenneth and Elizabeth
in gratitude

CONTENTS

ACKNOWLEDGEMENTS

I would like to take this opportunity to thank those who have patiently contributed to the slow development of this volume. I appreciate the generosity of Lord Derby, owner of the diaries, in making them available. I am, as before, deeply grateful. I would like to thank his successive librarians at Knowsley, and particularly Mrs. Brenda Burgess, the current Librarian, for friendly assistance. At Liverpool Record Office, Mrs. Naomi Evetts and other members of staff have provided highly professional guidance and cheerful assistance over a long period: I am grateful. For help with points of scholarship, I am indebted to Dr. Peter Gordon, of the Institute of Education, London, for his work on the Carnarvon diaries, and to the late Dr. John Leslie for his expertise on central Europe. For inimitable typing of a difficult manuscript, I thank Ms. Glenise Day and Mrs. Mary Tosh. To the Royal Historical Society, its officers, and perhaps particularly Professor Colin Matthew and Dr. John Ramsden, this text owes its very existence; without their considerate support it would still lie in oblivion. May what follows prove adequate thanks to the Society for its munificence.

ABBREVIATIONS

Bateman	John Bateman, *The Great Landowners of Great Britain and Ireland*. (new ed. 1971). *With an Introduction by David Spring*. Leicester University Press, 1971)
Cecil	*Life of Robert Marquis of Salisbury. By his daughter Lady Gwendolen Cecil. Vol. II 1868–1880*. (1921)
D.D.	Derby Diaries (when quoting from original not used in text) 1 Jan. 1870 (*et sim.*) form used for citing diaries published in this *Selection*.
GH	Nancy E. Johnson (ed.), *The Diary of Gathorne Hardy, later Lord Cranbrook, 1866–1892: Political Selections*. (Oxford: Clarendon Press, 1981)
H	*Parliamentary Debates, 3*
Later Diaries	*The Later Derby Diaries. Home Rule, Liberal Unionism, and Aristocratic Life in Late Victorian England. Selected Passages edited by John Vincent, Professor of Modern History, University of Bristol. Printed and published by the author ... 1981*
M. and B.	G. E. Buckle (in succession to W. F. Monypenny), *The Life of Benjamin Disraeli, Earl of Beaconsfield. Volume VI 1876–1881*. (London, 1920)
Speeches	*Speeches and Addresses of Edward Henry XVth Earl of Derby K.G. Selected and Edited by Sir T. H. Sanderson, K.C.B. and E.S. Roscoe. With a Prefatory Memoir by W.E.H. Lecky* (2 vols., London, 1894)
Stanley Diaries	John Vincent ed., *Disraeli, Derby, and the Conservative Party. Journals and Memoirs of Edward Henry, Lord Stanley 1849–1869*. (Hassocks, Sussex: The Harvester Press, 1978)
T	*The Times*

INTRODUCTION

The diaries

Edward Henry Stanley (1826–93), fifteenth Earl of Derby, the elder son of the Lord Derby who was thrice prime minister, served twice as foreign secretary in Conservative governments (1866–8, 1874–8). For most of his life, he was an assiduous, reliable, and copious keeper of diaries, selections from which follow for the period from September 1869, just before his father's death, to his resignation from Disraeli's cabinet in March 1878.

Derby, as the diarist will henceforth be called (he succeeded to the title on 23 October 1869) used Letts Diaries, in hard covers, printed, and with a page for each day. The diaries came in three sizes. For 1861–6, they were Letts No 8 Diary, described as 'note-paper size' or 7.50″ × 4.75″. For the years 1875 they were Letts No 1 Diary, described as 'letter-paper size', or 9.50″ × 7.75″. The diaries for 1876–93 were more impressive, leather bound, and 'foolscap size' or 12.25″ × 8″. Thus in the most important and busiest years of his career, 1876–8, Derby conveniently graduated to much more space per day. The prices of each size were, in 1876, 6s.6d. for 'note-paper' size, 10s. for 'letter-paper' size, and 14s. for foolscap. The diaries, hardly altered in condition or appearance since Derby's day, are written in a consistently clear hand. Formal cataloguing of the whole archive is not complete, but the reference for the diaries will be, as now, 920 DER (15). The Derby archives in Liverpool Record Office remain the property of the present Lord Derby. Enquiries about publication should be made to The Librarian to Lord Derby, c/o The Earl of Derby's Estate, The Estate Office, Knowsley, Prescot, Merseyside, L34 4AG (tel 051–489–4437) while archival matters should be referred to The Senior Assistant Archivist, Liverpool Record Office, Central Library, William Brown St, Liverpool L3 8EW (tel 051–225–5417).

This is the second volume of the diaries, taken in chronological sequence, but the third in order of publication.[1] Only the period April 1878–June 1885 now remains unpublished (in selection, there being nowhere where the diaries are published in full for a considerable length of time). The diary was kept continuously during the years 1869–

---

[1] The first published was John Vincent (ed), *Disraeli, Derby and the Conservative Party. Journals and Memoirs of Edward Henry, Lord Stanley 1849–1869.* Hassocks, Sussex: The Harvester Press, 1978. This was followed by a selection from Derby's diaries after he finally left office, *The Later Derby Diaries. Home Rule, Liberal Unionism, and Aristocratic Life in Late Victorian England. Selected Passages* edited by *John Vincent, Professor of Modern History, University of Bristol. Printed and published by the author ... 1981.* (An unpublished selection by the same editor for the years 1878–85 exists in typescript.)

78. It was as contemporaneous as well could be, being for the most part apparently written on retiring for the night. Sometimes it was written in intervals during the day itself, in a way suggesting that it was normally close at hand. There is nothing to show that his wife or private secretary ever saw it or even knew of it, and some internal evidence suggesting the opposite. Occasionally, Derby inevitably fell behind, and wrote up the diary two, three, or four days in arrears: very rarely more. Even when travelling abroad, the diary accompanied him. Desultory entries were rare, especially after taking office. Thus in 1875 there were only 47 such entries (out of 365) which were not well over half a side of foolscap, and these were concentrated in predictably uneventful months:

January	7	July	1
February	3	August	8
March	4	September	5
April	0	October	12
May	2	November	0
June	1	December	4

No days were left entirely blank. In addition to the pages themselves (which might overflow onto adjacent pages), the endpapers were used for an annual stocktaking of public and private affairs, with personal finance an important theme. The diaries are singularly free from revisions, additions, corrections, deletions, or mutilations.

Derby has hitherto left few footprints in history. Of all senior Victorian figures, he has long remained one of the least known. He has had no authorized biography and no modern academic one. So far as is known, none is contemplated, though an entry in the *New Dictionary of National Biography*, drawing on diary evidence, is in prospect. In place of a biography, Derby's executors prevailed upon his widow to look instead to publishing two volumes of his speeches.[2] Surprisingly interesting though these are on social questions, they tell us little of Derby the politician. Derby's father, wife, and brother have also slipped through the biographer's net, thus increasing the extent to which the view from Knowsley in the Victorian period is under-represented. The diarist's father, the prime minister, is the subject of a respectable academic biography[3] but not one based on family papers, and Lord Blake's definitive biography of the elder Derby is not yet published. As for Lady Derby, important though she obviously was in her own right, she – and her archives, which were always separate from those of her

---

[2] *Speeches and Addresses of Edward Henry XVth Earl of Derby K.G. Selected and Edited by Sir T.H. Sanderson, KCB and E.S. Roscoe. With a Prefatory Memoir by W.E.H. Lecky* (2 vols, 1894).
[3] W.D. Jones, *Lord Derby and Victorian Conservatism* (1956).

husband, the diarist – have vanished from view almost entirely. If her archives still exist, as they may well, they have escaped the attention of post-war historians, although the published book of letters[4] from her circle of friends in the 1860s is of high interest. Strangely, though the Derby diaries were known to exist, because they were cited, if at one point only,[5] by Disraeli's biographer, no recent diplomatic or political historian has made extended use of them.[6] The present volume is thus a useful corrective to a period of history often presented in mainly Disraelian (or Gladstonian) terms.

The nature of Derby's archive as a whole also enhances the value of the diaries. His other surviving papers are a disappointment, despite a few interesting individual items. The diarist weeded his papers ruthlessly in the early 1870s, as many diary entries then show.[7] This became a policy. 'Busy destroying old letters, of which in future I mean to keep hardly any ...'[8] Curiously, much of his non-official correspondence is limited to two or three letters per correspondent, almost as if a few letters were retained as a precaution against forgery. His official correspondence with Disraeli survives, but not their informal correspondence during their period of greatest intimacy, when mostly out of office. Only in the diaries, therefore, are we likely to get a full picture of the man, his outlook, and his habits of life and work.

The diaries, though known once to have existed, long remained in oblivion at Knowsley. Their great length and exceptional continuity, in particular, were not suspected. In June 1968, the position changed. A large part of Derby's papers, including some diaries, were moved from Knowsley to Liverpool Record Office. The division between what was moved, and what stayed at Knowsley, was somewhat arbitrary. Of the diaries, only the earliest section, going up to 1858, went to Liverpool, where it became all that was then known to exist.[9] The present writer began an edition of this earliest section in 1972. Then in 1976, during building operations at the estates workers' Knowsley Social Club, whose cellars adjoin the Muniment Room, workmen came across trunks containing the diaries of Derby from 1876 to his death. In autumn

[4] *A Great Lady's Friendships. Letters to Mary, Marchioness of Salisbury, Countess of Derby, 1862–1890. With Introductions and Notes by The Lady Burghclere* (Macmillan: London, 1933).

[5] M. and B. vi 266 (diary for cabinet of 27 March 1878).

[6] In that respect at least this text may add to the most exhaustive modern work on the Eastern Question, Richard Millman, *Britain and the Eastern Question 1875–1878* (Oxford: Clarendon Press, 1979).

[7] 29 Jan., 10, 21, 22, 24 Feb. 1871; 24 Jan., 26 May, 17 June 1873.

[8] 26 May 1873.

[9] Professor Linda Colley, then a Bristol student, first drew my attention to the early diaries at Liverpool, for which I am grateful: see L. Colley and J. Vincent, 'Disraeli in 1851; "Young Stanley" as Boswell', *Historical Studies*, vol 15, no. 59 (Oct. 1972), pp. 447–54.

1974, Professor D.B. Quinn of the University of Liverpool kindly informed me of this discovery. In summer 1976[10] the present editor located a further series of diaries running from 1861 to 1875. The complete set had now been found. The combined good offices of the Knowsley Estate Office and the Librarian made the newly traced diaries available for study and photocopying on the spot. Their later transfer in May 1980 to Liverpool Record Office, along with the remaining part of Derby's papers, made a more exhaustive study possible. Editions of selected passages followed in 1978 (for 1849–69) and 1981 (for 1885–93). Thereafter, it was a question of finding a publisher willing to take a selection whose value would necessarily partly lie in its very fullness, and therefore length.

Derby may well be unique in having kept a full diary while foreign secretary. Other candidates perhaps come to mind. One is Lord Kimberley, a known diarist, but an irregular one,[11] the other obvious one is Lord Malmesbury,[12] whose poverty and adventurous second marriage might have encouraged him to some degree of concoction. Until his printed text can be compared with original diaries, not much can usefully be said on this point. Perhaps it is safer to say that no foreign secretary has kept so full a diary during a prolonged and major European crisis, or placed foreign policy so firmly in its cabinet context. The diary is therefore a contribution to diplomatic history, to the history of central government, to the history of party, personality, and opinion, and to the social (and even economic) history of the Victorian landed class and its values.

The editor's object has been to include all matters of importance. All accounts of cabinet meetings are included in full. At times of diplomatic crisis, the political life of the foreign secretary has been placed, more fully than elsewhere, in its human context, however trivial. For an example, the crisis of April–May 1875 may be noted. In critical times, or where necessary to avoid confusion, the day of the week has been inserted editorially, without any remark in the apparatus. Spanish, American, and Italian affairs are omitted, though routinely reported in the diaries, because in the diarist's view they were unimportant and he had little to say about them not to be found in the press. In spring 1878, the diary is printed almost in extenso.

[10] When, by coincidence, over 50 volumes of diaries by another Lancashire Conservative magnate were awaiting editing, at the request of the family: see John Vincent (ed.) *The Crawford Papers. The journals of David Lindsay, twenty-seventh Earl of Crawford and tenth Earl of Balcarres 1871–1940 during the years 1892 to 1940.* (Manchester: Manchester University Press, 1984.)

[11] See John Powell, *Liberal by Principle* London, The Historians' Press, forthcoming, for Kimberley.

[12] See *Later Diaries*, 90–91.

The diaries for 1874–8 are a valuable correction to, and check upon, the Disraelian version of the process of cabinet government. They will become all the more important as a counterpoise, when in due course the great Canadian edition of Disraeli's letters weights the scale further in favour of the Disraelian angle of vision. But neither that consideration, nor the fact that Derby missed singularly few cabinets, exhaust the reasons for its special importance as a record of cabinet government.

The relative absence of other good diarists in the cabinet enhances the value of Derby's account. Cabinet diarists were few in 1874–80, fewer than in 1880–5, for instance, and not as thorough in their work as Derby was. Lord John Manners, who had long kept a journal, stopped on entering the 1874 cabinet, so far as one can judge from his biography.[13] Gathorne Hardy was indeed a persistent diarist, of undoubted honesty, but, lawyer as he was, he wrote as if to ensure that if his accounts of cabinet meetings fell into the wrong hands, no great harm would ensue. Sometimes indeed he mentioned nothing more of a cabinet meeting than the mere fact of its occurrence. (Selections, skilfully made, from Hardy's diary, have been published in an admirable modern edition.[14]) Carnarvon's diary, now being edited for publication, is intermittent during the period 1874–8, and increasingly so after his wife's death in January 1875. (Sandon's interesting cabinet diary, now published,[15] covers only May–August 1878.) In short, to obtain a primary record of cabinet proceedings under Disraeli, one has to conflate the various versions given in the diaries of Hardy, Derby, and Carnarvon (and in due course Sandon), and measure them against Disraeli's account in his cabinet reports to the Queen.[16]

As a diarist, Derby followed the same methodical routine that governed his daily life: personal post dealt with at home, exercise, the office, cabinets or meetings with diplomatists, the House of Lords, and then more often than not, a quiet evening at home. Comments on

[13] Charles Whibley, *Lord John Manners and his Friends*. William Blackwood and Sons: Edinburgh and London, 1925. 2 vols.

[14] Nancy E. Johnson (ed.) *The Diary of Gathorne Hardy, later Lord Cranbrook, 1866–1892: Political Selections.* (Oxford: Clarendon Press, 1981).

[15] *The Cabinet Journal of Dudley Ryder, Viscount Sandon (later third Earl of Harrowby) 11 May–10 August 1878.* Edited by Christopher Howard and Peter Gordon. *Bulletin of the Institute of Historical Research.* Special Supplement No. 10 (November 1974).

[16] See 'Cabinet Reports from Prime Ministers to the Crown 1868–1916' (Harvester microform), reel 2. No full comparison of Derby's and Disraeli's version has been made, but whereas Derby reports virtually all meetings listed by Disraeli, a check on the microform index for 1874 suggests that Disraeli may have reported only about half the meetings mentioned by Derby. Disraeli tends to report cabinet decisions even if trivial, whereas Derby reports discussions even where indecisive. A full collation should produce results very different from either source on its own, with Derby's version probably omitting or being very cursory with minor items of business in which he was uninterested.

matters of passing interest, or broad assessments of a situation, might close his account of the day; and thumbnail sketches of character were quite frequent.

Derby started his day early. His breakfast, if any, was a solitary affair, to judge by the absence of comment; work on his private post, especially estate affairs and begging letters, began the day, and indeed often occupied him, bar exercise, until noon. Prompt and meticulous application to the duties of a landlord, even in times of crisis, was never overridden by other claims on his time. He had no apparent secretarial assistance in this important area of his life. Begging letters, of which there were many, were scrupulously answered. Indeed, his study 'in its perfect neatness was more like a lady's boudoir than the workshop of a very busy man', wrote Lecky.[17] These tasks done, Derby, a keen pedestrian, often turned his mind to exercise, whether in town or country, the circuit of Regents Park being a favourite. The details of his exercise were carefully recorded; not so, of whatever sustenance he took in the middle of the day. He never seems to have lunched, and certainly not to have ever given anyone (other than family) lunch, or met people for lunch in the modern sense. On the contrary, this was the time of day when he attended the office and completed his daily business there, unless the cabinet met (as very often it did, from 12 to 1.30 or 2). His daily load at the Foreign Office was, in normal times and even sometimes during a European crisis, possibly lighter than his private correspondence and papers in the morning. Meetings with diplomatists reduced the time gained from an industrious routine; not so meetings with his under-secretary, Bourke, of whom he saw very little, or with his senior officials, who also figured little. His essential instrument in guiding matters was his private secretary, Sanderson.

Sanderson's place in Derby's life is a puzzle. He was a gentleman and a potential son-in-law, Derby pressing his suit. He was a constant walking companion, in town and country, and Derby's main male companion. He was to be Derby's executor. As such, it is certainly a gap that the diary completely omits any report of the conversation and views of this future peer and head of the foreign office. He was the recipient of Derby's generosity, as, more surprisingly, were his brothers after their City firm failed. He may have been the son Derby and Lady Derby never had; but this is speculation. In all respects, he lived essentially as one of the family, both in town and country.

As with Sanderson, we learn next to nothing of Lady Derby and her views on public matters, though her health is mentioned now and then. One cannot doubt that her involvement was considerable, as it had been in the 1860s. Only at the time of the formation of the government

[17] *Speeches*, xxxix.

in 1874, and perhaps briefly around December 1877, do we glimpse her at work. This rigorous excision of Derby's only two intimates can easily be overlooked, making Derby appear more solitary and self-contained than in fact he was, and the diary more comprehensively confiding than it really is.

The purpose of the diary, as so often, is uncertain. There is no clue as to whether it was written with an eye to posterity, except that Derby did not arrange for its destruction on his death. It is certain, however, that it had a mundane use, as a record of events for working purposes; Derby characteristically produced a day-by-day synopsis at the end of each volume for purposes of easier reference. On the other hand, it was altogether a more discursive and more literary composition than mere record required. It chronicles a life of integrity and dis-interestedness such as would be difficult to compose, in such great quantity, were it not true; and it records a daily timetable filled with duties to an extent which would have left little time for vagaries even had Derby wished. In fact, Derby's most pronounced taste was for an administrator's solitude of paperwork, just sufficient to occupy, but not enough to tire.

From opposition to government, 1869–74

On the death of his father in October 1869, Derby assumed a new and onerous role, but one well suited to his meticulous nature: that of manager of a great landed estate, though one burdened with debt which he considered it his duty to redeem (except for debts within the family). He approached estate questions with a sense of mission, combined with a native compulsion to save, while also carrying out the traditional duties expected of him, serving as chairman of the bench from 1856 to 1874, attending tenants' dinners and servants' balls, and preserving and shooting game on a large scale (he was an outstanding shot). Though in many ways withdrawing after his marriage from the business of life, where Lancashire was concerned he sought to uphold the semi-royal position of his family.

He cultivated Liverpool, civic and proletarian (Manchester rather less). He spoke to large Lancashire audiences, numbered in thousands. His popularity in the mean streets pleased and mystified him. He was enough of a local politician to be able to weigh his relative popularity in Bury (where a too masterful agent queered the pitch) and in Bootle.[18] He supported local charities, privately and as an expense upon the estate. Despite this apparent show of prominence, he kept his distance from the great middle class whom in the abstract he wished to see in

[18] 31 Aug. 1871

his party. Socially, his world consisted of Lancashire gentry, however obscure, and not Lancashire millowners, however eminent; these latter did not cross the doors of Knowsley. Derby's horror at his stepson's mésalliance with a middle-class woman indicated his deep sense of caste.[19] Only Cross, a fellow-Rugbeian and banker, whose election costs he offered to assist,[20] somehow passed muster,[21] though emphatically pronounced middle class by Lady Derby when addressing London society.

His management of his estates was an unqualified success. Few men repay inherited debts of £525,000. So successful was he, albeit with help from windfall sales to railway companies,[22] that all the temptations of steady accumulation grew upon him, and became a main object in life by the mid-1870s.[23] For the first time in living memory the Stanley estate received rather than paid interest.[24] His pleasure was perhaps enhanced by this being one field where he surpassed his father, who had left a muddle, with the estate office and accounts in confusion.[25] On inheritance Derby 'had not yet an idea what my income really is',[26] and to find out he had to become his own head agent, both his main agents being unsatisfactory in different ways.[27] He made large savings in household costs (house, stables, gardens, park, game) at Knowsley. These, in his father's last full year, were £36,000;[28] he aimed for £20,000, and achieved £25,000, despite the sharp rise in prices in the early 1870s. He got rid of horse breeding,[29] selling the racing stock for £4650.[30] The stud, which had cost his father £1300 p.a., was entirely abolished,[31] being a 'business I neither understand nor care about'. Likewise, he arranged to sell surplus fruit from the gardens,[32] and replaced flower-beds with less labour-intensive azaleas. His truly personal budget, of £5000 p.a., showed his frugality, for he saved £2000, much of the rest going on presents and private, as distinct from

[19] 17 July 1873
[20] Derby offered £500 if there was a contest, and £100 if not (27 Jan., 3 Feb. 1874). Cross was staying at Knowsley, 19–24 Jan. 1874, on the eve of his promotion to the cabinet.
[21] 'Every conversation that I have with Cross raises my opinion of his judgement and good sense' (7 Oct 1871).
[22] See below, 1875 flyleaf.
[23] 1 Jan. 1874
[24] 19 Jan. 1874
[25] 21 July, 15 Aug., 25 Sep. 1871
[26] 1 Nov. 1869
[27] 16 Aug. 1872
[28] 2 Nov. 1869
[29] 5 Nov. 1869
[30] 12 Mar 1870
[31] 6 Nov. 1869
[32] 3 Nov. 1869

INTRODUCTION 9

estate and local, charities. Of living like a lord there was no question.

Not all was parsimony, however. He improved Knowsley, which much needed it, despite expecting departure to somewhere more deeply rural 'which sooner or later is inevitable'.[33] He built two new cottages a year in the village.[34] His keeping a strong box at Knowsley in which he accumulated gold carried precaution to the limits.[35] He continued to acquire rural land, while selling urban property in Liverpool and elsewhere.[36] He had nothing more to do with equities, declaring 'a safe interest of four per cent is enough'.[37] With reason, Derby found much fulfilment in his role as a model landowner.

An early step, one contemplated by his father, was to rid himself of his Irish estates in Tipperary, which the diarist knew well.[38] These were sold for £160,000 to one V. O'Connor,[39] who himself left £300,000 in money and £200,000 in lands:[40] a portent of a changing Irish elite, akin to Lampedusa's portrait of a changing Sicily in *The Leopard*. Derby consistently held more unyielding views on Ireland than on anything else. He believed an Irish plebiscite would vote for independence,[41] he despised Butt,[42] and he took a minor acquittal as proof of Ireland being Fenian at heart.[43] However, on the Irish Land Act of 1870 he declined to take fright, expecting neither 'the good or the evil anticipated'.[44] In 1873, he argued that belief in Irish improvement was a delusion, the result of a stringent coercion act; and that the Irish University issue could not possibly be solved by compromise.[45] In the long term, the gradual reduction of the numbers of small tenants 'in a gradual, gentle, kindly, but yet effectual way'[46] was the only remedy for Ireland; a country not prominent in his diaries. Given such views, Derby's preference for an almost entirely Lancastrian estate was natural; yet even with his direct involvement in Irish matters behind him, Derby was anything but an inexperienced aristocrat with little practical

[33] 12 Aug. 1872
[34] 31 Dec. 1873
[35] 5 Feb. 1874
[36] 14 Sept. 1873
[37] 1 June 1872
[38] Derby however retained a strong personal tie with Ireland through his cousin Augusta, Lady Dartrey (néeStanley), wife of the whig lord-lt. of Monaghan and a friend of Derby since he was eighteen. On her death in 1887, her husband returned to Derby 'a vast bundle of letters written by me ...' (*Later Diaries*, 122).
[39] 24 June 1871
[40] 20 Nov. 1873
[41] 9 Mar. 1871
[42] 23 Sept. 1871
[43] 11, 15 Nov. 1871
[44] *H*, 16 June 1870
[45] *H*, 6 Feb. 1873
[46] *H*, 16 June 1870

knowledge of the questions of the day. Few others in the higher reaches of Victorian public life had such direct experience as Derby had in the four areas of urban artisan housing (as chairman of the Peabody Trust and similar bodies); urban criminality (as a Liverpool chairman of magistrates); travel outside Europe; and the Irish land question (and that in one of the worse areas) as it affected the practical management of estates.

There were none too many people in Derby's world. Northcote and Cross, of the cabinet, counted as friends. On the other side of politics, Lowe was a friend by marriage, and Granville, whom Derby was later to finance,[47] was becoming an intimate in the 1870s. Correspondence with old Lord Halifax involved an exchange of confidences with a wider Whig circle. Of the great families, the only one Derby saw much of, was that of the Dukes of Bedford and their kinsmen, including Lord Russell. By comparison, he saw little of Conservative grandees. His visits to Hatfield, once so frequent, dried up. With his poor relations on the Stanley side, he had nothing to do (beyond supporting them). With his wife's family, the Sackville-Wests, he could only note, from afar, their 'continuous and ceaseless quarrels'[48] and general proneness to disaster. His wife's brood of stepchildren, though living much under the same roof, excited little family feeling. His sister was a very remote figure. His mother, then living in London, he dutifully visited, but they moved in different worlds. Only with his much younger brother, towards whose career in politics Derby felt protective,[49] was the diarist potentially close; but in the way stood his brother's wife, Clarendon's daughter, who shared her father's ways. Constance, he noted, was 'full of gossip ... She makes mischief without meaning it.'[50] This trait probably led to Derby's sudden break with her in 1878, after which the brothers only met clandestinely and rarely.

Derby, after succeeding to the title in 1869 and still more after his marriage the following year, retreated into uxoriousness, the pursuit of health, the pleasures of frugality, the joys of commuting from a scenic Kentish retreat, and having 'no quarrel or dispute' on hand,[51] a matter to which he attached the highest importance. His wife's health gave increasing cause for anxiety: like him, but more so, she had become liable to depression,[52] having lost in five years her father, mother, first

[47] *Later Diaries*, 92–96.
[48] 3 Feb. 1870
[49] 1 Apr. 1873
[50] 24 Oct. 1870
[51] 1 Jan. 1871, 1 Jan. 1872. 'He withdraws more & more & feels his unfitness to lead men', Hardy noted (*GH*, 12 July 1876).
[52] 17 July 1873

husband, sister, and brother.[53] Only occasionally does evidence survive in the diaries of her playing the part of political great lady, as in the 1860s, and her links were much more with Liberals such as Lowe than with Conservatives: Derby knew much of what passed in Gladstone's cabinet, including details of legislation.[54]

Derby's view of religion was, in Disraeli's phrase, that of all sensible men. ('Sensible men never say'.) He might on occasion at this time attend church,[55] though rarely; in later life he was apparently a conspicuous absentee.[56] His scepticism, strengthened by Hume and Bishop Butler, had been perhaps a strong bond with Disraeli, as later with his Kentish neighbour Charles Darwin, whom he much cultivated; strong enough, at any rate, for distaste for the clergy and for zeal in religion to be one of his strongest emotions. He expected indeed to see England adopt the voluntary system:[57] Wales and Scotland, still more so.[58] His dislike of making benefactions to the clergy was keen. He was not altogether irreverent, however, for he brought back from Voltaire's garden at Ferney a pious souvenir to plant at Knowsley. In politics, he was allergic to the *parti prêtre*, as he called it,[59] and this governed many of his attitudes to the Conservative party.

Derby was bruised, it seems, less by the Conservative split of 1867, to which he hardly alludes, than by the events of 1868, when the Church party in the cabinet, led by Hardy, overrode any prospect of a reformist handling of the Irish Church question, and therefore of the 1868 election generally. The memory of 1868, and the renewed prominence of religious politics in the 1874 session, aroused in Derby a sense of physical aversion at the thought of leading the Conservatives. Derby's prejudices appeared in such matters as his dislike for Lord Sandon, 'a strong religionist' suffering from 'weakness and narrowness of brain'.[60] Since Derby's distaste for religion in practice meant distaste for popular protestantism, it brought him temporary support from Salisbury, who late in 1874 pressed Derby to succeed on any sudden vacancy, to frustrate the protestant party in the cabinet.[61] Derby found

---

[53] 10 Jan. 1870, 23 Apr. 1873; finally losing a son, to a wife from the middle classes (17 July 1873).

[54] In 1881 it was a matter for remark that 'no word ever reaches us of what goes on inside the cabinet' (Lady Derby to Halifax, 4 Feb. 1881, Hickleton MSS).

[55] e.g. 12 Jan. 1873 (at Knowsley), 25 Jan. 1874 (in London).

[56] *Later Diaries*, 23

[57] 14 Feb. 1870

[58] *Later Diaries*, 84

[59] He admired Mill, especially his *On Liberty*, 'one of the wisest books of our time'; Mill, whom Stanley tried to appoint to the Indian Council, spoke admiringly of the diarist (*Speeches*, xvii).

[60] 20 July, 19 Nov. 1874

[61] 2 Dec. 1874

it possible, slowly, to re-establish partial relations with the secular dissidents of 1867, Carnarvon[62] and Salisbury,[63] he never did so with the church party of 1868, loyal though its leader, Hardy, had been over reform. The religious wound never healed, interwoven as it was with the question of the Tory leadership.

Derby took books and reading seriously: 'with books and papers I can always enjoy myself.'[64] What he read, even in the relative leisure of 1870–3, is not easy to discover; though recording the details of his daily exercise, he hardly gave books a mention, perhaps because he hardly counted the literature of his own time as true books. He re-read Sallust and Persius;[65] read Hübner on Japan and China; read 'Juvenal through with some care' and tried Ovid;[66] and, nearer to his interests, read Renan on French politics,[67] went 'slowly and carefully through the greater part of Hume's essays – which well deserve the trouble',[68] and commented on Butler's *Analogy*, an 'old favourite' because it supported his anti-religious views.[69] There seems little enthusiasm, and much duty, in such reading.[70] It is not possible to say which newspapers Derby normally read. Derby certainly sought an alliance or understanding with the serious intelligentsia but one to be effected more by prominence in their affairs (such as London University Senate, or the presidency of the Royal Literary Fund from 1875) than by interplay with their ideas.

Derby travelled abroad three times[71] in these years, mostly for his wife's health. Each time, they went to France, the country he had come to know best; though he felt little enthusiasm either for it or for foreign holidays. After 'three years or more passed in travel',[72] mainly outside Europe, in his youth – Derby was more travelled outside Europe than any other British politician of his day – he was sated; indeed his lack of interest in the non-European world and in India is very evident in his diaries.

[62] 10 Feb. 1870
[63] 29 Mar. 1870
[64] 8 Nov. 1872
[65] 8, 11 Apr. 1873
[66] 20 Nov. 1871
[67] 19 Jan. 1872
[68] 20 Nov. 1871
[69] 27 Feb. 1870
[70] Yet Lecky described him as 'among the best-read men I have ever known. His private library was one of the finest in England ...' (*Speeches*, xlii.)
[71] 20–29 Feb. 1872; 14 Feb.–14 Mar. 1873 (missing the Irish Universities crisis); and 6–30 Nov. 1873. In addition, Derby was abroad 24 Mar.–10 Apr. 1876 in attendance upon the Queen at Baden, whence he returned via Paris where he spent a day on private visits.
[72] 24 Feb. 1873. The diarist was author of *Six Weeks in South America* (1850), *Claims and Resources of the West Indies* (1850), and *Further Facts connected with the West Indies* (1851).

In home politics, the diaries afford only glimpses of Derby's underlying aims. Much depends on whether stray sentences are seen as
typical or untypical. Was Derby's wish to 'assume a neutral position
for the time, waiting events'[73] linked to his refusal to succeed his father
as patron of N.U.C.A.;[74] or was he just too busy at the time? In 1870,
'in regard to politics my present position is that of a neutral, singularly
free from pledges or ties',[75] he wrote; but then, detached though this
may sound, it was pronounced in a year when the opposition were
themselves neutral on the main legislative issues like Irish land or
education (which latter Derby judged 'moderate in character' and 'as
fair a solution of the difficulty as can be found'.[76] Derby was not alone,
or singular, in lying low at this time. There is no reason to doubt that
in declining to lead the Conservatives in the House of Lords, he wanted
among other things 'a larger degree of personal independence than is
compatible with the position of being the mouthpiece of a party'.

It was not long however before he took a more distinctly conservative
and partisan view, again going with the national tide. He reacted
strongly against the 'conservative socialism' of the New Social Movement,[77] a sort of poor man's Young England, and in his speeches at
this time stressed that conservatism was about the free market economy,
or it was nothing. Housing for the artisan, he urged from deep
experience,[78] required no 'foolish and fantastic schemes' involving 'State
machinery' in order to depart from 'the fair market price'.[79] All thoughts
of Ireland brought out the conservative in him; he was never quite just
a centrist liberal who happened to be in the wrong party. He was
interestingly sensitive to the supposed threat from the First International.
Derby realised that an alternative had to be offered, distinctively non-
liberal but of some inclusiveness: 'I am convinced that the opportunity
is either come, or near at hand, for a ministry like that of Sir R. Peel.
But who is there to take advantage of it?' he wrote early in 1871. His
rousing welcomes from Lancashire crowds had taught him that popularity need not be only Gladstonian. These short hints of underlying
intention may mean as much as his own laborious self-analyses, entirely
in character though these were, or they may be random thoughts.

The 1874 cabinet was however as much Derbyite as Disraelian. It
was very different from Disraeli's first sketch of 1873.[80] It included

[73] 26 Oct. 1869
[74] 5 Nov. 1869
[75] 1 Jan. 1870
[76] 17 Feb. 1870
[77] 26, 27, 29 July, 6, 15 Oct. 1871
[78] As a member of five or six housing associations, returning about 5%.
[79] Speech to Liverpool Conservative Working men's Association, 7 Jan. 1872
[80] 25 Mar. 1873

Derby's Cross (who wanted Disraeli deposed). It no longer excluded Disraeli's foes of 1867, Salisbury and Carnarvon. It excluded possible Liberal renegades brought in as Disraeli's personal protégés, such as Harcourt, and some probably pliant minor Conservatives proposed by Disraeli earlier. In short it was not the cabinet Disraeli wanted, nor one he could expect to find easy to manage, still less dominate, and it justified Lady Derby's abundant satisfaction with the situation just after it took office. Disraeli had been tethered;[81] a fairly Derbyite cabinet stood by until the general prediction that Disraeli 'will not long bear the strain of parliamentary life' came true. In the meantime, Derby concerned himself not so much with foreign policy, as with consolidating the national position he had judiciously cultivated in his speeches[82] of 1870–73, by giving a strong lead on domestic matters life finance. When he discussed the budget with Northcote, he did so on equal terms, as might befit a future Peel; subject always to the electoral and party restriction that in bad times 'remission of taxation is out of the question, and estimates must not be increased'. In 1874–5, we see the cabinet constantly looking over their shoulder at the finance of the previous ministry.

Disraelian government under normal conditions, 1874–6

The year 1875 saw Derby at the height of his ministerial career. His satisfaction with life was much enhanced by success in his private affairs. By the end of 1875 he had repaid £510,000 of debt in six years, a task which on his father's death he had expected to take ten or twelve years.[83] That this was due less to his conscientious management, than to windfall sales[84] of land to railway companies, did not make 1875 any the less a landmark in the financial history of the Stanley estates.

Derby's health continued to be good, bar a short attack of depression in mid-September.[85] Though he noted 'deafness continually increasing upon me' on one public occasion, he hardly mentioned it again.[86] His attendance at cabinet was exemplary. The cabinet of 22 November

[81] In late Feb. or early March 1874 a 'happy, amiable, and confidential' Derby told his aunt Lady Cowper that 'Dizzy is a changed man' with 'a cabinet of the wisest people he can find and none of them subservient' (*Earl Cowper, K.G. A Memoir. Printed for Private Circulation, 1913*, 254, 265.)

[82] Derby himself noted, of 1873, that he had delivered 'a fair number of speeches on public occasions and have on the whole been as much before the public eye as in 1872' (1 Jan. 1874). Much more than most front-benchers, Derby had something to say to the new working-man elector of 1867.

[83] 20 May 1875

[84] The improvement was foreseen at the start of the year; see 1875 initial flyleaf.

[85] 12 Sept. 1875

[86] 26 June 1875

1875 was only 'the second I have missed since we took office'.[87] He
remained deeply uxorious, his brief separation from Lady Derby in
October being the first night spent apart in five years of marriage.[88]
The significance of his two Kentish homes was in part marital, Fairhill
especially being 'the only place where we can lead a really quiet life'.[89]
His enthusiasm for his recent purchase of Keston, near Bromley, in his
wife's native county, knew no bounds, both on the grounds of its
landscape, and because it assisted his increasing withdrawal from
London political society.[90] At Knowsley, he attended tenants' dinners,[91]
received foreign ambassadors, shot game in vast quantities, looked after
estate matters, entertained family and guests, most of them lesser lights,
and generally worked hard, with a continuous flow of boxes to deal with,
and his private secretary Sanderson usually close at hand. Knowsley, he
wrote, 'was really far less of a holiday than to be quietly settled in
London in attendance on my office'.[92] The diaries tell us remarkably
little of Lady Derby, as also of Sanderson, the two most important
people in Derby's life; but certainly she suffered from nervous strain
except when in the country,[93] where 'within an hour she seemed a
different person'.[94]

Only late in the year did Derby weary of his routine, serene and
emotionally undemanding, of visits from ambassadors during office
hours, uncontentious cabinet meetings, no committees, briefings of
journalists, and very often, daily commuting to and from Kent. 'I am
beginning to feel the incessant worry of this office, which hardly gives
one day of entire rest in the year',[95] he wrote shortly after the purchase
of the Suez Canal shares. More representative of his general mood in
1875, however, was his conclusion on becoming 49 that 'few men, I
suppose, have entered their 50th year with less regret for the past, or
more general contentment with the present.'[96]

In foreign policy in 1875 Derby was laborious but relaxed and
perhaps fatalistic. So far as the diaries enunciate any doctrine, it was
that 'to me it appears that when "isolated" we have generally been

[87] 22 Nov. 1875
[88] 5 Oct. 1875
[89] 20 Sept. 1875
[90] 12 May 1875
[91] 5 Jan., 7 Jan. 1875
[92] 2 Jan. 1875. 'I rather like shooting', Derby told Lecky, 'it prevents the necessity of
general conversation.' (*Speeches*, xliii.) Lady Derby's view of Knowsley was that 'I always
have the steady conviction that people must be so bored there' (to Halifax, 5 Nov. 1881).
[93] e.g. 8 Jan. 1875, following Disraeli's near-retirement.
[94] 28 Nov. 1875
[95] 10 Dec. 1875
[96] 21 July 1875

most successful.[97] There was little sign that he saw any need to cultivate party opinion on foreign policy, or anything else, or that he expected the cabinet to assist in forming foreign policy as it did in making the budget. On the other hand, he saw the need to cultivate a public opinion, whose emotionalism and potential for war fever he deeply feared, by means of the press: 'I intend if possible to have one editor at each large dinner we give: but they must not meet one another.'[98] Even in high summer, when out of town, he maintained contact with key editors like Delane and Levy by writing to answer their queries.[99] For all that, the 'intense desire for action' on the part of the public made Derby uneasy even at this early stage of his foreign secretaryship, as capable of lending itself to a 'cry for war'.[100]

The main diplomatic event of 1875 was the Franco-German crisis of April–May 1875.[101] This remains a mysterious episode. Derby's account, written as it happened, is unremarkable for foresight, conspicuous exertion, or excitement. Conversations with France were superficial, those with Russia, through the 'really able'[102] Schouvaloff, going altogether deeper. It was the Anglo-Russian aspect of the affair that mattered most for Derby, for he glimpsed a reasonableness at the heart of Russian policy, only awaiting Schouvaloff's manipulative skill.[103] As for the cabinet, the attention it gave to the European crisis at its meetings of early May was negligible.

Derby was not over-trustful of foreigners, whether statesmen or their ambassadors in London. The latter he did not dislike, but nor did he find their too frequent visits, breaking into his working day, something he valued or sought. None of them, except Schouvaloff in 1877–8, had the importance for Derby of Odo Russell in Berlin, or Lyons in Paris. The odd man out was Musurus, the Turkish envoy, of whom Derby took the common view that 'conversation with him was a mere waste of time'[104] since he was 'a muddle-headed person, which he cannot help'.[105] Münster and Beust, for Germany and Austria respectively, were pleasant enough company, but subject to the limitation of their being opposition politicians at home;[106] while the two Frenchmen, Jarnac and his successor d'Harcourt, went down well. Jarnac, Harrovian, Irish

[97] 6 Sept. 1875
[98] 20 Feb. 1875
[99] 21 Aug., 29 Aug., 30 Aug., 15 Oct. 1875
[100] 29 Nov. 1875
[101] First hinted at in the diary, 17 Mar. 1875
[102] 12 Mar. 1875
[103] 20 Apr. 1875
[104] 15 July 1875
[105] 4 Aug. 1875
[106] Münster, an English diplomatist told Derby, was 'no friend to Bismarck' and 'sent here to get him out of the way' (27 May 1875).

landlord, and long a member of London society, won a remarkable encomium on personal grounds;[107] his successor, d'Harcourt (sometimes written, confusingly, as Harcourt, like Derby's Cambridge friend, the Liberal politician) was seen as a worthy functionary, over-conscientious, but 'simple, frank, and unaffected'.[108]

Schouvaloff, the Russian, Derby found hardest of all to assess, a difficulty which the former's strange conduct did nothing to lessen, as in his pretence that he knew nothing of what passed in Russia.[109] Derby was not quick to trust him: 'it is impossible to rely on a Russian.'[110] 'But who can trust a Russian?'[111] Russians should be 'most distrusted when seemingly most frank'.[112] Such depth of suspicion applied to Schouvaloff alone among senior foreign diplomatists in London.

Among foreign statesmen, perhaps Decazes alone received qualified praise, as being 'moderate and sensible beyond most Frenchmen'[113] though Derby's disapproval of his supposed stockjobbing gradually hardened. Derby saw the Republic as the best regime for France.[114] As a power, however, France was 'tricky and unconciliatory',[115] its expressions of (unwanted) friendship being belied in Derby's eyes by its sharp practice in pursuing petty advantage in the matters of Annam, fisheries, and sugar, of the last of which Derby wrote: 'This is the third time that the French, in the midst of their professions of gratitude, have played us a trick'.[116]

Distrust of Bismarck was an axiom of British policy. Where France cheated, hoping to remain undetected, Bismarck's motiveless malignity was so transparent that it could never have been expected to deceive, and only won attention as a personal infirmity. 'The German game is evidently to promote disunion among European states' wrote Derby.[117] Bismarck apart, however, Derby thought that there was an inherent Anglo-German tension arising from difference of polity: 'There can never be entire cordiality between a military despotism, such as Germany is now, and a peaceable constitutional community like England.[118]

Derby was not well supported by English diplomatic talent. At the

[107] 23 Mar. 1875
[108] 10 July 1875
[109] e.g. 27 Jan. 1875
[110] 20 Mar. 1875
[111] 15 July 1875
[112] 27 Jan. 1875
[113] 10 Jan. 1875
[114] 6 Feb. 1875
[115] 5 Sept. 1875
[116] 17 July 1875
[117] 17 Mar. 1875
[118] 1 Sept. 1875

Foreign Office itself, 'the discipline of the office is not what it was in Hammond's time',[119] and Derby had to return careless drafting for correction.[120] At Constantinople, two English diplomatists were unfit for work.[121] Of the ambassadors, perhaps only Odo Russell in Berlin, and Lyons in Paris, were regarded with real respect; Russell, Derby wrote, 'is the best man we have'.[122] Somewhat below came Elliot, at Constantinople, more for his influence than for his insights: 'I doubt if at any time the personal influence of an English ambassador has been greater with the Porte.'[123] The elderly Sir A. Buchanan, in Vienna, was seen as 'a safe and sensible man' who did 'no more than he can help, and knows but little of what is passing'.[124] The 'pompous and tedious'[125] Loftus, at St Petersburg, was a less competent version of Buchanan, but as impossible to remove on mere grounds of inadequacy. Paget, at Rome, 'a most insatiable and querulous beggar for all that can be got',[126] was able but of marginal importance. On the periphery of diplomacy, Morier was viewed as 'an able, though restless and intriguing diplomatist'[127] while of the hyperactive Layard, then at Madrid, Derby held that 'diplomacy is the last profession he should have chosen',[128] and offered to move him to Lisbon,[129] having from the first thought him 'wholly wanting in discretion and tact'.[130] Lytton,[131] the future viceroy, then at Lisbon, Derby considered 'at all times dreamy and undecided'.[132] Money played its part, Derby assisting Tenterden, his senior official;[133] Sanderson, his private secretary; Sanderson's family; Lionel West, a minor diplomatist and his wife's brother, was handsomely supported;[134] while Odo Russell received £5000 from his (and Derby's) kinsman, the Duke of Bedford.[135] Morier, like Paget, was seen as esurient.[136]

[119] 28 May 1875
[120] 31 Dec. 1875
[121] 12 Sept. 1875
[122] 1 Nov. 1875
[123] 17 Mar. 1875
[124] 24 Aug. 1875
[125] 25 Nov. 1869
[126] 11 Mar. 1876
[127] 24 May 1875
[128] 22 Feb. 1875
[129] 26 Dec. 1875
[130] 27 Oct. 1869
[131] One of Lady Derby's correspondents. On his departure for India, he wrote to her outlining his expectations of a great historic role.
[132] 27 July 1874
[133] 12 Apr. 1870
[134] 2 Mar., 8 June 1873
[135] 25 Aug. 1873
[136] 2 Dec. 1873

In opposition Derby was no friend to empire. He agreed with Disraeli's view of 1870 that the white colonies could not be drawn more closely together. He opposed any extension to the north or west of India, which had 'at present as good a military frontier as could well be drawn.'[137] On Africa, he warned against 'a system of alliances and protectorates on the East African coast which could be of no possible advantage'. He was against conquering Ashanti,[138] considered the total abandonment of the Gold Coast,[139] and tried to avoid a protectorate in Fiji[140] (though later wavering).[141]

In office, Derby exercised a restraining hand. He held that 'having annexed land enough in Fiji and the Gold Coast',[142] further schemes should be resisted firmly. In 1875 this can be seen in his comments on Rajah Brooke's proposal to annex Brunei,[143] in his determination to arrest colonization in New Guinea, be it Belgian[144] or English[145] his opposition to involvement in local conflict in Siam,[146] his lack of interest in exchanges of territory with France in India and Africa,[147] and his deep misgivings, shared with Disraeli, about Carnarvon's forward policy in South Africa.[148] Military difficulties in Malaya,[149] the intermittent risk of war with China,[150] and possibly with Burma,[151] lent force to Derby's reluctance to give hostages to fortune.

Derby kept a close eye on the prime minister's prospects of continuance in office, following Disraeli's serious illness in autumn 1874. In the event, the premier's health stabilised, though age took its toll. At the start of 1875, Derby thought Disraeli 'capable of some years more work' and 'trusted and respected as never before' although outwardly 'old and feeble'.[152] In May, Derby noted that Disraeli fell asleep in cabinet for the first time in his recollection, during the discussion on trade union legislation (which, Disraeli thought, might have to be dropped).[153] In June Disraeli was 'wearied and out of

---

[137] *H*, 6 Feb. 1873
[138] 9 Sept. 1873
[139] 9 Nov. 1873
[140] 23 Feb. 1874
[141] 8 July 1874
[142] 21 Apr. 1875
[143] 21 Apr. 1875
[144] 13 July 1875
[145] 9 Aug. 1875
[146] 16 Jan. 1875
[147] 17 Apr. 1875
[148] e.g. 10 Feb., 13 Apr. 1875. For Disraeli, see 10 Sept. 1875
[149] 10, 11, 12 Nov. 1875
[150] Especially 28 Aug.–14 Oct. 1875
[151] 7 June 1875
[152] 1 Jan. 1875; also 25 Jan. 1875
[153] 29 May 1875

spirits.'[154] Summer saw an improvement; 'I think he has been at his
best lately',[155] Derby commented following the Plimsoll episode, which
he saw as showing Disraeli's indispensability. Disraeli concurred, saying
'I think I have another year's work in me',[156] and returned to work in
the autumn, as Derby observed, 'in good health and excellent spirits,
but visibly an old man.'[157]

Derby and Disraeli continued to exchange visits. Derby's last visit to
Hughenden was on Disraeli's birthday in 1869.[158] A haunch of Knowsley
venison also travelled south.[159] The Disraelis visited Knowsley in 1870;[160]
the widowed Disraeli, again on 13–15 October 1873.[161] Derby sent his
own portrait as a present to Disraeli, by request.[162] That was only one
aspect of their partnership. When in London, they conferred once a
month on average,[163] privately, mostly on governmental matters, but
also on appointments, peerages, and royal idiosyncrasies. (Narrowly
electoral matters, and questions of party organization, did not come
Derby's way.) Disraeli also corresponded with Lady Derby; how much
is unclear. Many of the meetings in London were at Disraeli's request.
Though there was remarkably little in the way of their dining together,
Disraeli could still credibly talk to Derby of their having a confidential
relationship unknown to the Queen.[164] If there were differences of
opinion on any issue in 1875 between premier and foreign secretary,
Derby was unaware of them, and Disraeli did not consider himself in
a strong enough position to pursue them.

Derby's claim that he was in no haste to succeed Disraeli should be
taken seriously. Aspects of the Conservative party filled him with
dismay. Noting the 'violent and reactionary temper'[165] shown by Tories
over the Judicature Bill, Derby considered that if Disraeli went, 'I do
not think I can go on with the rest of the party, either as leader or
follower'. Tory clericalism grated even more than Tory reaction pure
and simple, as his irritation with the parsonical Education Bill of the
otherwise harmless Lord Sandon showed. Of the two main Anglican
reactionaries in the cabinet, Salisbury remained in social contact with

[154] 23 June 1875
[155] 7 Aug. 1875
[156] 10 Sept. 1875
[157] 6 Nov. 1875
[158] 24 Dec. 1869
[159] 26 Aug. 1870
[160] 17 Oct. 1870
[161] 13–15 Oct. 1873
[162] 3 Nov. 1873
[163] In 1875, on 25 Jan., 1 Feb., 17 Feb., 18 Feb., 18 Mar., 13 May., 5 June, 12 Aug., 10
Sept., 3 Nov., 12 Nov., and 13 Dec.
[164] 21 Jan. 1875
[165] 6 Mar. 1875

Derby, but the other, Gathorne Hardy is so conspicuously absent from the diaries that one may infer continuing alienation, probably going back to the cabinet split over the Irish church issue in 1868. Since Hardy would have had to be Derby's strong right arm in any post-Disraelian government, this apparent aversion suggested marked unwillingness to cultivate party opinion in the way he cultivated the press and non-party centre opinion. Hardy, for instance, unlike Northcote and Cross, was never a guest at Knowsley. In 1875, however, with Disraeli's health more stable than in 1874, these issues were below the surface, if not far below, and the cabinet could unite on a programme of peace, retrenchment, and practical reform, Conservative administration thus meaning what Derby wanted it to mean; though as the cabinet discussions of 1875 on the budget showed, Gladstone's government remained in power if not in office.

Derby was fully in harmony with the social legislation of 1875, mostly the work of his nominee Cross (who in opposition had sought to remove Disraeli).[166] The session of 1875, Derby wrote, was 'justly thought dull, and unjustly considered as having been wasted.'[167] Derby intervened directly more over the budget, which as in 1874 was subject to repeated discussion in cabinet.[168] Policy-making here was to a remarkable extent a cabinet rather than departmental matter. It was the cabinet which overruled the Chancellor of the Exchequer on an important budget proposal,[169] and which subordinated the needs of defence to domestic political advantage, as in the decision not to fortify coaling stations, on which the navy now depended.[170] It was the cabinet, not a committee, which went through Cross's artisans dwellings bill clause by clause.[171] The strength of cabinet government also emerges in Derby's careful account of cabinet deliberations on the Suez canal purchase. Far from being chiefly a Disraelian coup, as myth once had it, no piece of business received closer cabinet attention[172] in 1875. Derby's concern for the general development of policy outside his own department was shown in his anxiety, shared with Disraeli, over Carnarvon's forward policy in South Africa, and indeed over Carnarvon's mental state itself.[173]

---

[166] 16 Mar. 1873
[167] 17 Aug. 1875
[168] e.g. 1 May, 25 June, 12 July 1875
[169] 10 Apr. 1875
[170] 1 May 1875
[171] 13 Jan. 1875
[172] The first news reached Derby on 15 and 16 Nov. 1875. Cabinets followed on 17, 18, 19, 22, 23 and 24 Nov. 1875; Derby missed the cabinet of 22 Nov., and the Canal shares are not mentioned in his report of 19 Nov. 1875. See Lord Rothschild, 'You Have It, Madam'. The purchase, in 1875, of Suez Canal shares by Disraeli and Baron Lionel de Rothschild. (London, 1980)
[173] 10 Feb., 13 Apr., 28 Apr., 10 Sept. 1875

Though Derby and Disraeli might consult, there is little sign of their bypassing the cabinet on ordinary government business. If the cabinet was indeed bypassed on the question of the Admiralty circular on escaped slaves,[174] that perhaps mainly reflected its normal autumnal dispersal. The two men, though conferring rarely and confidentially, had no specific area of business that they called their own.

Instead, discussion readily tended to drift to the topic of the Queen, Disraeli commenting that she wrote 'very wildly',[175] using 'Billingsgate' (Layard becoming 'Lie-hard')[176] and generally being, Disraeli thought, 'very troublesome, very wilful and whimsical, like a spoilt child'.[177] Later in the year, after her yacht ran down a pleasure boat with loss of life, Disraeli became 'uneasy as to her state of mind.'[178] The Eastern Question, and foreign policy generally, did not figure as dividing premier from foreign secretary. The Disraeli of 1875 who 'does not see how the power of the Sultan is to be propped up'[179] was not the Disraeli of 1877–8; whereas it was Derby who in 1875 made light of Turkish bankruptcy, presciently noting that the Turkish army and navy were as strong as its finances were weak.[180]

Unsurprisingly, the cabinet spent much time on trivia, partly because it had no committee system. (Derby only twice[181] noted the use of committees in 1875, one at least being a select committee; he served on neither.) It concerned itself with the Brighton Aquarium,[182] the living of Halifax,[183] the New Forest,[184] a peccant Dorset magistrate,[185] and artisans' dwellings in Battersea:[186] matters essentially local in scope. It anxiously contemplated Lord Henry Lennox's tenure of the Board of Works,[187] where his eventual departure under a cloud distracted cabinet attention at the start of the Bulgarian Atrocities controversy. The proposed tour of India by the Prince of Wales needed discussion in at least six cabinets,[188] this perhaps enhancing the lack of grip on the legislative timetable which contributed to the Plimsoll episode. Certain

[174] 7 Oct. 1875
[175] 11 Feb. 1875
[176] 17 Feb. 1875
[177] 21 Mar. 1875
[178] 10 Sept. 1875
[179] 3 Nov. 1875
[180] 1 Aug. 1875
[181] 13 Mar., 4 Nov. 1875
[182] 26 May, 12, 14, 16 June 1875
[183] 11 Nov. 1875
[184] 10 Nov. 1875
[185] 19 June 1875
[186] 14 Aug. 1875
[187] 27 Feb., 3, 26 June 1875
[188] 5, 9, 26 June, 3, 7, 14 July 1875

meetings of the cabinet dealt only with minor business.[189] The meeting which was fruitlessly spent 'discussing chiefly the question of Scotch banks in England, which seems a very puzzling one'[190] well catches the unbusinesslike atmosphere which Disraeli did little to discourage. The cabinet even sat as a quasi-judicial body, in the cases of the alleged poisoning of a British official by an Indian ruler,[191] of Col. Baker's alleged unwelcome attentions to a young lady in a railway carriage,[192] and in the matter of Dr Kenealy's right to petition the House of Commons against the judges in the Tichborne case.[193] In Irish matters, Mitchel's election, while a felon, for an Irish seat, came before the cabinet as a legal issue,[194] while the creation of Irish peers[195] touched on constitutional law as well as on policy.

With Ireland quiet and no Irish minister in the cabinet, the role of the cabinet was chiefly to endorse, unenthusiastically, the view of the Irish administration and to weigh Irish opinion. In an informal sense, Ireland enjoyed autonomy; it figured in perhaps only half a dozen cabinets in 1875, with Beach, as Irish minister, usually in attendance. When Beach presented 'a long list of bills which he wants passed',[196] one surely sees the Irish tail wagging the English dog, just as much as when Irish opinion carried the Education Bill despite Tory back-bench opposition.[197] Yet killing Home Rule with kindness was imposs-ible, in Derby's view: he saw 'not the slightest abatement in hostility to the Union',[198] and comparing the Balkans with Ireland, saw Home Rule in both cases as 'a compromise with which neither side will be content.'[199]

The line that Derby envisaged for himself in home politics in 1874–5, if necessarily somewhat lightly sketched out, was clear enough. He abhorred Anglican sectarianism. He did not wish conservatism to be confined to gentry traditionalism. He looked to a future in which science, including social science, played an honoured part (he was to be Darwin's pallbearer as well as Disraeli's). He cultivated the cooperative movement.[200] He sought to appeal to a non-radical intelligentsia and a

---

[189] e.g. 13 Feb., 5 June 1875
[190] 13 Mar. 1875
[191] 14 Apr. 1875
[192] 7, 11 Aug. 1875
[193] 8 Apr. 1875
[194] 13, 17 Feb. 1875
[195] e.g. 17 Feb., 27 Feb., 16 June, 19 June, 7 Aug. 1875
[196] 11 Nov. 1875
[197] 7 Aug. 1875
[198] 29 Mar. 1875
[199] 16 Sept. 1875
[200] Derby gave the Inaugural Address at the 1881 Leeds Co-operative Congress.

satisfied but politically conscious working class.[201] In his version of conservatism, there was room for almost all.

Thus not only did he nominate Cross, whom he knew well, for the cabinet in 1874, but the following year he pressed the claims of W.H. Smith, whom he hardly knew at all. His recurrent interest in honours and pensions for men of science and art says much,[202] as does his lending his Kentish retreat to Carlyle for August (and visiting him there).[203] His intimacy with his Kentish neighbour Darwin was in part political, not least on Darwin's side.[204] His election as Rector of Edinburgh University in 1874 symbolised the broader acceptability that Derby sought for conservatism. Even his firm approval of Captain Webb's swimming the channel[205] had as much to do with his views on social cohesion as it did with swimming.

In his own deep absorption in Home Counties landscape,[206] his youthful love of mountaineering, his inveterate pedestrianism, and his planting of two million trees,[207] he seems to hint at a new range of post-aristocratic, post-religious values. His public gestures aimed to occupy a broad middle ground between religious and political dogmatisms. His endowment of a chair of mining[208] at Owen's College, Manchester, and his Manchester address to the Society for the Promotion of Scientific Industry, sought to make 'Conservative progress', the Derbyite slogan of the late 1850s, into a practical urban reality. Urban, for while the diaries show the private Derby as a ruralist in retreat from urban pressures, his public preoccupations were with the people of the great cities. (As chairman of the Peabody Trust, he was by 1888 ultimately responsible for providing 11,000 rooms for 20,000 occupants at low but profitable rents.) His homilies on prisoners' aid, organization of charity, hospitals, artisans' dwellings, seamen's orphans, technical education, mechanics' institutes, the deaf and dumb, Thrift, and the Conduct of Life, would not have come amiss from Samuel Smiles. The lay sermon, he tried to show in his outdoor speeches of the early 1870s, had more to offer than the church one; and perhaps unlike most Victorian administrator peers, this conservative admirer of Mill had a message and needed an audience, though not a political one.

[201] The theme of his speech (17 Dec. 1875) to the City of Edinburgh Working-Men's Conservative Association, when he addressed 2000 in the Corn Exchange.
[202] 13 May, 18 Aug. 1875
[203] 31 July, 20 Aug. 1875
[204] 22 Dec. 1875
[205] 28 Aug. 1875
[206] 12 May 1875
[207] *Speeches*, xlii
[208] 17 June 1875

Disraelian Government under Stress

From very early in 1876 the nature of the diaries changes. They become much more the diaries of a foreign secretary than before. The Balkans becomes the central topic; and this well before the Bulgarian agitation[209] of August made it a domestic issue. 'The question of the East' generally became the peg upon which the European Powers hung their search for a new equilibrium to replace the one destroyed by the Franco-Prussian War of 1870; but equally it formed the ostensible agenda by reference to which conflicts of personality, style, and ambition within the cabinet came to be resolved.

In early 1876, a Balkan crisis did not appear the only possible outcome. Bismarck set on foot a brief but brisk courtship[210] of England, which came to nothing more than joint action against Spanish and Chinese misdeeds.[211] Briefly, again, Egypt and its finances seemed potentially explosive,[212] only to disappear from view. It was very much the dog that did not bark during 1876–8. Africa intruded, unsought, in the forms of Dahomey,[213] Zanzibar[214] and the Niger trade,[215] all 'foreign' and thus within Derby's sphere. His underlying attitude being that 'we have quite black men enough', as he was wont to say,[216] he was happy to defer minor extra-European issues until the August vacation,[217] when they figured on a list of chores. Such tasks apart, the world outside Europe hardly impinged, much less so than in 1875, and Derby was able to begin re-reading Aeschylus.

Domestic matters, too, fell into the background, though the budget and Queen's Speech were still very much cabinet matters, as before. Disraeli was in no state to impart momentum; he 'often appears half asleep, takes no part, and much time is wasted in loose talk.'[218] Derby, though at the height of his power, contemplated retirement should Disraeli not survive.[219] The Queen in all her aspects remained persona non grata with Derby, the Royal Titles Bill adding a further touch of frost on Derby's part; but then, as Disraeli now thought, 'she is very

[209] Derby initially suspected that the *Daily News* report of 'the massacre of 30,000 Bulgarians by Turkish troops' was 'one of those fictions by which insurgent leaders try to keep up the spirit of their followers.' (Derby to Ponsonby, 3 July 1876, Derby MSS.)
[210] 9 Jan., 8 Feb., 23 Feb., 7 Mar. 1876
[211] e.g. 23 Mar. 1876
[212] 10, 24 Mar. 1876
[213] 12 Apr. 1876
[214] 12 Jan. 1876
[215] 28 July 1876
[216] *Speeches*, xxxvi
[217] 16 Aug. 1876
[218] 25 Jan. 1876
[219] 6 Mar., 7 May, 24 June 1876

mad'.[220] As for colleagues, they raised few problems for the diarist, the exceptions being Carnarvon's 'tendency to rash and precipitate action'[221] and Lord Henry Lennox,[222] eased out under a financial cloud. Life in cabinet remained decorous, subdued, and highly departmentalized, if not quite friendly.

On foreign policy, so long as it was not an issue in British domestic politics, Derby had things his own way. His ability to thwart cabinet and premier so often in 1877–8 has to be understood in the context of his tremendous authority in 1876. In formulating policy, he was very possibly assisted by Sanderson, who had the advantage of propinquity and great ability, though this we do not know, and perhaps in some ways by Odo Russell in Berlin, who unlike Lord Lyons and Lord Tenterden was both a full member of the governing class and a family connexion. Foreign Office officialdom left little mark upon Derby's views, and he was almost unaware of the existence of his political junior, Bourke. The cabinet in 1876 did not decide or discuss policy, though Derby sought to induce discussion to educate them and to spite Disraeli by so doing. 'Among Disraeli's peculiarities' Derby wrote, 'is a dislike to allow foreign matters to be discussed in cabinet.'[223] The only sign of possible prime ministerial restiveness came from his unwarrantedly sharp criticisms of Derby's subordinates.[224]

On foreign matters, Derby and Disraeli worked as a team, but with Disraeli at times more obviously the junior partner than he can have wished. The Eastern Question of 1877–8 was partly a means of reversing this relationship. An extreme example of this was in early 1876, over the Andrassy note, which Derby wished to accept, seeing 'nothing in it dangerous to Turkey',[225] while Disraeli was opposed. The note was accepted without demur, Derby regarding Disraeli's submissiveness on this and other occasions as part of the natural order of things. Derby, by summer 1876, was acutely aware of profound differences between Disraeli and himself over the style and psychology of policy-making, saw fully the dangers, and expected that so long as cabinet, party, and public were not drawn into the Eastern Question, such perils could be contained.

The diaries for 1877 are almost too full in their accounts of cabinet divisions, albeit with human touches and literary skill adding something. In some respects, such as the Duke of Richmond's abject dependence on Cairns, new points emerge; but the general picture is familiar. More

---

[220] 3 Apr. 1876
[221] 21 Mar. 1876
[222] 26, 28 June, 15 July 1876
[223] 1 June 1876
[224] 8 Aug. 1876
[225] 4 Jan. 1876

interesting perhaps is Derby's assessment of the fluctuating European situation. This was only occasionally a military assessment – Derby was not a party to preparations for war – and more an assessment of the motives of foreign statesmen, and of Disraeli.

However, the most intriguing aspect is that they give Derby's record of business done with Schouvaloff, and the times and dates of their frequent meetings, together with some report of what Schouvaloff said (some of it highly unflattering to his masters). By a strange accident, we already know what 'Schou.' reported of Derby; now we have Derby's reports on Schouvaloff for comparison. These should make for an interesting comparison; it was 'Schou.'s' way to contrast his own finesse and assiduity with the torpor, procrastination, and fumbling of Derby. As 'Schou.' had his career to think of, being a possible successor to Gorchakov as Russian chancellor, it is important to bear in mind that there was nothing in his character which would have prevented embroidery in his reports. Derby indeed suspected that this might occur. It is rare, at any rate, to have both sides of a diplomatic relationship so fully in print as we now have with the Schouvaloff-Derby relationship of 1874–8.

Late in 1877, and early in 1878, the trail becomes especially confused. Speculation centres on four questions. These are whether Lady Derby, or even Derby himself, passed cabinet secrets to Russia; whether he had a nervous breakdown in early 1878; whether thereafter he remained only nominally in office, his functions being taken over by Salisbury and others, and whether Derby's character was deliberately blackened. The diary does little to resolve these questions in any final way, but it does suggest new lines of approach, and new reasons for caution.

First, the 'nervous breakdown' of January 1878. Derby was indeed seriously ill, perhaps from an infection; and then as on other occasions, nervous strain took its toll. He did however recover, and Hardy was soon to record with unconscious contradiction, 'Derby is so timid and irresolute that all the rest of the Cabinet cannot move him.[226] Whether one looks at the volume of business transacted by Derby in spring 1878, or at his continuing ability to overrule cabinet feeling (or deny its immediate execution), it is hard to see that the nature of his foreign secretaryship had essentially changed; and his policy, as explained in the diaries, had an altogether more rational basis than the inability of a stricken man to take any decisions. Central, perhaps, to his view of the situation was a fear that, before diplomacy could begin its work, an almost accidental conflagration between armed forces around Con-stantinople would make war for amour propre inevitable. Because a localised clash did not lead to war in spring 1878, this is not to say that

[226] *GH*, 22 Jan. 1878

Derby was wrong in seeing it as the most likely outcome, and one that made more grandiose diplomatic solutions at that time so much fine talk. The thesis of Derby as the 'lame duck' foreign secretary now looks questionable, especially in the extreme form in which it was put forward by Lord Salisbury's biographer.[227] Derby, like the others, was playing his hand, perhaps skilfully, and not just fumbling. There is a minor but serious reason for questioning orthodoxy: the conduct of Cairns, normally so close to Disraeli. In December 1877–February 1878, Cairns had moved back from bellicosity to supporting a pacific view. Only on the question of occupying a Mediterranean outpost did Cairns support the Disraeli/Salisbury view, and that strongly; and one can only suppose that this added to the charms of that policy, pressed so vigorously by Salisbury as the perfect shoehorn with which to eject Derby. Other issues might shift and blur; an occupation alone presented an issue on which it was known with certainty that Derby would resign. To some extent, therefore, Derby was almost a willing party to being tricked into resignation: but this all awaits investigation in other ministerial papers.

Were secrets betrayed? The answer is probably yes, but the question is by whom, and whether betrayal was the right word. Schouvaloff had access to a wide range of leaky insiders; Derby records his own strong suspicions in other directions. Schouvaloff had strong motives for exaggerating his knowledge to impress his masters. The diaries give almost no evidence as to Lady Derby's role, and one cannot well judge whether she elicited cabinet matters from Derby; he was certainly not privy to all that passed in her political life. She kept, among her personal letters, those from Schouvaloff, but she also kept those from other ambassadors of the day. What is clear is not who betrayed what, but who set the accusations on their rounds: Disraeli, basing his case on reports from Colonel Wellesley.

The latter would repay further consideration. He was not some sage servant of the state, grown grey with years of service, but a classic Victorian scoundrel: a fact not always taken into account when weighing his evidence. Financially desperate, fast in his tastes, he was open to any inducement: which does not mean that he received any. If a colonel in name, that was largely honorific. Wellesley was but a captain, recently promoted from lieutenant, when his posting to the Russian court brought such high honours his way, to meet the requirements of court etiquette. He was therefore not just a rogue but a young rogue, a Disraelian young man. He was moreover attached to the Court party, being an aide-de-camp to the Queen, and son-in-law of the ambassador to Russian, Loftus, who was a kinsman of Jane, Lady Ely, an influential

[227] *Cecil*, 209–11

friend at court. He was to be twice divorced, but before that, his resignation from the diplomatic service was precipitated, in 1879, by his winning the affections of one Miss Kate Vaughan, dancer and actress, from a sitting tenant, also a member of White's, a matter which gave the premier much delight. Up until this romantic episode, Wellesley seems to have played his cards well; on Salisbury succeeding Derby, Wellesley was promoted within the month to a plum posting. This promotion is all the more piquant, in that Salisbury had demanded Wellesley's dismissal the previous summer, charging him with corruption before the cabinet. Where so much turned on Wellesley's accusations, which provided perhaps the only and certainly the main evidence against Derby, one can but wonder at the assiduity with which they were used to blacken his name. One might even speculate whether he was in some way encouraged to provide evidence in the shape and sense desired. At any rate, delation by Wellesley is not something one would wish to hang a dog on, which is not to say that it might not be true for all that.

In the early months of 1878, the diaries discuss four main areas of foreign policy. These were the avoidance of an immediate collision over Constantinople; the tentative search for an Anglo-Austrian under-standing against Russia; the attempt to shift discussion of a Balkan settlement to a European congress; and the scheme for occupying a Mediterranean island either for naval use or simply by way of showing earnest. Over this last, Derby was to resign on 27 March 1878. Until then Derby faced a double difficulty. An Austrian alliance, to him, in theory made peace certain, once achieved; but no such alliance was likely to be achieved without a British demonstration that they meant business. Again, as Derby accepted, a European conference offered the best chance of restraining Russia; but if Russia were thus to surrender some of the fruits of its successes, it had to be demonstrated that Britain would risk war. The way to serenity, distantly glimpsed, lay through immediate confrontations which could readily flare into a war in which Europe, including Austria, might be a contented bystander. If Derby spent his energies more on stopping war than on creating peace, it was ultimately because the preconditions for a European settlement did not yet exist, either in Austria,[228] or in Bismarck's willingness to assist Austria's Balkan objectives.

The question of occupying a Mediterranean island was raised in cabinet on 14, 23, and 27 February, and 2, 7, 8, 16 and 27 March 1878. Schouvaloff knew that the topic was being discussed, as early as 26 February, while Beaconsfield told the Queen that the idea was first

---

[228] G.H. Rupp, *A Wavering Friendship: Russia and Austria, 1876–78* (Cambridge, Mass., 1941).

broached in cabinet on 27 February 1878.[229] Only on 27 March do the diaries specifically name Cyprus. Previously, they refer only to Mitylene as the subject of cabinet discussion, though in his private reflections as late as 24 March, Derby expanded this to Mitylene or Lemnos. Nowhere do the diaries show any awareness, at least before 27 March, that the seizure of an island might be linked to plans for a British sphere of influence in Asia Minor.[230]

Salisbury was clearly the most ardent supporter of occupation by force. From the time of the cabinet meeting of 2 March, he knew that this was the one issue on which Derby's resignation was almost certain. At that meeting, the cabinet agreed that the 'island scheme is to be carried out in detail'; on 8 March Salisbury, with help from Cairns, led the cabinet to resolve to 'take a naval station by force', though only if the congress did not go as wished. Until Beaconsfield's set speech in cabinet on 27 March, the premier played little overt part in the matter. On two occasions, however, each the day before a cabinet, the premier seemed to encourage Derby's dissidence. His private remark to Derby (26 Feb. 1878) 'that after consulting with the naval authorities, he had satisfied himself that an island would be of no use as a station', and his suggestion of 6 March that an occupation should be temporary and by consent appeared to depart (or were meant so to appear) from Salisbury's plans. Yet on the same day, 6 March, an anxious war minister found Beaconsfield 'bent' on an occupation '& seems to disregard military considerations'. The question of how and why this mildly peripheral issue became so politically central is one that might repay minute consideration.

The diaries are an intelligent interpretation of events as they occurred, seen from the best of all vantage points – the one where European and domestic politics interlocked. They have literary skill and articulateness; Derby's First in Classics at Cambridge stood him in good stead. They are not, as is all too easy to think, a record of Derby's whole existence, or even of his whole political existence, but of what he thought it fitting to record. But the impressions they leave, of a highly truthful man, meticulously linking his thought to his daily engagements, would be most difficult to concoct or even embroider on so large a scale. Thus in cabinet, Derby's effectiveness, and Disraeli's relative ineffectiveness, are well depicted. So, too, is the rather pathetic lack of impact of most of the would-be historic set speeches given by Disraeli to the cabinet when he meant to give a strong lead. The diaries are best however as a source for Derby himself. They show the predominance of calculation

---

[229] M. and B. 252

[230] For the development of policy, especially at military and expert level, see Dwight E. Lee, *Great Britain and the Cyprus Convention Policy of 1878* (Cambridge, Mass., 1934).

over indecision in Derby's approach, and his willingness to work happily with Disraeli while realising fully their difference in outlook. Minds as remarkable as those of Salisbury, Disraeli, and Schouvaloff, all had an interest in portraying the key to Derby's foreign secretaryship as indecision, rather than as a forceful and perhaps able intrusion of pacific, free trading mid-Victorian values into the alien world of honour and prestige. Thus are legends created and maintained.

The immediate family of the diarist

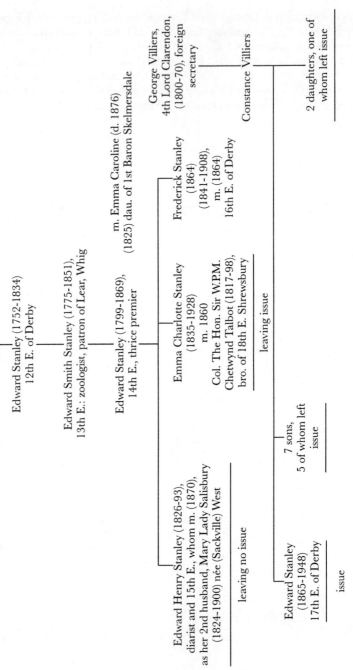

Edward Stanley (1752-1834)
12th E. of Derby

Edward Smith Stanley (1775-1851),
13th E.: zoologist, patron of Lear, Whig

Edward Stanley (1799-1869),
14th E., thrice premier

m. Emma Caroline (d. 1876)
(1825) dau. of 1st Baron Skelmersdale

Edward Henry Stanley (1826-93),
diarist and 15th E., whom m. (1870),
as her 2nd husband, Mary Lady Salisbury
(1824-1900) née (Sackville) West

leaving no issue

Emma Charlotte Stanley
(1835-1928)
m. 1860
Col. The Hon. Sir W.P.M.
Chetwynd Talbot (1817-98),
bro. of 18th E. Shrewsbury

leaving issue

Frederick Stanley
(1864)
(1841-1908),
m. (1864)
16th E. of Derby

George Villiers,
4th Lord Clarendon,
(1800-70), foreign
secretary

Constance Villiers

Edward Stanley
(1865-1948)
17th E. of Derby

issue

7 sons,
5 of whom left
issue

2 daughters, one of
whom left issue

The stepchildren of Mary, Lady Derby

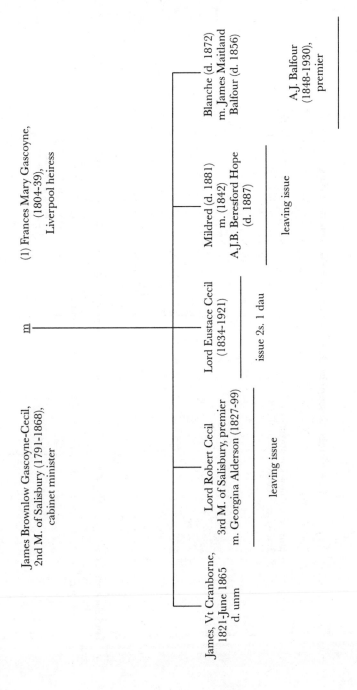

James Brownlow Gascoyne-Cecil,
2nd M. of Salisbury (1791-1868),
cabinet minister

m

(1) Frances Mary Gascoyne,
(1804-39),
Liverpool heiress

James, Vt Cranborne,
1821-June 1865
d. unm

Lord Robert Cecil,
3rd M. of Salisbury, premier
m. Georgina Alderson (1827-99)

leaving issue

Lord Eustace Cecil
(1834-1921)

issue 2s. 1 dau

Mildred (d. 1881)
m. (1842)
A.J.B. Beresford Hope
(d. 1887)

leaving issue

Blanche (d. 1872)
m. James Maitland
Balfour (d. 1856)

A.J. Balfour
(1848-1930),
premier

The diarist's stepchildren by his wife's first marriage

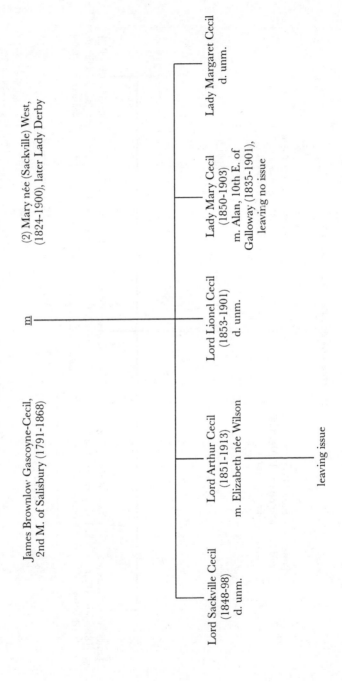

James Brownlow Gascoyne-Cecil,
2nd M. of Salisbury (1791-1868)

m

(2) Mary née (Sackville) West,
(1824-1900), later Lady Derby

Lord Sackville Cecil
(1848-98)
d. unm.

Lord Arthur Cecil
(1851-1913)
m. Elizabeth née Wilson

Lord Lionel Cecil
(1853-1901)
d. unm.

Lady Mary Cecil
(1850-1903)
m. Alan, 10th E. of
Galloway (1835-1901),
leaving no issue

Lady Margaret Cecil
d. unm.

leaving issue

1869

29 September 1869. With Moult[1] examining present state of debt on
the estate, I find it as follows:

To Rev. J. Cross	£28,000
J. Heywood[2]	£50,000
Ld Macclesfield[3]	£75,000
Legal & Gen. Assurance	£75,000
	£228,000 interest £8,920

Family charges:

Ld Wilton[4]	£26,000
Hon. C. Stanley[5]	£24,000
Ly E. Talbot[6]	£20,000
Mr Penrhyn[7]	£13,000
Hon. H. Stanley[8]	£12,000
Miss L. Hornby[9]	£6,600
Miss Hornby	£3,000
	£104,600 interest £4,410

Due to bank	£88,000 interest £4,400 at 5%
Total	£420,600 total interest £17,730

Moult speaks strongly as to the necessity of reducing expenditure
on the Kirkdale, Bootle, and Bury estates. ... The total charge is
heavy, but I shall be content within the limit of £400,000 capital,

---

[1] Estate accountant at Knowsley, working on the estate for more than 50 years; d. 3
Feb. 1876; 'an upright hardworking man: I shall miss him in many ways' wrote Derby
(diary, 4 Feb. 1876); succ. in the post by his son.

[2] Manchester banker, and holder of the estate's account.

[3] Thomas, 6th E. (1811–96): no relation.

[4] Thomas, 2nd E. (1799–1882), succ. 1814; his 1st wife a dau. of 12th Lord Derby:
sportsman, dandy, musician.

[5] Col. Charles James Fox Stanley (1808–84), 3rd s. of 13th Lord Derby.

[6] Emma Charlotte (1835–1928), the diarist's only sister, who m. 1860, Sir W.P.M.
Chetwynd-Talbot (1817–98), her father's former priv. sec., bro. of 18th E. of Shrewsbury.

[7] Edward Penrhyn of East Sheen, Surrey, chmn of Surrey quarter sessions; s. of Lady
Charlotte Stanley, e.d. of 13th Lord Derby.

[8] Henry Thomas Stanley (1803–75), 2nd s. of 13th Lord Derby: black sheep of the
family.

[9] The 12th E.'s sister m. a Hornby, as did the 13th E.

and £16,000 interest, which latter is only 10% of the gross returns.

2 October 1869. Knowsley ... Ld D[10] in the gout, but the attack is not severe.

Ld D. tells me of an arrangement he has made, by which F.[11] is to become tenant of Witherslack,[12] with option of buying the estate at any time if he thinks fit. I see no objection to this, as the property is completely detached, and too far from Knowsley to have any residential advantage.

3 October 1869. Stayed at home, my mind being full of a speech which I have to deliver on Tuesday and which relates to the rather delicate subject of Trades Unions. I began to make notes for it ... but at the cost of a headache. It is strange that with 20 years of practice, I cannot get used to these constantly recurring performances so as to become indifferent to them. They annoy me, more or less, for two or three days.

... Ld D. being in bed with gout, I read prayers in the Chapel.

4 October 1869. Ld D. still in bed, and worse rather than better, but not in much pain, nor is serious mischief feared.

5 October 1869. Went into Liverpool, and attended a dinner of the co-operative workmen ... A few words were said by me, on my health being drunk, in favour of co-operative industry. Thence ... to the Concert Hall, where a large meeting: I addressed them,[13] speaking more than half an hour, on trades unions and co-operation. Graves and Rathbone were both present and spoke also. What I said was

---

[10] Edward Stanley, 14th E. of Derby (1799–69), premier 1852, 1858–9, 1866–8; diarist's father.

[11] Frederick Stanley, 16th E. of Derby (1841–1908); diarist's heir and only brother; army career 1858–65; M.P. (Cons) Preston 1865–8, Lancs. N. 1868–85, Blackpool 1885–6; m. Lady Constance Villiers, Clarendon's dau., 1864; jun. office 1868, fin. sec. to war office 1874–7, fin. sec. to treasury 1877–8; sec. for war, 1878–80 (entering cabinet on brother's resignation), col. sec. 1885–6, pres. of board of trade 1886; cr. Baron Stanley of Preston, 1886; gov.-gen. of Canada 1886–93; while there, hoped for India, in diarist's view unwisely; in youth liable to depression, in age notably inattentive to business; succ. diarist as E., 1893; known as Col. Stanley, but in diaries as F.; see *Gov. Passion*, 257–8; *Later Diaries* 10–14, 72; *Crawford Papers*, 110.

[12] In Westmorland, 7m s.w. of Kendal.

[13] *T,* 5 Oct. 1869, 7f; 6 Oct 1869, 10 c. Derby had visited an ironworks (4 Oct.) erected by a building firm, many of whose shareholders were employees. To celebrate its completion, he presided at a workingmen's banquet (5 Oct.), then inaugurated the Operatives Trades Hall, intended to draw trade unionism from the pub. He commended unions as the only way workers 'can meet their employers on terms of equality'; condemned 'the indiscriminate outcry against them'; lauded the idea that workers 'shall to some extend share in the profit', and saw in co-operative production 'the best, the surest remedy' for industrial conflict; with 'nothing asked from the State except neutrality and fair play'. Samuel R. Graves (d. Jan. 1873), M.P. (Cons.) Liverpool 1865–73, and William Rathbone (1819–1902), M.P. (Lib.) Liverpool 1868–70, were leading local figures.

patiently listened to and in general well received. The audience were mostly, though not exclusively, working class.

6 October 1869. Ld D. still suffering a good deal.

7 October 1869. London by 9 a.m. train ... Some uneasiness is felt as to the state of French politics ... first, inasmuch as England can never expect to have a warmer friend or more faithful ally than she has had for the last 20 years, in Napoleon: and next because a violent republican outbreak cannot fail, if it occurs, to create a corresponding feeling here.

11 October 1869. London ... found a letter and a telegram, giving a bad account of Ld D. and requesting me to come down ... Gorst[14] has given him large quantities of opium to relieve the pain, and caused thereby a state of stupor, and then excessive weakness, and it is from this last symptom that the danger arises.

... Reached K. soon after 8. My father was lying in a state of partial unconsciousness, just able to answer the questions put to him by Miller,[15] but immediately relapsing into stupor...

About 11 ... Miller thought and said that the end was not far off; and my mother, brother, sister, and I, successively took leave of him, as we thought, kissing his forehead, as he lay breathing but insensible: a more painful and touching scene I never went through, and trust I never may again.

12 October 1869. The day has been one of anxiety, suspense, and agitation. ... His ordinary state is that of stupor ... from which he can be roused for a moment but falls back into it.

14 October 1869. I now despair, which as yet I have not absolutely done.

15 October 1869. I asked him how he was feeling: he answered with a good deal of energy, 'Bored to the utmost power of extinction.'

23 October 1869.[16] My brother, W.K. Hopwood,[17] and I, met at 11 to consider and discuss arrangements for the funeral to be settled, in accordance with my father's often-repeated wish, that it should be strictly private.[18]

[14] Local doctor.
[15] Specialist.
[16] Derby died peacefully at 6.55 a.m.
[17] Not traced under these initials. The Hopwoods of Hopwood Hall, Lancs., had intermarried with the Stanleys; Canon F.G. Hopwood was successively incumbent of Knowsley and Rector of Winwick, another Lancs. parish, both livings in the late Derby's gift: and four Hopwoods, including Rev. W. Hopwood, were in the family party following the hearse.
[18] Cf. *T*, 25 Oct. 1869, 8d, for the diarist's letter to Sefton, referring to his father's written instructions for a strictly private burial in Knowsley parish church, built by the deceased, and equipped by him with a family tomb designed for 24 coffins. (His predecessors since 1572 had been buried in Ormskirk parish church). At the funeral, a servant walked ahead of the hearse bearing Derby's coronet on a velvet cushion. The

25 October 1869. Walk with F. ... He volunteers to tell me, what I could not have asked him, that having the option between the possession of the Irish estate[19] and a sum of £125,000 (which I was aware of) he has decided for the money. I think in his own interest he is right, but where I am to find £125,000 in addition to existing debts is not easy to see. Probably however he will be content to draw the interest and let the principal lie. He talks sensibly about matters here, and says that the heads under which reduction ought to be made are the stables, the shooting, and perhaps the gardens.

26 October 1869. W.H.[20] called, and asked ... whether I meant to continue him in his office of comptroller? ... If invested with proper control over the servants, and charged with the exclusive payment of tradesmen's bills, he had no doubt he could make reductions to the extent of £3,000 or even £4,000 a year, and yet have the service as well performed as it now is.

In *Times*[21] of today, an article on my father's political life, and another on mine, giving me the very sensible advice to refuse the Conservative leadership in the Lords (which has never been offered) and assume a neutral position for the time, waiting events. This is what I shall most likely do.

27 October 1869. Layard[22] is announced as the new minister at Madrid: a questionable choice, since he is wholly wanting in discretion and tact ... Ld Clarendon[23] does not appear to make any secret of the fact that this appointment has been extorted from him by parliamentary pressure. Gladstone wants the place formerly held by Layard for Ayrton.[24]

... Talk with Moult in the office: settled with him that my private

congregation was restricted to tenants, servants, and family; the absent Disraeli sent a tribute. At the burial, the diarist was seen to be greatly distressed.

[19] For details of the Irish estate, which the deceased had recently wished to sell, see *Stanley Journals*, 343 (8 and 28 Sept. 1869). The Witherslack estate was made over to F. (diary 10 Nov. 1869): 'It is pleasant to see how keen his enjoyment; and not without reason, for the place is unusually picturesque, and it is the first land he has ever owned.'

[20] Sir William Wyndham Hornby (1812–99), K.C.B., J.P., D.L. Middx and Lancs.; admiral, ret. 1864; commr of prisons 1877; the 13th Lord Derby's wife was Hornby's father's sister.

[21] *T*, 25 Oct., 7e, gave a biographical sketch of the deceased, while a leader (6d) asserted that he was 'not a great man'. *T*, 26 Oct., 8c, had another disparaging leader on the late E.; another leader (8d) argued that the diarist was 'not a Conservative in any reasonable sense of the term'.

[22] (Sir) A.H. Layard (1817–94), author of *Nineveh and its Remains* (1848–9); M.P. (Lib.) 1852–7, 1860–8; under-sec. for foreign affairs 1861–6; 1st commr of works 1868–9; min. at Madrid 1869–77; amb. at Constantinople 1877–80.

[23] George William Frederick Villiers, 4th E. of Clarendon (1800–70); succ. his uncle in title, 1838; foreign sec. 1855–8, 1865–6, 1868–70, dying in office.

[24] A.S. Ayrton (1816–86), M.P. (Lib.) Tower Hamlets 1857–74; Bombay lawyer to *c.* 1850; parl. sec. to treasury, 1868–Nov. 1869; 1st commr of works 1869–73; judge advocate-gen. 1873–4.

allowance, or spending money, shall be at the rate of £4,000 a year: my grandfather allowed himself £6,000, and my father £5,000.

30 October 1869. Hornby was with me. I decided to confirm him permanently in his comptrollership. My reasons are (1) I feel unfit for the duty of minute supervision over servants and it is hardly the duty of a man in my position; (2) he will save his salary in stopping waste and extravagance, many times over; (3) he has no private means, and I should have at any rate to pay him two-thirds of his salary as a retiring pension. He undertakes, while keeping things in good order, and without undue narrowness, to manage house, stables, gardens, park, and game, for £20,000 a year. What the cost hitherto has been I do not know and do not wish to enquire, but probably half as much again. If I can reduce estate expenditure in the same proportion, there will really be means available for a large reduction of debt.

31 October 1869. Lowe[25] very full of a plan for taking life insurance into the hands of the State, whether by buying out existing offices or in competition with them is not clear.

1 November 1869. Agreed with Latter that he should continue secretary and librarian to me, as he was to my father: his salary is £240 a year. Set him at once to work on sorting and arranging a mass of old letters, found in Ld Derby's room. Talk with Hornby as to reduction of the household etc. I want, for this as for other departments, a regular estimate framed, which shall in some approximate degree represent the anticipated outlay of the year. ... Talk also as to reducing the excessive number of red deer, and doing away with some unnecessary roads. ... I have not as yet an idea what my income really is.

2 November 1869. Long conversation with Moult. ... The expenditure for 1868 ... is arranged thus:

	£
Interest of debt, taxes, family charges	36,000
Household, gardens, game, stables, park	36,000
Expenditure on estate, including agents	71,000
Other outlays[26]	18,000
	161,000

[25] Robert Lowe, 1st Vt Sherbrooke (1811–92), chanc. of the exchequer 1868–73; home sec. 1873–4; cr. vt 1880.

[26] His father's charities for 1868 came to £3,600, excluding those arising from the large Bury estate, the largest item being £1,000 for a church. Derby, the heir, proposed to fix his Lancashire and estate charities at £4,000 p.a., excluding London charities payable from his private purse. In 1868, Derby paid pensions of £680 to retired servants and labourers, and £300 to Dr Gorst for attending the poor gratis (diary, 8 and 11 Nov. 1869). For the late premier's efforts to see that want never went unrelieved in his London parish, see *T,* 1 Nov. 1869, 5e.

My estimate for 1870 is not easy to frame with certainty, but the deductions for debt, taxes, and family charges fall little short of £50,000. If I can reduce the household to £25,000 and the estate outlay, under all heads, to £45,000, I shall be able to lay by £30,000, after allowing £20,000 for unclassed outlay, including my own allowance. But to do this will not be the work of a day.

3 November 1869. In 1870 rental will be £170,000, deductions for debt and other charges £50,000. In 1880 rental ought to be £190,000, deductions reduced to £38,000, by the paying off of debt to the amount of £300,000. In 1890, whoever lives to see it, rental ought to be £210,000,[27] deductions reduced probably to £12–£15,000.

... Talk with W.H.[28] about selling surplus fruit from the gardens when the house is supplied. We have the means of producing a great deal more than we require. I see no objection to it.

... Talk with Hale[29] about building new cottages in the village ... in order not to lessen the effect of the economical injunctions which I have been giving, I arrange that they shall be paid for out of my private purse, and not from the estate fund.

4 November 1869. Received a letter from Statter[30] of Bury.... I foresee trouble in that quarter, as he has told Hale very fairly that he does not see his way to make the reductions which are required – in other words, he does not choose to do it. He defeated my father in a similar dispute, and may very possibly beat me. He has undoubtedly the excuse that while spending, as I must think, lavishly on the estate, he has increased the rental to an enormous extent. But I don't want an increased rental, and I do want to be out of debt.

5 November 1869. Write ... to Skelmersdale,[31] declining to succeed my father as 'patron' of the 'National Union of Conservative Assocns.' ...

6 November 1869. Talk with Hornby ... especially of the great breeding establishment kept up here, at a heavy loss, and which I shall at once

[27] In fact it was £243,716 p.a. (*Later Diaries*, 6).
[28] W. Hornby.
[29] Chief agent for the W. Lancs. estates; seen by Derby as too lax with tenants.
[30] Thomas Statter (1816–91), elder s. of Robert Statter, agent to E. of Derby; steward of Derby estates in Bury, Pilkington, Cheetham, Salford, Manchester, and Colne, 1841–91; laid out Bootle, planned Bury; bred pointers, grew orchids on a large scale, and was chairman of a gas co.; collected art treasures at Stand Hall, his home near Manchester; seen by Derby as being too hard on tenants and thereby jeopardizing the Derby interest politically.
[31] Edward Bootle-Wilbraham, second Baron Skelmersdale (1837–98); succ. grandfather 1853; held household office in Cons. ministries 1866–98; cr. E. of Lathom, 1880; m. Clarendon's 2nd dau., 1860; freemason. The diarist's mother was his aunt. The diarist told Carnarvon, when speaking of the Conservatives as a party shortly after his father's death. 'I shall certainly not tie myself to that dog's tail.' (Sir Arthur Hardinge, *The Life of Henry Howard Molyneux Herbert Fourth Earl of Carnarvon 1831–1890*, iii 46.)

get rid of: (it costs £1,300 a year, and takes up large parts of the park): but I am sorry for old Jim Forshaw, who was in charge of it, and served my father over 40 years. He has a pension of £50 left him by will ...[32] Still, I have no choice, for to go on with a business which I neither understand nor care about, would be madness.

Plan of substituting in the old garden leading to the kitchen garden, American plants, such as azaleas and choice kinds of rhododendron, for the bedding plants now there. The saving of labour will be immense, and the appearance not worse – perhaps better.

... Bright[33] and Gladstone[34] have been on a visit to The Grove[35] ... Bright seems to have taken the opportunity of enlarging on the necessity of breaking down overgrown fortunes, instancing especially, and by name, that of Ld Westminster,[36] and mine. This is at least fair warning, but John Bright is not the cabinet.

13 November 1869. London by 9.15 train.

17 November 1869. Walk, in a thick white fog, round the Regent's Park, for exercise. This is not precisely a cheerful occupation, but I always have thought and I do think that my poor father shortened his life by not taking any exercise when in London.

18 November 1869. Cairns[37] called ... He had decided to give up the lead of the Conservative party in the House of Lords for three reasons. (1) Because as an ex-chancellor he considered that his first duty was to sit and hear appeals, and this he could not do while retaining the lead, which occupied all his time. (2) Because in his opinion a lay peer and one of old standing or connection would be fitter for the post than a lawyer newly ennobled. (3) Because it was not convenient that that position should be held by the individual who if ever his party returned to power, must be Chancellor, and who in that capacity could not lead. Those were his ostensible grounds: but it was impossible not to see that dislike of the position had more to do with his retirement than any of these. He then discussed with me the expediency of my putting myself forward for the office. ... I declined any positive expression of opinion, but let it be clearly seen that I did not wish to be so brought into the thick of the fight.

[32] His pension was raised to £80 p.a. plus a house, and he was allowed to rent some paddocks in which to raise sheep for the Liverpool market.

[33] John Bright (1811–89), radical; president of board of trade, 1868–70, resigning on health grounds.

[34] William Ewart Gladstone (1809–98), premier 1868–74, 1880–85, 1886, 1892–4.

[35] Clarendon's house, Herts.

[36] Hugh Lupus Grosvenor, 3rd M. of Westminster (1825–99); succ. father, Oct. 1869; cr. duke, 1874.

[37] Hugh McCalmont Cairns, 1st E. Cairns (1819–85), lord chancellor 1868, 1874–80; cr. baron 1867, earl 1878.

22 November 1869. Called on Disraeli,[38] and much talk: he said nothing about what had passed between Cairns, Malmesbury,[39] and myself, though no doubt well aware of it: but discussed the state of Ireland. Thought the Queen both alarmed and angry at the open preaching of insurrection which has been going on for some time: said Ld Strathnairn[40] whom he had lately met, expected an outbreak or at least local disturbances, during the winter: believed nothing was settled as to the land bill: had met various people connected with the cabinet (Calcraft[41] being one) who seemed low and unhappy: they held the language that the difficulties of the Church bill were nothing compared to those which surround an attempt to deal with the land.

23 November 1869. Tait,[42] Archbishop of Canterbury, has been seized with an epileptic fit, ending in paralysis, and if he survives, which is doubtful, will be disabled from duty.

Assuming an increase of Knowsley rental to the extent of £2,000 yearly, I ought to be able to save as below:

1870–75	£30,000 p.a.	£150,000
1875–80	£40,000 p.a.	£200,000
1880–90	£50,000 p.a.	£250,000
1885–90	£60,000 p.a.	£300,000

Total in 20 years, if I live so long, £900,000. Which will clear the debt, and leave me with £200,000 in hand.[43] If I last the next 5 years, 1890–95, that would produce savings of £400,000 ... with which some great work of public usefulness or charity might be undertaken. But I must clear the estate first!

25 November 1869. Ld A. Loftus[44] called yesterday: he talked, as is his habit, in a pompous and tedious style ... Present danger of war was very slight. Bismarck friendly to England, but asks of what use are we? We should probably not fight even to defend Belgium, and how can we then expect to play a part in continental politics?

27 November 1869. Rather annoyed by an application from some

[38] Benjamin Disraeli (1804–81), premier 1868, 1874–80; cr. 1st E. of Beaconsfield, Aug. 1876.

[39] James Howard Harris, 3rd E. of Malmesbury (1807–89), foreign sec. 1852, 1858–9, lord privy seal 1866–8, 1874–Aug. 1876.

[40] Sir Hugh Rose, 1st Baron Strathnairn (1801–85), c.-in-c. Ireland 1865–70; Indian mutiny hero; cr. baron 1866, field-marshal 1877.

[41] Henry George Calcraft (1836–96), civil servant; priv. sec. to presidents of the board of trade, 1859–74; Mr Pinto in Disraeli's *Lothair* (1870).

[42] A.C. Tait (1811–82), archbishop 1869–82.

[43] By 1887 he had saved £700,000, as well as repaying half a million of debt (*Later Diaries*, 7–8).

[44] Lord Augustus Loftus (1817–1904), s. of 2nd M. of Ely; diplomatist, 1837–79; amb. to Russia, 1871–9; gov. of New South Wales, 1879–85; disliked by diarist also because of his Court connections through Jane, Dowager Lady Ely.

teetotallers at Bury for land to build a Temperance Hall on, which it appears Statter, in my father's time, refused, on no other ground that that he does not like the views, political and social, of the promoters. They appeal to me. I don't like to throw over an agent, or weaken his authority, but to refuse to allow a place of meeting to these gentlemen, merely because one does not agree with their ideas as to diet, is to me a rather startling assertion of power.

29 November 1869. Lowe appears confident that he shall be able to make some considerable reduction of taxes: and in addition to his scheme for enlarging the system of government insurances, is meditating one for making the State the national banker, by a vast extension of the post office savings banks, or some analogous machinery. ... He talked to my informant of this scheme as calculated to effect a large reduction of debt: but in what manner was not made clear.

15 December 1869. Lawrence[45] came. ... I directed him to draw for me a provisional will. It is very simple: £1,000 to my sister, £500 to Smith,[46] all the rest to my brother. If I live, other legacies will be added, but the above is enough, and will secure the personal property at Knowsley from dispersion.

21 December 1869.[47] To Hughenden,[48] where only D. and Ly. B.[49]

22 December 1869. Walk, morning and afternoon.

---

[45] W. Lawrence, family solicitor.

[46] Manservant.

[47] Disraeli's birthday.

[48] For details, cf. *Stanley Journals*, 346–7. For the impending vacancy in the Cons. leadership in the Lords, caused by Cairn's departure, see M and B, v 113; Disraeli had already written (12 Dec. 1869) that Derby could not be expected to take the post.

[49] Mary Anne Disraeli (1789?–15 Dec. 1872); cr. Viscountess Beaconsfield, Nov. 1868.

1870

1 January 1870. I begin a new year, with new duties and interests: living in London: my mother[1] remaining in this house[2] till Easter, when she sets up her own establishment in Cromwell Road. Estate and domestic business occupies more of my time than formerly, when of the latter I had none, and was only a looker-on as to the former, though to some extent allowed and encouraged to interfere.

In health I am well, though with a tendency to gout that requires some degree of care and prudence. In regard to politics my present position is that of a neutral, singularly free from pledges or ties. My inclination is rather to support than to oppose the government of the day, be it what it may, provided that those who compose it abstain from very violent or extreme measures.

The political state is: in Europe, all quiet internationally, and no present fear or expectation of war: the internal politics of France confused, and a strong republican feeling appears to have grown up there, but is nearly powerless from the disunion of its leaders: all depends on the Emperor: with decision and prudence he may still be master of the situation: of armed insurrection against his government there appears little prospect. In Germany, Russia, and Turkey, nothing excites special interest, except the late opening of the Suez Canal,[3] and the chronic dispute between the Viceroy of Egypt and the Porte, which for the moment diplomacy has succeeded in patching up. The Americans have revived the Alabama claims, in a tone sufficiently unpleasant: but they have disbanded their army and reduced their navy to the lowest point, indicating that however they may talk, they do not mean mischief.

Ireland remains as disturbed and excited as ever...

3 January 1870. Made up my private accounts for the last year: the general result is as follows: Lynn[4] has cost me £260: £500 ... a gift: £635 I have given to charities on public objects of various kinds: my whole personal expenditure is represented by £3,607. This is more than in any former year...

My private income ... will henceforth be £4,000, besides nearly

---

[1] Emma, Lady Derby (d. 26 Apr. 1876), d. of 1st Lord Skelmersdale; m. diarist's father, 1825.
[2] St James's Square.
[3] Opened 16 Nov. 1869.
[4] King's Lynn, the diarist's constituency 1848–69.

£500 from investments: of this I hope to lay by £2,000, leaving £2,400 to be divided between optional outlay and charitable claims. The latter head, however, will not include charities ... paid in Lancashire, and which are expected from me as a large landowner. For these I have allotted a separate sum of £4000.

... Called on Disraeli, whom found in the gout, on a sofa, wrapped up in a strange fashion, suffering some pain, but cheerful. He had no news.

10 January 1870. Ly Delawarr[5] died last night, in her 75th year ... Ly Salisbury[6] has in less than two years lost father,[7] mother, husband,[8] and sister[9] – all except the last, it must be said, in full age.[10] Ly D ... was induced, not wisely, to obtain from the personal friendship of the Queen a title for her second son,[11] and has left two peerages scantily endowed, instead of one, which would have been abundantly wealthy.

... Disraeli came to see me, and talked of France. He said the Rothschilds whom he had been visiting were now very confident that things would go smoothly; they thought the Emperor[12] had out-manoeuvred the Orleanists by adopting a constitutional system, and might look forward with confidence to the future of his son. He (D.) did not altogether agree, but thought the recent acts of the Emperor were evidences of failing energy rather than of prudence...

11 January 1870. I omitted yesterday to note a curious observation of Baron Rothschild[13] to Disraeli. He told him that whatever might be the condition of the Spanish government as regards money matters it could always raise funds (though at a high rate) in England. This is certainly not the result of the peculiar honesty of Spanish administration, but of a vague tradition of the ancient wealth of Spain...

[5] Elizabeth Sackville, d. of 3rd D. of Dorset; m. 5th E. De La Warr, 1813; cr. Baroness Buckhurst, 1864; m. of diarist's future wife.

[6] Mary Catherine née West (1824–1900), 2nd d. of 5th E. De La Warr; 2nd wife (1847) of James Gascoyne-Cecil, 2nd M. of Salisbury; widowed 12 Apr. 1868; m. diarist 5 July 1870; confidante of Wellington.

[7] George John West (from 1843 Sackville-West), 5th E. De La Warr (1791–23 Feb. 1869); father of diarist's future wife.

[8] James Cecil (from 1821 Gascoyne-Cecil), 2nd M. of Salisbury (1791–12 April 1868); succ. 1823, lord privy seal 1852, lord president of the council 1858–9; father of premier, and father-in-law of diarist wife; leading freemason.

[9] Arabella Diana (m. Sir A. Bannermann Bt) d. 10 Feb. 1869.

[10] Soon followed by the suicide of her bro., the 6th E. De La Warr, who d. unm. 23 Apr. 1873.

[11] Reginald Sackville-West (Sackville from 1871), 7th E. De La Warr (1817–96), briefly Baron Buckhurst (1870–3) between his mother's and his bro.'s death, the titles thereafter being united.

[12] Napoleon III.

[13] Baron Lionel Nathan de Rothschild (1808–79), M.P. City of London (Lib.) 1847–68, 1869–74.

13 January 1870. Bernstorff[14] called, he told me little or nothing, except that the fear of war has entirely disappeared. In 1867 it was the fashion among many people to sneer at the expedients by which diplomatists were trying (successfully as it proved) to prevent the then imminent quarrel between France & Prussia from breaking out into actual war. We said then 'In such cases to gain time is to gain everything: let 2 or 3 years pass, the existing irritation will have subsided, and people will be thinking of something else.' The result has so far justified that way of looking at the matter.

26 January 1870. A friendly, but singular letter from the Bishop of Gloucester and Bristol,[15] in which he expresses his hope that I shall assume the lead of the conservative party in the Lords, and his intention to give me all the support in his power.

Holwood[16] ... found Ly S[17] in a painful state of nervous agitation and illness, the too evident result of her long-protracted anxiety about Ly Delawarr. There are also family quarrels between the brothers, not serious, but disagreeable.

27 January 1870. Called on Disraeli: the latter full of the movement now going on in favour of systematic emigration and closer relations with the colonies; but, like most people, not seeing his way very clearly to what is to be done.

3 February 1870. Holwood ... Family differences continue ... There is something not quite consistent with sanity in the continual and ceaseless quarrels which arise in this family:[18] Ly S is happily clear of these.

7 February 1870. Dined with Lord Cairns and the Conservative peers at St James's Hotel: Salisbury[19] and Carnarvon[20] present, which was not expected. The speech was read and commented upon. Cairns

[14] N. German ambassador.

[15] Dr C.J. Ellicott (1819–1905), bishop of Gloucester 1863–1905.

[16] Near Bromley, Kent.

[17] Lady Salisbury, diarist's future wife.

[18] Of the offspring of the 5th E. De La Warr, the eldest, Lord Cantelupe (1814–50) d. unm. His brother, the 6th E., committed suicide, 1873. The next brother, the 7th E., produced an heir (who twice divorced). the 4th bro., Mortimer, 1st Lord Sackville, broke off all relations with his family, and sacked all his servants for, as he thought, trying to poison him. The 5th bro., Lionel 2nd Lord Sackville, sometime minister to Washington, never m., but kept a mistress, Pepita, d. of a Malaga barber, and their children, in a villa near Biarritz (see V. Sackville-West, *Pepita*); their dau. m. his nephew, 3rd Lord Sackville. Lady Derby suffered, by the 1870s, from chronic depression. Her sister, Elizabeth, m. 9th D. of Bedford, who shot himself (1891).

[19] Robert Cecil, 3rd M. of Salisbury (1830–1903); succ. 1868; p.m. 1885–6, 1886–92, 1895–1902.

[20] Henry Herbert, 4th E. of Carnarvon (1831–90); succ. 1849; col. sec. 1866–7, 1874–8, lord-lt of Ireland 1885–6, resigning in each case.

explained his reasons for wishing to withdraw from the leadership ...
He held out no hope of reconsidering his decision ... Nothing passed
as to the choice of a successor...

9 February 1870. Saw Disraeli, who well satisfied with the opening in
both Houses: he assured me that he had had little previous concert
with Cairns, which if accurate is singular, for he and Ld C. went over
exactly the same ground, and dealt with their subject in precisely the
same way. He says the impression is in H.C. that Bright's career as a
politician is ended, though he may recover from his present illness:[21]
he is still in London, unable to be moved or to see anyone. Lord
Clarendon lies in the gout, Gladstone is out of health, and there is
much speculation as to the latter breaking down.

... Heard in detail, from secret intelligence, the provisions of the
Irish land bill: but it will be public so shortly that there is no need to
note them for recollection.

10 February 1870. Carnarvon asked to speak to me, and we came
home together, he sitting here nearly an hour, going through the
colonial question, which he wants to raise on Monday next. He is
evidently bent on renewing our political and social relations, which
have been interrupted since 1867.

... Much talk in society about Bright's illness: it is not expected that
he will recover so as to be fit for business; and the question is who will
replace him as leader of the radical or democratic section? Some, of
conservative views, regret his break-down, thinking that he had gone
as far as he was likely to go, and would have been useful in repressing
the more ardent democrats of a later generation. Others believe, as I
do, that his dislike of the landed aristocracy was too inveterate to be
cured, or even softened, by office, and that as he was in the beginning,
so he would have remained to the end. He is respected for consistency
and personal disinterestedness: but his arrogant and domineering
temper prevents his having friends.

13 February 1870. Cairns came to me, and after some preliminary talk,
told me that the party was nearly unanimous in wishing to have me
for a leader[22] and that an offer would soon be made to me to accept
the post on my own terms. He dwelt a good deal on this, and left me
rather disturbed in mind.

... Met Calcraft, who gave me what I suppose is the official version
of Bright's illness: saying that he had been a long while out of health,
harassed with business, but would give himself no rest: that on the first
symptoms of his old complaint – some affection of the brain – returning,

---

[21] See K. Robbins, *John Bright* (1979), 208–10. Cf. T, 9 Feb. 1870, 9e, for the first news
of Bright's indisposition.
[22] *Vice* Cairns.

he became seriously alarmed about his condition, and put himself into the hands of the doctors: and that he will be at his post again in six weeks or two months.

In the papers, an odd story of a Mr Williams[23] of Caerphilly having left to Lord Bute,[24] with whom he is in no way connected by family, an estate of £3,000–£4,000 a year, and £200,000 in money. Lord Bute has a rental of about £150,000 of his own, and increasing.[25]

Lady Airlie[26] last night told me, what I was glad to hear, that the Carlisle property, which had been deeply dipped by the extravagance of the last possessor but one,[27] has been so put into order that when young Howard[28] (her brother-in-law) comes to it, the rental will be £60,000 a year,[29] and the encumbrances very few.

14 February 1870. In the Lords, debate on colonial policy,[30] raised by Carnarvon: he spoke fairly well, understanding his subject, and generally moderate in tone: but to my mind making the mistake of putting too large a superstructure on a very small foundation, and alleging against the colonial office more than he succeeded in proving. He also ended by a rather declamatory denunciation of a money-saving policy – which to me seemed unnecessary and imprudent. Granville[31] answered in a style which seems peculiar to him, and is not easily described: easy and conversational, never eloquent, sensible, and clear, but as it appeared to me, rather desultory, wanting method. (N.B. he never makes a note.) ... I made a short remark,[32] rather with a view to try what the room is like for speaking in than with any other object.

... Letter from Clark,[33] of Trinity, my old private tutor, who has lately renounced orders and returned to the status of a layman, enclosing

[23] W.E. Williams of Twyllypant House, Caerphilly, bachelor, had often expressed admiration for the benefits conferred on Cardiff by the Butes, whom he scarcely knew: T, 15 Feb. 1870, 8e.

[24] John Patrick Crichton-Stuart, 3rd M. of Bute (1847–1900), succ. 1848; Disraeli's Lothair.

[25] Given in *Bateman* as £151,305 p.a.

[26] Henrietta Blanche (b. 1830), d. of 2nd Lord Stanley of Alderley; m. 1851 5th E. of Airlie (1826–81).

[27] George Howard, 6th E. of Carlisle (1773–1848). The 7th E. (1802–64), the whig politician, died unm. and was succ. by his unm. bro., the 8th E. (1808–89), a Yorkshire rector.

[28] George James Howard, 9th E., b. 1843, succ. 1889; nephew of 8th E.

[29] Given in *Bateman* as £49,601.

[30] *H*, vol. 199 (1870), cols 193–233. Parliament reassembled, 8 Feb. 1870.

[31] Granville George Leveson-Gower, 2nd E. Granville (1815–91); succ. 1846; col. sec. 1868–70, for. sec. 1870–74, 1880–85, col. sec. 1886; Lib. leader in Lords.

[32] Derby, in his first Lords speech, stressed that recent defence cuts did not diminish Britain's responsibilities for imperial defence; and warned that U.K. involvement in European conflict could lead the colonies to seek independence and neutrality (*H*, vol. 199, cols 228–30).

[33] William George Clark (1821–78), Shakespeare scholar.

a pamphlet[34] in which he proposes his scheme of a church without articles of faith or tests, to continue in connection with the state. I answer this, expressing doubt whether such a plan would succeed in England, and intimating my belief that we shall come instead to the voluntary system,[35] though it may be a long while first.

16 February 1870. The land bill[36] is everywhere talked about ... The landlords appear on the whole inclined to think that matters might have been worse: and everybody agreed that there would be danger in putting off legislation to another year ... The provision most objected to, and as I think with reason, is that which gives to an evicted tenant, apart from all question of eviction for improvements, damages to the extent, in certain possible cases, of 7 years rent. This is in effect to make the tenant an owner to the value of one-third of the land. It is not easy to see by what arguments a transfer of property of this nature is to be justified.

17 February 1870. Saw Disraeli, and talk with him on the land bill. Saw also Colville,[37] who tells me that a meeting of Conservative peers is to be held tomorrow, and that the choice will fall on me without a dissentient voice.

... Forster[38] brought in his education bill, which appears moderate in character, and likely to be well received. He does not supersede existing schools, but supplies machinery to provide them where they are wanting. ... He retains the denominational system, but with a stringent conscience clause. This is on the whole, I believe, about as fair a solution of the difficulty as can be found, and Forster's personal popularity will help to pass the bill.

19 February 1870. To Grosvenor Gate: met Cairns and Hardy[39] there with D. and discussed the land bill at considerable length. It is to my mind objectionable in various respects: but the landlords are thoroughly alarmed at the height to which agrarian outrages have reached, they

[34] *The Present Dangers of the Church of England* (1870).
[35] Cf. *Later Diaries*, 28, 84, for his willingness to grant Scottish and Irish disestablishment in the 1880s. For his hostility to the Irish Church before disestablishment, see especially *Stanley Diaries*, 372 n. 28.
[36] Irish Land Act, 1870.
[37] Charles Colville, 1st Vt Colville of Culross (1818–1903); Scottish rep. peer 1852–85; mainly court career; cr. U.K. baron 1885, vt 1902.
[38] W.E. Forster (1818–86), M.P. (Lib.) 1861–86; junior office 1865–6; as vice-pres. of council, carried 1870 Education Act; conceded H. of C. leadership to Hartington, 1875; chief sec. for Ireland. 1880–2.
[39] Gathorne Gathorne-Hardy, 1st E. of Cranbrook (1814–1906), Cons. minister; M.P. 1856–78, when cr. peer; junior office 1858–9, pres. of poor law board 1866–7, home sec. 1867–8; war minister 1874–8, India Office 1878–80; lord pres. of council 1885–6, 1886–92; raised to earl, 1892; strong churchman, strong debater, and strong candidate to succeed Disraeli.

expected a more stringent and revolutionary proposal, and on the whole seem disposed to say, 'It might be worse'. In fact the power of eviction which the bill limits is one which few land-owners are able to exercise, in the actual state of popular feeling, and considering the prevalence of assassination on the most trifling pretexts.

... On coming home found Chelmsford[40] and the D. of Richmond[41] waiting for me. They came to report that the meeting[42] of conservative peers held today at the Carlton had been unanimous in choosing me for their leader, Salisbury strongly recommending that course: that there had been no dissentient voice, the D. of Northumberland[43] alone declaring that he would recognise no leader: but not expressing preference for anyone else. There was scarcely any discussion. Those present were about sixty in number: but the whole party had been communicated with. Lord Ellenborough,[44] I heard, was especially zealous in my favour.

I was prepared for this communication, but asked 24 hours for consideration.

20 February 1870. Up early, turning over in my mind[45] the offer of yesterday: but I was not, and am not, in any way excited or anxious about it.

Reasons against accepting I am new to the house. My voice is weak, and hardly equal to the effort of a long speech in that large room. I have not the offhand readiness of a practised debater, and speaking is disagreeable to me. My habit of mind is not that of a partisan, and when I have made party speeches they have generally been failures. I have much private business which I ought not to neglect. By accepting the leadership of one political party, I lose all hold over members of the other, many of whom now look to me. Lastly, the conservative

[40] (Sir) Frederick Thesiger, 1st Baron Chelmsford (1794–1878), Cons. M.P. 1840–58; sol.-gen. and kt 1844; att.-gen. 1845–6, 1852; lord chanc. 1858–9, 1866–Feb. 1868; replaced by Cairns on Disraeli taking office, Feb. 1868, much to his chagrin.

[41] Charles Henry Gordon-Lennox, 6th D. of Richmond (1818–1903); Cons. M.P. 1841–60; succ. 1860; pres. of poor law board 1859; pres. of board of trade 1867–8; lord pres. 1874–80; 1st sec. of state for Scotland 1885–6.

[42] *T,* 21 Feb. 1870, 9d, for the meeting of Tory peers in the Carlton Club library, Sat. 19 Feb., with Cairns, who had resigned the post, in the chair. The resolution, moved by Richmond and seconded by Salisbury, was carried unanimously. Cairns, who had come over from the South of France for the meeting of parliament, then returned to Mentone, 'where he remains till Easter', despite having led the House in the 1869 session.

[43] Algernon George Percy, 8th D. of Northumberland (1810–99); succ. father Aug. 1867; junior office 1858–9, lord privy seal (in cabinet) 1878–80; freemason, antiquary, scientist, Irvingite (m. dau. of Henry Drummond, Irvingite leader).

[44] Edward Law, 1st E. of Ellenborough (1790–1871); succ. as 2nd baron 1818 and cr. earl 1844; pres. of board of control 1828–30, 1834–5, 1841, and Mar.–June 1858 (resigned); Peel's 1st lord of the admiralty, 1846; gov.-gen. of India, 1841–6.

[45] For similar introspection, see *Stanley Diaries,* 140, 156–8.

party is in a minority which seems likely to be permanent.

Reasons for accepting The offer is unanimous, it comes unsought, and the acceptance of it gives me a political position which is conspicuous and important, and which hardly any change of parties can take away, unless by my own choice. The labour is not excessive, nor the hours trying to health, as in the H. of C. The post has been held by men who, like Lord Aberdeen,[46] were very indifferent speakers. Lord Granville is no orator, yet he gets through his work fairly. To refuse is to give offence to, or at least cause disappointment among, a large body of men now my friends, who will think themselves slighted, and this without the countervailing advantage of making friends on the other side, unless I were to join the radicals, which I am not disposed to do. What is the alternative? A seat on the cross-benches, which is insignificance: the position of a private member of the conservative party: or a junction with the Liberals, for which I am not prepared. The fact that a conservative government is not likely to be formed is to my mind a recommendation rather than otherwise, for the labour, anxiety, and worry of office are to me thoroughly distasteful. A few years ago, my opinions were wide apart from those of conservatives in general: but the questions on which we differed have been disposed of, and with the new school of radicalism I have no sympathy. I can be of use in discouraging opposition to measures which are either useful or inevitable: and perhaps in checking hasty legislation, of which we are likely to have a good deal. I have the hearty support of Cairns and Salisbury, and also, I believe, of Carnarvon. Nor is it wholly indifferent to me that by a fate which has never occurred to any other man in English politics, I replace my father in the position which he occupied without an interval. Want of readiness in speech is the difficulty which affects me most: but that is lessened by practice: the audience, though cold, is attentive: and I am conscious that without some external inducement I should not easily overcome my dislike to speaking, while such inducement is supplied by a position which makes silence impossible.

These are the main considerations which influence me on both sides. I weighed them carefully, and in the end decided to refuse, which I did in a note to Colville, of which copy is kept. Colville called upon me in the afternoon, and requested that I would write him a note for publication, which I accordingly did.[47] As far as it is possible to judge of one's own motives, that which most determined me was the wish to

---

[46] George, 4th E. of Aberdeen (1784–1860), premier 1852–5.

[47] *T*, 22 Feb. 1870, 7f, for Derby's letter to Colville, declining leadership as not something for 'which I am by habit or temperament well qualified' but hoping to take 'my full share' in debates.

retain a larger degree of personal independence than is compatible with the position of being the mouthpiece of a party. But to this feeling I have not alluded in either the public or private letter.

21 February 1870. Carnarvon called, to discuss the situation generally: very friendly and professing his entire willingness to have acted under me, had I accepted the lead.[48]

23 February 1870. The prevailing opinion seems to be, that Salisbury will act as leader: and I have caused him to be told that I am quite willing to act as mediator between him and Disraeli: supposing that personal intervention between the two, of a confidential nature, would not be agreeable to either.

24 February 1870. Heard that Salisbury after consideration declines to act as leader, and the D. of Richmond, though very unwilling, takes the place.

26 February 1870. Meeting at the Carlton, at which I was asked to attend, and second the motion, moved by Salisbury, that the D. of Richmond should take the leadership ... I did so in a few words; the Duke as briefly accepted: and in accepting begged, as a personal favour, that Salisbury and Carnarvon would take their seats on the front bench. They have hitherto sat below the gangway. This they agreed to, though Salisbury took occasion to say in a rather pointed way, that he was not to be reckoned with as a follower of Disraeli.

27 February 1870. In the last week I have read through with close attention Butler's *Analogy* – an old favourite of mine, but which I had not looked at for years. This last reading confirmed my original impression, that it is one of the most profoundly sceptical works in the English language – using the word sceptical in its true sense.

5 March 1870. Meeting at Grosvenor Gate, D. of Richmond, myself, J. Manners,[49] Patten,[50] Hardy, Dr Ball,[51] Sir J. Napier,[52] the last stone-deaf and therefore not of much use, Hunt,[53] and Disraeli. We consulted

[48] Not mentioned in Hardinge, *Carnarvon* (1925).

[49] Lord John Manners, 7th D. of Rutland (1818–1906), member of all Cons. cabinets 1852–92; declined both the chief secretaryship for Ireland, and the lord-lieutenancy (with a peerage), June–July 1866; declined chief secretaryship again, July 1868; declined Canada, Apr. 1868; declined viceroyalty of India, 1875.

[50] John Wilson Patten, 1st Baron Winmarleigh (1802–92); Lancs. M.P. 1830–74 and family friend; chanc. of duchy 1867–8; chief sec. for Ireland, Sept.–Dec. 1868, *vice* Naas; cr. peer, 1874.

[51] Dr John Thomas Ball (1815–98), Irish lawyer; sol.-gen. for Ireland, 1868; att.-gen. for Ireland, 1868, 1874; lord chanc. of Ireland 1875–80; M.P. Dublin University 1868–74.

[52] Sir Joseph Napier (1804–82), lord chanc. of Ireland 1858–9; vice-chanc. of Dublin University 1867–82; active in Irish church matters.

[53] George Ward Hunt (1825–77); M.P. Northants. N. 1857–77; fin. sec. to treasury 1866–8; chanc. of exchequer, *vice* Disraeli, Feb.–Dec. 1868; 1st lord of admiralty 1874–7; d. in office.

on the land bill, and agreed to try and modify some of its provisions. All the members of the H. of C. agreed that our friends there are inclined to accept the bill – some being in fear for their seats, others really thinking it a tolerably fair settlement, and all agreeing that they expected something worse. The point most disputed is the seven years rent given as a maximum compensation for the eviction of a small holder, and the alternative of a 31 years lease. I stated my opinion that (though not admitting the justice of granting compensation at all in such cases) yet if the principle were accepted (and if evidently will be so) a 21 years lease ought to be enough to give security, and five years rent should be the maximum allowed. I do not think the bill practically injurious, though doubtful as to its justice in principle.

Called on Carnarvon (the first time since 1867) and talk with him. ... Dined D. of Cambridge ...[54] I sat next Ld Ellenborough, and was well entertained. There is something about the old man that is unlike, and above, the common standard: he is the only statesman I know to whom English greatness, and the maintenance of our military and naval superiority, is an ever-present idea, and in whose mind the military aspect of all questions is the foremost. There is more about him of the Roman of classical times than of the character which seems to suit the politician of our peaceable and commercial community. His conversation is full of vivacity, notwithstanding his eighty years: his ideas often eccentric, sometimes striking, but almost always his own: his self-appreciation (I do not like to call if vanity) expressed without reticence or disguise: but there is nothing small or affected in it: he pays himself compliments, but invites none. He tells a story well, and enjoys a joke. I don't know when I have been more interested or amused.

12 March 1870. A very mild attack of gout. I am however able to walk, though rather lame.

... The racing stock at Knowsley has sold for about £4,650 ... It is more than double what I expected.[55]

The second reading[56] of the land bill, not being opposed except by a few Irish members, passed by 442 to 11. Whatever fight is made will be made in committee, but the Irish Conservatives (and many of the Whigs also) are too much afraid of their constituencies to offer serious resistance. They are moreover alarmed by the state of the country, and would gladly give up the rights which this bill takes from them, if thereby they could secure protection in the use of such rights as they still retain.

---

[54] H.R.H. George, 2nd D. of Cambridge (1819–1904); succ. father 1850; grandson of George III; c.-in-c. 1856–95.

[55] Part of Derby's retrenchments at Knowsley, begun as soon as his father died.

[56] *H*, vol, cxcix, col. 1853 (11 Mar. 1870).

... Walk to Grosvenor Gate, though slowly: saw D. well and in good spirits, having got his speech over: weak as he still is, he had been afraid of the effort.

15 March 1870. Rather an idle day, but in fact I have no work ready to my hands. ... Dined The Club, where Froude,[57] Merivale,[58] A.P. Stanley,[59] Stanhope,[60] Smith,[61] Murchison,[62] etc. Pleasant ... Talk with Froude as to the history of Ireland, from the battle of the Boyne to the Union, being unwritten – at least there is nothing trustworthy on the subject – and hinted that he might undertake it.[63] He seemed to like the idea. His interest in Irish matters is remarkable, and he has nothing else on hand.

19 March 1870. The education bill has passed its second reading, without a division: Harcourt[64] and Fawcett,[65] who represent the 'irreconcilable' section of dissenters, violent against it, but their supporters were few, as the whole body of conservatives would have backed up Gladstone. The bill is undoubtedly in its working very favourable to the establishment, especially in rural districts, where the majority will have everything its own way. Hence the anger of strong sectarians on the one hand, and of 'secular' educationists on the other. They may perhaps be right in the abstract, but in dealing with such a question it would be insanity to convert into enemies the country clergy and the landowners. In towns the dissenters will be strong enough to take care of themselves.

29 March 1870. Dined Travellers, with Carnarvon: I had walked up from the House with Salisbury, between whom and myself friendly

---

[57] James Anthony Froude (1818–94), historian; pub. *The English in Ireland in the Eighteenth Century* (3 vols., 1872–4); regius prof. of history at Oxford, 1892–4.

[58] Probably Herman Merivale (1806–74), civil servant and historian; perm. under-sec. for colonies 1848–59, for India 1859–; or his bro. Charles, cleric and author.

[59] Arthur Penrhyn Stanley (1815–81), dean of Westminster and biographer of Dr Arnold; broad churchman.

[60] Probably Philip Henry, 5th E. Stanhope (1805–75), historian, Peel's literary executor, and a main influence on the founding of the National Portrait Gallery and the Historical Manuscripts Commission; see below, 29 Dec. 1875.

[61] Possibly George Smith (1824–1901), publisher of the *Cornhill*, the *Pall Mall Gazette*, and the *D.N.B.*; introduced Trollope to Thackeray, 1860. If not, perhaps (Sir) William Smith (1813–93), classicist, and registrar of the Royal Literary Fund (1869), of which Derby later became president (1875).

[62] (Sir) Roderick Murchison (1792–1871), geologist; kt 1846, bt 1866.

[63] W.H. Dunn, *Froude*, ii (1963) gives no date for the commencement of Froude's Irish history.

[64] Sir William George Vernon Venables Harcourt (1827–1904); M.P. 1868–1904; sol.-gen. 1873–4, home sec. 1880–5, chanc. of exchequer 1886, 1892–5; led Lib. party 1896–8.

[65] Henry Fawcett (1833–84), economist and radical politician; postmaster-gen. 1880–4; M.P. 1865–84; blind.

relations are being re-established: but we shall never, I think, be on intimate terms again.[66]

12 April 1870. Sanderson called to tell me of Lord Tenterden's death, and Abbott's[67] consequent succession to the title. Abbott had himself written to me on the subject. In the afternoon, he, Abbott, called, and discussed with me his prospects. He has literally nothing except his pay as a clerk, his uncle having squandered the entire family fortune, about £4,000 a year, except the reversion of £1500 a year, which fortunately is so tied up that it cannot be touched, and may become available in a few years. He has therefore decided, sensibly, to keep his place in the F.O. and not to take his seat in the Lds, though assuming the title. ... Understanding from Sanderson[68] that the new peer was in difficulty as to present supplies, I offered a loan of £100, which was gratefully accepted.

13 April 1870. Read on the way down, a variety of pamphlets and essays by Congreve,[69] the head of that sect which takes Comte as its master ... What I could understand seemed to me by no means new; but it is unfair to judge a system hastily.

20 April 1870. Death of Julian Fane,[70] who retired from diplomacy two years ago on grounds of health. He was a little my junior: we were together at Cambridge.[71] In his profession he was singularly lucky, and counted one of the best of our rising men. With women he was popular: less so in male society, his manners, though pleasant, showing too obviously a higher opinion of himself than was agreeable to his acquaintance. He was remarkably handsome, which excused a little coxcombry. He had a strong fancy that his talents were thrown away in diplomacy (which was, on the contrary, exactly the proper sphere for them) and that he should some day earn a great literary reputation. This last hope he himself expressed to me, as being one of the motives which influenced him in his wish to retire: a wish which I combated as long as I could, but unsuccessfully.

26 April 1870. Called on Disraeli, and talk with him. He thinks it is

---

[66] Salisbury had refused office from Disraeli in Feb. 1868 (*Stanley Diaries*, 379).

[67] Charles Abbott, 3rd Baron Tenterden (1834–82); succ. uncle in title, 1870; entered F.O. 1854; asst. under-sec. 1871–3; perm. under-sec. 1873–82; freemason.

[68] Thomas Henry Sanderson, Baron Sanderson (1841–1923); F.O. career 1859–1906; priv. sec. to diarist 1866–8, 1874–8, to Granville 1880–5; perm. under-sec. 1894–1906; cr. peer 1905; rejected by Derby's dau. Margaret, he never m.; Derby's Monty Corry and executor; flautist.

[69] Richard Congreve (1818–99), positivist.

[70] Julian Henry Charles Fane (1827–70); s. of 11th E. of Westmorland; like diarist, educ. Trinity Coll., Cambridge; diplomatist, 1856–68; acting chargé d'affaires at Paris, 1865–7 and 1868; wrote *Poems* (1852) and translated Heine (1854).

[71] Where, like Derby and like Fane's close friend Harcourt, he was an Apostle.

too late to do anything that will unite the colonies more closely with England:[72] in which view I am compelled to agree. He agrees in the opinion I have long held that the Fenians will give far more trouble in the new character they are assuming of constitutional repealers than when they preached up armed insurrection: for the law cannot touch them – they are only asking for the repeal of an act of parliament passed seventy years ago – and yet for all practical purposes a parliament for Ireland is equivalent to an entire separation of the countries. – He thinks the government shaken and weakened, but that the best policy of the opposition is to keep quiet, and leave the differences of the Liberals to come to a head.

... Dined The Club, meeting Grote,[73] Sir H. Holland,[74] Murchison, Lowe, Stanhope, Bp of Winchester,[75] Reeve,[76] etc. Pleasant. Some talk with Lowe as we went away about reducing the debt, which he inclines to personally, but doubts whether he should have support enough.

28 April 1870. Agreed with Stanhope, as head of the Nat. Port. Gallery trustees, that the meetings shall be held at my house in future...

... The feeling is strong against the Greek government ...[77] The Times has seriously proposed a military occupation of Greece!

Dined Pender's,[78] meeting a large party, chiefly of artists. Sat next Dickens, and well amused.

30 April 1870. Dined at the Royal Academy dinner ... The dinner was dull, but sitting next Disraeli, I was well enough entertained.

6 May 1870. Called in Grosv. Street, and agreed, considering how many reports have gone about, which it is impossible to deny and awkward to admit, to tell my family and the world of the intended marriage between Ly S. and myself. Wrote accordingly to my mother ... and found that she was prepared for the news, and that it gave her pleasure.

... Informed F. & C.,[79] the Talbots,[80] A.C.[81] and Disraeli, thinking

---

[72] Cf. C.C. Eldridge, *England's Mission* (1973), 172–80. In his 1872 Crystal Palace speech Disraeli lamented the absence of 'some representative council in the metropolis'.

[73] George Grote (1794–1871), historian.

[74] Holland, (Sir) Henry (1788–1873), physician to the Queen and Prince Consort; bt 1853.

[75] Samuel Wilberforce (1805–73), s. of William; bishop of Oxford, then (1869) Winchester; 'Soapy Sam', noted anti-Darwinian.

[76] Henry Reeve (1813–95), Whig publicist; ed. *Edinburgh Review*, 1855–95.

[77] Following the kidnapping and eventual murder of British subjects by Greek bandits.

[78] (Sir) John Pender (1816–96), submarine telegraph magnate; Derby's chief friend in the business world; diarist presided over banquet in his honour, 23 Apr. 1888.

[79] Frederick and Constance Stanley.

[80] Derby's sister Emma Charlotte (d. 1928) m. in 1860 Derby's former priv. sec. Col. the Hon. Sir W.P.M. [Chetwynd-] Talbot (1817–98), serjeant-at-arms in the House of Lords 1858–98.

[81] Lord Arthur Cecil (1851–1913), s. of Mary, Lady Salisbury.

that due to near relatives and old friends. Well pleased that this business, to which I have been looking forward with a certain distaste, is over at last. It is disagreeable, but under some circumstances inevitable, to have one's private affairs the town-talk. But the content of my family, and especially of my mother, is very satisfactory. It seems that they have long anticipated and wished for this marriage.

7 May 1870. Dined Baron Rothschilds, meeting Disraelis, Sir R. and Ly G. Peel,[82] Ld Westbury,[83] B. Osborne,[84] Dr Quin,[85] and a variety of Rothschild cousins, great men in their way, but to me unknown. Fairly amused.

9 May 1870. The newspapers this morning announce my marriage.[86] Many congratulations in the Lords: not the least cordial being that of Salisbury, which under the circumstances I am glad of.

Much pleased also at Mary Cecil's[87] manner with her mother and me, we dining *en trio.* It is impossible that any girl should like, or should not be affected by, the remarriage of her mother: but it was impossible to show the feeling less than Mary did. I shall remember it to her credit.

10 May 1870. To Carlton, where a small meeting of Disraeli, Cairns, Hardy, Taylor,[88] Noel,[89] Colville, and D. of Richmond, to consider party (i.e. electioneering) arrangements consequent on Spofforth's retirement,[90] and Gorst,[91] the late M.P. for Cambridge, having taken his place. The fund wanted is £1,500 or £1,600 a year: I urged strongly endeavouring to collect in small sums from the party at large, instead of relying on the contributions of a small number of persons, which has been the rule.

14 May 1870. Read, with much amusement, a letter from Northcote[92]

[82] Sir Robert Peel (1822–95), eldest s. of premier; Irish sec. 1861–5.
[83] Richard Bethell, 1st Baron Westbury (1800–73), lord chanc. 1861–5.
[84] Ralph Bernal Osborne (1808–82), wit and Lib. M.P.
[85] Society doctor; probably Dr Frederick Quin (1799–1878), the first English homoeopathist; used by Disraeli to ask Granville to lead Tories in Lords, Feb. 1868.
[86] *T*, 9 May 1870, 11d.
[87] Mary, Lady Galloway, née Gascoyne-Cecil (1850–1903), wife of Alan, 10th E. of Galloway (1835–1901); see *Later Diaries*, 19–20.
[88] Col. T.E. Taylor (1811–83), M.P. (Cons.) co. Dublin 1841–83; chief whip c. 1860–68; chanc. of duchy of Lancaster, Nov.–Dec. 1868, 1874–6; chief commr. of works, 1876–80.
[89] Hon. Gerard Noel (1823–1911), jun. whip 1866–8, chief whip 1868–73; 2nd s. of 1st E. of Gainsborough; M.P. (Cons.) Rutland 1847–83.
[90] Markham Spofforth, Cons. agent 1859–70.
[91] (Sir) John Eldon Gorst, (1835–1916); after N.Z. career, Tory M.P. 1866–8, when anti-reform; party agent, 1870–77; M.P., 1875; refused junior post at board of trade 1875 (Hanham, *Elections and Party Management*, 361).
[92] Sir Stafford Henry Northcote, 1st E. of Iddesleigh (1818–87); M.P. 1855–85; pres. of board of trade, 1866, and sec. for India, 1867–8; gov. of Hudson's Bay Co., 1869–74; commr for Alabama claims, 1871; chanc. of exchequer 1874–80; cr. earl 1885.

to Disraeli: in which N. relates how during the Canadian difficulty at Red River, matters were unpleasantly complicated by the news that 'Sir John has broken out again': Sir John being the Canadian premier,[93] Macdonald, and his breaking-out the indulgence of a periodical fit of intoxication, which lasts over many days. It seems that he breaks out in this fashion once or twice in the year: and the habit is so well understood that no especial notice is taken of it – the grievance in the present instance being not that the minister should be drunk for a week together, but that he should not have waited till the urgent business on hand was disposed of.

19 May 1870. A strange story told me last night by Gladstone, about a letter purporting to come from the D. of Edinburgh,[94] and addressed to the P. of Wales,[95] having been published in a local (Shrewsbury) journal, professedly forwarded from India. It is questioned whether the letter is a hoax or real: if the latter, it has been surreptitiously obtained: if the former, Gladstone said, it must be the work of someone who is unusually well acquainted with the Prince, his ways of talking and thinking, and the habits of the Court here. From his description it would appear that the document is not very creditable to its author – but he gave no details.

20 May 1870. To a meeting at Disraeli's, chiefly on the subject of ballot,[96] attended by some 20 M.P.s and 5 or 4 peers. The whole party were for dividing against ballot on the second reading of the bill,[97] except Hunt, who thought it better to accept what is in the long run inevitable. Some talk also about game laws, and the excessive pres-ervation of ground game, of which the farmers complain, and in consequence of which it is maintained that in many counties landlord influence is diminishing. Walked up with Patten, who inclined to be desponding about affairs, and seems growing older.[98]

22 May 1870. Met M.[99] on the platform: with her to Hatfield ... luncheon nearly on the spot where in July 1855 we had held a conversation which led to a close friendship between us, never since interrupted.

23 May 1870. Went to call on the K. of the Belgians[100] at his request. Much conversation passed, but none of special interest. He was very

---

[93] Sir John Alexander Macdonald (1815–91), 1st premier of Canada.

[94] Alfred, D. of Edinburgh (1844–1900), 2nd s. of Q. Victoria; naval career to 1893, when inherited German duchy.

[95] Albert Edward, Prince of Wales (1841–1910), later Edward VII.

[96] Not passed until 1872.

[97] Attempts to stop the Ballot Bill reaching its 2R failed 220–110 (16 Mar. 1870), but it made no further progress.

[98] Then aged 68.

[99] Mary, Lady Salisbury.

[100] Leopold II (1835–1909), King of the Belgians (1865–1909).

complimentary to Lumley,[101] whom he described as universally popular: said he had no present apprehensions of reform from outside: but that the French authorities were fond of hunting for imaginary conspirators at Brussels (this Van De Weyer[102] also told me long ago). He spoke of the existing balance of strength between France and Prussia as favourable to peace, and especially as giving England the opportunity of effectual interference, as neither party would be willing to have us against them. ... I stayed with him at his desire about half an hour.

25 May 1870. To D. of Richmond, where met D. of Buccleuch,[103] Marlborough,[104] Malmesbury, Cairns, Salisbury, Hardy, Ball, and Carnarvon. We discussed the Irish land bill, Salisbury, Cairns, and I taking the principal part, and agreed on amendments to be proposed in committee. The tone of the meeting was moderate and prudent, the only exception being Salisbury, and he was not violent, nor inclined to press his individual opinions. We sat over two hours.

29 May 1870. Dined Ld Clanwilliam's[105] ... Ld Granville told me some amusing stories: among others he said that Ld Palmerston[106] never could be induced to see any talent or power in Lowe, and to the last persisted in considering Sir R. Peel much superior to him! This he ascribed to Ld P's sympathy with the somewhat noisy and blustering tone of Peel's public displays.

Col. Henderson[107] talked of the renewed activity of the Fenians: said they were active in the northern towns, more especially Newcastle and Darlington: they had laid in a considerable stock of arms, chiefly revolvers: they were all known and watched: he had expected an outbreak in the winter: their present scheme was to destroy the Times and Pall Mall Gazette offices, both of which he had been obliged to protect: the object was not clear, except to create alarm and keep themselves before the public. He said Burke ... was the only man of ability among them. Few of the leaders retained confidence long: and treachery was as frequent as in 1867.

30 May 1870. There is much talk (I hear) in the commons about Disraeli's retiring from the lead of his party: and it is possible that he

---

[101] U.K. minister to Brussels.
[102] Sylvain Van De Weyer (1802–74), Belgian min. in London 1831–67.
[103] Walter Francis Montagu-Douglas-Scott, 5th D. of Buccleuch and 7th D. of Queensberry (1806–84); succ. father, 1819; in cabinet 1842–6; the leading Scottish Tory.
[104] John Winston Spencer-Churchill, 7th D. of Marlborough (1822–83); M.P. 1840–5, 1847–57; succ. 1857; lord steward 1866–7, lord pres. of council 1867–8, lord-lieut. of Ireland, 1876–80; father of Lord Randolph Churchill.
[105] Richard Meade, 1st Lord Clanwilliam (1795–1879), diplomatist 1814–27; cr. U.K. baron, 1828.
[106] Premier.
[107] Sir Edmund Henderson (1821–96), chief commr of metropolitan police 1869–86; founded C.I.D.

may do so formally, as from want of health he has virtually abdicated during the present session. I do not believe there is any other reason: though in the actual state of affairs, there being no prospect of political success, and probably none for him at any time of return to office, he may naturally grow indifferent: the more so as he has won the great prize, and nothing can deprive him of the honour of having once been Prime Minister. His novel[108] is variously judged: the success of it has been immense, but that is explained by the writer's position: the style is characteristic: full of clever hits and graphic descriptions, original and eccentric, though not in pure taste. Many passages will be remembered and quoted. The fault most commonly found is a certain tawdriness,[109] and almost childish love of what is gorgeous and striking: the same oriental turn of mind that induces my friend like most of his race, to take pleasure in striking exhibitions of colour. Some one said, referring to the conversations in this book 'I don't know much about dukes and duchesses, but I should not have thought they talked so unlike other people'. There is in the book an ingenious and amusing, though rather overdone, exposure of the arts of the Catholic hierarchy, and their attempts to get hold of rich young men: which makes the ultramontane party describe it as the most immoral work which has appeared in our day, and has conciliated a certain amount of support among Protestant Dissenters and the old Evangelical party.

1 June 1870. Read in Blackwood a most savage article[110] on *Lothair*. It is reported, but God knows with what truth, to be written by the present Ly Salisbury,[111] who in bitterness of feeling and violence of language exceeds her husband.

2 June 1870. Pembroke Lodge for luncheon: Ld Russell[112] very old, and deaf, but less infirm than last year. Much friendly talk with him: amused to see how, whatever subject he begins upon, his mind immediately reverts to Whig politics. It is as though he had pledged himself never to let an hour pass without making a declaration of his political faith.

6 June 1870 (Whit Monday). Left for the Town Hall, Liverpool, where I was received by the Mayor ... Drove with him to the site of the new Stanley Hospital in Kirkdale – two acres of land given by me: the usual ceremonies of laying the first stone were observed, a prayer read, the

[108] B. Disraeli, *Lothair* (3 vols.) published 2 May 1870.
[109] Cf. A. Trollope, *An Autobiography* (1883), ch. xiii, arguing that of Disraeli's novels *Lothair* was 'undoubtedly his worst'.
[110] Actually by Sir E.B. Hamley (1824–93), commandant of staff college, Sandhurst, 1870–77; delimited Bulgarian frontier, 1879; see *Blackwood's*, 107 (June 1870), 773–93.
[111] Georgina, *née* Alderson, Marchioness of Salisbury (1827–99), wife of future premier.
[112] Lord John Russell, 1st E. Russell (1792–1878), premier.

Mayor said a few words, and I delivered my address ...[113] A crowd lined the streets all the way from the Town Hall, and I was cheered very frequently and loudly, as indeed was the case throughout the day ... At 2.30 I went with the Mayor to a flower show in the newly made Stanley Park.

... The scene of today has raised in my mind some curious thoughts. What is − what can be − the inducement to some thousands of persons receiving wages, and not too high wages, to pass several hours of one of their few holidays, in a crowd, hot, dusty, and generally uncomfortable, merely to see a few local notabilities pass? What makes them cheer such people? There is no motive for affecting enthusiasm, if it does not exist: yet what they have to be enthusiastic about is perplexing to me. It was the same when the P. of Wales and his brother were in Liverpool. One practical moral may be drawn − that in some inexplicable way, these public appearances of local magnates do give pleasure to, and create popularity among, the masses: and that therefore they ought not to be wholly neglected.

10 June 1870. Death of Dickens ... His literary failing was a tendency to run into mannerism and mere caricature. He was most at home in describing the middle and lower classes; never once has he represented what we conventionally call a gentleman ... Some years back he indulged in the incomprehensible freak of publishing in his magazine the details of a quarrel, ending in separation, between himself and his wife. ... His manner was more genial than that of Thackeray, who seldom became agreeable until thawed by much wine.

11 June 1870. Took occasion to say a few words advising moderation in regard of the Irish Land Bill.[114]

16 June 1870. The land debate began ... I spoke ... for about 45 minutes, with more ease and satisfaction to myself than usual, and well received. On the whole I was pleased, having said all that I meant to say. My argument was chiefly directed to show that the alleged protection to the tenant was illusory, and that the bill would operate, contrary to the professed intentions of its authors, in the direction of consolidating farms.[115]

19 June 1870. Correspondence ... about prospect of being able to sell the Irish estate, which I am more inclined to do since hearing these debates, inasmuch as it is plain that any fresh demand which the tenants may choose to make will not be long resisted. On the other hand, it yields nearly £6,000 a year net, with prospect of increase, and

[113] *T,* 7 June 1870, 12d.
[114] See above, 16, 19 Feb., 5, 12 Mar. 1870.
[115] *H,* 202, cols. 233–43 (16 June 1870).

I doubt whether the purchase money I could obtain under present circumstances would yield an equal return.

20 June 1870. Childers[116] is knocked up, and retires for a month. Bright is said to be better, but we know nothing certain. There is much curiosity and anxiety as to how Gladstone's health will bear the stress of heat, excitement, and overwork, which nearly killed him last year, the doctors then saying that a repetition of the attack from which he suffered would almost certainly be fatal.

23 June 1870. Dined at the House with Skelmersdale, and talk with him, as one of my trustees, about selling the Irish estate, in the expediency of which step I find he entirely agrees; which is lucky, since I could not do it without his consent. But I shall not sell at a loss. Ball told me the other day that in Tipperary twenty years value of the net rental was the common price: and on a well-managed estate it would be two or three years more.

27 June 1870. Heard early this morning that Lord Clarendon had died in the night, without pain, having lain during the last two days for the most part in a state of stupor. His family were unprepared for the shock, and indeed, though his health had long been failing, the end was very sudden. He was seventy years and six months old. He leaves his children, I fear, very badly off.

28 June 1870. Statter called, and gave a good report on the state of the business in and around Manchester. I impress upon him the advantage of buying lots lying within the estate, at any reasonable cost, and paying for them by the sale of chief rents, or small outlying fragments.

... The papers are, as might be expected, full of Ld Clarendon. (N.B. The few words I said about him last night are strangely misreported, and little better than nonsense.)[117] They praise him as is natural and just, but in an indiscriminate manner. His character was remarkable, unlike that of any other public man of our day, both in its good and bad qualities. In his family he was almost worshipped, and deserved to be so, for never was a more affectionate father. His wife had even in late years reasons to complain of him, which to the outside world were tolerably notorious, but either she did not know them, or consoled by the respect and devotion which he always showed to her, affected ignorance. The latest story of the kind, the facts of which are by a singular chance accurately known to me, is of so eccentric a kind that I am unwilling to set it down: but it was only the last of many.[118] In

[116] Hugh Childers (1827–96), Lib. minister; 1st lord of admiralty, 1868–71, resigning 1871.

[117] *H*, 202, col. 952, saying that 'to all the upper class of this country – Lord Clarendon set the example of a life of indefatigable industry passed in the service of the state'.

[118] A reference to Clarendon's *amitié* with the Queen of Holland, a friend of Lady Salisbury.

society Ld Clarendon was perhaps of all Englishmen of the present day the most agreeable companion. He was always ready to talk, and on all subjects his talk was equally playful, pointed, and full of good sense. He wrote as he spoke: a collection of his familiar letters would be well worth making, but they are in general of so unreserved a character that they could not appear in our time.

Connected with this taste for conversation and correspondence was one of his chief weaknesses – a great love of scandal and gossip, not without malice. He would attack friends and colleagues when their backs were turned, and that in no scrupulous fashion. Much of the absurd prejudice against the Queen, caused by her supposed relations with the man Brown,[119] was due to his delight in spreading or inventing tales concerning her. (She afterwards came to be aware of the fact, and never forgave it.) Yet, where the gratification of this peculiar taste was not concerned, he could be a warm and active friend: and it may be that what looked like a love of mischief was nothing more than pleasure felt in telling a good story, which certainly nobody did better.

In his relations with the outer world he was intensely sensitive: easily pleased, as easily offended, and neither lasted long. He was in general patient, but when annoyed could show his displeasure in a peculiarly disagreeable and even offensive manner. Of this Apponyi[120] used often to complain. He had strong personal likings, and as strong dislikes. In his private concerns I don't know whether it is praise or blame to say that he was utterly careless of money: a tendency of which he rather boasted among friends. His affairs have always been embarrassed, and of the family estates[121] but little remains for his successor. This arose from indifference, not from indolence: for activity of mind was one of his most notable peculiarities. He loved diplomacy, and was never so happy as when absorbed in negotiations. His way of working was singular, and to most people would have been inconvenient: he rose very late, often not till eleven, received foreign ministers and other visitors during the whole day, with boxes accumulating round him: wrote his private letters, an occupation which always gave him pleasure, and for which he managed to find time when most pressed: dined: and passed the night till 3 or 4 a.m. in clearing off the official business which anybody else would have transacted in the daytime. This regimen, accompanied by much tobacco, undoubtedly shortened his life, though in all respects except smoking he observed a strictly temperate diet. As a politician, his chief characteristic was strict adherence to party. It was

---

[119] John Brown, royal servant (d. 1883).
[120] Rudolph, Count Apponyi (1812–76), Austrian amb. to U.K., 1856–1871; amb. in Paris, 1871–6.
[121] Only £3741 p.a. in *Bateman*.

with him a point of honour to support his friends the more strenuously, the more they seemed in danger from the results of their own mistakes. No inducement would have prevailed upon him to leave them, and satisfied with having expressed his individual opinion, he never hesitated to vote with them even when in conversation most loudly condemning their proceedings – a state of things not rare in the years between 1860 and 1870.

As a diplomatist, I cannot judge him. He knew everybody and all that was doing: and certainly had every personal quality that could give success in that profession. I used to think him too restless, too fond of advising and interfering where silence and neutrality would have been preferable: how much of this tendency was the result of old habits and how much of personal temperament, I cannot pretend to decide. He could not endure inactivity: though well read, he had no literary turn: his life passed between conversation, correspondence, and office work. He might have lived longer if he would have taken rest, but as he told a friend of mine, he could not endure to be put on the shelf, and preferred to die in harness. The end came suddenly, but for many months his obviously failing strength had made his family anxious. He began his public career as an attaché in 1820 and had thus served, with little intermission, for half a century. His successor, Hyde,[122] is gentlemanlike in manners, and said to possess ability: but has never shown any disposition to use it.

2 July 1870. To attend Lord Clarendon's funeral at Watford ... The shops in Watford were mostly shut. ... Talk with Harcourt on the way there and back: he remarked on the singularity of the political situation: if anything were to happen to Gladstone there is not, he says, one member of the cabinet whom the H. of C. would accept as its leader. Lowe is too unpopular, Bright disabled, Childers, even if he recovers, not sufficiently strong, and he evidently has a low opinion of Cardwell.[123] He did not think Gladstone could stand more than 3 or 4 years, at the utmost, of his present life: he (G.) would give himself no rest, leave nothing to any subordinate or even colleague, but do all in person: the result being that he is overworked, and the rest not being employed, get into the habit of leaving everything to him. He told me a good deal about the Education Bill and the dissenters, whose organ he has become: how they will not recognise the Wesleyans as belonging to them, because these do not as a rule join in the political opposition to Establishments...

[122] Edward Hyde, 5th Lord Clarendon (1846–1914); held court office 1895–1905. See below, 18 Sept. 1871.
[123] Edward Cardwell (1813–86), sec. for war 1868–74; cr. vt, 1874.

5 July 1870. The Talbots came to breakfast: Lionel West, my 'best man', shortly after. At 11 I went with him to the Chapel Royal, where a certain number of friends had assembled: M. met me at 11.15, and we were married, the Dean of Windsor reading the service ... Delawarr gave her away. The Salisburys, Hopes,[124] Eustace Cecils,[125] and nearly all the West family were present. There was a crowd outside, and some cheering as we drove away. ... At 12.40 we got away finally, and driving through Bromley, reached Holwood about 2.30. The bells in Bromley were ringing, and there was a good deal of curiosity to see us as we passed.

13 July 1870. The weekly papers full of the war, about the iniquity of which there are not, nor can there be, two opinions: though Bismarck acted no better in 1866, and even now many persons believe that he purposely placed the French in the position in which they are, in order to provoke them to a rupture while keeping himself apparently in the right. Between him and the Emperor there is not much in point of morality to choose: the only difference is this, that Bismarck has at least acted in what he supposed to be the interest of Prussia, whereas with Napoleon the motive is purely dynastic.

19 July 1870. [Disraeli] gives me the Rothschild view of the war: his friends fear it will be long ... they think the Prussians well armed and well prepared; and that neither is a decisive result to be expected for the present, nor can either party acquiesce in a defeat which is not decisive. He said the cabinet had been completely taken by surprise: none of them knew anything of foreign affairs except Granville: and Gladstone really believed in Cobden's theory that men were growing too civilised for war. Hence the event found them astonished and perplexed. ... D. seemed excited by the novelty and importance of the situation: and better in health for the excitement.

20 July 1870. Left Euston by 10 a.m. train, having a saloon carriage: reached Edgehill by 3, where found cloth laid, the station ornamented, and a salute of fog signals fired. Much cheering from the crowd. We drove slowly (to Knowsley) and found a great collection of tenants and others assembled before the house. They made every possible demonstration of pleasure and good will: I thanked them briefly speaking out of the carriage. M. and I afterwards went out on foot: there was such curiosity to see her that we were almost mobbed, and her dress torn: but it was all done in kindness. The police and volunteers

---

[124] A.J. Beresford Hope (1820–87), Cons. M.P. and f. of *Saturday Review*; m. Mildred, d. of James, 2nd M. of Salisbury; thus bro.-in-law of Salisbury (the p.m.) and uncle of A.J. Balfour, premier.

[125] Lord Eustace Cecil (1834–1921), M.P. (Cons.) 1865–85; surveyor-gen. of ordnance 1874–80; 3rd s. of James, 2nd M. of Salisbury, by his 1st wife, and thus bride's half-brother-in-law (and bro. of future p.m.).

alone saved us from serious inconvenience. They – I mean the crowd – stayed till dark. A good deal of beer was drunk, and I heard of some drunkenness, but there was no row or quarrelling. Hornby had organised the whole thing very well. ... I have forgotten to note that at the bottom of the hill under the house the horses were taken out and we were drawn up by the people.[126]

22 July 1870. Lowe writes to M. confident that whatever may happen England will not get mixed up in the quarrel.

26 July 1870. The heat throughout England is said to have been greater than has been known for 20 years: temperature above 90° in the shade in many places. The drought is getting serious.

12 August 1870. Drove over to the fells ... It is on this part of the county that our family must fall back, if ever driven out of Knowsley by smoke and building. It is pleasant to live in, and our influence there is greater socially than in the south. I propose to buy land in these parts gradually, selling detached pieces in L'pool, Manchester etc. Indeed this is on my part no new resolution: I have often before discussed it...

13 August 1870. The Times is writing up, by very unmistakable hints, the deposition of the Emperor, and the calling to power of one of the Orleans princes. Q.: is this a result of Granville's influence with Delane?[127] He has always been said to be Orleanist in his views. The *Telegraph* and *Standard* are both Imperialist as regards French politics, the *Post* apparently the same: *Daily News* and *Pall Mall* republican.

16 August 1870. Weather still hot and dry. I have never seen the ponds so low...

17 August 1870. Busy sorting papers to send to the D. of Wellington, who has asked me for his father's letters and memoranda...

18 August 1870. Letter among others from Disraeli, who thinks the French utterly beaten: says that the Emp. brought all this on himself by taking up the doctrine of nationalities, which he did in the hope of securing Belgium: but Belgium is safe, and he has only created on each side of him a powerful rival in Italy and Germany. He speculates on the theory – common and popular among the Germans – that the Latin races are worn out, and that the future of Europe is Teutonic. Q.: will not the next great duel be between Prussia and Russia?

24 August 1870. Left Knowsley at 11, and drove into Bootle ... to lay the first stone of a hospital there, the site of which I have given. The Mayor and corporation attended, and presented me with an address.

---

[126] For Lady Derby's welcome, see *T*, 21 July 1870, 5f, and also a folio in the Knowsley Library, *Extracts from the Press on the marriage of Edward Henry, Earl of Derby* (1870).

[127] J.T. Delane (1817–79), ed. *Times* 1841–77.

I answered it briefly, laid the stone, and after the usual ceremonies, delivered a short speech,[128] which was not altogether easy, being in the open air, with a high wind blowing. A few words were said by others, after which we went to luncheon in a small public room adjoining. About 150 sat down, the Mayor taking the chair. My health was drunk, and I gave that of the Mayor. Then came the formal opening of the bazaar by M. and myself, which I performed by addressing half a dozen words to the crowd. We walked round the place, and bought a few things which we did not want, but it was expected. We got away by 3.30.

The roads were lined with people looking on and cheering, flags were hung out, and altogether we could not have been more warmly received if the occasion had been that of a royal visit. The enthusiasm was unbounded, and evidently sincere. It is strange, and to me perplexing, that this feeling should exist so strongly in a country of cheap newspapers and continual change: but the fact is there.

6 September 1870. Within the last few days I have received the proof from Hansard of my speech on the Irish land bill: which is such a mass of confusion and nonsense that I have written to the editor begging them he would omit it altogether, and declining to attempt its correction, which would in fact involve rewriting the whole.[129]

14 September 1870. All[130] drove in to Liverpool to hear Huxley's[131] inaugural address, delivered in the Philharmonic Hall. It lasted about $1\frac{1}{2}$ hours; the audience, between 2000 and 3000, very attentive, though they can have understood but little. I moved a vote of thanks, which was seconded by the Mayor.

4 October 1870. No event, and nothing in the nature of business to do. I have seldom been so entirely free from duties or obligations of a public nature.

9 October 1870. It is seldom that I have passed three months in such entire abstinence from political life, or indeed except in two or three cases, from public appearances of any kind. But apart from private reasons, I have been influenced by the consideration that, while this war lasts, nothing else can or will be attended to: and it will last some time longer. The next session will be full of plans for increasing the efficiency of the army, and more especially of the militia and volunteers.

---

[128] *T*, 24 Aug. 1870, 8b.

[129] Speech of 16 June 1870 (see above); not confused as printed.

[130] Those staying at Knowsley (12 Sept.-) were the Northcotes, Crosses, Stanhopes, Wilson Patten, Sir R. Murchison, A.J. Balfour, Sanderson, and Sackville Cecil.

[131] T.H. Huxley (1825–95), scientist and controversialist; 'Darwin's bulldog'.

17 October 1870. There arrived, the D. and Duchess of Cleveland,[132] with their daughter ...: Disraeli and Lady Beaconsfield: the Hopwood family – parents, two girls, and one son: Lds Camperdown,[133] St Asaph,[134] and G. Hamilton.[135]

... Talk with Disraeli on the state of foreign affairs: I find our views pretty nearly identical: he thinks the republic was inevitable in France whenever the empire collapsed, and if it was to come, that it could not come in a manner and at a time when it would exercise less influence in Europe: he sees no reason why we should not cooperate with Prussia as well as with France, or why Prussian predominance should be unfavourable to peace. He cannot explain the strong sympathy felt for France by many of the upper classes, and by those professing conservative opinions, notably by the *Standard*. He pities Napoleon personally, but remarks that he (N.) has always been though not unfriendly, yet a most troublesome ally: keeping us in hot water about Belgium, making the Crimean war, into which we were drawn, for dynastic purposes, and always ready to pick a quarrel with some neighbour rather than lose popularity with the army, on which he relied.

19 October 1870. Talk with D. as to a Conservative meeting, which I deprecate, partly because there is nothing to be said or done, partly because the Catholics are so much annoyed at certain passages in D.'s latest novel – that they would not join in any reception to be given to its author. This last point I touched on delicately, it was necessary to be mentioned, and I found he was aware of the existence of the feeling referred to, though probably not of its extent. He agreed as to the inexpediency of any present expression of opinion.

24 October 1870. F. and C.[136] came ... C. full of gossip, and fragments of stories of what she had heard had passed here, none of them well-founded. She makes mischief without meaning it, as all people must do who pass the greater part of their day in discussing their neighbour's affairs.

28 October 1870. Frederick and Constance left us. I thought F. out of spirits ... F. has hardly inhabited Knowsley since the change. C. also appeared to be changed, being irritable, inclined to find fault, and

---

[132] Harry George Powlett (formerly Vane), 4th D. of Cleveland (1803–91).

[133] Robert Haldane-Duncan, 3rd E. of Camperdown (1841–1918); succ. father 1867; educ. Eton and Balliol; 1sts in Mods and Greats; junior office 1868–74; Liberal Unionist activist, 1886.

[134] Either Dr Joshua Hughes (1807–89), first Welsh-speaking holder of the see in modern times; or his predecessor Dr T.V. Short (1790–1872), bishop of Sodor and Man 1841–6, and thus connected with the Stanley family. Hughes succ. Short, Jan. 1870.

[135] Lord George Francis Hamilton (1845–1927), 3rd s. of 1st D. of Abercorn; M.P. (Cons.) 1868–1906; under-sec. for India 1874–8; vice-pres. of council 1878–80; 1st lord of the admiralty 1885–6, 1886–92; sec. for India 1895–1903 (resigned); left £53,000.

[136] Lady Constance Villiers (1840–1922), Clarendon's eldest dau., m. diarist's bro., 1865.

generally out of humour: but her condition may account for disturbed
nerves. She, and her sisters also, feel very acutely the loss of social
importance which belonged to them as daughters of the foreign
secretary, trusted by him with his closest secrets, and acquainted with
everything that passed both at home and abroad. It would be unjust
not to add that her grief on other grounds has been deep, and is likely
to be lasting. To all three sisters their father, while he lived, was the
first object of affection: and as a father, he deserved to be so.

13 November 1870. Lowe called yesterday afternoon. I had a short
conversation with him, M. a long one.

17 November 1870. Ld Granville's despatch in answer appears in the
papers this morning: evidently drawn up by O. Russell.[137] It is temperate
but firm: in all respects what it ought to be.

... Lowe called in the afternoon: confident and sanguine: made light
of the fear of war: told M. that Gladstone, Cardwell, he himself, and I
think he added Ld Granville were determined not to fight, and that
without them the cabinet could do nothing. I hope he may prove right.

19 November 1870. Letters in Times from Mill[138] and Froude, against
a Russian war, Explanatory despatch from Gortschakoff[139] published,
which in some (but a slight) degree modifies the arrogance of the first.
It now remains to see what Austria, Italy, and above all Prussia will
do. The press discusses the situation with little difference of opinion. The
universal language is 'We don't wish to fight, but if this announcement is
meant as a challenge we cannot refuse it.' Not the least awkward part
of the complication is that American vessels will be fitted out under
the Russian flag, and the injury which they may do is incalculable.
The *Standard* and *Pall Mall* are crying out for instant war: the former
in the interest of France (it has now become almost avowedly a French
organ): the latter for no visible reason, but it has been protesting and
declaiming for a long while against a policy of peace.

24 November 1870. Cairns says that if parliament were now to be called
together, he has no doubt that the decision would be for war.

8 December 1870. Shooting in Rainford ... The guns were Ld Wilton,
Ld Sefton,[140] Moss, Hale, myself, Cecil Hornby (son of the rector of
Bury), Paterson. We killed 883 head, about 300 of them being hares.

[137] Odo Russell, 1st Lord Ampthill (1829–84), diplomatist; bro. of 9th D. of Bedford;
U.K. rep. at Rome, 1858–70; asst. under-sec. at F.O., 1870–71. In 1884 Derby wrote,
'Except Lyons, we have no better diplomatist ...'. (*Later Diaries*, 101.)
[138] John Stuart Mill (1806–73), philosopher.
[139] Prince A.M. Gorchakov (1798–1883), Russian foreign minister 1856–82, chancellor
1866–82.
[140] William Molyneux, 4th E. of Sefton (1835–97); succ. 1855; lord-lieut. Lancs. and
leading Liverpool Liberal.

Ld Wilton ... kept us in alarm by his reckless shooting. He hit one or two lookers-on, but none badly. We had with us a great crowd, not less than 300 at one time ... At parting they gave three cheers for Ld and Ly D. The sport is certainly popular among the neighbours, especially the colliers, pipe-makers, and working people in Rainford: nor do the tenants complain, for the game is liberally distributed among them. Still, there must be loss and damage to farmers, and I do not wish, nor intend, to continue preserving on this scale: but in respect for my father's memory, and from dislike to sudden and sweeping changes, I decided last winter that the reduction should be gradual. The cost of game for the present year will not be one half of what it was in 1868, which is at least a good beginning.

12 December 1870. The estates[141] have, practically, cost me £125,000, for that is the sum which F. accepted in lieu of them: I ought to be able to obtain, by a little waiting, £150,000, and at that rate the bargain will be a good one. They may be worth more, if Ireland remains quiet: but the political future of the country is not satisfactory, and it is scarcely worth my while to run risks in the hope of getting a little more.

15 December 1870. Unsatisfactory news in the papers as to the intentions of the Prussian government to annex Luxemburg. ... Gladstone, who was at Roby on the occasion of his niece's marriage, and had intended to stay over the night, left at once, and a cabinet has met today. He told his friends there that the insolence of Bismarck's language was such as he had never known before in diplomacy, and could not be submitted to.

17 December 1870. Wrote ... to Lord Halifax,[142] who had written to me a few days ago. Among other matters I mention army reform, and suggest the question of purchase being taken up in earnest.

22 December 1870. The subject of army reorganisation continues to fill the papers.

23 December 1870. Young Balfour[143] ... was variously judged by those who met him: to me he appeared to have some cleverness, along with much conceit, and a kind of self-assertion which is likely to be more useful to him at the bar than in society.

26 December 1870. Servants' ball in evening, which they kept up till 3 a.m. We dined early to give them more time.

27 December 1870. News that Otway[144] has left the F.O. (from which

[141] The Stanley estates in Tipperary. See above, 25 Oct. 1869, for diarist's bro. electing to take cash rather than Irish land.
[142] Sir Charles Wood, 1st Vt Halifax (1800–85), lord privy seal 1870–4; cr. peer 1866.
[143] A.J. Balfour (1848–1930), premier 1902–5; grandson of Lady Derby's first husband.
[144] Arthur John Otway (1820–), under-sec. for foreign affairs, 1868–70, after army career and Sandhurst education.

he ought to have been excluded by his folly and conceit) and is replaced
by Ld Enfield,[145] a sensible cultivated man, though not brilliant.

My speech of the 14th has given rise to a certain amount of newspaper
criticism, and is on the whole rather too peaceable for the actual state
of public feeling: which does not surprise me. There is in England a
curious desire, when war is going on anywhere, to take part in it, and
a doubt whether to look on without siding with either combatant be
not a cowardly proceeding. This disposition to fight, without well
knowing with whom or for what, is manifest just now; and the U.S.
government is unconsciously doing service, since the warlike part of
the community is restrained in great measure by the fear that if we get
into a European quarrel, we shall have the Americans upon us before
we can get out of it. In Lancashire the Liberals are divided, the party
represented by the *Manchester Examiner* being all for peace, the *Guardian* –
the organ of Palmerstonian Whiggism – all for fighting if any pretext
is afforded. The Conservatives are probably as a body rather disposed
for war, but not united.

Sent £5 to a London female reformatory, and to wrote to enquire
about an institution that takes in destitute boys.[146]

[145] George Byng, Lord Enfield (1830–98); styled Vt Enfield 1860–86, when succ. his
father as 8th E. of Strafford; sec. to poor law board 1865–6, under-sec for foreign affairs
1871–4, under-sec. for India 1880–3.

[146] Derby spoke 11 times in the House of Lords in 1870, of which six were brief
interventions in committee. He did not speak on foreign affairs, on India, or on the
Education Act. Two speeches, on Clarendon's death and on colonies, were brief and
unimportant. His speech on naturalization was in support of a technical measure based
on an Anglo-U.S. protocol he had signed in 1868. His only truly political speeches were
on the Irish Land Bill, and on the Peace Preservation (Ireland) Act, in both cases
resolutely opposing Liberal illusions.

1871

1 January 1871 (Sunday). The last year has been one of great importance and happiness to me. Marriage, and the settling down here as possessor of estates, have altered wholly the habits of my life: and I believe that few people have more enjoyments or fewer troubles than have fallen to my lot. My health, though requiring some care in diet and exercise, has been good on the whole: an inherited tendency to gout, and (as one of its consequences) a singular liability to cold and cough, are the inconveniences I have to guard against. In politics I have not been active, nor does the appearance of the political world attract me: but of local duties, such as attendance at meetings, sessions, etc. I have taken my fair share. My mother remains happily in good health and fair spirits. I have lost no friend, and am engaged in no quarrel or dispute of any sort.

As regards public affairs, attention is monopolised by the war. No one thinks or talks of anything else. Internal politics are in abeyance, and the only measure, or set of measures, that will attract any serious attention in the coming session will be that for the reorganisation of the war department. Cardwell is unpopular, it would be hard to say why, except that he is thought to be wanting in the energy required, and there are many rumours of his being superseded: but they do not seem to rest on any real foundation. The ministry in general is less strong than it was, chiefly from being thought too peaceable, for the present excitable temper of the nation: at the same time there is no rival candidate, and one does not see why they should not go on.

Church in morning.

25 January 1871. There called an Irish deputation, representing the tenants of Ballykisteen ...[1] They expressed regret at my intention to sell ... We discussed the possibility of several of them buying their own lands, and it seems likely that several of them ... will be able to do this ... The priest ... pressed me strongly to give long leases at the present rents (which are notoriously below the value) to all the smaller tenants − but I declined to give any pledge...

29 January 1871. Heard from F. that C. has a (5th) son: wrote to wish them joy. There is certainly no present fear of our name dying out in the land.

[1] Tipperary.

73

Weeded out old pamphlets, keeping only a few out of a vast accumulation...

1 February 1871. I received from Ld Granville an overture (it could hardly be called an offer) as to taking the principal part in a commission which he proposes to send to Washington in order to settle the Alabama business. I answered it by saying that I had grave doubts as to the policy of the proceeding, but would discuss it, if he wished, verbally. In my own mind I have no hesitation as to refusing: the personal inconvenience to me would be excessive: and living as I do close to the chief port whence Americans disembark, the result of forming a large transatlantic acquaintance would be that every week would bring a fresh visitor with introductions, whom I should have to entertain. M.[2] too must either bring her daughters with her, which would be undesirable, or stay behind herself. But apart from personal reasons, I think the step a mistaken one: England has done all that she ought, all that can be expected or reasonably asked, in proposing arbitration: and that offer having been refused, it is not consistent with self-respect that she should open a new negociation.

2 February 1871. Lowe called on M. yesterday afternoon, and talked much of the financial and political situation. He complained of the expense to which the nation was being put, unnecessarily, but in the actual state of feeling this could not be avoided. He took a gloomy view of the future – thought the republican party was gaining in strength, that there was an unpleasant feeling among the masses as shown by the popular objection to granting Princess Louise[3] a dowry, that the Irish measures had prepared people's minds for many things that would formerly have been considered violations of the rights of property – that corporation and church lands would be compulsorily sold, before many years were over. After that the great landowners would be attacked, etc. He was well satisfied as to the material condition of the country, and the prospects of a good revenue, but his budget would be spoilt by the increased military demands.

I called on Ld Granville at his request, and discussed the question of the Washington mission. I found him undecided as to what should be yielded and what insisted on, anxious to please the Americans, and as it seemed to me, by no means averse to throw on a public personage unconnected with his party and himself the responsibility of making unpopular concessions. He named Sir G. Grey[4] as the other proposed

---

[2] Diarist's wife.

[3] Princess Louise (1848–1939), the Queen's 5th dau., m. 21 Mar. 1871 Lord Lorne (1845–1914), who succ. father as 9th D. of Argyll, 1900.

[4] Sir George Grey (1799–82), home sec. in Lib govts 1846–52, 1855–8, 1861–6; retired from office 1866, but remained an M.P. until 1874.

commissioner and Tenterden as the secretary. He was anxious that I should read the papers that have passed between the two governments, and in good manners I could not give a positive refusal without doing so, but my language must have left him in no doubt that I meant to refuse. He said that both the President and Fish[5] are anxious to see this business disposed of: and that men of business in the States complain of the impossibility of getting over English capital until the cause of quarrel was removed.

5 February 1871 (Sunday). M. went to Chapel Royal: I stayed at home.

... Talk with Disraeli on the political situation. His language is that he does not wish to turn out the ministry, especially by the help of ultra-liberals, but that it may not be easy to keep them where they are. The ultras on their side are already hostile, and will embarrass them to the utmost of their power. They have lost three of their best men,[6] and are without a leader if Gladstone's health should break down. Gladstone has lost his prestige – Cardwell is discredited as a war minister: who is there to fall back upon? He (D.) had had enough of being a minister without a majority: and did not intend to try that position again. But it would be a session of great interest and excitement. He spoke kindly of the D. of Richmond, but said that his total want of political training made it difficult to discuss matters with him in a satisfactory way.

6 February 1871. In the newspapers ... the will of the late Mr Brassey,[7] the great contractor. He has left, besides landed estates, personal property to the value of six and a half millions, which is equally divided among his sons. This is believed to be the largest amount for which probate has been granted in England under any one will.

8 February 1871. Dined with the D. of Richmond and about 35 peers ... The speech was read ... Very wisely in the interest of his government, Gladstone does not this year touch the question of Irish education, which would infallibly break up the Liberal party.

9 February 1871. H. of Lds ... Westminster moved the address ... Ld Rosebery[8] seconded, showing much promise; if he gives up racing and sticks to business, he will do well.

10 February 1871. Occupied several hours, in examining and destroying old papers in the library...

... Dined with Ly Molesworth,[9] meeting Duc d'Aumale,[10] Apponyi,

[5] President Grant (1822–85), president 1867–77; Hamilton Fish (1808–93), sec. of state 1869–77.

[6] Clarendon, Bright, and Childers.

[7] Thomas Brassey (1805–70), railway contractor.

[8] Archibald Primrose, 5th E. of Rosebery (1847–1929), premier 1894–5.

[9] Andalusia, Lady Molesworth (1809–88), Lib. political hostess; widow of Sir W. Molesworth (1810–55), radical cabinet minister.

[10] Henri, Duc d'Aumale (1822–97), 5th s. of Louis Philippe; in England 1848–71;

the new Hungarian minister ..., Gladstones, Fortescue[11] and Ly Waldegrave.[12] ... Sat next Ly Waldegrave, who not very complimentary to
her husband's colleagues, nor well pleased with the state of things: but
magnified the successes of their Irish administration. She talked much
and eagerly about extending the powers of the B. of Trade, at the
expense of the H.O.

20 February 1871. Argyll[13] called and pressed me to serve on a joint
committee on ... Indian finance ... I reserved my decision, but shall
probably accept, for what else is there to do?

21 February 1871. Destroyed letters and old papers in the library
upstairs...

23 February 1871. Engaged part of the afternoon in destroying papers
in the library. I thought this work was done, but discovered a new and
large collection in the drawers of the table at which my father used to
sit. Few are of value, but there is one curious mem. of the date of 1855,
on a scheme of administrative organisation forwarded by Disraeli, in
the drawing up of which I remember to have taken part.

24 February 1871. Busy all the afternoon sorting and destroying old
papers, of which I burnt so many in my room (being private letters
addressed to my father, I did not like to give them to a servant) that
the smell obliged me afterwards to go and sit upstairs.

26 February 1871. Much talk of the debate on the Black Sea conference
... Gladstone at one moment is said to have so far lost his temper that
some unparliamentary explosion was feared, but he kept within the
recognized limits of debate. His performance has however renewed the
doubts as to his health enduring the wear and tear of his present life:
and people ask, who is to come next?

1 March 1871. Dined Stanhope's: meeting Disraelis, Hardys, Bp of
Gloucester and Mrs Ellicott, Mahons,[14] Froude, etc. Pleasant. Disraeli in
high spirits at the quarrel which has broken out between ministers and
their radical allies, and at the blunders which they have been making:

dedicatee of *Lothair*, for Disraeli, one of 'the two most richly cultivated minds I ever met'
(Blake, *Disraeli*, 431).

[11] Chichester Fortescue, 1st Baron Carlingford (1823–98) Irish sec. 1865–6, 1868–70;
pres. of board of trade, *vice* Bright, Dec. 1870–4; cr. peer, 1874; ld. privy seal 1881–5; ld
pres. of council 1883–5; lib. unionist 1886.

[12] Frances, Lady Waldegrave, *née* Braham (1821–79); m., 4thly, Chichester Fortescue;
Harcourt's aunt; Lib. political hostess.

[13] George Douglas Campbell, 8th D. of Argyll (1823–1900), succ. 1847; sec. for India,
1868–74.

[14] Arthur Stanhope, 6th E. Stanhope (1838–1905); as Vt Mahon (1855–75), M.P. (Cons.)
1868, 1870–5; junior office 1874–5; succ. father 1875; first church estates commr 1878–
1905.

also perhaps a little at his own success in two late speeches,[15] which has been very great. His attack on Gladstone's indiscreet speech about the Black Sea, delivered last Friday, exasperated the Premier so much that some unparliamentary violence was feared: and on Monday night he attacked the foolish proposal for a committee with great force, and to the evident satisfaction of the House. He now holds the language, that by availing himself of the overtures made by independent Liberals, he could at any time turn out the ministry, but as they would come in again from the impossibility of making up a rival cabinet that could stand, or adopt the alternative of dissolving, there is no use in making the attempt.

3 March 1871. The House is tired of Gladstone: inclined to magnify his mistakes, and find excuses for quarrelling with him. He was scarcely at all cheered during any part of his speech,[16] which to him is new.

5 March 1871. Reading Darwin's new book. ... Talk, everywhere, of fresh follies of the P. of Wales in the matter of women. There is a divorce case threatened in which he will be implicated if it comes on, but it may perhaps be stopped. Another trial like that of last year would most likely create, which does not yet exist, an acknowledged Republican party, bent on putting an end to the monarchy after the Queen's death. His folly almost amounts to insanity in this one respect: no warning seems to have any effect.

... Heard (secretly) that the C. of Ex. has a scheme for laying a new tax on gas, so much for 1000 cubic feet: he told my informant that it would yield 4 millions, but I suspect a mistake (I suspect £400,000). Also for equalising and simplifying the various duties on succession: by which he expects to get three quarters of a million. He had a plan for taking away the right of the Bank to issue notes, and giving this to the state, by which the reserve of 14 millions now kept by the Bank, might be utilised to pay off debt: but on consideration he has thought the Bank too strong to be meddled with.

9 March 1871. Debate on Ireland ... I dwelt strongly on the anti-English feeling of the lower classes in Ireland,[17] saying that we did not dare to let the press loose, nor should we venture to take a plebiscite on the question whether the union of the two countries should continue. Neither of these assertions appeared to be popular, nor will they be so: but neither was disputed.

10 March 1871. Patten[18] confirmed the views I had taken last night as to the state of Irish feeling: saying that in his belief it could not be worse than it was.

---

[15] *H.* vol. 204, cols 839–54 (Treaty of Paris) and cols 1003–8 (on Westmeath Committee), delivered 24 and 27 Feb. respectively.

[16] On Westmeath Committee, *H*, vol 204, col 1179 (2 March).

[17] *H*, 9 Mar. 1871.

[18] Briefly Irish sec. under Disraeli, 1868.

11 March 1871. Dined Portland place, meeting Odo Russell ... Russell amusing – told us of the utter contempt in which the German officers hold the French ... A general and his staff who came to Versailles to treat about the armistice arrived in so hopeless a state of intoxication that nothing could be done except to put them to bed. At dinner time they were roused, and invited to dine with Bismarck, but the general was in such a condition that when soup came round he began to wash his hands in it, smiling benignantly.

... I find the cabinet think O.R. went too far in his negotiations with Bismarck ... There is no love lost between him [O.R.] and Ld Granville, whom he accuses pretty freely of being incapable – but this only to friends, and in private.

14 March 1871. A Conservative gathering is being organized in Lancashire, which Disraeli is requested to attend ... I have declined to have anything to do with it, so far: partly because I see no use, and some inconvenience in these electioneering appeals made at a time when no election is in prospect: partly because the only articulate expression of opinion that has come from the Conservative side of late is in favour of a policy of war, increased armaments, and the retention of purchase in the army: three things to all of which I am opposed.

17 March 1871. The Army Bill passed through a second reading after six nights debate, without a division. Disraeli opposed it, but only in a guarded and cautious manner, not as if much in earnest.

22 April 1871. Wrote to Disraeli, suggesting opposition to the budget.

28 April 1871. Dined with Dean of Westminster and Ly A. Stanley, meeting Bruce,[19] F. Leveson-Gower,[20] Mme Mohl,[21] and a Russian author named Tourgeneff,[22] who told me that his writings had done more than anything to bring about the emancipation of the serfs. He talked well with immense volatility, and had the whole evening to himself...

29 April 1871. In H.C. the government was defeated last night by a large majority on a question of preserving Epping Forest to the public.[23] The state of the House is indescribable: ministers have managed to offend nearly every important interest in the country by some one of their measures, and collectively the opposition they have provoked is too strong for them. The army dislikes abolition of purchase: the

[19] H. A. Bruce, 1st Baron Aberdare (1815–95), home sec. 1868–73; cr. peer 1873; lord pres. of council 1873–4.
[20] Hon. [E.] Frederick Leveson-Gower (1819–1907), Granville's bro.; M.P. (Lib.) Bodmin 1859–85.
[21] Mary, wife of German orientalist; held salon in Paris, which Derbys visited (Feb. 1872).
[22] Ivan Turgenev (1818–83), novelist.
[23] Defeated, 197 to 97, on whig motion: *H*, vol 205, col. 1867.

publicans are furious at Bruce's bill: the country gentlemen think Goschen's[24] new plans of rating revolutionary: the middle class dread an increased pressure of income tax: the farmers have been warned by Lowe that he will tax their houses and carts if he could: the east end is disgusted by the (now abandoned) match tax: the dissenters have not recovered their good humour at last year's education bill; the clergy oppose the removal of university tests: and all the property-holding classes are uneasy at the proposed doubling of succession duty. There is no one of their proposed reforms that might not have been carried singly: but no government can fight the whole community at once. It is quite uncertain how the division of Monday next may go, and speculations are frequent as to what will happen in the event of a ministerial defeat.

... Meeting of Museum trustees, 12 to 1.30: came away with Disraeli, and talk with him about the situation. He is half disposed to think office again within his reach: and reckons on the dissatisfied Whigs for help. But in the same breath he says that he has had enough of being a minister in a minority – which I can well believe!

6 May 1871. From what I can learn of the state of public feeling, it seems as if something like a panic were spreading among the upper and middle classes. They believe that opinion among the masses is thoroughly revolutionary, that property will not be respected, that republicanism is gaining ground, and that our generation will see a general unsettlement of all opinions, social, political, and religious. I cannot discover what has created this vague feeling of alarm, which is not justified by either the composition of the existing H. of C. or the apparent strength of the ultra party outside: some part of it may be due 1) to the Irish land bill of last year, which was more revolutionary in principle than any act which parliament has yet sanctioned, though in practice it works fairly enough: 2) to the personal character of Gladstone, of whom his own colleagues are growing more and more afraid: they think that between impetuosity of temperament, zeal for the interests of the poor, and determination not to be outbid in popularity, there is no length to which he will not go: Bright himself being conservative when compared to him (this Lord Clarendon has said more than once in my hearing): 3) to the absence of any powerful or organised conservative opposition in the Commons: which annoys moderate Liberals the more, that it prevents their playing safely the old game of bidding for popularity by proposing what they know their opponents are strong enough to prevent being carried: 4) to the

[24] G. J. Goschen, 1st Viscount Goschen (1831–1907), pres. of poor law board 1868–71; 1st lord of admiralty 1871–4.

unsettled state of France, and the outbreak of the socialist party in
Paris: 5) to the supposed existence in the Universities, especially in
Oxford, of a party hostile to the Christian religion, at least as hitherto
understood: 6) to the agitation against the rights of landowners, at the
head of which Mill has put himself: 7) to the demand, likely to be
✓ conceded, for women's right to vote, which if granted will add a new
and wholly unknown element to the already very large electoral body.
There may be other reasons, but the above account for much of the
alarm which exists.

7 *May 1871*. Dined Ld and Ly Granville's ... Pleased with Ld
Lansdowne,[25] one of the few young men of his class whom I have met,
who seemed at once industrious and sensible.

10 *May 1871*. Received notes from Ld Sandon[26] and Mr Rathbone,[27]
asking me to help in promoting a company in Liverpool for providing
labourers with decent houses. I answered that I would make enquiry
before answering, as I know nothing of the parties in whose hands the
undertaking is, but that I heartily sympathised with the object. Probably
there is no place on earth where dirt, drink, and disease prevail as they
do in Liverpool. The great demoralisation of the town dates from the
Irish famine...

29 *May 1871*. The insurrection at Paris has been suppressed ... A
large proportion of the combatants were foreigners, belonging to the
international secret society of whose existence there seems little doubt,
though its precise nature is not known...

1 *June 1871*. To the rooms of the Law Association, Liverpool, at 2
p.m. to take the chair at a meeting for the promotion of a company to
put up improved dwellings for the labouring class. The amount of
overcrowding which now exists is greater than probably in any other
town in England. According to Dr French, the medical officer, 150,000
persons, or nearly a third of the whole population, are living in houses
sublet so that each family has only a single room. Hence drunkenness,
disease, and an enormous mortality. The meeting was attended by
about 200 persons, all of the respectable class. ... I spoke about half
an hour.[28]

5 *June 1871*. Disraeli called: talked of the treaty, and of Northcote,
whom he had seen. Also of the state of France.

[25] Henry Petty-Fitzmaurice, 5th M. of Lansdowne (1845–1927), succ. 1866; Lib. junior
minister 1869–74, 1880 (resigned); governed Canada and India, then Unionist statesman.
[26] Dudley Ryder, 3rd E. of Harrowby (1831–1900), M.P. 1856–60, 1868–82; succ. 1882;
as Vt Sandon, vice-pres. of council 1874–8 (outside cabinet); pres. of board of trade 1878–
80; lord privy seal 1885–6, both in cabinet.
[27] William Rathbone (1819–1902), Liverpool merchant, philanthropist, and Lib. M.P.
[28] *T*, 2 June 1871, 12c.

6 June 1871. Tenterden called, and vindicated the treaty[29] in a conversation of more than an hour. I said little. He is evidently proud of it, and considers it as his personal work. I hear he had an unpleasant reception from Hammond,[30] and having been in his own eyes little less than an ambassador, he does not like the transition to a clerkship.

7 June 1871. Meeting at D. of Richmond's to discuss the American treaty. Present, Cairns, Salisbury, Carnarvon, Redesdale,[31] Malmesbury, Chelmsford, and myself. All, except Salisbury were against voting for Ld Russell's motion;[32] and he spoke doubtfully. We agreed to criticise the treaty, but confine ourselves to discussion.

8 June 1871. Northcote called; he did not enter much into discussion on the treaty, but talked of the U.S. generally. He said he liked the people better, and the institutions worse, than he had expected.

9 June 1871. Letters: one asking for help to repair the chapel of Trin. Coll. Cambridge, which I can scarcely avoid subscribing to, but the money might be better employed.

11 June 1871. General complaints as to the impossibility of getting any business done in the H. of C. ... To some extent the present delay is ascribable to Gladstone's want of tact in dealing with the House. He tries to drive instead of leading, threatens to sit on till September if necessary, to hold more frequent morning sittings etc. forgetting that he can do none of these things without the cooperation, not only of his colleagues, but of his party, and even in some degree of his opponents.

13 June 1871. Heard from Lord Cowley,[33] who knows the fact, that the Emperor,[34] so far from being, as was supposed, in danger of poverty, has private means to the extent of £20,000 a year.

... Sat next Ly Clanricarde ...[35] She told me that not long ago she had been talking of Irish affairs to Gladstone ... On her asking which among the Irish Liberal M.P.s he did regard as his friends, he named three as those whom he most especially respected and looked to as reflecting national opinion. They were – Maguire, Murphy and Macar-

[29] Treaty of Washington (8 May 1871), submitting *Alabama* claims to arbitration.

[30] Edmund Hammond, 1st Baron Hammond (1802–90), perm. under-sec. at F.O. 1854–73; cr. peer 1874.

[31] J. T. Freeman-Mitford, 2nd Baron Redesdale (1805–86), cr. earl 1877; chmn of ctees. and dep. speaker in H. of L. 1851–86; 'narrow, prejudiced, and utterly unaware of what is going on in the country' (Disraeli, 1880). Derby refers to 'his laborious habits and honesty in dealing with private bills' but also to 'his obstinacy and ill manners and the many enemies he has made' (Derby diary, 28 Aug. 1876).

[32] Russell opposed the Washington Treaty (12 June); *H*, 12 June 1871.

[33] Henry Wellesley, 1st E. Cowley (1804–84), amb. at Paris 1852–67.

[34] Napoleon III.

[35] Dau. of George Canning, premier; mother of Lord Dunkellin, whose motion destroyed the Russell ministry of 1865–67; wife of Palmerstonian Galway landlord.

thy Downing![36] all of whom have since been in opposition to him, and who hold the most extreme nationalist view.

16 June 1871. The English representatives of the 'International' democratic association have signed an address which is in substance an apology for the acts of the Commune of Paris, including the murder of the Archbishop. To this address are affixed the names of Lucraft,[37] a member of the London School Board, and Odger,[38] whom the Liberal press has continually recommended as a candidate for the H. of C. ... The manifesto will produce a great and probably a lasting effect on the middle class ... The Association boasts of having supporters in every country in Europe, and threatens to begin the war again before long – which is likely enough to happen.

17 June 1871. With Disraeli in afternoon: talk about army bill, ballot, the American treaty, state of Ireland, and Paris: he agrees in thinking the repeal movement serious, now the priests have joined it. He points to what has passed, as justifying the opinion expressed by him many years ago as to the influence of the secret societies. He spoke as if it would be in his power to induce Canada to break off the fishery treaty (which I doubt, for colonists do not want to be encouraged by English sympathy before expressing their opinions on their own affairs) but shrunk from the responsibility, though feeling something must be said. He thought the real explanation of Gladstone's want of success in managing the House was, apart from his deficiency in tact, that the House having done what it was returned to do as regards the Irish church and land, was not disposed to initiate fresh reforms, its members being individually conservative, alarmed at the state of feeling abroad, and the rich radicals very few.

D. seemed in fair spirits, but rather wearied with long sittings which is not strange.

23 June 1871. Debate last night in H. of C. on ballot: which was marked by little novelty, but in the course of a preliminary discussion Gladstone spoke of the expediency of reconsidering 'at an early period' both the question of franchise and that of the distribution of seats, neither of which, he said, had been settled in a manner altogether satisfactory.[39] This expression of opinion had reminded the world that

[36] John Francis Maguire (d. 1873), mayor of Cork 1861–4; f. (1841) and ed. *Cork Examiner*; R.C.; M.P. Dungarvan 1852–65 and Cork C. 1865–72; N. D. Murphy, M.P. Cork C. 1862–80, solicitor; McCarthy Downing (1814–79), M.P. Cork Co. 1814–79, solictor.

[37] Benjamin Lucraft (1809–97), trade unionist and radical leader; member of General Council of First International 1864–71, and of London School Board.

[38] George Odger (1820–77), pres. of First International 1870; leading trade unionist and working man's candidate.

[39] *H*, vol. 207, col 406 (22 June 1871): 'There is the question of the franchise. Many of us may think that great question may advantageously receive, at any early period, further attention'.

he gave in his adhesion, last year, to the principle of universal suffrage: but it was done in so offhand a manner that he was not thought to have spoken seriously, or at least with premeditation. Now we have a threat of renewed agitation and fresh changes, uttered at a moment when both parliament and the country desire nothing more than rest. Disraeli naturally did not lose his opportunity, and his reply is said to have been singularly happy. The effect of Gladstone's announcement on his own supporters was a kind of displeased surprise, plainly indicated (as I am told) by looks and silence.

24 June 1871. Letters from Hale ... as to the Irish estates. I accept Mr O'Connor's offer of £160,000, which with Ryan's £6000, and the backrents, makes a fair, though not a brilliant settlement of the matter. I gain from £2000 to £2400 yearly income, and lessen the burden of debt on the English estates by more than $\frac{1}{4}$th.

26 June 1871. Walk with Carnarvon ... He looks on the existence of the 'International Society' and the principles put forward by it, as a new fact in history, unlike anything that has gone before, in which I cannot agree with him, for surely socialism, in some form, is as old as civilisation.

3 July 1871. Cairns called: discussed the Army Bill with him: he agrees with me as to the impolicy of opposing it: Carnarvon takes the same view: but Richmond has the feeling of an old guardsman on the question of purchase: and Salisbury is always for fighting.

4 July 1871. Meeting at D. of Richmond's on Army Bill, attended by Cairns, Carnarvon, Salisbury, Redesdale, Ld Strathnairn, Ld Hertford,[40] Ld Hardinge,[41] and one or two more: how selected I have no clear idea. No agreement was come to, nor was it likely: Cairns and Carnarvon, with me, pointed out the danger and inexpediency of trying to throw out the bill: seeing that purchase cannot be permanently maintained, and that the officers are never likely to get equally good terms again. Salisbury and Redesdale were strongest on the opposite side: dwelling chiefly on the political aspect of the question, the risk of breaking up the party by declining to give expression to their views, the discredit of yielding to the fear of agitation, and so forth. The Duke at first inclined strongly to the latter opinion, but was a good deal shaken by the discussion.

8 July 1871. Talk with Disraeli, who thinks the Ballot Bill likely to break down in the Commons, very many of the Liberal M.P.s being averse to it in their hearts, though compelled by the double pressure

[40] Francis Seymour, 8th M. of Hertford (1812–84); army career; became general (1876).
[41] Charles Hardinge, 2nd Vt Hardinge (1822–94), M.P. (Cons.) 1851–6; succ. 1856; under-sec. for war 1858–9.

of the ministry and their constituents to vote in its favour: hence they are willing to make objections, and not disinclined to see time wasted by useless speeches. But in last night's sitting, he says, the objections suggested were so serious as to compel the withdrawal of the clause discussed, and the work of committee has to be begun over again. The old constitutional Liberals are averse to have the question settled, because they are at the end of the reforms with which their training has made them familiar, and neither see clearly what new controversies are about to be entered into, nor like the prospect before them. What is vaguely feared is legislation, or demands for legislation, in the Socialist or Trades Union sense: which does not suit a House essentially of the middle class, and very wealthy.

11 July 1871. T. Hunt[42] called: I urged him not to allow threatening or violent articles to appear on the Army question, as such demonstrations are the surest way to prevent the bill passing through the Lords.

18 July 1871. Much talk in the world about Salisbury's speech ...[43] If he is acting on any other motive than that of gratifying an unhappy temper, the object must be to provoke a collision between the two Houses – but for what purpose I cannot see.

21 July 1871. To Lincoln's Inn to sign a paper relating to the amount of personal property, which from £200,000 is reduced to only £70,000, by unpaid bills and the balance against me at the bank. It is unintelligible to me how my father, with his habits of business, could have endured the financial muddle in which I have found everything. But a year or two will see me out of it.

To D. of Richmond, where met Cairns, Carnarvon, Salisbury, and discussed the situation. It was agreed not to throw out the bill, so far as it provides compensation for the officers, but to accompany it with a resolution condemning the conduct of the government. We were all agreed on substance.

24 July 1871. Disraeli talked freely and eagerly of the situation, which he does not like. He sees that Gladstone has reconciled himself with the ultras, though at the cost of alienating the Whigs: thinks that he (G.) is prepared to go all lengths to be the man of the people, and that the next attacks will be on the H. of Lds and the land. (I remember

---

[42] Thornton Leigh Hunt (1810–73), journalist.

[43] On army regulation bill, 17 July 1871, *H*, ccvii, 1849–59, urging rejection of bill on general grounds of refusing to pander to democratic opinion, though Salisbury also praised purchase as procuring 'an easy Army retirement and a pure system of promotion'. Earlier in the debate Derby, in opposition to his party, had urged 'Get rid of it now' before it became an election issue. He had privately pressed the government to abolish purchase: 'I believe you could hardly take up a more popular question'. (Derby to Halifax, 17 Dec. 1870, Halifax MSS.)

that G. said last year to Clarendon, 'If I am to be baited much longer
in this way, I will take off the gloves' – which is what he is doing.) D.
repeated an expression which Delane had used to him, and which, he
added, 'as it is not flattering to me, I suppose was sincere': to the effect
that there was no reaction of public feeling in favour of any individual,
but that there was a strong reaction against one – namely the Premier:
this D. went on to say, he thought was about the truth. He objected to
make any move against the government, on the ground that a vote of
censure proposed by him, or at his instigation, would not be supported
by the Liberal malcontents: they could not join in it without risking
their seats: but if (as is now the common talk) a vote of confidence
were proposed as an answer to the expected censure of the peers, they
might easily stay away, or even oppose it. He wished to see a motion
of that kind, as among other results it would certainly prevent the
ballot from passing.

26 July 1871. Letter, among others, from Pakington,[44] asking to see
me: I telegraphed in answer, and he came down about 4 p.m. His
object was to ask me to join in a plan for creating a committee
or commission (self-appointed) composed of Conservative peers and
landowners, to consider sundry demands of the artisan class, as stated
by their leaders. The idea of such a committee appears to have
originated with Scott Russell,[45] the shipbuilder, lately a bankrupt. The
idea of the men, or rather of those who represent them, is to work on
the feelings or party-interests of the landed class, as against the
mercantile and manufacturing employers: an ingeniously conceived
scheme, which seems to have succeeded to some extent, for J. Manners
takes it up warmly, Carnarvon rather approves, Pakington is hot for it,
and Disraeli sees in it a new method of outbidding the Whigs, or rather
Gladstone. The demands which they put forward are vague, the
language used admitting of being construed in various senses: which
does not arise from accident: the principal are limitation of hours of
labour to eight, right to take land compulsorily for workmen's dwellings,
wherever wanted: sale of articles of consumption (as I read it) on State
account, thereby suppressing the small tradesman: establishment of
technical schools: increased public provision for recreation and pleasure:
and some minor details, which I do not clearly make out. Pakington
explained these at length, and seemed to approve. I tried to point out

[44] Sir John Pakington (né Russell), 1st Baron Hampton (1799–1880); M.P. (Cons.) 1837–
74; cr. peer by Disraeli on losing seat, 1874; involved with diarist in social reform in 1850s
(*Stanley Journals*, 143–5).
[45] John Scott Russell (1808–82), shipbuilder; sec. to the society of arts 1845–50; jr. sec.
to Great Exhibition, 1851; with partners, bought the Exhibition building; bankrupt 1861,
annulled 1862; F.R.S. 1849; wrote *Systematic Technical Education for the English People* (1869),
and works on naval architecture.

to him that the compulsory limitation of hours of labour for adults involved in principle something like an economical revolution, and that the whole scheme pointed in one direction – to the suppression of the capitalist, which would very soon be followed by that of the landowner and fundholder: though these latter parts of the Socialist programme are, for prudential reasons, kept in the background at present. In fact the plan, as he laid it before me, is that of the Socialists, as lately stated by themselves in a manifesto called *Rights and Wrongs of Workmen*, only with the part relating to the land left out.

I endeavoured to impress on P. the gravity of the questions with which he is playing: but not, as far as I could judge, with much success. He is intoxicated with the prospect of being one of the regenerators of society, and reconciling the people with the aristocracy.[46]

27 July 1871. Many letters, chiefly to beg, but among them one from Carnarvon enforcing the view taken by Pakington, and begging me not to decide against it. I answered him, expressing doubt whether I understood P's whole scheme, and dislike of what I did understand, but observing that he had not asked me to give any decision for or against.

29 July 1871. I answered Pakington declining to join his committee, but giving as my chief reason the impossibility of attendance, and saying nothing as to the merits of the scheme in itself.

1 August 1871. Letters, papers etc: morning idle, yet busy: destroying letters, throwing away parliamentary papers, etc.

Holwood by 5 p.m. train. Walk after arriving there ... The advantage and pleasure of having this place of retreat while detained in or near town by business, is not to be exaggerated.

5 August 1871. Drove with M. to Chiselhurst to call on the Emperor[47] and Empress: they received us together in a pleasant sunny room, where however they had a fire, and which smelt strongly of cigarettes. I should hardly have known the Emperor again: he is grown very fat, and walks with an obvious lameness, but otherwise appears in perfect health, his features are as little expressive of intellect as in the days of his power, but neither is there any sign of weakness or despondency upon them: the anxieties and misfortunes of last year have not left a visible mark. The expression is that of a kindly, good-natured, rather indolent man of the world. He talked freely and pleasantly, for the most part about England, but making no allusion to France. ... We stayed with them about half an hour.

[46] For a summary of press reports on the New Social Movement, see *Ann. Reg.* 1871, 117–20.
[47] Napoleon III.

15 August 1871. With Moult in the office, looking over receipts of last year from each estate separately, but not with much satisfaction, for there are many things which I fail to understand, and though I am far from distrusting anyone employed here, I yet feel disagreeably the extent to which I am in their hands.

17 August 1871. Wet morning, with east wind, which brings the smell of St Helens into our windows more strongly than I have ever observed it before. The neighbours say it is an increasing nuisance, and if it continues to grow upon us, it may possibly decide in my lifetime the question of removing from this part of the world: which sooner or later is inevitable ... North Lancashire is evidently our place of retreat, as nearly all the family estates, and all the prestige of the name, lie in this county, and to leave it would be a mistake in every way.

20 August 1871. Since coming down (to Knowsley), I have resumed the practice of gymnastic work, moderately in quantity, but not omitting it altogether on any day: and am conscious of increased health and energy in consequence. I owe the first adoption of this device for securing exercise to Dr Ferguson, who recommended it to me in 1857, and for several years I practised it assiduously, at Harrison's rooms in the Haymarket: but increasing occupations, and some dislike to the publicity of the place, made me gradually leave off attendance there, and until this house became my own, I had no opportunity of putting up the requisite machinery at home.

22 August 1871. East wind, and the smell of St Helens again very perceptible. I will write to the inspector of alkali works if I can get his address.

Parliament prorogued yesterday, and the newspapers are full of comments on the session. It has undoubtedly left Gladstone and his colleagues in a weaker position than they were in at its commencement: the prestige of success which belonged to them in 1869–70 is vanished and in departmental administration they have managed badly. Bruce is a failure at the Home Office: the Admiralty has been (to say the least) unlucky, and the reforms introduced by Childers appear to have done more harm than good: Cardwell, rightly or wrongly, is thought to be ill suited for the War Dept: the Church and Land Bills have not put an end to disaffection, nor conciliated the Irish: the American treaty is accepted as patching up a quarrel which all the world wished to see settled, but the conditions are such that it cannot be a matter of pride or congratulation on our side: the Black Sea arrangement has undone the main result of the Crimean War, and made it clear that we shall not again fight for Turkey: the budget began with a blunder, almost ridiculous, and was only amended by Lowe adopting an expedient which a week before he had condemned as unjust, and which Fawcett denounced as an undue concession to democratic prejudices:

in a word, no department has come out of the trial of the session with credit, except those like the India Office which attract scarcely any public notice. In regard of parliamentary action, the session has not been as barren as is the fashion to call it: the abolition of University Tests, and of purchase in the army, are important changes, and a ballot bill[48] has for the first time been carried through the H. of C. But these results have only been accomplished by sacrificing a host of minor, but still important measures, the Licensing and Rating Bills being the most conspicuous. It is admitted on all hands that Gladstone has lost his influence in the House: his friends do not dispute the fact, but account for it by ascribing to the members middle-class and plutocratic prejudices, and saying that the working class electors know him better: which may or may not be true, for nobody can tell.

26 August 1871. The papers are full of the East Surrey election,[49] which on all sides they regard as significant, no Conservative having sat for that district since 1841. The causes are variously stated. The licensed victuallers will not easily forgive Bruce's licensing bill: the Liberal landowners dislike Goschen's rating bill: the action of the government as regards enclosure of commons had dissatisfied a certain class: but the main reason is that neither the Premier nor his colleagues hold the position in public estimation which they held two years ago, while Gladstone's determination not to allow himself to be outbid for the lead of the Radical section has alarmed the Whigs.

Note. I might have added that the acts and manifestos of the 'International' have thoroughly alarmed the well-to-do classes, and created a vague, but powerful feeling of resistance to revolutionary movements, or what may be thought such. I am convinced that the opportunity is either come, or near at hand, for a ministry like that of Sir R. Peel. But who is there to take advantage of it? Disraeli is disliked by many, and not much trusted even by those who like him best: nor can I wonder at it, for his way of looking at things is peculiar to himself, and the Reform Bill of 1867 cannot be forgotten. He has been unalterably faithful to his party connection, but with him a temporary success is an end in itself: he either does not care, or thinks it useless to struggle, for distant results: and indeed will sacrifice these for the advantage of the moment, as has been often seen. Hardy is honest, sincere, and has a kind of ability, but I do not think he has sufficient range or breadth of mind to manage the H. of C. And there is no one else.

31 August 1871. To Bury for an agricultural meeting ... I was well received in the show yard ... but I do not think the popular feeling

---

[48] Defeated in the Lords 97–48 (10 August 1971).
[49] Cons. gain by 3912 to 2749 (26 Aug. 1871); in 1868 the Libs won by 384.

was as strongly shown as at Preston or Bootle. Statter's merits as an agent are great, and I see them more and more clearly: but his present unpopularity is obvious (I cannot wonder at it) and some part of the blame falls on me.[50]

3 September 1871. Ld Shaftesbury,[51] having taken the lead in throwing out the ballot bill, is gone down to Glasgow, where for several days he has been addressing popular audiences, always well, and at times enthusiastically received.

4 September 1871. Long interview with Hale ... in which I desired him to take any opportunity that may occur of selling outlying pieces of land in Liverpool, to help in paying off debt. I do not propose to touch the bulk of the estate in Kirkdale, and still less in Bootle: but only the fragments scattered about Liverpool, which may collectively be worth £250,000.

6 September 1871. Gladstone, to whom rest seems impossible, has delivered two speeches to country audiences: one at Wakefield, one at Whitby:[52] the former is harmless enough ... : the latter (first in order of date) contains observations which have been severely criticised. ... More important is the indication given of Gladstone's readiness to raise a cry against wealth and the upper classes. His increasing use of ultra-democratic language is noted on all sides, and it is believed that his own colleagues are seriously uneasy. The common talk is that he leans more and more to socialist ideas: but singularly, the radical party does not appear to trust him, and follows his lead unwillingly. His family tendency to mental excitement is well known, and I have heard of bets being laid on his going mad before the next general election.

18 September 1871. C.[53] talks of her brother Clarendon: thinks he will do nothing in public life: he dislikes exertion, and is entangled with a woman (this I knew before): he is better off, she says, than anyone believed, having £12,000 a year after all debts are paid, and not including Ly Clarendon's life-income.

... C. says F. is subject to fits of depression and low spirits, which last for days, and from which it is not easy to rouse him.

23 September 1871. Begun again gymnastic exercises ... The effect of the quickened circulation which they produce on my nerves and spirits is curiously marked. A few minutes of strong muscular effort will remove for a day the feeling of languor which is caused by being shut up at home on a wet day. I used to find the same effect from cutting

[50] Hence the unbroken Liberalism of Bury, so untypical of Lancashire towns.
[51] Anthony Ashley Cooper, 7th E. of Shaftesbury (1801–85), philanthropist.
[52] 2 Sept. 1871, taking strong radical line.
[53] Constance Stanley née Villiers, Clarendon's daughter.

trees with an axe. But it is a stimulant which like all stimulants, should not be too freely used.

Butt[54] has been returned for Limerick, unopposed: indeed no one could have stood against him without great personal risk, so excited were the mob. He is notoriously a man of bad character, venal, having left the House under a cloud, oppressed with debts: in politics he has belonged to all sides: personally he has nothing in his favour except a florid kind of oratory, with little either of taste or power . . .

25 September 1871. The discrepancy between nominal rental and actual receipts has often puzzled me: it exceeds £8000 a year: I think now I have made out its cause. The arrears practically irrecoverable, or which for some reason are remitted, come to one half of this amount, at £4000: a large deduction, but possibly inevitable on an estate like mine. The other £4000 of apparent deficiency is due to the practice of letting building land, and entering it in the account as let at such and such a price, although the payment of rent is not required until the building to be put upon it is actually in existence. It represents in fact future but not present income. I am glad to have cleared this matter up, as it caused me some perplexity.

27 September 1871. Another speech by Gladstone, the subject this time being the 'Home Rule' movement, which he condemned strongly enough to satisfy English feeling, hinting at the same time at concessions to the priests on the subject of education. The place was Aberdeen.[55]

6 October 1871. Sir R.[56] and Miss Gerard went away. He says that he can control 500 votes in S. Lancashire, and told M. that they would be given to the candidate whom I support, but that he had no confidence in Disraeli.

Pakington has been delivering an address at the 'Social Science' gathering, much in the sense of the ideas which he pressed on me in July at Holwood: what he means exactly is not easy to make out, and perhaps he does not know it himself: but his language is justly commented on by *The Times*[57] as giving encouragement to wild theories. He seems to have said among other things that the State was bound to provide the workingmen with lodging at fair rents and wholesome

[54] Isaac Butt (1813–79), Irish leader; professor of political economy, Trinity College, Dublin, 1836; protectionist, 1849; entered parliament, 1852, as Derbyite; led Irish home rule party 1870–9; cf. *Stanley Journals*, 322, describing Butt as 'now a pauper, and with a ruined character'; protestant.

[55] *T,* 27 Sept. 1871, 6 a-f. Reprinted in John Vincent, 'Gladstone and Ireland', *Proceedings of the British Academy*, lxiii (1977), 232–6.

[56] Sir Robert Gerard, 1st Baron Gerard of Bryn (1808–87), cr. peer 1876; R.C., with estates, mostly in S. Lancs., worth £43,000 p.a.

[57] *T,* 5 Oct. 1871, 12c. Pakington stressed English technical backwardness, as laid bare in Scott Russell's recent pamphlet, and urged a great extension of education.

food at reasonable prices: rather a vague and dangerous doctrine to lay down. The explanation of the matter is that P. with some activity and public spirit has much vanity and not a very clear head, and thus he enunciates principles which he has not cared to work out to their results.

7 October 1871. Cross[58] talks much with me on the wish of the local Conservatives to have a party meeting some time in the winter. We agree in disliking the idea, partly because for a party in opposition, and likely to continue so, it is disadvantageous to be compelled to announce a policy – their proper course being to lie in wait for, and profit by, the mistakes of their opponents: partly also because Disraeli must be invited to make the principal speech, and no one knows, or can guess, what he is likely to say. If he confines himself to criticism on the events of last session, the subject is worn out: if he lays down a programme for the future, we do not know what we may find ourselves pledged to. I mentioned to Cross my suspicion that he was inclining to the semi-socialist ideas of 'Young England' of which Pakington has just given us a sample: and he also thought this probable. Still I said if the local leaders insisted upon it, the thing must be, and I could not refuse to attend, unless absolutely aware that the language to be held was contrary to my views. Every conversation that I have with Cross raises my opinion of his judgement and good sense.[59]

15 October 1871 (Sunday). Church: walk in the afternoon with M. ... A Mrs Brooke has given in one lump to the N. Counties Idiot Asylum, £30,000 ... Calculations have lately appeared in the papers to the effect that in the last two years alone, £100,000 has been contributed to public uses in sums of not less than £1000 each. I take these unusual displays of liberality to be in a great degree the result (though not consciously on the part of the givers) of the uneasy feeling which prevails on the subject of the poorer classes. Everybody is saying, 'Something must be done for them' and for most people the most obvious expedient is to draw a cheque.

The papers during the last few days have got hold of, and been busy with, the programme of workingmen's demands which Pakington communicated to me on the 25th of July last: and naturally see in it an attempt at coalition between Conservatives and Socialists, on the basis of 'Young England' ideas of twenty-five years ago. How far Disraeli had to do with the business I do not know, and do not care to

[58] (Sir) R. A. Cross (1823–1914), Lancastrian; M.P. Cons. 1857–62, 1868–86; educ. with diarist at Rugby and Trinity, Cambridge; bar, 1849; home sec. 1874–80, 1885–6; cr. vt 1886; Indian sec. 1886–92; lord privy seal 1895–1900; banker, social reformer, private financial adviser to the Queen; on local bench with Derby.

[59] See below, 9 and 18 Feb. 1874, for Derby's influence on Cross's promotion to cabinet.

enquire. It is not unlikely that he may have played with the movement, and encouraged it to some extent, while keeping clear of it personally.

28 October 1871. The only book of any importance which I have been trying to study is Maurice's *Essays*: and they leave me utterly in the dark as to his meaning. After several attempts, I can make nothing out of them: I suppose from natural inaptitude (of which I have always been conscious) for metaphysical thought.

29 October 1871 (Sunday). Church: read and wrote: Northcote and Sir M. Beach[60] came over to luncheon – the first by invitation – and were persuaded to stay for dinner. ... He and Sir M. are in Liverpool on a commission of enquiry into Friendly Societies, in which they have already detected a good deal of rascality – the very poor being as usual the victims.

31 October 1871. The political world is busy with a speech delivered by Gladstone at Greenwich last Saturday,[61] which has undoubtedly in part removed the unfavourable impression produced by his ill temper and bad management during the session. ... One extraordinary blunder is attracting general notice. The Premier quoted some verses, very indifferent as compositions, in favour of self-help: in the verses themselves there is no harm, but they are extracted from a book called the *Secularist's Manual* or some such name, which is full of indecent parodies of religious and scriptural writings, being indeed compiled with the express object of bringing these into ridicule.

11 November 1871. In Dublin a fresh indication has been given of the strength of the feeling of disaffection which prevails. A man named Kelly has been tried for shooting in the street one Talbot, a detective officer who had given evidence against the Fenians ... yet a jury carefully selected have unanimously acquitted the prisoner. Butt was leading counsel for the defence ... No event during the last four or five years has more clearly shown the tendency of popular feeling.

15 November 1871. The acquittal of Kelly has been celebrated with bonfires and rejoicings in various parts of Ireland: being regarded as a Fenian victory, which it is.

20 November 1871. I know not if it be worth noting that in the last fortnight – having no active occupation, or next to none – I have been renewing acquaintance with the Latin classics. I have read Juvenal through with some care, Persius more slightly, and the Epistles of Horace (but these last I knew well before): and attempted Ovid, whose

[60] Sir M. E. Hicks Beach (1837–1916), 1st Lord St Aldwyn; Cons. M.P. 1864–1906; junior office 1868; chief sec. for Ireland 1874–8, 1886–7; col. sec. 1878–80; chanc. of exchequer 1885–6, 1895–1902; cr. vt 1906, earl 1916.

[61] At Blackheath, 28 Oct. 1871.

smooth and monotonous verse did not encourage me to go on. Reading of this kind gratifies and perhaps improves the taste, but I doubt whether it adds much to the stock of ideas. I have also ... gone slowly and carefully through the greater part of Hume's essays − which well deserve the trouble.

25 November 1871. I was shown a kind of circular, in print, calling on Ld Romilly[62] to resign his office of Master of the Rolls. It is alleged, I believe truly, that he cannot keep awake on the bench, and that thus cases are decided on a very imperfect hearing of the evidence or argument.

2 December 1871. Received and answered a letter from W.H.[63] about the meeting of Liverpool Conservatives, which some of the promoters are anxious to turn into a county demonstration. This being contrary to the understanding come to, and altogether impolitic, I say that if it is permitted I shall decline to take the chair or attend.

13 December 1871. Talk with Cairns as to a regency: he thinks the Princess of Wales should be regent, if the necessity should arise:[64] the only other possible contenders are the D. of Edinburgh and the D. of Cambridge. But the first of these is successor to the foreign Duchy of Coburg, which is an objection: the latter is not very near to the Crown, and neither young nor a good life. To the Princess, the objections are her foreign birth, little acquaintance with English ways of life, deafness, and the doubt which exists whether her impenetrable reserve is the result of discretion, or of the absence of interests and ideas. *Per contra*, she is nearest in relationship, can have no interest other than that of her son, is young, handsome, and will attract a great deal of interest and sympathy.

Talk also as to ballot, on which Cairns evidently thinks, as I do, that it is useless to make further opposition. He thinks it will do the Conservative cause no harm in England, and in Scotland there is none to be done: the doubt is as to Ireland.

He has an idea, which I cannot see the policy of, that it might be well to move an amendment to the address, expressing in strong terms the devotion of parliament to the monarchy, and its determination to maintain the Irish Union. Surely this is giving too much importance to Sir C. Dilke[65] and Mr Butt!

31 December 1871. The gross rental of the Galloway estates is £31,500.

---

[62] John Romilly, 1st Baron Romilly (1802–74), master of rolls 1851–73.
[63] W. Hornby, comptroller of Derby's household.
[64] P. of Wales nearly d. of typhoid, 8–14 Dec. 1871.
[65] Sir C. W. Dilke (1843–1911), 2nd Bt; M.P. (Lib.) 1868–86, 1892–1911; notorious republican in early 1870s; for. under-sec. 1880–2; pres. of local govt board 1882–5 (in cabinet); ruined by scandal, 1886.

This is reduced by fixed local charges to £28,500, or thereabouts. The debts are £170,000 which at $4\frac{1}{2}$ p.c. make a deduction of £7650 for interest, leaving in round numbers nearly £21,000 a year. But there are temporary charges, and Ly Galloway's jointure, which will be £3000, so that on the whole estimate that Garlies[66] will have an income of £15,000 is not far from the mark.

---

[66] Alan Stewart, 10th E. of Galloway (1835–1901), succ. father 1873; previously Lord Garlies; m. Derby's step-dau. Lady Mary Cecil (1850–1903) 25 Jan. 1872; d.s.p.

1872

1 January 1872. I begin this year in good health and spirits, engaged in no quarrel or dispute, nor exposed to any annoyance in public or private life. During 1871 I have taken a fairly active part in politics, and delivered a good many speeches[1] on social questions, especially during the months of Sept. and Oct. To me personally the chief event of the year has been the sale of my Irish estates, a step contemplated by my father in his later days, and to which I was led by various considerations. First, the annoyance of the land act, and the attitude of the tenantry, making it practically impossible even to change the boundaries of a farm without the consent of the occupier: next, the effect of the church disestablishment, which would have thrown on me, as nearly the largest proprietor in Tipperary, the burden of supporting half the Protestant clergy in that country: thirdly, the general feeling of disaffection which prevails throughout the south of Ireland, making it impossible to look forward to a safe future: and lastly, the wish to diminish encumbrances by the sale of an estate which gave me neither pleasure nor influence. The price I have received, though not high, is sufficient to increase my net income by at least £2000: and with this I am content.

I have repaired, enlarged, and ornamented my house in London, at a cost of nearly £4000: in Knowsley I have made no change. Some progress has been made in reducing the debt, but I shall not know for some weeks how I stand financially.

My life has been one of great, though quiet, happiness: and there is in the last 12 months no action of importance on which I look back with regret.

2 January 1872. I copy ... my note of last year's expenditure on private account.

Public institutions, charitable & other, received

---

[1] Outside parliament, Derby had spoken, or otherwise pronounced upon, the following issues in 1871: on national defence (*T*, 9 Jan. 1871, 5b), on armed services (*T*, 16 Feb. 1871), on charitable relief (*T*, 23 Mar. 1871, 6d), on working-class housing (*T*, 2 June 1871, 12c), on discharged criminals (*T*, 26 Aug. 1871, 12c). He also spoke at Bury (*T*, 1 Sept. 1871, 3f), at the Manchester and Liverpool Agricultural Society, and laid the foundation stone at Liverpool Seamen's Orphan Institution, (both *T*, 13 Sept. 1871, 8f). He spoke on Art Education at Birkenhead (*T*, 28 Sept. 1871, 3e), on the New Social Movement (*T*, 18 Oct. 1871, 6b), on national defence (*T*, 18 Oct. 1871, 6b), and on opening Manchester Grammar School (*T*, 26 Oct. 1871, 5e).

from me	£980
Donations to individuals, not being presents to friends, were	£284 nearly
Presents to friends & relatives, including help to H.S.	£249 nearly
Making total given away, in round numbers	£1513
Books and works of art cost me	£373
All other private expenses amounted to	£638
Total expended in the year	£2524 nearly

I have a reserve stock of £2600, and investments in safe securities to the amount of £20,000: besides some shares of uncertain value. ... I have laid by in 1871 about £600 added to reserve, and £2000 invested.

For this year, I am free to spend about £5300: of which I propose to lay by for investment £2000, and add to reserve stock £400.

8 January 1872. Messrs Lee and Nightingale came for notes of my speech to be delivered tomorrow, which I gave them.

9 January 1872. Dined at 5.30, and set out after dinner to attend a meeting in Liverpool, got up by the Conservative Working Men's Association. It was held at the Amphitheatre, near Lime Street, and attended by about 3000 persons, as far as I could judge. I was very well received, spoke $1\frac{1}{4}$ hours, much impeded at times by loss of voice and hoarseness, from which I have seldom been free on such occasions of late, but got through without missing anything that I had intended to say. My speech[2] ranged over a great variety of topics; it had been carefully considered: and I introduced into it enough, and only enough, of party spirit to make my advice go down. I deprecated taking office again without an assured majority, and pointed out the influence which Conservatives might exercise, in the divided state of the Liberal party, even without being a majority of the whole House. ... Home, weary, but well satisfied.

13 January 1872. Disraeli's view of the state of politics as expressed to me yesterday, is briefly as follows. 'It is not desirable to take office. We cannot hold it while in a minority of 100, and it cannot reasonably be expected that a dissolution though it may reduce this minority, will turn it into a majority. Nor are the party now anxious for the patronage of office, for of that they had a vast share in 1866–8. They can afford to wait: and if Gladstone resigns our course ought to be, to refuse to take his place, and advise a reconstruction of the present cabinet. He will then have to go on for another year with the present H. of C. and

---

[2] See *T*, 10 Jan. 1872, 10a. Derby also spoke 9 times in H. of Lords during 1871 (3 of them in ctee); he did not speak on the Ballot Bill, and avoided party controversy. His topics were Fenian prisoners, the Tichborne claimant, the Treaty of Washington, army purchase, criminal law amendment, and Abyssinia.

before he dissolves it is probable that he and his colleagues will have been a good deal lowered in public estimation. We may therefore attack the ministry, beat them if we can, and drive them to offer their resignations, but allow them to resign. It is likely enough that G. may choose, seeing the difficulties before him, to be defeated, and go out on some minor point. He cannot dissolve in the present state of feeling, and with a House not four years old'. The above is the substance of what D. said. He seemed well, eager, animated, altogether different from what he was twelve months ago.

19 January 1872. Reading Renan's new essay[3] ... on the state of France: very original and striking. Renan, like many others, is politically a conservative, while rejecting the ancient faith: dreading and disliking the sceptical spirit, which no one has done more to encourage. In this respect he resembles Disraeli, who personally incapable of religious belief, yet holds (so far as I can judge, quite sincerely) that a nation which has lost its faith in religion is in a state of decadence.

25 January 1872. Delane uneasy about the American business: says that the claims are monstrous in amount ... The talk of the arbitrators being bribed is in everybody's mouth, though it can only be a matter of suspicion.

Disraeli considers that all other questions have become unimportant in comparison, and evidently expects a crisis.

28 January 1872. Saw Disraeli, and discussed the state of affairs generally. ... D. tells me that he reckons the Conservative strength on which he can rely at 274: at the beginning of the parliament it was about 260. He is confident of winning both the vacant seats – Nottinghamshire and the W. Riding.[4]

30 January 1872. The Queen sat with me, and had a long talk on many subjects, but keeping generally clear of home politics: she asked especially why with such enormous growth of wealth, there is as much distress as ever among a certain class of the poor? I could give no very satisfactory answer – drink, improvidence, misdirected charity, and the tendency of all who have failed or come to grief in any way to migrate to London, seemed the most probable solutions.

1 February 1872. Long visit from Disraeli, who discussed the situation, but exclusively with reference to American affairs, which he considers have rendered every other question insignificant. He thinks the U.S. govt. must be called upon to withdraw their demand for compensation for indirect injuries, and on their declining, which they almost certainly

---

[3] E. Renan, *La Réforme Intellectuelle et Morale* (1871).
[4] Both were Cons. gains; the only Lib. defeat in W. Riding N. in the whole life of the constituency (1865–85).

will, that the negotiations must be broken off. He says it is a vexatious and unsatisfactory state of things, but will not lead to war, since neither desires that. He believes the treaty to have been purposely worded in an ambiguous style by the American commissioners, so that these new claims might be advanced under it, without our suspecting any such intention until it was too late to recede. He had seen Northcote, who takes this view, and who advised at an early stage of the negotiations, that matters should be settled by the payment of a sum down, as the least dangerous expedient. But of this Gladstone and the cabinet would not hear.

8 February 1872. Much writing in the press on Alabama claims. *The Times, Post* and *Standard* all agree in supporting the view I have taken of the treaty (i.e. that it must be admitted to be ambiguous but admits of our construction as well as that put upon it by the Americans, and is void if it was understood by the parties concerned in two different senses) against that of Gladstone.

Lowe called yesterday, and talked freely to M. of his chief. He says that G. if driven out of office will be 'the reddest of the red': that the tendency of his mind is all in that direction: that most of his colleagues would be glad to be out of their troubles by resignation after a hostile vote: that the opposition could turn them out if they pleased: that the West Riding election is significant: other constituencies will do the same: the Whig, or moderate Radical, will be squeezed out between the Radical on the one side and the Conservative on the other: he thinks that state of things dangerous, since the war will be one of classes, or at best one of parties not shading into one another as now, but sharply and directly opposed.

... Reeve, Delane, and Hayward,[5] all express satisfaction with my statement of the English case: they think Gladstone has gone too far: and Kimberley implied the same thing, though naturally he would not say it. Northcote, as one of the Commissioners, says there is not a pretext for asserting that the question in dispute was left open or unsettled: on the contrary a clear understanding was come to as to the rejection of the claims now advanced, and he cannot consider the renewal of them under these circumstances.

10 February 1872. B. Museum ... Walked home with D. who says Ministers will be pressed on the Collier question,[6] but will have a majority, as he supposes, of 20 or 25.

12 February 1872. Heard with sorrow of the death of poor Mayo,[7] by

[5] Abraham Hayward (1801–84), man of letters.

[6] Using a technicality to circumvent his own statute, Gladstone placed Sir R. Collier, attorney-gen., on the judicial ctee of the privy council; hence 'Colliery explosion'.

[7] Richard Bourke, 6th E. of Mayo (1822–72), Irish sec. 1852, 1858–9, 1866–8; gov.-gen. of India 1868–72; styled Lord Naas 1849–67.

assassination ... Mayo was of all public men whom I have known, the one who most thoroughly united the solid good sense of an English gentleman with the geniality and humour of the best sort of Irishman. As a companion, always pleasant: as a colleague, he said what he had to say simply, going straight to the point, yet managing to make his advice remembered by some stroke of wit, or unintended quaintness of expression, which relieved a dry discussion. He was not an eloquent, nor even a fluent speaker: the matter good, the delivery seldom effective. Tact and judgment were his strong points: high spirits and unfailing good humour disarmed opposition: and in India the higher qualities of his mind appear to have had full scope. It was only since his appointment as Gov. General that he had taken in public estimation the place which he deserved. Indeed the selection of him was thought a doubtful act; and often imputed to Disraeli as a job. But the event has fully justified it.

13 February 1872. Lowe says to M. 'Gladstone is mad, but he is cleverer in his madness than almost any other man in his sane mind'.

14 February 1872. B. Cochrane[8] called ... he deprecated strongly the making of any attempt to take office, which I find to be the general Conservative feeling.

17 February 1872. Coleridge[9] (the Att. Gen.) talking to A. Russell[10] says 'The dissenters want to turn out Gladstone, feeling sure that if they do, he will within two or three years head the movement for dis-establishment of the English church. They think that he is moving in that direction, and that many of the High Church party will go with him'. And C. who is a personal friend of the Premier, seems to have thought their calculation might be justified by the result.

18 February 1872. Saw Disraeli, and much talk. It is clear to me that he is sanguine as to the prospect of forming a new government, though not at once. He said several times that other matters were unimportant, it was the American business that would destroy Gladstone. Motions ought to be made in both Houses. I must bring one on in the Lords, he would do so in the Commons, etc. He thought the result of our Thursday's division[11] would do no harm, perhaps the reverse, for there were many Radicals who disliked the Collier job, but would still more

---

[8] A.D.R.W. Cochrane-Baillie (or Cochrane-Wishart-Baillie), 1st Baron Lamington (1816–90), author, member of Young England, and M.P. (Cons.) intermittently 1841–80; cr. peer 1880.

[9] Sir J.D. Coleridge (1820–94), att.-gen. 1871–3; cr. judge 1873, 1st Baron Coleridge 1874.

[10] Lord Arthur Russell (1825–92), bro. of 9th D. of Bedford, Lady Derby's bro.-in-law; M.P. (Lib.) Tavistock 1857–85.

[11] Stanhope's resolution condemning government abuse of its judicial patronage in the Collier case was defeated by ministers, 88–87 (*H*, 209, cols 375–462, Thursday 15 Feb. 1872).

have disliked seeming to back up the Lords: whereas now no such feeling could exist.

Among the peers who voted for ministers on Thursday was Ld Foley,[12] who is imbecile, requiring to be watched, and incapable of managing his own affairs. He was brought in by his uncle Ld Howard of Glossop.[13] Ld. Cowper[14] was brought back from Italy by a telegram.

20 February 1872. Left London by 7.40 train from Charing Cross, crossed from Dover to Calais...

24 February 1872. The North Nottinghamshire election ... has been won by the Conservative candidate, the majority being as 5 to 3, though a close contest was expected. This following on the W. Riding victory, looks more like a real Conservative reaction than anything we have yet seen.

26 February 1872. Called with M. on Mme Mohl ... met Ernest Renan and Leon Say.

29 February 1872. Left Paris early ... London about 6 p.m.

2 March 1872. Answered a letter from Mathew,[15] the minister at Rio, now going back to his post: I made my answer dry, he being a pushing, intriguing person whom I do not wish to encourage. I named him to his present post in 1868, but it was less for his sake than to facilitate other arrangements.

... Called on Disraeli, whom I find apparently unwell, looking pale and ill, but in good spirits: he says the state of things is quite as unfavourable to the ministry as it was, they are aware of the fact, and that they may any day be driven out: perhaps indeed they rather wish it, in order to escape from Alabama liabilities: the Conservatives, excited by success in recent elections, are growing eager: they want us to take office, and dissolve immediately: he dissuades them to the best of his power, but finds them no longer willing to listen to moderate counsels.

6 March 1872. Talk ... with Hunt (Ward Hunt) and I find with some surprise that he is favourable in principle to the purchase of railways by the State.

8 March 1872. Letter from Mr C. Stanley,[16] repaying me £20 which

[12] Henry Thomas Foley, 5th Baron Foley (1850–1905); succ. father 1869; d.s.p.

[13] Lord Edward George Fitzalan-Howard, 1st Lord Howard of Glossop (1818–83), 2nd s. of 13th D. of Norfolk; cr. peer, 1869.

[14] Francis Thomas De Grey, 7th E. Cowper (1834–1905), succ. 1856; lord-lieut of Ireland 1880–2 (resigned).

[15] (Sir) G. B. Matthew, min. to Brazin 1867–79.

[16] Probably C. Stanley (d. 1877), 'my unlucky cousin in Ireland. He was the best of that lot, having always kept a decent character, and not been very importunate in his demands for assistance: but like all the rest of them, he was either incapable or unwilling

I lent him in the winter: the first person who ever did so to me, and I think there will not be many others.

9 March 1872. Talk with Disraeli, who says the Dissenters made a very weak case, but that their feeling was stronger than ever. Nothing has been done on the part of ministers to conciliate them. It is noticed that Gladstone did not speak in the debate, though often appealed to, and many think that his silence indicates an intention of throwing his colleagues over.

11 March 1872. Cross dined with us: he is well pleased with the political situation: thinks a general election would reduce the majority against us by 50 at least, possibly more: wishes it could take place now: inasmuch as the blunders of the ministry cannot well be greater than they have been, and with time they may be able to raise a new cry which will restore their popularity. Talk of a threatened High Church secession, to come off if some projected changes are made in the Church service − I believe the omission of the Athanasian creed. Gladstone is reported to be deeply interested in this.

13 March 1872. Much discussion with M. as to the advantage or otherwise of my attending the meeting at Manchester at which Disraeli is to deliver a manifesto. To stay away, may look either like jealousy of D. (which I should be sorry were it supposed to exist) or indifference to politics altogether. On the other hand, if I go, it cannot be as a listener only : I must speak: and then the meeting is not exclusively in honour of D. − besides which if our language is different, or can be made to appear so, comments to that effect are sure to be abundant. The question is complicated by the existence of a section of the party who would follow me, but who will not follow D. What their number may be I have no means of guessing.

Dinner at the Rothschilds' house: a large and pleasant gathering.

14 March 1872. Spoke to Cross and Patten about attending Disraeli's meeting at Manchester: they both see the objections, but think that the local feeling is strong, and that my absence will cause more disappointment than the thing is worth. This was my own conclusion, after reflection: and I have agreed to be present. But I have said that the meeting being in D's honour, not in mine, I would take no part beyond a short speech of a complimentary kind, if that was desired.

20 March 1872. Wellington College meeting at 11, where a large attendance of governors, I think 20: the chief subject of discussion being a disagreement between the Head Master[17] and some of the

---

to do anything towards his own support.' (D.D., 25 Apr. 1877, on his uncle Henry's eldest son.)

[17] Edward White Benson, 1st head of Wellington Coll. 1859–72; archbp of Canterbury 1882–96.

governors, which we had to decide. Three boys had got into trouble about a woman, one of whom became infected: Benson thought it necessary that all three should be withdrawn: the governors present at the last meeting (when I was in Paris) insisted on his reinstating the two younger lads: on which he took the opinions of five other head-masters, and appealed in a privately printed pamphlet to the whole body of the governors. The case came up for consideration today: and by a majority of 13 to 6, we determined to accept his view, I voted in the majority. There was some feeling shown, especially on the part of Talbot,[18] who for personal reasons seems to have determined to make him resign. They have long been jealous of one another: Benson stands up for the independence of his position in matters of discipline: Talbot, who has given a good deal of time to the affairs of the college, inclines to treat him too much as a servant. In the present instance I have no doubt that Benson was right. We sat nearly three hours.

28 March 1872. Much conversation yesterday and the day before with Kimberley, who seems to wish for more acquaintance. I like him, for though he talks too much, he talks well. He speaks highly of Jessel,[19] the new Sol. Gen. and confirmed a remark of mine that he (Jessel) though a professed Liberal in politics, is not extreme, and indeed leans to a conservative view of matters with which he has to deal.

Vague reports of cabinet differences: Hartington[20] is said not to be well pleased with the very Liberal policy of his colleagues, or with their ultramontane sympathies. He is the natural leader of the old Whigs. Lowe told M. the other day that he had opposed sending out of the Washington mission from the first: he spoke of Ld Ripon[21] with the utmost contempt: but to speak so of colleagues is habit with him, and proves nothing.

The budget appears popular...

... Very idle, which yet I cannot help, there being nothing to do.

30 March 1872. At 1 to Grosvenor Gate, where talked with Disraeli over his coming speech. I found him very nervous, more so than I have known him to be on any occasion of late years: he said he did not like his visit to Manchester, it had been forced upon him by importunity continued ever since the last general election (this I know to be true) and at last he was obliged to give way. He gave me an

[18] Cf. John Chandos, *Boys Together* (1984), 286–7.

[19] Sir G. Jessel (1824–83), sol.-gen. 1871–3; master of the rolls 1873–83.

[20] Spencer Crompton Cavendish, 8th D. of Devonshire (1833–1908); styled Lord Hartington 1858–91; elected Lib. leader in H. of C. unopposed, Feb. 1875; p.m.g. 1868–71, Irish sec. 1871–4.

[21] George Robinson, 1st M. of Ripon (1827–1909), chairman of Alabama commission, 1871; cr. M. 23 June 1871; in cabinet 1863–6, 1868–73, 1886, 1892–5, 1905–8; gov.-gen. of India 1880–4.

outline of what he meant to say: thought he should occupy two hours
at least: admitted that he was anxious about the chance of any ill-
considered phrase escaping him in so long a speech: his memory of
subjects and facts was good, but he had always found verbal preparation
impossible – unlike Lytton[22] in that respect.

He talked of the reform bill of 1867, which he intended to vindicate:
would contend that it only restored to the working classes the electoral
privileges which they had before 1832 in the boroughs where scot-and-
lot vote existed: which Ld. Grey's bill took away, and the loss of which
he said had caused the chartist movement. He said he had gone
carefully into the figures with Lambert:[23] the gross total of registered
electors in the U.K. is (as lately published in the papers) 2,500,000: but
deductions to be made for double returns, deaths, etc. which he is told
reduce the effective total to 2,250,000 or thereabouts: in other words
of the adult males throughout the country, not much more than a
quarter have votes – and this is the system which by opponents on
both sides is said to be a near approach to universal suffrage!

3 April 1872. Left for Manchester about 3 to attend the meeting in
Free Trade Hall where Disraeli is to speak. ... To the Hall a little
before 7: much trouble in getting inside, the crowd being immense:
within there were said to be 6,000 persons, but I do not think the
number was so great: the building was full, and the heat was oppressive.
D. spoke from 7.30 to nearly 11: 3 hours and 20 minutes: the first two
hours were occupied with a kind of essay on the British constitution,
ingenious, but to my mind somewhat unreal: most of his argument
would not have been difficult to answer had anybody cared to take the
republican side. He went on to speak of the condition of the labouring
class, and of current affairs: this part of his speech was the best: but it
was delivered to an audience already exhausted, and in a weaker voice,
not heard throughout the entire room. On the whole, the oration,
though a remarkable intellectual feat, being admirable in point of style,
and delivered without reference to a note, fell flat, being much too
long: of which D. himself was quite aware. He ought to have cut it in
two, and delivered it on two successive days to different audiences. I
followed briefly and repeated the advice I gave in January, not to be
in haste to take office. The length of D's speech caused me to miss the
11 p.m. train, and it was nearly 3 a.m. before I got to bed, very weary,
but glad that this business is over.

2 April 1872. News of Disraeli having had a very good reception at

[22] (Sir) E. Bulwer-Lytton, Bt, 1st Baron Lytton (1803–73), novelist, cabinet minister,
noted orator; cr. peer 1866.
[23] Sir John Lambert (1815–92), perm. sec. to local govt board 1871–82.

Manchester: the horses taken out of his carriage, which was drawn some way by the crowd: at the station he was mobbed so that for some minutes he could not get out of it: but all in good humour...

6 April 1872. The local and London press is (naturally) full of criticisms on Disraeli's speech, which on the whole was not a success, partly from its length, partly from the want of any definite purpose ... a manifesto of policy being inopportune. But in fact Disraeli's peculiar powers do not lie in the direction of popular oratory. He wants a cultivated audience, and is never so much at home as in the H. of C. The enthusiasm shown by those who come to receive and to see him has surprised all parties – Conservatives not less than Liberals. There has been nothing like it in my recollection.

13 April 1872. Heard with regret that Mr Alexander, the owner of Holwood, intends to live there, and that we must give it up in June 1873. Perhaps this is as well for we should never have left the place of our own accord...

16 April 1872. Meeting at the D. of Richmond's, Salisbury, Carnarvon, Cairns, Malmesbury, Marlborough, and myself: to consider a motion of which Ld Russell has given notice on the American negotiations ... Walk with Carnarvon, who volunteers to express satisfaction at the political condition of affairs, saying it was very different from what he and others had expected: and praises Disraeli's late speech in very high terms. So that quarrel is ended. He has been living in the country, and not under Salisbury's influence of late. He talks at length of his (or rather Ly C's) recent accession of fortune:[24] which is for a long time to come more nominal than real, for the Chesterfield estates are encumbered almost to their full value. Ly C. and her mother allow the present Ld Chesterfield £2000 a year out of them. He is in some way under a cloud and does not appear in the world. He tells met that he has just sold an estate in Wiltshire which gave him a net return of £4000 a year for £190,000: and has cleared off all his debts.

24 April 1872. Disraeli called on M. yesterday, and with much agitation confided to her his fear that Ly Beaconsfield is dying. She will not allow herself to be ill, and struggles on to the last, but he does not expect her to last many months.

A crisis was expected last night in the H. of C. on Fawcett's motion,[25]

---

[24] George Stanhope, 7th E. of Chesterfield (1831–71) d. unm. of typhoid. His mother Anne, Lady Chesterfield née Weld (1802–85), widow of the 6th E. (1805–66), became after 1873 Disraeli's confidante. On her son's death in 1871, the Chesterfield estates, but not the title, passed to his sister Evelyn, Lady Carnarvon (1834–75) who m. Carnarvon in 1861. The distant cousin who inherited the title, George Philip Stanhope (1822–83) was an Ulster squire of little note.

[25] Fawcett's motion on Irish universities was talked out by the govt; *H*, cccx, 1813– (24 Apr. 1872).

reports having been spread that if beaten upon it ministers will resign: but the report is thought to be of their own framing, and not much believed, except on the hypothesis that they wish to make a show of going out, in order to be called back again: a device which if successful always strengthens a cabinet.

25 April 1872. Cairns asked me to his room to discuss the Chancellor's appellate jurisdiction [bill] with Lds Westbury, Penzance, and Colonsay.[26] All agreed in condemning the bill, but in the end, it was settled to let it go to a select committee.

26 April 1872. Received a note from Cairns, in which he announces his decision to oppose the Chancellor's bill at once, and directly: which is contrary to the resolution come to yesterday, and (I think) a mistake.

27 April 1872. Wrote to Cairns, expressing my hope that if he does throw out the Ld Chancellor's bill on a second reading, he will take care that his rejection of it is based, not on the necessity of maintaining the appellate jurisdiction, but on the elements of the bill itself. But I fear he has a strong personal feeling in the matter, which will bias his judgment.

28 April 1872. Called, among others, on Disraeli: he thanked me warmly for having come to the Manchester meeting, spoke of his visit with pleasure, but described the fatigue as almost past endurance. His entertainers would not allow him a minute of rest. We discussed the immediate future: he is against forcing on a crisis, thinks a dissolution now would give us very large gains, but not a majority: 30 to 40 seats most likely, making 60 to 80 votes on a division, which is good, but not enough. He is not afraid of what some friends say, 'that he is missing the opportunity by not dissolving now'. The same thing was said in 1839, but it did not prevent Peel from coming in with a vast majority in 1841.

He seemed calm, not agitated or anxious, but in low spirits: which remembering his conversation with M. I could account for.

Gladstone has in the last week pledged himself to household suffrage for the counties:[27] which in any other prime minister would be thought a singular proceeding, but from him it excites no surprise. He last year declared for universal suffrage, without limitation of town or country.[28]

29 April 1872. Saw Patten at his request: he is rather disquieted in mind about the proposed formation of a farmers' club in Lancashire: dislikes the plan, fears it will do mischief, but fears also the unpopularity of not taking part in it, and the things getting into bad hands if he and the other gentry stay away...

[26] Judges and peers.
[27] *H,* cccx, 1907–12 (25 Apr. 1872). Gladstone spoke of 'the present condition of the county franchise, which cannot long continue' but declined to take action.
[28] Cf. above, 23 June 1871.

He tells me Gladstone is growing intensely unpopular with the House: much more so this year than the last: which he ascribes to his (G's) increasing irritability and violence, itself the effect of overworked brain. The Liberals would most of them prefer Forster for a leader ... Bouverie[29] has been talking to him, eager that we should take office: pledges himself that the Whigs will do nothing factious, on the contrary, will support us – the old story: they would use us until their quarrels among themselves are made up, and then turn us out. But we know better than to play at that game again.

2 May 1872. Dinner at Ld Granville's to meet the K. of the Belgians ... Mrs Gladstone[30] talked much to me after dinner, and in very singular strain, about her husband: her fears for his health, anxiety that he should be relieved, the difficulty of dealing with a Liberal majority, and his disposition to do his colleagues' work as well as his own: all quite true, but odd from her, and to me.

3 May 1872. Cairns says that the Ld Chancellor,[31] who used to be thought a singularly kind and amiable person, has quarrelled for different reasons, with most of the judges, so that they will not speak to, nor do business personally with him. He named especially Martin and Cockburn. The wish that he should be succeeded by Sir R. Palmer[32] is universal on both sides of the House: and the change would probably have been made, but for the wish to retain Palmer for the arbitration at Geneva, if it ever comes off.

5 May 1872. Saw Disraeli ... but did not stay long. He was in a nervous and depressed condition, expecting Sir W. Gill's visit to Ly B. I fear the end is not far off.

10 May 1872. To dine with the Van De Weyers, meeting there K. of the Belgians, Stanhopes, Disraelis, C. Fortescue and Ly Waldegrave, Sydneys,[33] etc. Pleasant evening.

Ly Beaconsfield was at the dinner, pale and ill, but showing her usual energy, though she is believed to be dying. She tells her friends that she will go on to the last, and utterly refuses to be an invalid.

... W. Harcourt, whose attacks on Disraeli were unmeasured in their vehemence, so as almost to exceed the recognised limits of parliamentary and literary war, has now turned round, and begun to court him assiduously. Harcourt is clever, though unpopular from the general

---

[29] Edward Pleydell-Bouverie (1818–89), Lib. M.P. 1844–74; pres. of poor law board, 1855–8.

[30] Catherine Gladstone, née Glynne (1812–1900).

[31] William Page Wood, 1st Baron Hatherley (1801–81), lord chanc. 1868–72.

[32] Sir R. Palmer, 1st E. of Selborne (1812–95), lord chanc. 1872–4, 1880–5; cr. baron 1872, earl 1882.

[33] (Sir) John Townshend, 3rd Vt Sydney (1805–90), succ. 1831; courtier.

arrogance of his manner: radical as far as he has any convictions, but mainly bent on making a great personal name for himself. His last move is evidently to establish a Tory-Radical alliance – if he can.

11 May 1872. To a meeting of the cotton famine relief fund, which has now £80,000 in hand, Patten being in sole charge of the money...

... Saw Cross after luncheon: he thinks the negotiations over, the Liberal party altogether disunited, and the resignation or defeat of the Ministry probable. He holds that we ought not to lose the opportunity, but come in, and dissolve at once.

12 May 1872. Busy most of the morning with notes and applications of various kinds – nine-tenths, as usual, being about matters with which I have nothing whatever to do.

... I did not vote in most of the D. of Richmond's divisions, which I do not regret. He appears to have taken the amendments suggested by the licensed victuallers without choice or discrimination. It was right to support them, for they support us: but the thing might have been done with a little more disguise.

13 May 1872. Meeting of Richmond, Salisbury, Cairns, Chelmsford, and myself at the Carlton to consider the situation today, and also the reception to be given to the ballot bill, the second reading of which we decided not to oppose, Salisbury only having doubts.

16 May 1872. M. went again to Holwood, and returned with news of the sudden death of her step-daughter, Ly B. Balfour,[34] who had long been in weak health and was not expected to live long: but there seemed no special reason why she should die at this particular time. She appears to have passed out of existence without disturbance or pain, while supposed by those who were watching her to be asleep. Her life for many years past had been that of an invalid, and signs of mental eccentricity had appeared at times.

Meeting of N.P.G. trustees at my house, as usual: both Gladstone and Disraeli were there, but nothing of importance was done.

27 May 1872. Death of D. of Bedford[35] announced, at the age of 62. He had been for many years in bad health, unable to walk, and seldom leaving London. His wealth gave him no enjoyment. The management of his estate he left to his successor, H. Russell,[36] but retaining a power over it, and expecting to be consulted. His rental exceeded £300,000: certainly the largest fortune possessed by any landowner, though in the next generation Ld Westminster will have more. He saved much, and

[34] Lady Blanche Balfour, née Cecil, 2nd d. of James, 2nd M. of Salisbury, by his 1st wife; m. of A.J. Balfour, premier, widow of J.M. Balfour (1820–56).

[35] William Russell, 8th D. of Bedford (1809–72), succ. father 1861; d. unm.; recluse in later life.

[36] (Francis Charles) Hastings Russell, 9th D. of Bedford (1819–91); succ. his cousin, 1872; m. Elizabeth Sackville-West (who d. 1897), sister of diarist's wife, 1844.

spent little, in which he will be imitated by the new Duke.

31 May 1872. Talk with Cairns, Disraeli and others about what is to be done if the treaty fails. We cannot pass the matter over in silence: it is difficult to comment upon it without moving a vote of censure: and if the ministry, seeing themselves in trouble, made that the opportunity of resigning, what would be our position? Should we refuse office and let them come in again, strengthened by our refusal? Should we accept, and dissolve at once? Cairns is strongly for the last course, and there is no doubt that we should gain strength by it: but whether we should turn a majority of 100 into a minority is doubtful, and to go out again without facing a parliament of our own summoning (for the second time in four years) is not a desirable position.

1 June 1872. Heard from Coutts that my remaining shares in the Fairbairn[37] Engineering Co. are sold a little above par. This particular speculation has paid me well: but I have seen enough of such things to wish to have no more to do with them. A safe interest of four per cent is enough.

4 June 1872. Making notes for a speech on the treaty ... Ld Russell made his motion, speaking over an hour, with great force and energy for a man of 80, who has never been physically strong: desultory at times, but on the whole able and dignified. Ld Granville followed, weak, as I thought, and confused: he is evidently in bad health, much harassed by anxiety and worry, and his usually excellent temper now often fails him.

7 June 1872. It is announced that Ld Pembroke[38] – brought up as a Peelite, while that party existed – has joined the Carlton. It is expected that a Conservative will be returned for Bedfordshire – the county squires would have allowed a Russell to sit, though not agreeing in his politics, but A. Russell[39] will not leave his seat at Tavistock, and there is no other, Amberley[40] not being popular either in the county or his family. The present Duke of Bedford, while in the H. of C., professed rather extreme ideas, and let himself be surrounded by a clique who toadied him: but I hear that his accession has in many ways modified his views. As owner of the largest income in England (above £300,000 rental, with no debt of any kind) he cannot ally himself permanently with men whose chief object is the destruction of all such exceptional

---

[37] (Sir) William Fairbairn (1789–1874), engineer.
[38] George Herbert, 13th E. of Pembroke (1850–95); s. of Sidney Herbert; succ. uncle as earl, 1862; left Eton, 1867; surprise appointment as under-sec. for war, 1874; house guest at Hughenden, Whitsun 1874; m., Aug. 1874; resigned, 1875, for 'health reasons' (*D.N.B.*), never regaining office.
[39] Lord Arthur Russell, M.P. Tavistock 1857–85.
[40] Viscount Amberley (1842–76), s. of premier, father of Bertrand Russell.

positions as his. And his radicalism has never prevented him from looking very sharply into expenditure: the yearly savings on the estate have been of late years £100,000 and upwards, all of which he inherits.

10 June 1872. Heard, through M., a painful and melancholy story of Ld Hardwicke.[41] His son Royston is in debt to the extent of £200,000 if not more, making it impossible that he should ever live on his estates, or be otherwise than very poor. All this debt has been contracted by gambling and other follies. Ld H. has during the greater part of a long life been engaged in working off the encumbrances on his estates (which he has done) and will leave an unencumbered rental of £26,000. Now his work is destroyed, at least for the life of his successor. The old man takes his misfortune quietly, and says that his duty must now be to save his grandson from being involved in the ruin.

12 June 1872. Heard with some regret that young Gerard, Sir Robert's son, just returned from an Indian tour, has won £6000 on the Derby: which will probably confirm him in gaming. He is a foolish youth, and has been continually in debt.

17 June 1872. A quarrel broke out between Bath[42] and the Chancellor, other peers taking part, and some rather sharp words passed: the provocation was a very singular proceeding on the part of ministers: they had objected to a proposal by Lord Shaftesbury: Cairns objected to it also: Ld Shaftesbury insisted on a division, when seeing that the clause could not be carried, all the members of the government turned round and voted for it, for what reason is not obvious, unless they thought that their popularity would suffer by having taken the opposite course five minutes before. Naturally this curious manoeuvre produced some sharp comments: whence the quarrel.

18 June 1872. Great heat continues ... Walk for exercise, briskly, in the middle of the day. Bathed and dressed afterwards, cool and comfortable in consequence. I am satisfied that with my constitution, free and frequent perspiration is the first condition of health: missing it I become unwell, or at least uncomfortable.

19 June 1872. To see the Salisbury's new house ... very spacious and fine it is, comfortable too ... but ... I should have preferred having kept the £60,000 which it has cost already: and even now the decorations are not nearly finished.

... Talk with Sir H. Maine, the first time I have seen him since his

[41] Charles Philip Yorke, 4th E. of Hardwicke (1799–1873); p.m.g. 1852, lord privy seal 1858–9 (both in cabinet). His s., also Charles Philip (1836–97), formerly styled Lord Royston, held court office 1866–8, 1874–80, though best known as 'Champagne Charlie', a social celebrity. The grandson, left penniless, became a sleeping partner in a firm of stockbrokers.
[42] John Alexander Thynne, 4th M. of Bath (1831–96), succ. 1837; high churchman and tory malcontent.

Indian experiences: he says the climate has improved instead of injuring his health: and so his looks say also.

20 June 1872. Long conversation with Disraeli on general state of affairs: he wishes the Ballot Bill to drop through for the year, thinking that no interest is felt in it, and an agitation on the subject will be impossible.

... Talk with Salisbury on the question of state purchase of railways. We both see the gravest objections to the measure, financial, as indefinitely increasing debt, and constitutional, as creating in various forms an enormous patronage: but the idea is gaining strength, and will probably come to the front when the next election compels candidates to look out for new subjects.

26 June 1872. Wellington Coll. half-yearly meeting: about 20 governors present. We sat two hours, and did some business, but in a strange confused way: chiefly by the fault of our chairman, the D. of Wellington, who is deaf, absent, and unused to affairs, so that half a dozen subjects are talked about at once, and perhaps nothing decided as to any of them.

Lowe informs M. last night that the American business is settled: but gives no details.

4 July 1872. Ly Bulwer called on M. in good health and spirits. She has about £40,000 of her own, untouched, but will be obliged to put her husband's affairs in Chancery, as he has left more debts than his property will cover.

... The Bp of Winchester told a story of the Ashburton treaty, which I heard too imperfectly to set down, but the purport of it was that Ld Ashburton had given Daniel Webster a cheque for £10,000, on Webster's own suggestion, to help the passage of the treaty through the Senate. The treaty did pass, and Ld A heard no more of the money, which he paid out of his own pocket. But he always believed afterwards that the Senate had been a pretext, and that the money had gone into Webster's own pocket.

I have not noted that Disraeli has been delivering another speech to the Conservative party: this time at the Crystal Palace (as they call it) at Sydenham. He was not so long as at Manchester, but the performance was not reckoned a success. In fact he had nothing to tell his friends that was either new or important. His chief point was that the Liberals represent cosmopolitan, the Conservatives national ideas.

6 July 1872. Drage called ... he reports well of my health, and says that but for exercise and care I should not have escaped a fit of gout.

... Examining the income and property of Winchester College: the lands include about 30,000 acres, much scattered ... The present gross income is £17,600 ...

7 July 1872. Not very well pleased at the position of public affairs. The amendment making secret voting optional has been rejected, as a matter of course, by the Commons: and the question is again before us for consideration. The present feeling of the majority of the House is in favour of persevering: and if a vote passes in this sense, either resignation or dissolution must follow. Both would be inconvenient, and the ground is not well selected (in my opinion) for an appeal to the constituencies. ... It is quite on the cards that a crisis of a very disagreeable kind may be impending.

Lytton called, to express his dislike of the whole business, and his determination not to vote for the amendment, even if he did not vote with the government, which he was half disposed to do. I could not differ from him, but said that personally I was pledged to the D. of Richmond, Cairns, etc. It is clear to me that we cannot go on permanently as we are doing now: Richmond, though sensible by nature, has never studied political matters, and his want of knowledge is painfully apparent in debate: Salisbury destroys by violence the effect of his undoubted ability: and Cairns, whose character and capacity make him the proper Conservative leader, if he would accept the post, is rather too much disposed to dwell at length on details – the usual lawyer's fault – and so to weaken his admirably skilful arguments. But besides all this, there is no concert or communication, and each of the three takes a line of his own.

8 July 1872. To the Lds ... House very full, above 300 present ... The only speech of interest was that of Ld Russell: a vigorous attack on secret voting generally, very pointed and able as to argument ... The amendments[43] were lost by 19:157 to 138. The result was doubtful to the last: many peers remaining, as I believe, undecided even when they came into the House. It was a common remark that the worst thing that could have happened to us would have been a very small majority: with a large one, we might have faced a dissolution: but when almost equally divided ourselves, it would have been difficult to resist a large majority of the H. of C. Both sides appeared relieved that the crisis was averted. Our decision, however, had it gone the other way, would not necessarily have been final: a conference between the two Houses is always possible, and would serve as an excuse for concession or compromise.

13 July 1872. Called on Sir S. Fitzgerald,[44] just returned: but did not see him. His administration at Bombay has not been a success: he managed the Abyssinian expenditure wastefully, as far as his share of

[43] To Ballot Bill.
[44] Sir Seymour Fitzgerald (1818–85), Cons. M.P.; under-sec. for foreign affairs 1858–9; chief charity commr, 1875.

it was concerned, and is thought to have done a good many jobs for friends and dependents. He was deep in debt when he went out, so much so as to have some trouble about leaving the country: and I fear he is not much better now.

18 July 1872. Stanley of Alderley[45] called, I could not well make out why: he has grown very deaf, and grey, though not yet 45. He is not less eccentric and dirty-looking than formerly, but takes pains to impress on his acquaintance that he is a changed character – rather conservative, and ostentatiously religious. He used to call himself a Mahometan, and now leans to the Catholics, having a wife of that creed. I do not think him entirely sane: yet he has cleverness of a certain kind.

21 July 1872. My 46th birthday. Just half my life has passed since I was for the first time the guest of Ld & Ly Salisbury at Hatfield, July 21 1849.

30 July 1872. Lowe told M. lately in conversation – the questions thus answered having been suggested by me – that he expected a new crisis in finance, but less severe than that of 1866, inasmuch as it was anticipated, and would be to some extent provided for. That he saw no present reason why his surplus should not be as good at the end of the financial year as it promises to be now. That he expected the American award to be moderate in amount – perhaps a million or so – and intended if the cabinet allowed to pay it out of the balances. That he certainly would not consent to buy the Irish railways – which Gladstone is notoriously willing to do. That he is now much alarmed at the strikes, and rise of wages in general, but thinks the dearness of coal exceeding serious, as tending to break down our manufacturing superiority.

Much talk with M. as to certain reductions to be made in our establishment, which though cut down, is still far larger than we require either for convenience or dignity. The supply of hothouse fruit is larger than wanted and much of it goes to waste: the rise in coals moreover gives a fair opportunity of reducing expenditure in that department. The shooting may be gradually cut down a little more: perhaps another beat be given up: and the number of servants be lessened by two or three.

1 August 1872. At 3 o'clock, while in committee, we heard a very loud explosion, like the firing of a heavy gun: the cause was not known, until in the House we heard that Gladstone and Lowe had been trying experiments with dynamite in the garden behind the Treasury: and the force of the explosive compound having been under-estimated, most of

---

[45] Henry Stanley, 3rd Baron Stanley of Alderley (1827–1903), succ. 1869; buried with Moslem rites.

the office windows above them were broken. They do not seem to have suffered in person.

2 August 1872. The Customs report for 1871: it shows a degree of prosperity which has never yet been reached, and one is disposed to say that it must be too good to last.

3 August 1872. Heard at Chevening that the D. of Cleveland has bought up the reversionary claim to his estates, of the two Milbankes, father and son: they being both hopeless scamps, and drowned in debt, so that all would have gone to ruin. He is now free to dispose of his property (Raby included) as he likes: the redemption having cost him, according to Ly Stanhope, about £15,000 a year. It is a wise act on his part, made possible only by many years of previous saving.

10 August 1872. Mr Maclure ... speaks of the difficulty of finding a suitable candidate for S.E. Lancashire, the present member, Mr Henry, having ruined his health by drink: indeed he is never sober now. They want Mr R. Callender (Disraeli's late host) to stand, but he does not like to leave his business.[46] Mr M. thinks the success of the last general election ought to be retained, if not improved, at the next, in all parts of the county: says the well-paid artizans are growing conservative in great numbers...

12 August 1872. Talk (not for the first time) of the possibility of resigning possession of the estates and house to my brother, when all debt is cleared: keeping for myself a liberal life income, say £40,000 a year, which out of a clear rental of £100,000 (as it ought to be in 7 or 8 years) will not be too heavy a tax. We neither of us care for social display, and would not be sorry to devolve local duties on to the shoulders of our successors. But this is a castle in the air! The step once taken is irrevocable, and ought neither to be taken without the fullest deliberation nor so much as hinted at to any relative or friend. In Jan. 1875, if I live, and all goes well, I shall be free of the bank debt: in Jan. 1880 of the mortgage and family debts, except my brother's £170,000, which will merge in the rest of the estate, on my death, or on my giving up to him.

13 August 1872. The session has ended tamely. I see our press – the Standard and Globe – expresses discontent at the inaction of Disraeli, and at what it describes as the loss of great opportunity. In the case of D. it is probable that his wife's approaching death may have indisposed him to exertion: but apart from personal causes, I think he has acted wisely. The great opportunity never really existed. Ministers might have been driven to resign, but they would have come in again, unless we

---

[46] J.W. Maclure (1835–1901), chief exec. of cotton famine relief cttee under elder Derby, and chmn Manchester Cons. Assocn (1868–); J.S. Henry, M.P. (Cons.) S. Lancs. 1868–74; W.R. Callender (1825–76), M.P. Manchester (Cons.) 1874–5.

had dissolved immediately on accepting office: and though by a bold move of this kind some seats would undoubtedly have been gained, I do not think we could have expected to turn a majority of 80 to 90 (as it is now) into a minority. The country, as far as I can gather its wishes, does not desire a change of men, but does desire a cessation of violent and exciting legislation changes: the feverish restlessness of 1866–70 appears to be allayed: and Gladstone has had the sense to see this. In truth, except ballot, which was a foregone conclusion, very little has been effected. The licensing bill and health bill have been pared down to nothing: the army bill was a necessary sequel of the abolition of purchase: the Scotch Education Bill is the chief result of the year, and this only interests 3 millions out of 30 millions of people. The Washington treaty was only saved by the action of arbitrators, in spite of the follies and blunders of both governments: nor do we yet know the result. The extraordinary material prosperity of the country has kept all classes in tolerably good humour: and the working men have been more occupied with attempts to raise their wages than with political questions. On the whole the cabinet has got through its difficulties safely, but not triumphantly: having escaped defeat rather than accomplished success.

... The debates in both Houses have been, I think, below the average: the best speech of the year, to my mind, was that of Cairns on the Chancellor's law reform bill. Lowe has abstained in a rather marked manner from taking part in questions which did not touch his special department. Gladstone has been less excitable than in 1871, and has several times let drop phrases which seemed to imply that he neither expected nor desired his tenure of power to be much prolonged.

Long talk with W. H.[47] on household affairs ... I say that if (as is likely) prices of all articles rise, we must reduce establishment in proportion, as I will not exceed the limit of expenditure actually fixed.

14 August 1872. Laid the first stone of a new school ... I praised the actual arrangements for popular schooling under the Act of 1870, which I could honestly do, for I believe them better suited to our state of society than any other would...

16 August 1872. Discussed ... various points of G. H.'s[48] conduct towards me with which I am not altogether pleased. He is honest, gentleman-like, and trusted by the tenants: which is much: and I believe him to understand his business: but from ill health, or from other causes, he has grown very indolent: leaves letters for weeks unanswered: and either from this cause, or from dislike to be interfered with, it is nearly impossible to induce him to act on instructions. E.g. Neilson's business, in which no step has been taken: the intended sales in

[47] Hornby, comptroller of Derby's household.
[48] Hale, the chief agent for W. Lancs.

Liverpool, to which the same remark applies though I have pressed them for some time: the building of cottages, delayed for nearly two years, and then begun on a site different from that which we chose together: the refusal, without reasons assigned, to let Mossborough farm ... I will taken no hasty step, but watch with care to see how much is due to mere laziness ... and how much to a fixed purpose of having his own way, which I strongly suspect...

22 August 1872. Walk ... with Skelmersdale ... He says the out-turn of coal will diminish next year. The men will only work 3 days a week, very few work 4. They can earn £2 a week, some more. They never save, as far as he knows; are dainty in their eating, and much goes in drink.

27 August 1872. Ld Russell very deaf, but full of energy and animation: he is 80 this week. Talks much of the session of 1873, and of a great attack on the landed interest which he hears Gladstone is meditating, I suppose in the form of a bill for dealing with rates and local administration generally. He thought the landed interest in the Commons too strong to allow any very violent measure to pass: but shook his head doubtfully when I asked what such men as the D. of Devonshire would do. He is also very strong against Ld F. Cavendish,[49] who represents the W. Riding, acting as Gladstone's secretary: says that the Yorkshire constituency, still the most important in England, has a right to expect that its representative shall be able to vote independently, which as an official subordinate he cannot do.

1 September 1872. Letter from L. West[50] asking whether I advise his acceptance of the Buenos Ayres mission offered him by Lord Granville. I recommend him to refuse as by going there he runs the risk of being forgotten in Europe: and will acquire no reputation by anything that can be done in that obscure and remote corner. The expense of living is great...

2 September 1872. Ld and Ly Russell left us. ... Lord Russell,[51] in the week that he has passed with us, has conversed abundantly and freely with M. and myself. He is full of interest in the politics of the day, those of Europe as well as of England: his mind appears as active as in his earlier years: the only drawback to the enjoyment of his society

---

[49] Lord Frederick Cavendish (1836–82), M.P. W. Riding 1865–82; Hartington's bro.; m. to Gladstone's niece; assassinated.

[50] Lionel Sackville-West, 2nd Baron Sackville (1827–1908), succ. bro. 1888; diplomatist 1847–88; U.K. minister in Washington 1881–8; when alleged intervention in U.S. elections led to resignation; bro. of diarist's wife; usually referred to by diarist as Lionel West; promoted by diarist to Madrid, 1878, from Buenos Aires (1872–8); unm., but for his irregular private life see above, 1870, n. 18; generously financed by Derby.

[51] Former premier.

is the great deafness which makes it impossible for him to hear unless one shouts at his ear. We both noticed that he talked of nothing with much pleasure except what related to public affairs: social or literary topics appeared indifferent, except where historical literature was in question: when they were introduced, intentionally or casually, he would listen, but return in a minute to parliamentary recollections. I cannot affirm that we got from him any anecdote of interest that I had not heard before: he spoke without bitterness of past statesmen, with the single exception of Canning, who he said was an intriguer and not to be trusted: he did not much praise Brougham, except as an orator, and described him as unequal even in that character: Sir R. Peel he mentioned slightly, but with respect: the period to which his mind seemed oftenest to revert was that of the first reform bill, but on the whole he was less retrospective than old men in general, and speculated eagerly on the prospects of 1873.

He told M. frankly that in 1868 he thought he ought to have been sent for, though he would have withdrawn his claims in favour of those of Gladstone.

He twice expressed strong dissent from the prevailing tendency to treat the economical or material side of questions as the most important: with civil and religious freedom assured, those matters, he thought, would always take care of themselves. He had been reproached, he said, by financial friends on his own side for having said once that if necessary, England would be prepared to double her debt: but he meant it, and thought that we might do so with no great harm, if it were required for our safety or honour.

22 September 1872. Curious talk last night of Gladstone, carried on by Harcourt, Pender, and Massey:[52] Lowe present, but not taking part. Instances were given of his humane, but singular, practice of picking up women in the streets, taking them to his house, preaching to them, and sending them away again: nothing more is imputed to him, but the practice, in a person situated as he is, shows singular imprudence, for among the people, how many would believe in his innocence who heard one of these stories? Harcourt says they are a good deal circulated, and have made him unpopular, not that the lower-class London world is particular about morality in the abstract, but that they think a public man whose habits are not moral should not make such vehement professions of religion.

Pender believes that he, Gladstone, is dependent on Glyn's bank for money: that he has lost heavily in speculations, is active in buying and

---

[52] W.N. Massey (1809–81), Lib. M.P. 1855–63, 1872–81; financial member, govt of India, 1863–8; historian.

selling on the exchange (of course through brokers) and certainly he told stories that seemed to confirm this belief.

I gathered from Pender that Lowe had been consulting on two projects – one simple, the sale of waste lands belonging to the crown – the other more important and complicated being an attempt to throw open the system of banking in Scotland ... Lowe also told me that he had a scheme by which to lessen the national debt to the extent (he said) of some 32 or 34 millions, but he did not explain it further, and I could not press him.

24 September 1872. Left Minard[53] with Pender, Mr & Mrs Lowe .. Much pleased with both Mr and Mrs Pender: nothing can exceed their civility and attention: nor have I ever seen a self-raised man, become a millionaire by his own exertions, so free from any trace of ostentation or vulgarity. His father lived in a cottage in the Vale of Leven, and was as I gather, a weaver, having also a farm. ... He went as a boy to Glasgow, convinced as he says that he should some day make his fortune: and appears to have advanced steadily, with but little check or interruption. He married early, has a son by that marriage, and became a widower within the year. The second Mrs P. ... is an heiress: he would not touch her fortune: she had £40,000, which in his hands, kept as a separate fund, has grown to £120,000. He has 10,000 acres round Minard: and expects to be able to buy out two of his neighbours, impecunious lairds who are not unwilling to sell. Meanwhile his Manchester business brings in a very large return (I have heard from others £50,000 yearly): and he is continually speculating on a vast scale. ... Long story of his share in founding the Atlantic telegraph and also the Indian telegraph, both of which I believe to have been mainly his work. Various persons connected with the Atlantic line were rewarded, but he got nothing: which at the time could not well be helped, for he was in the thick of an election scrape which led to the disfranchisement of Totnes: and later it would not have been easy to reopen the question. He has since sounded Gladstone on the subject, but got no encouragement. What he wants is a baronetcy.

25 September 1872. In singular confirmation of the stories we had heard at Minard, the Lord Provost told Pender, who repeated it to me not an hour afterwards, that the Premier had been very active in stock exchange speculations, and had lately employed him (Watson).[54] Very strange – but what motive had he to invent the story if not true?[55]

[53] On 17 Sept. 1872 the Derbys left Greenock by steamer for Minard, the W. Highland estate of the millionaire industrialist Pender. The party included the Lowes, C.P. Villiers, the orientalist Sir H. Rawlinson, Leighton the artist, and Sir W. Thomson, the engineer.
[54] Sir James Watson (1801–89), Glasgow stockbroker, lord provost of Glasgow 1871–4.
[55] Cf. *Gladstone Diaries*, vol. 7, cix–cx.

2 October 1872. Retirement of Lord Hatherley finally announced. As a Chancellor, his resignation is a gain to the ministry. His speeches were confused, tedious, and inconsecutive; his plans of law reform feeble and unpopular, and though respected both as a judge and in private life, he was a thoroughgoing and not very scrupulous partisan. Sir R. Palmer, who succeeds him, has the good opinion of all parties: and though his refusal of office when the demolition of the Irish church was in progress, really involved no sacrifice, but on the contrary a considerable pecuniary gain, he was adroit enough to make it appear a political martyrdom, and attained unbounded sympathy from both sides.

... The public accounts for the last half year point to no decrease, as yet, of the general prosperity ... But the coming check will make itself felt within the next few months.

5 October 1872. To Preston, for the first meeting of a new farmers' club, got up in the first instance by some of the tenantry in Cheshire and South Lancashire, and joined by the leading landowners to keep it out of bad hands. We met in the Town Hall, about 300 present ... My opening address occupied about 50 minutes ... Talk of state of feeling about landowning among the tenantry – Hale & Wyatt agree that it is not hostile, but that since the Irish legislation they have been led to expect some change in their condition, they do not themselves exactly know what.

12 October 1872. Received among others a cool request from an Austrian resident at Trieste, who describes himself as ruined by gambling, gives no references, and asks for a loan of £1000 or £1200 to set him on his legs again.

25 October 1872. Visit of the Queen to Manchester ... The people were very cordial in their reception of us, M. and I being constantly cheered.

28 October 1872. Drove with the Queen ... to meet the 11 a.m. train ... Her suite is of 14 persons ... ... There is compensation in the pleasure which the neighbours feel in being asked to meet a Queen. In this way she has enabled us to lay in a stock of local popularity which is always useful.

5 November 1872. The contest for Tiverton ended yesterday by the return of Massey by a very small majority (577 to 547). ... He has held very radical, and indeed very violent, language, and swallowed every pledge required by his party. ... At Minard he told me, unasked, and in the plainest language, that his feelings were now those of a Conservative: and that he should declare himself one, but for his dislike to break old personal ties. Pender also spoke of him to me as one who would, if elected, do his utmost to resist Radicalism.

7 November 1872. The Duke[56] showed me his estate accounts, which are kept with admirable minuteness and order, so that every item of expense or receipt can be found in an instant under its separate head: they are perfect in their way, but must involve a considerable expense in the keeping up.

The rental for 1871 was £353,000, including receipts of every kind: the outlay £272,000.

8 November 1872. My visit to Woburn has been made under favourable circumstances, the party whom I have been asked to meet was agreeable and well-chosen: nothing has gone wrong in any respect: yet the feeling of relief with which I return to my own house and my own pursuits convinces me that my dislike to visiting and to mixed companies – though in my position a misfortune – is incurable. With books and papers I can always enjoy myself: in conversation, I am wearied by much listening and I fear to weary my neighbours by much talking. It is however true that I have not been altogether well of late, and my present feelings may be coloured by that circumstance.

13 November 1872. To the commission on science in its relations with the State: D. of Devonshire[57] chairman ... I was questioned, or rather argued with, for about an hour and a half: my view as expressed was in favour of State aid to science, but against a scientific council to assist and advise the executive, which is with some persons a favourite scheme.

14 November 1872. M. went with the Queen of Holland to Watford, the Queen having expressed a wish to see the place where Lord Clarendon is buried! M. being pressed to go, could not well refuse, though not much liking the journey.

17 November 1872. Much talk in the world of a marriage between Eliot Yorke,[58] younger son of Lord Hardwicke and one of the Rothschilds, a daughter of Sir Antony. She remains a Jewess: receives at her marriage £200,000, and will probably have ten times as much when her father dies.

In the *Spectator* of this week, a curious article stating the sums left during the last ten years by various well-to-do people: the number selected is 124, of whom 10 leave amounts exceeding a million. The largest is Mr Giles Loder,[59] a Russian merchant, who figures for £3,000,000. The above relates to personalty, the value of landed estate not being officially declared. At the usual rate of 30 years purchase,

---

[56] Of Bedford.

[57] William Cavendish, 7th D. of Devonshire (1808–91), succ. 1858.

[58] Eliot Yorke (1843–78), 4th s. of 4th E. Hardwicke, Derby's cabinet colleague, m. (Feb. 1873) Annie, 2nd dau. of Sir Antony de Rothschild.

[59] W.D. Rubinstein, *Men of Property* ... (1981), 44, gives Loder as the 3rd largest Victorian fortune, actually bequeathed; yet not in *D.N.B.*

the D. of Bedford would be estimated at £10,000,000, and I, or rather the family of which I am for life the representative, at £5,000,000.

14 December 1872. Letter from Chelmsford, in which referring to an old conversation between us, he urges me not to give up political life, and dwells a good deal on the absence of confidence in Disraeli: which remembering the transaction of Feb. 1868 is natural.[60]

15 December 1872. Talk of Patten, who is in family troubles: his only living son is drinking himself to death: he was sent round the world in hope of curing him, but without result: and he cannot now probably live more than a year or two. He had another son, who went the same way, and is dead.

... Heard in afternoon of the death (long expected) of Ly Beaconsfield: a heavy blow for Disraeli, and one from which he will probably never altogether recover. New habits are not easily formed at 67: his life was eminently domestic: though not attractive to most people, Ly B. was to him a singularly devoted wife: nor do I doubt the reality and strength of his attachment to her.

27 December 1872. Report sent by Stanhope, of which I do not believe a word, that Gladstone is to resign on personal grounds, being weary and worn out: the D. of Argyll[61] doing the same on the ground of health. The story has probably arisen from Gladstone's frequent allusions in his speeches to the cares of office, and to his own weariness – which sayings are probably sincere enough, but do not mean much.

28 December 1872. Met Lord Lindsay,[62] and long talk with him on what is called spiritualism: he very frank and open in the expression of his views: he does not believe in spiritual or supernatural agency in connection with the phenomena which he has seen – or supposes himself to have seen – but thinks that there is some force, or series of forces, at work, of which as yet we know nothing. He told me, quite seriously, that he had seen Home[63] fly out of a window eighty feet from the ground, and in at another on the same floor: that he had seen him elongated by 11 inches while lying on the floor, and measured the growth: that he had seen chairs, standing on a lawn out of doors, fly up in the air and remain there some time, no person being near: that he had held a redhot coal in one hand, at the bidding of a medium, without its burning him: that thinking there was some trick he had touched it with the other hand, and burnt his finger sharply (he showed me the mark of the burn, which was visible enough): that he had

[60] Replaced by Cairns on formation of Disraeli's 1st ministry; only minister thus dropped.
[61] George Campbell, 8th D. of Argyll (1823–1900), succ. 1847; Indian sec. 1868–74.
[62] Ludovic Lindsay, 26th E. of Crawford (1847–1913); succ. father 1880.
[63] Daniel Douglas Home (1833–86), spiritualist.

entirely satisfied himself that no imposture, or form of conjuring, could have produced the effects he had seen: that he thought the subject worth more enquiry than it had received, but had no theory of his own about it. ... Ld Lindsay has some talent, with a good deal of oddity no doubt, but he has a taste for scientific inquiry, and some knowledge of practical science. But I suspect latent unsoundness.[64]

[64] Derby's contributions in parliament in 1872 were few and non-partisan: Kew gardens, the Treaty of Washington, landownership statistics, the Indian princes of Delhi, and appellate jurisdiction. Outside parliament, he spoke on English improvidence (*T*, 1 Feb. 1872, 5e), on education (*T*, 15 Aug. 1872, 3f), on the labour question (*T*, 30 Aug. 1872, 3f), on the land question (*T*, 7 Oct. 1872, 11a) and on discharged prisoners (*T*, 20 Dec. 1872, 10b).

1873

1 January 1873. I begin this year with no other anxiety, private or public, than such as arises from Ly Derby not having been, during the last month or six weeks, in her usual health: the cause of which is known, and is, as I hope, easily removable: in every other respect I have nothing to ask for or wish for.

Public affairs are quiet, both in England and the Continent: general expectation points to a quiet and inoffensive line of policy as likely to be that of the ministry: and this expectation, though resting on no other foundation than that of popular belief, seems to show what is the general wish. It is thought that the diminished popularity and weakened health of the Prime Minister make them indifferent to a long continuance in office: and he has certainly talked a good deal in that sense of late.

The country is still prosperous to an extraordinary degree, though the bad harvest, and signs of an overdone trade, point to the possibility that 1873 will not see a continuance of the advance made in 1872. This is perhaps as well for nothing except a check in the demand for labour can prevent the rise of wages to amounts never known before. Indeed they have risen already beyond all previous experience.

We have in the house Arthur and Lionel Cecil, Margaret C. and no other guests.[1]

3 January 1873. Heard last night of the death of Lord Galloway,[2] who has long been imbecile; he appears to have suffered little. He was 72 years of age. It is believed that his affairs are in great confusion, though the estate is fine, the rental not being much below £30,000.

5 January 1873. Sent £25 to H. Stanley,[3] for the quarter, ignoring a hint which he gives me as to paying his debts.

... Wrote to Sir C. Adderley[4] on a plan which he forwards to me, for dealing with the question of local taxation.

11 January 1873. It is singular that of all my relations, scarcely any

---

[1] Diarist's stepchildren. Derby was at Knowsley until 18 Jan., apart from a visit to his mother at his brother's house, Witherslack, N. Lancs. (2 Jan.). On 15–17 Jan. he chaired Kirkdale quarter sessions, then returned (18 Jan.) to London.

[2] Father-in-law of diarist's stepdaughter, née Lady Mary Cecil.

[3] Henry Thomas Stanley (1803–75), diarist's uncle.

[4] C.B. Adderley, 1st Baron Norton (1814–1905), cr. peer Apr. 1878; pres. of board of trade 1874–8.

except the Stanleys of Cross Hall seem to come up to the average of mental capacity.

12 January 1873. Church: called at the Hales ... Talk with him about Burkitt, my sub-agent for the Fylde, who is nearly, if not quite, past his work: I suggest he should be replaced by a young man, acting as assistant to Hale in his general work, which seems to be rather more than he can manage. I know that H. had proposed to abolish his place, which is not now wanted, all the costly improvements of the last 20 years in the Fylde being ended. No decision was come to, but when Burkitt retires something of the kind must be done.

... Wrote at length to Hunt on the plan which he left with me for reform in the Excise. ... What I suggested to Hunt was to accept the plan proposed as to the spirit duty: to repeal the licences on sale of beer, wine, and tobacco, whenever opportunity suited, without providing an equivalent, and for the the others, gradually to lessen the number, striking off those that yield least, and reducing the others by degrees.

18 January 1873. News of the sudden death of Graves, one of the Conservative members for Liverpool. He was only 54 or 55 ... His loss will be felt, for he was both hospitable and laborious: worked for his constituents and entertained them. He attended meetings of all sorts punctually: and both in public and in private talked good sense, though in a heavy pompous manner. His opinions were moderate, and his whole character suited to the position which he filled.

19 January 1873. Death of Ld Lytton announced, which was quite unexpected, for he had not reached the age of 67 ... But his health for many years past had been bad, and his strange ways of living did not improve it. He smoked much, used opium, took little exercise, and sat up most of the night. He had made a considerable reputation – inherited a fortune – and acquired a peerage: all things which he valued, yet he seemed to enjoy them little. ... In the H. of Commons he delivered one singularly fine speech, that on reform in 1859: but was with great difficulty induced to make it, and in the Lords, where he sat five years, he never spoke at all. Deafness prevented his taking much part in politics, which were not, as I conceive, to his liking at any period of his life, though he used them as a means to an end. He was above all things a literary man, valuing the reputation of an author above every other.

20 January 1873. Meeting of the Winchester Coll. governing body ... We discussed the matter on which we had met for nearly 5 hours: and a minute was agreed to from which I was the only dissentient. ... We avoid either approving or censuring the Headmaster's conduct ... The minute then goes on to review the practice of allowing prefects ... to inflict bodily punishment on their juniors, and though a legal opinion taken at my request condemns it as indefensible by law, the minute

sanctions and defends it ... Dr Vaughan[5] was most active in bringing
about this result; I opposed it strongly, but was almost alone. In
conclusion I protested against the decision, as being one which if called
in question in Parliament I could not undertake to defend.[6]

22 January 1873. Household expenses, according to a return which I
have this morning received, were in 1871, £22,108; in 1872, £24,174,
the difference being due to the general rise in the prices of all articles.

Met Cairns, who talked of Disraeli, whom he has seen. He (D.) is in
better spirits than was expected, the long illness of his wife having
lessened the final blow. Talks of taking rooms in a hotel for the year,
the house in Grosvenor St having gone away from him. ... D. has no
idea of giving up public affairs, and will probably appear on the first
night.

Anxiety of Cairns that I shd open the debate in the Lords: I asked,
why not Richmond? He says the Duke has never spoken on these
foreign questions, knows little of them etc., and he himself does not
wish to be the chief speaker, lest it should be thought that the objections
which he is prepared to take are those of a lawyer only.

23 January 1873. Funeral of Graves ... very largely attended: all
Liverpool seems to have gone into mourning. Though aware that he
was popular, and deservedly so, I did not know how deep and general
was the feeling in his favour.

24 January 1873. Wet morning: stayed at home, and arranged and
destroyed old papers, which I find almost always useless...

... Sir Henry Holland calls, and tells me among other things that
Keston Lodge,[7] Mr Toone's place, is to be sold after his death, which
as he is 84, and very infirm, cannot be distant. But that the price in
that neighbourhood will be enormous, I might gratify M.'s taste by
buying it.

27 January 1873. Much bustle and excitement as to the Liverpool
election: the Liberals offered the candidature to Robertson Gladstone,[8]
who declined, then to Fitzjames Stephen,[9] who also declined; and
finally, to a Mr Caine[10] of whom I know nothing, but who appears to
have been active among the teetotallers. He accepts, and will stand.

29 January 1873. Much talk and writing about the Liverpool election.
The Orange or ultra-protestant [section] have seceded from the Conservative candidate, as not going far enough for them; *per contra*, the

[5] C.J. Vaughan (1816–97), headmaster of Harrow 1844–59.
[6] Derby resigned, 21 Jan. 1873, followed by Northcote. Cf. John Chandos, *Boys Together* (1984), 244–5; excessive zeal by a prefect had excited controversy.
[7] Near Bromley, Kent.
[8] Premier's brother.
[9] (Sir) James Fitzjames Stephen (1829–94), legal member of council in India 1869–72.
[10] W.S. Caine (1842–1903), zealot: not M.P. until 1880.

licensed victuallers will to a man oppose Mr Caine, who is one of the apostles of the U.K. Alliance.

30 January 1873. Agreed ... to invest £200 ... in a Preston company for building a new public hall. It ought to pay, but in any case such local objects have a certain claim upon me.

1 February 1873. Saw Cairns, in afternoon, and discussed with him at some length various points connected with the American case.

2 February 1873. Sale of Northumberland House and the adjoining property wh. belongs to the Duke: he gets from the Metrop. Board £500,000, wh. is not excessive considering the situation. Besides an addition to his income of £20,000 a year, he is relieved from the burden of a London house much too big for any requirement of modern life; saving both ways: but he probably will not think so. The price is probably the largest ever given for a single house.

4 February 1873. Saw Disraeli for the first time since his loss: he talked freely and naturally: his spirits are better than I had heard they were, but it is easy to see that he has suffered and that it is with him an effort to take an interest in anything. He said he had wished to retire, but did not see who was to do the work: Hardy would not hear of taking the place of Leader, and who else was possible?

5 February 1873. Dined with D. of Richmond, meeting a party of Conservative peers. The speech was read as usual: it is quiet and subdued in line, saying comparatively little on domestic subjects.

6 February 1873. Up early, rather nervous and uncomfortable in prospect of a speech ... Clarendon moved the address ... I followed, speaking about 45 minutes: with satisfaction to myself the whole: well listened to throughout.[11] Ld Granville's reply was singularly feeble and confused, so much so as to be a subject of general remark. ... Very well pleased that this business is over. My dislike to making speeches certainly does not diminish with time.

7 February 1873. Saw F.[12] and advised him to take up in parliament the case of the merchant seamen, as to which an enquiry is to be asked for. (It is alleged that hundreds of lives are sacrificed yearly, by

[11] *H*, ccxiv, 16–26 (6 Feb. 1873). Derby declared that Irish improvement was illusory (despite a coercion act 'the most stringent and severe passed within my recollection') and saw no hope of settling the Irish university question. He warned against 'a system of alliances and protectorates on the E. African coast which could be of no possible advantage', and deplored any idea of extending India's frontiers ('that country has at present as good a military frontier as could well be drawn'). He was strongly critical of the legal basis of the Alabama settlement, as laying down trouble for the future. He noted that 'the battle between capital and labour never was fiercer'; that the record price of coal threatened U.K. industry; and that buoyant revenues came mainly from drink. 'We have drunk ourselves out of the American difficulty'.

[12] His brother.

overloading ships ... A Mr Plimsoll,[13] M.P. for Derby, has lately written
a book on the subject...)

... Satisfied with the effect which my speech of yesterday appears to
have produced. Disraeli, who like me had been prompted by Cairns
on the various points of international law, spoke in exactly the same
sense. Called on him, hearing that he had shown signs of illness in his
speech and closed it abruptly, as though from exhaustion. Found him
much relieved, and cheerful: he acknowledged to me that his nervousness had been so great that he did not think he could get through
with it, but the plunge having been made, the rest was easy.

8 February 1873. To British Museum. Business lasted till 2: Duke of
Somerset in the chair. ... We discussed the possibility of getting hold
of Sir T. Phillips's[14] collection of MSS, one of the most valuable existing,
which is held in trust under the provision of a very eccentric will ...
The trustees are without funds. (Among the provisions of the trust are
these, that no fire or warning apparatus shall be allowed within the
building where the MSS are kept: and that no R. Catholic nor
bookseller, shall be admitted to see them ...) ... The MSS are
beginning to decay from damp and neglect...

... Disraeli dined with us, and much affected, and nervous, on seeing
M. for the first time: but he rallied, and talked in his usual strain. He
said a good deal to her about the discomforts of his present life: and
left on her mind the impression that he was likely to marry again. He
criticised Thackeray, whom he has always disliked, saying that the
whole secret of his success lay in having closely and even servilely
copied Balzac, who was very little known in England...

Some, though not much political talk, in which I was glad to find
that he agreed with me as to the inexpediency of again taking office
while in a minority, and with the present parliament. He did not exactly
think a crisis probable, but it might happen, and it is well to be
prepared.

9 February 1873. A. Balfour[15] came to luncheon: on his way to Egypt,
for health: he seems intelligent, has his mother's look and manner, but
pale and thin to an extraordinary degree. His father, uncle, and aunt
died of consumption: his mother died at 45 or thereabouts, after long
illness.

10 February 1873. Dined with Lord Russell ... Bought a little more
eastern china ... there is a great want of all such ornaments at
Knowsley, the house having been cleared out in my great-grandfather's
time, as I have always heard, and the losses never made good.

[13] Samuel Plimsoll (1824–98), M.P. (Lib.) Derby 1868–80.
[14] Sir Thomas Phillipps (1792–1872), bibliophile.
[15] A.J. Balfour, later premier.

11 February 1873. Ld Halifax[16] called: in conversation he said that the local taxation bill of this year would be a small measure, chiefly preparatory: abolishing exemptions, consolidating rates, and in some cases rearranging the dues of taxation. He thought the Irish plan would be abused on all sides, but accepted in the end on the ground that no better substitute could be found.

12 February 1873. London U. Senate where a long debate as to whether Greek should be made optional for the matriculation examination, instead of compulsory as it is at present. Hutton[17] moved the resolution to that effect. Lowe supported it strongly. Maine was the chief opponent, and Twisleton.[18] In the end it was carried by 10 to 8. I voted for it, as did Lord Granville.

13 February 1873. My speech of this day week, in so far as it condemned the Washington Treaty, has been generally approved by the Whigs: Ld Romilly spoke of it to me as 'unanswerable'. Ld Russell said ... that he was ready to take his place in the 'Derby Dilly',[19] and other expressions of the same kind have reached me.

... Patten mentioned the wish of some persons connected with the Idiot Asylum in N. Lancashire, that their building at Lancaster should be formally opened by the P. of Wales, and that I should invite him to Knowsley for that purpose. This I at once declined, for several reasons: I do not like the system of continually calling on members of the Royal Family to parade themselves on public occasions, and as regards the P. of W. I see no advantage in cultivating his acquaintance. He can be of no use to me, would expect more attention than I am disposed to give, and neither he nor his friends are the kind of people I wish to have to do with.

Dined The Club: meeting Reeve, Walpole,[20] Ld Romilly, Bp of Winchester,[21] Van De Weyer, Sir H. Holland, and one or two more.

14 February 1873. Last night ... Gladstone spoke 3 hours on his plan of Irish university education: I have heard nothing of the effect. It does not on the face of it appear to be framed in an ultramontane sense, and the Premier disavowed having had any connection with the R.C. hierarchy...

We dined at 7, and left at 8.30 for Dover, where we put up at the Lord Warden Hotel.[22]

[16] Sir Charles Wood, 1st Vt Halifax (1800–85), Whig min., ending as lord privy seal, 1870–4.

[17] R.H. Hutton (1826–97), co-editor of *Spectator* 1861–97.

[18] E.T.B. Twisleton (1809–74), member of public bodies.

[19] Whig secession of 1830s led by the elder Derby.

[20] Spencer Walpole (1806–98), Derbyite home sec. 1852, 1858–9, 1866–7.

[21] Wilberforce.

[22] Derby's tour of France, Switzerland, and Italy, with Lady Derby's depression in mind, lasted from 15 Feb. to 14 Mar.; thus he missed Gladstone's defeat on the Irish

15 February 1873. To Paris by 9.30 boat, arr. Paris 6.30. Put up at Hotel Westminster. Saw L. West with his Spanish news.

16 February 1873. Saw Ld Lyons:[23] no details, then received by Pres. & Mme Thiers at Versailles.

... After dinner the President took me apart, and after some compliments began to talk over affairs. He congratulated England on having settled affairs amicably with Russia: said he was convinced that the Russian cabinet had no designs on India: they knew the difficulties too well: they had territory enough, and knew it: what they wanted was increase of population. He believed the Czar was thoroughly peaceful: and his personal will was everything. He was more powerful since emancipation than before: the people, besides their former half-superstitious worship of him, knew that he had given them liberty and land.

He talked of Spanish affairs: seemed to think that the struggle would lie altogether between the republicans and the carlists: there was another difficulty in the future – supposing the republic was established what form was it to take – centralised or federal? The latter was the wish of the extreme party and in some of the provinces they would find support. He spoke of possible designs on Portugal: I ventured to say that the Spaniards would find no sympathy among Portuguese of any party, as far as I had always heard; but he was not sure of that. He rather hinted at than expressly mentioned the possibility of a joint understanding between England and France for the protection of Portugal, and took occasion to express an earnest hope that the British government would not adopt the ideas of 'the Manchester school' which he thought Gladstone was too partial to.

Turning to French affairs, he said he was busy with the reorganisation of the army, which was the one thing essential for France, if she was to recover her lost position in Europe: but the object was not war: no: the quarrel should not come from the side of France: but it might be that very serious events would happen before long, and France must be ready to take her part. He thought a breach probable between Germany and Bavaria: Bavaria had joined the German empire only on certain conditions: & would Prussia observe these? He thought it very doubtful.

He talked of the doctrine of nationality, which he believed to be an essentially false one: it had been invented by France, he said, for the benefit of the Poles, in the first instance, and the result had been the

Universities Bill (11 Mar.) on hearing of which he wrote, 'I do not suppose that a Conservative Government is either possible or desirable'.
[23] Richard Lyons, 2nd Baron Lyons (1817–87), succ. 1858; amb. in Paris 1867–87; cr. vt 1881, earl 1887; offered F.O. by Salisbury 1886; R.C. convert 1887.

creation of the Italian and German powers, against the interests of France. The French had had the honour of the phrase, but rivals had gained the advantage of the thing.

I mentioned a report which I had heard as to the French communists exerting themselves actively at Madrid: the President did not seem to believe it: he thought they had had enough of violence: in France they were looking to the elections, and hoping to gain their object by parliamentary means, which was legitimate: their loss during the siege of Paris had been at least 50,000: 30,000 'par le feu' – the rest ... at this point he was interrupted by someone coming to take leave, and did not resume the subject.

I found an opportunity of expressing my conviction (which I could do sincerely) that in England all parties wished for his continuance in power, believing that no serious mischief could be done while he was there. He was extremely cordial, and made me promise to come again on my return from the south, which I must do if possible.

He asked me how it was that the Emperor had created so strong a feeling in his favour in England? adding that he had no friends left in France. I said his popularity was rather personal than political: we knew that he liked our country: and we were indebted to him for the commercial treaty. But I added that I did not believe there was any sympathy with the Bonapartist party.

22 February 1873. Called on Lady Bulwer[24] who as I find from M. is solely persecuted on account of her late husband's debts. Disreputable people start up in all parts of Europe with claims upon him real or imaginary: and threaten exposure if not paid. Lord Dalling,[25] though not without public spirit in his way, had no scruples where money was concerned: and but for the vigilance of her trustees his widow would have been robbed of her own fortune.

23 February 1873. Wrote to Disraeli, chiefly to know what is doing, and indicating what seems to me the weak point of the Irish scheme.

24 February 1873. Nothing seems to have passed in parliament of the slightest political importance. ... There has been no further discussion of the Irish bill; nor do either radicals or conservatives seem anxious for serious fights. I cannot regret my absence, though personally I should be glad of some occupation beyond sightseeing, to which three years and more passed in travel have made me perhaps more indifferent than I ought to be.

25 February 1873. According to the English papers, there is much

[24] Georgiana, née Wellesley, Lady Dalling and Bulwer (1817–78); a Cecil on her mother's side.
[25] Amb. at Constantinople 1858–65; cr. peer 1871. There was a twofold link between him and the Cecil interest. His mother-in-law was a dau. of the 1st M., while his bro. m. the sister of the 2nd M. of Salisbury's 1st wife.

controversy going on as to the cause and probable consequence of the coal famine, and an opinion is beginning to find favour with many people, that the State should buy up all the collieries ... A more reasonable proposal would be to lay a tax of 1s. a ton on all coal raised, applying the proceeds, between £5 and £6m., to paying off debt. But even for this measure of foresight it is questionable whether opinion would be ripe.

27 February 1873. Letter from Burton,[26] to the effect that he is tired of Trieste, at which I am not surprised, and wants to be employed in Central Asia. It has more than once occurred to me to send him out at my own expense, which on public grounds would be well worth doing, and I should not miss the £2000 which it would cost ... He has absolutely no private means, and though I might be willing to pay for his journey, I could hardly undertake to maintain Mrs B. in his absence: nor would he accept it.

28 February 1873. Letter from Disraeli, in answer to mine. He says there are rumours in the House of ministerial defeat on the Irish bill. A resolution is to be moved on the second reading, which is equivalent to throwing out the bill.

1 March 1873. Two letters from Lionel West contain a hint that he is likely to marry a young lady, a Jewess connected in some way with the Rothschilds: the family respectable, and fortune believed to be £200,000. But it does not seem clear that there is any certainty of the event coming off.

2 March 1873. Talk last night with M. about the affairs of her brother Lionel. It seems that he has been long embarrassed, to what extent is unknown: the Duchess of Bedford has just helped him to the amount of £2000, and he wants £2000 more, as he says, to enable him to leave Paris. I agreed that M. should advance £1000 of this, which I will repay her ... The rest he may probably be able to get from his brothers. The marriage with the Jewess is evidently desirable, if it can be brought about. The beginning of the mischief was a connection of many years standing with a Spanish woman, I believe, originally a dancer, by whom he has a family left on his hands to maintain. She died last year. It is an awkward business altogether.

10 March 1873. To Ferney ... Walk in the garden, saw the terrace where V[oltaire] used to sit: and picked up horse chestnuts ... for planting in England.

12 March 1873. Nor is it easy to see how they can resign, in a parliament where the Liberals have so large a majority: for what other cabinet can be formed? One possible solution is that the Premier –

---

[26] Sir Richard Burton (1821–90), explorer; consul at Trieste, 1872–90.

who has for a long time been talking in all consequences of his wish to retire – will make himself the scapegoat, and withdraw in favour of Ld Granville, with Cardwell or Forster to lead the Commons.

14 March 1873. Paris to London ... Arrived about 6 p.m. Called at once on Disraeli, and heard from him in detail the story of his negotiation with the Queen: she appears to have been sincerely friendly, offered to dissolve at once if he wished it, and as he says, showed evident reluctance to the idea of Gladstone's return to power. D. however remained firm in his refusal, as to which he knew that both Cairns and I agreed with him, and as far as I can make out his colleagues in the H. of C. take the same view.

Passed the evening very busily, with letters and papers, of which I have a roomful to examine.

15 March 1873. D. asked me to call in the afternoon, and showed me a long letter[27] which Gladstone has written to the Queen, in a tone of repressed but very visible anger, denying in effect the right of the Opposition to refuse office after they have brought about the rejection of a bill which the cabinet have announced that they treat as a question of confidence. We discussed it and I drew a mem. showing what seemed to me the weak points in his argument: this at D.'s request, that he might embody it in a letter to the Queen. We both agreed that the evident dissatisfaction of G. at the course adopted by the Opposition is strong evidence that the decision was right.

16 March 1873. Saw D. again at his request: and went with him over his letter to the Queen, in which he has embodied the substance, and mostly the words, of the mem. which I gave him.

Saw Corry[28] and Barrington:[29] who agree that the party in general are satisfied with our refusal of office under the circumstances.

Saw Cross, who tells me at some length that I ought to take Disraeli's place, inasmuch as the constituencies have more confidence in me than in D. – which may or may not be the fact, but what he proposes is impossible.

The talk today is that partly in anger and partly from considerations of health, G. will not take office again.

... F. dined with us. He holds the same language as Cross, and does not see that I am the last person who can move in such a matter.

[27] Printed, with Disraeli's riposte, in P. Guedalla, *The Queen and Mr. Gladstone* (1933) i, 399–402.

[28] Montagu ('Monty') Corry (1838–1903), Disraeli's priv. sec. 1866–81; cr. Baron Rowton, 1880.

[29] George Barrington, 7th Vt Barrington (1824–86); sometime priv. sec. to Derby when premier; held minor offices, 1874–80, 1885–6, 1886; cr. Baron Shute, 1880; succ. father in viscountcy, 1883; intimate of Disraeli, who however called him 'stupid and uninteresting'; but one of v. few to whom Disraeli chatted on front bench.

17 March 1873. Letter from Delane, asking whether it is true that I am forming a government. A question easily ansd.

... H of Lds in afternoon, where we were told that Gladstone has undertaken to reconstruct his cabinet.

20 March 1873. Went to hear Disraeli, whose speech was singularly ingenious and happy: one of the best, I think, for its purpose that he has ever delivered.

23 March 1873. L. West and Sanderson dined with us. West said nothing as to his marriage ... He tells me, which I am sorry to hear, that there is at F.O. a party for & against Tenterden, and that the new clerks – those of the last 2 or 3 years – do not work well with the seniors.

25 March 1873. Mr J. E. Gorst, the election manager for the Conservative party, called at my request: I had asked him through Cross: he said ballot had done neither harm nor good, nearly all the voters said beforehand what candidate they would support, and by the result it was found that they told truth, the numbers coming out in accordance with the list made out from the promises. He believed we were as well prepared for an election as we ever should be, and that for that reason the cabinet would put off dissolving as long as they could – some thought, even till 1875. I begged him to call whenever he had anything to tell or ask, coming between 10 & 11.

Disraeli called, and we occupied ourselves in drawing out a list of the future cabinet...

Disraeli	Treasury
Cairns	Chancellor
Derby	Foreign Office
Northcote	Exchequer
Hardy	Home Office
Richmond	Ld President
Carnarvon	India Office
Buckingham?[30]	Colonial Office (or J. Manners?)
Hunt	War Department
Pakington?	Admiralty
Stanhope?	Privy Seal
Malmesbury?	Post Office
J. Manners?	Board of Works

Besides these, there are Cross, Patten and H. Lennox[31] who have a claim to moderately high office.

---

[30] Richard Grenville, 3rd D. of Buckingham (1823–89), succ. 1861; chmn., L.N.W.R., 1853–61; pres. of council 1866–7, col. sec. 1867–8; gov. of Madras 1875–80 (previously offered to Lytton); reputable s. of reprobate father.

[31] Lord Henry Lennox (1821–86), Cons. M.P. 1846–85; whip 1852, 1858–9; sec. to admiralty 1866–8, where seen by diarist as talented; when young, close to Disraeli; 1st commr of public works, 1874–6, resigning after financial scandal; bro. of D. of Richmond who sat in Disraeli's cabinet.

Stanhope might be satisfied with something done for his son: and Malmesbury may not care to serve again. Cross and Patten would be more useful in cabinet.

The above was sketched out on paper by Disraeli and myself, March 25, not as final, but for consideration.

27 March 1873. I notice that Hardy, and our friends generally, are eager to dissolve...

29 March 1873. Rather uncomfortable in prospect of a speech, though one of no consequence. It is always so, with me, and will be to the end.

... Dined with the Inst. of Civil Engineers ... I observe that the engineers and those who attend their dinner are of a very conservative disposition.

1 April 1873. Disraeli called: thought a fresh crisis, and a dissolution probable: speculated on the future: thought V. Harcourt might be secured, which I doubted or rather doubt his being of value if we got him, as he would lose in the change what character he has. He said he should like F. to be secretary to the Admiralty, which I shall be heartily glad of if it can be managed.

2 April 1873. Dined D. of Cambridge: a large party, all Conservative...

... D. of Cambridge very free in his comments on the new short-service system, which he does not like: he says what soldiers really care for is the prospect of pension, the idea of being provided for: short terms of service lead to nothing, and they quit the army unfit for other occupation. He thinks we shall have either to return to the old plan of long engagement, or adopt conscription in some shape, for which he evidently has a liking, though aware that it would be unpopular.

3 April 1873. F. and Cross came to consult me about a landlord and tenant bill now going through H. of C. I advised accepting it for the most part, but resisting steadily the clause which forbids the landlord & tenant agreeing to contract themselves out of it. In this they both agreed.

6 April 1873. Disraeli dined with us, alone: we thought him in low spirits.

7 April 1873. Budget ... Lowe's speech was dry ... but the substance of his plan was good, and will be popular. He has, in round numbers, a surplus of £4,800,000: which he applies (1) to paying off half the American indemnity (2) to taking off half the sugar duty (3) to taking a penny off the income tax. This division seems fair as between direct and indirect taxation, and the income tax at 3d. is as low as it ought to be. The other changes are matters of very small detail.

... The feeling of the House was evidently one of relief at the decision not to pay off the whole American debt in the present year.

They did not seem to care much about sugar, but appreciated the reduction of income tax.

8 April 1873. Began in afternoon to read Sallust, which I have not done since leaving Cambridge.

11 April 1873. Finished Sallust, whom I read with ease, but with less pleasure than formerly. Began the satires of Persius.

16 April 1873. Wrote to Disraeli on the budget, expressing approval of the postponement of half the American payment, and of the division of relief given between direct and indirect taxation: but I suggested a doubt whether the estimate is not too sanguine, as Lowe reckons on their being no falling off ... Many signs ... point to an impending commercial crisis, or at least to a slackening in the rate at which we have been lately going ahead.

23 April 1873. Home, where found a telegram, received by M. to the effect that Delawarr, who was staying at the Bull Hotel, Cambridge, is missing, and there are fears for his life.

24 April 1873. Lord Delawarr had gone out ... leaving letters behind him from which it is inferred that he intended to destroy himself. ... The body had been found in the river ... The motive is a mystery. He was well in health, habitually cheerful, temperate in his habits, fond of society in a quiet way, though detesting the bustle of London life: his affairs were not embarrassed, and by economy and good management he was rapidly putting the family estates into order. Few men seemed to enjoy life more. He had some little oddities, but not of a serious kind, and nothing in the nature of insanity was ever suspected.

M. much stunned and almost bewildered...

25 April 1873. Later news tells us that the cause of poor Delawarr's act was the recent death of a woman to whom he had been attached: for which, in some way not explained, he seems to have considered himself responsible. The impulse must have been sudden: for had there been premeditation, he would not have gone down to an inn at Cambridge ... His journey there was on business ... M. tells me that when excited by family troubles, of which in earlier years there were many, he would discuss them calmly and quietly in the evening, go to bed, pass a sleepless night, and come down in the morning excited by want of rest and his own thoughts, so that his language & manner then would be in complete contrast with what they were a few hours before.

26 April 1873. Evidence at the inquest ... The woman was a Miss Nethercote ... her death was caused by drink ... poor D. felt it deeply: and probably his idea of being responsible for her death arose from a notion that he had either not exerted himself enough, or exerted himself injudiciously, to check her propensity.

6 May 1873. Carnarvon consults me as to raising £60,000 or £80,000 for working coal, of the existence of which he appears to feel pretty sure, on his Notts. estates. I strongly dissuade him, saying that he can lease them, or form a company, and so take part of the risk, but that he should not take it all; nor is it worth his while. He seems to agree.

9 May 1873. Death, at Avignon, of J.S. Mill, aged 67. He was certainly of our time the thinker who has exercised most power over public affairs. His democratic sympathies were intensely strong: but until the last four years, he had the skill (perhaps unconsciously) to veil them under an appearance of impartiality ... In parliament, though respectfully listened to, and though his speeches were sure to contain something worth hearing, he had no considerable success: voice, manner, and that indefinable peculiarity which distinguishes a student from a man of the world, were all against him, and he seemed to lose self-control when actually engaged in political conflict. Those who most respected his abilities and position regretted most to see him mixed up with vulgar agitators such as Odger, Bradlaugh,[32] etc. But in whatever he may have failed, he has left no man of equal literary or philosophical eminence behind him. I remember with pleasure my offer to him of a seat on the India Council, in 1858.

10 May 1873. Talk both with Disraeli and Northcote, separately, on the political situation. They agree in saying that the cabinet is demoralised: Gladstone is known to be weary of the whole business: and they both seem to think it likely that he may take the opportunity of some trifling or casual defeat to resign again. In that case, what should we do? I cannot but agree with them that under the circumstances supposed, we should have no option except to take office and dissolve. The time is more convenient than in March: the work of the session is over: and if we refuse the challenge now, can we hope for a more favourable opportunity hereafter?

Stansfeld's bill on local taxation is harmless, being cautious even to feebleness: strange that he, who entered public life as the friend of Mazzini, should be far more timid and safe than Goschen, whose plans frightened all the country gentlemen two years ago, and contributed to the present reaction.

14 May 1873. Met Northcote, walked with him, and talk of finance. He seems against farther reductions in customs or excise duties, considers the lightening of the rates to be a more urgent matter, and had a scheme which I did not well understand, but what I understood of it I disliked, for subsidising friendly societies and savings banks, by allowing them a higher interest for deposits than the State itself can invest at. But he explained it briefly, and I may have mistaken his meaning. I rather pressed, instead of plans of this sort, a fresh attack

[32] Charles Bradlaugh (1833–91), free-thinker.

on the debt, by means of a new creation of terminable annuities. N. is evidently aware that he is to be C. of Ex. if we come in.

15 May 1873. Called on Darwin[33] at his house near Down: sat half an hour with him, talk on general subjects, but I could carry away nothing of special note.

16 May 1873. Called on Gladstone, in consequence of communications from Mr Arnold:[34] discussion with him: he condemned strongly the notion of holding a meeting in support of the memorial to Mill, on the ground that it would almost certainly lead to difference of opinion – nobody could answer for what might be said or done: he would have nothing to say to it for one. He laughed a little at Mr A.'s enthusiasm. I agreed entirely as to the meeting – which in fact I had made up my mind not to attend if it were held – and we settled that its abandonment should be advised – that a limited committee should be formed to promote the memorial on which both he and I should serve, with if possible some neutral person at its head – he suggested Ld Russell, as being now retired from affairs – and that we would recommend a portrait, bust, or statue, for the N.P.G. and in addition if funds sufficed a scholarship or prize to be founded at the London U. – I am perhaps wrong in speaking of the application of the fund as settled between us, for it was only talked of: the other matters were decided, and Mr G. undertook to write to Mr A. That gentleman however followed me to the H. of Lds, and I told him what had passed. He at once consented to give up the meeting.

19 May 1873. Received from Gladstone a note, containing a copy of a singular letter which he has written to Mr Arnold. In this letter Mr G. refuses to have anything to do with the Mill memorial,[35] until a charge made against Mill in a printed, but unpublished, circular is explained away. This charge is that he, Mill, as a young man, was concerned in circulating papers recommending intercourse between men and women so guarded that no children should follow. The date of the alleged act being fifty years ago. The author of the circular is said to be Hayward. The vehemence of Mr G.'s language in reference to a matter of so old a date, and amounting at most to the foolish promulgation of a theory notoriously held by his whole school of economists, is perplexing: and it is impossible not to think of the extreme horror with which Catholics condemn all such devices.

... Dined Grillions ... Rather dull, Lowe and D. being apparently afraid of one another, or at least mutually disinclined to talk.

20 May 1873. Note that Lowe told M. 'they' (I suppose the cabinet)

---

[33] Derby was a pallbearer at Darwin's funeral.
[34] (Sir) Arthur Arnold (1833–1902), progressive publicist.
[35] See Morley, *Gladstone*, ii 543–4.

had made up their minds that the rest of the sugar duties must go: and probably if there is any surplus, this will be done in the next budget.

23 May 1873. Saw Ly Cowper, who very anxious about M's health.

26 May 1873. Request from Mrs H. Stanley for help: it is not yet 2 months since her husband[36] asked for £50 and got it.

... Busy destroying old letters, of which in future I mean to keep hardly any, after a year or two. One never refers to them, and they only take up space to no purpose.

2 June 1873. ... East wind, and St Helens again disagreeable.

8 June 1873. Wrote agreeing to be surety for L. West's loan of £5000 from an insurance co. ... Deductions from his salary over 7 years will set him free ... (The talk of his marriage is merely talk...)

12 June 1873. ... Talk with Ld Lawrence[37] last night: I asked after his eldest son: he complained that he (the son) though a good fellow, and active in his way, will not take to any kind of work: I laughed, and asked whether he (Ld L.) would have gone out to India, and led the life he did, if he had had £2000 or £3000 a year secured to him? He said with a good deal of energy 'If I had been sure of only £100 a year in England, when I was young, I would never have gone east.' This is like the D. of Wellington wishing to give up military life, if he could have obtained a small situation here at home.

... Talk about the Shah's visit: Ld L. says from what he knows of orientals, he does not believe in any result following from their seeing European civilisation: it merely puzzles them: it is odd and new and that is all...

13 June 1873. H of Lds, where ... met Richmond, Cairns, & Salisbury to discuss a new registration bill, which comes on next week, and is much objected to by our people.

14 June 1873. Old Mr Robertson,[38] of Ladykirk, is a peer: the reason not explained. He is old, out of health, and a thoroughgoing partisan: but in the House he has never made any position for himself, and outside his own county he is unknown.

... Meeting of Richmond, Malmesbury, & self at Disraeli's, to discuss the registration bill. We agreed to throw it out, but it is put off for another week. D. thinks a crisis probable – Irish and nonconformist members both alienated, and ministers cannot now reckon on a majority.

Dined Carnarvon's, at his new house in Bruton St, which very

---

[36] Diarist's uncle.

[37] John Lawrence, Baron Lawrence (1811–79), Gov.-Gen. of India 1863–Sept. 1868.

[38] David Marjoribanks (Robertson from 1834), 1st Baron Marjoribanks (1797–1873), 4th s. of a Scottish laird; became London merchant; M.P. (Lib.) 1859–73; lord-lt. Berwickshire 1860–73; peer, 12–19 June 1873 (died), title becoming extinct.

handsome and comfortable, and I cannot conceive why Ld Granville should leave it. ... Pleasant enough: but I have been out so little of late that I felt as if unused to a large party, and indeed I am always glad to be at home again after an hour or two passed in society.

16 June 1873. Passed 2 hours in tearing up all except a few of my letters of 1869 and 1870: a tedious business, but which the accumulation of papers made necessary, and it is done once for all. Those of 1871 and 1872 may wait a little longer.

18 June 1873. M. much knocked up by heat. It is more and more apparent to me that a London life is impossible to her. Even a fortnight of London seems to affect her health.

23 June 1873. Curious story of the late Ld Marjoribanks having left a large fortune (some say £120,000) to the Gladstone family. As he was rich, enthusiastically devoted to Gladstone, and left no male heir, the thing is not improbable in itself, nor does it imply any dishonourable bargain: but the coincidence of the legacy (if it be true) with the peerage, cannot fail to lead to unpleasant suspicions real or affected, and the more so as the premier's indebtedness to the Glyn family has been matter of common talk ... There is one way of escape: to refuse the legacy: but that is a heavy sacrifice for a man who if not poor is certainly far from rich.

Lady Stanhope talks of Lord Dysart, who is 79, eccentric to the verge of madness: lives in two rooms, which he never leaves, somewhere in or near the Strand: has £70,000 a year, and his sole pleasure is in accumulation: he lately desired his agent to bring him a note for £100,000, which the man did in a few days, apologising for the delay, as notes of that value were scarce: in fact, he said, the Bank had of late years issued only one, and they did not know in whose hands it was. 'Don't they?' said Ld Dysart, 'it is in this box.' Ham House, with its magnificent collections, going to decay: the son dead (he was insane in the later part of his life): only one grandson to succeed to all, and he of feeble health and of weak brain: a boy of 10 or 12.

24 June 1873. Sat next to D. of Argyll, who talked of the new school of economists, of which Prof. Cairnes[39] is the type, with some alarm. He says their leading idea is to draw all wealth into the hands of the state, a system which is that of semi-barbarous countries...

27 June 1873. In the Lords last night, Cairns exposed the blunders of the Registration Bill in one of his very best speeches, as to which I hardly know whether I listen to them with more pleasure in the skill displayed, or dissatisfaction at the hopelessness of equalling it.

28 June 1873. Cross called: he thinks a crisis probable (he may be right, but he has often told me the same, when nothing came of it) he

[39] J.E. Cairnes (1823–75), economist; prof. at Univ. Coll. London from 1866.

wants to know whether I think the time favourable for dissolving? I say yes, the ministry are weak & discredited, they have just renewed their quarrel with the nonconformists, they may gain by delay, and can hardly lose. Personally I should not like a dissolution just now, but it is clearly the interest of the party.

Called on Disraeli, but he had been ill in the morning, & was asleep.

30 June 1873. Mr R. Turner, of the Charity Organisation Society, called: he gave curious details as to the extent and magnitude of frauds committed by means of forged letters of recommendation ... In one instance a single impostor, working with a gang of which he is the head, had netted for his own share £40 weekly for several weeks past. In another case a woman, slightly but not seriously out of health, had contrived to raise a large sum to get her admitted into one of the hospitals for incurables, which she kept for her own use, her husband being in good employment ... He named several of the smaller hospitals and refuges as being mere pretences – enough done to make a show, no accounts kept, or at least produced, and the bulk of the money contributed going to the secretary.

2 July 1873. Talk with Edwards-Moss, whom I met, about the representation of Liverpool, Ld Harrowby's age and health making an early vacancy probable.[40] The local leaders want a man of note in parliament – their system being that one member should be allotted to the affairs of the town and the other give it dignity in the H.C. by his political importance: but such a man is not easily found, and in general prefers a more quiet seat. Plunket[41] was named, & H. Lennox, but qu. as to either?

3 July 1873. Visit with M. to Mr Carlyle[42] at Chelsea. His house, small and plain, but comfortable: many books: a few paintings and prints: he showed with especial pleasure a portrait of Luther and an engraving of John Knox. He shook and trembled a good deal at first, and is evidently growing very old: after a little he rallied, and talked with a good deal of energy. He said he had given up writing, being unable to use his hand much, and not finding it easy to dictate.

6 July 1873. The political event of the moment is the separation of the nonconformists from the bulk of the Liberal party: on the ground that the education bill of 1870 is opposed to their principles, and that the proposed amendment of it in the present session does not remedy their grievance. It has undoubtedly worked, in the main, for the interests

[40] Lord Sandon's father in fact lived until 1882.
[41] David Plunket, 1st Baron Rathmore (1838–1919), M.P. (Cons.) Dublin Univ. 1870–95: cr. peer, 1895.
[42] Thomas Carlyle (1795–1881), author.

of the establishment, and so far they are right, but their complaint is not so much that they have been injured by what was done, as that an opportunity has been lost of striking a blow at their rivals. It remains to be seen whether this split will be general: if so, a Conservative majority at the next election is certain: a thing of which I have never yet seen much appearance, though it is commonly predicted: but the unwisdom of such a course, from the point of view of Liberal politicians, is so manifest that at least a partial reconciliation will probably be arranged.

7 July 1873. .... Walk with Carnarvon on the terrace for an hour: he inclined to take up the Euphrates valley line, which appears to be in some way, not clearly explained, connected with Reuter's schemes for Persia: I dissuaded him: it is possible (though for my own part I do not see it) that the thing might succeed, but without the guarantee of the British parliament, it could not be attempted, and it is quite certain that under present circumstances no such guarantee will be given.

11 July 1873. In H of Lds, I talked to Cairns, Salisbury, and Richmond, urging the settlement of the difficulty about the Judicature Bill, on which we have been met by Gladstone in a conciliatory spirit. They seemed aware of the inexpediency of throwing the Bill out, which indeed would be a foolish waste of public time.

17 July 1873. A. and L. Cecil[43] came bringing a piece of news more surprising than agreeable: viz. that A. has engaged himself (at 22) to marry one of the sisters of Mr Wilson, the farmer and land agent with whom he is staying. The lady is 30. It does not seem that the Wilson family have any knowledge of the affair. M. is naturally much disturbed in mind: the object with us must be to gain time, and prevent anything being done in haste. Much talk after dinner both with A. himself and with his brother: which ended in their seeing the necessity of delay.

18 July 1873. Passed the morning at home, chiefly discussing Arthur's affairs. I wrote a letter to Mr Wilson ... expressing regret at the engagement on the ground of unsuitableness of age, and suggesting that on every account nothing should be done without ample time for consideration. I made my letter purposely civil, avoiding all reference to want of fortune or connection, and expressing my conviction that he knew nothing of what was going on. This letter I showed to Arthur and it was agreed that he should go down and meet Mr W. at Newcastle tomorrow, taking it with him.

19 July 1873. Short walk with M. early, and rather anxious talk about her health, which has never recovered the succession of shocks to which

---

[43] For Arthur (1851–1913) and Lionel Cecil (1853–1901), Lady Derby's sons, see *Later Diaries*, 15–17. The mésalliance went ahead.

it has been exposed. Mary and Margaret both out of health − Arthur's accident of last year − her own complaint of last winter − the death of a brother in April − and now this last trouble: are quite enough to explain the depressed state of spirits in which she mostly is, and the morbid state of nervous sensibility of which I cannot help seeing the growth. ... Much of the depression is due to a merely bodily cause. From weakness of the heart, fatigue, and a sense of extreme despondency, come on about 2 hours after breakfast: passing off again with rest after a little while. In the afternoon there is little or none of this peculiar sensation.

20 July 1873. A. Cecil came back ... He was reserved on the subject of his communications with Mr Wilson, but enough passed between them and his sisters to make it clear that no suspicion of his intentions had crossed Mr W.'s mind.

21 July 1873. Letter from Mr Wilson, thoroughly sensible and honourable, saying just what he ought about Arthur's youth, his expectations, and the folly which he has committed. I wrote to him again to express my sense of his fair dealing in the matter, and regret at the annoyance caused to him and his family.

23 July 1873. Arthur went up to see Salisbury, who as head of the family is the most proper person to remonstrate with him: but, though I do not think his feelings are deeply concerned, he is so entirely satisfied of his own wisdom that I am not sanguine of advice doing any good: and unluckily he is master of his property, which though not large is enough to marry on. Mr Wilson's conduct in the matter has been perfectly fair and straightforward, which is the only satisfactory part of this unlucky business.

24 July 1873. Letter ... from Salisbury, who says it is useless to talk to Arthur Cecil. 'He is not of the sort that take advice', and that he 'values the young lady, among other reasons, because she will protect him from good society', in which last remark I am afraid there is some truth.

... H. of Lds. Judicature Bill discussed, and passed, Redesdale dividing against it. Salisbury and Carnarvon stayed away, Cairns, Richmond, and I voted for the bill. There had been previously some discussion between us. I found Cairns undecided, half inclined to throw out the bill, which we could have done with ease had we been so minded: indeed the difficulty was the other way, for if there had been a full attendance I doubt whether it could have been got through. Nearly all the Conservative peers dislike it, and a good many Liberals.

26 July 1873. A. is come back from the north, having seen the young lady, but has been made to understand clearly that her family will have nothing to say to him ...

27 July 1873. Passed our last and on that account rather a melancholy day at Holwood ... Called in the afternoon on Mr Darwin, but found him surrounded with his family, and had little talk.

28 July 1873. Left Holwood with a real feeling of pain, more than I can account for by the fact that we have lived there three years, and that we can never find another equally enjoyable. ... In 1870, all was bright, the present and the future: now, M.'s health shaken and her spirits affected, partly by illness, but more by mental shocks: Mary and Margaret both suffering: Arthur on the eve of committing a folly that will be the regret of his life: M. West and Buckhurst in open quarrel: Delawarr dead by his own hand: L. West struggling with debt and going abroad for many years: in short, but for our entire happiness with one another, the prospect is not cheerful.

31 July 1873. Dined with the Salisburys, meeting Sir H. Holland.

12 August 1873. M. having again spoken to me about Keston Lodge, I wrote ... saying that I would give £20,000 for it ... Looking to the possibility of Downing St, we require a villa near town: and besides the absence of a house fit for use at Fairhill, M. thinks the distance by rail too great for her to go up and down. I should be content with hiring a villa at Wimbledon or Roehampton: but M. has set her fancy on this place, and I am willing to gratify it if the sacrifice is not absolutely unreasonable.

Ayrton having resigned his post of the Officer of Works, accepts that of Judge Advocate General, which was abolished three years ago as being useless, and a sinecure. A strange performance for a cabinet which piques itself on rigid & minute economy.

18 August 1873. In the papers is noticed a gift, by one of the Baird family, the great Scotch ironmasters, of £500,000 to the Scotch Kirk. ... The sum is the largest ever given at one time: the Peabody is now equal in amount, but it was made up by three different contributions, the last being a legacy.

20 August 1873. Began to read Baron Hubner's book on Japan and China ... He has more faith in the slow but persevering Chinese, whom he believes to be gradually adopting European ideas, and who will retain them more firmly because they do not adopt them in haste. I am the more pleased with this opinion, because it has long been mine, and in general Europeans take an opposite view.

25 August 1873. Odo Russell is grown very unwieldy, and seems out of health. They declare that they cannot do the necessary cost of receptions etc. at Berlin on the salary allowed, and had last year to draw £5000 from the D. of Bedford to meet their expenses. They would evidently prefer Paris. I think however that R. does not mean to rest satisfied with diplomacy ... his ambition is to take the management of F.O....

4 September 1873. Mr and Mrs Lowe left us early – not much to my regret. Nobody talks better than the new Home Secretary, but though amusing, he is hardly agreeable.

9 September 1873. Among the letters I wrote was one to Disraeli on the Ashantee war, expressing doubt as to the utility of a movement on Coomassee, the climate being believed to be the worst in the world, and neither gain nor glory attainable in the event of success.

11 September 1873. Disraeli writes to M. (not having received my letter) and is anxious to know what I think on Spanish affairs, recommending at the same time an article upon them in *Revue des Deux Mondes.* Does this mean an attempt to conciliate the R.C. priests, by affecting to patronise the Carlist party? I suspect it, but perhaps without adequate reason.

13 September 1873. Letter from Disraeli in answer to mine: he talks of the possibility of a vote being required, and a session to be held in the autumn in consequence. He describes himself as having passed the last few weeks in entire seclusion at Hughenden, like a prisoner of state, adding that 'it is a dreary life, but society is drearier'.

14 September 1873. It is impossible to feel sure that land near Liverpool will maintain the artificial value which from circumstances it has acquired, and if it does not what remains? There is no natural beauty, no residential enjoyment, and the possession of a few hundred acres more or less does not in any degree affect the social position of the family.

18 September 1873. Walk with Pender ... His own friends, strong Liberals up to the present date ... believe that Gladstone, half out of ambition and half out of sentimental sympathy, is ready to throw all the influence of the state into the scale against the employer. But while they dislike Gladstone, they are equally suspicious and afraid of Disraeli: they think him the enemy of the capitalist class ... He ... thought that if I were leader the party would gain a great accession of strength. Ld Strathnairn held the same language to me at night, though not assigning the same reasons. I gave a similar answer to both – that D. was a personal friend and an old colleague, and that I was therefore the last person who could entertain the idea of superseding him. Besides, who is to manage the H. of C. if he retires?

19 September 1873. In the papers, death of Ld Hardwicke announced. It had been long expected. His life has been long, respectable, and unfortunate. As a naval officer, he was disappointed of the promotion which he claimed, and felt the disappointment to the end of his days: as a politician, he neither aimed nor attained any considerable success, though he had a seat in the cabinets of 1852 and 1858: in private life, he laboured with energy and perseverance during many years to clear his family from a burden of debt, and was rewarded by the discovery that his eldest son has involved himself to an extent which he can never recover. With limited intelligence and a hasty temper, he was not popular in the world: but he honestly and consistently did what seemed his duty, and was respected as he deserved.

... In evening came Dr Taylor, a shrewd able man ... ... We talked much of Scottish administration: he thought, and I agree with him, that Scotland ought to have a minister[44] in the cabinet, instead of the work being done by a lawyer in large private practice, who must neglect either his professional or his official duty. But I told him that it was useless to expect that parliament would make a change of this kind, involving expense, unless it were asked for by those whom it concerned in a way to show that they really wanted it.

21 September 1873. Pender talks as if thoroughly alarmed at the state of the labour market, and influence of unions: he believes the iron trade especially will be driven away altogether.

23 September 1873. News of Dover election being won by the Conservative candidate, which was not expected, the Liberal, Fowler, having great influence owing to his connexion with the L.C. & D. railway,[45] of which he is general manager or secretary ... This really looks like winning at the general election if we make no blunder.

30 September 1873. Reached Alnwick ... Found there a large party, none known to us before: it is the custom of the Duke and Duchess,[46] as I am told, not to invite parties made up beforehand, but to ask all their friends to stay with them in passing: a hospitable and convenient custom, but which is apt to make a dull house, as it is left to chance whether the guests are or are not congenial. They remain at home from August to January, receiving in this way: which to persons not of an eminently sociable turn, must be a laborious kind of existence. We sat down to dinner some 25 persons...

5 October 1873. Talk with W.H. who says that the expectation of our coming into office is universal: adding that the party wish me to take the lead: the old story: 'We don't trust Disraeli'.

9 October 1873. Bath election come off yesterday, and contrary to expectation was lost by the Conservatives ...[47] I am afraid that the result was due in part to a foolish & violent letter written by Disraeli to Grey de Wilton, which he evidently intended as a manifesto, and which for both manner and matter, was in very bad taste. In it he accuses the present ministry of 'blundering and plundering' ... The

[44] Created Aug. 1885.
[45] London, Chatham, and Dover.
[46] Of Northumberland.
[47] Bath returned 2 Libs. in 1868. In byelections (May 1873 and June 1873) there were 2 Cons. gains; hence the surprise over the third byelection.

production is curiously unfortunate ... as its tendency must be to drive away the moderate liberals and middle class 'indifferents' who are frightened by Gladstone and wish to get rid of him but who cannot sympathise with the policy of absolute reaction which appears to be indicated by D. I say 'appears' for I do not suppose that he had any real meaning except that of encouraging the party by any address calculated to excite their zeal: though its effect will be in an opposite direction.

10 October 1873. Letter from Ld Granville, telling me that Hammond has resigned, and asking my opinion as to the appointment of Tenterden in his place. I give it in T.'s favour, as there are obvious inconveniences in bringing in a stranger, and among the clerks I know of no one better qualified, or who has stronger claims.

11 October 1873. Disraeli and Sanderson came.

12 October 1873. Church: walk there with Sanderson: walk in afternoon with Disraeli.

Wrote to Hammond on his retirement, and to Ld Granville in favour of Sanderson, who is better qualified than anyone I know in the office to succeed to the place vacated by Tenterden.

Much talk in the afternoon with D. as to possible appointments: I find him in a quite natural and collected state of mind, not excited, not confident of immediate success, but saying, as is undoubtedly the truth, that it is necessary to be ready for any event, and that there would be something even ridiculous in being taken unprepared. He spoke a good deal about the Catholic movement abroad, and its near relative, the Ritualist movement at home: and I was glad to see that he felt the unpopularity of both, and the inexpediency of seeming to support either. He said he thought the English Ritualists would before long make some decisive move to test the strength of their position: he did not know what it would be, but they were boasting everywhere of their strength, and that 7000 of the clergy belonged to their party. He was quite prepared to go against them if necessary.

Talk of Acheen,[48] Ashantee, etc. Letter from Cairns, raising what seems to me captious objections to the war, and ignoring the obvious fact that it was at least in the first instance a war of mere defence. Thinks the allowing the Dutch to occupy the rest of Sumatra a great mistake and source of danger to our trade: which I cannot see.

13 October 1873. Wrote to congratulate Tenterden on his appointment: which I find he considers as only temporary, his ambition being to serve on a mission, and afterwards to take his seat as a peer, which while a permanent official he cannot do.

Disraeli left us: A. Balfour came in the afternoon: he is a candidate

[48] N. Sumatra.

for Hertford,[49] and goes there in the next few days: he seems intelligent, but I doubt his having health for the work of parliament. I sketched out for him the outline of a speech to be made at a dinner which he is to attend, and where he is to make his first experiment in that line.

15 October 1873. Letter from Ld Granville, civil and friendly; he thinks Sanderson too young to be assistant under-secretary, and that his promotion would cause jealousy in the office: which indeed is possible.

16 October 1873. Making notes for a speech at Liverpool,[50] and rather uncomfortable in consequence. Time and practice have little effect in destroying, or even mitigating, the disagreeable sensation of nervousness which with me precedes all public appearances. I suppose it is constitutional, and will never leave me. My father had it quite as strongly.

... Spoke with perfect ease and satisfaction to myself ... I dwelt entirely on two subjects: the state of the labour market, and the Ashantee war.

23 October 1873. Shooting ... We killed 668 head.

... Very weary at night, and nervously excited, not in the way of irritability, but a peculiar sense of nervous exhaustion, by the constant noise of guns, and bustle: I had this feeling as a boy, at times painfully, and never entirely lost it ... and I think as I grow older it has gained strength.

24 October 1873. Walk with Sanderson in afternoon.

Salisbury came for one night. He talked of his Liverpool estates,[51] which appear to be managed in a singular way, by a local architect and a solicitor, without any regular agent: they yield, I believe, £15,000–16,000 yearly. Not much passed between us on any political subject.

Heard with regret that one of the Wellesleys, a son of Ld Cowley, is killing himself with liquor, the craving for which in his case amounts to disease. It is strange that in my limited acquaintance, there are three such instances: Patten's eldest son, whose death is expected every day:[52] and the eldest son of Beresford Hope, who was sent to America to cure him – unsuccessfully.

28 October 1873. Kirkdale for sessions ... Cross took the second court, and came to Knowsley with me afterwards. We sat from 10 to 6.

29 October 1873. With Cross to Kirkdale.

... Ld Salisbury sends details of his outlay to M., from which it appears that his gross rental is about £70,000, burdens about £17,000, or 25% nearly.

30 October 1873. With Cross to sessions...

---

[49] Returned unopposed.

[50] *T,* 17 Oct. 1873, 10a.

[51] Cf. *Bateman,* which notes Salisbury as having 1796 acres in Lancs., yielding £7999.

[52] Patten's eldest s. Eustace d. Dec. 1873. Cowley's sons lived to 1895, 1916, and 1931.

31 October 1873. Sat with Cross and others to try appeals, 10 to 5.30.

2 November 1873. Heard with regret a story of young —— of the F.O.: that he lives with a woman who keeps him and has paid his debts. I am afraid it is likely enough to be true, but will not set his name down even in this book till I know more.

... The political event of the week is the failure of the French plan for a Legitimist restoration, owing to the refusal of the Comte de Chambord to give any guarantees. It looks as if he thought the chance of success not worth the risk ... He has lost nothing, having nothing to lose: the party really compromised is the Orleanists, who have sacrificed their separate position as a political party (the only French representatives of constitutional monarchy) for the sake of a fusion which has come to nothing.

3 November 1873. Read, with regret, the death of Chief Justice Bovill:[53] a good Conservative and amiable man, though perhaps hardly equal in point of ability to the requirements of his great place. His successor will be Coleridge, who has more eloquence and less law.

... Paid Miss Hawkins £25 for copying the picture of me by Sir F. Grant,[54] as a present to Disraeli, he having expressed a wish for a copy of it.

4 November 1873. Much pleased with a speech of my brother, delivered at Preston ... He had a few hints from me, but in the main, it is his own work. Wrote to him to express satisfaction, and encourage him to persevere, for I see that unless stimulated by approval he will never have confidence enough in himself to go on.

5 November 1873. Called ... on old Mrs Grote.[55] I found her full of Mill's newly published autobiography, believing it on the whole as a narrative of fact, but evidently intending, if she lives, to supplement it by a narrative of her own. She says that the praise bestowed on Mrs Mill is extravagant to the last degree ... Of the elder Mill she speaks as having been a domestic tyrant: the wife a simple, illiterate woman, so much oppressed as at one time to have taken steps to obtain a separation: without influence on her children. All the children, except J.S. Mill, showed little ability: and their brother could not endure them.

6 November 1873. Left St James's Square about 7.20, Charing Cross 7.40. Dover about 9.45. ... Reached Paris about 6.10 ... between 11 and 12 hours door to door. ... We find the Bazaine trail going on, and the Assembly in full crisis: on which grounds we decide to stop a day longer than intended.

---

[53] Sir W. Bovill, chief justice 1866–73.
[54] Sir Francis Grant (1803–78), president R.A. 1866–78.
[55] Harriet Grote (1792–1878), bluestocking, widow of George Grote (1794–1871), radical.

7 November 1873. Dined at the embassy. ... Sat by Lytton. He tells
me of two unfinished plays and many unfinished novels left by his
father: also of an essay on conservative forces in politics, or something
to that effect, which L. is thinking of publishing: and of a novel by the
present C.J. Cockburn, apparently sent to the late Ld Lytton in MS
for criticism, and never returned. He says that Cockburn expressed no
interest in it when told of its being still in existence: which seems a
proof of good sense. He has also a large number of Disraeli's early
letters, written from the east, which he says are like a page of *Lothair*:
the same florid style, and pleasure in describing the details of a luxurious
life. On the whole, Lytton's way of talking gave me a higher idea of
his judgment than I should have formed from his writings.[56]

Conversation with Col. Connolly, the military attaché: he says France
will certainly not be ready for war within 3 years, if so soon: the
difficulty is not to put men in the field, but to replace the enormous
quantity of military material taken or destroyed: this they are doing,
and have about 1800 guns already, but other articles are still wanting.
They could put into the field 400,000 well-trained soldiers, but could
not arm nor equip them. They expect ultimately to have available as
the result of the new law of universal service, 1,200,000. All the officers,
he thinks, know that a German war now would be an insane attempt,
and they will not press for one.

The garrison of Paris, including all troops within a day's march, and
the gendarmes, he estimates at 120,000, being a slight reduction on the
number just after the war, which was 150,000.

9 November 1873. Two letters in *The Times* by Lord Grey[57] on the
Ashantee war ... what he contends for is the revival of the old system
as set on foot by him in 1847–51, or the total abandonment of the Gold
Coast. As to the former alternative, it is enough to say that it broke
down in a few years' trial, owing to the unwillingness of the chiefs to
submit to taxation, or to combine for purposes of common defence.
The latter seems an extreme measure, though it may be the best way
out of the difficulty in the end.

10 November 1873. I forgot to notice that Ld Lytton assured me the
other day that in the spring of 1871 there had been a movement in the
south of France to break off from the north, and form a Ligue du
Midi, including, I think, Lyons. The object being a purely local one:
to escape liability for future German wars, which do not concern them.

[56] Among Lytton's papers in Herts. County Record Office are MSS of 3 complete
plays and 3 fragmentary novels. The unpublished essay 'Our political state and its
prospects' (bundle D/EK W 46) may be the item mentioned by his son. Many Disraeli
letters appear in the lives of Lytton by his son and grandson. I am indebted to Andrew
Brown of C.U.P. for this information.
[57] Henry George Grey, 3rd E. Grey (1802–94), succ. 1845; col. sec. 1846–52.

12 November 1873. Discovered the villa bought by L. West for the lady with whom he lived. It is still his property, but in some way settled on the children.

14 November 1873. Reached Bayonne ... We saw the Villa Caradoc, which Ld Howden built (it is said) here at a cost of £50,000 for a woman with whom he lived there during many years.

18 November 1873. A quarrel with the Turkish government, which bankrupt and defenceless as it is, nevertheless aims at the conquest of Arabia, and is now threatening the Lahej tribes near Aden, which we are bound to protect. It is inconceivable that the Turks should push matters to a rupture, but their military ambition, hastening on the inevitable result of bankruptcy, is doubly inconvenient to us, as creditors and as neighbours.

20 November 1873. Hale writes that Mr V. O'Connor, who bought my Irish estates, left £300,000, which with the land makes him possessor of £500,000.

25 November 1873. To Toulouse...

News of the death of T. Baring,[58] whom I have known well, though never intimately, for more than 20 years. He had long been in weak health, and was 73. No man was more respected in the H. of C. where his position as head of a great mercantile house gave him authority as a speaker. He spoke rarely, and always with a certain effect. He leaves some natural children, but it is not known to whom his large estates will go. He might have been Chanc. of Ex. in 1858 if he would have accepted the place, and a peerage was offered him more than once: but he preferred to both his independent and irresponsible position in parliament.

Disraeli has delivered his Lord Rector's address at Glasgow, about the success of which he was nervous when at Knowsley: it appears to have been well received: he made two other speeches, not political, and which were as good as speeches about nothing in particular can be expected to be.

25 November 1873. Wills: Sir E. Landseer leaves £160,000, Sir H. Holland £140,000.[59]

27 November 1873. Request from H. Stanley[60] for £200 to pay his debts...

2 December 1873. Mrs Morier came to luncheon: she has been asking F.O. for an increase of her husband's pay (£1400) on which he says he cannot live, all prices in Germany having risen enormously. She

---

[58] Thomas Baring (1799–1873), head of Barings 1828–71; see *Stanley Diaries*, 350, n.34.

[59] Artist and doctor respectively.

[60] Diarist's uncle.

says that diplomatists without private means cannot now maintain themselves: and as the service in its actual state does not attract men of private fortune, one does not see what is to be the end.

... Morier[61] does not conceal his bitter disappointment at failing to get the place vacated by Tenterden: which however I should doubt his having health for.

5 December 1873. Sent through Statter £25 to a Bury Temperance Hall, a concern of which I have no great opinion, but it is got up by my tenants.

9 December 1873. In consequence of a complaint against him which proved to be well-founded, I decided to pension off my old servant, Ralph Smith, giving him his full wages to retire upon. He has served me for 22 years – ever since my return from India – but of late has become almost useless from failing health, aggravated I fear by drinking spirits. His going is a relief to me, but I did not like to remove him absolutely without fault on his part.

12 December 1873. Papers are full of the marriage of the D. of Hamilton[62] to Ly M. Montague:[63] he was all but bankrupt a few years ago, and put his affairs into the hands of one Padwick, a racing man better known than trusted: but the choice appears to have been less bad than it seemed, for it is now said that the financial difficulties are over, and that the rental has risen to £140,000 yearly.

18 December 1873. Note that Brett[64] speaks of Coleridge with unusual bitterness: he, being a very good-natured man in his general judgments: thinks him false, malevolent, and a pretender, with little ability except his ready and agreeable flow of speech.

19 December 1873. All our party left us ... I took especial note of G. Hamilton, knowing that he is looked upon as one of the rising men on our side, and the results of conversation with him was to satisfy me that he is quite fit to represent a department – say the F.O. – without risk of compromising it either by stupidity or indiscretion.

Tavistock[65] seems good-humoured, and has some degree of cultivation: but I judge him to be indolent and not likely to interest himself warmly in anything.

Lord Aberdeen,[66] young, simple, and natural in manner, seems fairly

[61] Sir R. Morier (1826–93), diplomatist; in Germany 1853–76; promoted by diarist to min. at Lisbon, 1876–81; see A. Ramm, *Sir Robert Morier 1876–1893, Envoy and Ambassador* (1973).

[62] William Douglas-Hamilton, 12th D. of Hamilton (1845–95), succ. 1863; contents of Hamilton Palace fetched £400,000 (1882).

[63] Dau. of D. of Manchester.

[64] W.B. Brett, 1st Vt Esher (1815–99), judge 1868–97; cr. baron 1885, vt 1897.

[65] George Russell, 10th D. of Bedford (1852–93), styled Lord Tavistock 1872–91, when succ.; M.P. (Lib.) Beds. 1875–85, but never prominent.

[66] John Hamilton Gordon, 7th E. of Aberdeen (1847–1934) succ. 1870, on drowning of

well informed: has an odd nervous way of talking: of his two brothers, one shot himself at Cambridge, the other was lost at sea after several years wandering over the world as a common sailor. The family is odd, to say the least.

21 December 1873. Announcement of new peerages ... Monsell's promotion is simply ludicrous.[67] He has failed as an administrator, and been compelled by failure to resign: he has never achieved in parliament even a moderate success, and his sole claim to a political position is that he has been the agent of Gladstone in his negotiations with the Irish R.C. hierarchy. The choice is inexplicable except as evidence of the extreme value which G. sets on the good will of that body.

22 December 1873. Agreed ... to give £20 to the Alkali Act extension association, which has constituted me its president.

25 December 1873. ... In the papers, will of T. Baring: he leaves £1,500,000 personalty, the bulk of which is equally divided between Northbrook[68] and two other relatives.

26 December 1873. The receipts from rents alone, in the year ending June 30th, were £177,711: against £174,756 in the year preceding ... Of this £1900 comes from arrears: so that as last year, the receipts exceed the rental due: a state of things which cannot continue.

30 December 1873. Application from C. Stanley, son of H.S.,[69] for help to educate his brother's children. I refer it to F. Hopwood. The family are not well off, but their own statement of their affairs cannot be relied upon without confirmation.

... Made some notes for Manchester speech: but want of exercise produced its invariable effect of making me sleepy, heavy, and unfit for mental exertion.

31 December 1873. At 3 p.m. went into the coachhouse, where found the Knowsley and Huyton tenants assembled, and at the end of their dinner. My health was drunk: I made the usual speech, and one on behalf of Ly D. All very cordial and friendly. I told them it was my intention to build at least one pair of new cottages in the village every year for several years to come, to replace those which are getting unfit for use.

Endpaper, December 1873. Expended in the year just ending on private account, £2977

[76] bro.; other bro. d. in shooting accident (G.E.C.); respected public figure, governing Canada and Ireland; wife of his s. not only in trade, but had first m. when her 2nd husband was only two.

[67] William Monsell, 1st Baron Emly (1812–94), (Lib.) Limerick 1847–74; p.m.g. 1871–3, when postal finances questioned; R.C. convert 1850, but Unionist, 1886.

[68] T.G. Baring, 1st E. of Northbrook (1826–1904), s. of 1st Baron; succ. 1866; Gov.-Gen. of India 1872–6; cr. earl 1876.

[69] Diarist's uncle.

Of which, presents to relatives and friends	£437
Charitable donations to individuals	£328
Public objects of all descriptions	£501

In all, given away	£1266
Books, prints, works of art	£722
Travelling	£706
All other items	£283

For 1874, I purpose to retain on private account only 1) Presents (2) Books & art (3) Travelling (4) Miscellaneous. Donations & subscriptions being all thrown on the general, or estate, account. And in partial substitution for these, I pay all the cost of the Knowsley library, to which hitherto the estate has contributed £200.

Assuming that I receive, as hitherto, from Moult, £4000, and as interest of investments £1000, or rather more, I have £5000 to spend. Of this £2000 is to be laid by, leaving £3000 for use. Allow for (1) miscellaneous £300 (2) presents £300 (3) travelling £600: there remains for my favourite objects of books, drawings, and objects of art £1800, which is more than I have yet thought it right to spend.

I have invested on private account £24,000.

In reserve £4000. Total laid by, £28,000.

Note of the debts on the estate

Hon. F. Stanley[70]	£170,000	
Hon C. Stanley	£24,000	
Hon. H. Stanley	£12,000	making total due
Miss Hornby	£10,000	members of the
Lady Derby (d.)[71]	£9,000	family £240,000
Lady Derby[72]	£15,000	

Legal and General Insurance Co.	£30,500	
		£105,000
Lord Macclesfield's Trustees	£75,000	

... Receipts from various estates, year ending 1 July 1873:

East Lancashire

Bury	£34,166
Colne	£828

[70] Diarist's only brother.

[71] Dowager Lady Derby, the diarist's mother.

[72] In a will made Feb. 1874, Derby left his wife £20,000 cash and a life interest in Fairhill. To Talbot, Hornby, and Sanderson he left £1000 each; to Moult and Statter, £500 each. To his servants, he left 2 months wages for each year of service, 'as in my father's will'. All the rest he left to his brother.

Pilkington £33,180

£68,174

Liverpool
Bootle £12,012
Kirkdale £14,603
Liverpool £11,806
Walton £ 50

£38,471

Home estates
Knowsley £5273
Huyton £2757
Roby £2874
Whiston £ 26
Eccleston £633
Rainford £7059
Bickerstaffe £10,575
Ormskirk £1828
Burscough £6941
Newborough £1286
Bispham £1455
Halewood £6157
Melling £ 540
Mossborough £ 287

£47,690

Outlying estates
Macclesfield £4852
Hope £ 43
Preston £2780
Bolton £1445
Weeton £2553
Trayles £5053
Thornley £1859
Sowerby £2063
Milthorp £ 847
Inskip £1252
Chippin £ 615

Expenses

	1871	1872	1873
Compulsory deductions	£49,300	£46,700	£40,300
Estate expenses	£44,500	£46,200	£48,200
Household	£25,000	£25,000	£25,000

Self, benefactions, etc.   £12,300   £14,900   £15,900
... There is an annual saving varying between £40–£50,000: available for cancelling of debt or purchase of land.

1874

1 January 1874.[1] I begin the new year in good health, Ly D also being well, and neither of us suffering from any annoyance or anxiety. The last year has been the least happy of my married life, though solely from external causes: the illness of two daughters, the death of poor Delawarr by his own hand,[2] the embarrassed circumstances of one brother[3] and the almost public quarrels of two others,[4] added to Arthur's folly,[5] having naturally affected Ly D's spirits, and consequently mine. Matters however are mending: L. West's affairs have been patched up: the family lawsuit is settled by arrangement: Arthur's marriage, though slightly ridiculous, has in it nothing discreditable, and we have become reconciled to the idea: Mary and Margaret are both fairly well, and though delicate, there is nothing in their condition to cause uneasiness.

For myself, I have had no troubles, nor have I any cause of complaint: all that I have taken in hand has prospered, though not owing to special skill on my part. The debt on the estates is being rapidly lessened: the Fairhill[6] purchase is a success: and if some pending negotiations end satisfactorily, I may by the year 1876, if living, be entirely freed from mortgages or other permanent changes.

... I have made a fair number of speeches[7] on public occasions and have on the whole been as much before the public eye as in 1872 ... I have no great scheme on hand, except sales to railway companies ... Improvements of Knowsley go on steadily, and as debt lessens, I can push them more rapidly forward. The house must be dressed up, new glass etc. put into windows, and minor changes made: but the heavy work of draining is finished. No. 23 wants some new furnishing and internal cleaning; Fairhill the same.

Left early for Preston ... took the chair at sessions...

2 January 1874. Application from C. Stanley (of Kinsale) for help

[1] Derby was at Knowsley 4 Dec. 1873–25 Jan. 1874.
[2] See above, 23–26 Apr. 1873.
[3] See above, 2 Mar. 1873, for West's finances.
[4] Lords Buckhurst, and Delawarr *fils*.
[5] Lord A. Cecil's mésalliance; see above, 17–26 July 1873.
[6] Near Tonbridge, Kent, bought 24 Apr. 1873.
[7] Lord Derby had spoken actively outside parliament in 1873, nearly always in Lancashire. He spoke on thrift (*T,* 10 Mar. 1873, 8a), on pauperism (*T,* 12 Jun., 5a), on railway nationalisation (*T,* 14 Jun., 5d). He spoke at Lancaster (*T,* 9 Oct., 7e), at Liverpool (*T,* 17 Oct., 10a), and at Manchester (*T,* 18 Jan., 5f); and to the Lancs. Rifle Volunteers (*T,* 30 Jan., 10c), and the Manchester International Fruit Show (*T,* 4 Sept., 6e).

from me to pay the schooling of his brother's children: which I will consider.

... A.[8] is to be married next week. M. naturally suffers, not so much from the parting, as from the event which is to come off, and the uncomfortable relations which it will probably create.

4 January 1874. News of the death of Ld Charteris,[9] Elcho's son, on his return from the African coast: killed by fever, he was heir to the title and estates. His elder brother shot himself in a fit of insanity.

6 January 1874. Received ... a singular application from Lord Denbigh,[10] asking me to draw up a mem. or paper on the state of Ireland for the use of the ecclesiastical authorities at Rome! ... Of course I declined...

7 January 1874. Shooting ... Mr Blundell[11] talks of his family, which has made itself comparatively poor by selling land in Lancashire to buy in Dorsetshire: he himself has retrieved its affairs considerably by letting land: he has six miles of coast (so he says) near Southport. He appears something of a scholar and artist, having cultivated tastes and some literary knowledge, but has never come to the front in any public capacity. He is a strong Catholic, and lives almost exclusively among Catholics.

Sir H. de Trafford[12] cares for little, as I am told, except farming, hunting, and shooting. He lives mostly all the year round at his place close to Manchester: never reads, and visits little. He draws a very large income – certainly not less than £40,000 a year, and probably much more – from building land, and if he were willing to give up his house and park, and live in some more agreeable situation, he might increase his rental indefinitely.

10 January 1874. Long letter from Sanderson on Acheen,[13] as to which it is clear that I am in no way compromised, the arrangements discussed in 1868 having been entirely different from those since adopted.

11 January 1874. Settled to fill up the old ice-house, now disused for 20 years...

19 January 1874. Business in the office ... For the first time in the memory of anyone living here, Heywood[14] is paying interest to the

---

[8] Lord Arthur Cecil.

[9] A.D.C to Sir G. Wolseley in Ashanti War. Lord Elcho (1818–1914), the Adullamite, thus styled 1853–83 until he succ. his father as E. of Wemyss, lost his eldest s. 'in a revolver accident', 1870 (*G.E.C.*).

[10] Rudolph Feilding, 8th E. of Denbigh (1823–92), succ. 1865; R.C. convert, 1850.

[11] Probably Nicholas Blundell of The Hall, Crosby; succ. his father, 1845.

[12] Sir Humphrey De Trafford, 2nd Bt (1808–86); succ. father 1852.

[13] Native kingdom in N. of Sumatra, a subject of electoral controversy following an allusion in Disraeli's manifesto to the (geographically distinct) Straits of Malacca being put at risk by Liberal indifference over Acheen.

[14] Manchester banker.

estate for money in his hands, instead of the estate being in debt to him.

Cross came for the sessions.

20 January 1874. Kirkdale[15] for sessions: all day in court: Cross came out with me, and took the second court ... Sat till 6.20.

21 January 1874. Kirkdale in sessions: all day in court ... We adjourned at 6 ... Cross had the second court.

The D. and Duchess of Northumberland came. Lady Sefton dined with us, Ld S. being away.

Received Irish emigration papers; the emigrants are in 1873, 90,000: in 1872, 78,000 ... tending to prove the oft-repeated paradox that more leave the country in good times than in bad...

22 January 1874. Kirkdale with Cross ... Walk in with Cross most of the way, the carriage not being ready; walk with him again in the afternoon.

23 January 1874. Kirkdale for sessions ... Ended about 4 p.m. Cross and I home together. D. and Duchess of Northumberland left us.

24 January 1874 (Saturday). Report in the *Liverpool Post* that Gladstone has decided on instant dissolution ... It is useless to comment on this story until we know whether there is any truth in it or not.

... Cross left us for his home: he told me in conversation that while in London he managed to secure an average walk of nine miles daily, chiefly by living a long way off, and walking in and out twice a day.

... Telegram from Disraeli asking me to come up as soon as possible, which I accordingly settle to do tomorrow instead of Tuesday.

To the Conservatives, I see no loss in this sudden summons: they are confident, well organised, and have been long preparing ... On the whole I incline to think Gladstone has made a mistake.

25 January 1874. Church ... Left in afternoon ... Reached St J. Square about 10: very busy with letters and papers.

26 January 1874 (Monday). Disraeli dined with us alone: I thought him in better spirits than last year: he has secured a house of his own, the want of which used to make him uncomfortable. He gave an amusing, but probably coloured description of the circumstances which led the cabinet, or rather the Premier, to take this sudden step. He ascribes it to their having made various unsuccessful attempts to agree on a policy as to county franchise, education, etc.[16] On all subjects they found the extreme section bent on having its own way, the moderates equally uncompromising, and no option seemed left except to resign or dissolve. Gladstone is believed to have been anxious to bring in his budget before dissolving, but this was found impossible...

[15] N. Liverpool.
[16] Interesting, as showing Disraeli's ignorance.

D. did not seem either sanguine or eager, as to the result: he seems to think the majority either way will be narrow, but not to expect that we shall win. Still he is turning over in his mind the appointments which must be made if we come in.

27 January 1874. A circular which asks help for the election in S.W. Lancashire: I sign a guarantee for £500, in the event of a contest: Turner is ready to pay on his own account up to £4000: Cross being a poor man, is to be brought in for nothing if possible.[17]

Heard that the D. of Marlborough's freehold house in this square is to be sold for £55,000.

28 January 1874. Leicester Square is being set to rights at last: Albert Grant,[18] of all people, having bought up the rights of the various persons having an interest in the area of the square, and presented it to the public. In any man this would be called an act of public spirit: in a disreputable speculator, who has more than once narrowly escaped prosecution for fraud, it is an ingenious device for putting himself right with the world. And in that point of view it will be a very good investment.

29 January 1874. Wrote to guarantee £500 for expenses in S.E. Lancashire. Wrote to Skelmersdale that I will help the Carlton fund, but will not name a sum until I see how matters go in my own country.

... Agreed to pay £80 a year to help in educating the children of my cousin E. Stanley,[19] who was killed in India. This to continue until they come of age, when they are entitled to legacies of £1000 each.

... Called at the F.O. and looked over Acheen papers with Tenterden. ... Wrote a short note to *The Times*,[20] contradicting a short statement made yesterday by Gladstone on the Acheen treaty.

My mother dined with us, the first time since we married...

2 February 1874. Speech of Disraeli on Saturday at Aylesbury,[21] very clever, sensible and right as to finance, dwelling too much on that petty Malacca business, and perhaps too personal in reference to Gladstone: but for this there was provocation.

[17] Cross and Turner returned unopposed.

[18] Albert Grant (1830–99), company promotor, gave the square to the metropolitan board of works, 1874; M.P. (Cons.) Kidderminster 1865–8.

[19] Henry Edmund Stanley (1840–67), army capt. killed in fall from his horse in India; 3rd s. of Henry [Thomas] Stanley (1803–75), the diarist's reprobate uncle; according to *Burke's Peerage*, d. unm., but the diarist refers to some offspring, whom he assisted.

[20] *T*, 30 Jan. 1874, 9f, arguing that Derby's draft treaty of 1868 with Holland merely recognized existing Dutch interests in Sumatra, purposely excluding all mention of Acheen, whose status in U.K. eyes was unaffected until the Liberal treaty of 1871.

[21] *T*, 2 Feb. 1874, 5d, for Disraeli's speech of 31 Jan. in Aylesbury Corn Exchange.

... Telegram from F. to say that he is returned without opposition. ... On receipt of this news, wrote ... to Skelmersdale saying that I will give £1000 to the Carlton election fund.

3 February 1874. I promised to give £100 towards the expenses incurred by Cross, in the event of there being no contest: the guarantee given for £500 not applying to that case.

5 February 1874. Bought yesterday a strong box, and transferred to it my reserve of gold: the box, and gold together, are too heavy for any burglar to remove (even if he knew of its existence) without disturbing the household.[22]

6 February 1874. Carnarvon dined with us ... Talk with Carnarvon about Salisbury, whom C. thinks he can secure.[23] I have my doubts.

7 February 1874. Lowe called on M. and did not conceal his dislike to Gladstone's intended budget. He would have preferred taking one penny off the income tax, and raising the limit of exemption. He seemed to think that the whole of the sugar duties must be removed, owing to the inconvenience of discriminating between different qualities: though why this should be greater now than formerly is not obvious.

Walk early with M. Talk about office, etc. I arrange that of my £5000 a year, she shall have £800 for dress and other expenses belonging to the position, and I intend £200 for Sanderson. ... F. having been returned unopposed, the dissolution has cost me comparatively little. The Carlton fund has received £1000, W. Lancashire and Bury each £100, and I am liable to the extent of £500 for S.E. Lancashire, which however will probably not all be wanted. I shall contribute to F.'s expenses, but the whole will be covered by £2000, or nearly so.

8 February 1874 (Sunday). Called on Cairns, and much talk on the situation. He is in favour of a direct vote of no confidence, in the event of Gladstone not resigning, rather than of a trial of strength on the choice of a Speaker: the latter course being invidious, and votes being likely to be lost to us, owing to the natural reluctance to displace the existing Speaker, who has done his work well.[24]

He agreed with me that to reduce the income tax by one penny, leaving it at twopence, and to raise the limit of exempted income, say, to £200, would meet all reasonable expectation on that subject: and I have reason to think that this is also the view taken by Lowe.

---

[22] Visiting Knowsley in 1913, Lord Newton saw 'an iron box with a slit in it, through which he [Derby] constantly inserted a sovereign. When he died, the box was found to contain no less than £11,000'. Lord Newton, *Retrospection* (1941), 199.

[23] Carnarvon saw Salisbury the following morning, without success. Salisbury had returned to England on the 7th after wintering abroad. See *Cecil*, 43–4.

[24] Sir H. Brand, 1st Vt Hampden (1814–92), speaker 1872–84, cr. vt 1884.

Salisbury dined with us: nothing was said as to his joining which I thought too delicate a subject to touch upon, but my impression is that he will prefer to remain a free lance.[25]

9 February 1874. Disraeli called: list of proposed cabinet discussed: he wishes it small. It is as follows, but open to alteration. Disraeli, Treasury: Cairns, Chancellor: D., Foreign Office: Hardy, H.O.: Northcote, Exchequer: Hunt, War Dept.: Carnarvon, India: J. Manners, Colonies: D. of Richmond, Ld President: Malmesbury, Privy Seal: Admiralty remains for Salisbury's acceptance (but he will certainly refuse): on his refusal, try D. of Somerset.[26]

I advised some reference to old Lord Russell, who is very friendly,[27] and might encourage young Whigs to come over: and pressed for the admission of Cross to the cabinet, to which D. seemed averse.[28]

I also, though with reluctance, advised against J. Manners having so high a post as that proposed. He is amiable and excellent, but hardly equal to a great place.

10 February 1874. I ought to have noted that Cairns on Sunday spoke strongly in favour of keeping up an economical system as regards the services: arguing that whereas formerly we never knew what the Emperor of the French might do next, we had now nothing to fear from France, and no probability of a quarrel with Germany. Indeed if such a quarrel occurred, the French would for their own sakes be only too willing to help us.

11 February 1874. Disraeli dined with us alone: I never saw him in a mood which promised better for the conduct of affairs: not excited nor elated, but calmly hopeful, and busy in forming his ministry.

He talks of an earldom for Skelmersdale, he having been active and useful, and it being difficult to find anything else. Court places seem to give more trouble than others, as everybody feels himself qualified for them. D. of Beaufort[29] for Master of the Horse. Possible objections of

---

[25] Salisbury commented to his wife, 'He [Derby] hinted much but said nothing directly. I gathered that they had not quite given up the idea of his having the first place. As far as I could, I encouraged it, for it would undoubtedly solve many difficulties.' *Cecil,* 44.

[26] Edward Adolphus Seymour, 12th D. of Somerset (1804–85), Whig; minor office 1835–41, 1850–1; in cabinet 1851–2; 1st lord of admiralty 1859–66; styled Lord Seymour until 1855, when succ.; offered, by Disraeli, 1st refusal of col. office, *vice* Carnarvon (see below, 30 Jan. 1878); see below, 19 Mar. 1874.

[27] Cf. 13 Feb. 1873.

[28] Cf. *GH,* 7 Dec. 1874: 'Reeve told me that Lord Russell expressed his "great relief" at the general election!' See also *Cecil,* 47 for Lady Derby saying (14 Feb.) to Salisbury 'they had a scheme for offering (as a compliment) a place in the Cabinet to Lord Russell – and trying through him to get the Duke of Somerset to join.'

[29] Henry Somerset, 8th D. of Beaufort (1824–99), succ. 1853; P.C. 1858, master of the horse 1858–9, but replaced in 1874–80 by Lord Bradford, K.G., and lord-lieut., Monmouth.

the Queen, as his life is not the most respectable. D. of Richmond[30] having one place for himself, and another for his brother, wants one for his son March also! H. Lennox: doubts as to his fitness for Ireland. He is not much trusted by any one, though rather clever.

Sir S. Fitzgerald: what to be done with?

Patten: any office?

Cross: more talk about his admission to the cabinet.

Question of the offer to Salisbury, which must be made, but I see plainly that D. does not expect it to be accepted, nor greatly desire that it should be.

12 February 1874. Northcote called: talk about the situation generally, and especially about finance. I pressed the expediency of taking only one penny off the income tax, with the addition of a higher limit of extended incomes – say, from £150 to £200 – and the necessity of relieving indirect taxation to an equal extent. In both of these he seemed to agree, but doubted as to my farther suggestion to dispose in the present year of only 3 out of the 5 millions available, paying off debts with the rest, so as to ensure an ample surplus next year, when we must deal with the subject of local taxation. He thought Gladstone would not wait for the meeting, but resign at once, as we did in 1868.

Sir Erskine Perry[31] called ... He warned me confidentially against Seymour Fitzgerald, saying that his administration at Bombay had not been a success, and that there are ugly stories of his hands not being clean in money matters.

13 February 1874. Various letters ... One, from G.A. Sala[32] of the *Telegraph*, the meaning of which obviously is that he wishes to open communications with me.

... F. tells me that there is a strong feeling at the Carlton that the income tax – or at least schedule D – should be got rid of: which is natural, but I regret it.

14 February 1874 (Saturday). On returning to St James's Square, I found Salisbury with M. He wished to see me, and some conversation passed in her presence. S. wished to know, first, should we support a bill restricting hours of labour to 9 in the day? I said certainly not, as far as I was concerned, in reference to the labour of adult males: the only nine hours bill of which I knew anything was one limited to the case of women and children, in regard to whom the principle of restricting hours of labour is already conceded, and the obvious reason, that they are as a rule dependent on others, whereas men can protect themselves.

---

[30] Charles Gordon-Lennox, 12th D. of Richmond (1845–1928), styled E. of March 1860–1903; M.P. (Cons.) 1869–88; freemason; Eccles. Commr 1885–1903, but never held political office.

[31] Sir T.E. Perry (1806–82), Indian judge; member of council of India, 1859–82.

[32] G.A. Sala (1828–96), leading *Daily Telegraph* journalist.

S. then went to the question of franchise, which however he dismissed as not urgent: we both agreeing that it was undesirable, and indeed impossible, to take up the question of franchise in the current parliament. Some discussion arose about income tax, which S. appeared to care little about, saying he should acquiesce in whatever was agreed upon: he seemed to me to parade a certain indifference to financial subjects. He discussed county financial boards, which he seemed to dislike, but without absolutely saying that they must be resisted: then passed on to ecclesiastical matters. He must have, he said, an assurance that nothing would be done to extend the limits of the church by altering terms of subscription: and though disliking the ritualist party, whose folly he thought had done great mischief, he felt anxious that no step should be taken against them that might lead to a breaking up of the church. As to these matters I referred him to Disraeli, saying that they were not in my line – that I wished to have as little as possible to do with controversy – that I should never willingly stir these subjects, but did not like to give any pledge as to what it might or might not be necessary to do in regard to them.

In this interview I purposely avoided expressing any personal wish or feeling as to S. rejoining us: partly because I really doubt whether his presence or absence will give most strength, and partly because with his temperament, I know that the expression of a desire that he should do a certain thing would probably drive him in the opposite direction. He left me without any expression of opinion except that he will see Disraeli on Monday.[33]

15 February 1874 (Sunday). Walk early with M. Called in Cromwell Road.[34] F. dined with us. No event.

16 February 1874. Cairns called: talk of India, of local taxation, the budget, etc. He proposes a commission to enquire into the working of the Criminal Law Amendment Act, the Master and Servants Act, and the law of conspiracy. I agree, for they are all complained of, and apparently not clear, decisions upon them being often contradictory. ... Disraeli dined with us.

17 February 1874 (Shrove Tuesday). Disraeli told us last night, on what he assumed to be good authority, that the Queen had decided the question of resignation by expressing a strong wish, or rather giving it as her command, that Gladstone should retire at once. To this decision no reasonable objection can be taken, for under all the circumstances it is probably a wise one for the cabinet to adopt: but the reason given is that the Queen did not choose to have the trouble of changing her

[33] Cf. *Cecil*, 46–7, for Salisbury's version, and his dissatisfaction with Derby's reply on ritualism.
[34] Mother's home.

ministers at the moment when she would have occupied in the reception of a new daughter-in-law![35] A good instance of the way in which a court personal considerations go before those which concern the public.

Talk of changes – J. Manners is not to be a Sec. of State: and H. Lennox cannot be trusted to go to Ireland – so D. thinks: he is too much mixed up in companies not of the best sort.

R. Bourke[36] thought of as Irish Secretary.

Ld Russell having been communicated with, writes to D. of Rich. very civilly as regards the party, but much the reverse towards Disraeli.

It is understood that Cardwell and Fortescue are to be peers ... Why Cardwell, who was considered as the next Liberal leader of the House, after the disappearance of Gladstone, should retire from active public life, is not so easy to understand.

... Salisbury dined with us.

18 February 1874 (Ash Wednesday). Last cabinet arrangements are: Disraeli, Cairns, Northcote, Richmond, Malmesbury, Derby, as before: Hardy War Office, Hunt Admiralty: Cross Home Office: Carnarvon, Colonies: J. Manners, some minor office. If this stands, the promotion of Cross will be my doing, and I don't regret it. So will the lower position given to J. Manners, which I only regret on private grounds, for it is a right step. Salisbury having India increases the number to twelve.

... Salisbury dined with us: in good humour, seemingly quite indifferent about politics, and chiefly concerned to know what sort of bishops D. is likely to make.

19 February 1874 (Thursday). Saw Disraeli, calling there early with M. He very weary, said he had hardly been able to sleep, but satisfied with his reception by the Queen: the arrangement as noted yesterday stands. ... But it is possible that Malmesbury may refuse. The arrangement is, to my mind, as good as can be made.

... Disraeli dined with us: still exhausted, but in good spirits. He goes to Windsor tomorrow.

20 February 1874. Ld Strathnairn called by appointment: he talked of various matters, at considerable length (to which he is addicted) and in a discursive way ... He says recruits are being passed whom the medical inspectors reject, as too young or weakly: the W.O. dares not refuse them as not knowing where others can be found: lads of 15 or 16 volunteer calling themselves 18, and though the deception is obvious,

[35] Princess Marie Alexandrovna (d. 1920), only dau. of Alexander II, m. Alfred, D. of Edinburgh, in St Petersburg, 23 Jan. 1874.
[36] Robert Bourke, 1st Baron Connemara (1827–1902), s. of 5th E. of Mayo and bro. of Lord Mayo, Indian viceroy (d. 1872); Cons. M.P. 1868–86; undersec. for foreign affairs 1874–80, 1885–6; gov. of Madras 1886; cr. peer 1887; m. dau. of Lord Dalhousie, Indian viceroy; see *Later Diaries*, 137.

it is left purposely unnoticed. Deserters, not being marked, cannot be traced: and the deserters in 1873 were between 7 and 8,000. He ascribes this to the abandonment of long terms of service, and the loss of hope of a pension, which was formerly the soldier's chief inducement to stay on. I thought he did not allow enough for the natural effect of high wages in civil life...

21 February 1874 (Saturday). Called on Ld Granville by appointment: he had mistaken the hour of leaving for Windsor, which made our conversation short ... Left for Windsor between 1 and 2 ... At the Castle the ceremony of swearing in was short ... We were back in London between 4 and 5.

... Returning home, G. Hamilton, my intended under-secretary, called in some disturbance of mind, saying that he is not fit for the place, as he cannot speak a word of French:[37] which certainly is a serious objection. I told him I would consult Disraeli, and asked him to call tomorrow. M. Corry came to see me on the same subject: with him I went to D. and we agreed that Hamilton shall have another place. I want R. Bourke[38] instead (he was going to the India Office) and it is arranged that if possible I shall have him.

Criticisms on the new cabinet are generally, I may say, universally favourable: it is thought that D. has made the best use of his materials, and that the materials are good.

22 February 1874. I called on Disraeli: he asks D. of Northumberland[39] to go to Ireland, after refusal of D. of Marlborough. Tells me Sir R. Peel[40] wants an embassy! the most unfit man in the world for one. D. of Buckingham[41] refuses a court place, but is very friendly. ... Endless trouble about court appointments – the only part of the affair the Queen now cares about.

23 February 1874 (Monday). Sanctioned a telegram by Carnarvon ... on Fiji questions, warning the commodore there, who seems to have assumed general control of the islands, not to compromise us by announcing a protectorate, to which he seems disposed.[42]

Saw Bourke, my new under-secretary in the place of G. Hamilton. He was my original choice for the place, and I am thoroughly satisfied with the appointment.

[37] Result of Harrow education.

[38] Recent house guest at Knowsley; lacked public school educ., but went to T.C.D.

[39] Cf. M. and B., v 290–1. Northumberland, the third to be offered the post (for which Lord H. Lennox and Lord Beauchamp were also considered) declined, Lord Abercorn, the first choice, finally accepting (1874–6). Northumberland held no post until 1878, when he entered the cabinet.

[40] Palmerstonian minister, 1861–5.

[41] Gov. of Madras, 1875–80.

[42] Cf. Carnarvon to Robinson, 23 Feb. 1874 (tel.), in C.C. Eldridge, *England's Mission: The Imperial Idea in the Age of Gladstone and Disraeli, 1868–1880* (1973), 154.

25 February 1874. Short brisk walk early: bought two fine Dresden vases, cost me £30: walk later with M. Office at 12. Business chiefly routine ... Saw Malet,[43] just returned from Pekin: he says Chinese affairs are more generally quiet than they have been for generations, and the condition of the country is rather one of slow progress than of decay.

Cabinet at 5: sat till near 7: discussed first the news from Ashantee, which is indecisive: but nothing can now be done in the way of sending out fresh troops: they would not arrive till the healthy season is over.

Discussion, next, of Indian famine: here again little is possible except to confirm orders already given: Salisbury talks of a loan of 6 or even 10 millions being necessary to meet expenses incurred. The stock of grain is probably sufficient: the difficulty is to find means of transport.

Question of budget raised by Northcote: surplus is fully five millions, as estimated: what shall we do with it? General feeling that income tax should be reduced, not abolished at once: also that either something should be done at once in regard of local taxation, or a surplus held over till next year, and a promise given to apply it to that purpose. I suggested that indirect taxes should be dealt with in same proportion as direct, which Hunt supported, but nobody else.

F. is financial secretary to the War Dept.: an office which he likes, and which suits him: it gives £1500 a year. ... Home for dinner: worked most of the evening. Rather overdone with the suddenness of the change from idleness to constant occupation.

27 February 1874. Discussion with Bourke, Tenterden, and Lister[44] on Sir B. Frere's[45] plan (taken up to some extent by the late ministry) for suppression of East African slave trade.[46] The scheme as laid before me involves an outlay for several years of £250,000 yearly, falling chiefly on Admiralty: I think we may reduce a good deal of it, and postpone most of the rest till the estimates of 1875 are being prepared.

... Interview with Brunnow,[47] who much broken in health and spirits: his wife is dying, and he does not seem likely to survive her long. He said, 'Ma carrière est finie.' Tears were in his eyes while he talked, which he did in his old rambling way...

4 March 1874. Death of Lytton's only son, which extinguishes the title

[43] Sir Edward Malet (1837–1908), amb. in Berlin 1884–95.
[44] T.V. Lister, Clarendon's priv. sec.
[45] Sir Bartle Frere, 1st bt (1815–84), gov. of Bombay 1862–7; sent to Zanzibar to suppress slave trade, 1872.
[46] For Derby's qualms, cf. above, 6 Feb. 1873.
[47] Ernst Philipp Ivanovitch, Count de Brunnow (1797–1815), Russian minister in London 1840–54, 1861–74; cr. count 1871.

unless he has another. He has another child ill, supposed dying, and is in great distress.[48]

... Remarkably little business in the office.

... Cabinet at 4: all present: Queen's speech considered: no draft of it was before us, but we went through various subjects deciding which should be dealt with.

Cairns brings forward a Transfer of Land Bill, and one for extending the jurisdiction of the new Appellate Court to Scotland and Ireland. Cross introduces a bill for amending the Licensing Act: not a large one, but such as may remove the defects most complained of in the working of the present measure.

A Royal Commission is to sit on the law of conspiracy, the Crim. Law Amendment Act, and the Master and Servant Act.

We discussed the question of touching railways, but agreed on the whole to leave them alone.

We also agreed not to mention Home Rule in the speech. Sat from 4 till about 6: no serious difference of opinion in any quarter. Salisbury singularly eager, and almost violent, in supporting the largest possible concessions to the licensed victuallers: I do not well know why, except that the teetotal party are for the most part dissenters or freethinkers.

6 March 1874. Disraeli asked me to call, which I did. I found him looking ill and exhausted, about to start for Brighton, but anxious to be informed of the state of the Central Asian question. It seems that Salisbury has sent round the cabinet, in a circulation box, a letter written by Ld Northbrook about the first two or three days of Feb. when he (Ld N.) had received notice of a Russian expedition against Merv[49] supposed to be in preparation, and had not heard of the remonstrances addressed to the Russian government by Ld Granville and the consequent assurance of the Czar that no such expedition is intended. The result is that some of our colleagues are alarmed, and want a cabinet, which will do no good.

Some talk afterwards on the budget, as to which I find his ideas nearly identical to mine.

Saw Mr Vivian,[50] who has left this office for a diplomatic life, and starts for Bucharest in a few days. As he asked for general directions, I told him to send us as much information as he could, to engage in no local intrigues of any kind; if questioned about treaties to say that when we had once entered into an engagement we were pledged to it, and there was no use discussing the question of whether it ought to

[48] Lytton's e.s. d. 1871, aged 6; his 2nd s. d. 1 Mar. 1874, aged nearly 2. The 3rd s. inherited and was acting viceroy of India, 1925.

[49] Cf. *Cecil*, 70: 'Russia must advance to Merv ultimately, and we have no power or interest to prevent it.' (Salisbury to Northbrook, summer 1874).

[50] Sir Hussey Vivian (1834–93), clerk in f.o. 1851–72; agent at Bucharest 1874–6.

have been entered into or not (this being the simplest way of meeting all hints that we may not feel bound by the treaty of 1856): and above all to remind the Rumanians that while united to Turkey they had together with complete local independence, the protection of a European guarantee, which they certainly would not have if they set up for themselves.

9 March 1874. Dinner for the new Duchess of Edinburgh in St George's Hall,[51] about 150 present. Gladstone there, we talked foreign affairs, he denounced Ignatieff[52] in the most unmeasured language.

11 March 1874. Wrote to resign the chair of the Kirkdale quarter sessions, which I have held since 1856.

12 March 1874. Cabinet at 3: sat till 4.30: all present. Went through the Queen's Speech, and struck out of it one paragraph promising legislation on the landlord and tenant question: chiefly on the ground that there was no time to consider a bill before the session, and that the other measures proposed are sufficient to fill up the session.

Received ... a telegram from Constantinople, announcing in hardly courteous language the refusal of the Porte to release a prisoner whose liberation has been asked for. ... The tone of the Turkish government is curiously altered since 1868, when nothing could exceed their humility or their gratitude. Is this the doing of Ignatieff? or the mere natural arrogance of an ignorant soldier, promoted by the caprice of his master to the highest place in the empire?

Dined Buckingham house ... I asked the Queen about sending F.O. papers to the P. of Wales which has been the custom of late years. She sanctions its being continued, but observes that he is in the habit of keeping them a long while, and that they lie about...

14 March 1874. Hunt called, in distress at the decision of the cabinet not to put the landlord and tenant bill into the Queen's speech: he thought himself compromised by the refusal, being deeply pledged to his former constituents. We talked the matter over, and I think he went away better satisfied. He talked ominously of the state of the navy, and the need of larger outlay.

15 March 1874. Accounts from Constantinople are very unsatisfactory. The Turkish government is borrowing at 55 per cent to meet its immediate necessities: and the new Grand Vizier, formerly Minister of War, is well known to be under Russian influence, and strongly hostile to England. He is supposed to have been directed by Ignatieff in the policy he has adopted in Yemen: viz. to assure the English Amb. that orders would be given to withdraw the Turkish troops, to send out

[51] Windsor.
[52] Nikolai Pavlovich, Count Ignatiev (1832–1908), seen in U.K. as embodying Russian expansionism; at Paris peace conference, 1856; amb. at Constantinople, 1864–78.

such orders for form's sake, but to accompany them with a hint that they are not meant to be obeyed.

18 March 1874. Cabinet at 5, settling answers to questions in the H. of C. and departmental bills. Nothing of much importance, but Hunt talked in an alarming way about the naval requirements for next year.

19 March 1874. H of Lds at 5 for opening of the session ... D. of Somerset attacked Gladstone with great and telling effect: I have seldom heard a speech more bitter, though delivered with calmness...

21 March 1874. Sir F. Goldsmid[53] called to ask help for the Jews in Roumania, who seem to be a good deal ill-used. I promised to do what we can: which is very little.

Cabinet at 2, which sat till near 4, to consider the budget. We agreed pretty well as to repeal of the sugar duty, reduction of the income tax by one penny, and a larger subsidy in aid of police: but questions arose in connection with Northcote's plan of doing away the duty on horses, and of partially exempting from income tax all incomes under £500. The latter scheme I opposed, as unnecessary, and as tending to a graduated income tax: the most dangers of all fiscal expedients. The surplus is £5,400,000 according to Northcote's statement: the largest, I suppose, ever known in England.

25 March 1874. Cabinet at 4, where the budget was again discussed, with only the result of unsettling what had appeared to be settled on Saturday. Northcote has yielded to the pressure of the brewers: who want the duty on their licences taken off: and the extra half-million thus disposed of has unsettled his calculations. No final arrangement was come to, but opinion seemed to lean towards dealing with tea instead of sugar, in which case the budget would stand nearly as follows:

Income tax, one penny taken off	£1,500,000
Tea duty, reduced from 6d to 4d	£1,100,000
Railway and horse duty, about	£1,000,000
Brewers' licences	£ 400,000
Increased subsidy to police	£ 600,000
Total revenue sacrificed	£4,600,000

I doubt the policy of this change, and opposed it, but the matter is still open to discussion.

28 March 1874. Cabinet at 2: where to my satisfaction I found that Northcote had taken advice, and reverted to his original scheme, or nearly so. His plan now stands:

Sugar, repeal of duty	£2,000,000
Income tax, one penny	£1,500,000

---

[53] Sir Francis Goldsmid, 2nd bt (1808–78), 1st Jewish barrister and Q.C., M.P. (Lib.) Reading 1860–78; pres. of senate, Univ. Coll. London; philanthropist.

| Houses & railways | £1,000,000 |
| Subsidy to police | £   600,000 |

Total of remissions   £5,100,000

Far from diminishing, as the financial year comes nearer its end, the surplus increases. Northcote now reckons on £5,800,000, a figure never reached before in English finance.

Two other questions were to be discussed – the honours to be assigned to Sir G. Wolseley,[54] and the proposal of the bishops to legislate for the repression of ritualistic practices. Nothing was concluded as regards either subject.

11 April 1874. Questions now pending.
1. Fiji: annexation, protectorate, or what?
2. Gold Coast: what to do with?
3. Central Asia, Russian advances in.
4. Turks in Arabia: their claims to be resisted.
5. Canada and U.S. reciprocity treaty.
6. Suez canal, tolls upon.

15 April 1874. Cabinet at 3. Here we discussed the budget again, and it assumed its final shape: which was pretty nearly that indicated in my letter of the 5th: (though this of course is merely a coincidence): we take off income tax one penny: repeal sugar duty, take off duty on houses, and if the state of the revenue allows, give a million or thereabouts in aid of lunatic asylums and police rates. Northcote estimates for £5,400,000, which I think is sanguine, but he has strong assurances from the revenue officials in support of his view. There is besides an item of about £500,000 yearly, being repayment of advances by the State, which the Audit Office insists on treating as revenue, though it never was thought so before: this Northcote very properly applies to the extinction of debt, and with it creates a terminable annuity which will extinguish 8 millions of debt in 1885.

18 April 1874. I hear vaguely that there is likely to be a court quarrel, out of which F.O. must be kept if possible, as to the rank of the Russian lady. We call her 'Royal Highness': she claims to be 'Imperial' ... I hear also much talk as to Disraeli and his state of health. Many of his friends think he has lost his energy (though his speeches of last Feb. showed no trace of any falling off) and will not long bear the strain of parliamentary life.

... Musurus[55] called, talking in a rather confused way about Bahrein and other pending questions. It is almost useless to discuss these with

---

[54] Sir Garnet Wolseley (1833–1913), conqueror of Ashanti.
[55] Musurus Pasha (1807–91), Ottoman minister 1851–6, amb. 1856–85.

him, as he is too much afraid of his own government to report to them anything that may be likely to displease.

19 April 1874. Despatch from Lyons, pointing out the probable danger of a close alliance between Russia and France, and the results on the eastern question of the Franco–German quarrel. It is not a pleasant prospect for Turkey. Either France or Germany would sacrifice the Porte without hesitation, if by so doing they could secure Russian help in the fight to which they both look forward. The Czar knows this, and can, if he pleases, encourage them to bid against one another.

21 April 1874. Sent F. a note, telling him that I will pay his late election bill, which is only £350...[56]

25 April 1874. Long talk with Tenterden as to printing in the office, which I want to increase, so as to do away with much of the copying, and at the same time to circulate important despatches more freely among the various missions than is possible at present.

... Cabinet at 4: sat till 6: talked of a rating bill, but it is not yet ready for discussion: of railways, and in the absence of any plan to which we could see our way, agreed to let Ld Delawarr have the commission for which he asks: of the new grant to the police rates, how it is to be paid: of the constitution of the British Museum: of a grant to the troops engaged in Ashantee, value £12–13,000, which is not objected to on its own account, but there is a doubt as to the precedent which it will create: however the troops are to have it: of the Archbishop's bill,[57] which he is to be asked to put off for a time: and of a bill to be proposed by the Lord Advocate, for doing away with patronage in the Scotch Kirk: this is to be taken in hand, if we can obtain the consent of the leading Scotch proprietors, which is expected. While the cabinet was sitting, a telegram came to me announcing that Lesseps has given way, and that the Suez canal difficulty is over. This was a relief to everybody, most of all to me, for the affair was growing serious.

29 April 1874. In cabinet, rating bill discussed: Northcote undertaking to bring it in. No disagreement except on minute details.

Conversation on the Nine Hours Bill: which Cross thinks can be so modified, as in the main to satisfy both parties. I hope he is right, but have my doubts.

Cairns explained his Judicature Bills, which we accepted in faith rather than on knowledge.

Hunt asked for a supplementary estimate of £250,000, saying that he should like £300,000 if he could get it: we all objected in various ways, and in the end he agreed with good temper, though with obvious reluctance, to take £150,000 and ask for no more.

[56] For his uncontested return in N. Lancs.
[57] Abp Tait's bill against ritualism.

2 May 1874. Letter from the King of Siam, addressed privately to me, complaining of Knox,[58] our consul there. His chief grievance is that Mr Knox on one occasion told him there was nobody to talk to in Siam: that they were all like children, and that life in Bangkok was like being in prison.

4 May 1874. Cabinet at 2 p.m. Discussed the Nine Hours Bill, which we support, but extend the hours from 54 to 56: the Archbishop's bill, which is to be supported on the second reading: Irish fisheries: Irish Sunday closing: and some minor matters. Sat till 3.30.

9 May 1874. Cabinet at 3: sat till past 5. Archbishop's bill discussed at great length, with little result: though all present wished to come to an agreement: I never before realised so clearly the absence of union, and indeed the activity of hostile feeling, between the two ecclesiastical parties.

Carnarvon sketched out his own scheme for the Gold Coast: agreed to.

Rating bill discussed again, but in a hasty manner.

Grant agreed to for Livingstone's family.[59]

16 May 1874. Cabinet to 2 p.m. – Shannon drainage: juries bill: factories bill: archbishop's bill: the chief subjects. We sat an hour and a half.

19 May 1874. Received a letter from Disraeli, complaining of not having had in due time a telegram announcing the fall of the French govt. There was some delay, and he is right in finding fault, but his language shows an irritability quite unusual with him: and he goes out of his way to attack Ld Lyons, who could have nothing to do with the matter. I half suspect a wish to remove Lyons, of whom he has complained on several occasions for no particular reason that I could see.

20 May 1874. Another letter from D. about the delay of the telegram on Sat. evening. This is odd, for the event was one on which no action could be taken, and whether the news reached us at 10 p.m. on Sat. or next morning at breakfast could be of no practical importance to anybody. But it is D's way to treat small matters of form as having more importance that we commonly ascribe to them. And from what I hear of his language on other subjects, and to various people, I am afraid that work and late hours are telling on his nerves. No wonder, considering what the life is.

30 May 1874. Gave the usual official dinner ... ... party afterwards where from 1500 to 1700 persons came. This is the fourth we have

---

[58] (Sir) Thomas George Knox (1824–87), consular official in Siam since 1857; consul-general, 1868; promoted to agent and consul-general (1875–9), kt 1880.

[59] David Livingstone (1813–73), African missionary; buried Westminster Abbey, 1874.

given: none of our predecessors, I believe, went beyond two. But the expense is considerable: not less than £500 for each ... Home about 1 a.m., rather tired, but glad that these social duties are finished for the season.

3 June 1874. Derby day: holiday at the office.

16 June 1874. Disraeli wrote to ask me to call: I found him in the gout, on a sofa: he was uneasy as to the state of the party in H. of Lds, which he thought to be thoroughly disaffected: Richmond, he said, was alarmed and perplexed: and he had received warnings from other persons. I told him, what is the exact truth, that I believed the loss of the appellate jurisdiction was unpopular, as might have been expected: and that there may be some feeling against Cairns in consequence: that the abolition of patronage in the Scotch Kirk is also disliked by some Scotch lords, and that Richmond has mismanaged the late debate on Scotch and Irish peerages, possibly giving offence to Ld Inchiquin,[60] and one or two others. But of more deep-seated causes of discontent I know nothing, nor did I believe that they existed.

24 June 1874. Cabinet: Endowed Schools Bill considered, and it was agreed if the necessary arrangements can be made to continue the Commission for another year. Other business of minor importance.

27 June 1874. Cabinet at 5: several members absent: discussion on Endowed Schools Commission and Bill: also on Rating Bill, which is disliked by some of our supporters: they accepted it willingly last year, but are now less disposed to be reasonable. We sat about an hour, but on the whole there seemed no reason for the sudden summons.

8 July 1874. Cabinet, where the question of accepting the sovereignty of Fiji was discussed: Carnarvon opening it in a clear and concise statement: there was much talk, but no difference of opinion: we all agreed that the offer actually made to us, hampered as it is by various conditions, cannot be accepted: that on the other hand the proposal of cession is not to be absolutely declined: what we must do is to try and induce the natives to explain more clearly the terms which they insist upon: and with that view Sir H. Robinson,[61] the governor of New Zealand,[62] is to be sent to treat with them. ... As a naval station the place might become important.

11 July 1874 (Saturday). Cabinet at 1: the most interesting we have

[60] Edward O'Brien, 14th Baron Inchiquin (1839–1900), succ. 1872; Irish repr. peer 1873–1900.
[61] Sir Hercules Robinson, 1st Baron Rosmead (1824–97), col. governor 1859–80; negotiated cession of Fiji, 1874; high commr for S. Africa 1880–9, 1895–7; cr. peer 1896.
[62] *recte* New South Wales (1872–9).

held yet. The subject was the Bishops Bill, about which public feeling, at first indifferent, has been growing more and more excited, until those who like it least, as Hardy and Hunt, admit that they have never known the H. of C. so strongly moved by any measure within their recollection. Northcote said, and the cabinet seemed to agree, that if a vote were taken on the second reading, the majority for it would be nearer 300 than 200. Disraeli told us plainly that the question was not now whether we should let the bill pass or not, but whether the House would not take matters into its own hands and pass it, possibly strengthened, with or without our help. The immediate question which we had to consider was, whether to give another night for the second reading, and after that for the committee: which in the end we agreed to do. The argument which weighed most with those who dislike the bill, was that if it were thrown out, the cabinet must necessarily pledge itself to bring in one of their own next year: and was there any chance of our being able to agree on one? We all felt that there was not, and that probably the question would break us up. – Speaking generally, Cairns, Cross, and I supported Disraeli's view that we should take up the movement and put ourselves at the head of it if only to be able to control it better: while Hardy, Hunt, Salisbury, and in a lesser degree Northcote, leaned to an opposite policy. They however gave way before the obvious necessities of the position, and it was satisfactory to see that whatever the personal differences of opinion, there was a marked desire to keep together. Salisbury especially showed an inclination to conciliate: which is not his nature, and particularly not where ecclesiastical questions are concerned.

12 July 1874. Received a rather strange letter from Lytton, who seems to wish to retire from diplomacy, unless he can be assured of going as minister either to Rome or Lisbon. I neither could nor would give any such promise, but wrote an answer which was complimentary and vague. He (L.) is at all times dreamy and undecided (so his friends say): and just now much disturbed in mind at the death of his only son.

14 July 1874. Called on old Mrs Grote at her request: she wants a nephew got into F.O.

17 July 1874. Fiji in H. of Lds: Carnarvon told his story with his usual accuracy and clearness:[63] but not as I thought with very good judgment: seeming to represent the cession as more of a thing decided than it really is (for we don't know that the chiefs will accept our terms) and also making the best of it as a natural advantage in itself: which is questionable: our real defence being that in the circumstances of the

---

[63] *H*, ccxxi, 179–87. Carnarvon said U.K. would only accept 'unconditional cession' with crown colony status, Sir H. Robinson to be sent to convey this. Fiji was annexed 10 Oct. 1874.

islands, with a white population of several thousands, chiefly British, whom we can neither allow to massacre the natives, nor to be massacred by them, it is easier to keep order by a direct assumption of sovereignty than by the exercise of consular jurisdiction, or the constant presence of ships of war.

20 July 1874. Cabinet at 2 on Endowed Schools Bill, as to which Sandon & the D. of Richmond appear to have gone further than anybody expected or wished: the fault being with the former, who though laborious and not incapable, is obstinate and a strong religionist. We discussed the matter, and agreed to some modifications, but they were not important, and probably will not satisfy the House.

24 July 1874. Cabinet at 12, which ended by agreeing to pass so much of the Endowed Schools Bill as has got through committee, dropping the rest: the main point being carried, which transfers the power of the late Commissioners to the Charity Commission. All felt that the other clauses could not be gone on with (indeed they are so ill drawn that they would sanction much which we never intended: and deserve a good deal of the blame they have received): the only difference between us was that some wished the whole bill dropped, and the subject taken up again next year. In the end we were all of one mind, except Salisbury: Hardy acquiesced reluctantly but did acquiesce. Salisbury is doubly dissatisfied, at this and the Bishops Bill: and I think regrets having joined the cabinet: but he has been consulted and made much of so that there is no such unpleasantness of feeling as existed in 1867. ... Locock[64] I had a good deal of talk with him, and found him intelligent and sensible. ... Of Turkish finance, he speaks just as Elliot[65] does: the crash must come soon.

25 July 1874. Northcote shows me a letter from his brother-in-law,[66] confidential, and not meant to be shown, in which Adderley's unfitness for this work is complained of. He is represented as willing, industrious, and popular by his good nature and readiness to learn: but he simply cannot master the questions which come before him, and if he continues, some mischief will follow. I am afraid this is likely enough to be true.

28 July 1874. I went to Disraeli at his request, and settled with him about Balmoral. He says he finds the Queen 'very wild': is rather uneasy about her: she declares she will not receive at Balmoral any of the Ritualist party, as she calls them, in the cabinet. D. tries to quiet her, and flatters himself that he succeeds.

---

[64] Probably Sidney Locock (1834–85), sec. of legation at Constantinople.

[65] Sir Henry George Elliot (1817–1907), amb. at Constantinople 1867–77, at Vienna 31 Dec. 1877–84; granted leave of absence on health grounds from Constantinople, Feb. 1877, when replaced de facto by Layard.

[66] (Sir) T.H. Farrer, 1st Baron Farrer (1819–99), perm. sec. at board of trade, Adderley's dept., 1865–86; cr. peer, 1893.

29 July 1874. The Dean of Windsor[67] called here yesterday, and talked about the Queen in the same vein as Disraeli had done: has never seen her so excitable: said of the family 'they are all mad' making one exception, I think, for P. Arthur:[68] Lady Lorne[69] become very eccentric and unmanageable. Talk in London of the Queen refusing to see her daughter, the Crown Princess, for more than an hour or so, and that in public, though there is no open quarrel.

1 August 1874. Cabinet 1 to 3: settled the speech: discussed, but could not decide, a rather wild proposition of Carnarvon's...

2 August 1874. Disraeli writes asking if I see any political objection to the scheme of a tunnel under the Channel, as the partners have found money enough to begin with, but will not go on if we dislike the project. I say, no objection, provided they don't expect government help: in a military point of view it leaves us where we were: since it can be drowned at either end in a few minutes. Commercially it may do some good, but the rates will probably be too high for ordinary traffic: politically, it brings more foreigners into England, which may not be altogether a gain, but it is too late to imitate Japan.

3 August 1874. Hardy tells me of odd things in his relations with the Queen: a fancy of hers to have her name conspicuously printed in the Army list, on the first page, with a page to itself and some note implying that she is the head of the army: with her A.D.C.'s names given in the next page, before any mention of the Sec. of State or C.-in-C. Duke of Cambridge anxious to resign, but absolutely forbidden, as she is determined to keep the place for P. Arthur, that it may not go out of the family. Late attempt to issue an order, contrary to regulation, with no mention of its being approved by the Sec. of State. He definitely thinks there is some craze in all this, and there may be: but there is design also, and the question may yet give trouble.

26 August 1874. Abergeldie is leased by the Queen from the Gordon family, for a term of 40 years: Birkhall is owned by the P. of Wales: and Balmoral itself, about 10,000 acres, by the Queen. The three together give the family command of about 40,000 acres, besides which they have leased the shooting on the opposite side of the Dee, from Farquharson of Invercauld.

28 August 1874. Hot close day, with east wind and smell of St Helens. Church: Seftons met us there: Sefton walked home with me: talk of Towneley,[70] where he has just been: a fine estate, £40,000 to £50,000

---

[67] Gerald Wellesley (1809–82), dean of Windsor 1854–82.
[68] Prince Arthur (1850–1942), 3rd s. of Queen; cr. D. of Connaught, May 1874; freemason, field marshal.
[69] Formerly Princess Louise, 4th dau. of Queen.
[70] Hamlet, s.e. of Burnley, Lancs.

a year, but partly coal: the place spoilt by the town of Burnley close to it: the old man[71] growing feeble, and rather childish: has been singularly hospitable, and is so still: keeps open house both in London and country: his married daughters all live with him etc. A nephew succeeds. Talk also of magistrates: Sefton gives himself much credit for refusing all appeals to make them from political partisans: and I believe he may say this with truth.

... By an odd fancy, the Queen had the stations through which she passed on her way down cleared of the crowd which had come to see her, except at Aberdeen: the result being discontent and absolute silence instead of cheers. One is reminded of George IV who in his latter days had a morbid horror of being looked at. Is this an indication of growing eccentricity?

30 August 1874. All the people in attendance are weary of Balmoral. There is nothing to do indoors, and they are never allowed to go out, even for half an hour, till 4 p.m. in case it should occur to the Queen that she might want any of them. They are naturally disgusted, and talk of the great lady's selfishness...

Lady Biddulph[72] says that the Queen has of late years taken, in her private conversation, to exalt beyond measure the virtues of the poorer classes, and speaks with extreme bitterness of the London world, the aristocratic and fashionable part of it. This way of thinking has grown upon her, and it is ascribed in part to her recollection of the reports spread about her and John Brown,[73] which she has never forgiven: in part the feeling common among royal personages, which makes them like best those who are farther removed from them in point of rank and station, and whom therefore they consider as most dependent and submissive.

12 September 1874. Walk with M. to Balmoral, and there called on Disraeli, whom we found in his room, not at all well. He related with much of his characteristic humour a conversation he had had with the Queen, in which she sketched the characters of different members of the royal family, as he says, with real discrimination. Of the Duke of Edinburgh, she said that his wife would never have much influence over him – no woman could have over a man who was so thoroughly selfish – but that he would lead a domestic life. She praised the Prince of Wales's gentleness and willingness to take trouble, but added that neither he nor the Princess could live without excitement: it was impossible for them to be quiet at home, or long in one place. She had

[71] Charles Towneley (1803–76), succ. 1846; educ. Oscott; F.S.A., F.R.S., B.M. trustee.
[72] Wife of Sir T.M. Biddulph (1809–78), courtier.
[73] John Brown (1826–83), Queen's personal attendant.

tried to induce the Princess to read a little, telling her that she was ignorant of many things which it would hereafter be very inconvenient to her not to know: but the Princess answered that she had been promised that she should have no more lessons after she married! an answer which the Queen thought conclusive.

22 September 1874. Walk to Girnock with Cairns and round the hill after breakfast. He uneasy about Disraeli's Irish visit,[74] both on the ground of health, and of what may be said: thinks he was badly advised to undertake it. Talk of Whiteside,[75] who being Chief Justice, wants the Chancellorship of Ireland, intending to hold it only long enough to qualify for a pension, and then retire on £4000 a year to live in London. This Cairns thinks a job. Anxiety about ecclesiastical questions for next year: fears an attempt to renew the Endowed Schools Bill, and that it may break up the cabinet. Especially distrustful of Salisbury: thinks Hardy moderate where his own judgment is concerned, but fettered by his connection with Oxford. Wishes that Gladstone could have that seat again: thinks he, G., would certainly be preferred for it if an election were to take place: and that it would be the only seat which he would have a chance of securing. Talk of the Queen: says her mind has been full of the notion of being proclaimed Empress of India: an idea obviously suggested by the royal marriage. Agrees with me that her peculiarities are increasing with years, and expects them to grow troublesome. Notices her growing habit of imagining that she wants rest after everything: even after an interview with one of her own children: her dislike of all society: strange fancies of various kinds: supposes that she will be what her predecessors since George III inclusive have been, if her life extends to old age. Talk of patent law amendment, for which he has a plan ready: of land transfer, of judicature bill: thinks we must do something about game and also about unexhausted improvements.

Talk of the Highlanders, among whom he has lived every year for a month or six weeks: he denies that they are a hardy race...

7 November 1874. Despatches from Berlin ... Bismarck talked to Odo Russell of the Arnim[76] trial ... he denounces Arnim in violent language, says he deserved not imprisonment but hanging, that he has speculated in the funds, used his official and secret information to help him, and falsified despatches (I suppose those received by him) to suit his private

---

[74] See M. and B., v 345 for Derby's letter (15 Sept.) to Disraeli strongly advising against the Irish tour.

[75] James Whiteside (1806–76), M.P. (Cons.) 1851–66; lord chief justice (Ireland) from 1866.

[76] Harry, Count Arnim (1824–81), Germ. amb. in Paris, 1872–; arrested 4 Oct. 1874, and tried.

objects. He adds, what seems strange, that Decazes[77] has gone shares
with him in these transactions.

... Rather alarmed and uneasy at a note which M. has received
from Disraeli: refusing an invitation on grounds of health, and hinting
clearly that in his own opinion he will not be long fit to undergo the
labour of office.

10 November 1874. In cabinet, the whole programme of next session's
work was gone through: the principal subjects were judicature bill: land
transfer: patents: Irish coercion acts (to be renewed or not?), endowed
schools (feeling seemed against touching the question again): game
(doubt whether it should be dealt with): tenants' improvements (a bill
may be introduced): local govt board: sanitary legislation; improvement
of dwellings: assaults, fresh penalties upon: university revenues: railway
accidents: law of master and servant: army exchanges: juries: and some
others. Out of all these, which are work for several sessions, we have
to choose.

Questions decided were 1. Shall we send out an Arctic expedition?
Cost will be £100.[78] Agreed that we cannot afford it next year, but
hope may be held out for the future. 2. Shall we buy up Ocean
Telegraphs? Decided against, partly on grounds of expense and partly
that the offer made is a bad one. 3. Public buildings. Are we to buy
the whole block between the new offices and Great George St? Cost
will be about two millions, but it might be done out of terminable
annuities. We decide that also in the negative.

Disraeli in the course of discussion expresses himself strongly in
favour of keeping up income tax at its present rate. He says and I think
truly, that people do not now complain of taxation, and are not asking
for fresh remissions. Northcote says he expects a surplus of about
£500,000 for this year, but is uneasy about next year when the expense
will be increased by the charge for police and lunatics, which has come
only partly into operation as yet, and when the return from income
tax will be diminished. Balances also are weak, in consequence of the
drain upon them for local loans.

11 November 1874. Ld Cairns dined with us: nothing passed of much
interest, except that he described with some humour a ball at Balmoral
given to the servants, at which the Queen sat till 1 a.m., John Brown
being master of the ceremonies, and addressing her continually without
any mark of respect, such as 'Your Majesty' or the like.

12 November 1874. Cabinet at 3: Northcote explained the financial
situation, which is good for the present year, unsatisfactory for 1875–6.
He expects to end with a surplus of £500,000 more or less: but next

---

[77] Louis, duc Decazes (1819–86), French foreign min. Nov. 1873–77.
[78] *Sic.*

year will bring increased expenditure for police and lunatics, and a falling off in returns from income tax: the two together making a difference of £1,300,000 as compared in 74–5: which if there be no increase in the revenue would land us in a deficit of £800,000. The natural growth of revenue may bring us round, but if we can get a balance on the right side it is all we can do: remission of taxation is out of the question: and estimates must not be increased. Disraeli appealed to Hunt and Hardy to cut down theirs, but got no encouragement. Both seemed willing, but declared themselves unable. We discussed the government of London: all agreed in rejecting the plan of Elcho and Mr Beal,[79] which is to create one vast municipality out of all London: this we object to 1. as politically dangerous 2. because between different parts of London there is no community of interests, and but little local intercourse. We agreed that the bill must be opposed, and that we cannot legislate next year on the subject.

Agreed to do nothing about endowed schools: nor about game: to bring in a bill for compensation to tenants for improvements: and some minor matters. We reconsidered, and reversed, our decision of the other day as to an Arctic expedition: believing that it is desired by the navy and by men of science: the cost will be £40,000 this year, £36,000 in 1875–6, and a little more afterwards. We sat two hours.

Home about 6 ... The Chief Justice talked of Kenealy,[80] and his scurrilous paper *The Englishman*: in which everyone who has taken part against his client Orton[81] is accused of corruption or something equally bad. He is the more annoyed because he patronised Kenealy, though knowing him to have got into trouble, thinking that he ought to have a chance to retrieve his character: he has letters of K. written to him in terms of abject adulation: when the trial came on K. did all in his power to insult the judges, hoping to be committed for contempt of court, which he thought would make his fortune with the attorneys: he failed and has never got a brief since. He is now desperate and is throwing mud in all directions. Cockburn[82] thinks that in the interests of justice he ought to be prosecuted, and has spoken to Cairns on the subject.

13 November 1874. Doyle[83] sent me a curious pamphlet, now selling in the streets, recommending the abdication of the Queen, on the ground that she cannot or will not do her proper duty. It is not violent, nor

---

[79] James Beal (1829–91), London radical.
[80] Edward Kenealy (1819–80), barrister, counsel for Tichborne claimant; M.P. (Ind.) Stoke 1875–80.
[81] Arthur Orton (1834–98), Tichborne claimant.
[82] Sir Alexander Cockburn (1802–80), lord chief justice since 1859.
[83] Sir Francis Doyle (1810–88), belletrist.

abusive, nor especially foolish, except in saying that the Queen has £10,000,000 laid by out of income.

14 November 1874. Saw Mr Gorst, who rather alarmed at what he calls the sore feeling of a large section of the clergy, especially in the south of England, at the Public Worship Bill. They have always been used, he says, to do what they liked in matters of service and ritual: and the prospect of being in any degree controlled by their congregation is a grievous offence to them.

... Cabinet at 2: sat till 4. Cairns gave us notice that he must raise the question of Dr Kenealy before long, but did not go into it. Nearly all our time was occupied with Cross's scheme for improving dwellings in London. He cited precedents of what had been done at Edinburgh and Glasgow, and went fully into detail. All the cabinet agreed in the principle of his bill. Speaking of the Battersea project, he told us that on 36 acres 15,000 persons could be well and comfortably lodged without overcrowding. In fact the model houses save space. They will hold easily 1000 persons to the acre. The worst back slums in London seldom lodge more than 400 to the acre.

17 November 1874. Cabinet discussed in part Irish affairs: Ball attended: he pressed the necessity of amending the Juries Act, which at present, as he said, leads to a total failure of justice: the peasant-juryman now put on will not convict, and the trials are a farce. Ball thought we could do without the Coercion Acts, but as he put it himself, they have succeeded so completely that they have destroyed the evidence for their own necessity. Some provisions as to arms will in any case have to be renewed.

Our discussions were less to the purpose than usual: dealing with many questions, and not in a very business like way. Cross explained a bill which he has in preparation on explosive substances: and Carnarvon began a statement of S. African matters, which we agreed to hear farther on Thursday.

19 November 1874. Read a mem. by Sandon, circulated to the cabinet, on compulsory education: in which he speaks with a kind of pious horror of the growth of school boards in country places. It has confirmed me in the opinion I had formed of his weakness and narrowness of brain: though he is assiduous and I believe accurate in business.

Pender told ... a strange and rather confused story of some person, professing to be an agent for some member of the govt, telling him that his baronetcy was secure if he would pay £20,000 ... It is probably a mere swindling trick: but the mere suspicion, however groundless, of such practices, is mischievous. I am certain that in the cabinet there is no man who would sell his influence: in the inferior posts there are one or two of whom I should be less sure, but they have none to sell.

... Cabinet at 3 ... We discussed South African matters at considerable length, the question most in dispute being what to do with a chief[84] named Langalibe [sic], or something like it, who having shown some tendency to revolt was seized, justly enough, and very unjustly sentenced by a court which had no authority to try him, for the offence of murder which he had not committed. He is now a prisoner at the Cape. It is not just to keep him, nor safe to let him return to his tribe. The expedient probably resorted to will by temporary surveillance under friendly control. The governor, Sir B. Pine,[85] to be recalled, and his acts annulled.

Cairns brought before us the case of Dr Kenealy, whom the judges, especially Cockburn, want to prosecute. He is every week issuing the foulest libels upon them, the jury, counsel, and all concerned in the Tichborne case. His paper has a large circulation, and nothing can be more offensive. But if prosecuted for libel, he would be entitled to call as defendants the persons whom he has libelled, and insult them at pleasure (for great latitude must be allowed to a prisoner defending himself): thus the scandal would be intensified: and if proceeded against, as the Att. Gen. seems to think possible, for conspiracy with others to bring the judges into contempt, it is likely that the prosecution would fail. On the whole it was thought better to leave him alone, and we were all of one mind.

The Lord Advocate[86] laid before us a programme of Scotch legislation: he has bills ready, or preparing, on roads, education, game, hypothec, power to owners of entailed estates to borrow, courts of law, and one or two more. But it is clear that of all these subjects few are ripe for consideration.

20 November 1874. Cabinet at 2. We sat exactly 2 hours. We discussed South Africa again: coming in the main to the same conclusion as before. Cross called attention to the question of flogging as a punishment for brutal assaults, saying that a great majority of the judges, stipendiary magistrates, & others consulted were for it. No decision was asked or expected. I have my doubts as to the wisdom of making this change, unless it is very carefully limited.

Cairns told us of an unwise speech made last night in the Temple, where Cockburn on his health being drunk adverted to the Kenealy business, & complained in strong terms of the Att. Gen. not doing his duty in vindicating the character of the judges by a prosecution.

... Hardy took occasion to mention that contrary to the general belief the recruiting is going on satisfactorily as regards the army in

---

[84] Given a life sentence, col. office despatches declaring this illegal being ignored.

[85] Sir Benjamin Pine (1809–91), gov. of Natal 1873–5.

[86] E.S. Gordon, Baron Gordon (1814–79), lord advocate 1867–8, 1874–6; lord of appeal 1876–9.

general, but not in the Guards – the pay being now equalised, London expenses heavy, and men of the requisite size not easily obtainable.

23 November 1874. To Buckingham house at 1 p.m. to attend the christening of the Edinburgh child ... Disraeli was to have been there, but gout kept him at home.

28 November 1874. Disraeli has been ill during the last few days with gout and bronchitis: a disagreeable combination. He stays at home and sees no one. Reports are current as to his not being able to go on long: a prospect which for many reasons I do not like to contemplate.

29 November 1874. Disraeli is rather better, but in bed, and sees no one.

1 December 1874. Disraeli is mending, but still weak and unfit for business.

2 December 1874. Lytton sends me a letter ... he mentions that the President [of France] had a conversation with him, Lytton, in which he expressed opinions very unfavourable to the republic: something to the effect that he did not understand anyone wishing to see it established in France, except those who wished to see France humiliated. This is the most decisive intimation we have yet had of his personal opinions, which as a rule he keeps to himself.

... Letter from Salisbury, who has got in his mind the notion that there is in some quarters a project for making the D. of Richmond the next premier, when Disraeli's health compels him to resign: an event which Salisbury evidently considers as not far distant. He protests against this, says it must not be allowed, that the Duke is unfit for the post, that his appointment would justify the title of the 'stupid party' as applied to us, and that in the event of a vacancy I must assert my claim to the position. He writes in a very friendly tone, and I am bound to suppose his wish sincere, for why else should he have written at all? I answer in a similar spirit, but cautiously, agreeing as to the unfitness of the Duke, saying nothing as to my own possible claims, but pointing out that the weakness of our position is in the want of a competent leader in the H. of C. I did not enlarge on this, but it is impossible not to see that Hardy, with abundant fluency and rhetorical power, wants judgment, and that Northcote, whose judgement and sound sense can be relied on, is too heavy a speaker to be an effective chief.

I am inclined to think that Salisbury's aversion to the notion of having Richmond for chief, is due to the fact that the Duke is entirely under the influence of Cairns. S. being a strong high churchman, fears nothing more than that Cairns, who is low, should virtually make bishops and guide ecclesiastical policy: he would prefer a neutral, like myself, whom he might hope in some degree to guide.

The Queen talked to me at some length after dinner: she said that Carnarvon wanted to alter the name of the Fiji islands to 'Oceania' or 'Windsor islands': which she laughed at, and disapproved. I agreed with her.

6 December 1874. Disraeli reported improving, but he is far from well.

7 December 1874. The *Observer* yesterday hints at an understanding having been come to by which the D. of Richmond should take the lead if Disraeli cannot go on. It is not stated when, where, or by whom this arrangement was made, and probably the whole story has no other foundation than vague report: but it explains Salisbury's letter of the other day, and shows that there is a party who wish R. to succeed. He no doubt represents the average country-gentleman's view of things, better than either Salisbury, Cairns, or I. But the crisis is probably now postponed.

17 December 1874. I have been seriously considering the question whether or no it will be expedient to protest against the advance of the Russians to the line of the Atrek,[87] which the Persian govt desires. My decision is against it, for various reasons. The protest will be useless: nothing can come of it unless we were prepared to back up our words by acts, which in such a matter we are not: the Persians are not to be trusted as allies, any prospect of momentary advantage, or a bribe offered to their statesmen, would induce them to throw us over while we were engaged in fighting their battles: and on the question of right it is not easy to say that the Russians may not be justified in occupying a desert tract, inhabited only by wandering tribes, who own no allegiance, and live by plunder. The Persian territory is neither attacked nor threatened: and we are in no way pledged to protect the independence of nomad Turcoman hordes.

22 December 1874. Shooting in Mossborough wood ... killed over 700 head: Russian ambassador very keen about sport, but no great performer...

23 December 1874. Much wearied with the noise and bustle of these two days, and rather unreasonably worried at the arrears of business inevitably caused by my being out all day.

... I have had, in a desultory way, a good deal of interesting talk with Count Schouvaloff,[88] but little of it remains with me distinctly enough to be worth writing down. He is evidently a man of considerable acuteness: talks admirably in French: shows great eagerness to catch the ways, and adapt himself to the manners of the country he is staying in: a more agreeable guest it would not be easy to find. Like most

---

[87] River rising in N.E. Persia, entering S.E. Caspian.

[88] Pyotr Andreyevich, Count Shuvalov (1827–89), Russian amb. to London 1874–9; served in Crimea; former head of political police.

Russians that I have met he is extremely frank and unreserved in appearance, but when you come to think over what he has said it comes to little. He does not seem to like the French: ridiculed Thiers, whom he described as a sort of actor: of the German statesmen he said little or nothing. He talked of the internal state of Russia; said the emancipation of the serfs had worked differently in different provinces: towards the north it had lessened the value of estates: in the south he thought the landowners were better off than before ... He complained of the excessive number of functionaries required under the Russian system: wished the landlords could be utilised as in England to do unpaid work...[89]

[89] Derby spoke little outside parliament in 1874: at Liverpool (*T*, 15 Jan. 1874, 5d), at Manchester, on scientific industry (*T*, 17 Jan. 1874, 5c), at the Society of Arts (*T*, 18 Feb. 1874, 93), and at University College Hospital (*T*, 11 Feb. 1874, 12d). He was however elected Lord Rector of Edinburgh University (*T*, 16 Nov. 1874, 9f; 25 Nov. 1874, 9f; 1 Dec. 1874, 8c) for the coming year, and gave five F.O. receptions (*T*, 1 Apr. 1874, 9e; 17 Apr. 1874, 9f; 23 Apr. 1874, 9f; 25 Nov. 1874, 9f; 1 Dec. 1874, 8c).

1875

[1875] Flyleaf

Notes of debts on the estates

... Total debt on Jan. 1st 1875	£262,000
Total interest on debt	£11,345
Total debt on Jan. 1st 1874 was	£345,000
Showing diminution in the year of	£83,000
Receipts were in the year ending June 30, 1872, from rents	£174,756
Same, in year ending June 30, 1873	£177,711*
Same, in year ending June 30, 1874	£175,223

*This includes a more than usual proportion of arrears paid up. Increase of rent may be reckoned at £1000 certain, on an average of years, £1500 probable, and £2000 not absolutely improbable ... I take £1500 as a safe estimate, one year with another.

Expenditure has varied in various years, but it may be assumed as not likely to fall much below, or rise much above, the following estimate.

Estate, £45,000. Household, with park, gardens, stables, game & c. £25,000. Benefactions, private allowance, & incidental, £20,000. Total, £90,000. This is rather high, and £85,000 might be a sufficient average. ... Taxes come to £6000: quitrents, over £6000 (these are in course of gradual extinction): annuities charged on estate, £4000: interest of debt, say £11,500; my mother's allowance £6000. Total £33,000, making total outgoings between £120 and £125,000 ... Hence there is a surplus of £50 to £55,0000, applicable to purchase of land or accumulation in money. If I prefer land, I may add to the family estates 1000 acres yearly, on an average ... In Oct. next I am to receive from the L. & Y. Co.[1] £50,000. Next year there will be due from the same co. a sum which is to be fixed by arbitration, but according to Statter, it cannot be less than £50,000 and may be double that amount.

There is another negotiation going on for sale of land near the station at Bury, about 7 acres, for which we ask between £60 and £70,000. And Hale is asking the Cheshire R. Co for £40,000 or thereabouts ... It would seem probable that I may reckon next year on receipts to the amount of £140,000 or possibly a good deal over.

1 January 1875. I begin this year without trouble or disturbance of

---

[1] Lancs and Yorks Railway Co.

any kind, except what arises from Lady Derby's health not being as strong as formerly, or as I could wish: there is however no actual illness, and I have good hope of amendment when the cold and dark time is past. ... My own health is good ... I have no quarrels private or public: and politically speaking I have nothing to wish for. The Foreign Office with a majority of 50 or 60 in the H. of C. and without the personal labour of attendance there, is perhaps as suitable a post as I could find. Disraeli, though aged and growing feeble, is capable of some years more work: and he is certainly trusted and respected by the country as he has never yet been.

Europe is quiet, except in Spain...[2]

2 January 1875. The post brought 6 boxes, in addition to 8 left over from yesterday: very busy upon them ... I find that to be here with the necessity of receiving guests, attending to them, going on shooting expeditions and the like, is really far less of a holiday than to be quietly settled in London in attendance on my office.

Hale came to see me: I discussed with him the possibility of farther reduction in the quantity of game, as there is really more shooting than I can get through, and it becomes a labour rather than a pleasure. I wish also to cut down the ground-game, but as the tenants themselves don't desire a reduction, and everybody else has an interest in keeping it up, that is not an easy matter. ... In my room all day between breakfast & dinner: biscuits only for luncheon.

3 January 1875. Made up private account ... Sent H. Stanley £25, on his renewed request. Talk with Hopwood of his affairs, which H. agrees with me are hopeless, so far as the chance of getting the old man to live on any regular allowance is concerned.

4 January 1875. Shooting ... We killed 218 hares, and in all 521 head.

5 January 1875. Very busy all morning with boxes ... Walk early with M. & with Sanderson later. Tenants' dinner at 3.30, where I had to make the usual speeches.

7 January 1875. Second tenants' dinner: attended and spoke again. Walk later with Sanderson. In the evening arrived two cyphered telegrams, which cost Sanderson & me nearly half an hour to make out: and when made out they were of little importance.

8 January 1875. Disgusted ... to see the mischief done by rabbits ... The sight confirmed my determination to extirpate them altogether ... I spoke to Hale about this, and instructed him to get warreners from outside to do it – the keepers will not, as they like rabbits for themselves, and shooting for their friends when I am away.

... Walk ... with M. She has seen Bickersteth again, and he says

[2] Spanish internal politics, copiously mentioned in the diaries, have been omitted from this selection, as not bearing on U.K. or international affairs.

she is suffering from nervous strain, must have complete rest, and so
on. The best thing to do is that she should go abroad for a month as
soon as is conveniently possible.

10 January 1875. General hope that Decazes will stay where he is,
and I share it, for he is moderate & sensible beyond most Frenchmen.
... Harcourt[3] sends me his late speech at Oxford; it is clever and
skilful: he is laying himself out to be the leader of the Whig, or moderate
Liberal party ... and with his ability and ambition, he seems not
unlikely to succeed.

11 January 1875. London by early train ... Sanderson came up with
us.

12 January 1875. Cabinet at 2: sit till past 4: all present except Hardy,
who is kept away by the death of a daughter.[4] We began by talking
over the Brussels conference:[5] I explained the course taken, which was
approved: and also the situation of Spain, as to which questions were
asked.

We then went into the real business, finance: Northcote expects for
the end of this year a surplus of about £600,000: which though not
large is enough to justify his estimates. But for 1875–6, after deducting
what has already been promised in anticipation, we have hardly any
surplus at all: £80 or £90,000 on a moderate computation: and he is
pressed with demands which if granted would involve a deficit of more
than a million. The first of these is for the navy. Hunt wants £300,000
over the estimate of last year: he stated his claim at length, and certainly
it is a strong one. But where is the money to come from? We cannot,
without absurdity, put on the penny on the income tax which was
taken off last year: nor without serious unpopularity begin raising taxes
which our predecessors during the last five years have been occupied
in reducing. These arguments which I had embodied in a brief note to
Disraeli before the cabinet began, were pressed by Cairns, Salisbury, &
myself, Disraeli assenting: the entire cabinet was against increased
outlay, with the single exception of J. Manners, who thought that a
policy of liberal expenditure was expected from us, and would be
popular! We parted without settling anything, but in good humour.

13 January 1875. At 3 in the cabinet, which sat till 5.20. The only
business was going through Cross's bill for the sanitary reconstruction
of towns: which was carefully discussed clause by clause. A bill of his
for the prevention of violent assaults was also gone through, but in a
more general way, it being less important. All present except Hardy.

[3] Friend of Derby at Trinity, Cambridge, where both Apostles.
[4] Hardy's dau. Edith d. 8 Jan. 1875.
[5] On the usages of war, under chiefly Russian auspices and chairmanship (July 1874–);
no important results ensued (*London Gazette*, 24 Oct. 1874).

14 January 1875. Cabinet at 3, which sat till past 5. We again discussed army and navy estimates. The two services jointly require an increase over last year's estimate of £350,000: they would like twice as much, but this sum they consider indispensable and certainly Hunt and Hardy made out a strong case. The increase of 6d. in the spirit duty would give £500,000, but it is an inexpedient move, if we can avoid it. To increase the income tax again, after lowering it last year, is not to be thought of. In cabinet, Hardy paid a high compliment to F. Both he and Hunt were moderate and good-tempered, though firm, in their demands: seeing and admitting our difficulties, and only asking that we should admit theirs.

15 January 1875. In the papers, a letter from Gladstone to Ld Granville, formally resigning the leadership of the party. ... Forster, Harcourt, Göschen, Lowe, are pretty equal in parliamentary position: Hartington, inferior in ability to all of them, is thought likely to be selected as a nominal chief, by way of compromise between rival claims: a possible, but doubtful, policy.

... Cabinet at 12: sat till 2.30. Much business done, but not of a very interesting kind: Merchant Shipping Bill, Local Govt Bills, and a variety of similar measures discussed.

16 January 1875. Saw Mr Mason, consul for Siam in England, who came in consequence of an alarm of our intended interference in the civil war now going on. (The 'second King' has taken refuge in the British consulate, and a gunboat has been sent to protect British subjects if necessary.) I assured him we would leave parties in Siam to fight it out, and only wished to secure our own people. He is apparently an American by his speech.

17 January 1875. Jarnac[6] called early, with despatches & letters about the Podgoritza affair[7] – a trifling affray between Montenegrins & Turks which has been swelled to vast dimensions by consular interference – which show that Decazes either feels, or thinks it expedient to affect, considerable alarm at what may come out of this dispute. It seems that Russia & Austria have taken it up seriously; and this is the more important, as the thing itself does not justify the importance given to it: there is therefore the appearance of a deliberate design to pick a quarrel. It is in that light that the French F.O. professes to see the matter. The French want us to act with them, but I can give no answer until our own telegrams arrive: and it does not seem that Elliot thinks it as serious as they do, else he would have telegraphed before now.

The subject of the moment is Gladstone's retirement. Most people

---

[6] Philippe Chabot, Comte de Jarnac (d. 22 May 1875), French amb. 1874–5; Harrovian, with estates in Kilkenny.

[7] Small fortified town 19 m. N.E. of Cetinje, Montenegro.

think ... he will come back again ... Some believe that he wishes to shake himself clear of the old landed Whig party, which he has always disliked, and to lead the radicals only: but this is mere conjecture. The remark most commonly made is that if he is in earnest about resigning his leadership, he ought to leave the H. of C. – since his importance there is too great to allow of his sitting as a private member. ... On the whole, his resolution is not taken very seriously: no one doubts that it is sincere, but scarcely any one expects it to be permanent.[8]

18 January 1875. Russell[9] writes that Bismarck's anti-clerical policy is more strictly enforced than ever ... No expectation of war this year, as the German military organisation will not be complete till 1876.

21 January 1875. By a letter to M. from Disraeli I learn that Tennyson has refused the offer of a baronetcy, in a letter which D. describes as 'impertinent', at the same time referring to a promise which he alleges was given him, that his eldest son should be made a baronet in his place. D. is sensitive and Tennyson is credited with extreme vanity: but the story of the promise is incomprehensible ... There must be some misunderstanding to be cleared up.[10]

22 January 1875. Elliot begins the new year with a survey of Turkish finance and administration. His judgment is altogether unfavourable. He says that the financial prospects of Turkey never were worse. The deficit of the year just ended will be greater than ever before – persons acquainted with the subject say 8 or 10 millions sterling. The reckless outlay on places and ironclads continues. Appointments are given to men selected without respect of fitness, who have gained favour with some favourite of the Sultan.[11] The Grand Vizier[12] can do nothing. The Sultan personally is the cause of all. The Turks are beginning to speak of him as out of his mind. It is hopeless to alter his habits of extravagance: they are formed and inveterate. Turks in high position say that Elliot ought to use his influence. France has none: Russia, Austria, and Germany are all considered as hostile. He alone, they think, can interfere: but he himself believes that whatever influence he has gained arises solely from the habit of not interfering needlessly: and moreover that if he were to open the Sultan's eyes to the conviction that matters are going wrong, the only result would be the removal of

[8] *T,* 15 Jan. 1875, 9f for letters between Gladstone and Granville.

[9] Odo Russell, amb. in Berlin.

[10] Cf. *Alfred, Lord Tennyson, A Memoir by his Son* (1897), ii 161–3. Tennyson believed that Gladstone had promised a baronetcy to be conferred on his s. after his own death; he thrice declined a baronetcy, but was cr. peer, 1884.

[11] Abdul Aziz (1830–4 June 1876), sultan 1861–76; deposed 29/30 May 1876; succ. by Murad v (May–Aug. 1876) and Abdul Hamid (31 Aug. 1876–1909).

[12] Perhaps Mahmood Pasha, or Mahmut Nedim Pasha (1817–83); cf. above, 12 Mar. 1874.

the Grand Vizier, whose hands he wants to strengthen. Elliot thinks the Grand Vizier clear-sighted, resolute, and friendly to England, for all which reasons he is cordially disliked by Russia. Aarifi,[13] the Foreign Minister, Elliot considers as indolent and incapable: (but he has now been removed.) On the whole the picture which Elliot draws is not a pleasing one.

25 January 1875. Called on Disraeli, whom I found in excellent spirits: apparently quite restored in health, and fit for work. We discussed Spanish matters, and some others.

Lady Carnarvon, who had been dangerously ill for a fortnight, died this morning: a great loss to the party ... She will be regretted by many, being hospitable and social in disposition.

26 January 1875. Winmarleigh called, in trouble about the Labour Law Commission, which is divided: the C. Justice, he says, having changed his mind at the last moment.

27 January 1875. Schouvaloff called, with a singular request. He says his govt tell him nothing, that he receives neither instructions nor information, and he will be obliged to me to let him know when anything is doing that concerns Russia. I promised, of course: but am puzzled to know whether what he says is to be taken as truth. It is not in itself improbable, for Gortschakoff[14] is his enemy and it would be quite in accordance with Russian practice to discredit a colleague with the Czar by refusing him the means of doing his duty: and Schouvaloff who is not by profession a diplomatist, may be simply speaking out his mind. But it is the penalty which a Russian must pay for his nationality, that he is most distrusted when most seemingly frank. He told me that in his belief the origin of the Brussels conference was the feeling of repugnance created in the mind of the Emperor and his entourage by the severities exercised in France by the German army. He himself (S.) had thought the conference harmless, but not likely to lead to much result.

28 January 1875. Cabinet at 12, which sat till 2.30. ... In cabinet Irish bills discussed. We agree on a Judicature Bill, reducing in some degree the number of legal appts: also on discontinuing the greater part of the coercive laws of 1871, which appear not now to be required: but with a proviso that they will be re-enacted if the freedom thus granted is abused. The press laws, which were extremely stringent, are said by Sir M. Beach to be practically inoperative. I did not well understand why: and there is, he says, as much anti-English writing as ever. We discussed a bill for putting all prisons under central management: there are twice as many of them as necessary, and a superfluity of officers to

---

[13] Aarifi Pasha, grand vizier 29 July–18 Oct. 1879.
[14] Prince A.M. Gorchakov (1798–1883), chancellor 1866–82.

each – the result of local jobbing. We discussed the demands of the
school-teachers, who want an additional grant of £240,000: where are
they going to get it? There were some minor measures, which I do not
well recollect.

Mr Levy[15] of the Telegraph called for information, which I gave him.
He is very friendly, says we have everything our own way, and can do
what we please – that there is no Liberal party, and so forth.

29 January 1875. At 12 to cabinet, which sat to consider the Queen's
speech. We read it twice, and made many verbal alterations, but left
the substance as it stood.

31 January 1875. Wade[16] sends a long letter from Pekin, which might
be supposed to proceed from Constantinople, so similar is his language.
He takes a gloomy view of the future of China: sees signs everywhere
of increasing disorganisation: if the war with Japan had not been staved
off, insurrections would have broken out over half the empire. The
Chinese were utterly unprepared to fight, and know it: yet with their
usual conceit and stolidity, they will not show any gratitude to Wade
for having got them out of the scrape. He thinks (but does not give his
reason for thinking) that Russian agents were busy stirring up the
Japanese to fight, and advising the authorities at Pekin not to give way.
If true, this is exactly their policy in Turkey.

1 February 1875. Sir B. Frere came to talk over the Sultan of Zanzibar &
East African slave trade. Called on Disraeli at his request: found him
not over well pleased, at being summoned down to Osborne for
tomorrow, at short notice, he does not know why, and at the imminent
risk of catching another chill. He wanted to talk over with me the
language that should be held on foreign affairs in the event of a
debate...

... The Podgoritza, or Montenegro, business, which alarmed Jarnac
so much a fortnight ago, is announced as settled: and there is nothing
else important or dangerous.

... The object of Russia is not to renew the Holy Alliance, but to
check the progress of German influence by detaching Austria from
Germany. It is in fact a part of the same policy as that indicated in the
almost excessive civilities shown by Russia to France. Bismarck does
not like the arrangement: thinking that the three – Russia, Austria &
France – may at any time combine against him.

Schouvaloff, in a recent conversation, hinted at something of the

[15] Edward Levy-Lawson, 1st Baron Burnham (1833–1916), ed. *Daily Telegraph* from 1855;
assumed name of Lawson 1875.
[16] Sir Thomas Francis Wade (1818–95), min. at Pekin 1871–83; for Derby's view of, see
below, 28 Aug. 1875.

same sort: saying that the basis of the Russian alliance with Austria was – No Polish movements on the part of Austria: No Sclave propaganda on the part of Russia: Mutual consultation on affairs outside the two empires.

3 February 1875. ... In a party point of view, our good fortune during the last twelve months has been extraordinary: if we lose our position, the fault is our own. Finance is our weak point just now: though not by the fault of Northcote, who is industrious and able.

... Telegram from Disraeli that the Queen wants alterations made in the speech, for which it is now rather late. I answered that before assenting I must know what was objected to, and on what grounds.

5 February 1875. ... Salisbury came home with us to dinner. ... In both Houses the opening was quiet, and the interest in the proceedings feeble.

6 February 1875. Breakfast at Grillions, or rather at the new rooms in Regent Street where the club now meets. About thirty came together.

... Cabinet at 3: sat till 5.30. We again discussed naval and military matters, but chiefly the first: and came to the conclusion, reluctantly, but at last without disagreement, that an increase of £500,000 in the estimates was not to be avoided. Some other matters were discussed, but of less importance.

... In our cabinet today, it was worth notice that though nobody was pleased at the decision which we were forced to come to, not even those who pressed it most strongly (for it makes an increase of the spirit duties, or something of that sort, inevitable) there was not a trace of hostile feeling, or of ill humour. From first to last, in this as in our earlier meetings, all have been anxious to come to an understanding: there has been no division into parties: and no foolish talk. It is the first time since I have held office that I remember business got through in a really satisfactory way.

... The internal govt of France is not a matter in which England can interfere: but I have never concealed my personal opinion that the Republic is for France the best possible alternative, and the restored empire probably the worst. ... But the best Republic for France would be one that should have a Marshal for President.

8 February 1875. D. of Bedford told me last night that his London estate ... is less than 130 acres in extent. His whole acreage is 80,000 acres. He declares the ordinary expenses, together with taxation, absorb 50 per cent of the rental: which I cannot understand...

10 February 1875. Cabinet at 3: sat till 5.30. We discussed South African matters, which I am afraid Carnarvon is trying to manage with too high a hand: Froude's influence over him is not good in that respect. He seems to wish to take from the settlers in Natal all control over native affairs: which may be more just as regards the natives, but is not prudent, as it will certainly make disaffection in the colony. But for the moment we are all agreed as to what shall be done.

A discussion followed on educational matters. Sandon being called in: he is very strong for compulsory schooling, I did not at first see why: but he is against school boards, and thinks that if more children can be forced into the existing schools, they can be kept up as at present on the voluntary system, to the great content of the local clergy. Hence his zeal. He says the various acts which restrict the labour of children are inadequately enforced. That which relates to agricultural children especially is a dead letter. He told us that there was provision for teaching 2,800,000 at present, that if every child without exception were in school, and for as long as it ought to be, room would be wanted for nearly 4,000,000: that 2,200,000 are actually on the books and that the average attendance on each day is about 1,600,000. The great trouble of the department seems to be irregular attendance.

We went through various clauses of the tenants' improvements bill, but did not finish it.

11 February 1875. Last night, I had from the Queen an odd rambling letter ... She is in an excited condition ... ... Disraeli says she writes to him nearly every day, sometimes oftener, and very wildly.

... Loftus[17] writes that Schouvaloff has been sending home reports on the state of parties and of opinion in England, which are much admired: (as S. speaks no English, & hardly understands it, his reports must be founded more on imagination than knowledge): he has enemies at home, and his profession of entire ignorance, made to me, can only be a pretence, either to draw out my views, or to excuse himself for giving no opinion of his own: probably the latter, as he is new to diplomacy, and afraid of committing himself. He, Schouvaloff, is considered as the probable successor to Gortschakoff ... This is from O. Russell.

Curious position of the great Powers: Russia, jealous of German power, is showing more & more sympathy for France: Bismarck sees this, and redoubles his attentions to the Russian govt to prevent a hostile alliance between the two: and they both pay court to Austria, which is equally afraid of offending either.

13 February 1875. Cabinet at 3: sat till 5.30.

... The cabinet occupied itself partly with Irish affairs, the coercion acts being discussed: partly with the question whether a commission shall issue to enquire into alleged corruption at Boston, which was decided in the negative: partly with a bill sketched out by Salisbury for dealing with the surplus revenues of Oxford University and the colleges: partly with the question what shall be done when Mitchel,[18] the escaped

---

[17] Amb. to Russia.

[18] John Mitchel (1815–75), Irish nationalist; twice elected for Tipperary, 1875, but seat awarded to Cons. opponent.

convict, claims to take his seat for Tipperary. (He is certain to be elected, probably without contest.) The law officers were called in, and it was argued that by law he is disqualified as a felon. If he had served his full term, or been pardoned, the disqualification would have ceased: but as neither of these things have happened, it continues.

17 February 1875. Cabinet till 3: sat till 4.45. Salisbury and Malmesbury both absent from illness. We discussed Mitchel's case: and again called in the Law officers, to settle course of proceeding: we discussed a plan which Carnarvon has much at heart, of extending the power of giving colonial pensions, so as to include the case of Gov. Eyre.[19] All present were against moving in the matter, and C. withdrew, at least postponed, his proposition. Details of the Irish peace preservation act were gone into: and the question of keeping up or doing away the convict prison at Gibraltar was raised, but we could not agree, and postponed it.

Disraeli tells me of a letter he has from the Queen, violent against Layard[20] to an extreme degree: she says he ought to be called 'Lie-hard': and applies epithets of abuse to him which D. said 'I can only describe as Billingsgate'. He has passed the matter over with no more notice than was inevitable: but he thinks her in a strange excited state of mind.

18 February 1875. Münster[21] called ... he said among other things that Saldanha[22] had seriously proposed to him that Germany should interfere in the Spanish civil war, with a proposal to divide Spain, allotting the northern provinces to Don Carlos, the rest to Alfonso! Münster naturally laughed at the idea: but the old man was quite serious. His object was looking at the matter from a Portuguese point of view, to have two weak neighbours instead of one strong one.

... A message from Disraeli asking to see me: I went to his house, found him anxious & uneasy: Cairns at the last moment has doubts as to the legality of the course to be taken about Mitchel, and suggests agreeing to the appointment of a committee. This might have been done in the first instance, and may still be done if the House show an inclination to it; but it clearly cannot be proposed by us, after having given notice of a different course.

20 February 1875. There dined with us, D. & Duchess of Bedford ... Mr Levy of the Telegraph ... 18, besides our two selves. I intend if

---

[19] E.J. Eyre (1815–1901), col. governor; gov. of Jamaica 1864–6, when recalled for undue severity.

[20] Min. at Madrid 1869–77.

[21] Georg Herbert, Count von Münster (1820–1902), German amb. in London 1873–85; amb. in Paris 1885–1900.

[22] Joao Carlos duque de Saldanha (1790–1876), Portuguese amb. to London; twice Portuguese premier.

possible to have one editor at each large dinner[23] we give: but they must not meet one another!

22 February 1875. Wrote again to the Queen ... She has not treated me to any of those explosions of temper which Disraeli talks of. I admit to her what is not to be denied, that Layard is wanting in tact and diplomatic smoothness: indeed diplomacy is the last profession he should have chosen.

24 February 1875. Cabinet at 3, sat till 4.40. Talk of various subjects as to which there is a motion in the House: division of the bishopric of Winchester: etc. but our chief business – dull, though useful – was to consider a bill by Cross for amending the law respecting the storage and transport of explosive substances.

27 February 1875. Cabinet summoned at 12, chiefly to discuss the state of the B. of Works: Lennox, as head of it, having contrived to quarrel with everybody ... Nothing was settled, as he has not answered the letter telling him that his complaints of Treasury interference are unfounded: indeed I believe he has not received it: but seeing that the cabinet felt some delicacy, the D. of Richmond being there, in saying what was evidently in the minds of all, I expressed plainly the opinion that while Lennox remained in his office, the quarrels which have disorganised it cannot be expected to end. I smoothed this over with compliments to his abilities, and suggestions that he might be transferred to another place: which is barely possible, but civil to say. Disraeli sensibly closed the discussion by saying that till we had his answer, we need not consider ulterior measures.

Sir M. Beach was called in, and we considered some Irish measures. One of the political prisoners released in 1871 has come back to Ireland, contrary to the pledge given: agreed to arrest him again. Some talk about Irish schools: agreed that further help from the Treasury is not desirable, unless on the condition of local support: at present the Treasury does nearly all, the localities benefited contribute little or nothing.

4 March 1875. The meeting of the Lords yesterday at the D. of Richmond's was hostile, the feeling against Cairns's Judicature Bill being all but unanimous: Redesdale, the Duke says, being very offensive in his language: Ld Shrewsbury equally so, but so mad that he only raised a laugh. The end of it is that the question is to be postponed till after Easter, and in the meanwhile the sense of the H. of Commons tested by a motion which some independent member will make. This looks unpleasantly like surrender: but with nearly all the Conservative

[23] Frederick Greenwood (1830–1909), ed. of *Pall Mall Gazette*, 1865–80, dined with Derby, 10 Mar. 1875, the D. of Richmond and 3 other peers (and Sanderson) present.

peers against us, and half the Whigs, the position is difficult, and it
may well be that no other course was possible. Disraeli is not, I think,
quite in sympathy with Cairns: it is one of the peculiarities of his mind
to dislike lawyers, and men of the middle class: and he is a little jealous
of colleagues who are not closely tied to him by personal influences.
Hence I suspect that he has not been unwilling to abandon the bill: as
indeed he showed last year, when both this and the Land Transfer Bill
were dropped for want of time – many people thought, without
adequate reason.

6 March 1875. Cabinet at 12 ... In Cabinet, we went through the
Agricultural Holdings Bill, making some few alterations. But our main
business was to consider how the Judicature Bill shall be dealt with.
Disraeli opened the subject with a long statement of the situation,
Richmond related what had passed at the meeting, & said, I have no
doubt with perfect truth, that it was useless to attempt to persuade the
Lords to part with their jurisdiction, all the Conservatives would be
against it and many of the Liberals. I spoke strongly against the plan –
which in the first instance seemed to offer a fair escape out of the
difficulty – of encouraging a motion in the Commons on the subject.
It was a bad precedent, and would expose us to charges of double-
dealing: since the motion would be supported by all our friends, and
by some members of the govt, while it was in effect one directed against
a measure which we had ourselves lately brought in. I put this strongly.
Hunt, Northcote, & Cross took the same views. Salisbury was for going
on with the motion. We had much discussion, but all friendly, every
one feeling that the situation is awkward, and trying to find a practicable
solution. In the end we decided that the simplest course was the best:
that as we could not carry the bill, we had better drop it, saying why
we did so: and ask time to consider what should be done, as the whole
question of judicature is at present in a provisional condition. This in
reality postpones our difficulties instead of settling them: but no other
arrangement seems practicable.

Acquiescing in what has been done, as best under the circumstances,
I am disappointed at the result. Not only have we let drop a useful
measure, and reopened an old controversy supposed to be settled, but
the evidence of a violent and reactionary temper on the part of our
supporters is a bad omen for the future. Should Disraeli, who to a
certain extent is able to control the H. of C., abandon his post, I do
not think I can go on with the rest of the party, either as leader or
follower.

8 March 1875. In the Lords, Cairns withdrew his Judicature Bill with
a brief explanation ...

9 March 1875. Saw Mr Levy, and talked over many things in a way
which may be useful.

10 March 1875. Cabinet at 12, which sat till 1.30. The sole question discussed was the course to be adopted on the Judicature Bill[24] – or rather, the Bill being dead, on what is to be substituted for it. We had a sharp, though quite amicable discussion, in which I took a good deal of part – indeed I think the principal part: Disraeli reserving himself as usual, and Cairns being less decided than from his position & interest in the subject it might be expected. We settled nothing finally, but it seemed to me pretty well agreed that the Act of 1873 – temporarily suspended – shall be allowed to come into operation in November, so that the English appeals shall pass to the new court. The Scotch & Irish appeals will remain for the present where they are. Walpole's motion to be if not actually withdrawn, at least indefinitely suspended, which is practically the same thing.

12 March 1875. Saw the Russian ambassador, just returning to Petersburgh. He has asked to see me, and to discuss the question of our relations in Central Asia: which we did at considerable length. I have made a note of the conversation. As usual, he professed to be without instructions, which is a convenient excuse for knowing & telling nothing. He enquired as to many points, apologising for indiscretion, etc. My answers were, as may be supposed, general and cautious: their purport as follows: 'We have land enough, and do not wish to advance our frontier in any direction: least of all to the westward: Afghanistan is a poor, half-savage & warlike country: we wish to be on good terms with its ruler, and to exercise over him the influence of an ally, but designs on his independence we have none. The same is true of Baloochistan and of Kashgar. The stories of our supplying the native chiefs in those two countries with arms & military instructions are fictions. If the Russians keep quiet, we shall keep quiet: but an advance on Merv would lead to a counter advance on our part against Herat, which would lead to complications, and place the two armies very near one another.' Our talk was accompanied on the Russian side, as to the entire frankness with which his govt desired to act, the impolicy of a system of mutual distrust, and so forth. I believe Schouvaloff to be really able, and like most able men, he sees the advantage of telling truth as a general rule: but it is impossible to rely on a Russian.

13 March 1875. 3, when cabinet. We sat till 5: discussing chiefly the question of Scotch banks in England, which seems a very puzzling one. In the end it was agreed to appoint a committee to examine it. We also talked of the exchanges proposed between France and England in W. Africa, but did not settle anything, except to consider them again.

---

[24] A judicature bill failed to pass in 1874. Reintroduced in 1875, it passed its 2 R. in H. of Lords, Feb. 1875. A reactionary caucus led to its withdrawal, and a new measure was introduced a month later.

We received a message from the Queen, to the effect that she considered Ltd Lyttelton's[25] bill about new bishoprics as an invasion of the prerogative: which I am afraid was received with some laughter, for it is absolutely free from objection on that score, whatever its other faults may be.

15 March 1875. Much social scandal about the P. of Wales, who has broken out in the old line. The object of his present attentions is a Miss Farrer, an Irish lady, said to be handsome, fast, and not too respectable to suit princely tastes. They are a good deal together, publicly and privately, the family not objecting.

The D. of Edinburgh is open-mouthed against the Queen who, as he declares, has turned him and his wife out of Buckingham house because he objected to shake hands with John Brown. There is nothing intrinsically improbable in the story, and it is certain that he lodges at the Charing Cross Hotel when in London: but his statements are not to be taken to be accurate.

... Lowe talked of the growing corruption of the press. When he first wrote for the Times, he said, editors never thought of going out in 'society': they held to their own position, which if obscure socially, was independent. Now all is changed: from Delane downwards every editor reckons on invitations to great houses as part of the perquisites of his office: the result is that they cannot write honestly about men & things. He instanced the adulation of Gladstone in the Telegraph: which certainly was fulsome enough: and specified Fortescue as a man whose position had been entirely made for him by the newspapers. He, or rather Ly Waldegrave, invited & courted all the journalists, so that whatever Fortescue might do, not one of them would write against him. I thought what Lowe said perfectly true...

17 March 1875. From Paris I hear that there is a good deal of vague apprehension, caused in part by the German note to Belgium, in part by the recent prohibition to export horses from Germany: which is considered as a sign of impending war. The German embassy disavows all military objects in connection with this decree, saying that it is for the sake of farmers, and to prevent Germany being drained of horses: but this is not believed, nor perhaps meant to be.

... The German game is evidently to promote disunion among European states. The German empire is stronger than any one of them singly, on land, and fears nothing except a combination: the Czar is known to be, though friendly, yet jealous of any increase of German power: and will not allow France to be crushed. This view, which is Loftus's, is confirmed by what I hear from Berlin ... At Constantinople, the three eastern Powers act as one, under the direction of Ignatieff.

[25] George Lyttelton, 6th Baron Lyttelton (1817–76), strong churchman.

Thus they can obtain their object, so far as it can be obtained by a demonstration of union & strength. But the result of this combination is that if the Turks are alarmed, and feel their weakness, which they do, they also feel that we, the English, are the only friends they have, and I doubt if at any time the personal influence of an English ambassador has been greater with the Porte than it is now. The fact that we do not care to use it for purposes of our own makes it all the greater.

18 March 1875. I have three letters from H. Stanley, who declares that his son is paralytic and must be brought home. Knowing that this has long been the wish of both father & son, who know that if in England he must be supported by me, I am a little sceptical, but promise enquiry...

O. Russell has had a curious conversation with Bismarck, marked with his usual affectation of perfect unreserve, which however we understand sufficiently not to be taken in by it. ... He praised Schouvaloff highly: said he was honest, truthful, inclined to peace, and would be the best successor to Gortschakoff. ... We should find Russian influence exerted against us in all quarters, especially as regards the Suez canal ... ... He spoke also of the danger to Germany: Russell asked from what quarter it could possibly come? He said from the union of France, Austria, & Russia...

... Now what is the meaning of this carefully prepared warning from Bismarck? It may be sincere, but more likely it is part of his plan to keep the Great Powers separate, by making each jealous of the other: and he has not improbably given the same caution to Russia to beware of our designs. In any case, I thought it wise to express gratitude for his advice: if honestly given, he deserves thanks: if not, the more we affect to be deceived the more we shall see into his game.

... Disraeli called to prepare me for a new scheme by Cairns on the judicature question: he did so with many professions of his confidence in my judgment, his wish to do all that I approved and nothing else, & so forth – partly sincere, for we are old friends, but partly, and very evidently, dictated by an apprehension that I should disapprove the plan. Thus his visit rather increased than lessened any feeling of distrust which I might have entertained. But our talk was confidential & cordial.

20 March 1875. Busy at home till 12, when a Cabinet, which sat not quite two hours. We discussed briefly the report of the Labour Laws Commission: the state of the finances, as to which Northcote's prospects are better than I had supposed, for he has good hope of being able to do without new taxes: an excess of £140,000 in naval expenditure which is discreditable to the department, and as to which an inquiry is to be set on foot, to know who is responsible: and Cairns's new plan for dealing with the Judicature question. This is, in substance, to set the new court of appeal as created by the Act of 1873 in motion, with some amendments of detail, which have been pointed out as necessary, and which it is supposed will not raise any objection: but he leaves in existence the final appeal to the H. of Lds, and to the Judicial Committee, suspending the operation of the Act as to these for a year, so as in effect to reserve the decision of the pending question till the session of 1876. Some conversation followed, but we all reserved our judgments, and in truth mine is not yet formed.

21 March 1875. Amused, at this audience, with Lytton: the Queen questioned him about French politics: he answered well enough, bringing in one or two things which are circulating about Macmahon[26] ... the Queen affected to be amused, but evidently without in the least understanding what they meant. She detests a joke or a sharp saying: a peculiarity I have often noticed: I suppose it is a kind of royal instinct: whatever approaches to satire is felt by princely persons as uncongenial and dangerous.

Disraeli talked yesterday about the Queen's correspondence with him: saying he was sure she had no idea that we were on intimate terms, and that like George III, she wanted to separate us and play us one against the other: it may be so, but I own this seems to me like over-refining. I asked if he had seen in her any trace of hereditary tendencies, in the way of eccentricity? He said not, he did not think she had altered much: he saw nothing unsound in her mind: she was very troublesome, very wilful and whimsical, like a spoilt child: not without sympathy for others, but totally without consideration for their feelings or wishes. All this is very much in accordance with my own observations. She complains to him often of the ingratitude of her children, who fear her, and dislike her: the P. of Wales gets on best with her: she has just sanctioned his going to India in the winter, which it was supposed she would resist vehemently.

23 March 18/5. The death of Count Jarmac, caused by cold weather acting on a weak constitution, is a real loss. Living in Ireland & London, he was at least half English: and knew Englishmen as well as they knew themselves. He had not, I think, eminent abilities: but he had perfect manners, tact, and experience of affairs: in the whole diplomatic service there was no man whom it was so easy to do business with, or so pleasant to talk to. I never found him unreasonable, and have no reason to believe that he ever deceived me.

24 March 1875. Gortschakoff has followed the example of his representative in London, and held a long and confidential conversation with Loftus on Asiatic affairs: half complaining that we don't trust him: protesting that Russia wants no extension of territory: and saying that

[26] Marshal MacMahon (1808–93), president 1873–9.

it is the press which has created the distrust which exists between the govts. Probably he refers to articles which have appeared in the M. Post: a journal to which Russia seems to attach more importance than belongs to it: perhaps because it was once inspired by Ld Palmerston.

... From Berlin O. Russell writes, that in his belief there is no fear of war for the present year. Bismarck is not likely to attack France while the French remain passive, and show no sign of making new alliances. R. does not think the Belgian business serious: it is only a sort of warning addressed to the clerical party all the world over ... He holds that if Germany engages in a new war, it is more likely to be against Austria...

... The Belgian govt are ... a little agitated by Bismarck's remonstrance ... ... Two objects are ascribed to the German govt – one, to find a plea for withdrawing gradually from their guarantee of Belgium – the other, to crush ultramontane resistance to German policy, even in foreign countries. I suspect the latter to be nearer the truth of the two: if indeed the whole proceeding is not more an effect of temper than of calculation.

26 March 1875. O. Russell writes, informing me that the Emperor of Germany had again taken the opportunity of warning him against unfriendly influences at Petersburgh: at the same time praising Schouvaloff in high, & even exaggerated terms. There is some intrigue going on here which I cannot make out. I suspect that whatever mischief is being made is rather at Berlin than in Russia.

29 March 1875 ... I see not the slightest abatement in Irish hostility to the Union. It is less demonstrative than formerly, because hopeless of success: but not less deeply felt.

30 March 1875. An amusing letter from Disraeli: it seems there is a great dispute about the P. of W.'s Indian journey: the Princess insists on going with him if he goes: the Queen will not hear of it, & regrets having given her consent, which she says she did under a misunderstanding. D. has been obliged to promise to bring the matter before a cabinet. I answered, saying that in my judgment the Princess ought not to go ... her going will double the expense: a consideration not to be lost sight of if India is to pay: besides, whether she goes or not, the P. is sure to run after women, and the scandal will be less if he does so in his wife's absence than if she were there.

31 March 1875. Left for Windsor ... ... Torrington[27] takes the foreigners over the armoury ... He (Ld T.) talks seriously, and with alarm, of the P. of W., who is gone off to Mentone on the plea of health, but travels with a certain Mrs Murieta ... who has made herself

[27] George Byng, Viscount Torrington (1812–84), lord-in-waiting 1859–84.

abundantly notorious in London. The thing is so openly done that it can hardly fail to make a scandal: T. says London is full of it...

2 April 1875. News by second post of the death of H. Stanley[28] in a letter from the widow. ... Considering the life led by my poor uncle the only cause for surprise is that it did not come sooner. His whole history is a puzzle to me. I have heard my father say more than once, that 'Henry' could have done more than he, if he had tried: his ability when young was certainly considerable: his power of pleasing, by all accounts, singularly great: and he had warm and active friends for many years after he had ceased to mix in society: but they dropped off at last, worn out by importunity, and disgusted by finding confidence betrayed. I believe that my grandfather and father have paid for Henry Stanley first and last not much less than £100,000. He played high, and in bad company: he was obliged to retire from the army, I believe in consequence of drunkenness: but the circumstance that finally cut him off from the world was his marriage with a woman whom he had literally picked up in the streets, and whose attachment to him was certainly not exclusive. Why he did this, whether in sheer weakness, or to spite his family, I never knew: after the marriage he gave up all show of respectability. In earlier years he used to have a strange habit of disappearing for weeks and months together, leaving no address with any friend: on one of these occasions I remember that my father employed the police to find out where he was: this for some reason he treated as a grave offence. He was always in debt: lived at Boulogne and Brussels for some years: was once at least (I think twice) in prison: and exhausted the patience of friends by continual demands upon them: not always accurate as to fact. My father seldom passed a month or six weeks without some application from him: though he had given £12,000 in a lump as a provision for the family which now goes to his children: besides paying debts again and again. On me his claims were moderate, and I am glad to think that they were never refused. On the whole, I imagine that few men have had more chances in life, and very few have so thoroughly muddled them away.[29]

Of his three sons, one is dead, leaving a widow and children; another, childless and I believe never married, lives in Ireland, and has lately talked of emigrating to S. Africa: he is in bad health, feeble, and not

---

[28] Henry Thomas Stanley (1803 – 2 Apr. 1875), 2nd s. of 13th E. of Derby; m. Anne Woolhouse, 1835, having issue Edward (1838–?), Charles (1839–77) who had issue, Henry (1840–67), who left a widow and children, and Charlotte (d. 1872). Henry's widow was to prove even worse in her improvidence.

[29] Cf. Robert Blake, *Disraeli* (1966), 71–3, for one such episode, for which Derby (the premier) blamed Disraeli.

likely to do either good or harm: the eldest was set up in business in Manchester, failed discreditably, with cooked accounts, married an actress or singer, at one of the minor theatres: went to Australia: came back: went out again to New Zealand, and is there now. He is hopeless: resembling the father in character, but without his social charm: the other two have done nothing discreditable, though both poor creatures. There is a daughter, who died imbecile some time ago. Of the grandchildren I know little or nothing. There is at Knowsley a portrait of Henry Stanley...

5 April 1875. Morier sends a report, very wordy as usual, but curious, of the system of spying established by Bismarck: the German ministers are watched, and their reports compared with those of the secret agents, who are the more trusted of the two. Nothing like it, according to Morier, has been seen since the days of Fouché – if then.

... Morier's description of the German, or rather Bismarckian, system is confirmed indirectly by what reaches me from many quarters. It seems impossible to doubt that the possession of almost absolute power, acting on a nature always impulsive & violent, has developed in the German statesman a tendency like that shown by the first Napoleon between 1805 and 1812: a tendency difficult to describe in exact terms, but which is the disease of despotism. Not only can he bear no opposition: not only is resistance to his wishes a crime, even on the part of foreign & independent States, but mere acquiescence in his authority is not enough. It must be exercised and felt at every moment and in every place. Nothing must be done in Europe in which he does not at least seem to take the lead. ... I suspect the anti-English feeling which is evidently strong at Berlin. We are not dependents – therefore we are suspicious, and to be watched. I note these things for future use.

6 April 1875. Called on Disraeli at his request: found him in high spirits, confident of the future, and chiefly perplexed about the business of the P. of W.'s Indian tour, which seems likely to end in a quarrel between mother & son. According to D.'s story, the Prince said a few words to him on the subject in an offhand way, and then obtained the Queen's consent by alleging that his plan had the warm approval of the Prime Minister and the cabinet – this on the strength of a mere civil expression of hope that he would enjoy his tour ... The Queen is aware of the trick, and furious. But this seems her normal condition where her family are concerned.

Col. Mansfield[30] called: just returned from Warsaw, where he has been 10 years, and wants a change. He is a man I think well of,

[30] Lt-col. (Sir) Charles Edward Mansfield (1828–1907), min. to Rumania 1876–8, then S. American posts until ret. 1894.

cultivated, shrewd, and refined in manners: which a good many of our consuls are not.

8 April 1875. Cabinet at 12: we discussed the Chancellor's plan of dealing with the Judicature question: I was specially appealed to by Disraeli, & was compelled to say that though not much liking it, I saw no alternative. We then discussed some minor questions of no great moment: among them that of how the H. of C. should deal with a petition accusing Cockburn of corruption and partiality in the Tichborne trial. To our great surprise, both the Speaker and Sir E. May[31] were for refusing to receive it: but it is a monstrous doctrine that the House is not to listen to a charge of misconduct against a judge, who can be made responsible to no other tribunal. We all agreed that it should not be rejected, especially as Kenealy is about to bring on a motion on the subject.

Then came the budget: Northcote is satisfied with the results of last year: he has got a surplus of half a million over estimate, and of £600,000 over expenditure. For next year, he estimates income at £75,585,000: expenditure at £75,263,000: giving a surplus of more than £300,000. He will make no changes in taxation, except a small rearrangement of stamps on offices, and of brewers' licences: but he has two schemes, one for fixing the rate of income tax for 3 years, the other for setting apart a fixed yearly sum for interest of debt and sinking fund together, so that the larger may increase. Both are well intended, but I doubt whether either one or the other will work. It was mentioned in the course of our conversation that income tax now gives £1,900,000 for each penny: and that the natural rate of increase in revenue, apart from the effect of reductions of taxation, is £2,000,000 in a good year, and £1,600,000 in one of rather dull trade. This is the calculation of Mr Welby.[32] I cannot however but think that the permanent revenue officials are rather unduly sanguine. I thought so last year, and am confirmed in the opinion. The prosperity of the last 30 years has been so great that its continuance is regarded as a law of nature.

... Saw Gavard ...[33] I tried to impress upon him, what the French will never see, that the German military preparations are quite as much the result of fear as of fresh aggressive designs...

9 April 1875. Saw Ld Lyons: he reports the French much alarmed, & expecting or at least fearing war: but he cannot say why.

... Münster came, and told me that Bismarck is much agitated by the preparations which France is making: that he is convinced the

---

[31] Sir T. Erskine May, 1st Baron Farnborough (1815–86), clerk of H. of Commons 1871–86; cr. peer 1886.

[32] R.E. Welby, 1st Baron Welby (1832–1915), Treasury official; cr. peer 1894.

[33] French chargé d'affaires.

French meditate a new war, and that soon: that in 1876 or 1877 their army will be in its highest state of efficiency, and then they will make their attack: that Gambetta and the war party are now virtually in power: that Germany deprecated a war, having got all that war could give but, if the attack was to be made, it would never do to let the enemy choose his own time: in short, his govt thought the situation serious. I combated these views to the utmost of my power, saying, as I really think, that whatever ideas of revenge to be obtained at some future period the French nation may entertain, they do not dream of going to war with Germany singlehanded. I pressed this strongly, but without much effect. It is plain that Bismarck is disposed to resent as a menace any attempt on the part of the French govt to re-assert their claim to a place among Great Powers – which is not satisfactory in the interest of peace.

10 April 1875. Cabinet at 12. The chief subject discussed was the budget. We rejected Northcote's proposal of trying to secure the income tax for 3 years, as contrary to recent practice, and certain to provoke opposition, while it might even turn out inconvenient to ourselves, in the event of our wishing to make any alteration. In the discussion on this scheme I took the lead: all, I think, were of one mind: and Northcote gave way with excellent temper. His other plan about the debt seems ineffective, but is well intended, and harmless: no one objected to it, and he will do as he likes. We discussed the Tichborne petition again, and the Prince's visit to India.

13 April 1875. Walk and talk with Carnarvon whom I caution as to his plans for dealing with the S. African natives. They are large and well-meant, but he hardly allows enough, as it seems to me, for the strength of colonial opposition.

14 April 1875. Cabinet at 3, which sat till 5: we discussed some matters of detail, but were chiefly occupied with the case of the Gaicowar[34]: a sufficiently perplexing one. He was tried on a charge of trying to poison the Resident, Col. Phayre: the commission being composed of three Europeans, and three natives: the former were all for finding him guilty, the latter for acquittal. Consequently no decision was come to. The evidence is strong against him, and he has been guilty of various other offences, as to which there is no dispute. What is now to be done with him? Ld Northbrook & all his advisers say he must be deposed: all the Council being with him except Sir H. Maine. This view the cabinet concurred in, though feeling the awkwardness involved in thus seeming to reverse the decision of the commission of inquiry. We can however do it in such a manner as to show that his deposition is on the general ground of long-continued misgovernment, not on the specific charge

[34] Gaekwar of Baroda, deposed 1875.

of poisoning, which has not been proved against him.

16 April 1875. Saw Münster, who was authorised to give assurances as to friendly intentions towards Belgium: but he again began to talk about French armaments in a vague, disquieting way: professing on the part of his govt uneasiness which it is impossible he should really feel. One thing said by him in part explained this anxiety. I had contended that whatever might be the preparations made by France, Germany would still be the stronger power: this he did not dispute: but he said, look at the difference of the situation of the two countries. France has virtually only one frontier to defend ... we are assailable on all sides. 'Well', I answered, 'but you can send 700,000 men across your frontier in any direction.' (I wanted to see whether he would admit this.) 'Yes', he said, 'in a few weeks we could: 500,000 at first, and the rest to follow.' 'And', he added, 'our men are all there: the French forces are half on paper'. It did not seem wise or necessary to point out how this last, evidently sincere, utterance, contradicted the former professions of alarm.

17 April 1875. The Belgian minister came to ask if I had news of the state of the dispute between his govt and that of Germany: he did not seem alarmed or uneasy. I could tell him nothing that he did not know before.

Cabinet at 3: sat till 4.30. The chief business discussed was Carnarvon's favourite project for an exchange of territory with the French in Africa: they taking over the Gambia, we receiving in return their settlements on the Gold Coast, and some small ports which they have near Sierra Leone. The strongest argument in favour of the arrangement is the risk of war with the tribes near the Gambia, if we keep our possessions in that part.

We settled also that Kenealy shall have a day assigned for his motion against the judges, which he is evidently anxious to keep on the paper as long as possible without bringing it on.

18 April 1875. Letters received from Lumley,[35] who is evidently uneasy at the state of the Belgian controversy with Germany...

... Russell wrote some days ago that Bismarck has contrived to make the Emp. & Crown Prince believe that France meditates an invasion of Germany through Belgium. He, Russell, does not believe in war, but says that half the diplomatists do. The beginning of the disturbance he ascribes to anger at the reconciliation of Italy & Austria, which puts an end to the German game of playing off one of these states against the other.

19 April 1875. Statter came, and talked of various negotiations with

---

[35] Min. in Brussels.

railway companies to which he is attending ... ... In all £180,000 at least, but I don't know when I shall get it.

20 April 1875. Saw ... Gavard, who came to talk about China, Greece, etc. He said little about the Belgian business.

... Received late at night an extremely satisfactory telegram from Loftus, to the effect that the Czar has sent out instructions to his general in Central Asia to abandon the plan of establishing a fort on the Atrek, to make no move in the direction of Merv, and generally to abstain from all demonstrations of a warlike nature against the Turcoman tribes. The reason assigned for this order is the wish to do nothing that can excite the 'jealous susceptibility' of the English, which the Emperor wishes to respect, though not admitting that it has any reasonable basis. This order is the work of Schouvaloff, and does credit to the sincerity of his pacific assurances. I conceive it also probable that the Russian govt is well aware of the risk of a general war in 1876, and does not wish to have any part of his army engaged in Asiatic operations, at a distance from the real scene of action.

21 April 1875. Cabinet early: announced the Russian telegram, which gave general satisfaction: discussed a question raised by Rajah Brooke,[36] whether he shall be allowed or encouraged to extend his territories in the direction of Brunei, as he desires: we decided in the negative, having annexed land enough (Fiji and Gold Coast) and fearing to create disturbance in those parts. The course of the Kenealy debate on Friday was talked over, and details of some bills settled, but nothing of much moment. We sat from 12 to 1.30.

... Dinner to 42 persons at F.O. and party afterwards. About 2200 invitations went out, and perhaps half the number came.

... Talk after cabinet with Disraeli about Pembroke: he never goes near his office, partly from ill health, partly from indolence: and ought to resign. It is a pity, for he has ability, but habits of work seem wanting. I recommend Cadogan[37] for employment.

22 April 1875. H. of Lds ... committee on tenant right bill, which was well and carefully discussed in detail. The subject was familiar to most peers present, and I never heard a better or more thorough sifting of the clauses of a bill. No long speeches, and very little nonsense. Entire absence of party feeling: a listener with eyes shut would not have known from which side the various speeches proceeded. The Whigs being all landlords, dare not try to outbid us in concessions to the tenants.

---

[36] Sir Charles Brooke (1829–1917), 2nd Raja of Sarawak; succ. uncle, 1868.

[37] George Cadogan, 5th E. Cadogan (1840–1915), succ. 1873; under-sec. for war, *vice* Pembroke, 1875; for colonies, 1878–80; 1d privy seal 1886–92; lord-lt of Ireland (in cabinet) 1895–1902; for Hardy on Cadogan as his junior min., see *GH*, 359.

23 April 1875. Saw Beust:[38] long and interesting conversation ... did not believe in a new French war ... but hinted that Austria is more likely to be the object of attack. Thought Bismarck very likely to be swayed by personal impulses and caprices, and that his sayings and doings were not always to be considered as the result of a calculated policy. Was glad that the policy of reconciliation with Italy had been adopted: had himself advised it long ago ... he (Beust) talked of the effect the reconciliation had produced at Berlin, and evidently considered it the cause of the late war-panic.

24 April 1875 (Saturday). Wrote to Sir B. Frere to offer his son a diplomatic appointment, if he chooses for him that ill-paid and wearisome profession.

Walk with M. early. Office between 1 and 2. No diplomatists. Cabinet at 3, but we had scarcely any business, and what there was related to H. of C. matters, as to which the peers present had little to say. Some uneasiness caused by proceedings of the Viceroy. He has sent a telegram *en clair*, pointing out the differences between his views and those of the home authorities: and as the whole previous correspondence has been in cypher, it is difficult to avoid the suspicion that this change has been made on purpose. He has not managed the business of the Gaekwar judiciously, and seems to wish now to throw the responsibility on us. However, the Whigs cannot attack us without attacking him, which they will hardly do: and indeed we know that the Indians in parliament, Halifax, Argyll, Grant Duff,[39] and Sir G. Campbell,[40] are all favourable to the course we have taken.

Left D. St. about 5: walk to Cromwell Rd: dined at home, and quiet evening.

25 April 1875 (Sunday). Keston with Sanderson: London again at 3: called in Cromwell Rd. Mary Galloway and Sanderson dined with us ...

... More letters from Madrid, in the same strain as before ...

26 April 1875 (Monday). Balances received from Moult ...

Many letters: walk early for exercise. Levee at 2: got away about 3: office till 5: then to H. of Lds, expecting a motion by Ld Russell on Belgian affairs, but he had to put it off ... All ended early.

There dined with us at home, old Ly Westminster, her daughter Ly Theodore, and the Galloways. At Berlin, the panic has subsided: and the fashionable language is to abuse the press for having created it: said press having acted strictly up to their orders. The Emp. wishes for

[38] Austrian amb. (until 1878).

[39] Sir M.E. Grant Duff (1829–1906), Lib. M.P. 1857–81; under-sec. for India 1868–74; for cols. 1880–1; gov. of Madras 1881–6.

[40] Sir George Campbell (1824–92), lt-gov. of Bengal 1871–4; Lib. M.P. 1875–92.

peace, but he is old & feeble: his son is too weak to resist Bismarck: in short the minister is Emperor, and will do as he likes. The German people prefer peace, but will be easily persuaded that another war is necessary to finish the work of consolidation.

27 April 1875 (Tuesday). Many letters & boxes: but nearly clear by 11. Walk with M. in the park. Fine hot day. Office about 1.

Agreed to appoint three attachés, as they are wanted: Balfour, a son of Ly Blanche, & brother of the present member for Hertfordshire: Otway, a son of the late undersec. who is recommended by Ld Wilton, Cochrane, & others: and Frere, son of Sir Bartle.

... Saw M. Gavard: no other diplomatists called. Wrote to O. Russell, and to Adams at Paris.

News that the Sultan had suddenly, and without apparent cause, dismissed his Grand Vizier, Hussein. The change is on the whole a loss: Hussein, an ignorant Turk, a soldier and nothing else, originally hostile to the English, and indeed to all foreigners, but fairly honest for a Turk, and of good natural capacity, had gradually come to be very friendly, and our own relations with him were of late as satisfactory as we could wish. His overthrow is probably the result of a Russian intrigue: but no details are known.

H. of Lds, which adjourned in half an hour; walk with Sanderson by the new embankment to Chelsea.

Dined The Club ... ... Pleasant evening.

28 April 1875 (Wednesday). Signed 17 leases in Bootle & K[irk]dale, giving exactly £200 new rent. Many letters & papers: nothing specially important.

Walk with M. in the park: Cabinet at 12: we sat till 1.30. The chief business done was the consideration of a proposal by Carnarvon for the confederation of the various South African colonies, including the two independent states of the 'Orange Free State' and 'Transvaal Republic'. He thinks it may be possible to induce these to join in a common policy as regards the treatment of the native races: and as a first step he proposes to summon a conference of representatives from the colonies to consider the matter, inviting the two republics to do the same. His scheme was sharply criticised, and I think no member of the cabinet quite likes it: but the proposal for a conference does not seem dangerous: the worst that can happen is that it should fail. – I cannot but see with some apprehension a tendency in Carnarvon's mind towards the revival of the old authoritative, or absolutist, system in dealing with colonies: a disposition no doubt encouraged by Froude, who able as he is, has caught something of Carlyle's liking for 'enlight- ∨
ened despotism': I have cautioned him on the subject as far as could be done without offence: and I can perceive that my apprehensions are shared by several of our colleagues.

... Letters and despatches from Adams:[41] he represents Decazes as very uneasy, which is not difficult to believe, and as saying that the Germans seemed to regard it as a *casus belli* that France should have either an ally or an army. 'Europe ought to interfere to put a stop to such outrageous pretensions' – easier said than done.

Walk with Sanderson late in the afternoon: quiet dinner and evening.

29 April 1875 (Thursday). Walk with M. in Kensington gardens. Bought a drawing in the Strand ... Office at 1. Received the Argentine minister, newly arrived. No other diplomatic visitor. Routine business, but nothing important. Easy day. H. of Lds at 5, and stayed till 8. Long speech from Ld Selborne on the Judicature Bill ... ... Mary Galloway and young Ld H. Russell dined with us.

Sudden death of Ld Hobart[42] announced last night: Salisbury tells me today, rather to my surprise, that he has offered the post to Lytton ... Lytton is quite fit for the place, as far as brains go: but he has weak health, no great love for business, and is much devoted to his wife and children, whom he could hardly take with him. I expressed wonder at Salisbury's choice, which he vindicated on the ground that it was desirable to have a man of rank in that position, and one accustomed to the conciliatory habits of diplomacy, as he would have trouble in his relations with the Gov. Gen. on one hand, and with the permanent officials on the other.

Talk with Carnarvon who rather alarms me: saying the power and popularity of the H. of C. is diminishing, that of the Crown is increasing: in the event of a struggle the Crown would have the people on its side, and more to the same effect: which to me seems little better than nonsense, but it is an unsafe sort of nonsense to be talked by a minister.

30 April 1875 (Friday). No letters of importance. Business till 11, then walk for exercise, sharply: office a little before 1. Saw there Gavard & Münster, but they both came about matters of detail, and had nothing new to tell me. Decazes, it seems, is easier in mind for the present, but apprehensive as to what may be coming next year. I could not say he had no reason for anxiety: but I pointed out two things for consideration: one, that assuming Bismarck to intend a new war, the chances were much in favour of Austria, not France, being the victim: Austria having German provinces to lose, France no territory which Germany could hope to hold, except by sheer force: the other, that the Russian govt, though unwilling to interfere, would not see with pleasure the whole equilibrium of Europe disturbed for the aggrandisement of Germany.

Peabody meeting at 4: Gen. Schenck & Sir C. Lampson: we settled

[41] (Sir) Francis Adams (1826–89), acting min. at Paris 1874–81, when Lyons absent; min. at Berne 1881–8.
[42] Gov. of Madras 1872–5.

to begin building on the Grosvenor Road estate, 7 blocks to be extended
hereafter: cost, including land, under £5000 per block: expected return
about $3\frac{5}{8}$ per cent.

Home at 5, and there being nothing in the Lords to require my
attendance, drove with M. to Hampstead Heath, where we walked &
sat for more than an hour, the evening being warm & pleasant.

1 May 1875 (Saturday). Wet cold day: letters & papers, of which I have
many, till near 12, when to cabinet.

We discussed the state of parliamentary business: which in H.C. is
getting confused. The budget debate is expected to bring out Gladstone
and the opposition leaders, and to last two nights. The Irish have
succeeded in their object of wasting time, and the Coercion Acts are
not yet passed. There is to be a discussion on privilege, raised by Ld
Hartington, which will probably not give trouble, but will take time.
Altogether things look as if the session would be neither easy nor short.

Hunt proposed to us a loan of a million to fortify various coaling
stations, now unprotected, in the colonies. He said with truth that ships
were now wholly dependent for warlike purposes on coal: and that a
squadron might be crippled by an enemy burning its supplies. We
talked the matter over, but all agreed (I leading the opposition) that to
come forward with a proposal to borrow money, just after launching a
scheme for lessening debt, would be absurd: reviving all the worst
features of the old sinking fund: so that whether the thing ought to be
done or not, it ought not to be done with borrowed money, nor at this
time.

The rest of the business was a discussion on clauses of the land bill,
and on Sunday closing of public houses in Ireland.

Talk with Salisbury: Lytton refuses Madras on account of his children,
as I expected: his refusal is a good escape, for with weak health, absence
of mind, and no taste or fitness for executive action, he must have been
a failure. He is just in his place at Lisbon. I suggested Layard, who
though rough, is ready and able: Salisbury talked to my utter surprise,
of Bath: who though rather sharp, has no habits of business, no
experience of any kind, strong prejudices of rank and class which make
him unpopular at home, and an amount of personal conceit which is
offensive. I protested strongly, and I hope not without effect. As an
alternative choice to Layard, I named Ld Bury:[43] he is a late convert
to the Conservative party: one of some importance on account of his
old Whig connexion, which may lead others similarly circumstanced

[43] William Keppel, 7th E. of Albemarle (1832–94), styled Lord Bury 1851–91, when
succ. father as earl; raised to Lords, 1876; under-sec. for war 1878–80, 1885–6; Lib. M.P.
until 1874; R.C. convert 1879; m. dau. of Sir A. McNab, Canadian premier.

to follow: he has held minor offices and I have a distinct recollection of his making an excellent speech in H.C. many years ago. He would be I think both a competent & a popular governor.

Home early, & working there: Academy dinner, the usual party, a whole batch of royal people, ministers, ex-ministers, and miscellaneous celebrities. Matthew Arnold made a neat little speech in his peculiar vein, which pleased me, though I could not hear all. Disraeli was happy also: he said little enough in substance, but said it with his peculiar felicity of phrase.

2 May 1875 (Sunday). Keston by 10.25 train with M. The woods in special beauty, but yesterday having been wet, there was no sitting about possible, and after visiting our old friends, the Holwood lakes, we returned by 3 p.m. We had meant to stay on till 5 p.m. ... Called in Cromwell Rd. Sanderson and Mary dined with us.

3 May 1875 (Monday). Up early, rather nervous and uncomfortable at the prospect of an unusually busy week. At work by 8. Walk round Regents park, sharply, for air and exercise: busy on letters & papers till 1, when to office.

... Office 1 to 5: no visitors, except the Belgian minister, who came to leave with me the reply of his govt to the German demands.

In Lds, question by Ld Russell about Belgium, which I answered in as cautious & guarded a manner as I could.

... Wrote to Loftus, O. Russell, and Morier: despatches & letters from all parts of the world. They are not altogether satisfactory as to the prospects of peace. Moltke openly says that France ought to be summoned to disarm: that the Great Powers should advise the French govt in that sense ...   ... Bismarck's own language is that the French assurances are satisfactory: but the 'officious' press, which ... is notoriously directed by B. continues as menacing as before.

Lumley writes from Brussels that the state of affairs is critical: that German officers talk freely of the approaching campaign: that it is thought if war breaks out Bismarck will occupy Belgium as a military measure ... – The situation is perplexing and dangerous: something may be hoped from Russian intervention, for it is not the interest of Russia to allow Germany to domineer over the whole Continent.

4 May 1875 (Tuesday). Up early, at work by 8: cleared off all business by 10: then walk for exercise. Office at 12.

Newspapers all mention the little debate of last night: and approve the caution of the answers given.

... Meeting of the Cotton Famine Relief Fund to settle the new scheme for a convalescent hospital, which has been before Chancery. It has taken a long while, but the money is rolling up.

In Lds, moved the second reading of the International Copyright Act, but only spoke five minutes. No debate.

... Dined at home, & quiet evening.

5 May 1875 (Wednesday). ... Drawing room: got away early, and office by 4 p.m. Found there only routine business to dispose of: and finished all there was. Cabinet at 6, which sat till 7: the question discussed was one which has lately excited the H. of Commons a good deal, as to the power at present vested in any one member to exclude strangers. ... Hartington lately raised the question of exclusion and proposed resolutions, which however were obviously defective: Disraeli opposed them, in which he was right: but he provided no substitute, and seemed inclined to leave matters as they were, which will not do. Since the discussion he has found out his mistake: and this cabinet is called to repair it. We agreed to an expedient which will probably serve the purpose: allowing any member to move for clearing the galleries, on which, if opposed, a division shall be taken without debate. All present agreed, after much talk, and it was rather disorderly talk. I think I have noticed that cabinets held late in the day seldom go off well: men come tired with other business, and impatient to finish: they are more disposed to gossip & less willing to listen.

6 May 1875. Letter from the Principal of Edinburgh University, asking for my promised donation of £1000: I sent it to him.

... Stayed at home all morning, working on army papers: office only for a short time: I forget whom I saw, except Gavard, who came in a state of much alarm and excitement. I reassured him as well as I could, but it was not much use: in fact I could not deny the apparent reality of the danger. I could only say that one of two things was clear: either that Bismarck means war, or that for some purpose of his own, he wishes it to be thought that he does: and that the latter alternative seemed to me to be the more probable.

The papers are full of these rumours of war ... ... Yet whether Bismarck means it or not, there is no doubt that the whole military party at Berlin wish it, and only regret that time is being lost.

Angry scene in H. of C., Disraeli having declared, perhaps in rather too strong language, that he meant the measures of govt to pass, however long the session might last. Gladstone rose in fury, and talked violently, probably being aware that most of his former colleagues (though not Ld Hartington) have combined with the Irish members to waste time, in the hope of preventing legislation: when they will have a cry about the session being barren of results.

7 May 1875. In the Commons, Gladstone, who seems to have quietly taken again his old post as leader, attacked the budget with unusual vehemence: Northcote answered ... and in the judgment of the House, had the better of the wrangle.

Conversation with Disraeli ... on prospects of war & peace: the Queen eager to do something, & pleased with my letter, as he says.

8 May 1875. Letter from O. Russell, brought by Schouvaloff, who is just returned from Berlin. He brings the thoroughly satisfactory news that the Emperor of Russia, who will be at Berlin on Monday, is determined to insist on peace being maintained, even at the risk of a rupture with Germany. This, as Russell says, is a heavy blow to Bismarck, and it remains to be seen whether he will accept the situation quietly, or break out in some unexpected way. The humiliation is the more severe if, as is alleged, Austria joins with Russia: Austria, whose subjection to Germany was treated as a matter of course: and the ultimate absorption of whose German provinces is an object steadily kept in view at Berlin.

... Ld Lyons called, to ask if it was necessary that he should go back at once? I said no, for as matters stand there is nothing urgent...

... Saw Lytton ... He says he never thought of accepting Madras: health & children made it impossible.

Cabinet at 3, chiefly on Irish business, but I read and got sanctioned a telegram to O. Russell, instructing him to support whatever efforts the Emperor of Russia may make at Berlin for the preservation of peace. We sat only till 4.30. I thought Disraeli tired and ill. He said he had a little gout.

9 May 1875. Madras is at last given away: to the Duke of Buckingham,[44] whose acceptance of it is singular, for he is well off, having nearly £30,000 a year, and has not shown anxiety for public employment. I think he is the first Duke who has served in India. The appointment is fairly good: the Duke is a man of business,[45] and will keep things in order: but he piques himself too much on doing things for himself, attending to details which are better left to subordinates, and he is not conciliatory to the persons he acts with. At least such was the impression he left behind in Downing Street in 1868.

... In the afternoon Schouvaloff called by appointment: he confirmed the news sent by O. Russell as to the intentions of the Czar: adding many curious details. The impression left on his mind by his conversations with Bismarck evidently is that B. is suffering from over-excitement caused by labour, excitement, and imprudent habits of life. He says that B. complained to him of being often unable to sleep the whole night through, and told him that the doctors had said that unless he retired he would not be alive, or would be disabled, in a year or two at most.

10 May 1875. Wrote to Gen. Ponsonby,[46] giving in fuller detail than above an account of Schouvaloff's conversation.

The Queen has decided to write to the Emperor of Russia asking

---

[44] Governor 1875-80.
[45] Chairman, L.N.W.R., 1853-61.
[46] Sir H. Ponsonby (1825-95), Queen's priv. sec.

him to do what he can to preserve peace ... ... I doubt whether the expression of her personal wishes would go as far with the Czar as she supposes, even if the matter were not already settled.

... Carnarvon came: in a fidget about the question of war & peace ...

11 May 1875. Telegrams from Berlin gave entirely satisfactory assurances as to the maintenance of peace: and I had no hesitation in authorising Bourke to say to the H. of C. that all danger of war is over.

Cabinet at 6, but the business was not important, nor much concerned the peers, as it related almost wholly to the progress of bills through the H. of Commons.

12 May 1875. The purchase of Keston has certainly embarrassed my finances during the last six months as far as money goes: but the inconvenience if it can be called one is only temporary: and I do not regret the purchase, whether I consider the pleasure it gives to M., or that which I myself derive from it. Though less than 100 acres, it is so completely shut in that ten times the extent could hardly give more privacy: the natural and artificial beauty of the ground is greater than I have seen in any other place: the land immediately adjoining, Holwood & Keston Common, adds to the enjoyment, being picturesque and little visited: and the nearness to London makes it possible to pass a few hours there, when even Fairhill would be out of reach.

13 May 1875. Settled that Sanderson, who has been working rather too hard, shall go down to the house at Fairhill next week while we are at Knowsley, with his brother, and take a holiday there.

... Talk ... with Disraeli about rewards to scientific men: a matter with which I think he might advantageously deal. He seemed well disposed.

15 May 1875. Knowsley by 10 a.m. train ...

16 May 1875. Church ...

20 May 1875. Anyhow, in 5½ years I shall have cleared away more than £460,000 of debt ... And if I am paid honestly, I shall clear off by Dec. £50,000 more, making £510,000 in 6 years, and finishing the work which when I succeeded, I thought must inevitably occupy 10 or 12 years.

Andrassy excuses himself from joining in our movement at Berlin by saying that he had personally received from Bismarck such assurances of peaceable intentions, that he could not in good manners make any fresh representation on the subject. An ingenious come-off, the fact being that he is afraid of his neighbour. He talks a good deal of Bismarck's state of mind, and seems to think him troubled with something like monomania on the subject of conspiracies to murder him, and plots against the German empire.

French gratitude is loudly and warmly expressed for our exertions to help France in the late crisis. These expressions are in part no doubt sincere, but they are also intended to make it appear in the eyes of Europe that we have taken the French as against the German side, instead of simply intervening to keep the peace, as is the fact. Decazes however is behaving sensibly, and has induced the minister of war to renounce, or at least to postpone, a projected increase of army estimates. The intention to raise a new loan is also abandoned.

The German press continues to write against Belgium ... ... Some of the German papers write up the annexation of Holland with a slice of Belgium – France to have the rest as compensation for the loss of Alsace & Lorraine. Others have discovered that it is only Prussia which guaranteed Belgian independence and that as Prussia is now merged in Germany, the guarantee has ceased to exist.

There is something comic in the language mutually employed by Gortschakoff & Bismarck in speaking of one another and of the recent interview.

Gortschakoff declares his success to have been complete, and says that his object now must be to prevent an undue feeling of humiliation on the part of Germany, that it is enough to have succeeded, without boasting of success, etc.

Bismarck speaks with extreme irritation of Gortschakoff, describing him as a vain old man, long become unfit for affairs, and who with one foot in the grave, has nothing better to do than to *poser* in the part of peacemaker before Europe, affecting to have prevented a war which nobody meant to make.

At the same time he (Bism.) does not retract what he had said about French intentions. He thinks that they mean to have their revenge, but says that his language will be not like, like Moltke, 'Up and at them', but 'Let them come on if they will'.

O. Russell has been impressed with the Czar's earnestness in talking of his wish to maintain peace, and friendly relations with England. He believes him sincere in both respects, and certainly appearances point in that direction. Gortschakoff too is very cordial in his language towards England: volunteering to tell O.R. that Bismarck has been trying to make mischief between the two countries.

Bismarck, after laying the blame of the late panic on the shoulders of Moltke, now says that it has been got up by the press and by stockjobbers. The former assertion is partly true, but he ought to have added that the journals which are in fault were those notoriously inspired by himself.

I think the above are the points of most importance in my official correspondence of the week.

21 May 1875. The park especially is in better order than ever I saw it. I began to work upon it, though with limited authority, in 1860, and

15 years have certainly changed its appearance to an extraordinary degree.

... Sefton came to stay ... He is as talkative as ever – more so he cannot become, for where he is no one else can put in a word: this habit makes him unpopular in society, and reasonably so: but I have always found him a good neighbour, and in his duty as Lord Lieut. he has been impartial and discriminating, especially as regards the selection of magistrates. I wish him well, and like him: but it is possible to have too much of his company.

23 May 1875. Dined early. By rail from Huyton at 4 p.m. – London 9.30. Sefton with us.

24 May 1875. Saw ... Beust ... He gave the same excuse for the inaction of Austria that had been reported by Buchanan ...[47] It would have been simpler to say, what every one knows to be the truth, that he is afraid of saying or doing anything that can give offence to Germany.

... Forster came with a complaint from the Bradford people about some intended remodelling of the Austrian tariff ... He threw out a suggestion that it would be well to send out a special commission to Vienna and other capitals to see what was doing in regard of tariffs, and suggested Morier as a fit person: an idea worth considering, as it may be of real use, will at any rate conciliate the manufacturers, and will give suitable employment to an able, though restless and intriguing diplomatist.

26 May 1875. Saw the Italian chargé d'affaires, who called to read me a despatch explaining the course taken by his govt in the Berlin business. It was identical with what I had heard from Paget.[48] The Italians are as anxious for peace as we are, but afraid of giving offence in any quarter.

... Cabinet at 3: I was obliged to leave it sitting at 4.30, in order to return to Fairhill: we discussed the Brighton Sunday opening case, which is likely enough to make a noise: and the new bill for dealing with Labour Laws, which is not likely to pass quietly. Employers and men have directly opposite interests in this question, or at least think so, and one or other must be dissatisfied, probably both.

27 May 1875. Saw Adams, some talk with him. He confirms a report which I have heard lately, that Decazes is much addicted to speculating on the Stock Exchange, and has lately lost heavily: which is a pity, for he is able and sensible.

... Adams told me that Münster[49] is no friend to Bismarck: indeed

---

[47] (Sir) Andrew Buchanan (1807–82), amb. at Vienna until 16 Feb. 1878, when retired.
[48] Sir Augustus Paget (1823–96), min. (1867–76) and amb. (1876–83) to Italy.
[49] Formerly in Hanoverian service.

has ambitious hopes of succeeding him by the favour of the Crown Prince: and has been sent here to get him out of the way...

28 May 1875. H. of Lords, where answered a question ... as to the Geographical Congress ... (Note that on this subject I received a mem. from Staveley,[50] entirely misleading, he not having seen half the papers that related to it: the discipline of the office is not what it was in Hammond's time: no wonder, for Ld Granville neither worked himself nor made anyone else work.)

29 May 1875. Cabinet in afternoon: we sat $2\frac{1}{4}$ hours, discussing the bills which relate to the law of master and servant, and to the law of conspiracy: differences arose on points of detail: in principle all were agreed, Salisbury & Carnarvon saying that they dislike the proposed legislation, but agree that it cannot be avoided. Disraeli seemed to doubt whether there would be time to go on with the bills this session, and indeed it is late, but we are so pledged to them that they must not be given up without absolute necessity. Both at this and the last cabinet, D. has appeared much exhausted: and today he fell asleep and remained so some minutes: which I never saw him do before. The work is too heavy for a man of 70.

30 May 1875. Sanderson tells me, to my great regret, of the impending, though not absolutely certain, failure of his brother's house in the City...

31 May 1875. Heard that the Sanderson house in the City has been obliged to stop payments.

1 June 1875. Walk with Sanderson: whose cheerfulness under the heavy blow that has fallen on his family is very creditable. I know few people who would have borne trouble equally well. His brothers, two of them in partnership, were making £30,000 a year as bill-brokers, having started with very little capital 17 or 18 years ago. Now all is swept away, and they have to begin again. Such is life in the City.

3 June 1875. Much talk with M. about helping the Sanderson family, but I hardly see how it is to be done except by increasing the allowance I made to T.S. from £400 to £600 a year.

5 June 1875. Cabinet at 3: sat only till 4.15. Much was discussed, but nothing at great length: the commission on vivisection: report of recent committee on election trials, which we all agree in disapproving: it is proposed to have two judges sitting in each case instead of one, which would involve the creation of more judges, if the work is to be got through: a bill for removing difficulties connected with old Scotch entails: the reception of the Sultan of Zanzibar: Delawarr's motion for a committee on the transport of cattle: Salisbury's bill about pollution

---

[50] T.G. Staveley, F.O. senior clerk.

of rivers, which we agreed to cut down & try to pass part of it this year, I and some others objecting on the ground that we cannot get it through, and had better not waste time over it.

Disraeli said in cabinet he wished to send a commissioner to the Philadelphia exhibition: privately he told me that the person is H. Lennox who had broken out again into violent quarrel with his subordinates and must resign sooner or later. He ought never have been allowed to withdraw his resignation when offered in the spring. The proposal to send him to the States is intended as I presume to give him a decent excuse for retiring: but he will not be a creditable representative of England.

The Prince of Wales's Indian expedition was discussed: D. read a letter from the Queen, sensible enough in substance, but written with so much violence and so little dignity, that to hear it read with gravity was impossible. She said that 'no young friend' was to go with the P. on any account: talked of his 'questionable and bad' acquaintance: fell especially foul of Ld Carington & Ld C. Beresford,[51] the latter 'a halfcracked and most objectionable person, addicted to practical jokes': in short, she is determined that his tour shall be a grave official progress, while he means to take a bachelor holiday and enjoy himself. Another question which has arisen is about presents ... Such gifts are always returned to the full value ... We all agree that (as in the case of Indian officials) the presents should be a mere form, being sent to the Indian treasury when received by the Prince: but he has thrown out hints that he does not like this arrangement, and it may not be easy to get them back out of his hands. Altogether, I seem to foresee trouble out of this journey.

6 June 1875. Two new field-marshals[52] have been made, both men of nearly 90. I asked Hardy the explanation of what seems a singular choice, and why generals who have done real work, like Strathnairn, are not selected, in preference. Hardy's answer was that the system had appeared to him as strange as it did to me, but he could not alter it, the difficulties were too great. The men chosen (Ld Tweeddale & Gen. Forster) had done good service in Spain with the Duke, and it was held that they could not be passed over. He added that it was impossible to employ a field-marshal on actual service, his staff being so expensive: which is strange. I did not think he sounded well satisfied with his own reasons, but probably he had no choice.

---

[51] Charles Carington, 1st Earl Carrington (1843–1928), succ. 1868; gov. New South Wales (1885–90); cabinet minister; cr. M. of Lincolnshire, 1912; and Ld Charles Beresford (1846–1919), admiral.
[52] George Hay, 8th M. of Tweeddale (1789–1876), leading freemason; cr. f.m. May 1875; and W.F. Foster (d. 1879, aged 80), military sec. to D. of Cambridge 1869–71; general, 1874.

7 June 1875. The chief object of Bismarck has been & is to conceal the failure of his attempt to obtain Russian support.

9 June 1875. Cabinet at 12: sat till 1.30. We discussed in part the Agricultural Bill, as to which the county members seem puzzled and not sure what they want: the tenants also seem not to like the notion of 'letting value' being discussed in a court of law, probably because they think that enquiry of this kind would bring out the wide difference between rents actually paid and rents that might be obtained under a system of competition, as in Scotland. We considered also the prospects of a Burmese war, which are unsatisfactory enough: and the Prince's Indian journey. He has been got hold of by all sorts of foolish people on this subject, and having at first contemplated a holiday tour, now wishes the thing to be on a scale of magnificence which parliament probably would not, and certainly ought not to sanction. He talks of half a million being required! Salisbury & I both spoke in strong terms against any such outlay, and the cabinet in general agreed that £100,000 divided between England & India should be the maximum of outlay. But if war breaks out, the tour must be put off.

... Saw ... Münster ... He said, as I expected, that Bismarck had been hurt by our proceedings at Berlin, as they ascribed to him designs which he never entertained etc. I answered in conciliatory tone, which I could do with truth, for whatever my personal opinion may be, I have in public treated the dispute between Germany & France as a mere misunderstanding which explanation might remove. I made our conversation into a draft.

11 June 1875. The revenue returns of the year so far have shown a rate of growth which considering the dull state of trade, and falling off of exports, is extraordinary. ... I am not sure that a large surplus is desirable, for the army & navy will both be clamorous in their demands, and backed by a considerable amount of public feeling will most likely eat it up.

Cross has brought in his bills on the Labour Laws, a difficult subject, as to which opinion is divided: but his speech was a remarkable success, the best proof of which is that Lowe has praised it loudly & publicly. He has effectually vindicated his appointment.

Letter from Lumley, now in London, very alarmist in tone: he is convinced that Bismarck has designs on England, and that his object in bullying the Belgians is eventually to draw us into a quarrel: this seems to me far-fetched & improbable, and though not doubting that B. cordially dislikes England & the English, I see no adequate motive of policy for breaking with us. He adds, what I am more ready to believe, that in some late rows which took place in Belgium in connection with religious processions, German agents were found by the police to be active on both sides – setting Catholics against Liberals, and Liberals against Catholics.

12 June 1875. Work till 12 at home, when to cabinet. We then discussed again, and at length, the question of the P. of Wales' Indian tour: his suite is limited and fixed, the naval expense of sending him out and bringing him back will be £40,000, and we ask parliament for a grant of £50,000, mainly for presents and personal expenses. His travelling in India itself will be paid for out of Indian revenue. He is greatly disappointed, having contemplated an expenditure of half a million, as his friends say, and being encouraged by them in these exorbitant demands. Some hints were also given as to increasing his income, but to that we do not listen. Amendments in the agricultural bill, desired by our friends in H.C. were then discussed, and some minor matters. We called in Sclater-Booth[53] who is anxious to press on the Pollution of Rivers Bill: but from the reception which this has met with in the Lords, and the force of the opposition which it will have to meet, we clearly see that it must either be dropped, or reduced to a mere fragment of what was originally proposed.

We had a long and unsatisfactory conversation over the business of the Brighton Aquarium, which we see no way out of. The courts of law have decided that it cannot be opened at all on Sunday, for money, even without music and the other accompaniments. This decision is opposed to the general feeling, but to attempt to amend the law relating to Sunday opening would lead to such a storm of controversy that no other business could be finished, and we cannot abandon all our bills, or sit through the whole autumn. We came to no conclusion except that we did not see our way to present action. We sat a little over 2 hours.

14 June 1875. Cross sent me a mem. which had previously gone to the Chancellor, to the effect that he thinks we ought to hold out some hope at least of being able to give relief during the present session to persons who like the managers of the Brighton Aquarium, find Sunday legislation turned against them in a way which was not intended ... Opinion is almost unanimous on the subject: and we are likely to get into more trouble by avoiding the difficulty than by facing it. I returned his box with a brief note entirely agreeing, and encouraging him to persist.

15 June 1875. Letters and despatches from O. Russell, but little in them beyond what we know already. Bismarck is gone to Varzin: he expresses himself through Bulow[54] pained and disappointed at our want

---

[53] George Sclater-Booth, 1st Baron Basing (1826–94), pres. local govt. board 1874–80; cr. peer 1887.
[54] Bernard Ernst von Bülow (1815–79), sec. of state in the F.O., Berlin.

of confidence in him, and especially at my statement in the Lords having contained no expression of sympathy with Germany, or with him personally! Surely a strange ground of quarrel, the more so as I took pains to ignore the almost menacing language which he had held, and to represent the difference with France as a mere mutual misunderstanding.

In his private letter O.R. speaks of 'barefaced lying' as one of B.'s characteristics. Hence his dislike of English debates, which make mystification difficult, if we choose to expose it: but hence also we have a hold upon him, for the German press, however open to influence, cannot suppress what is said in the English parliament.

16 June 1875. Cabinet at 12, sat till 2. ... News of the Suffolk election being carried by a Conservative, 2700 odd to 1000 odd ... We had the seat before, and never expected to lose it: but much had been said about the discontent of the farmers: the Liberals were sanguine of at least cutting the majority down to a small figure: and instead of that, it is greater than ever.

Sir W. Lawson's liquor bill was lost in the Commons by a larger vote than has yet been given: 371 to 86: majority 285. Another indication of the present set of popular feeling.

Our cabinet was not especially interesting: Carnarvon, who seemed very ill, coughing incessantly, got leave to bring in a bill concerning Canadian copyright, which I do not much like, foreseeing trouble from it, but there are difficulties all ways: the Aquarium case was again taken up, and we agreed that Cross shall bring in a bill giving him power to remit penalties in such cases, which will stop vexatious proceedings at law: a question then rose about the salary due to Ld Penzance as judge under the Ecclesiastical Act of last year, which was deferred for further information: we then called in Sir M. Beach, who has a new Irish education bill in hand: we discussed it, first with him, then with one another, but ended by putting off the decision till Saturday.

17 June 1875. An application has been made to me to help in endowing Owen's College, Manchester, with a professorship of geology and practical mining. The sum required is in all about £12 to £15,000. The D. of Devonshire has promised £1000, and I have done the same: partly as thinking the thing likely to be useful, partly because being much in the habit of refusing clerical applications, I do not wish to get the reputation (which in such cases the parsons are very willing to confer) of undue parsimony.

19 June 1875. Received particulars of the Witley estate, in Surrey ... The area is about 1000 acres: country singularly pretty, but land poor: the owners ask £33,500, besides timber ... Small isolated estates of this kind have the disadvantage of requiring to be looked after, & costing in superintendence more than they are worth: on the other hand, they tend to increase constantly in value, and if I thought fit, would make an excellent provision for younger children of my brother. The chief drawback to such acquisitions is the multitude of petty demands which they invite from the neighbourhood, in which one settles: small in aggregate amount, but giving an infinity of trouble.

Cabinet at 12: we discussed the state of business, which is not altogether satisfactory: according to calculations made, we can reckon only on 28 days allotted to govt business between the present time and the 14th of August, and we shall require 33, not allowing for accidents, to get through the bills to which we are absolutely pledged. The House is friendly enough, and has been steadily supplied with work: but friends will talk for the pleasure of talking, opponents encourage them in order to defeat us by delay, and it is impossible to prevent much waste of time.

The Chancellor brought before us the case of a Mr Cox, an agitator, who is also a magistrate: and who, on the occasion of a late assault case at Sherborne, arising out of Arch's [55] meetings, wrote to the person convicted a letter expressing sympathy, condemning the magistrates for over-severity & partiality, and reflecting in rather violent terms on the unpaid magistrates as a class. Cairns seemed to think that Mr Cox ought to be dismissed from the magistracy: but to this we all objected: first, because removal would make him a martyr, which is probably what he wants: next, because although his language is unseemly and offensive, there is nothing in it either libellous or offensive as regards individuals or seditious in tendency. It is only, in substance, what any M.P. might say who might move for the general substitution of stipendiaries for unpaid magistrates.

Irish education was again discussed, & Hicks Beach called in: he pleaded so strongly the pledges which he had been allowed to give, that we sanctioned (rather reluctantly) his bringing in a bill to indicate the nature of his scheme, though not with any idea of carrying it.

The question was raised of a resolution to be moved by Stanhope, advising that no more Irish peers shall be created. We all agreed, I mean those of us who sit in the Lords, that it will certainly be carried if moved: and recommended its being accepted. Disraeli seemed averse: talked of prerogative, and said he would consult the Queen.

We had a curious conversation on the state of the War Office buildings. It appears that they have of late been overcrowded & ill ventilated, and the Queen has taken up the matter very vehemently. Repairs have been made, and the mischief is set right: but the complaints still continue, and the Queen presses them. We were puzzled at first, but the thing is now explained. The D. of Cambridge and his staff

[55] Agricultural trade unionist.

want to get back to the Horse Guards, where being in a separate building, they will appear to the public to constitute a separate dept, not dependent on the Sec. of State. The object is political, not sanitary, and it is part of the game, which has been played by the court ever since I can remember.

21 June 1875. Worked at home with Sanderson: by special train to Windsor, with the Sultan of Zanzibar and his Arab suite ... The Sultan talked freely in Arabic, cracked jokes, and generally showed himself much more alive than orientals usually do: he is more of a gentleman, according to our notions, than either the Shah or the Turkish Sultan: his face rather heavy, and lips thick, as if from some intermixture of negro blood, but his manners are pleasant, and he converses with a good deal of animation. ... He is himself very devout, stopping to pray several times in the day, wherever he may be: but in the matter of food he has invented a formula which sets his conscience at ease: saying that he is among friends, and is sure they would not ask him to eat anything unlawful.

23 June 1875. Cabinet at 12: we sat till a little past 1: Salisbury not present, being unwell: I thought Disraeli looking wearied and out of spirits: he took less part than usual in the discussion. We considered a bill for enlarging Dover Harbour, at a cost of about a million, but it had to stand over till next year for want of time. We went at some length into amendments on the Artisans Dwellings Bill, and talked over the state of business in H.C. which is not satisfactory: time cannot be found or made for all, or nearly all, that there is to do. We agreed to allow Sir J. Whitworth[56] to pass a private bill, by which he gives his estates in Derbyshire in trust to support certain engineering scholarships, which he now maintains at a cost of £3000 a year: he is in bad health, and if he gave the land by deed, and died within 12 months, the gift would be void: hence his wish for a bill.

26 June 1875. Saw ... the new French ambassador, Marquis d'Harcourt,[57] and arranged for his audience at Windsor.

... Cabinet at 3, not interesting: we discussed some fresh demands by the P. of W. to have more money for presents, and public precedence over the Viceroy: both were refused. Then came the question of continuing or suppressing the second judgeship in the Land Court, Ireland: which we agree to continue, there being really a good deal of work to do, and all the Irish unanimous. Next came Adderley's Merchant Shipping Bill, which we decide to push on as regards one

[56] Sir Joseph Whitworth (1803–87), engineer.
[57] Bernard-Hippolyte-Marie, Count d'Harcourt (1821–1912), amb. in London; called Harcourt by diarist, and thus only distinguished from U.K. politician of same name by context.

half of it, dropping some clauses which for want of time are sure not to be passed. Then the question of reorganising the Office of Works, which is still in a state of utter confusion, H. Lennox having quarrelled with everybody: we agreed to appoint a departmental committee, on which F. is to serve with three others.

We agreed to have a commission on copyright: the rest of our business was of no interest. ... Dined Marlborough House ... I find deafness rapidly increasing upon me, and I suspect other people are aware of it too.

27 June 1875. *The Echo*, a popular & rather well-written paper of strong Liberal opinions ... is bought by Albert Grant, and is to be turned into a Conservative organ. The change in public feeling has influenced the press. The *Telegraph*, though in the main Liberal, is friendly to the present cabinet ... the *Daily News* alone keeps up the old traditions of its party, and that in a subdued and temperate fashion. But the position which Albert Grant is making for himself and us will be difficult. He has done too many dirty acts to be whitewashed: and too many that are useful to be neglected. Probably some day he will ask for a baronetcy.

2 July 1875. Office ... with Ly D. received the Queen of the Netherlands[58] who came with Ly Cowley, Reeve, and her suite to see the statue of Ld Clarendon: she complained of it as unlike, talked to us about Ld C.: and seemed much affected.

3 July 1875. ... Cabinet at 3: sat till 4.30: as they were just ending, and all important business over, I left, and with M. by 4.45 train to Fairhill, where a quiet evening.

The chief business in cabinet was the visit of the P. of W. to India, as to which he becomes more unreasonable every day, backed by the D. of Sutherland,[59] Ld Carington, and his intimates. He now talks of taking with him 60 friends instead of 16 in his suite: wants innumerable carriages, horses, and other requirements of travel, provided at the public expense: and in addition to his transport there and back, which is paid for by the Admiralty, and to the actual cost of travelling in India, which the Indian govt will defray, he sends in a demand for £100,000 for presents and casual outlay. The allowance made at a previous cabinet, which certainly does not err on the side of parsimony, was £50,000. We agreed, with some reluctance, to increase it to £60,000, but absolutely declined more, and this is to be conveyed to him with the further information that the cabinet is unanimous and

---

[58] Sophie, queen of the Netherlands (1818–77), wife of William III (1817–90).

[59] George Sutherland-Leveson-Gower, 3rd D. of Sutherland (1828–92), succ. 1861; host to Garibaldi; accompanied Prince to India.

the decision final. The P. has not shown to advantage in this business: he grasps at all he can get, presses on Salisbury and Disraeli with an unbecoming importunity, and is not very truthful in his statements of fact: e.g. he told the Queen he had the consent of the cabinet to his going, whereas they never had been consulted.

Our other business was the discussion of various bills before the House: chiefly Cross's Labour Laws Amendment Bill, which it is proposed to alter in detail: but we keep to the original draft if we can pass it.

7 July 1875. Busy at home till 12: then cabinet: we sat $1\frac{1}{2}$ hour: the business not urgent, nor of much importance. We discussed the interminable subject of the visit to India: nothing more was said about money: but the Queen has revived her objection to the personal composition of the Prince's suite, and insists on his having someone of rank and authority to keep them in order. This is easier said than done...

We discussed Cross's bill for amending the labour laws again: and made some verbal amendments. We talked about judicial arrangements, in regard to which the H. of C. has played us the curious trick of insisting on three more judges than we considered necessary, which annoys Cairns, and is not very creditable, the thing being done entirely by the lawyers present, who want more prizes for their profession: the Attorney Gen. opposed feebly enough.

8 July 1875. Called on Lear[60] who has set up a sort of private exhibition of pictures and drawings at his lodging: I bought 8 watercolours, cost me £96: they will do very well for Fairhill.

... Office ... Col. Morris, just returned from Vienna. I saw him, and he explained the state of the Austrian army: its weak point, he says, is the artillery, which is all in the old style, and must be replaced: 2000 fieldguns are wanted: to be made on the Krupp system, but at an Austrian factory. Till these are supplied, the army is not fit for a campaign. Of the cavalry he could not speak too highly ... The infantry he praised also, saying that for activity and endurance there was none better ... ... The force available for service beyond the frontier was comparatively small: not more, he thought, than 300 to 350,000 men...

9 July 1875. House of Lords: Stanhope moved a resolution having for its object to put a stop to all future creation of Irish peers: Cairns opposed it on a point of form ... Salisbury resisted it on other grounds, but was not successful: in fact no one could be so, for the House was absolutely unanimous, and I am bound to say, I think they were right. Richmond made a poor speech, and in the end gave way. It would have been better if we had in the first instance agreed to accept the

---

[60] Edward Lear (1812–88); as author of *Book of Nonsense*, linked with diarist's boyhood, when employed by his grandfather.

policy indicated, for there is really no argument against it: but Disraeli, when the matter was raised in cabinet, objected on the ground of prerogative, and said the Queen was opposed to the charge. We have tided over the difficulty for this year, but it will revive in 1876.[61]

10 July 1875. Cabinet at 12: which turned entirely on the conduct of H. of C. business. We agree to push the Labour Laws Amendment, Agricultural Holdings, Land Transfer, Judicature, and some other bills: those relating to patents, pollution of rivers, local loans, and a variety of others, must be dropped for want of time. Merchant Shipping we are not willing to sacrifice if it can be helped: but Adderley has blundered it throughout: the shipowners are hostile and powerful, and I doubt whether any part of it has a chance of passing.

We sat only a little over an hour. I thought Disraeli ill and feeble, and he himself said that he was not well, but he rallied and talked with a good deal of energy and vivacity. He dines out a good deal, and I hear that his appearance is much noticed: he seems at times half asleep, and it costs him an effort to speak.

... The French Ambassador called ... M. d'Harcourt is simple, frank, and unaffected: I think him inclined to be fidgety, as Buchanan warned me he was: he seems possessed by a conscientious fear of leaving anything unsaid or undone that belongs to his duty: a natural feeling for a man who has only come into the diplomatic line late in life.

12 July 1875. To Arlington St. for a party, and was well enough amused. I think I ought to go out more: with the life I lead during the day, it is impossible for me to see friends & acquaintance any other way.

14 July 1875. Cabinet at 4: the subjects most discussed were the labour laws, and sundry amendments proposed to Cross's bills: as to which we agreed pretty well: and next, the eternal topic of the Indian journey. Mother & son have been quarrelling again, and D. takes credit to himself for having stopped an angry letter from the former. The fact is that the Prince has been persuaded that his tour ought to be a royal progress: and he wanted a detachment of Guards to escort him. These ideas have been put into his head by the toadies who hang about him, and who find that to inveigh against the parsimony of the cabinet is a cheap road to favour. The Queen shows sense & firmness in refusing to humour him: she thinks the thing a folly, dislikes it as coming from him, and does not conceal her jealousy of the royal attitude which he wants to assume. He has contrived to get a good deal of support in the press, and it is believed, in the House also: letters appear every day to the effect that the £60,000 which we propose to vote ought to be

---

[61] No Irish peerage was cr. between 1868 and 1898 (Curzon), and none thereafter. A bill preventing new creations passed the Lords, but failed in the Commons.

doubled. It is almost comic that we, who have been over and over again attacked for extravagance, should now be complained of for an opposite fault. But I believe the outcry which has been got up on the subject is confined to few persons, and neither the middle nor the working class join in it.

15 July 1875. Saw Schouvaloff, who is going away on leave: talk with him about the late debate in parliament, the 'intermediate zone', etc. He is friendly, profuse in pacific assurances, and I believe they represent his real feeling: but who can trust a Russian? Musurus called, and chattered as usual: he is never told what is passing in his own country, which makes conversation with him a mere waste of time: and it is useless to warn him of impending troubles, as he makes a point of affecting to disbelieve the possibility of anything going wrong.

... There is no question of importance pending, yet I have seldom been more pressed for time than during this week.

17 July 1875. Mr Ritchie M.P. called on the sugar question. It appears now that the French, after giving solemn assurances that the system of refining in bond should come into operation as soon as the convention lately held on the subject at Brussels was signed, are proposing to put it off till next spring, so as to secure for 9 months longer the advantages of the bounty which they have undertaken to discontinue ... This is the third time that the French, in the midst of their professions of gratitude, have played us a trick. They have made a treaty with Annam which is unfavourable to British interests, and contrary to the rule always hitherto acted on by them and us of giving equal commercial rights to all European countries: and have passed the ratification of it through the assembly in haste, while assuring us that nothing should be settled till our representations had been considered. They have given very unconciliatory & dangerous instructions to their naval officers on the Newfoundland coast, which we only knew by the officers having frankly communicated the purport of them to ours: and this while assuring us that their orders should be in an exactly contrary sense. And now comes this sugar business. One would think that they had not so many friends that they could afford to alienate any: but their diplomacy has always been sharp – to use the mildest phrase.

Letter from Lumley, relating a conversation with the King of the Belgians: in which the King expresses a wish that Belgium should have a colony somewhere, as an outlet for the enterprise of the people, and names New Guinea as a desirable country in which to look out for one. I refer this letter at once to Ld Carnarvon: stating my belief that it will not do. The Australians would take very ill the planting of a foreign settlement in a country which – unexplored and unknown as it is – they already half consider as their own. The King's reason for wishing for colonial possessions, if sincere, is an odd one: he argues that they would draw men's minds off from religious quarrels! Surely a sanguine speculation!

20 July 1875. Explanations in House yesterday as to state of business: Disraeli, with his usual and curious dislike of telling a plain story in a plain way, seems to have made a sort of mystery about it, talking as if all the bills on the table were to be carried: which is contrary to what we settled, and on the face of it impossible.

21 July 1875. My 49th birthday. In point of health, mental and bodily activity, and outward circumstances, I have nothing to complain of: and few men, I suppose, have entered their 50th year with less regret for the past, or more general contentment with the present.

... Cabinet at 12: Disraeli opened it, speaking with unusual animation, and describing the state of things as critical. He complained of the treatment which the Agricultural Tenancies Bill had met with by our own friends: said we must decide whether to drop that or the Merchant Shipping Bill: and rather inclined to go on with the latter, as being more certain to pass. In this suggestion however no one agreed: Salisbury, Cairns, and I all contended strongly against it, pointing out the danger of leaving the tenants' claims unsettled, and so of having an agricultural agitation in the recess: while in the case of the other bill, no such agitation is possible, the subject not being one to admit of it, nor would it lead to danger if by any chance public feeling were stirred upon it. We pressed the further objection that if the one measure were dropped, it was by no means certain that we should succeed in passing the other, considering the muddle which Adderley had made of it: and if both failed, our position would be intolerably absurd. In the end Disraeli gave way, and it was settled to call a meeting of the party for tomorrow.

22 July 1875. F.O. before 12, to attend a meeting of the party held there: Disraeli addressed them in a speech of half an hour, which for tact and dexterity was nearly perfect. He reminded them that the fate of the Agricultural Bill was in their hands: that if they persisted in vexatious amendments, it must drop: that if it dropped he would not take it up again: and that the danger was great of an agitation which might lead to much larger demands being made by the tenants, and to these being conceded by the Liberals, who would be only too happy to profit by our failure. Salisbury said a few words in the same sense: Cairns explained some provisions of the bill which seemed to have been misunderstood. The appeal made by Disraeli succeeded: no discontent was expressed, and it was agreed without difference that the bill should be supported: Sir G. Jenkinson[62] alone making some hostile comments, which did not please.

---

[62] Sir George Jenkinson, bt (1817–90), M.P. (Cons.) N. Wilts. 1868–80.

... Fowler[63] the engineer called ... He talked also of his Rossshire lands, 45,000 acres, where, he says, he has planted between 5 and 6 million of trees, the soil being fit for that, though for little else: a good example.

23 July 1875. In the Commons last night, a strange and unpleasant scene.[64] ... Plimsoll ... got up violently excited ... and so conducted himself that a motion was made by Disraeli that he should be reprimanded. ... It is variously explained, but the general belief is that the outbreak was calculated, and that it was Plimsoll's object to get himself put into custody, so as to revive interest in his agitation, of which people are growing tired.

26 July 1875. Found telegram saying that a cabinet had been summoned at 2 ... straight to Downing St, where arrived at 2.30: we sat till 3.30: all present except Richmond, who is at Goodwood. The reason for our sudden meeting was, that there is growing up in H. of C. a strong feeling that some part at least of the Merchant Shipping Bill should be saved if possible: Plimsoll's vehemence, real or simulated, has attracted attention to the subject, and it was thought that the opposition might take this opportunity – the last they will have – of making an organised attack. Gladstone has come up, and is in council with their other leaders: the story goes that a vote would have been proposed, condemning the sacrifice of the M.S. bill, and the pushing on of the agricultural bill: but for Ld Granville, who objected, I suppose as thinking the move impolitic and premature. The Liberals are really sore and angry, and with some reason, for they reckoned confidently on the failure of the agricultural bill, in which case the cry would have been raised that it was never meant to pass, and every effort would have been made to stir the farmers against their landlords, and so break up the Conservative strength in the counties. Many, too, of the Whigs dislike it on the merits, and would have been happy to throw it out even if it had come from their own side. – It was decided with no difference of opinion to endeavour to bring in a bill of a provisional kind, which might supply the chief deficiencies in the existing law till the whole question can be dealt with next year. Adderley, Mr Gray,[65] and Mr Farrer[66] of the Board of Trade were called in. Much discussion, and the difficulties appear great. But we saw our way enough to be able to decide on doing something: and a notice was given accordingly.

... Cairns brought in the bills dealing with labour laws in an excellent speech, addressed to 16 peers who formed his audience.

[63] (Sir) John Fowler, 1st bt (1817–98), pres. of Institution of Civil Engineers 1866–7.
[64] Over decision to drop Merchant Shipping Bill.
[65] Thomas Gray, civil servant; asst sec. for marine dept board of trade.
[66] T.H. Farrer (1819–99), perm. sec. to board of trade 1865–86.

27 July 1875. Cabinet at 12: we settled the general purport of the provisional Merchant Shipping Bill, and sent it on to be drafted. We sat only about an hour.

29 July 1875. Heard from J. Manners that Adderley had brought in the new M.S. bill yesterday afternoon, after making strong personal objections to do so: as mostly happens when a minister introduces a measure which he does not like, he made an indifferent speech. But (according to J.M.) the feeling of the House is in favour of getting out of the difficulty, and consequently in favour of the bill.

... Called on Carnarvon in consequence of a note from him: found he was anxious if possible to postpone the conclusion of the question of West African exchanges till next year: there being scarcely time now for parliamentary discussion, and he, fearing that we may be accused of having kept it back till an expression of adverse opinion was impossible. In this I partly agreed: at any rate, it is more his business than mine: I therefore wrote to M. d'Harcourt, and wrote and telegraphed to Lyons.

30 July 1875. In H. of C. yesterday Mr Plimsoll apologised ... The sudden excitement created by the M.S. question was as little expected by the House as by the cabinet, and all are equally concerned in coming to a decision.

Cabinet at 12: Disraeli reviewed the situation, of which he spoke hopefully: said great attempts had been made by the opposition to get up an agitation: they had sent round circulars to call workingmen's meetings everywhere: but the success had not been great: the announcement of a new bill had checked the movement, as he thought effectually: there had been an intention of making Plimsoll a hero, bringing him down to the House in triumph, but he had declined to be made use of in that way. The Liberal agents were telling voters to be ready for an immediate dissolution: so confident had they felt of carrying some vote hostile to the ministry: but their confidence had much abated in the last 24 hours. He was confident that all would go well. – We discussed at length what amendments could be accepted, and what must be rejected: and agreed without dissentients that the new bill should be placed in charge of Sir S. Northcote. His being in the cabinet, and Adderley out of it, would be reason enough, and Adderley's feelings need not be hurt: though it is in great measure from his inefficiency that this trouble has come.

31 July 1875. We have lent Keston for a few weeks to Carlyle, the author, who is unable from weakness to travel, suffers in the close air of London, and either cannot afford or dislikes to hire a house in the country. The old man is much pleased, and the house could not be put to a better use.

*

1 August 1875. Letters from Lyons ... Decazes has been much put out by our postponement of the West African arrangement, (from which he evidently expected credit & popularity), but has taken the disappointment well, and is disposed to meet our wishes.

... Letter from Elliot ... ... Elliot evidently thinks that bankruptcy, total or partial, cannot be long delayed: and that the Sultan personally is the chief cause. ... On the other hand, it seems really the fact that the Turkish army is more efficient than it has been for a hundred years past: and the navy, though badly manned and commanded, has many fine ships, which under foreign officers might hold the seas against the Russian fleet...

3 August 1875. H. of Lds ... Carnarvon took the opportunity to say a few words about West African exchanges of territory, giving at once notice that negotiations are going on, and assurances that nothing shall be done till parliament has met again next year.

4 August 1875. Troubles in Herzegovina continue, and seem to be increasing, but unless the insurgents are backed up by Austria or Russia, or both, there is no serious danger.

... Saw G. Hornby,[67] the admiral, who wants to get his son into the rifle brigade. I wrote to Hardy on his behalf.

... Saw Musurus ... ... I was very guarded in my answers, not from distrust of him for which there is no cause, but because I find that he generally manages to misunderstand or misreport my answers, not intending it, but being a muddle-headed person, which he cannot help.

5 August 1875. Saw ... Ld A. Loftus, who discoursed at length on the politics of Europe, with some sense, but more pomposity: the Russians have evidently persuaded him that a cordial agreement on Asiatic affairs is possible between Russia & England. I complimented him highly on his success in obtaining information: which I might justly do, for he is the head of mission, and responsible: but it has been managed by young Wellesley.[68]

6 August 1875. Dinner to Ministers at the Mansion House on Wednesday: Disraeli took advantage of the occasion to deliver an ingenious and able speech in vindication of the general results of the session. If the thing was to be done at all, it could hardly be done better: but it

---

[67] Sir Geoffrey Hornby (1825–95), lord of admiralty 1875–7, c.-in-c. Mediterranean, 1877–80; his father (ld of admiralty 1852) was bro.-in-law of 13th E. of Derby.

[68] Col. F.A. Wellesley (1844–1931), British military attaché in St Petersburg; s. of Lord Cowley (1804–84); s.-in-law of Ld. A. Loftus, amb.; 'incurable spendthrift, which does not concern the public' (Derby diaries, 13 May 1876); offered Warsaw, at Cowley's request, by Derby, June 1876, but declined; hence renewed for 2nd term of 5 yrs in Russia by Derby, Aug. 1876; secret emissary between Tsar and Disraeli, behind Derby's back; twice divorced, his 1st m. (1873) to Loftus's dau. ending 1882.

is not to the advantage of govts, or of public men, that they should be perpetually called upon to talk about what they are doing.

7 August 1875. In H. of C. last night, Hartington delivered a carefully-prepared and not unskilful criticism[69] of the session: which has done more than any of his former performances to justify his selection as leader. He was followed by Disraeli, whose reply was in his happiest vein: indeed notwithstanding all that is said of failing health, I think he has been at his best lately: only he requires the excitement of an attack, or of an emergency of some sort, to rouse him.

... Cabinet: we discussed and settled the Queen's speech, paragraph by paragraph. The criticisms upon it were all verbal.

We then had to consider the Irish education bill, which has justified the predictions of Hicks Beach, in so far as that it passed through the Commons without a dissentient voice: the Irish peers however dislike it, and Bath who without any particular right, has constituted himself their spokesman, has written to Salisbury a violent and foolish letter upon it. The Irish M.P.s on our side are said to dislike it greatly: but their constituencies not being of the same mind, they have prudently kept their opinions to themselves. The question of withdrawing the bill was raised, but it seemed clear we could not give way to a few Irish lords, who have not even expressed their opinions in public, nor to Irish M.P.s who have felt themselves compelled to vote for the bill which they want to get rid of. The conversation disclosed what I had suspected before, that there is not a very cordial feeling between the Ld Lieut. and the Viceroy:[70] the usual difficulty of Irish administration.

We dealt next with the case of Col. Baker,[71] who obviously cannot remain in the army, after his conviction & sentence, but the question is how he shall leave it? There are three alternatives – dismissal, permission to resign his commission unconditionally – i.e. without receiving the price of it – and permission to sell out in the ordinary way. The last alternative was rejected as too lenient, finding no supporters except Richmond & Salisbury: the other two alternatives were more carefully discussed – Cross & Hunt being for the more severe course, the rest of us generally inclining to think that compulsory retirement with the loss of £5000 was punishment enough. Nothing was absolutely settled, and it was agreed to consider the matter again on Wednesday.

9 August 1875. Talk with Carnarvon about a letter he has sent to F.O. suggesting the creation of a settlement in New Guinea. His object is to

---

[69] *H*, vol. 226, col. 652–67 (6 Aug. 1875).
[70] Confused; 'between Ld Lieut. and Chief Sec.' intended.
[71] Valentine Baker (1827–87), later in Turkish and Egyptian service; guilty of unwelcome attentions to lady in railway carriage.

please the Australians, with whom this is a favourite idea: but it is a crude and premature proposal, for we know nothing of the country. I told him that the first step was to send out a surveying expedition, which might be easily done, pledged us to nothing, and would in any case be useful, while it served to keep the colonists quiet. To this he assented.

11 August 1875. ... At the cabinet, we settled Col. Baker's case. It seems that this is not the first offence of the kind that he has been guilty of, there being a former conviction recorded against him in Ceylon: this fact, not known to us before, put an end to all question of treating him with exceptional leniency: and his dismissal was decided on.

Northcote read, and we criticised, the proposed instructions to the B. of T. officers as to the working of the new Act.[72] It is impossible not to be uneasy at the large powers which must be left in the hands of surveyors, and the opportunity for corruption which will be afforded: but the powers are necessary, if the Act is to work at all.

Discussion on the B. of Wks: Capt. Galton[73] has resigned, and has received a special pension of £1000 a year. The office not to be filled up. It seems that in the departmental committee some one said that he was 'a fifth wheel on the coach'. F. added 'yes, and a fifth wheel at right angles to the other four'. Hardy quoted this as a good thing.

12 August 1875. ... Talk with D. about Adderley & the B. of T, which it is quite evident must be in other hands. I suggested Smith of the Treasury, who however will be hard to replace: D. is thinking of moving Beach from Ireland, and sending Chaplin[74] there. About the necessity of a change there is now no question.

Talk with D. also about honours or pensions to men of science: something done in this line would be popular, and useful. He asked me to put my recommendations into a letter, that he might consider them.

Talk with Cross about the police: it costs in all about £2,500,000, of which Treasury pays half: if we could make up our minds to centralise it, paying the other half from national rates, the relief to rates would be considerable, and there would be a great saving by getting rid of divided authority, and enabling the police of one district to act in another when required. But the local opposition would be considerable.

D. of Richmond on our way back talked a good deal about P. of W. who has lately been his guest at Goodwood: does not like his ways:

[72] Merchant Shipping Act.
[73] (Sir) Douglas Galton (1822–99), director of public works (1869–75); kt 1887.
[74] Henry Chaplin, 1st Viscount Chaplin (1840–1933), M.P. 1868–1916; devotee of rural sports and representative of agriculture; cr. peer 1916.

very high play goes on every night, he has lost more than £1000 at a sitting: is uneasy and bored if he cannot have his amusement: the taste is growing on him: he also bets heavily on the turf. The Duke is no gossip, nor censorious, which makes one think more of what he says in such a matter.

Disraeli tells me that the Queen frequently expresses her conviction that he will never live to reign: that she shall survive him: that he is destroying his health etc.

The Queen at today's audience received Layard with marked civility, though she continues to speak very bitterly of him to me: hoping that he might have as long a leave as possible, so that he should not go back[75] to do mischief sooner than could be helped – and other like speeches.

... To Fairhill ... heartily glad that the session is ended.

14 August 1875. At the cabinet on Wednesday, a discussion on first admissions to the Navy. The Chancellor and I brought it on by agreement, finding fault mildly with Hunt for having done away with limited competition and replaced it by nomination, without consulting his colleagues: we invited him to consider whether the former state of things could not be restored. Hunt excused the action he had taken as an inadvertence, said he had not attached much importance to it, and promised reconsideration.

Cross brought on his plan for putting up workingmen's buildings on the waste ground near Battersea park, which for many years has been lying idle. It was originally meant for villas, but none have been built nor is it likely they ever will. Northcote quite agreed, and we consented.

Carnarvon pressed hard for an increase of military force at the Cape, which was disliked, and disputed, but in the end a partial concession to his wishes was made.

Northcote brought before us the financial position, which he does not represent as satisfactory: but it was evident to me that he made the worst of it in order to check extravagant tendencies in the spending depts. He told us that if all our plans were to be acted upon, the increase of outlay would be two millions, whereas on the most favourable estimate we could hardly count on more than $1\frac{1}{2}$ millions increased revenue. I do not remember exactly how he made it out: sinking fund is £300,000: automatic increase in various depts, £400,000: education, £300,000: land for new public offices, £300 to £400,000, and there were other items. I suggested, & Disraeli agreed, that the purchase of land for public offices is a fair charge to be spread over several years, and the money for that might be raised by terminable annuity. But the other items do not admit of being treated in the same way. The moral

[75] As amb. to Madrid.

was – no increase is possible on army & navy. Neither Hunt nor Hardy approved this declaration, but they said nothing.

15 August 1875. The trouble in Herzegovina continues, and seems to grow more serious: at the outset, it might have been put down with the loss of perhaps 50 lives: now, it will cost at least 1000, and probably many more. The Austrian govt is showing itself more friendly to the Turks than could have been expected...

16 August 1875. The Herzegovina troubles seem rather to increase than diminish: the surrounding govts are acting honestly, doing what they can to prevent assistance being given from outside: the Turks do nothing for themselves ... ... in fact the Porte is the chief ally of the insurgents.

17 August 1875. The newspapers have all delivered their criticism of the session just ended; and for the most park speak of it as barren of result. I cannot agree. No measure such as the Irish church act or land act has passed: none such was expected or desired: but Judicature, Land Transfer, Artisans Dwellings, Labour Laws, Army Exchanges, Tenant Right, and Public Health, are large subjects, and in regard of each of them something not inconsiderable has been done. But journalists, and the public too, want excitement: what they look to is not the importance of the law when passed, so much as the noise made in passing it: and as the year has been marked by no great debates, by no explosion of party zeal, by no danger to the govt, and no victory to its opponents, it is justly thought dull, and unjustly considered as having been wasted. No progress has been made by the Liberal party towards a reunion ... the difficulty still remains of finding a policy to unite upon, and a leader to follow. Hartington has done, as a stopgap, better than was expected: but his heart is not in the work: he does not attend regularly, nor is he ready in debate when present. I can see no question other than that of reduction of county franchise on which the party can unite: and half of them are afraid of raising that cry, some lest it should endanger the class to which they belong: others because they believe that household franchise in the counties would make the Conservative landowners all-powerful.

Besides, the farmers are against it to a man, especially since the formation of agricultural trades unions.

18 August 1875. Wrote to Disraeli at some length on the question of honours or rewards to men of science: I recommended the selection of Darwin and Owen,[76] or of Darwin alone, for the present, leaving for another occasion the recognition of such claims as those of Huxley, Tyndall,[77] Stokes,[78] Thomson,[79] etc. I advised that a pension should be

---

[76] (Sir) Richard Owen (1804–92), naturalist; kt 1884.
[77] John Tyndall (1820–93), scientist and populariser.
[78] Sir G.G. Stokes (1819–1903), physicist; Cons. M.P. 1887–91; cr. bt 1889.
[79] Sir W. Thomson, 1st Baron Kelvin (1824–1907), physicist; kt 1866, baron 1892.

offered to Darwin, and either a baronetcy, or, better, a K.C.B.

20 August 1875. To Keston with M. to see Mr Carlyle, who is settled there. . . . Found the old man out of doors, he seemed feeble, but talked readily, as of old. He had been reading Michelet's *France*, which he praised, but said he was never sure how much of what he read was true, and how much was only the author's imagination. He said he himself had been accused of treating French history without sufficient seriousness and sympathy, but there are many scenes in it which it was difficult to treat in that way: he went on to say, in his own style, which I cannot reproduce, that the French endeavour after better institutions had failed, & would fail, because they believed in nothing: the priests and the philosophers between them had destroyed all faith in a real Providence and in the laws by which the world is governed.

21 August 1875. Received & answered a letter from Levy, of the *Telegraph*, about Herzegovina, giving him such information as I safely could.

22 August 1875. Among office papers today is a telegram from Elliot, saying that the three northern powers have agreed to send consuls as delegates to the insurgents in Herzegovina, to warn them they will get no support from outside: and to advise them to lay down their arms, and state their grievances in a peaceable manner. The Porte accepts this offer gratefully, and asks England to join: a request which can hardly be refused, but I thought it best to write to Disraeli to obtain his consent before acting. Whether the Turkish acceptance is wise may be a doubtful matter: but their acquiescence removes all possible scruple on the ground of interference in their affairs.

24 August 1875. . . . Sir A. Buchanan called to take leave: we talked of Herzegovina: he, Sir A., is a safe and sensible man, but at no time has he been very efficient, and now the natural apathy of age, and the absence of inducement to work, lead him to confine himself to routine duty. In plain words, he does no more than he can help, and knows but little of what is passing. But as his failings are of the negative kind, I cannot well get rid of him, and he will not resign while he can help it.

. . . Received Disraeli's answer about the Turkish mediation proposal: he does not like it, but sees that it is inevitable. I accordingly settled with Tenterden a telegram and despatch authorising Elliot to join with the other ambassadors.

26 August 1875. London: chiefly to see my mother, whose strength is diminishing . . .

28 August 1875. In the papers, a strange letter from old Ld Russell, offering a subscription of £50 in aid of the Herzegovina insurgents. His letters to me were not at all in the same sense: but I imagine that while a certain restlessness remains he has now very little recollection of what he may have said or done even a few weeks ago. In Servia it seems that there is growing popular excitement, and the Prince may be dragged into the quarrel whether he will or no.

... An uncomfortable, but vague, telegram from Wade, warns us to be prepared for the possible necessity of sending out an expedition against the Chinese. I am inclined to think that ill health and shaken nerves have not been without their influence on his judgment.

... A merchant captain called Webb[80] has swum the Channel ...

... He is of course to have a testimonial, and I shall join willingly: for such displays of exceptional strength and courage, even if no direct use, have an effect which is good in many ways. They keep up abroad the opinion of English hardihood: and stimulate men to cultivate bodily energy more than in an age of sedentary & industrial employment they might otherwise care to do.

29 August 1875. Wrote to Delane & Levy on the present state of the Turkish disturbance: which the tendency of our press is to represent as much more serious than it has yet become. Insurrections are always apt to look bigger at a distance than they really are: I remember that in America, in 1848–9, I was frequently asked in a serious and not unfriendly manner, about the Fenians and their chances of success: and this not by ignorant or foolish persons.

30 August 1875. Wrote to Levy on Spanish arrest in Porto Rico, as to which he is misinformed, and is writing up a quarrel with Spain...

... I have before me a mass of papers on the Turkish insurrection, but no definite result is to be drawn from them: and they are for the most part superseded by telegrams. ... Elliot himself thinks the conduct of Austria equivocal and open to suspicion: and I am compelled to agree.

1 September 1875. In Berlin much alarm is felt as to the probable result of the struggle. Bulow is reserved and uncommunicative, it is difficult to get at his real opinion, but it seems clear that he, & Bismarck also, has been taken by surprise: that the affair has grown into proportions which they did not expect: and that they suspect Russia of meaning to take her own course, shaking herself clear of past alliances & engagements. There appears to be in official German society a strong feeling against England: the tone of the German press is strongly hostile to us, and flattering to Austria. The reason is not clear. ... There can never be entire cordiality between a military despotism, such as Germany is now, and a peaceable constitutional community like England: still neither of these reasons appears adequate to account for the extreme irritation which prevails...

---

[80] Matthew Webb (1848–83), drowned swimming Niagara.

5 September 1875. Busy enough ... with papers left over from the last few days. Among these is a proposal to renew the negotiations begun in 1858 for territorial exchanges in India: the French getting an extension about Pondicherry, keeping one other port, and ceding all their smaller settlements. The transactions would be an advantage to both sides, but it may be a question whether the time is suitable. ... The conduct of the French govt in the matters of Annam, New-foundland, & the sugar negotiations, has not been such as to encourage the hope that we shall find them reasonable in other affairs. They have shown themselves tricky and unconciliatory.

6 September 1875. Letter from Hardy, who tells me that the Queen having been occupied exclusively by the accident caused by her yacht,[81] and having talked of nothing else, is now getting excited about Turkish matters: fearing lest England should be 'isolated', which is the continual dread and horror of diplomatists. I must wait to hear more: but to me it appears that when 'isolated' we have generally been most successful. We were so in the Cretan war,[82] and carried our point: we were equally so in declining the Russian proposition of last year[83] about usages of war, and in that instance it is probable that our resistance will cause the whole scheme to collapse.

7 September 1875. London early: moved into 4 Carlton Ho. Terrace, which we have taken for the winter, No 23 being under repair.

... Accurate intelligence of what is passing in Herzegovina & Bosnia seems unattainable. There is much skirmishing, with little result: each sides accuses the other of acts of barbarity, & probably in the main the charges are just: but details cannot be relied on. ... But neither side really wish to negotiate...

10 September 1875. London soon after 2 p.m. Called by appointment on Disraeli: he was in good spirits, satisfied with the work of the year, and sanguine of the future: but I thought him visibly more feeble: rather deaf: he walked like an old man: and though speaking of his own health cheerfully, he said at parting 'I think I have another year's work in me': as though not feeling sure on the subject, and not choosing to look farther.

He tells me that the Queen is strangely excited about the collision in the Solent: that she telegraphed & wrote about it several times a day: wanting him to do sundry impossible things: he thinks she is now calming down: but was at one time uneasy as to her state of mind.

He talked of Turkish affairs, but chiefly asking my opinion: said that

[81] The royal yacht, commanded by a royal relation, ran down the schooner *Mistletoe* (18 Aug. 1875), with loss of life.
[82] *c.* 1866–8.
[83] At the Brussels conference.

the Empress of Germany[84] has sent several mysterious messages to the
Queen, warning her to be on her guard, lest the Eastern Question
should be settled without England being consulted: this he does not
understand, nor do I: but it explains Hardy's letter of last week: most
likely it is an intrigue against Bismarck, in which we are invited to join.

We spoke of honours to men of science: he proposes to offer the
K.C.B. once more to Carlyle, and in the event of his accepting, then
to Darwin also: failing any arrangement of this kind, it is always possible
to offer a pension.

... Talk also of Carnarvon, whom he considers, as I do, inclined to
be too hasty in his action, & wholly under the influence of Froude:
though up to this time all has gone well. His view of C.'s policy &
temperament coincided curiously with mine.

11 September 1875. Received a corrected return ... ... The outlay is:

Compulsory deductions ... in round numbers		£ 38,000
Debt paid off	say	£ 84,000
Estate expenses	say	£ 55,000
Household	say	£ 19,000
Miscellaneous	say	£ 22,000
Total	say	£218,000

... 'Estate' is considerably in excess of what it should be, and I have
told Hale so: £45,000, or 25 per cent on the gross rental, ought to
cover all. The amount of debt paid off is satisfactory, being the largest
sum I have yet cleared in one year.

12 September 1875. Nothing especially noticeable, except that I am
troubled with a passing fit of low spirits & nervousness, of which I
cannot imagine the cause, but which is disagreeable enough while it
lasts. I have not been often troubled in that way of late years.

... Walk early with Sanderson: serious talk about state of the
Constantinople embassy: Moore is dying, but does not know it, and
quite unfit for work: and Hughes, probably from disease of the brain,
is in a state of excitement approaching insanity, and not unlikely to go
altogether crazy. Neither is of any use to Elliot, and a change must be
made somehow.

16 September 1875. Received from Adams[85] a letter to the effect that
Decazes is very anxious to know our opinion as to the settlement of
the Bosnia & Herzegovina business: and that he inclines to the idea of
a conference, so as to ensure all the powers being consulted. He at the
same time frankly admits that he is ready to adopt almost any plan,
and that his object is to keep up the appearance of France not being

[84] Augusta, Empress of Germany (1811–90), wife of William I; hostile to Bismarck.
[85] Min. in Paris.

left out in the framing of any scheme of settlement that may be adopted. This is thoroughly characteristic of French vanity and regard for appearances rather than reality. I have answered to the effect that till the insurrection is put down it is premature to propose anything: that I do not think any administrative reforms will satisfy the malcontents, who want to get the Turks out of the country altogether: nor have I faith in schemes of local autonomy, where the population is divided in religion, and the two sectors are naturally hostile. At the same time, the Porte should be pressed to redress grievances etc. – The truth is, local autonomy will satisfy no party. The Porte will not concede it, except under pressure such as to be equivalent to compulsion: and the insurgents do not care about it, as what they want is a separate nationality, and entire separation from Turkey. Nor would it please Austria, to whom the prospect of a chronic religious war on her frontier cannot be agreeable. It is like Home Rule in Ireland, a compromise with which neither side will be content.

17 September 1875. In the papers today appears an unwise letter written by the Queen's order through Ponsonby, intimating to the yacht squadron that all yachts are to be kept out of the way of the Royal steamer in future: which is an indirect way of throwing the blame of the late collision on the vessel which was run down. ... The effect of the whole is ungracious and unpleasant.

20 September 1875. Left Fairhill with regret: it is the only place where we can lead a really quiet life...

21 September 1875. Left for Knowsley ...[86] Margaret & Sanderson travelled with us.

22 September 1875. Carnarvon came, on his way southward from Balmoral. Very little business from the office, which is as well, for I had enough to do otherwise.

23 September 1875. The gardens are in perfect order, but Harrison complains that along one wall his fruit-trees are blighted, and have lost nearly all their leaves, which he ascribes to the vapours from St Helens. I am afraid he is right: today the smell has been disagreeable all over the place. Mentioned this to Hale, with a request that he would look at it himself, and report to the inspector.

Walk in afternoon with Carnarvon, and talk with him about New-foundland, S. Africa, Gambia etc. I see with regret that his health is weak: he can bear neither heat, nor cold, nor wet feet, nor walk faster than an old man, and seems generally feeble. But his spirits are good,

---

[86] At Knowsley, 21 Sept.–1 Oct., then with Ly D. and Sanderson to hotel (on Pender's property) near Llandudno, until 5 Oct.; at Knowsley (where saw Fr., Germ., and Russian ambs.) 5 Oct.–3 Nov.; then to London, 3 Nov.–16 Dec., when to Edinburgh to speak; at Knowsley, 18 Dec. 1875–11 Jan. 1876.

and he talked with energy & eagerness. He could give no satisfactory report as to the prospect of a settlement on the Newfoundland question, saying indeed that the colonists were ready to make concessions, but when we came to discuss them in detail, they proved to be little more than the formal recognition of rights which the French have long *de facto* asserted, and which they will certainly not pay for by the surrender of other rights which they regard as equally their own. On the whole, I do not see any light on this old and perplexed dispute: but as in 100 years it has never yet led to a quarrel, and as the French are not in a position to quarrel with anybody if they can help it, we may hope that no mischief will follow.

24 September 1875. Death of Robertson Gladstone[87] announced in the papers: he was not above 70: and appeared to be in good bodily health, though eccentric to the verge of insanity. He was sincere and not unkindly: the violence of his political language was regarded on both sides as a result of peculiar temperament, and did not make enemies, though it often excited ridicule. He had been an extreme High Tory in early life, and when converted, went as far in the opposite direction. He took an active part in local affairs: indeed he might be considered as the most prominent member of the Liberal party in L.pool: his brother's position giving him a certain influence, and his own energy and independence of character doing the rest. I have never known a man so nervously excitable: when making a few ordinary remarks at quarter sessions he would shake and tremble all over: and at times he was medically advised to abstain from business, lest mental disturbance should follow. In private he was, by a not uncommon combination, generous and penurious: willing to part with large sums for purposes which he approved, and at the same time grudging petty expenses: like the late Ld Westminster.[88] He will be missed in L.pool, where he was regarded with kindly & respectful feeling, both for his family's sake and his own.

4 October 1875. ... Wolkenstein[89] has seen Bourke on the subject of Servia: and asks us to interpose to prevent the Servians breaking out into a war with Turkey. I direct him to answer that we are already doing all we can in that sense...

5 October 1875. Left ... for Knowsley ... ... I left Lady D. by her

[87] R. Gladstone (1805–75), elder bro. of premier; for infirmities, see *Stanley Diaries* passim.

[88] Richard Grosvenor, 2nd M. of Westminster (1795–1869), succ. 1845.

[89] Anton, Graf von Wolkenstein-Trostburg (1832–1913), Austrian diplomatist 1858–1913; served in London 1868–9, May 1870–Dec. 1876, by when 1st sec.; amb. in Russia 1882–94, in France 1894–1903.

own request,[90] that she may have as much as is possible of the sea-air: it is the first time since our marriage that we have been separated for 24 hours.

7 October 1875. Speech[91] in the L.pool Town Hall at a dinner given to Ly D. & me by the Mayor. I spoke about half an hour: too long, but I had much to say. Well received, and pretty well satisfied with my performance.

... In the speech, I dwelt on the foreign policy of England, pointing out that though we had not now the exceptional position acquired by us during the last few years of the old Napoleonic war ... we were trusted, our opinion looked to, and our policy watched & criticised jealously, even by those who are always declaring our influence to be gone. I spoke of China & Turkey, describing the position of matters in each country: and took an opportunity of announcing the suspension of the Admiralty circular about escaped slaves,[92] which has caused a noise very disproportionate to its real importance. This had been settled between Disraeli & myself by letter. I also dwelt a little on trade matters, taking a sanguine view of finances on the whole, but explaining that an increase of expenditure as well as of income must be expected. (This speech appears by subsequent notices in the press to have been approved by the public as a whole, especially in that part which related to China.)

9 October 1875. In afternoon Schouvaloff came, according to agreement. I had a conversation of 2 hours with him, chiefly on Turkey: he dined, but went away at 10.30 to catch a night-train. I made this conversation into a draft: it contained in substance nothing except what I had previously heard from Elliot: the reason why he was specially charged to speak to me was that the Emperor of Russia is specially anxious as it appears, that his moderation in regard to the eastern question shall be known and appreciated. Certainly nothing can be more conservative than the language held both by Schouvaloff here, and by Ignatieff at Constantinople: the cause of this moderation is not so clear: it may be that foreseeing future complications with Germany, the Czar is not anxious to provoke hostility or to engage his forces in Turkey: it may be that the great cost and small return of the Central Asian annexations has disgusted him with the notion of further territorial extension, at least for the time: it is equally possible that he thinks Bosnian insurgents more likely to look to Austrian than Russian protection, and that jealousy of Austrian influence, and the dislike of

[90] In N. Wales.

[91] *T,* 8 Oct. 1875, 7f.

[92] An Admiralty circular on fugitive slaves, issued (31 July 1875) without cabinet knowledge, reversed policy by countenancing slavery; discovered by *Daily News,* 9 Sept., public outcry ensuing.

playing a secondary part, has thrown him on the Turkish side. It is possible, though considering the character of the man less likely, that he prefers to play a waiting game, and thinks the longer the delay, the surer will be the collapse of the Turkish empire: and that he prefers this should happen of itself, without interference on his part.

Ignatieff is undoubtedly vexed at the determination of Austria to outbid him with the native Christians: and there is apparently some pique, as well as policy, in his sudden change, and obvious wish to support the Turkish cause.

In Schouvaloff's conversation one passage only was remarkable: he expressed his belief that the Austrian government had no wish for an extension of territory, if that territory were occupied by a Sclave population: they had trouble enough, he said, with their existing Sclave subjects, and wanted no more: he then went on to quote a phrase which Andrassy had used, as summing up the policy of the two states: 'We will raise no Polish question: you will raise no Sclave agitation: and as to the eastern question, we will agree to defer it to the Greek kalends.'

He talked, among various other subjects, of the serf emancipation: which he seemed to think had not been altogether a success. It was right to have given them land, but they had received too much: and would neither as a rule work for others, nor yet cultivate what they held. They would moreover as a matter of course divide it among all their children, and would, he thought, be in a condition little above pauperism after a generation or two.

10 October 1875. Nothing yet from China, and we are waiting in some anxiety to know what the decision of the Chinese will be.

13 October 1875. Into Manchester to make a speech to the 'Socy for promotion of scientific industry'...[93]

14 October 1875. News from China at last satisfactory: it is vaguely worded, and to my mind does not prove that we may not have more trouble hereafter: but for the moment there can be no war. Wade avoids details, and between the brevity of his telegrams (perhaps inevitable, as they don't come in cypher) and the enormous length of his despatches, which exceed all human powers of reading, it is not always easy to make out what he is doing. – I am not sure that news will be well received by the press, though satisfaction must be professed: it is strange how strong the desire of fighting seems to be even where nothing is to be got by it, either in gain or glory.

15 October 1875. The newspapers are full of the repudiation, or rather bankruptcy, of the Turkish govt ... ... The English creditors deserve little pity: they speculated with their eyes open ... and having mostly

[93] *T,* 14 Oct. 1875, 10d.

bought at a very reduced price, they will get a fair return out of their investment even at the reduced rate of interest. ... Levy, of the D. Tel., wrote to me on the subject, and I answered him frankly to the effect that I do not see what there is to do though quite willing to meet the general wish as far as I can.

19 October 1875. Decazes is nervous and fidgety about the Turkish bankruptcy: very anxious that something should be done for the bondholders ... ... The Italians are also inclined to complain: and for a curious reason. The clericals have on principle declined investing in Italian securities, lest they should strengthen the new Italian kingdom: consequently their savings are largely placed in Turkey: and the govt is anxious to conciliate them where it can without any compromise of principle.

... It is significant that the Bulgarians, in general a quiet and easy-going people, are said now to wish for independence, and to be ready to join in the movement if Servia had led the way.

25 October 1875. Wrote to ... O. Russell ... chiefly to mention the fact of Münster's[94] absolute silence on foreign affairs, which considering the usual diplomatic habit of talking over such matters in and out of season, is singular.

... There came in afternoon, the French Ambassador, with wife and daughter ... Cross & Mrs Cross ... ... In all with ourselves 24.

27 October 1875. Shooting ... ... We killed, I think, something under 400 head.

29 October 1875. Shooting ... ... We killed 555 head...

31 October 1875. Ignatieff continues his game of denouncing the Austrians, & taking credit to Russia for defeating their schemes.

1 November 1875. Letter from O. Russell, in which he answers a question I had put to his brother, relating to the reports current in his family that he is tired of Berlin. He denies all wish or intention of the kind, which I am heartily glad of: he is the best man we have.

2 November 1875. Talk with Sanderson, whose brothers are now talking of setting up in business again after their failure: I offered a loan, not exceeding £5000, the terms to be hereafter settled, in case they see their way to start afresh. I afterwards put this on paper, that there might be no mistake.

3 November 1875. London by 11 train from Edgehill, reaching St J. Square about 4.40 p.m. ... Disraeli called about 6 and we talked over the situation at some length. He is full of the Turkish business, thinks the end is coming, does not see how the power of the Sultan is to be propped up: agrees with me that we cannot treat the case of the

---

[94] Guest at Knowsley since 18 Oct.

bondholders as in any way exceptional, but thinks the bankruptcy will affect English feeling about Turkey so as to make a continuance of the old policy impossible.

He explained that he had been obliged to keep Adderley at the B. of T. after having turned him out of it, but negotiations with Cave,[95] who was the intended successor, had failed, Cave standing out for a seat in cabinet, which D. objected to. Cave thereupon resigned altogether (he is in bad health, which makes the loss less important, though a sound sensible man): and his place is to be taken by G. Bentinck:[96] E. Stanhope[97] replacing him as second to Adderley. The arrangement is good: Stanhope is able, popular, and deserves promotion: Bentinck, who is much the reverse, is pushed aside into an office where there is nothing to do – and without affronting him, for in form it is promotion.

Talk of peers: he is much pressed, says he must make some: thinks of Tollemache, Gerard, Sturt, Ormsby Gore, and perhaps Gerard. Of these Ormsby Gore has no son: Tollemache, Sturt and Gerard are all of old family, and large territorial wealth: in every way fit: except that Gerard[98] is ultramontane, and that his son is a bad sort of fool, there seems no objection to any.[99] He is pressed to make Ld E. Hill[100] a peer, for which there appears no adequate reason: and Cochrane,[101] which is absurd. Legh[102] of Lyme would also be glad of promotion: but he has hardly earned it.

D. was in high spirits, as he has reason to be: the promotion of Baggallay[103] to be a judge has vacated Mid-Surrey, a large & formerly very democratic constituency: but though they have tried hard, the Liberals can find no one to contest the seat.[104]

---

[95] (Sir) Stephen Cave (1820–80), Cons. M.P. 1859–80; paymaster-gen. and vice-pres. of board of trade, 1866–8; paymaster-general and judge advocate-gen., 1874, resigning latter post, Dec. 1875, to go on special mission to Egypt.

[96] George Cavendish Bentinck (1821–91), parl. sec. to board of trade 1874–Nov. 1875; judge advocate-gen. 1875–80.

[97] Edward Stanhope (1840–93), 2nd s. of 5th E. Stanhope; parl. sec. to board of trade, Nov. 1875–Apr. 1878; under-sec. for India, 1878–80; cabinet min. 1885, 1886–92; Fellow of All Souls, with First in maths.

[98] Old R.C. Lancs. family, with s. on the turf.

[99] Four commoners were cr. peers, Jan. 1876: (1) John Tollemache, 1st Baron Tollemache (1805–90), Cons. M.P. 1841–72, (2) H.G. Sturt, 1st Baron Alington (1825–1904), Cons. M.P. 1847–76, (3) J.R. Ormsby-Gore, 1st Baron Harlech (1816–June 1876), Cons. M.P. 1837–41, 1859–76, (4) Robert Gerard, 1st Baron Gerard of Bryn (1808–87).

[100] Lord Arthur Edwin Hill (Hill-Trevor from 1862), 1st Baron Trevor (1819–94), Cons. M.P. 1845–80; cr. peer, 1880.

[101] Member of Young England; cr. peer, 1880.

[102] William John Legh, 1st Baron Newton (1828–98), Cons. M.P. 1859–65, 1868–85; cr. peer 1892; cf. *Stanley Diaries*, 239.

[103] Cons. solicitor-general.

[104] Cons. returned unopposed, 24 Nov. 1875.

4 November 1875. Cabinet at 12: all present except J. Manners: we sat 2¼ hours. We had a long discussion as to the Admiralty instructions about fugitive slaves, and agreed, without difference of opinion, to remodel them, as Cairns does not agree with the law officers in the construction which he puts on the law: and he is of the three more likely to be right. Their withdrawal was therefore decided, and a committee of cabinet is to frame the new orders.[105]

Long discussion afterwards about the case of collision between the *Iron Duke* and *Vanguard,* in regard to which it is thought that the public and the profession are dissatisfied with the decision of the Admiralty: Hunt however defended it, making, as seemed to me, a pretty good case, and anyway we have no choice now except to uphold his judgment.[106]

5 November 1875. Cabinet at 2: sat till 4.15: various subjects discussed: we sketched out a list of bills for next session. D. expressed himself as not anxious to have a large programme, but wishing to carry all that we brought in: which was generally agreed to.

The bills approved merchant shipping: public prosecutors: marine insurance: court of final appeal: universities: militia ballot: factories and workshops: juries: consolidation of laws of evidence: and one or two more which were only talked about, but not settled.

Long discussion as to B. of T. arrangements for working the m. shipping bill of last year. They are difficult, for all turns on getting surveyors who are both honest and competent: their opportunities of roguery, if they are otherwise than honest, being considerable: and if incompetent, they may give great annoyance to shipowners without advantage to anybody.

Talk about cattle disease which is disturbing the minds of farmers: but nothing was settled. Talk about new public offices: agreed to give notice for the land between G. George St and the present offices: the cost will be £1,500,000, and £1,000,000 more for building.

Talk about Dover harbour, where great outlay is desired by the naval authorities: agreed to put if off for the year. Long conversation about gunboats for service in China: Hunt says we have scarcely any fit for service: he wants twelve new ones: cost about £250,000. We agree to wait till we see how finances are. Northcote is not sanguine: the last quarter has not been satisfactory: the revenue is coming in badly: and every department wants money. He thinks that if he can escape from

[105] Derby's Liverpool speech (7 Oct.) announcing suspension of the circular, had argued that it was legally correct. This Disraeli, writing to the Queen, called 'an indiscretion in policy' (M. and B. 398).
[106] H.M.S. *Iron Duke* sank H.M.S. *Vanguard* in fog (1 Sept.). An Admiralty minute exonerated the Admiral commanding the squadron, while dismissing, undefended, a lieut., reversing previous court-martial verdicts.

the necessity of putting on new taxes, that is all we can expect.

... Saw Delane, who came to ask about Turkey and China.

6 November 1875. Cabinet at 12: sat till 2: our business was chiefly to consider the Chancellor's proposal for a court of final appeal: we all agreed to his plan, which is perhaps as little unsatisfactory as a compromise can be: I do not entirely like it, but acquiesce, having nothing better to propose.

Northcote brought forward a scheme for creating a new class of clerks, intermediate between the present highly paid clerks on the establishment, and the mere copyists: it was much debated, and not favourably received: we agreed to discuss it again later.

Disraeli threw out hints as if one more cabinet would be enough: but this notion was not approved, and Cross mildly hinted that there were still many subjects to consider. D. is unequalled in his judgment as to what line the public will expect us to take on a difficult question: and his skill is also conspicuous in getting out of all embarrassment: but he dislikes detail, is easily wearied by it, and cares little about the preparation of bills while the session is still distant. He is in good health and excellent spirits, but visibly an old man.

9 November 1875. Lawrence called[107] ... talk with him about investments etc. He does not advise mortgages, saying that it is not always easy to find them for the exact sum wanted, that the security depends on the title to the estate mortgaged, as to which mistakes may and do happen: and that in the event of payments failing, it is necessary to collect the rents oneself: a troublesome business. He likes railway debentures, but says they are hard to get for large sums. Thinks Indian securities too high, in which I agree. Funds are safe, but they may fall, in which case part of the capital is sacrificed. Land pays little, but is safer than anything else.

... Dinner at Guildhall ... Disraeli discussed foreign affairs at some length, and in a safe cautious tone. He was less effective than I have heard him, but judicious and sensible, which is the main point.[108]

10 November 1875. Cabinet, from 2 to 4.15: various matters discussed, but not in a businesslike way, Disraeli being evidently exhausted from last night & not paying much attention. We called in the Lord Advocate, who has bills on various questions: education the chief, but there were several others: one for letting improvements on Scotch estates be paid for in the same way as is provided by the English bill of last year. We had in Sclater Booth, & discussed his plans: he has 4 bills in hand: pollution of rivers: poor law amendment (including the power to create or dissolve unions to be vested in the L.G.Bd): one which I forget: and

---

[107] Derby's solicitor.
[108] Cf. Zetland ed., *Letters to Lady Bradford* (1929), i 300–301.

a highway bill, over which we had a long conversation, Salisbury & one or two others fearing lest it should take away power from quarter sessions. Cross asked & got leave to consolidate the burials Acts, which are many & confused. We talked of Irish peerages, and of new arrangements for the New Forest: but nothing was settled on either of these matters. We talked of the disturbances in the Malay peninsula, which threaten to become serious: and agreed on telegrams to be sent sanctioning the sending thither of troops from India.

11 November 1875. Cabinet at 2: sat till 3.45: Carnarvon, rather agitated, pressed us at once to remove Gen. Colborne,[109] who has gone from Hongkong to take command against the Malays: he (C.) believing him to be unfit for the work. This we refused to do without hearing what the War Office had to say. Hardly is ill, and could not attend. A discussion followed about the living of Halifax, which in the end we agreed must be referred to a committee. Sir M. Beach was then called in, and gave a long list of bills which he wants passed: the subjects (1) judicature (2) powers of chairmen of counties (3) jury laws (4) reform of Irish prisons. He had other plans, but we all agreed that the above were enough for one session. We discussed the Sunday opening of public houses, as to which we were nearly beaten last year: he suggested a possible compromise, that of leaving it optional with the magistrates, in all cases of transfer or renewal of licences, to issue them for six days only. This was left over for consideration. He told us that in the north there is a bad feeling on the land question. The Ulster custom, legalised by Gladstone's act, is vague: and the tenants seem to have expected much more than the courts have given.

... Schouvaloff called to compare notes on the eastern question: he took great pains to assure me that his Emperor was anxious only to keep things quiet, and avoid a general disturbance. Certainly the acts of the Russian govt correspond so far with these professions: and they may be true, for the Emperor's character is peaceable, and he has trouble enough at home: but who can trust a foreign diplomatist, and who can trust a Russian?

12 November 1875. Cabinet: we settled after some discussion that no change shall be made in the position of Gen. Colborne, but that Gen. Ross shall go as his second-in command. The rest of the time was taken up with a scheme that Cross has for altering the law of enclosures. At present all is at a deadlock: H. of C. will sanction no enclosure bills, however unobjectionable, and much inconvenience ensues.

Talk with D. about the Indian gov. genship, which Northbrook wants to give up: and will probably do so in a few months. Who is to be the successor? Carnarvon was thought of, but would not go: nor do I feel

[109] Gen. (Sir) Francis Colborne (1817–95), 2nd s. of 1st Baron Seaton.

sure, able as he is, that the choice would be a good one: D. of Buckingham is not equal to the place: Ld Lyons was thought of, he would certainly refuse, and is fitter for his present employment: Napier of Magdala[110] is possible, but has the reputation of being reckless in financial matters: Sir B. Frere is open to the same objection: I could at the moment suggest no one: but have since thought of Ld Dufferin,[111] who might be disposed to accept, and is probably competent. Though a Liberal, he is serving under us in Canada, and his promotion is not therefore like the selection of an opponent.

We have two other difficulties: the choice of a solicitor-general, for which place there is really no one well suited now in parliament on our side: and that of a charity commissioner. Disraeli proposes for the latter Sir S. Fitzgerald, who is looked upon with suspicion as a man whose hands are not clean: I never heard that anything had been proved against him: still a mere suspicion, if widely spread, is enough to throw discredit on such a choice for a place which involves large dealings with money.

... I forgot to note that before the cabinet I attended with Richmond, Northcote, Cairns, & Cross, in the Exchequer Chamber, where the judges were assembled, to settle the list of sheriffs. This rather useless ceremony (for all is arranged beforehand) occupied an hour.

13 November 1875. With Sanderson ... to Haslemere station to see the Witley park estate. ... We ... managed to walk over the greater part of the estate, which took my fancy.

14 November 1875. Carnarvon dined with us, alone: I was struck with a change in him which I can scarcely describe. He talked incessantly, in a rapid excited way which is new with him, except that he has done the same once or twice in cabinet. Ly Derby was impressed as I was by his manner, it seems as if since his loss he had thrown himself into work with a feverish activity, not quite healthy or natural.[112]

15 November 1875 (Monday). Very busy, chiefly with routine work. Mr Greenwood[113] of the Pall Mall Gazette called with a story that the Khedive is going to sell his share in the Suez canal[114] to a French company, which I don't believe, but telegraphed to Cairo to make sure.

16 November 1875. Worked on letters & papers till 11: then with Sanderson to Waterloo: reached Witley at 12.45, and passed the time till 4 in walking over the estate and on to the adjoining Hindhead

---

[110] R.C. Napier, 1st Baron Napier of Magdala (1810–90), conqueror of Abyssinia, 1868, c.-in-c. India 1870–6; cr. peer 1868.

[111] Frederick Blackwood, 1st M. of Dufferin and Ava (1826–1902), gov.-gen. of Canada 1872–8, gov.-gen. of India 1884–8.

[112] Carnarvon's 1st wife d. 25 Jan. 1875. He m. 2ndly Dec. 1878.

[113] Frederick Greenwood (1830–1909), ed. *Pall Mall Gazette* 1865–80.

[114] See Lord Rothschild, *You Have It, Madam* (1980).

common. ... I left the place much inclined to make an offer, but will
do nothing in haste.

Home, & busy most of the evening. The report of the Khedive
wishing to sell his interest in the canal to a French company appears
to have some truth in it.

Despatches from Petersburgh ... ... The Austrian plan of Turkish
reform has been considered at Pet. & rejected: we do not know exactly
what it was, but it is clear that Russia & Austria are not agreed...

... From Berlin, I have a remarkable letter: Russell thinks that
Bismarck is keeping purposely aloof feeling uncertain what Russia will
do, & not wishing to be prematurely committed. The Russian & German
relations are evidently neither confidential nor cordial. Bismarck wishes
all to be settled by the three empires, believing that he can influence
Austrian action, and so get his own way: on the other hand Gortschakoff
wishes to bring in France, England, & Italy: confident that France will
do what he wishes, and hoping to be able to settle terms with England.
Bismarck has never forgotten, or forgiven, the joint action of England
and Russia in May last: which took him by surprise, and the more so,
as he had taken great pains to create mutual distrust between the two.
He now says that Russia has betrayed him ... The Turks, Russell
thinks, have no friends in Germany: and the German people would
not care if England were to occupy Egypt.

17 November 1875 (Wednesday). Cabinet at 12, sat till 2. I brought on
the question of the Suez canal: it was agreed without dissent that we
could not allow nearly half the shares to pass to a French company, as
that would set M. Lesseps free from all control: and we determined to
instruct Stanton[115] accordingly to protest against the sale intimating that
we are ready to buy if reasonable terms can be obtained. This is an
important decision, it will give offence in France, though not reasonably,
for we only act in self-defence, and they have tried to steal a march on
us, and nearly succeeded. It remains to be seen if terms can be come
to.

We then discussed the question of education, as to which we are
likely to be pressed in the session. Hardy and Salisbury want one or
both of two things: that voluntary schools may in some shape receive
help out of the rates, so as to put them on an equal footing with school
board schools: and that children may be compelled to attend them in
the same way as they are where school boards exist. I opposed both
these proposals, Cross supporting me, and Disraeli though he said little
taking the same side. We separate without any conclusion come to.

18 November 1875. Cabinet at 2: we called in Ld Tenterden and Col.

---

[115] Edward Stanton, U.K. consul-general in Egypt.

Stokes[116] on the Suez canal affair: by telegrams received this morning it appears that the Khedive has no intention of selling his interest, though he has decided to mortgage it as the only means of getting a loan of which he is in urgent want: consequently nothing can or need be done, beyond watching the transaction. He offers to give the British govt the refusal if he should decide to sell, which is fair, and all that we could ask. He holds $3\frac{1}{2}$ million sterling, out of 8 millions of original capital: which has since been swelled by loans by 14 million. It is singular that the shares of 500 fcs ($\pounds$20) are at a premium (685 fcs) although no dividend has at any time been paid except out of capital. But the traffic is growing, and in the end it will be a paying concern.

Education bill discussed afterwards, we agreed on requiring that all children working for wages from 5 to 13 should have to have a certificate of being able to read, write, and cypher: but numerous exceptions will be necessary.

19 November 1875. Saw ... Mr Greenwood, who came with some further information as to the Khedive's debts ...: Levy, who came to ask news, and got what I had ... Cabinet at 4: Cairns read his draft of amended Admiralty instructions, which was provisionally agreed to, but the Law Officers object to it in principle, and on that ground we delayed settling anything till they have reported again. We then discussed the Merchant Shipping Bill, not in much detail, for it must be gone over again later with Adderley, but so as to consider the general lines on which it shall be drawn. ... Troubled with a heavy cold.

20 November 1875. Saw Schouvaloff, who discussed the situation in Turkey, which he thinks is becoming more serious. He wishes the question of how the Christian populations are to be treated, to be discussed by all the Powers, and not by three only: and expresses fear that if the war continues until the spring, it will be impossible to keep Servia & Montenegro from taking part. The meaning of this is that his govt does not like what the Austrians are doing, & thinks that a conference would be the most effective way of keeping them in check. – Home early from office, being unwell with a heavy cold, & hardly fit for business.

21 November 1875. Stayed at home, having a heavy cold upon me. ... I have not been thoroughly well for some time past...

22 November 1875. Much troubled with cold, and excused myself from attending a cabinet in consequence: the second I have missed since we took office. Saw M. Corry, who came from Disraeli to talk over Suez canal matters. D. seems now to see the difficulties attendant on a direct

---

[116] Sir John Stokes (1825–1902), engineer; on Danube commission 1856–71; U.K. commissioner on Suez canal dues, 1873; director of Suez canal 1876.

purchase by govt of the Viceroy's interest: and wishes the thing done through some mercantile house, Rothschild or Baring.

... The newspapers, possibly in want of other subjects, are full of the eastern question: and appear to exaggerate the imminence and extent of the danger. The situation is as follows: Russia, for whatever reason, is holding back, giving moderate and judicious advice to the Porte and apparently is in earnest in wishing to put an end to the insurrection. But the official article published in the Russian papers, though probably addressed only to Russian opinion, has frightened the Porte, and Ignatieff's known and habitual looseness of speech, to call it nothing more, increases the distrust felt: he has been so often found saying what was not true, that he cannot now get credit for sincerity. – Andrassy is planning some large scheme of reforms, which the Porte is sure to reject: the Emperor of Russia has apparently forced him to withdraw one project of that kind, and he is now elevating another. He vehemently disclaims all intentions of annexation, and all idea of a military occupation of Bosnia: which nevertheless is the design generally attributed to Austria.

Bismarck remains obstinately silent, waiting events, & perhaps not seeing his way, jealous of Russia, and more so since the commencement of a better understanding between Russia & England. The French govt would accept any policy, or act with any ally, rather than appear to be shut out: provided France can appear to have regained some of her influence in Europe, they care little for the rest. We are simply watching and waiting. Meanwhile the Sultan has ordered sundry reforms, and seems more than usually willing to listen to advice: the trouble is, to find men competent to execute them...

23 November 1875. Cabinet in afternoon: being the last for some time, we sat over three hours. Suez canal again discussed: and Egyptian affairs generally. We did not come to any definite result, nor do I see how we could: but another telegram was sent to Stanton, desiring him to prevent if possible the sale of the canal shares to either of the companies with which the Khedive is negotiating. We then discussed a mem. by Hunt on the state of the navy, in which he draws a gloomy picture of its condition, and insists on an increased outlay of £413,000. He is backed up by all the naval authorities, Milne, Hornby, and Ld Gilford.[117] We came to no conclusion on his demand as a whole, but authorised the building of six new gunboats, which in the ordinary course would not have been sanctioned till next April. It is clear now that even with estimates as they are, there can be no surplus: and Hardy has a large additional bill for army expenditure, which he says

[117] (Sir) A. Milne (1806–96), admiral, junior naval lord of admiralty 1872–6; Sir Geoffrey Hornby (1825–95), lord of admiralty 1875–7; Capt. Lord Gilford, lord of admiralty, 1874.

cannot be deferred. The question seems to be, not whether new taxation shall be put on, but whether the amount shall be a penny or only a halfpenny extra in the income tax.

24 November 1875 (Wednesday). Richmond talked to me seriously yesterday of Hunt's unpopularity with the public: he has been unlucky, and a series of accidents coming one after another has made the world think him incapable – not with justice, as I conceive, but prejudices of that sort once taken up, are hard to be shaken off. Richmond went so far as to say that the party would not support him: and that Disraeli ought to put someone else in the place: but the step would be a harsh one, and hardly generous where there is so little real ground of complaint: and what is quite as much to the purpose, there is nobody that I can see to take his place. It is one of the weak points of our cabinet that we have scarcely any competent men outside to fill vacancies if they should occur.

Received in the course of the afternoon a telegram saying that the Khedive has been offered 100 million francs (£4,000,000) for his Suez canal shares, by Lesseps, but would give us the refusal of them at that price. A cabinet was called in haste to consider the offer, for an answer is wanted by tomorrow: all attended, except J. Manners: after short discussion we agreed to accept: subject, that is, to the consent of parliament. Rothschild undertakes to find the money, and takes the risk of parliament refusing the bargain, which is not likely to happen: there was no difference of opinion among us, Northcote being as ready as any. I telegraphed accordingly.

25 November 1875. Delane called yesterday on Lady Derby and spoke seriously, as if alarmed, at the growing unpopularity of the Queen. Her conduct after the accident in the Solent was much blamed: she was thought to show a want of feeling toward the sufferers by it, and an undue eagerness to screen her officers: then came this foolish business of old Brown's funeral,[118] and her following it on foot, which she must needs put into the court circular. The thing is in itself a trifle, but it is noticed that of all the relations and friends whom she has lost, from the Duke of Wellington downwards, she has never attended the funeral of any: and it is not thought decent that the sole exception made should have been in favour of a Highland farmer. There is no doubt but that she is growing every year more wilful and selfish, and that she is fond of saying that the only people really loyal to her are the Scottish peasantry about Balmoral.

Telegram from Cairo that the bargain with the Khedive is concluded, and the contract signed. Northcote called, and discussed details with me, at length.

[118] *T*, 21 Oct. 1875, 9e. Of deceased's five sons, four were in the Queen's service.

26 November 1875. Heard with regret, but not with surprise, that Disraeli's idea of appointing Seymour Fitzgerald to the vacant Charity Commissionership is likely to be extremely unpopular. Fitzgerald has been all his life an embarrassed man, and though I could never ascertain that any definite charge was made, he has lain under suspicion of corrupt dealings during his governorship of Bombay.

... Northcote & Disraeli agree in wishing Cave to be sent out to Egypt to advise the Khedive. I had suggested Lowe, who is willing to go, and would command more confidence in the City, after what he has done this year on the Loans Committee...

27 November 1875. Office: saw there Harcourt,[119] and explained to him fully all that had passed about the Suez canal. He was quiet & moderate, as he always is, but said his people would be rather sore. I laid stress in talking to him on the fact that no surprise was intended on our part: the suddenness with which the thing was done being a necessary condition of its being done at all.

... Münster ... is much delighted with the Suez transaction, chiefly because of the annoyance which he thinks it will give in France.

28 November 1875. Left with M. early for Keston ... ... Effect of the change of air on M. in regard of health & energy was marvellous: within an hour she seemed a different person.

29 November 1875. So far as I can make out, the purchase is universally popular. I might say even more, it seems to have created a feeling of something like enthusiasm far in excess of the real importance of the transaction. It is a complete political success: yet the very fact of its being so causes me some uneasiness: for it shows the intense desire for action abroad that pervades the public mind, the impatience created by long diplomatic inactivity, and the strength of a feeling which might under certain circumstances, take the form of a cry for war. It shows also what guess-work the management of an English administration is. A few years ago, such a proceeding as the purchase by the State of shares in a foreign company would have been thought absurd, and the minister who proposed it ruined in public opinion.

2 December 1875. News from Stanton that the Khedive is contemplating a fresh sale of his interests in the canal: this time what he wants to part with is his right to 15 per cent on all profits over 5 per cent: a very shadowy kind of property, but which may have its value. He asks for it two millions sterling, which he says the French are willing to offer, but he had rather deal with us. I am a little sceptical as to the French proposal, and consulting with Cairns and Northcote, both of whom are in town, I found they agreed that the offer was not desirable to be

[119] French amb.

entertained. It is a bad, at least a very speculative investment: it would make the French believe that we shall not be satisfied unless the whole canal is in our hands, which is contrary to the language we have always held, and calculated to create jealousy: and I think it is questionable whether parliament would approve. There are already signs of a reaction from the first enthusiasm with which our action of last week was received.

... Talk about calling parliament together at once: Cairns is for it, Northcote against, I am inclined to be against but have hardly as yet been able to decide.

6 December 1875. Despatches ... Bismarck, the Emperor, the German court, and the German public, are all equally pleased with the Suez business: I suppose because they consider it a blow to France.

Gortschakoff talks of the good relations between England & Russia (to O. Russell) in a marked way, as if something was wanted to be got out of us. He speaks frankly enough of Turkey: saying two alternatives are possible, one a real reconstruction of the east, which is a more serious business than any govt seems willing to take in hand: the other a patching-up ('replâtrage') which may last for some years, and about which he thinks there ought to be no difficulty. The latter is the course he is prepared to adopt, if the Emperor agrees.

10 December 1875. I am beginning to feel the incessant worry of this office, which hardly gives one day of entire rest in the year...

13 December 1875. Worked at home till 1, when called on Disraeli. Much talk with him on many subjects. He has offered Lytton the Gov.-Gen.ship of India:[120] a questionable choice, for L. has weak health, and not energy for so hardworking a place, though there is no question of his talent. It is still in doubt whether he will accept.

D. of Abercorn wants to retire from Dublin, but it is not easy to find anyone to take his place: Beauchamp[121] has been named, but his ritualism would be unpopular with the protestants, and his pedantic stiff ways peculiarly objectionable to the Irish. Ld Percy[122] has thrown up his court post, saying he wants a working place, but as he has never worked, nor shown any aptitude for work, this is a wish not easy to gratify. ... D. talks of the Queen, says she has been quiet of late, not

[120] Previously declined by Lord Powis, Lord John Manners, and Lord Carnarvon.

[121] Frederick Lygon, 6th E. Beauchamp (1830–91), succ. bro. 1866; pres. of Oxford Union, fellow of All Souls; member of council, Keble Coll.; Cons. M.P. 1857–66; a lord of admiralty 1858–9, lord steward 1874–80, ld-lieut. Worcs. 1876–96, paymaster-gen. 1885–6, 1886–7. Cf. Derby Diaries, 30 Jan. 1878, 'We talked of Beauchamp as a possible minister; he is cultivated and has some capacity, but is a prig, and generally disliked'.

[122] Henry Percy, 7th D. of Northumberland (1846–1918), styled Earl Percy 1867–99, when succ. father; Cons. M.P. 1868–85; P.C. Mar. 1874; treasurer of the household 1874–5, holding no further ministerial office.

violent nor excited: is very eager to be declared 'Empress of India' which was her fancy last year, but it then passed off: much disgusted also at the D. of Edinburgh, who has run into debt, to the extent of £80,000, with an income of £50,000 a year, and no particular reason for expense. ... D. seemed well, and said that he had been resting in the country.

15 December 1875. Saw Beust, who expects his long-waited-for note[123] next week: I settled to go up to town from Knowsley to see him.

16 December 1875. Left for Edinburgh...

17 December 1875. Inaugurated as Rector.[124] I delivered my address, which lasted nearly an hour. The room was quite full: about 1600 were said to be present.

... At 8 I went with the Lord Adv. to a workingmen's meeting, where more than 2000 had assembled ... I spoke to them for about $\frac{3}{4}$ hour ... ... My speech was well received from first to last ... ... My argument was all directed to one point – that there is no reason why workingmen should not be conservative in regard of politics, since they have ... nothing more to get or to expect from agitation. Following the same line of thought, I noted the various points on which Liberals are not agreed among themselves...

18 December 1875. Received the freedom of the city. ... I spoke about half an hour ... ... Luncheon with the Lord Adv. and left for Knowsley at 2.10 with Sanderson.

19 December 1875. Walk early with Sanderson: busy all the rest of the day.

20 December 1875. M. arrived from Woburn...

22 December 1875. Read a letter by Darwin addressed to M. on the occasion of my Edinburgh address, which gave me more pleasure than compliments usually do, for three reasons: because it need not to have been written, and therefore is probably sincere: because it comes from one of the very few men who are eminent as thinkers, not only in their own country, but throughout Europe: and because the passages which he has selected for praise are those which refer to science ... ... The three speeches of last week appear collectively to have succeeded with the public...

... Heard from Disraeli. He has been reproached by the Queen for letting the secret of the D. of Edinburgh's debts get out: she sent him 7 telegrams, he says, in one day: but he was able to justify himself: the fact is the Duke has been running about telling his affairs to all the world, and trying to raise the sum he wants. Schouvaloff is not altogether ill pleased, for the matter will be settled by the Duke going

[123] Andrassy Note, not received by Derby until 4 Jan. 1876.
[124] Of Edinburgh University.

on a cruise for 3 years, during which time he may economise.

23 December 1875. The Khedive is talking of selling his right to 15 p. cent of the surplus income of the canal over 5 p. cent, to a French company. We cannot object in principle to the transaction, but I have telegraphed to advise against it. He is to receive £2,000,000, but to pay 9 per cent interest upon it if the returns of the investment do not amount to so much.

24 December 1875. Despatches from Constantinople. The promised reforms are published, and seem plausible enough, if their execution could be guaranteed. The Austrian opposition to their publication continued to the last, but the object of it was too obviously personal: Andrassy wished that nothing should be done of which he has not the credit, and therefore urged delay: Ignatieff pressed on the publication mainly, as would appear, in order to mortify Andrassy.

25 December 1875. Margaret asked this morning to speak to me, and explained that (as we had long seen) an intimacy had been growing up between Sanderson and her, which had led to his making speeches of which she could not misunderstand the meaning. An explanation between them followed, in which she seems to have spoken her mind with great frankness and even some roughness. What she said was that he was not to entertain the hope that she would marry him either then or at any future time. He is disappointed, and not unreasonably, for she undoubtedly gave him a good deal of encouragement, more than she ought: but she has no experience of the world, and was naturally pleased with his attentions. ... She repeated to me three times ... that her mind was made up, and that she should not change it, but on that point I am not so certain. If she did so, want of means need be no obstacle, for I have enough for both: and S. is a man thoroughly to be trusted: but in any event a London life and a moderate income would be hard to bear, for she has always lived in great houses, and likes nothing so well as the country. I am not sure that the matter is ended yet.

26 December 1875. Wrote ... to Layard to ask ... whether he would like to move from Madrid to ... Lisbon. My reason for doing this is that I know he was trying last year to negotiate an exchange with Sir C. Murray.[125] If he accepts, I shall probably put Morier into his place, and dispose of Munich to Rumbold,[126] who is miserable and discontented in Chili, and appears to have pleased the Chilians as little as they please him.

... Hearing that Sanderson's brothers have as yet found no employment, I made an excuse to give him the £100 now which I should

[125] Sir Charles Murray (1806–95), min. at Lisbon until 1874.
[126] Sir Horace Rumbold (1829–1913), min. in Chile 1872–8, in Switzerland 1878–9.

have paid in April. He is apparently supporting the whole family, but that state of things cannot last long.

28 December 1875. Arthur Cecil and his wife arrived: she has never been at Knowsley since their marriage. She is large and plain, but not vulgar, at least no more so than many women in society, and has a look of good sense. Her husband is as young, as boyish, and as well satisfied with himself as ever. Except in the latter particular, he curiously resembles Eustace.[127]

Talk with M. about Margaret's business: I pressed her not to throw any obstacles in her way, if her daughter really liked Sanderson: indeed I do not know where she could find a better husband for her, and I am certain that for a girl of rather passionate and romantic temperament, a marriage of convenience and reason would not be a success: though it has answered well enough in her sister's[128] case ... ... She professes indifference to him, but her manner does not indicate it. I said that if the marriage were to come about I would settle upon them jointly ... an annuity of £2000 a year for both their lives, which with her fortune and his pay, would make a joint income exceeding £3000. There is of course no question of pressing the marriage upon her, if she shows no marked preference.

29 December 1875. I have not noticed the death of Lord Stanhope,[129] announced some days ago ... ... He had been failing in health and spirits ever since the loss of his wife 2 years ago ... ... He has filled a considerable place in society for many years. His house was always open to literary men: his own books, though showing no great mental power, are laborious, accurate, and readable: and though he took little part in politics, he had the knack of selecting subjects which when attention was called to them, proved ripe for action. Thus he induced the H. of Lds virtually to abandon the use of proxies: got the division lists printed & published: induced the govt of the day to omit the political services from the prayerbook ...: and by raising last year the question of Irish peerages, has probably brought about the abandonment of the rule established at the Union, that their number shall be kept up to 100. None of these are great successes, but in each case the thing which he proposed has seemed to the public the right thing to do. In private life I have known Stanhope so well, and been so often his guest, that I am no fair critic. He owed much of his social position to his wife: his manner was somewhat pedantic, and by many persons his conversation was thought tedious: but if never original, he was always well-informed: in French and English literature there were few

[127] Lord Eustace Cecil.
[128] Mary, Lady Galloway.
[129] See above, 1870 n. 50.

works of any note or merit published in our day with which he was not familiar: and he gathered round him men celebrated in literature & politics, both English and foreign, without respect to party or in general to opinion. He was an industrious collector of scraps and fragments of knowledge: always storing up memoranda of whatever interested him: I do not know what their value may be, but their bulk must be considerable.

31 December 1875. Sent off 7 office boxes ... I was obliged to mark several drafts as requiring to be rewritten. There is a good deal of careless drafting in the office, about which I have had to speak more than once.

1876

Flyleaf, 1876 ... When I succeeded, in Oct. 1869, I found mortgage debts to the value of £327,000: my brother's claims were £205,000 more: £114,000 was due to the bank as overdrawn balance: and legacies and succession duty made up the whole charge to about £680,000. I have thus cleared myself to the extent of £460,000 in six years: and though it is true that I have parted with the family estates in Ireland, yet land has been bought in Lancashire or in Kent worth more than £120,000...

... My present object is to lay by £40,000 yearly for the next four years, so as to make up £200,000 invested, in 1880. Beyond that date I do not form any definite plans; but at the same rate of saving I might in 1890, if alive, have £700,000 laid by.

I am in expectation of receiving from railway companies various large windfalls in the next 12 or 18 months. Collectively they ought not to fall short of £150,000...

1 January 1876. Wrote to S.[1] ... telling him that I will increase his personal allowance to £600 a year, to continue while we remain in office ... His position is trying: his brothers ruined, after having had brilliant prospects in the City: one other brother a curate: all the family apparently on his shoulders, and he has only his pay and what I allow him. Then on top of all comes this love affair ... I have never seen more courage and cheerfulness shown under difficulties than by him in the last few months.

... Looking through a notebook of personal expenditure, I find that I have spent in the year just ended about £3200, of which more than three fourths is works of art, china, plate, drawings, pictures, or books.

In the history of the last twelve months there is little to note. My life has been mainly occupied by the incessant business of the Foreign Office, which leaves little leisure for other pursuits. In official life I have had perhaps fewer worries and troubles than fall to the share of most ministers: what speaking I have had to do has been in general a success rather than the contrary: and the two chief actions of the year, the intervention to maintain peace in May, and the Suez purchase, have both been approved. In China[2] too matters have gone well so far,

[1] Sanderson.
[2] In 1875 the Yunan Mission was attacked and a UK consular official, A.R. Margary,

though it is too early to feel confident that we shall have all our demands conceded.

The ministry has apparently lost no strength: our majority remains unlessened, one or two defeats being balanced by gains elsewhere: there is no open disaffection, though probably some secret disquiet, among our friends: and the Liberal chiefs are too little united even to desire an early return to power. It is not probable that the cabinet will survive the next general election: but that event is distant: and at present no serious danger has shown itself.

In point of health I have nothing to complain of: that of Ly D. though not as strong as I could wish, does not get worse: indeed is better than at the beginning of last year ... But I accept the good fortune which has hitherto followed me with a full sense of its uncertainty, though not aware of any probable cause for a change.

Beust writes to me that his long-expected note is due next week, and wishes for an interview: I put him off to the week after: as we have been kept waiting for this document since the early part of Dec. there can be no such urgent haste to decide upon it now.

2 January 1876. Disraeli wants me to find a place as consul for a Mr Johnston,[3] an Irish Orangeman of extremely violent opinions, but as is said having considerable influence in Ulster: I do not like the job, and shall excuse myself if possible. Luckily no consulship of any value is now vacant.

3 January 1876 A. Cecil and his wife left us. She is plain, middle-aged, very fat, and wholly without attraction: so that one does not see how the marriage came about: but not vulgar and seems to have sense. M. is not ill-pleased with her, thinking that she will keep her husband out of scrapes. He is unaltered: high spirits, good humour, good manners, and boundless conceit: but she can do with him what she pleases. They travel with a dog, a parrot, and a baby: and as she is 33 and looks all her age, whereas A. is young for his, one would hardly take them for man and wife.

... Settled ... requests for land to be let cheaply, or given, for the benefit of schools or chapels. I have made it a rule in such cases not to reduce the full rent by more than one-half, or less than one-quarter.

4 January 1876. Telegram from Wade, in a tone of alarm: he thinks the Chinese are playing with us, and wants the squadron reinforced. But he is at all times nervous, and possibly a week hence may telegraph that his fears are removed.

---

murdered. After much negotiation, Derby secured from China an inquiry, with Britain represented, to discover and punish the offenders.

[3] William Johnstone (1829–1902), Orangeman; M.P. 1868–78, 1885–1902; inspector of Irish fisheries, 1878; imprisoned, 1868, and dismissed, 1885, both for extremism.

The long-expected Austrian note[4] is come: I read it rapidly, and with satisfaction, for in tone and general purport it appears moderate, and I can see nothing in it dangerous to Turkish power ... Wrote about it to Russell, Harcourt,[5] Delane, and Levy...

... Shooting from 10.30 till 4 ... we killed 666 head, chiefly pheasants.

5 January 1876. Walk with Sanderson: talk with him about Margaret ... I told him that I have been aware of and quite approved his wishes: that I was prepared to hear of a marriage: – that I regretted his want of success, but did not see why he should consider it as necessarily final: I told him the story of Mary Galloway, and her many vacillations ... I said that if the lady changed her mind, want of means would be no obstacle ... In short, I encouraged him to persevere.

6 January 1876. The appointment of Lytton to India is noticed in most of the papers[6] favourably: the objections to him, weak health and a dreamy absent habit of mind, are not known to the public. Disraeli has been happy in his choice of men so far: but in this case I have doubts. Northbrook is to have an earldom: his reasons for retiring are not clear, but are probably various: four years of exhausting labour must have told on his health: there is some domestic scandal about a son of his in India which I know only in a vague way, and do not care to know better: and having come into a large fortune at the death of T. Baring,[7] he is now in no want of money.

... The Portuguese cabinet is again seized with one of its periodical panics as to the danger of invasion by Spain.... As usual, what is wanted is a promise of protection from England: but there is an obvious awkwardness in undertaking beforehand to do certain things in a wholly uncertain contingency.

Beust having expressed a wish to talk over the Austrian note, I asked him down here,[8] but our discussion is put off till tomorrow.

7 January 1876. Walk early with Beust, and conversation with him: whether from really having little to add to what is already known, or from dislike of the business, he did not speak in a very definite or decided way: dwelling chiefly on the dangers of leaving things as they are, and avoiding discussion of the particular reforms proposed. In consequence of our conversation I wrote to Disraeli: expressing my opinion that we must in some form adhere to the movement made by the three powers: France will certainly join them, so will Italy, and if we stand aloof we shall be isolated in Europe. That might matter less, if we were sure of support at home: but English opinion is likely to go

---

[4] Andrassy Note (30 Dec. 1875), accepted by Turkey, 13 Feb. 1876.
[5] Diplomatists.
[6] E.g. *T*, 6 Jan. 1876, 5d.
[7] Thomas Baring (1799–1873), financier.
[8] To Knowsley.

entirely against Turkey. I pointed out that if we decline to join, and
the Porte accepts (though under pressure) the reforms proposed, we
are placed in the foolish position of being more Turkish than the Turks:
if on the other hand the Sultan is by our abstention encouraged to
refuse, the whole responsibility of defeating what is at least a promising
attempt at pacification will fall upon us. Whether the insurgents will
come in on any terms is a separate question: and also whether the
whole fabric of Turkish administration is not so rotten as to make
all attempts to patch it hopeless, but these are matters in regard to
which certainty is unobtainable beforehand: we can only try. I added
that I have given no intimation of opinion which can compromise the
cabinet, though not concealing my personal satisfaction at finding
that the Austrian proposals are more moderate than I had been led
to expect.

8 January 1876. Letter[9] from Salisbury on eastern matters, long and
able: the purport of it that we ought to accept the Austrian reforms in
the lump, but take care not to engage ourselves in such a manner as
to be drawn into further proceedings which may be contemplated by the
three Emperors: he assumes that a military occupation is contemplated,
ending in Austria being made the catspaw, and in the extension of
Russian territory. I am not sure that I agree in his anticipations but his
practical conclusion is pretty nearly that to which I had already come.
We must however see what Disraeli has got to say.

9 January 1876. Opinion seems utterly confused and divided on
the eastern controversy, and the only thing clear is that no real
settlement is possible: only a temporary delay. Meanwhile we gain
politically: petty questions of administration, and small subjects of
criticism, are pushed into the background when a European
complication occurs: and with tolerable management it is always
possible to keep opinion favourable.

I have had by me for some days a secret despatch from O. Russell:
reporting a remarkable conversation with Bismarck. He (B.) expresses
his earnest desire for a frank and frequent interchange of ideas with
us: and would be glad to know our views, so as if possible to ensure
united action. He did not, he said, agree with those who consider the
state of Turkey hopeless: in his opinion Turkey might yet be kept
together by mutual forbearance and cooperation. Russell naturally
answered that on our part there had been no reluctance to discuss
affairs: all the reserve and reticence had been on the side of Germany.
Bismarck excused himself on this score by saying that he did not
know what Andrassy's plans were: personally, he attached but small
importance to these plans, which were all alike in substance: but he

[9] Not in *Cecil.*

did wish to know what the Austrian and Russian politicians were contemplating. Germany had no special interests in the east, and on that account he was more free to support those of England. He, Andrassy, and Gortschakoff were for the present acting cordially together, but there were ambitious men in both countries who might interfere. ... Germany could not afford either to allow Austria and Russia to become too intimate behind her back, or to let them go to war. If they were to quarrel, Germany must take part: if against Russia, then would follow a Russo-French alliance hostile to Germany: if against Austria, the existence of the Austrian empire would be endangered, which was not in the German interest. He did not wish France excluded: on the contrary, he thought it well that she should occupy herself in the east, rather than brood over plans of revenge for the late defeat.

... The overture which it contains is important, not to be accepted as sincere, nor yet rejected as obviously false. It is clear that Bismarck does not trust his allies, and I see no reason to doubt his meaning what he says when he professes to be anxious for our support. It seems also probable that he has other plans in contemplation, the nature of which is not yet disclosed.

10 January 1876. Letter from Disraeli, on the Austrian note. He is against accepting, on the ground that all the reforms of importance asked for in it have been anticipated by the Porte, except two – local taxation and waste lands – which are of doubtful merit and value. That if the Porte accepts, and the insurgents refuse, or if from whatever cause the negotiation fails, some ulterior measures must be contemplated by the Powers, and we might be bound to concur in them by what we had already done, or at least should find considerable difficulty in drawing back.

These reasons seem to me excellent – as against the Austrian note in principle ... but out of place now. The Austrian note is a fact: wisely or foolishly, it will be sent in, and backed by Russia or probably by Germany: the only question that remains is whether the Porte incurs less risk by accepting them than by rejecting the advice so offered him. In this sense I have answered, briefly: reserving fuller discussion for personal intercourse.

11 January 1876. London by 11 a.m. train. ... Despatches from Berlin. Russell hopes we shall join in the Austrian proposals, as matters will be simplified if we do. He thinks that Bismarck's offer of alliance is made in earnest, and that it ought to be accepted: 'an ambitious, irresponsible, unaccountable genius with a million of soldiers at his back' is a friend worth having. Russell thinks him sincere, and explains his change of front (for he certainly did not love us last year) by a conviction on his part that the Alliance of the three Emperors is a failure. He, Bismarck, got it up, intending to play the leading part: but Austria and Russia have drawn together, and last spring the Russian government had the satisfaction of binding over Germany to keep the peace. He feels the check, and would be glad to repay Russia in kind: which he would be able to do, if with the help of England he checked Russian aggression on Turkey. This explanation is conjectured only, but it is probable and natural. It is worth noting that while Gortschakoff frequently boasts of having established with England more confidential relations than ever existed before: rather exaggerating the real facts: Andrassy on the other hand expresses a deep distrust of English policy. No one knows why, but such appears to be the fact.

... The Czar has had a confidential conversation with Gen. Leflo, the French ambassador ... He expressed confidence in Andrassy, but had doubts as to the efficacy of the reforms suggested.

12 January 1876. Saw Tenterden, Lister, Münster, Schouvaloff, Levy (now calling himself Lawson) and Mr F. Hill,[10] of the *Daily News*. Greenwood also called, but came away hearing that I was engaged. An editorial levée. Mr Hill's was a first visit, he came for information. I made him a little speech, disclaiming all wish to bias his judgement, but expressing willingness on public grounds to supply him with facts ... I told both that no definitive answer could be given to the note until next week, after the cabinet had met. Read a mass of Zanzibar papers: Kirk[11] has been on the brink of going to war with Egypt on his own account: but the Egyptian force having been recalled, one may hope there is no further risk of collision.

13 January 1876. Saw Harcourt, who talked of the Austrian note, anxious that we should join in pressing it on the Porte: I gave him the only answer in my power ... he must wait for the cabinets of next week. I went however rather fully into the pros and cons of the question, wishing that he should see that it is being seriously considered. He said that Decazes looked with great alarm on the extension of the war: thinking that it was the object of Germany to extend it, in order that Austria and Russia might have their hands full in the east, and Germany be free for another war with France. He was convinced that Bismarck would not be satisfied till he had brought about that result. I pointed out that Bismarck's present conduct did not fit in with that theory, since he, B., was as eager as anybody to see the note accepted, and the plan of pacification tried. But he was not convinced.

Musurus came next, and talked extravagantly. The note was an insult: to accept it would be suicide: better war, or the loss of a province:

---

[10] Frank H. Hill (1830–1910), ed. *Daily News*, 1859–86. Cf. *Stanley Diaries*, 256, for Derby's cultivation of editors.

[11] Sir John Kirk (1832–1922), consul-gen. at Zanzibar 1873–80.

the Sultan would not be safe on his throne ... If the two powers were at war, no third party intervening, Turkey was the stronger of the two. I asked him if he meant this seriously? He said he did ... This kind of talk did not promise much, and I did not prolong it.

Greenwood called, and discussed the whole subject thoughtfully and calmly.

14 January 1876. The only diplomatist seen today was Beust, who came in consequence of a conversation with Martino.[12] That talkative Italian has been to Hatfield, and while there contrived to engage Salisbury in confidential conversation: in the course of which S. appears to have told him more than was necessary or desirable: both as to the Austrian propositions, and the view which he, Salisbury, was disposed to take of them. The information so gained Martino has been busy in diffusing, with large additions of his own: and it was to counteract some of the misunderstandings so put about that Beust come to me. ... The only thing he said which was new had a personal reference. He explained that he was more than usually anxious to succeed in this business, because it was imputed to him both in Austria and here that he disliked Andrassy's policy: and his enemies would be ready, if the negotiation failed, to lay the blame on his indifference or ill-will.

Hardy had sent in to the cabinet a minute asking for £265,000 to be added to the Army Estimates. The increase of men which he wants is 3000, and this increase accounts for £149,000 of the demand: the remaining £116,000 is desired to be expended in little advantages and comforts to the soldier ... It was proposed to increase the man's ration of meat from ¼lb. to 1lb.; but ... the added quarter of a pound weight in the daily ration would cause an increased cost of £250,000.

15 January 1876. Disraeli dined with me ... he told me of the Queen's last fancy, which is to be declared Empress of Great Britain, Ireland, and India. The reason of it is that her daughter will have imperial rank, and she cannot bear to be in a lower position ... The effect of the change would be bad...

Talk also, at some length, about the Austrian proposal: which D. is not inclined to accept: we argued the matter pretty fully, and at some length: he objects that England ought to lead, and not to follow: that the plan of pacification embodied in the note is likely to fail: and that we shall be, or may be, drawn into ulterior measures as a remedy for the failure. I asked what he would wish to do if we are not to accept the note? He said, ask for a conference, or a congress. To this I answer, first that the other powers will not agree, but will look upon the suggestion as merely an expedient to gain time: next that if they do agree, the conference will not prevent the war going on ... thirdly that

[12] R. de Martino, counsellor at the Italian legation.

... France would certainly follow the lead of Russia, and we should find ourselves entirely isolated, except so far as the promised support of Bismarck can be counted on: and he is not one of those persons who can be trusted implicitly, even by his best friends. I do not think my arguments had much effect on D. nor had his on me.

17 January 1876. Wrote to accept the presidency of the Literary Fund, offered to me on the death of Lord Stanhope ... I am already the largest yearly subscriber...

Montagu Corry, D.'s private secretary, called, and I explained to him for repetition to his chief, the reasons for adhering to the Austrian project, and against a conference. I afterwards saw D. himself in his bedroom, ill with a cold: the end of our talk was that he came round to my view, or at least consented to waive his own. Every govt in Europe is anxious that we should join, and even the Porte, disliking the whole thing, but aware that it is inevitable, would rather that we did not stand aloof.

I saw Beust, Musurus, and Harcourt ... The language of Musurus has remarkably changed from that which he held on Thursday last. Beust intimated that his govt was ready to give way on the questions of local taxation and waste lands, if we were bent on pressing our objection to these points: and on the other hand to promise that our acceptance of the note should be followed by a strict observance of neutrality on the frontier.

In the press, Times and Telegraph are favourable to the Austrian project, D. News and Post against...

18 January 1876. Cabinet at 2, sat till a little past 4: I brought on the question of the Austrian note, arguing it at some length, and concluding decidedly for acceptance: I might have spared my breath and my colleagues' time, for there was no dissent, nor questions raised. A few observations were made on points of detail by Cairns, Salisbury, and Carnarvon: but that was all. Disraeli expressed concurrence, and it was settled that we give a general support to the note. I telegraphed this decision to our ambassadors, and wrote it to the ambassadors here: informing also Delane, Lawson, and Mr Hill of the *D. News.*

Hardy raised the question of the army estimates. He obtained without trouble his extra £265,000: but our faces were blank at the news that in addition to these new charges, the estimates would exceed those of last year by half a million: total £770,000. Part of this increase is inevitable, and indeed not under control, arising from cost of food, fuel, forage, and the like: a good deal has been caused by the unfair policy, as I must call it, of our predecessors: who put off every item of expenditure which by any contrivance it was possible to postpone ... Hunt has also an enormous bill to send in: and I do not see that new taxation can be avoided, though it will be unpopular, and reasonably so.

... The Turks say that the insurrection is wholly fed from beyond the frontier, chiefly from Montenegro, and that there are not above 500 or 600 insurgents actually in arms in the disputed districts ... Ignatieff has been playing his old game, telling the Greeks, through their minister, to be ready to use their opportunity when it comes, and warning the Sultan against our designs on Crete! ... It is noticeable that Russia is now very unpopular at Athens: the confidence formerly felt in Russian sympathy and support being transferred to England.

19 January 1876. At 3 went into cabinet, which sat till near 5. We discussed at length the state of finance: which appears to justify Northcote's prediction: he will have for the present year a surplus of about £1,000,000: but the demands of the army and navy for 1876–7 land him in a deficit of £1,700,000, taking the present revenue as the basis for calculation. This is more than the natural increase can be counted upon to cover, and unless Hunt and Hardy can be brought to lower their demands, which they seem very unwilling to do, we shall have no option except to raise the income tax again. Opinions varied a good deal: Northcote was for adding an entire penny, which would give him £2,000,000: the surplus above his requirements being applied to reduce local taxation: others, I among them, thought this dangerous, as it brings the claim of the ratepayer and of the small income tax payer into direct and invidious collision: Cairns and Salisbury both suggested an increase of the spirit duty, which was not approved. J. Manners wanted to tax coal exported, which nobody agreed to: I advised leaving local taxation alone, on the ground that we had no surplus to dispose of: and adding one halfpenny only to income tax: this was doubtfully received, the members of the H. of C. thinking that to leave local taxation alone is to put it into the hands of the opposition as a weapon to be used against us. They may be right: on such a question a peer is no fit judge. We settled nothing, but all agreed in pressing Hunt and Hardy to cut down their estimates, of which there seems little hope.

We discussed Cross's bill for dealing with enclosures, and Northcote's plan for the civil service.

20 January 1876. Musurus ... talked, not very wisely or coherently, but in a calm quiet tone, quite unlike his language of ten days ago. What he now said was in substance that the Porte would be willing to listen to any advice offered in a friendly spirit: the main point was to save appearances, that the Sultan might not be humiliated in the eyes of his Mussulman subjects. This seems sensible, and I said that I would do whatever might be in my power to ensure the advice given being made as little unpleasant, in point of form, as possible.

Cabinet at 3: sat till 5: Sclater-Booth was called in: and explained a new plan for dealing with highways, which I did not well understand, but it was variously received by the representatives of the farming interest: Salisbury against it, Hunt in favour.

Cross then brought forward a scheme, for putting all prisons in England and Wales under the direct management of the Home Office. There are 116 of them, and of these it is reckoned that 50 may be shut up as not required. The cost to the state will be £300,000 a year in round numbers, the saving to the rates over £400,000. The adoption of this plan must depend on financial possibilities: but in principle the whole cabinet approved it, though several thought – Hardy especially – that there would be much opposition from the dislike of the local magistracy to part with any portion of their power.

... J. Manners told us, to my satisfaction, that the Post Office is considering a plan for doing away with the clumsy inconvenient system of P.O. orders, and substituting that of the 'Cheque Bank', which collapsed from want of funds, but which while it lasted was a great convenience for small payments.

21 January 1876. Reached Osborne a little after 6 ... The Queen sent for me ... I expected to be asked about eastern affairs: but she scarcely mentioned them ... She was in high good humour ... in fact indulged herself in a real gossip, showing minute acquaintance with the families and personal history of the diplomatists...

22 January 1876. Talk last night with Ponsonby about the Queen: he thinks her in a quiet mood, not excited or worried: I sounded him about the 'Empress' question, but he knew, or affected to know, nothing, and said he thought that was all over: it was an idea she had entertained some years ago, but had dropped it of late. I think however he had heard more on this matter than he cared to repeat.

23 January 1876. Letters from Berlin: it appears that much anxiety was felt about our adhesion to the Austrian note, and the announcement has given general satisfaction. The Austrian language there as elsewhere is, that the business of pacification will not be difficult ... From Petersburg also I hear that Gortschakoff is confident of the result. Loftus believes him to be sincerely anxious for peace...

24 January 1876. Saw Sanderson: who is in fresh trouble: his sister-in-law having gone out of her mind ... Saw Schouvaloff: he gave a striking account of the railway accident on the G.W.R. in which he was ... describing himself as having nearly succeeded with others in extricating some wounded passengers from the carriages destroyed in the first collision, when another express came by, passing over the wreck and smashing all that was under it. He escaped, he says, only just in time, and fell into the ditch at the side of the line, which saved him.

... Saw Major Starkie[13] M.P. ... He came to tell me that he had
refused the offer of a baronetcy from Disraeli, not thinking it worth his
acceptance: he wanted a peerage: and asked my support to obtain one.
He is a large landowner, rich, active in the service of his party, and
has political influence: but rather stupid and loutish ... I could not
think him exactly of the stuff from which peers should be made: but
many peers are made from the same sort of material.

Cabinet, which sat from 3 till 5. We agreed to the appointment of a
commission on the questions raised by the late Admiralty circular, in
regard of slaves, which may prevent these questions being raised by
the opposition, or at least so raised as to cause serious trouble. We
agreed to telegraph to Cave not to give his sanction, without our
previous knowledge, to a scheme which the Khedive has devised for
getting rid of his debts, partly by the help of an English company, but
which as we understand it, seems to imply partial repudiation, and also
the appointment of British commissioners to control the application of
the finances of Egypt: a kind of authority which we do not desire, and
which would give reasonable offence to other Powers. Salisbury raised
some questions connected with the Oxford University Bill, which were
settled: Hardy being the chief objector.

25 January 1876. Layard refuses the transfer to Lisbon, as I expected,
and Morier must now go there. ... Münster called: he expressed
considerable doubt as to the success of the Turkish intervention, and
hinted that Bismarck thought as he did.

... Cabinet at 3: talk about the Queen's wish to style herself Empress.
We agreed that the title would be absurd, as regards Europe, or if
applied to her in ordinary public documents: but if confined to India,
there was no harm done. Discussion on the Merchant Shipping Bill
occupied some time, but the details are very technical, and I suspect
that few of us understand them. Cross talked of making a new bishopric
of Cornwall if £30,000 can be raised by subscription: some wise person
having already given £1200 p.a. for the purpose, and the bishop of
Exeter being ready to sacrifice £800: Cross would go on if he could
get £3000 a year in all. We sat 2 hours: but I think I observe that
there is less order and method in our cabinets than there used to be:
Disraeli often appears half asleep, takes no part, and much time is
wasted in loose talk.

26 January 1876. Cabinet at 2: the first business discussed was Cave's
proceedings in Egypt. It is clear that he has gone beyond his instructions,
and is mixing himself up more than might be wished with the plans of
speculators who are trying to make a good thing out of the Khedive's

---

[13] Probably L.G.N. Starkie (1828–99), who had land worth £19,500 p.a. and military
credentials: or J.P.C. Starkie, M.P. (Cons.) Lancs. N.E. 1868–80.

difficulties: he has obtained the information which we wanted, or most of it, and on the whole we were all agreed that his return was desirable. It was settled therefore that he should have notice to wind up his mission, and I telegraphed accordingly. The rest of our work was a discussion of two rival highway bills: useful, but not interesting. We sat two hours. As yesterday, a good deal of time was wasted.

28 January 1876. Saw Musurus at his request, but as usual he had nothing to say ... The want of a really able Turkish ambassador at a time like this is serious. Musurus is, I believe, honest in his way, and wishes to keep things straight: but he writes home exactly what he thinks his govt will like best to hear: he knows little of what is passing here, or of the state of opinion: and very little of what is going on in his own country. The telegrams which he brings me from time to time are barefaced fictions: but for these he is not personally responsible.

Saw the new Gov. Gen. Ld Lytton: and was better pleased than I expected to be. His manner was modest, not elated: not affected, showing some natural apprehension of the responsibilities of his new office: but without fuss or nervousness. ... In speaking of the selection of a military secretary, said very emphatically that he would not have one of the D. of Cambridge's people, but if possible some officer trained in the school of Sir G. Wolseley. This looks like business.

30 January 1876. Ignatieff is violent against the Austrian note, says the Powers will repent having sanctioned it ... it is not clear why the open opposition to Gortschakoff which he professes is tolerated ... whether there is some secret design to be served in having two opposite opinions put forward in the name of one govt. It seems odd diplomacy, nor is the object clear. I think I have noticed that in diplomacy, when we reflect at all on the motives of others, we are apt to over-refine, and ascribe to deep-laid policy what is, as often as not, the result of mere laziness or blunder.

31 January 1876. Walk early in to Bromley: and by 10 o'clock train to London. Working at home till about 1, when to office. Saw there Beust, who had only stale telegrams to read to me ... Sent a telegram to Elliot to urge him to see the Sultan ... and protest against a change of G. Vizier just now.

... Nothing important from Austria or Germany, though despatches in: Bismarck is ill, and Bulow has nothing to tell (he never has).

Cabinet: we sat two hours, exclusively occupied in framing or rather editing the Queen's speech. I am not sure that we improved it. I took little part. Disraeli was more alive than last week, though suffering from his throat.

Returned to Keston by 6.5 train, bringing Sanderson with me.

1 February 1876. Very lame, as I have often been of late, I suppose from some sort of gouty or rheumatic affection in the right foot, which has made itself felt of late pretty constantly, and is increasing.

... The French ambassador called, to talk about the Gambia exchange: but I could only tell him that I would consult the cabinet: Carnarvon has several times altered his plans, and I do not know what he now proposes.

Greenwood called: he says the attack of the Opposition will be chiefly directed against Cave's mission: in which if it is so, they will show sense, for it is a more vulnerable point than the Suez Canal purchase.

... White[14] reports that both Servia and Roumania swarm with Russian secret agents, who say 'the time is not come yet, but Russia sympathises as much as ever with Sclave aspirations – only wait, etc.' On the other hand I hear from many quarters that the state of Russian finance is such as to put a great war out of the question, and to make even a partial bankruptcy probable.

3 February 1876. Cabinet at 3: I raised the question of the Gambia exchange, and it was agreed that in one or other form the decision of parliament should be taken before anything is done. This enables me to give an answer to the French Ambassador, which is what I want. A joint committee of the two Houses was proposed, but peremptorily rejected by Disraeli, who seemed out of humour about it, I don't know why.

Hunt brought on the question of Capt. Welch,[15] of the Queen's yacht: he was reprimanded by the Admiralty for his conduct in the matter of the collision in Sept. last: he ought to have been tried by courtmartial, but this was not done because the Queen interested herself personally for him: and it was understood, she being a consenting party, that he was to be let off with a private reprimand on condition of his giving up command of the yacht. This she now declines to allow, saying that he is her servant, and must be protected against popular prejudice. Strong feeling has been excited about this matter, small as it is: chiefly owing to Welch's own blustering & foolish talk, & to the injudiciously displayed partisanship of the Queen – prompted, it is said, by Brown. We shall have debates in H.C. if he is not removed. Disraeli undertook to do what he could to induce her to give way: but he is too submissive & given to flattery in such matters.

4 February 1876. Despatches just received from Elliot ... The caprices of the Sultan seem to increase ... In fact he seems to have lost his head altogether, and to have no sense of the difficulty of his position. It is thought he would have been assassinated or deposed before now,

---

[14] Sir W.A. White (1824–91), consul-gen. in Servia 1875–9.
[15] Responsible for *Mistletoe* incident.

but for the fear which is felt of giving excuse for a foreign intervention.

6 February 1876. The English 'Domesday Book'[16] is out at last: the general result is that in England and Wales, London being excluded, there are landholders under an acre 703,289: above an acre, 269,547: total 972,836 ... The number of large estates is smaller, and that of small estates greater, than anybody supposed...

7 February 1876. To see Disraeli, who had also asked for Northcote: we went over the various subjects that will be discussed in the two Houses tomorrow.

The Roumanian govt have announced to some of the Powers ... that they have been compelled to arm by the fear of a Turkish invasion: one of those fictions which deceive nobody ... Their agent at Vienna says more frankly that they want three things: their ruler to be a recognised king, with royal dignity & title: the tribute due to Turkey to be capitalized and paid off: and their independence to be secured by a European guarantee. In short, they wish to be an eastern Belgium.

8 February 1876. Opening of parliament by the Queen ... The precaution had been taken of keeping Brown out of the way ... A conversation between O. Russell & Bismarck in which the latter professes warm friendship, and anxiety for British cooperation in eastern affairs. He has held the same language before, and supposing that he really means it, the offer is well worth accepting: but can we trust him?

9 February 1876. Saw B. Hope,[17] who came to ask a consulship for his intending son-in-law...

Letter from the Queen in reference to a proposal from Bismarck for a free unreserved interchange of ideas between the German and English govts on the eastern question. This has been put forward by him more than once, and I have always received it with the warmest professions of satisfaction & acquiescence: but the real drift of the overture is not clear to me. When Bismarck offers us German assistance to carry into effect an English policy, what does he want in return? It is not diplomatic custom, and certainly not his, to give much for nothing: and until we can ascertain what object he has in view, I am against giving him anything more than fair words. Russell, I ought to add, considers him sincere: thinking that his desire is to shake himself free of the Russian connection, or at least to be in a position to turn against Russia if he thinks that expedient. He must be encouraged & treated with apparent confidence: any other course of action would be wantonly throwing away chances: but the darkness is too thick for us to step forward.

[16] Parl. P. 1874, lxxii (England and Wales), collated in John Bateman, *The Great Landowners of Great Britain and Ireland* (1876). The return had been requested by Derby in 1872, with a view to proving the widespread nature of landownership.

[17] Beresford Hope, Salisbury's bro-in-law.

10 February 1876. Much talk with Bourke about business in parliament.
Bourke is not methodical, nor a good man of business, and gives little
help in the office: but he seems to know the temper of the H. of C.
and manages it well, which after all is his chief business.

11 February 1876. Odd speech[18] of Bath last evening in the Lds – he
said, laughing, but in a tone that meant something, that I might settle
the Turkish difficulty well enough if I would send him to Constantinople.
He lately wanted Madras, as a stepping-stone to Calcutta. His ambition
is inconvenient: with great local influence and some cleverness, his
vanity and weakness are such as to make him impossible. He patronises
his brother-peers, and scarcely recognises any one as fit to be spoken
to who is not a peer or a great landowner. But he has 30,000 acres,
spends freely on elections, and must not be made an enemy if it can
be helped.

Butler-Johnstone[19] perplexes me by writing to say that he is going
back to Constantinople on private affairs, but wishes to be recognised
as a sort of semi-official representative of the views of govt. This won't
do – he speaks of being on cordial terms with Elliot, who wrote home
to complain of his ways of going on. I answered him civilly, but so that
he might understand that what he had asked was impossible.

... Saw Beust, who called to take leave ... Saw Münster ... about
Bismarck's overtures, which I acknowledged warmly, & explained that
if we had not developed our views as to Turkey, it was not from
distrust, but because in the actual confusion & uncertainty as to what
might happen, it was impossible to lay down a plan.

12 February 1876. Windsor for a council ... & cabinet at 4. We sat till
5.30 ... At Windsor Queen civil and in good humour to all the world.
Ponsonby says that she is pleased the opening went off so well ... She
talked chiefly about Bismarck's overtures, and agreed in the view I took
of them...

Dined Disraeli's ... Corry, who sees all his chief's correspondence,
talks about the Queen: thinks there is no flaw anywhere in her intellect,
which is shrewd and acute: but that she is selfish and despotic beyond
measure: that if her power were equal to her will, some of our heads
would not be on our shoulders: that she never forgave opposition to
her will: with more to the same effect. He says she discusses all sorts
of matters with Brown, and that he, Brown, has been mainly the cause
of her unreasonable conduct in the matter of Welch...

As well as I can gather, the session has opened favourably for the
government...

13 February 1876. After frequent consultation with Tenterden, I have

---

[18] Not traced in *H*.
[19] H.A. Butler-Johnstone, M.P. (Cons.) Canterbury 1862–78.

decided on strengthening the office by the addition of a third under-secretary. Northcote to whom I spoke wisely and in a friendly manner made no difficulty about the extra £1500, and I found Tenterden and Lister both well pleased at the notion of having help, which indeed they require. I propose to try and induce Sir. H. Maine[20] to accept the post. Of his fitness there can be no doubt, and besides being permanent, which a seat in the Indian Council is not, the place would give him £300 a year more than he has. On the other hand the work is likely to be a good deal harder.[21] The Col. Office has three under-secretaries, and the work there is far less than ours. We are not strong in men just now: Tenterden, though indefatigable, and excellent in all respects, is obliged since a severe illness to give himself more rest than he used: Lister, with many excellent qualities, is not very fond of work, nor has he a strong constitution: of the senior clerks, Anderson[22] is disabled by long illness, Woodford[23] I have just been forced to remove, and Wylde,[24] though very willing, is not very capable.

14 February 1876. Saw Musurus, who came to tell me, what I had heard before from Elliot, that the Porte accepts the Austrian proposals as to 4 out of the 5 stipulations which they contain: reserving the 5th, which is that which deals with local taxation, as to which both Decazes and I have expressed our doubts.

... Saw Morier,[25] and offered him Lisbon, which he accepted with much appearance of gratitude. He was evidently not prepared for the offer, having taken up a wholly unfounded opinion that I was prejudiced against him. He is able, active, full of zeal, a copious writer, though much too diffuse in style, and good linguist: he has suffered in his profession from over-eagerness to push his way, which sometimes takes the form of intrigue: and from want of social tact: a defect which I see in him clearly, but should not know how to define.

... A singular application from Lytton for the K.C.B.

... Letter from O. Russell ... he ... agrees with me in distrusting

---

[20] Fellow Apostle from Derby's Cambridge days.

[21] New post of legal assistant under-sec. went to (Sir) Julian Pauncefote, 1st Baron Pauncefote (1828–1902) who held it 1876–82, becoming perm. under-sec. 1882–9.

[22] (Sir) Henry Percy Anderson (1831–96), entered F.O. 1852; senior clerk 1873; asst. under-sec. 1894–6; kt 1885; 'glad to see returned', Derby noted, 'his second, Stevens, being altogether incompetent' (D.D. 12 June 1876).

[23] John W.G. Woodford, senior clerk.

[24] William Henry Wylde, superintendent of commercial, consular, and slave trade depts. 1869–80.

[25] Minister at Lisbon 1876–81. D.D., 5 Apr. 1875, noted that Morier 'had been in the sulks ever since his failure to obtain Lisbon. Though vain, egotistical, and given to intrigue, he is too able to be spared from diplomacy, where we have few men of even average capacity. His despatches are full of useful intelligence, but immoderately long...'

Bismarck, but for various reasons thinks him at present sincere in his wish to maintain peace.

15 February 1876. Letter from Hale, laying before me a plan for the office work at Knowsley. Young Moult is to succeed his father, at the same salary ... Hale only to sign cheques: besides the weekly balances I am to have a monthly summary of receipt and outlay. This is all right enough, but in addition I shall require an independent audit.

16 February 1876. Called on Disraeli, at his request, to consider a proposal made by Decazes, for a kind of joint management by England & France of Egyptian finances. This I strongly opposed, as did also Northcote who was present, and Disraeli came round to the same opinion. In the first place, the Khedive would not agree to it ... We should not go on for six months with the French without a quarrel. their restless vanity & spirit of intrigue makes them dangerous allies at best: and we have a precedent in the state of Tunis, where the representatives of the two countries keep up an incessant wrangle.

18 February 1876. Peabody trust meeting ... We lodge nearly 1900 families ... they pay about 3 per cent net, the latest giving the largest return ...

19 February 1876. Saw the French ambassador[26] ... I find him dry and reticent, but scrupulously accurate, and all that he tells me seems sense.

Cabinet at 4: chiefly occupied with details of H. of C. business: Hunt raised the question of giving compensation to the owner of the *Mistletoe*, which he said, and Disraeli confirmed him, the Queen is strongly opposed to ... We were all of opinion that it was better to give them freely than after a trial in which many unpleasant things would be said.

The Italians having proposed to send Gen. Menabrea[27] here with the rank of ambassador, which involves our raising the mission in Rome to an embassy, I brought the matter before the cabinet, who agreed without dispute that it should be done.

20 February 1876. Rather weary after a week of bustle: slept on the sofa before dinner, which I hardly ever do. I have dined out two days running, and these social gatherings knock me up more than any work, I hardly know why.

21 February 1876. Letters ... from O. Russell, who has seen Bismarck ... He trusted Andrassy entirely, but could not be sure that he would always have the upper hand ... He found he had given offence to the

[26] Seen by Lyons as 'straightforward, timid, not brilliant' (D.D. 24 Mar. 1875); and by Derby as 'a worthy honourable man, and I suppose believes what he says: but where can he have lived?' (D.D. 15 Nov. 1877).
[27] Luigi Federico, Count Menabrea (1809–86), Italian amb. in London 1876–82, in Paris 1882–92; 'a new diplomatist, and scrupulous to excess in matters of form' (D.D. 8 Sept. 1876).

Austrian emperor by taking up the cause of Andrassy too warmly. He repeated what he had said before, that England & Germany were the Powers that could best deal with the eastern question, their sole interest being the maintenance of peace. He wished if possible to settle matters as we were doing now, by the union of the Powers on the basis of the territorial status quo: but if that failed, as it might, the next thing to do was to try and settle in a friendly way the changes that might become necessary, rather than go to war about them.

These words may mean much or little: Russell thinks that B. has no fixed plan ... What he most fears is a too close intimacy between Austria & Russia: since these Powers united could at any time reckon on help from France, and so make a coalition against Germany.

... The U.S. govt is in difficulty what to do with the Alabama compensation, which far exceeds all claims upon it that can be made, after admitting every one that can be supported by even questionable evidence.

23 February 1876. Matters look as if France were in a fair way to settle down. I have never understood why a republic should be difficult to establish, in a country where social equality is pushed very far, and where dynasties have lost their influence: nor why it should not be conservative, when the general feeling of the nation so evidently is so.

... Either the Russian govt is playing a double game, or Russian officials act strangely. At Ragusa, the consul has made his house a kind of headquarters for the insurgents ... I have sent reports of these proceedings to Petersburgh, to hear what the Russian govt will say about them.

... Saw Lawson, who very angry with Lowe ... Lowe appears to have said that the London press was always in favour of a spirited policy, because ... war increased the circulation of newspapers: Lawson vehemently denies that the press has anything to gain by war: alleging that the expenses more than eat up any profits due to increased circulation.

... Saw Münster, who came about Chinese pirates ... It seems as if Bismarck were bent on showing the sincerity of his offer of cooperation by asking our help & advice on all matters small + great: and this is a tendency to be encouraged.

25 February 1876. In H. of C. last night, Whitbread's resolution condemning as unnecessary the appointment of a commission to treat the question of escaped slaves, was lost by 45 – 293 to 248 ... The opposition had the advantage of a popular cry, and used it: their defeat shows our position to be very solid, and leaves them with no other convenient subject of attack.

... Saw Schouvaloff, who is anxious for direct intercourse between the Gov. Gen. on one side & the Russian commandant in C. Asia on the other. I say this must be referred to Salisbury.

26 February 1876. Cabinet at 12: some talk about the Burials Bill, or rather about the resolution which is to be moved by O. Morgan in lieu of a bill: on this question the Irish and Scotch members side with the nonconformists, and they nearly had a majority last year. Disraeli evidently expects to be beaten, but feeling among a section of the party is too strong to make it possible for him to give way.

We had then a long discussion on a point raised by Cairns ... The peers present were all in favour of Cairns – the commoners doubtful or hostile ... We came to no conclusion...

27 February 1876. I shall ... arrange to pass Mondays as well as Sundays in the country: going up early to town and returning at night: this rather on M.'s account than my own, for even a few hours of country air have a singular effect on her health and spirits.

... My mother[28] had had a violent attack of illness in the night ... I cannot shut my eyes to the ... improbability of her life being long protracted ... I cannot, even as a child, remember the time when she could walk a mile without fatigue .. no one who knew her would have predicted that she could reach the age of 40.

28 February 1876. Cabinet at 11, where after much discussion, we agreed to leave the admiralty circular alone, as to modify it again is not easy,[29] and indeed would answer no purpose, while its withdrawal would seem an act of weakness. We were, I think, all agreed at last, though the decision was contrary to my first impressions and to those of others of my colleagues.

29 February 1876. Carnarvon came, much fidgetted and perplexed by what he says is the great unpopularity of his proposed committee on the Gambia exchanges. I do not ... entirely believe it, & Carnarvon is nervous and excitable to excess ... At his request, I agreed with Tenterden to write to Paris to ask the French govt to define more exactly than they have done what they proposed to give in exchange. Great difficulties are being raised in France to the transaction, chiefly among the mercantile class, and it is possible that Decazes may be glad on his side of any excuse for suspending negotiations.

Carnarvon began by being too sanguine, and underrating the obstacles in his way: I well remember pointing them out to the cabinet, but he would have the matter gone on with: but I have from the first taken care to keep a door open, saying that we could not proceed with the exchange if public feeling declared against it.

[28] D. 26 Apr. 1876, at her home in Cromwell Rod., London, and bur. at Knowsley.
[29] Revised version (Dec. 1875) of fugitive slave circular had not ended controversy.

3 March 1876. H. of Lds. ... where found Carnarvon fidgetty & excited about the Gambia affair as is his nature to be when anything goes amiss: but I quieted him down enough to prevent his doing or saying anything foolish.

Appellate jurisdiction bill passed ... almost without criticism ... Cairns has been adroit & lucky in getting his compromise accepted. But it is strange to see how the peers are satisfied at retaining the name of the H. of Lords in connection with the new court, though it is a name only, and they have no more to do with it than with the Court of Chancery: except that the judges are made life peers, which is an innovation formerly much objected to.

4 March 1876. The Empress of Austria wants to visit the Queen on Monday. I send the telegram saying so to Ponsonby: and got a brief note from him declining the visit on the part of H.M.: which will not make matters pleasanter between the two royalties.

... Cabinet at 12: but not much business done: discussion, rather desultory, on the general state of affairs: of which Disraeli thinks well: he says the week has been a rough one, but successful: he sees no more rocks ahead: is satisfied on the whole: but he looked very weary and half asleep. His friends are becoming anxious that he should leave the H. of C. and take a peerage. His absence would no doubt be a loss: but he cannot go on long as he is: and his colleagues must learn to manage the Commons without him. The probable alternative is that he must give up altogether, or break down.

6 March 1876. Letters from Berlin ... O. Russell reports all quiet, nothing doing: the risk of complications is thought to be diminishing, and the relations between him & Bulow are excellent. He finds Bulow 'all attention, civility & confidence': exactly as Münster is here.

... Queen's levée at 3 ... Short talk, while there, with Disraeli, in reference to something which lately passed between M. and him, about his removing to the H. of Lds. He wishes it, being now physically unfit for the strain and late hours of H. of C. life: but is afraid, naturally enough, of leaving things there to get into confusion. He also talks vaguely of retiring altogether: but that cannot be, unless his health were so far to break down as to make his continuance in public business impossible.

... It is clear that the opposition, though they can scarcely see their way to do any serious mischief, are bent on giving all the trouble & annoyance possible. Gladstone has returned, & though not nominal chief, seems to push Hartington into the background whenever anything is to be done.

7 March 1876. Saw C. Münster, who expressed to me the strong desire of govt to act with ours in Chinese affairs: as to which he again repeated that Bismarck foresaw trouble. I said what was proper in reply, and said it sincerely, for joint action in China is very desirable, and the German interests are identical with ours.

9 March 1876. I cannot sleep at nights as I used.

... Office ... Ld Denbigh came with a heap of papers about Turkish affairs: he is full of the Urquhartite[30] craze, which is that Russia has corrupted the public men of all European countries: his chief point today seemed to be that Beust & Andrassy were both in Russian pay.

10 March 1876. To Disraeli's house ... where met Northcote, Cave, & Stokes: discussion on the state of Egyptian finance, and what can be done for the Khedive. The dilemma is awkward: if we let all alone, there will be a financial collapse before the end of the month, and this following close on Cave's mission will be awkward for the govt and even a little ridiculous. On the other hand, if we do interfere, by what means are we to obtain an effective control of the finances without interfering with the independence of the country?

11 March 1876. Malmesbury sends me a letter from Paget, written in much alarm lest he should not be allowed to continue at Rome when it is raised to an embassy. Paget is not one of our worst men, but he is a most insatiable and querulous beggar for all that can be got: increase of pay, higher rank, honours, etc. In this his wife backs him up, & being good-looking, she has formerly helped him: but influences of that kind do not weigh much at F.O. as things are now.

... Cabinet at 12, sat till near 2: we discussed various subjects: one of them Egyptian finance: another an impracticable proposal by Sandon about religious education: a third, Scotch game laws, as to which there has been a defeat of the govt in H of C on Wednesday last ... It was agreed that we should take up the bill thus carried against us, and amend it in committee.

12 March 1876. Despatches from Turkey: Ignatieff has written to the Greek minister, warning him seriously, and in much detail, of English designs on Crete. He continues to hold language opposed to that of his govt, and is especially eager that the insurrection shall not be allowed to end without something being done for Montenegro.

14 March 1876. On all divisions we have had good and steady majorities. I am however uneasy about the royal titles bill: which though carried through its second reading in H. of C. is universally disliked, and with some reason.

16 March 1876. Saw the editor of the 'Echo', who was admitted, he being friendly to govt, but I did not like his ways. He wanted to know the contents of Cave's reports,[31] and as I declined ... he pressed his request. Considering his connection with Albert Grant, I felt bound to

---

[30] After David Urquhart (1805–77), diplomatist, crank, and pro-Turkish agitator.
[31] Report by Mr Cave on the financial condition of Egypt, *Parl. P.*, 1876, lxxxiii.

be specially careful: and indeed I have no doubt but that he wanted the information for stockjobbing purposes.

17 March 1876. In H. of C. last night, the royal titles bill ... was carried into committee by 305 to 200. Many Liberals stayed away, and many Conservatives also, disliking the bill, but equally disliking to oppose it, the Queen's personal interest in the matter being so well known. It is a stupid business altogether, but being so deeply involved, there was and is no option but to go on.

... Over to No. 10 to see Disraeli, Northcote, Cave & Stokes on Egyptian finance: I took Tenterden with me, and he was useful. No progress has been made in any plan of settlement, and I do not see what we can do ... There is moreover the inconvenience of acting with the French, who are sure to intrigue, and oppose all that we suggest, as they did and do in Tunis...

18 March 1876. Cabinet at 12, sat till nearly 2: discussion on the royal titles bill, which though it has passed so well in parliament, is generally disliked: talk of various amendments likely to be proposed, of possible alterations in the style of the coinage, and of the general wish that the Queen should repudiate the imperial title in England & Europe, reserving it only for the east.

We then had a long discussion on Egyptian finance: Cairns & I pointing out the difficulty of farther interference, Carnarvon in favour of it: but the question solves itself for there is no practical proposal put before us: the financiers will do nothing for Egypt without something in the nature of a guarantee by England, or some other leading Power, and that we clearly cannot give. It was agreed that Cave's report should not be published without the Khedive's sanction.

Talk of making Lds Justices, when the Queen goes abroad, whether that is necessary as a matter of form or not. Agreed that the D. of Northumberland shall have a committee on noxious vapours, which he is anxious for. J. Manners rather sore about a proposed enquiry into the working of the postal telegraphic system, which he thinks we ought to have resisted, but the enquiry will be useful, and it conveys no censure. We smoothed him down, which was easy, for no man has less of touchiness in personal matters.

Cross raised the question of vivisection, but does not see his way through it, nor does any one else. He would leave it alone if he could, but that is impossible.

19 March 1876. I am not sure that this continuance of internal troubles in Spain is altogether a disadvantage: the arrogance of the nation is so unbounded, and has been so often shown where British interests are concerned, that as soon as they are free of internal dangers, they will probably do something that will lead to a rupture.

21 March 1876. Cabinet at 12: we again discussed Cave's report and the position of the Khedive: it is becoming more and more clear that no English financier will lend him the money he wants, nor does it seem as if they would be wise to do so. ... A compromise, and general reduction of interest, seems the only resource.

Carnarvon, to my great surprise, started a project which would be most unpopular in parliament, and amount to a reversal of one of the most important decisions of the late cabinet: but he named it to us as a matter which he took for granted we should consent to. He wishes to revive the policy of quartering troops of the line in various colonies, from which of late years, the rule has been to withdraw them as far as possible: and would have begun by sending a regiment to Victoria: where, as I told him, there is not an enemy within 3000 miles. He said rather emphatically that he had made overtures to the colonies, and that to refuse to sanction them would be a reversal of his policy. I took the lead in opposing his scheme, which I did strongly, and at length. Cairns, Richmond, & Malmesbury agreed with me: Salisbury took a middle view: Disraeli defended Carnarvon in principle, but said that the time was not opportune, even if the cabinet has been agreed.

... The high wages of a colony make desertion on a large scale inevitable: and that while soldiers are sent out from England, no effective colonial militia is even likely to be formed.

I told C. that I should not object to officers (of whom we have plenty to spare) being sent out as instructors, nor to artillery being supplied if necessary: & this modified concession the cabinet seemed inclined to adopt.

C. has shown much ability in his office, and more energy than he was thought to possess: but success, and perhaps overstrain from work, have developed in him what I never saw before – a tendency to rash and precipitate action, and a kind of restlessness, which have already led to one or two failures. The Gambia exchanges have collapsed: the South African federation plan hangs fire: and a quarrel between Canada & B. Columbia, in which he offered to arbitrate, remains unsettled, his decision not having been accepted by the parties.

23 March 1876. Lawson and Cross called: talk with the latter about our cabinets, which are less careful and businesslike than they used to be, chiefly from Disraeli's indifference to detail and dislike of discussion.

... singular letter from Col. Office to F.O. requesting us to declare the right of England to all territory in S. Africa lying south of the Portuguese possessions: which on the west coast includes about 1200 miles of coastline beyond our present frontier. This without previous notice or communication of any kind. I sent Lister over to C.O. and arranged an answer, putting off the affair: but it is a strange freak!

24 March 1876. Unsatisfactory debate in H.C. last night: Disraeli

seems to have talked rather wildly & foolishly on the royal titles bill:
for which indeed it is not easy to say anything sensible: he represented
the assumption of imperial title as a measure of precaution, and as a
demonstration that we intended to resist Russian advances in Asia: the
logic of which is not clear.

... Question raised by Tenterden, Sanderson, & also by Disraeli,
whether in the present state of matters it will be possible for me to go
abroad, as proposed, in attendance on the Queen. ... The Egyptian
business seems to have reached a crisis.

25 March 1876. Cabinet at 12: we discussed and settled the budget.
... In round numbers, he has to meet a deficit of a million ... To meet
this, he proposes to add a penny to income tax, at the same time
relieving all incomes under £150 altogether, and all up to £300 to the
extent of £150. He also proposes to introduce an intermediate scale in
the wine duties ... The loss by this change is insignificant. We all
agreed in approval, except as to one detail. Northcote at first proposed
to carry his partial exemption from tax as high as incomes of £500.
This I opposed. Salisbury seconded me, on the ground that it is going
too far in the direction of a graduated income tax, the most revolutionary
of all schemes, and the cabinet seemed to approve our objections: the
point was left undecided.

We next discussed Egyptian finance again: and called in Tenterden.
A draft was read, framed to meet the latest state of affairs, & being
approved has been sent off.

There was a conversation as to whether I ought to leave England or
not in the present state of business. I put myself in the hands of
my colleagues: they agreed, and I think rightly, that to change the
arrangements at the last moment ... would create an impression of
difficulties & dangers ahead which do not exist ... The fact is that the
Queen ought not to leave England while parliament is sitting: it is a
thing hardly ever done before ... Personally, I am rather glad to go: it
✓ would have been disagreeable to me to speak in favour of the titles bill,
which I opposed in cabinet...

Saw Münster on question of fines inflicted by Spaniards on foreign
ships, as to which we agree to act in concert.

... Saw Carnarvon ... very friendly, our little difference of Tuesday
having left no unpleasantness. I gave him some hints for his speech on
the titles bill, which I had meant to use if obliged to speak.

26 March 1876. I will pay Mrs H. Stanley £100 a year ... She does
not deserve help, but for the sake of the name, my uncle's widow ought
not to be writing begging letters to all the people she knows: though
for that matter she has a clear £500 a year for life.

27 March 1876. Reached Brussels ... Lumley is an artist, and his
house is full of paintings, old tapestry, & works of art...

28 March 1876. To Frankfort ... Telegram from Tenterden to say all well.

29 March 1876. Reached Baden. ... The Queen arrived ... about 2 hours after us...

31 March 1876. Saw Ponsonby ... The Queen writes to ask an appointment for a Mr Maude, connected somehow with the Biddulph family: as there is an attachéship vacant, I give it to him, but warn the Q. that if he has no private means, diplomacy is not the profession he ought to choose.

1 April 1876. Turkish matters are going on as ill as ever: they cannot change for the worse: nobody is paid, the troops starve, and the insurgents seem very little inclined to make their submission. In truth it is not easy for them to go back and live in peace with their Mahometan neighbours, whose houses they have burnt ... It is this feeling of local hostility, much more than abstract dislike of Turkish rule, that makes pacification difficult. By the middle of May, we shall see whether Servia can be kept out of the fight: if yes, it may continue for a long time on the frontier, without any general mischief being done: if the Servians join, matters will grow serious, and probably an Austrian occupation must be the next step.

2 April 1876. I have not seen the Queen, except passing in her carriage: and from what Ponsonby says of her state of mind I do not think it is desirable that I should. She arrived here in bad humour, and has been so much excited about the titles bill, that though Ponsonby brought me a message of enquiry from her on the subject, he accompanied it with a caution that I had better answer as vaguely as possible, 'for fear', as he said, 'of setting her off again': a phrase which explains itself.

... Received a letter conveying the resignation of Mr Chirol, one of the junior clerks in F.O. – he was a Catholic, and appointed at Ld Acton's request. The cause of his retiring is debt: he has raised money in all directions, and in some instances by false statements, which might lay him open to prosecution ... There is also an ugly report as to his having tried to sell secret information about Egyptian matters, which he did not possess...

3 April 1876. Cross sends me a minute of the last cabinet, at which the budget was finally settled: Northcote writes also. The proposal to deal with the wine duties is dropped for the present ... The effect is that we estimate for a surplus of more than half a million. He makes a remission in the duty on servants, which was not mentioned before, but it costs only £30,000. The question of partial exemption from income tax is compromised by carrying it as far as £400 of income, which is halfway between Northcote's original suggestion of £500, and mine of £300. The owners of incomes below £400 are allowed to deduct for purposes of taxation £120: how this figure was got at I don't understand.

... Trouble between Tenterden & Bourke ... about a report of a bullfight to be held at Lisbon on a Sunday, when the P. of W. is to be there: the pious would take alarm, and Bourke in a fuss wanted to telegraph out in my name & get it stopped without consulting the P. This evidently would not do, and Tenterden objected: the matter was referred to Disraeli and by him decided: he telegraphed to the P. on his own behalf, and the matter ends. But I see, and am sorry to see, that Bourke has less judgement than I credited him with: as has been shown in various instances. He is nervous, easily frightened, and ... will act hastily & rashly rather than seem to do nothing.

4 April 1876. Ld Shaftesbury's resolution ... against the titles bill is negatived[32] ... So end the debates on this ... I cannot think of it otherwise than as a piece of harmless but unnecessary fuss. In the country it is rather unpopular than otherwise, but I do not believe the feeling about it is either deep or real. It is a royal whim indulged, and that is about all the comment it requires. Disraeli would have acted with more judgement ... if he had resisted the pressure put upon him ... ... He might have told H.M. that he would consult his colleagues, and if he had expressed his own opinion that the thing was unwise they would have been ready enough to agree ... I notice that the people about court − Ponsonby, Ly Churchill, & the rest − do not conceal their dislike of the innovation.

5 April 1876. Letter from Tennyson the poet asking that one of his sons may be allowed to compete for a clerkship in F.O. − which I agree to: and one from Ly Beauchamp, in which she asks for a place for an old servant of her father & mother. This I cannot refuse, and I all but promise the next vacancy.

A rather alarming telegram from Wade to effect that he wants the squadron sent up to Shanghai: but it does not appear why.

6 April 1876. The budget appears by the papers to have been well received, or at least without much objection, which is all one can expect where increase of taxation is in question.

... The Russian game is more difficult than ever to understand. It is inconsistent with the Czar's personal character, which is truthful, to suppose that he has instructed his agents to hold exactly opposite language in private & in public: yet either this is so, or they act for themselves, in a manner which is utterly inconsistent with official discipline.

[32] A motion asking the Queen not to use the title of Empress was defeated 137 − 91 (*H* vol. 228 cols 1039–94).

Morier called on his way to Lisbon ... We talked of Delagoa Bay, which Carnarvon seems to have told Morier the Portuguese might be willing to sell: but I believe this is a mistake: of the Portuguese claims to the Congo river & adjoining districts, which we have never recognised, but as to the justice of rejecting which I am not yet entirely satisfied: of the wine duties & commercial treaties to be made: and of the continually repeated request of the Portuguese govt that we should pledge ourselves to protect Portugal against Spanish invasion. As to this last matter, I told Morier that he had better avoid giving anything in the nature of an absolute guarantee, but anything short of that he might say in the sense of our wish to defend Portuguese independence.

7 April 1876. Went to see the Queen at her desire: she talked eagerly ✓ about the titles bill, and asked me as to the expediency of holding a council at once on her return to England, at which a proclamation should be settled, stating her new title: this in order to anticipate a motion on the subject of which Fawcett has given notice. I had no hesitation in advising her to abandon this idea ... She was in apparently good humour, & disposed to gossip.

8 April 1876. Left Baden...

9 April 1876. We reached Paris ... M. went to see her old friend Apponyi ... also Madame Mohl. I went with Ld Lyons ... to call on Decazes. The latter received us very cordially, and discussed foreign affairs for an hour and a half. He talked, as I thought, remarkably well ... Egypt was naturally the chief subject: and the arguments for and against sending out a commissioner were gone over.
... We talked also of the Herzegovina, where Decazes thought, as I do, that affairs are as bad as they can well be. He agreed in thinking the Russians & Austrian govts sincere, but doubted whether they are well served by their agents.

10 April 1876. Crossed by Boulogne ... Bismarck ... has begun talk of the necessity of an Austrian occupation of the disturbed districts. Those who refine on the motives of public men are apt to think that he has from the first been pressing the Austrian govt to take this course, with a view to embroil them with Russia ... It may be so, but the simple explanation is equally probable – that Bismarck thinks interference in this shape the only step which can put an end to the existing civil war. ... Meanwhile the Russian govt has been holding plain and even peremptory language to Servia & Montenegro – much to the disgust of Ignatieff. ... The Empr. of Austria is trying to get Ignatieff out of his place...

11 April 1876. Saw Disraeli, and talk with him about the Queen: he says he cannot make her understand that it would have been impossible to withhold the papers in the *Alberta* case ... We talked of ... Schouvaloff's way of discussing public questions ... I was glad to find that D.'s experience was the same as my own, that he talks, though cleverly, yet in so very discursive a manner that it is nearly impossible to catch his exact meaning, or to note it afterwards. This may be a Russian peculiarity, for it was also that of Brunnow,[33] but in his case I ascribed it to the rambling way in which old men are apt to talk.

Talk with Cross ... He generally satisfied with affairs, thinks our troubles are over, but I can see from his way of talking that he considers Disraeli to have lost the confidence of the House. His singular declaration about Russia, in the debate on the titles bill, has done harm. As to the bill itself, Cross thinks as I do that it is unpopular in society, but that the general public, though rather disliking it, does not care much one way or the other.

12 April 1876. Met Northcote: walk & talk with him: he like Cross thinks well of the state of politics: believes there is no real feeling about the titles bill (in which opinion I should be glad if I could agree) ... Thinks a time of financial depression is coming, but his estimates are so moderate that he runs no risk.

... Talk with Tenterden about ... a quarrel with the king of Dahomey. He has ill-used a B. subject, and the commodore on the coast has fined him to the value of £6000 – a rather excessive sum. The question now, shall we approve the commodore's action? I desire the papers to be printed for cabinet circulation, the matter being too serious for me to deal with singly.

13 April 1876. I forgot on Tuesday to note that Disraeli talked much of the Queen in regard to the titles bill and the admiralty business: and said in conclusion, 'There is only one way of explaining it – she is very mad.' This is contrary to his impression of last year, and to mine, but I suspect there is truth in it: though much of her unreasonableness is rather that of a spoilt child, arguing at finding the least difficulty in getting in its own way, than of an insane person.

... Saw Musurus, who talked vaguely and foolishly of the excellent army now in Herzegovina, the certainty that the insurrection would soon be put down, the wicked conduct of the Austrian and Russian govts. I thought it well to let him know my opinion of the state of matters, which is unfavourable enough, and everybody to whom I talk seems of the same mind. But it was quite useless. The poor man is probably half aware that the official reports which are his brief and from which he is bound to speak are lies: and does not want to have his eyes opened. This is natural, as he can do nothing to mend matters: but then he need not invite discussion. Two things he said which had a little sense in them. Ones that the Porte had been nearly as hard pushed in the Cretan war, and yet had come through without loss: the

[33] Russian amb. in London 1861–74.

other, that it would be better for the Sultan that the war should be allowed to go on without interference on either side: since the loss of a province or two would not be utter ruin, if the worst came to the worst, whereas the continuance of the present troubles made all improvements hopeless. But in this he did not allow for the natural tendency of all insurrectionary movements to spread. How long would Bulgaria remain quiet or Greece be content with its present limits, Bosnia being once independent?

The circumstance which makes conversation with Musurus a mere waste of time is that he does not dare to report home anything that would offend or annoy his employers: his despatches are few, and from what I have heard of their contents they are more fitted to mislead than to inform.

Send Tenterden over to the Admiralty, and settled that all further steps against Dahomey shall be postponed, till the cabinet has an opportunity of reading the papers and judging. I cannot make a war, even an African war, on my own account.

15 April 1876. Finished the *Life and Letters* of Macaulay ... I have always felt a strong intellectual sympathy with his character & a warm admiration for his career ... Even his faults: his unmeasured aversion to social display, with its accompanying *ennui* and waste of time: and his habit of treating stupidity as something like a crime: are those to which I feel myself most easily inclined.

17 April 1876. In Turkey, things are worse than they have yet been ... There is a marked, yet not unfriendly divergence between the Austrian & Russian views: & no doubt Bismarck will do his utmost to keep them from uniting ... It is clear to me that the attempt at pacification has broken down. What next?

19 April 1876. Two letters from Layard, one about the P. of W.'s intended visit to Madrid, which was not expected, & seems to have been a sudden thought: in the actual state of our relations with Spain it is unlucky. Much talk at Madrid of a certain Madame Murieta, well know in London society, who has gone by appointment to meet the P. at Seville: she is too proud of the honour to keep it to herself: and, according to Layard, lodgings have already been taken for the P. under an assumed name: so that while the utmost publicity has been given to the meeting, there is enough affectation of mystery to affix to it a questionable character.

Layard's other letter is a long & formal enumeration of our causes of complaint against Spain[34] ... He suggests that we should withdraw

---

[34] A number of small incidents concerning shipping, taxation, and the acquittal of the murderer of a U.K. subject, were causing concern, and had been taken up in a parliamentary campaign by Serj. Simon.

him, if justice is not to be had, and give the Spaniards three months to settle the matters in dispute: failing which – war.

20 April 1876. The visit of the P. of W. to Madrid is officially announced, and has been settled apparently between him & the Spanish govt. We know nothing of it, and I regret that it should take place, for it may encourage the Spaniards in their present line of conduct. Disraeli telegraphed a warning to the P., and I added a telegram...

22 April 1876. While sitting up this afternoon, M. being in the room, my mother took a pen and paper, and wrote a note addressed to her, which ... expresses hopes for our happiness ... Nothing in all this miserable business has touched me more. Her last written words have been words of affection for us – affection undiminished when the mind has too clearly failed.

26 April 1876. Heard at 6 that the end had come ... I rose more depressed in spirits than I remember ever to have been.

27 April 1876. Bismarck has been ill & invisible: and Bulow being in the same state, there is little to report from Berlin. O.R. believes the German govt to be entirely absorbed in the question of railways, and not much concerned in what is passing in the east.

29 April 1876. Cabinet at 12, sat till 2. We discussed clauses of the merchant shipping bill, especially those which relate to foreign vessels ... If we exempt them ... we are giving the foreign shipowner an undue advantage: if we exercise the same control over their ships as over our own, we invite retaliation: and an inspection ... would in Spain, Portugal, & South America become a mere engine of extortion. We felt the difficulty, and argued the matter over at length: calling in Tenterden. In the end we fell on the expedient of leaving the application of the law ... in the hands of the consul of the country concerned, and leaving the said consul a veto: which may, and would be, an effectual check on abuses, though it may prevent the law being very efficiently applied. Some discussion followed on the American extradition question, as to which we were all of one mind.

30 April 1876. To Euston, and Knowsley by 11. Sanderson with us.

1 May 1876. Talk with Hopwood[35] about a consulate for his son, now a clerk in F.O. and who wants to marry: but he seems to think the young man better where he is, & possibly he is right.

2 May 1876. Funeral at 11 ... the church was nearly full. ... By 4 p.m. train to London ... Troubled with a heavy cold, & unwell, which was so far an advantage that it seemed to deaden mental pain.

3 May 1876. Much troubled with cold in head ... Cabinet at 12: we went over Cross's prisons bill, but the rest of our time was mostly taken

---

[35] Lancs. kinsman of diarist.

up with discussions on the state of business in H. of C. ... We have only 9 government nights before Whitsuntide, and the usual block is beginning.

Last night in the House, a violent attack by Disraeli on Lowe ... for having said at Retford that the titles bill had been proposed to two ministers by the Queen, and that they had refused to have anything to say to it. ... He denied Lowe's statement on the Queen's own authority, which he had her leave to do. This completed his victory: but the denial must be taken with some reserve. That it is literally true I do not doubt: probably no definite proposal has been made to any minister on the subject: but it is certain that several of our predecessors have been sounded, and that they were given to understand that the Queen would like the thing done.

... The Turkish question is the only one which presses ... Gort-schakoff, with the Emp. of Russia, is to be at Berlin next week, and Andrassy will meet them: so we shall know more as to the designs of the three Powers shortly. ... Bismarck & Bulow are both reserved: they think, as most people do, that Andrassy's plans of pacification have failed ... I am no philo-Turk, nor much interested in the quarrel: but there is an absence of fair play in all this which jars on English feeling.

Sent off 35 boxes to the office between morning & night: the largest number, I think, that I have dealt with in one day. Sanderson dined with us.

4 May 1876. About the will: all is left to my sister: it will be a little over £15,000. ... Lawrence answers a question ... about 'The Oaks', my great-grandfather's villa in Surrey. It was sold in 1833 ... for £11,000 ... it is now again in the market, and £30,000 is asked. ... Cold still very troublesome.

... Telegram from Andrassy to the effect that Austria & Russia are entirely agreed in eastern matters: which is notoriously the reverse of the truth: but it is the fact that they are doing their best to keep together, so far as divergent interests & ideas will allow.

Schouvaloff discoursed, as his manner is, at considerable length: his chief points that the Andrassy note had failed as a means of pacification: that there must either be a fresh offer to the rebels or an Austrian occupation: the latter would settle nothing, and would be objectionable in many ways ... His personal impression is that nothing would satisfy the Herzegovinans except to be put into the same sort of position as Servia. He said Gortschakoff & the Emperor both were anxious that whatever is done shall be done by all the six Powers, and not by three only.

5 May 1876. Saw the new Italian ambassador, Gen. Menabrea, an intelligent and agreeable person ... I noticed however that he asserted in a rather marked manner the interest which Italy by her geographical position must take in the affairs of her Turkish neighbours.

... Saw Col. Mansfield, just about to return to Warsaw: he summed up briefly and clearly his impressions as to Russian policy. These are in substance that sensible Russians have given up the idea of acquiring and holding Constantinople: they know the difficulty and cost of distant conquests, and Russian finance is not in a position to make a great war. What they want is not to absorb Turkey, but to weaken it: so as to have on their southern frontier a circle of weak and dependent states, such as Servia and Roumania.

He further observed shrewdly, that the chief gainer by the war of 1870 has been not Germany, but Russia. Russia has now an ally always ready against the Germans: and Bismarck lives in continual fear of a Russo-French coalition.

6 May 1876. ... Letters and papers till 12, when cabinet. We passed nearly an hour in talking over the question of releasing the Fenian prisoners still under sentence, which it seems the Irish govt is disposed to do, thinking the step likely to be popular. Sir M. Beach was called in: it however appeared that in his judgement, no good would be done by a partial remission: all ought to be included or none: indeed he thought a partial release would increase the existing agitation – if it can be said to exist – by recalling attention to the subject. He farther told us, on a question put by me, that those for whom the popular feeling is strongest are the two who were sentenced to penal servitude for life for deliberately murdering a constable in Manchester. These men we all agreed could not be set free: and the matter was therefore allowed to drop.

7 May 1876. Walk early with M. Long and serious talk as to possibilities of retirement for the time from official life. I feel the consistent pressure of business upon me exhausting. I do not do the work as I used to or as I ought, and shall probably grow worse in that respect instead of better: nor does it give me pleasure. Disraeli complains of over-fatigue, which as leader of the H. of C. he well may: and seems to wish to throw it all up. If he does, it is on the cards that the succession will fall to me, and I do not believe myself well fitted for that post: or that the Queen may prefer someone else (Richmond for instance) in which case I am free to decline retaining my present place. If I go, it will not be either essential or desirable to shut the door against a possible future return. Health is excuse enough for withdrawal, and though mine is not bad in general, the nervous disturbance which a speech always causes me, and the incapacity of bearing extra fatigue, are real disqualifications.

10 May 1876. Cabinet at 12: sat till 1.30 ... We discussed some points concerning the application of the Titles Bill to the colonies: the release of the Fenian prisoners, which is evidently much in Disraeli's mind (I presume he has been told that it will influence the Irish vote): and then at some length the question of Sir W. Hewett's[36] action against Dahomey. The conclusions come to were in substance, that the Commodore had acted hastily, and that he ought to have referred home for instructions ... that the thing being done, we could not get out of it, and that the blockade must be sustained in case of non-payment, but that time should be given to the king to think better of his refusal: that all active operations against Dahomey shall be left alone, & the blockade only sanctioned. From some of Sir. W. Hewett's despatches it is clear that he has determined on a war if one can be got up – in the interests of civilisation of course, but which will cost a great deal of money, & can serve no English interest. Some talk on the question of dissenters' burials followed, but leading to no result. We did not do much business: Disraeli was evidently preoccupied with the motion[37] that is to come on tomorrow.

There is a partial rising in Bulgaria: & things look more warlike than they have yet done. All tends to show treachery on the part of Russia and Montenegro, and great credulity on that of Austria. The Austrian influence is lost in Servia: Prince Milan talks openly of his indifference to threats from Vienna, & of the probability of war, though he adds that he will not take the first step. ... Altogether it is less easy than ever to see what will be the end of all this.

11 May 1876. Statter called ... alarm is felt at foreign competition in articles where it never existed before: ironwork is brought in from Belgium: American cloth ... is selling in Manchester itself: and ... bricks are being carried into London ... from Japan. They came at first as ballast, now as cargo, and for goodness & cheapness, are said to beat ours.

... Settled with Admiralty to send such ships as we can spare to Smyrna ... Elliot is alarmed, thinking a Mahometan rising against the Christians possible, & that there is no force to repress it.

12 May 1876. Harcourt came ...... I said that I agreed with Decazes on two principles ... the first, to settle all matters ... among all six Powers if possible, and not among three only: the next, to refuse to go into a conference without having the basis of it clearly defined beforehand.

13 May 1876. Went to Disraeli at his request: he had however nothing special to say, & only asked generally about eastern affairs.

... Cabinet at 3.30: sat till past 5. We discussed first a resolution

---

[36] Sir W. Hewett V.C. (1834–88), naval officer commanding W. African station.

[37] A motion by Sir H. James regretting that the Royal Titles Act inadequately prevented the use of the Queen's new title outside India, was defeated 334–226 (*H* vol. 229 cols 370–474). Disraeli spoke briefly (cols 455–62).

on Sunday opening of public houses in Ireland, which was carried
last night in H. of C. over our heads: and agreed not to oppose
the second reading of the bill which will be based upon it. Cross
seems inclined also to give up the practice, introduced by Gladstone, of licensing grocers to sell spirits: which is attacked by a
combination of the publicans & the teetotallers ... We agreed that
another gunboat shall go up to Constantinople, in case of disturbances: & that the squadron after stopping to coal at Smyrna,
shall go on to Besica bay. We decided that unless the Khedive
materially alters his scheme, we cannot sanction it by appointing a
commissioner to overlook his distribution of the revenues ... We
talked, with little result, of the Burials question: and of the steps to
be taken to punish the persons guilty of bribery at Norwich &
Boston.

14 May 1876. Letter from the Queen, through Ponsonby, asking to
be kept informed of all that passes in regard of eastern matters. I
answer, promising: but in fact she already has all the information that
reaches me, sent on only a few hours later.

Paget reports the K. of Italy to have talked in a warlike style about
eastern affairs: saying rather simply 'that it was his nature to be doing
something, he could not bear rest' ...

15 May 1876. At No 23 saw Tenterden, & Disraeli shortly afterwards
at his house, about a new proposal settled between Russia, Austria, &
Germany ... The proposal is for an armistice of two months, and for
a new negotiation between the Porte & the insurgents, on a basis which
does not seem fair or satisfactory. I stated my objections to it in convn
with the three ambassadors ... The last paragraph is remarkable. ...
The Powers are to agree, if the present scheme fails to bring about a
pacification, upon ulterior measures to be taken by them in union: in
other words, the insurgents are told that if they will only refuse the
conditions offered, better terms will be made for them by the Powers!
Of course they will take the hint, and the scheme will fall through like
the Andrassy note. It is not easy to imagine with what view it can have
been framed. Possibly, as the result of a compromise, and merely to
gain time. A simple proposition for an armistice might have a better
chance. Disraeli in talk with me took an odd line: he seemed to care
very little about the plan itself, whether good or bad, but wished me
to profess indignation at our not having been consulted earlier. 'We
are being treated', he said, 'like Servia or Montenegro.' I agreed with
him to some extent, but tried to point out that this was only a secondary
consideration, & that we could not reject a good plan, if one were
brought before us, merely because we had not been the first to
be consulted. In the end he partly acquiesced. Münster did not conceal from me that Bismarck expects nothing from this move: and

Schouvaloff, truly or otherwise, declared that he had never heard a word of it.

16 May 1876. Cabinet at 1: we sat only an hour, and discussed nothing except the Berlin note. All agreed that it will not do, the plan proposed being impracticable, unfair towards the Porte, & certain to fail in effecting its supposed object ... At the cabinet Disraeli produced a written statement of his opinion, & reasons for it, which he read to us: I never knew him, or any minister, do this before. I do not remember to have seen a cabinet which was so entirely of one mind: this is lucky, for our decision will be much criticised, though I believe on the whole it will be popular.

17 May 1876. Saw ... Lawson, who appears to be in communication with Andrassy, and is aware of all that is going on. Rather an easy day, which I observe often happens when there is a diplomatic crisis going on.

18 May 1876. Saw Beust ... The object of Beust in calling upon me was to ascertain whether I would support a proposal by the Powers for an armistice simply, not accompanied by any special basis of negotiation ... Beust then expressed a hope that if I did not support the armistice I would not oppose it. I told him ... That I should not encourage the Porte to resist it, but if asked my opinion, I could only say what I thought. I added, that it was useless to talk of wishing to put down the insurrection unless the Powers were prepared to enforce a real observance of neutrality by Montenegro. This he seemed not indisposed to admit.

... I have begun again the reading of Aeschylus, partly to divert my thoughts, partly to see if I have forgotten my Greek...

19 May 1876. Gen. Menabrea called about the Berlin note ... He told me frankly that he agreed in my view as to the effect of an armistice at the present moment.

... Münster ... takes especial pains to make me understand that Bismarck is not the author of the plan before us, and that it is the result of a compromise between Austrian & Russian ideas...

... Sandon's speech in moving his education bill was a success ... Sandon has ability, and puts his heart into his work more than most young men of quality ... : it is a pity that he is so much under parsonic influences as to be hardly fit for any office that would give him power in a cabinet.

20 May 1876. Cabinet put off till Monday, Disraeli being unwell. ... Visit from Beust ... I told him plainly that I did not see how the Porte could be expected to accept the terms of the Powers ... He came, as it seemed to me, not expecting any result...

21 May 1876. I am more & more pleased with the solitude, quiet, & charm of Keston...

22 May 1876. Despatches: Greek govt alarmed and uneasy thinking a crisis is coming, and wishing that the status quo had been maintained for a few years longer, when Greece might have been in a position to profit by it.[38]

... Cabinet at 12, sat till 1.30. Discussion turned entirely on Turkish affairs. It was agreed that the fleet in Turkish waters shall be strengthened, which is right enough: but Disraeli, who was unwell and rather excitable, indulged in strange talk as to the Turkish navy: how we ought to seize it if necessary, as that of Denmark was seized in the old war, rather than let it fall into Russian hands: how it ought to be officered by English officers, so that we might have control over it as over our own. I pointed out that all this was premature, that the Turkish ships were good and numerous, but the crews worthless, and there was no money to pay them. To my surprise, Carnarvon was nearly as eager as the Premier for some action to be taken: but for what purpose, or against whom, I do not think either of them know. Cairns took the opposite, or cautious line, as did I.

23 May 1876. Despatch from Decazes, deploring our abstention ... I don't doubt the sincerity of the writer: he accepted the Berlin proposals without having even seen them except in a telegraphic summary, and is naturally disgusted that we have not thought fit to follow his lead. ... I did not doubt the Emperor's sincerity (I said) but if he wanted to put an end to these troubles, why was Ignatieff kept at Constantinople? Weakness might be as dangerous as bad faith.

24 May 1876. Cabinet at 12, sat till 1.30, Turkish affairs again: they are no doubt urgent and important, but not to the degree of superseding all other business. They have however taken hold of Disraeli's mind and he can talk of nothing else. We agreed to some strengthening of the fleet, and should have agreed to much more, Northcote being unable or unwilling to fight his own battle, but I objected to deciding such questions when we did not know what the expense incurred would be – telling my colleagues that I would not sign blank cheques – and got most of the proposed augmentations put off. Carnarvon and Malmesbury were both away: C.'s mother is dying, and M. has only just buried his wife.[39] Disraeli has gout, and we met at his house.

Saw Musurus, who rambled as usual. I told him – for which intimation he was quite prepared – that the Porte must not suppose that we could fight for Turkey again as in 1854–56: times were changed: feeling here had altered, especially since the bankruptcy: and instead

---

[38] See E. Kofos, *Greece and the Eastern Question 1875–8*.

[39] Carnarvon's mother d. 26 May 1876; Malmesbury's wife d. 17 May 1876. Carnarvon's wife d. 25 Jan. 1875.

of having France as an ally, we had Europe (nominally) united in one policy. He took this well.

27 May 1876. Cabinet at Disraeli's house: he has gout in both feet, and can hardly walk, but has little pain, and his mind & temper are unaffected. We discussed what is to be done in the cases of Norwich & Boston, both of which have been reported against for bribery, by commissions sitting upon them: we agreed in each case to disfranchise the guilty parties, and in that of Norwich to suspend the issuing of the writ for the present parliament.

We then went into eastern affairs again: Hunt had a plan for getting several more ships ready, at a cost of £220,000, which would require a supplementary estimate, and involve a party fight in H.C. The cabinet were at first apparently inclined to support this proposition, but it was strongly opposed, I taking the lead, and Northcote seconding me. I argued the absence of necessity, as we are already much stronger than any other Power, and don't want to fight all Europe united: the mischief we might do by exciting suspicion of our designs: the unpopularity of increased taxation, especially after what we had already done in that line: the certainty of strong parliamentary opposition: and the probability that speeches would be made about Turkey that would do far more harm ... than our additional force could do good. These last arguments prevailed with Disraeli, and he expressing agreement with me, the matter dropped.

Carnarvon & Malmesbury were both absent. Ly Carnarvon is dead: he has lost wife & mother within 14 months.

Harcourt called with a proposal from Decazes that if the Berlin proposal is rejected by the Porte – as it certainly will be – we should ask for a conference, or that France would. This is the last Russian dodge: for France is now a diplomatic dependency of Russia. I gave no immediate answer nor was one expected.

28 May 1876. Disraeli writes to tell me of the French intention to propose a conference ... He is in favour, and calls it a diplomatic victory that we have in this way got rid of the Berlin note. May be so, but a conference will involve us in quite as much responsibility, and the chances of union seem small.

29 May 1876. Talk with Sanderson, whose health has failed of late: gave him £25 for expenses, that he may take a week's holiday...

30 May 1876. ... News of the deposition of the Sultan ... Saw Gennadius,[40] the Greek, who wanted to know what Greece was to get as a reward for behaving so well, in the event of a general breakup in the east? I gave him no answer...

... I am growing very weary of the turmoil & bustle of this life,

---

[40] M.J. Gennadius, Greek chargé d'affaires.

which not [only] allows no leisure, but for the most part makes it impossible to do any one thing at a time, or to give the proper amount of care & thought to it.

1 June 1876. Cabinet, which met for no very obvious reason, & sat only an hour. We talked a good deal about the east, but in a rather vague way. Disraeli characteristically said he was afraid the late revolution had not been made by Elliot: it ought to have been his work. I proposed that we should at once recognise & congratulate the new Sultan,[41] which was agreed to. D. complains about not getting enough information from Elliot, which indeed is what he says of all our diplomatists. He expressed uneasiness as to the admiral having no detailed instructions as to what to do with his squadron, saying it was a similar state of things that had brought about the battle of Navarino. I reminded him that in the days of Navarino there were no telegraphs. Both he & Cairns seem alarmed about the Russian fleet, which I vainly try to explain does not exist. In the end, to satisfy my colleagues, I agree that we shall tell the Powers that strict orders have been given to our fleet to do nothing that can ever be misconstrued as a violation of treaties, and that we hope and expect that similar instructions have been issued by them. This is needless, but it is also harmless.

Talk about a local dispute at Halifax, where the vicar has some right, lately referred to a committee, of levying a rate on the town for his support. The people will not pay, he cannot make them, & the substituted payment which the committee propose is more objectionable than that now in force.

Office ... A busy, harassing day ... To all I said ... that I thought it only fair to give the new Sultan a little time to look about him, before pressing any particular reforms upon him.

7 June 1876. Letter from Millais[42] the painter, asking for a nomination for his eldest son. I answer, nearly, but not quite, promising him the first vacancy. ... Keston by 5 p.m. train.

8 June 1876. To my new estate of Witley ... I do not know of any situation within 40 miles of London at once so secluded & so accessible: nor any better fitted for residential enjoyment, at least for those who like woodland and a wide range of common behind.

9 June 1876. Passed the day quietly at Keston. Walk alone for exercise only: later drive & walk with M.

... Letters from Elliot ... The Russian embassy has double reason for disliking the revolution: Ignatieff, or his suite, speculate in stock: and calculating on the effect of the Berlin note in producing a fall, they

[41] Murad V (30 May–Aug. 1876).
[42] Sir John Millais (1829–96), artist.

had made their arrangements to gain by it. The Sultan's deposition
has caused a considerable rise instead, & they have burnt their fingers.

... Our rejection of the Berlin note, our naval display of force, and
the general attitude assumed by England has been a success. We are
more respected & consulted than has been common of late years: and
by a singular chance, our policy is as popular in France & Germany
as at home. Fear of Russia is the predominant feeling on the Continent
... and to oppose the Czar seems a rare and unexpected display of
independence. Yet one does not see why it should be so. Russian
finance is very bad, the Russian navy hardly exists: the army is ill-
officered and weak for aggressive purposes ... The Czar dislikes war
on principle: and in his present state of health – asthmatic, weak, &
depressed in spirits – would probably rather abdicate than fight. So
well is his feeling known, that Bismarck says openly it will be better to
settle the eastern question in his lifetime than with his son, who is
thought to be warlike, & known to be anti-German.

10 June 1876. London by early train ... To Disraeli at his request.
He was anxious that I should see Schouvaloff, which I will do some of
these days: S. had made a communication to him which he wished
repeated to me: I did not clearly make out its purport from D.'s
statement.

Cabinet at 12, sat till 1.30. We discussed a proposal made by Musurus,
that we should buy three half-finished ironclads now in England, which
were being constructed for the late Sultan: Hunt advised against it on
the ground that they do not contain the latest improvements, and I
because we don't want them, because we have not got the money to
pay for them, and a supplementary estimate would be almost fatally
unpopular. In the end we all agreed. I was asked to give some
explanations as to the state of the Turkish business, which I did. We
then discussed the extradition difficulty with America, as to which
Cairns & Cross were not entirely agreed: nothing was settled: we discuss
it again on Monday.

Münster and Beust both called: Beust bringing the rather important
news that the Czar has warned P. Milan that if he persists in going to
war he will have neither support nor sympathy from Russia ... The
language I held to both was the same: that we were bound to let the
new Sultan see if he could arrange terms with the insurgents: that if
he succeeded, well: if he failed, which was more likely, it must then be
seen whether he had power to put them down: at present, I did not
see much hope of a solution, for it was certain that the insurgents
wanted autonomy, and equally certain that the Porte would not grant
it.

... White sends from Belgrade a very unsatisfactory report: believes
the war party to be uppermost, the govt not strong enough to resist it:

and Russian agents incessantly pressing the Prince to take the decisive step.

... Despatches from Zanzibar, to effect that the Sultan has prohibited the land traffic in slaves throughout his dominions: this is a decided step on his part, for he has not the least power to enforce his order, and it will be very unpopular among the Arabs: it amounts to his putting himself wholly into English hands, and we shall be bound to support him. My prediction in 1873, when Frere's mission went out, that alliance with Zanzibar would lead first to a protectorate, & then to annexation, seems on the way to be realised.

12 June 1876. Cabinet at 12, sat till near 1 only, discussing extradition: in the end we agreed without difference on the part of any one present that we had better hold our ground. It was the general observation that Fish's last despatch is curiously, and as would appear, intentionally offensive in style. Carnarvon was alarmed & uneasy at the possible effect on Canada, if our present extradition treaty breaks down, and the Americans will not agree to a new one. But they will suffer as much as the colonists, and something is sure to be arranged before long.

... Schouvaloff's conversation is long, & I shall have to make it into a despatch. We parted mutually satisfied. The substance of what I told him is that we don't distrust the Czar, we know that he is for peace: but we do distrust many of his agents ... We have no system or policy of isolation: we agreed in the Andrassy note without having much faith in it ...

15 June 1876. Settled that Sanderson shall have a week at Fairhill with his sister, as he wants rest. Promised Mrs Grote a second nomination for her nephew ... who nearly came in at the last competition.

... The editor of the *Standard* called for news: I talked freely with him, but did not form a high opinion of his ability.

Not much is known of the character of the new Sultan. He is though to be a mild quiet person, not very able, & likely to be guided by his ministers. ... I had hardly written the above, when Musurus P. called with news of the murder of Hussein, the war minister, & Raschid, the foreign minister, by a Circassian officer. The act is supposed to be one of private revenge ... I called on Disraeli, who after his manner had convinced himself that the affair was a plot, intended to lead to a fresh revolution: but of this there is not a particle of proof.

17 June 1876. Saw Schouvaloff, who came to read me a despatch ... the contents did not seem very material. ... The chief argument seemed to be that it was dangerous to allow fighting to go on anywhere in Turkey, lest insurrection should spread, and the whole empire collapse: a result for which Europe was not prepared.

... The K. of Dahomey consents to pay the fine of £6000 ... thus saving us the necessity of another African war. 'All's well that ends well': but it is awkward that a naval officer should have in his hands the power of involving his country so seriously, without special authority from home.

18 June 1876. Reading for the second or third time George Sand's life...

20 June 1876. My only diplomatic visitor was Beust, who came with a proposal that we should advise the Porte to make overtures to the P. of Montenegro: hinting at a cession of territory in the event of his discouraging the insurrection. I received this suggestion favourably, but said I must consult Disraeli upon it. Till lately, the Austrian govt objected to any extension of Montenegrin territory: it may be presumed that a sense of increasing danger has led Andrassy[43] to change his mind. The idea is not in itself a bad one, for Montenegro is the centre of the insurrection: but I doubt whether it does not come too late. The Servian news is more and more warlike ... everything is ready as far as it can be made so: but there are very various opinions as to whether Servian troops will fight or not. ... Montenegro & Servia ... are rivals rather than friends: and it is on this natural jealousy that Austrian politicians appear to count. Beust also read me a despatch ... The argument was the same as that employed by Russia, viz. the danger of a general conflagration extending all over the east...

21 June 1876. Saw Schouvaloff at some length. He read a despatch stating the Russian views as to advice to be given to the Porte. I discussed it with Tenterden afterwards, and ordered it to be put into print. The concessions advised are 1) territory including a port to be ceded to Montenegro 2) a district often asked for, Svornik, to be given to Servia 3) administrative autonomy to be given to Bosnia & Herzegovina ... Schouvaloff cited the instance of Finland ... I of course gave no answer offhand ... Reading Ld Amberley's posthumous work on religion[44] with much interest.

22 June 1876. I have not noted the receipt of a letter from Gen. Ponsonby on the eastern subject. It is dictated in substance by the Queen, and evidently under Russian or German influence. She expresses her confidence in the Czar, and hopes we are not going to be too Turkish in our policy. I answer vaguely, but in the sense that as regards continental statesmen, we can trust none of them: Bismarck has his special designs: Andrassy does not know his own mind for a week together: the Russian emperor may be, and probably is, sincere in wishing to keep the peace, but if sincere, it is plain that he is not

[43] Julius, Count Andrassy (1823–90), Austrian foreign min. Nov. 1871–9.
[44] *An Analysis of Religious Belief* (2 vols, 1876) by John Russell, Vt Amberley (1842–76), e.s. of 1st E. Russell.

master in his own house. I sent this letter and my answer to Disraeli.

... Lawson called, but I had not much news for him ... Menabrea came, to discuss Egyptian finance, in which his govt appears to take a singular interest ... From Belgrade a very warlike telegram: the entire militia & reserves are called out ... No explanation is given of this sudden change: possibly it is a mere demonstration, suggested by Russia...

23 June 1876. Cabinet at 12: we discussed almost exclusively Merchant Shipping Bill, which comes on tonight for 2nd reading in H. of Lds. Office 2 to 5 ... Saw Beust, & told him that I accepted the Austrian scheme of encouraging Montenegro to negotiate direct with the Porte on the basis of receiving a small grant of territory ... It is worth the Porte's while to buy off its most dangerous enemy.

24 June 1876. Disraeli has seen M. and confided to her that he is going to tell the Queen that he cannot go on with the H. of C. which has become too laborious for him: he intends to come up to the Lords, taking the place of Malmesbury,[45] who is out of health, and has resigned. The vacancy in cabinet will probably be filled by Hicks Beach: but that remains to be settled. The arrangement is a good one in all respects. Malmesbury, from failing health, had become a merely nominal representative of the govt: and his loss will not be felt in a public sense. Irish business suffers from the absence of the Irish secretary when it is discussed: Cross has his own work to do, and cannot properly attend to it. The only department which ought to be represented in cabinet, and is not, besides Ireland, is the Board of Trade: and while Adderley remains there, his promotion would serve no useful purpose. Disraeli's partial retirement is matter of necessity, not choice, unless he were to retire altogether, which would be inconvenient in many ways.

... Saw Musurus, & pressed upon him the same advice as to M.negro which I have already given through Elliot: pressed him to telegraph what I said...

25 June 1876. In air most of the day, walking or sitting with M. Convn with her at night about health & low spirits. I urge German baths, or a visit to the sea, for I cannot but see that a sort of constitutional melancholy gains upon her, not dependent on any external cause, & not capable of being reasoned away. I have long observed this, but it has grown in a marked manner within the last 12 months.

Ominous hints reach us from Greece that the Greeks will not remain quiet if Servia & Montenegro go to war. ... Everything now points to

[45] Lord privy seal; resigned Aug. 1876, his post going to Beaconsfield, while Sir M. Hicks Beach, chief sec. for Ireland, entered the cabinet without change of office. The board of trade remained unrepresented in cabinet.

the probability, if it is not certainty, of war: & all we can hope for is that it may be localised.

26 June 1876. Cabinet at 12, sat till 1.30: chiefly on the state of business in the H. of C.: it seems to be doubted whether all our bills can be carried, and each minister stands up for his own. We also discussed the position of H. Lennox, who has got into serious trouble by his connection with the Lisbon Tramways Co., a bubble company, promoted by Albert Grant. He is charged with having helped in promoting this scheme, under circs which leave no reasonable doubt that he must have known it to be a swindle. ... Lennox never had much character to lose ... enough is proved already to make it impossible for him to continue to hold office. Disraeli sees this, but between good nature and weariness, has hitherto done nothing in the matter, and questions are going to be asked in parliament.

28 June 1876. Called on Disraeli ... I told him my conviction that war was now inevitable. Talk also about H. Lennox: I stated plainly my conviction that he must be induced to resign, & that without delay: if he did so at once, admitting indiscretion in regard to his connection with Albert Grant & the company, I thought nothing more would be said, & exposure as to the graver charges might be avoided: Disraeli agreed with me, said he had communicated with L. but so far to no purpose: L. had answered in a swaggering tone, and enclosed an attorney's letter which was to the effect that nothing could be proved against him. D. said nothing as to his own retirement from H.C. though he authorised M. to tell me of it. He wants, I believe, to be able to say that he has not communicated with any of his colleagues on the subject: anticipating some opposition or at least discontent, on the part of Hardy, who will not like serving under Northcote.

To office, where saw Harcourt: he showed me a despatch from Decazes, reporting at secondhand what Schouvaloff says I have said to him: as might be expected, it is for the most part a wild fiction: which is possibly as much the fault of Decazes as that of Schouvaloff. Having made this conversation into a despatch, I was able to send Harcourt a correct version...

... Saw Schouvaloff ... and had with him another long discussion the substance of which I dictated to Tenterden immediately afterwards. I told him that of the three points mentioned in Gortschakoff's despatch, we agreed with his govt on one, that relating to Montenegro, and had already acted in the sense of recommending concession ... I did not disguise my opinion that our exertions were too late, the Servian govt having evidently decided on war: but I did not say as I might, with truth, that these exertions were never meant to succeed on the part of Russia.

30 June 1876. At 1, with Tenterden to the Ch. of Exchequer, to take the yearly oath as to the disposal of S.S. fund. ... The excitement here is considerable. It surprises O. Russell, who says that at Berlin no interest is felt in the affair. He notes as I do the growing divergence of Austria & Russia.

1 July 1876. Very busy till 12, having 15 boxes to send off. Then to cabinet. No business of much interest, and what was to be done was discussed in a lazy sort of way. I volunteered a statement about foreign affairs, knowing that some curiosity is felt, and that reports have been spread, without reason of any kind, of differences between Disraeli and myself. These reports have their origin in the obvious difference between our respective points of view and our style of handling such subjects: D. being a little too anxious to excite interest, to astonish or puzzle his audience by an air of mystery, and generally to put on an appearance of greater activity than is either really being shown or than there is need of. I on the other hand am supposed, perhaps with justice, to be disposed to make as little as possible of what we do. But in regard to the action to be taken we are absolutely as one: and I see no reason why we should not continue so. Among D.'s little peculiarities is a dislike to allow any foreign matter to be discussed in cabinet: he always discourages even questions as to passing events: knowing this, and knowing also that some of our colleagues are dissatisfied (not altogether without cause) I asked whether any one desired to put questions, and explained what was doing abroad.

The subjects discussed were: Indian troops employed in the Malay peninsula, who is to pay?: management of Scotch business – shall we have a Scotch under-secretary? an idea generally approved: Halifax vicarage, an utter and hopeless muddle: Admiralty circular, which we agreed not to issue immediately, but to wait till more pressing business is dealt with, as it may lead to a debate. There were one or two smaller points which I forget.

... Saw Schouvaloff, who wished to know whether he was right in supposing that we should maintain an attitude of non-intervention in the Turco-Servian war: I said we should, as long as other powers did the same: but we could not pledge ourselves farther.

2 July 1876. ... Telegram in afternoon gives news that both Servia & Montenegro have declared war: which however important was so fully expected that it could create no surprise.

3 July 1876. Called on Disraeli at his request, and well satisfied with his way of talking. I told him that there was no fear now of our policy being thought weak – what I apprehended was rather that if we did not hold moderate language, it would be called a policy of sensation and swagger: above all things, we must guard ourselves from the imputation of being too Turkish, and relieve the public apprehension as to a possible disturbance of peace. To all the above D. assented willingly enough.

4 July 1876. Beust called ... It is evident that the Austrian authorities are now getting really alarmed ... and with some cause. What they fear is ... a fairly powerful Sclave state ... ... This state ... will not rest until it has got access to the sea ... It would not take much to break up the ill-compacted empire, & it is suspected at Vienna (though I believe wrongly) that Bismarck wants the German provinces, and would help in the work of demolition. But if these calculations are well-founded, why has Andrassy done so much to encourage the insurgents? What was to be gained by it? The more I think of the matter, the less intelligible it all seems. Vacillation, carelessness, & a sanguine temper, are imperfect explanations, but I can find no better.

6 July 1876. Saw O. Russell: ... I want him to see Bismarck at Kissingen when he goes back, and ascertain how far he, B., is prepared to call upon Russia to observe neutrality in the Servian fight. The only real danger that we now have to fear is lest Russian feeling should grow so strong in the event of a Servian defeat as to lead the Czar to intervene. All accounts are unanimous in describing him as averse to war ...

O. R. has been talking to Ly D. of the inefficiency of Buchanan at Vienna. Andrassy says he can do no business with him: and the old man himself evidently has no idea of retiring, but does as little as he can. In present circumstances, this is a serious drawback. Elliot's health also is failing at Constantinople ... A desirable combination would be – Paget to go to Vienna, Elliot to Rome, Layard[46] to Constantinople, Thornton[47] to Madrid: Washington might be adequately filled by several persons, L. West being one of them.

7 July 1876. O. Russell called to take leave ... I put it to him whether he thought his going would do good or harm? He said, certainly good: & so I agreed to the journey. But he goes on his own personal account, & without instructions.

Saw for the first time the new American minister, Pierrepont: ... I liked the man better than I expected, & decidedly better than his predecessor, Schenck.[48]

8 July 1876. The English newspapers are beginning to take sides: *Pall*

[46] Replaced Elliot in all but name, 31 Mar. 1877.

[47] Sir Edward Thornton (1817–1906), min. at Washington 1867–81; offered Madrid by Derby, 21 Oct. 1877, though not expecting him to accept 'the most disagreeable post in Europe'; declined by Thornton in person, 24 Oct. 1877, 'preferring to wait for an embassy'.

[48] Edwards Pierrepont (1817–92), U.S. minister in London May 1876–Dec. 1877; R.C. Schenck (1809–90), min. May 1871–Feb. 1876, resigning under a cloud; authority on poker.

Mall, Telegraph, Standard, M. Post, and *Sat. Review* more or less Turkish, or rather anti-Russian: *D. News* violent for the insurgents, *Spectator* the same, *Times* inclining in the same direction, but more moderately.

... Cabinet, sat from 12 to 1.30: Hunt raised again the question of buying the Turkish ironclads, which we finally declined: they have been offered again at a reduced rate, the Porte being in urgent want of money. This matter led to a general conversation, or discussion, on foreign affairs, which I purposely encouraged knowing that some of my colleagues are inclined to think that they are kept in the dark: and it is true that (for whatever reason) Disraeli does not like to have these subjects debated in cabinet. Not much came of our talk, but it served to remove the feeling of unsatisfied curiosity. Some conversation followed on the state of business in H.C. and we then proceeded to discuss H. Lennox's affair. The D. of Richmond with good taste retired, as he said, because we should talk more freely in his absence. Cairns and Northcote took the lead: the end of it was, that H. Lennox says he has a complete defence, is confident of its effect, and professes himself anxious for the whole affair to be brought before the House: which it will be. He may be right or wrong in the view he takes, but it is clearly impossible for the cabinet to condemn him unheard by requesting his resignation. This we all felt, and there was no difference of opinion. But it is a bad case.

9 July 1876. Letter from Ponsonby: the Queen objects to the employment of bashi-bazouks by the Turks, on account of the cruelties they commit. True enough, but if we don't fight for the Turks we can hardly tell them how they are to fight their own battles.

... F. Wellesley declines Warsaw, having found out that he cannot hold the post together with his military pay: he had previously tried to keep his military attachéship at Petersburg together with the consulate: both would have been gross jobs, and were impossible. He is extravagant in money matters, and has been put up to these proceedings by his father-in-law Lord C. Loftus, who is himself deep in debt.

10 July 1876. Met Beust, who had a rather unsatisfactory telegram. The two emperors (Austria & Russia) have met and have agreed to maintain an attitude of non-intervention: if occasion appears fitting, they will again try to obtain joint action of all the Powers. As Beust truly said, the difference between their ideas is not now wide: they have the strongest possible interest in acting together, and Austrian interests & feelings are a guarantee for their acting independently.

Saw at office ... Disraeli who wanted an answer for a question to be asked today.

H. of Lds at 5, where question by Granville about alleged acts of cruelty in Bulgaria. No business of importance. A similar question was asked in the Commons. It is now clearly the policy of the opposition

to get up an anti-Turkish cry & support the Servian insurrection: but
they may very possibly come too late.

Work again on extradition ... Rather nervous about speech on
Thursday, for it is rather a legal than political question.

11 July 1876. Rather nervous and uncomfortable about speech on
Thursday ... The Liberal papers, D. News in particular, are beginning
to work the so-called 'Musulman atrocities' ... We have no news on
which it is possible to rely...

... To Windsor with the U.S. minister ... I am inclined to like Mr
P.: he is straightforward, shrewd, courteous without fuss or ceremony,
and does not seem (but it is early to judge) to have as much of the
American touchiness as his countrymen in general.

13 July 1876. Working on extradition, but less than I ought. ...
Saw Beust, who showed me a despatch by Andrassy on the policy
of Austria, which is not to go in a blue book. It was frank &
outspoken, but contained nothing new. It referred to the special
position of Austria, exposed to danger from Sclave ambition, and
at the same time obliged to conciliate the Sclave populations lest
they should be driven to look wholly to Russia. He points out the
expediency, not to say the necessity, of keeping on good terms with
Russia ... My only criticism upon it was that it assumes us to be
more Turkish than we really are.

14 July 1876. Letter from Elliot ... the Sultan's health is causing
anxiety: something serious is the matter with him & nobody knows
what: the Grand Vizier is equally invisible...

Deputation[49] on the eastern question: John Bright headed it, & about
150 were present, picked out as representing important towns. They
spoke several in succession, all briefly. I answered them, speaking nearly
half an hour, in part without preparation: my speech was decidedly a
success as far as the audience was concerned: what it may be to the
public I don't know. The general line of what I said was to show that
we did not contemplate, and never had contemplated, intervention
between Turkey & Servia. This I could say with entire safety, and
luckily none of the questioners raised the more difficult question, 'What
will you do if Russia, or any other Power, were to interfere, & so violate
the treaty of guarantee?'

... Long talk with Carnarvon on W. Indian affairs: he alleges that
parliamentary govt works badly in these communities of mixed race,
since if the franchise is narrow, you have an oppressive oligarchy of
colour: if wide, you have mere demagoguism & anarchy. This was Lord

---

[49] From the Peace Society, urging the government not to over-react to the news of
atrocities; Derby's reply enabled Bright to stand aside from the issue in coming months.
See K. Robbins, *John Bright* (1979), 223.

Grey's[50] view, and there is something in it: but Carnarvon is by nature inclined to absolutist as against parliamentary theories of govt.

15 July 1876. Extreme hot weather ... At home till 12, when to cabinet. We sat till 1.30. Nothing was said of foreign affairs, except that Cairns & Cross expressed approval of my speech of yesterday: one or two others did not, I think, especially Hardy, but that may have been my fancy. Disraeli said nothing. He could not quarrel with the substance, but the style would not be such as to suit his taste. Our chief business was to consider the case of H. Lennox, about whom questions are to be raised in the House next week. It is not disputed that he has been mixed up with Albert Grant & other speculators in a company which turned out a mere bubble, and supposing him not to be imbecile, he must have known as a director that a fraud was being practised on the public. Other & more direct charges of fraud are made against him, but these rest on no evidence that is before us, & may be calumnies. It seemed to us all that we could not take on trust his vindication, though he still maintains that it is complete, & will satisfy the House: and that he must be told that he had better resign in the first instance, so as to speak as a private member, & not to compromise the govt. It will then remain to be seen what sort of a case he can make: whether a committee shall be appointed to inquire etc. If entirely cleared, supposing that possible, he might even be re-employed: but his resignation must be the first step. The only dissentient from this view was J. Manners, & he did not persist. The Duke entirely agreed, adding significantly that he was afraid it would not be of any benefit to his brother to ask for a committee.

Hunt brought on again the question of the Turkish ships, which he very evidently wishes we would buy, though he will not take the responsibility of saying so: Carnarvon & one or two more were for the purchase: I strongly against it, on political grounds: how could he tell the public we expected peace, while taking steps whose only justification was the probable imminence of war? In the end we all agreed – for the third time – to reject the offer. The rest of our business was unimportant.

16 July 1876. Weather still very hot ...

17 July 1876. Weather intensely hot ... The king of Greece called ... He talked exactly as he had done 9 years ago, during the Cretan war. He wants Thessaly & Epirus for Greece, and said naively that he thought his people would be discontented if they got nothing for their good conduct ... I tried to explain to him that Thessaly & Epirus were not mine to give. ... This he would assent to ... but he came back to the same subject in a few minutes as if nothing had been said upon it. Now, as in 1867[51] he left on my mind the impression of having been instructed beforehand in what he should say ... His manners are pleasant and gentlemanlike, but do not seem to indicate much ability.

In the Commons, H. Lennox announced his resignation, and vindicated his character, in a speech which seems to have been judicious and to have impressed the House favourably.[52]

18 July 1876. Saw Beust, who ... told me that the Whigs, a party of whom he met at Strawberry Hill, are much discomforted at my statement of last week: they had reckoned on being able to attack us as too warlike, & now find the ground cut from under their feet. Saw M. Lesseps,[53] a vivacious gentleman, extremely polite ... Heat continues so as to make walking disagreeable ...

19 July 1876. There is a strange mystery about the new Sultan: some think he is dangerously ill: others that he is out of his mind: others that he is nearly always drunk: the one thing certain is that he remains invisible, & no satisfactory explanation is given ... It matters little: the best thing that can happen is that his ministers should be free to act without interference.

20 July 1876. Sent £100 to Disraeli's secretary, Corry, to meet the expenses of the two parties given at F.O.: this being the arrangement between us. ... From 88 to 90 in the shade has been common in the last few days ...

... Short cabinet ... from 12 to 1, to consider what bills should be dropped. The progress of business in the Commons is not satisfactory – by whose fault does not appear. They muddle away time as some people muddle away money, without having anything to show for it. We shall pass the Education Bill & Appellate Jurisdiction: but the rest of our measures are in danger, even the Prisons Bill may be lost. It seems impossible to keep the House together after the second week in August: which indeed is not surprising.

21 July 1876. My 50th birthday: the first of many which has brought me no letter from a mother. In regard of health, domestic happiness, & outward circumstances, I have nothing to complain of, except that the wear & tear of office is sometimes oppressive: but the loss of this Spring can not be repaired, and has tended to lower spirits which are never very high.

Lawrence called to draw a new will for me: I leave to M. the option of Keston or Fairhill for her life, and a sum of £20,000. To Mary &

---

[51] See *Stanley Diaries*, 315.
[52] Cf. *GH*, 283: 'extremely well done in few well chosen words ...' Lennox never held office again. See *H*, vol. 230 cols 1481–4.
[53] Builder of Suez canal.

Margaret £5000 each: to Sanderson also £5000: to my sister as much of the £20,000 as may remain unpaid ... Some smaller legacies ... This disposes of £60,000: whatever else I leave goes to my brother, with the estates.

... Day very hot ... Musurus ... brought a long list of Roumanian demands, including one for a cession of territory: I advised him, or rather his govt, not to refuse to consider these, and so bring on a fresh war, but to discuss the proposals made, & so gain time ...

House at 5 ... I don't know what the reason may be, but it is clear that the front bench opposite – the official opposition – is getting angry, and anxious for any opportunity of making itself unpleasant. Possibly they are sore at the loss of any plausible ground of attack on foreign affairs: which since my answer to the deputation a week ago has become difficult: and disgusted that the session should have passed as it has without giving them any advantage.

I hear from Disraeli that H. Lennox objects to have his resignation considered as definite, and thinks he ought to be reinstated after his defence: not seeing that it is in consequence of the atonement made by giving up his place, that the House & the public have agreed to condone his indiscretions, & that if restored to office he would infallibly be attacked again.

23 July 1876. White from Belgrade gives the best account of the Servian campaign I have seen. ... The reports from correspondents of newspapers, and the official despatches on both sides, are chiefly fictions.

... Telegrams from Elliot: one to the effect that the new Sultan is more or less out of his mind: but there are hopes that he will get right.

24 July 1876. At home till 12, when cabinet: chiefly on the state of public business. The Education Bill has been delayed by Sandon's acceptance of certain amendments relating to the dissolution of school boards in certain cases, in which I see no great harm, nor much importance, but Sandon's language is not always judicious, and his very evident, and rather fanatical religionism makes him not well fitted for the place he holds.

... The Queen has written one of her singular letters about the Vivisection Bill: in which she says she cannot trust herself to speak or write about 'that horrible subject': that the medical profession has 'greatly lost her confidence' by the line it has taken on this question. The object of her writing was to prevent the bill dropping through: which if seriously opposed, it must, from want of time.

25 July 1876. Saw Lawson, who congratulates on the success of the Turkish papers, saying that the Opposition find no fault with them, and will not attack. I observe that there is in the press hardly any hostile criticism, and that of the mildest kind.

26 July 1876. Letter from Disraeli, who explains that he has at last settled to leave the H. of C. He does not say who his successor will be, but from previous communications I have little doubt but that Northcote is the man.

... I have never yet noted any details of Odo Russell's interview with Bismarck and the Emperor, more than a fortnight ago. Going round by Kissingen, as was agreed, he found B. who had just been sent for in haste, by the Emperor, and was naturally much disturbed at the interruption of his cure. He asked Odo to go with him to Würzburg, where the Emperor was: the invitation was accepted, and they travelled together. B. appeared excessively irritable and nervous, complaining of the Emperor, and saying that he must resign. B. had his audience, and Odo followed. He found the old sovereign full of the wildest ideas as to our policy, inspired evidently by Russia: he believed that we contemplated a *coup de main* on Constantinople, and desired a war with Russia. He lamented over the blindness of the world, which would not do justice to the disinterested philanthropy of the Czar, and said that the Czar was broken-hearted at the suspicions of which he was the object. Much more in the same stream followed, but in the end Odo brought him round to more rational views, to the great relief of Bismarck, who thanked him warmly for what he had done. Bismarck's chief fear appears to be that a quarrel may break out between Austria and Russia, which would displace Andrassy, and put the Sclave party in power.

28 July 1876. Discussion at the office about a stoppage of trade on the Niger by some of the local chiefs, who dislike steamers going up, as they lose the profit which they formerly had as middleman, when direct communication is established between the sea & the interior: the traders have complained, and we agreed that Commodore Hewett should be telegraphed to, with orders to send up a gunboat if one can be spared from the Dahomey blockade. Hunt, Tenterden, Sir A. Milne settled this between us. We did not consult the cabinet, for the steamer leaves Madeira this evening, and by missing her a month would be lost.

Saw Lawson who has got hold of a story about a secret treaty between Germany & Russia, but I think it is a canard.

The war drags on, without decisive or even important results:[54] the

---

[54] On 16 June 1876, Serbia and Montenegro signed an alliance, and on 30 June and 1 July respectively declared war on Turkey. By early August, Serbia (whose army was led by a Russian general) was clearly unsuccessful, Prince Milan appealing for a ceasefire on 4 August. On 28 Sept., Serbia resumed hostilities, meeting decisive defeat at Aleksinat on 17 Oct., following which Turkey sought to impose harsh terms. Faced with a Russian ultimatum (31 Oct.), Turkey accepted an armistice, leading to peace on the basis of the status quo (28 Feb. 1877), Montenegro however remaining at war.

Servian attack has failed, and that on the side of Montenegro has not succeeded. ... Nor does there appear any sign of rising in Bulgaria, as was expected. There is much and apparently genuine enthusiasm in Constantinople, and Christian volunteers are said to have freely enlisted. I should have doubted as to this last statement, but Elliot vouches for it. On the other hand, the new Sultan seems likely to follow his predecessor. ... He is invisible, and can do no business. These are not times when an imbecile sovereign is possible in Turkey.

Meeting today in favour of the Servians, got up by Farley,[55] A. Arnold, Freeman,[56] & a few enthusiasts of that sort: Auberon Herbert[57] active among them. Ld Shaftesbury in the chair. I do not gather that the proceeding created much interest. It is odd that Ld Shaftesbury was one of the hottest supporters of the Crimean war, 22 years ago: he did not refer to it, nor seem to see any inconsistency in his position. The most excited of the whole party was Freeman the historian – who has taken a violent antipathy to me, and loses no occasion of expressing it. It is on purely abstract grounds, for I never saw him to the best of my recollection.

29 July 1876. Cabinet at 11, to settle details of business in H. of C. The last few days there have been wasted in angry debates to no purpose, consequent on an amendment proposed by a private member, which is intended to give facilities for dissolving schoolboards where they have worked badly. There is nothing ... unreasonable in the idea ... However, the amendment was proposed on one side, and resisted on the other, with the view of getting up a fight, and in this both parties have had their way. Sandon, to [do] him justice, has managed matters with ability, and his language seems to have been in general temperate: but he cannot prevent his strong religious bias from showing itself, and that is never agreeable to the House. ... The loss of time caused by this unexpected quarrel has made the sacrifice of the Prisons Bill inevitable: which is regrettable, but less important since its principle is accepted, and it will probably pass next year without opposition.

Menabrea called ... He is able, courteous, and agreeable: but his diplomatic zeal brings him to the office about three times a week, which is more than his share.

30 July 1876. Despatches from Greece and Turkey ... Mr Wyndham[58] believes that if Servia had had a success, it would have been impossible

[55] J.L. Farley (1823–85), writer on Turkey; led deputation to Derby, 14 July, seeking help for eastern Christians, Derby rebuffing him strongly. For the meeting in Willis's Rooms, see *T*, 28 July 1876, p. 10; R. Shannon, *Gladstone and the Bulgarian Atrocities Agitation 1876*, 43–8: meeting proposed full autonomy for Turkish Christians.
[56] E.A. Freeman (1823–92), medievalist; regius prof. at Oxford 1884–92.
[57] Carnarvon's bro.
[58] (Sir) Hugh Wyndham (1836–1916), sec. of legation in Athens 1875–8.

to keep the Greek people back. Russian money is being spent freely to get up an agitation. The feeling is not so much one of hostility towards Turkey, as of fear lest the Turkish empire should go suddenly to pieces, without Greece getting her share of the fragments. What the politicians of Athens most dread and dislike is the creation of a powerful Sclavonic state protected by Russia, which would be fatal to their views of aggrandisement, and dangerous to their independence. They are therefore more than ever inclined to lean on England as a counterpoise to Russia. In the event of a conference they mean to claim an extension of territory. What they will do however is uncertain, for the present ministry has been nearly a year in office, and naturally cannot last much longer.

Elliot describes the Sultan's health as very bad (in fact reports of his death are current), gives sundry details as to alleged massacres, says the R. Catholics of Bosnia are all for the Porte, disliking Greek heretics worse than Mahometans – and notes that all the Montenegrins, some thousands in number, who usually work for wages in the capital, have gone home undisturbed, though it is known that they go to join in the war.

31 July 1876. Debate in H. of Lds on eastern question.[59]. ... Ld Granville followed, reviewing all the transactions of the last nine months in a very temperate & candid style, agreeing with us in substance, and only indicating dissent on some points of comparative detail.

... Made preparations for the end of the session, and the break-up of the London establishment. It has not come too soon: though seldom exposed to severe fatigue, I have never, since Baden, been wholly free from labour and anxiety, and in the long run these tell. I want rest and country air. When official life ceases, will the excitement of it be missed? I hope not, yet I doubt, for mere reading scarcely satisfies, and of country pleasures I have few.

1 August 1876. To Witley. ... The scenery ... surpassed my expectation. There are miles upon miles of wild heath, picturesque hills, admirable views ... I have already 930 acres, and it is believed that several of my neighbours think of selling, so that I may not improbably extend myself a good deal more. ... The place is within easy reach of London & will be to me a continual amusement. Fairhill has its own merits ... and the two will not interfere: they are like pictures of different schools, but each by eminent masters. ... Found on getting home a vast accumulation of boxes ...

2 August 1876. Saw Schouvaloff, who is going home. He recapitulated

to me the substance of the report which he says he is going to make
when he gets home, as to the ideas of the cabinet & parliament on the
eastern question. It was accurate enough, & I said so. Schou. is not to
be trusted, for he is a Russian, & an incessant talker, which last habit
makes a man loose-tongued: but I am inclined to believe that he is
well disposed as to the maintenance of peace...

... I have been reading Gladstone's speech of Monday, and Disraeli's
reply.[60] The former was effective, as his speeches always are: but it is
curious to note that now as in 1853–4 his argument and his practical
conclusions disagree. Before the Crimean War he denounced the
Turks so vehemently that one would have expected him to resist any
proposition of fighting for them: yet he concurred in making the war:
now he holds language nearly of the same kind, but as before, shrinks
from the obvious inference that England ought either to side with the
insurgents or stand aloof altogether. In fact his criticism ended in a
vote of confidence, for he condemned nothing that had been done,
and only gave advice for the future.[61] Altogether the conduct of the
opposition in both Houses – whether due to moderation, to a wish not
to embarrass the course of negotiations, or to a sense of weakness, has
greatly strengthened our hands. A certain divergence between Disraeli's
language and mine has naturally been made the most of: but it involves
no difference of opinion on any practical question, and is really a
matter of style and taste.

4 August 1876. It is to Sir George Campbell, influencing Gladstone,
that we mainly owe the passing of the Irish land act of 1870 in its
present shape – the one really revolutionary measure which parliament
in my time has passed.[62]

7 August 1876. ... Cabinet at 12: where settled Admiralty instructions
on the slave business, mainly from a draft by Cairns, though with some
verbal amendments: thence proceeded to consider the Queen's speech,
which we went through. My paragraphs were accepted as proposed ...
We had no difference as to the general tone & purport of the language
to be held.

8 August 1876. Letter[63] from Disraeli, rather sharp in tone, complaining
of the F.O. and Sir H. Elliot for misleading him about the massacre in

---

[60] *H*, vol. 231 (Monday 31 July). Gladstone 'still desired, if possible, the maintenanc
of the territorial integrity of the Turkish Empire' (col. 172) and poured cold water on the
idea of a S. Slav state; Disraeli used the phrase 'coffee-house babble' about certain
atrocity stories (col. 203).

[61] Gladstone recommended the peaceful achievement of home rule for the Turkish
Christians, achieved by force of European opinion.

[62] See E.D. Steele, 'Ireland and the Empire in the 1860s; imperial precedents for
Gladstone's first Irish Land Act', *Hist. Jnl.* xi (1968), 64–83.

[63] M. and B., 46. Cf. Disraeli's earlier complaint to Derby, 14 July 1876, ibid. 44.

Bulgaria, by want of sufficient information. There has been a debate[64] on the question in H. of C. yesterday: in which Bourke appears to have spoken well, with tact and judgement. I cannot see that D. has been either misled by false information, or inadequately supplied: the truth is he has got into some trouble with the House by making too light of the affair in the first instance, and lays on his informants, the blame of his own careless way of talking. I have not been in haste to answer him.

In fact, I did not answer him, for we met later at the H. of Lds, where I found him uneasy at the prospect of having the discussion renewed. I agreed to his proposal that we should meet in cabinet tomorrow, and discuss the whole matter.

9 August 1876. Lawrence brings me a paper showing all the transactions between the trustees and myself since I succeeded to the estate. I have sold land to the value (including a small amount of accruing interest) of £508,691: of which £262,000 has gone to pay mortgage debts, and £241,000 in purchase of other lands, leaving a small surplus. The properties in Kent and Surrey have together cost me £121,621.

... Cabinet at 10.30, sat about an hour, discussing foreign affairs exclusively: with substantial agreement, but there was on the part of Disraeli a determination to find fault with Sir H. Elliot, which I thought unjust, and said so. He is however evidently nervous, and uncomfortable about the Bulgarian business, which may be an excuse. I think also that it is an annoyance to him that ambassadors should be permanent officials: he would like to have them changed with every change of ministry: in fact he persuaded Malmesbury in 1852 to revert to this, which was the old system: with the effect of raising against Malmesbury an outcry which made him unpopular, and from which he never quite recovered.

... We settled to send somebody as a consular agent into Bulgaria – not that he will be of the least use – but to satisfy people that there is not going to be any repetition of the acts of the bashi-bazouks. Also to telegraph to Elliot, to warn the Porte as to keeping discipline among the Turkish troops when they invade Servia. For this the opportunity is favourable, for we have just got news of the taking of a place called Zaitchar, which is understood to imply the abandonment of the Servian line of defence. It is evident that the position of Prince Milan is unpleasant. He has been forced into war by popular feeling, probably against his own better judgement, and under the influence of fear lest his rival, Karageorgevitch, should be put in his place: extravagant hopes of success were entertained, the Servians thought they had only

---

[64] *H*, vol. 231, cols 722–46. For Bourke, who read out Baring's initial report, confirming the atrocities though on a lesser scale than first thought, see cols 734–42.

to show themselves in Turkey to produce a rising, and that the Turkish troops would not fight. They now find that they have been mistaken in both calculations: the subject populations have not stirred, the Servian campaign has been a failure, and the sacrifices made by the people – undoubtedly very great – appear to have been thrown away. Of the enthusiasm of the Servian population there is no question: but where a whole people is suddenly armed and sent into the field, there will be many who show no fight: it is reported that wounds in the hands are suspiciously numerous, and we hear of officers and men shot for running away.

10 August 1876. Talk with Carnarvon: he has been told of Disraeli's intention to retire, and fidgets over it, saying that it is political suicide. He also declares that it will be very unpopular with the public, which I see no reason to think.

11 August 1876. Debate[65] in H. of C. on the Bulgarian business: which passed off without damage to the govt. ... No one seemed much disposed to blame the F.O. Bourke spoke at length ... Disraeli with great tact & skill.

12 August 1876. It is useless to criticise Disraeli's retirement from the H. of C. as a political move. Obviously he loses influence by it, and the cabinet is weakened: for though Northcote, Hardy, and Cross are all capable both as administrators and debaters, they do not replace their chief. But health left him no choice, and it is better that he should have done as he has than resigned altogether. I have given him the same advice throughout. There appears, contrary to expectation, to have been no difficulty in persuading Hardy to acquiesce in the lead of the House being given to Northcote. Both are good speakers: Hardy, for a dashing, slashing party speech by far the better of the two, but he wants tact, and his somewhat extreme devotion to clerical interests – increased by his Oxford connection[66] – is against him. His elevation would have been regarded as a triumph of the high church and ultra section. Northcote is safe, moderate, makes no enemies, and never discusses any subject of which he is not master. In the Lords we still have a superfluity of strength – Disraeli, Cairns, and Salisbury, are each of them an overmatch for any peer on the opposition side, except perhaps Selborne.

13 August 1876. Well pleased that the session is over & well over. We end our third official campaign without having lost any credit or shown any sign of decreased strength. There are few cabinets in late years of

[65] *H*, vol. 231, cols 1078–1147. Bourke made a vigorous defence of Elliot (cols 1111–1119). Disraeli wound up, saying 'our duty ... is to maintain the Empire of England ...' (col. 1146).
[66] M.P. Oxford Univ. 1865–78, when cr. peer.

which the same can be said. We have carried fewer bills than might have been expected: for this perhaps equal blame should be given to both parties. It was a folly on our part to bring in the royal titles bill: it was equally foolish in the opposition to waste weeks in trying to throw it out. Never was more fuss made about a matter so utterly unimportant. The resignation of H. Lennox, being supposed voluntary, has stopped all attacks on him, and he has even gained credit for a delicacy of feeling which he was not expected to show. Malmesbury's resignation was anticipated, and does neither harm nor good: he took no part in debate, but little in cabinet, and his health was quite broken down. No reputation has been made in the session, but none has been lost: Northcote has gained steadily in the confidence of the House, and in debating power: on the other side, Hartington has shown more aptitude for leadership than he was generally thought to possess. Gladstone has interfered but little, and succeeds in maintaining the difficult position of semi-retirement. Of young candidates for distinction there is a great dearth: not one of the under-secretaries has come forward as a really effective debater: Bourke does what he can, with tact and skill in general, but he is not forcible nor eloquent: Hamilton succeeds in every speech that he makes, but appears to want ambition: my brother dislikes putting himself forward, and is absorbed in his office,[67] in which he has gained a high reputation for administrative talent...

14 August 1876. At 3 p.m. to H. of Lds where answered a question by Stratheden[68] on Roumanian affairs: he represented the entire opposition, and on our side there were about five peers present. Great heat continues.[69]

Received from my sister a large collection of my own letters of former years to my Mother, most of them from abroad. I destroyed nearly all of them, not having the curiosity to look at many again. Those that I did read seemed to me fairly well written, but meagre and uninteresting. Much as at one time I liked travelling, I never had the qualifications of a traveller, who ought to be a minute observer of details, and to mix freely in all sorts of society.

In consultation with Disraeli, I decided today to telegraph to Belgrade, to the effect that H.M.G. are not disposed to offer mediation, but if P. Milan thinks fit to apply for our good offices, the request will be favourably entertained. The telegram is to be communicated to all the Powers.

16 August 1876. Heat still extreme ... I do not remember such a

---

[67] Fin. sec. to war office 1874–7.
[68] William Campbell, 2nd Baron Stratheden (1824–93), succ. 1860.
[69] Temperatures reached 96°F in London in the shade.

summer: 1868 and 1870 were hot, but not for so long together. Complaints of the want of water are beginning, the earth is cracked and gaping for yards in depth.

Here are some of the questions pending at the F.O., & which must be dealt with in the recess. Extradition – U.S. Fisheries – U.S. Three Rules – question likely to be raised by Mr Fish. Fisheries, Newfoundland, question with France. Sugar Convention. Renewal of commercial treaties with France, Austria, Italy & c. Roumania treaties. New Guinea, claims of foreign states upon, if any. Sooloo, Spanish blockade of Grosvenor mission & general negotiations with China. Protected tribes at Aden. Zanzibar: numerous small matters connected with slave trade. South Africa, relations with Portuguese both on east & west coast. Dahomey, blockade of coast. Niger river, protection to trade in. Spain, numerous complaints & grievances, chiefly connected with shipping. Talisman case in Peru. Egypt and the new tribunals.

17 August 1876. Went out with the intention of taking a walk, but the heat was too great & sent me back ... ... I have three or four hours employment daily with the papers that come down.

18 August 1876. Comparatively cool ... ... Wrote to Carnarvon on New Guinea, advising him not to lay claim on the part of England to the whole island, which except as regards those parts claimed by the Dutch he seems disposed to do: but to consider how much, if any, of it is really wanted, & consult the cabinet as to occupying that. The parts nearest Australia are described as islands, and might possibly be separated from the rest.

19 August 1876. Gortschakoff ... ... is not unwilling to listen to proposals for a conference ... ... Gortschakoff has for years made it an object, before he retires, to preside over a European congress. An odd form of vanity: but I have heard the story from so many persons who have the best means of knowing that I cannot doubt the fact.

22 August 1876. London by early train ... ... Saw in succession Beust, Schouvaloff, Harcourt, & Musurus. ... Schouvaloff ostensibly wanted an explanation of certain passages in our last published despatches, but his real object seemed to be to talk over the state of affairs.

23 August 1876. In the *D. News* of today is an article, or rather letter, by Mr Freeman the historian personally directed against me, and so exceptionally violent that I shall cut it out and keep it. Intellectual antipathies of this kind, felt against persons unknown except by their public utterances are, I suppose, common: to me they are easily intelligible, having known the feeling myself: I had it to a degree which I could never quite explain to my own satisfaction, against the late Duke of Newcastle:[70] a dull decent respectable man, whose chief faults

[70] Henry Clinton, 5th D. of Newcastle (1811–64), cabinet minister.

were his toadying of the Prince Consort, and his tendency to overrate his own abilities.

... Telegraphed again to Elliot on Servian matters, desiring him to warn the Porte of the danger incurred by a continuance of the war, in consequence of the growing excitement in Russia, and of the bad effect produced in England by Bulgarian events.

25 August 1876. Drove with M. to Maidstone ... On our return, about 4 p.m. Sanderson met us with news that the Servians are prepared to ask for mediation – in fact, Prince Milan has done so, addressing all the foreign representatives collectively. I sent off at once three telegrams: one to White, saying that we will do what we can to bring about an armistice, another to the embassies asking what view is taken by foreign powers, a third to Elliot, in terms as strong as I could use, warning the Porte of the danger of losing this opportunity of ending the war. I wrote briefly to Disraeli, telling him what I had done. Nothing more seemed possible at present.

26 August 1876. In the evening a shower of telegrams, answers to mine: the purport of all is favourable to mediation, but as no mention is made of terms, the real difficulties are untouched. The Turks would like to be able to reoccupy Belgrade & the other fortresses, which is impossible: the Servians ask for the status quo, & considering the danger which Turkey incurs by the continuance of the war, I think it would be wise to grant it, however reasonable in the abstract may be the demand that they should pay some penalty for an unprovoked war.

The Liberals are evidently bent on making capital out of the Bulgarian massacres, and several meetings have been held on the subject. It is not clear what the promoters of these meetings wished or expected that the British govt should have done: but it is natural that popular feeling should be strong, for the cruelty of the Turkish troops seems to have been great & unprovoked, and the existence of this feeling greatly complicates the situation.

28 August 1876. London early, with Sanderson ... The first point is to ascertain whether the P. of Montenegro is willing to join in asking for an armistice. He is supposed to be, but has said nothing definite yet. France, Italy, Russia, are willing to mediate: from Austria & Germany we have no answer, ostensibly because Andrassy & Bismarck are both in the country, really, I suppose, because they wish to consult together before answering.

29 August 1876. Sent Elliot another telegram, confidential & for his private guidance. It is to the effect that the events in Bulgaria have destroyed entirely the sympathy felt in England for Turkey: so much so, that if Russia were to take part openly with the Servians, & declare war, it would be practically impossible for us to interfere. The position in that case would be humiliating for England, and unsatisfactory generally: peace is therefore essential: and the strongest pressure must be applied to the Porte to induce consent to the conditions which Europe might agree on.

30 August 1876. Wrote to Disraeli in answer to a suggestion made by him some weeks ago as to replacing Elliot & Buchanan: my answer was, that for the moment I thought Elliot must be left where he is. If we displaced him now, when there is a cry against him on account of his alleged backwardness to report the misconduct of the Turks in Bulgaria, we should seem to be making a scapegoat: a thing which never pays ... ... The necessity of the moment is to make peace: when that is done, a change, if still thought desirable, is easy & free from objection, and Elliot could then retire with credit to himself. As to Buchanan, I said nothing. His removal is no doubt desirable, for mediocre at all times, he is now becoming incapable of work from old age: but there is nothing urgent about the matter.

I received today notice that the P. of Montenegro consents to ask for a suspension of hostilities: and accordingly framed a telegram to Elliot, directing him to ask, in the name of his govt, for an armistice, to be general for all the combatants: the term not to be more than a month, and immediate negotiations for peace to follow. He is to tell his colleagues of the step he has taken, & to ask their support. I kept this instruction back, in order to be able to communicate with Disraeli, & also to have official assurances of the cooperation of the German govt which I have not yet, though not doubting that it will be given.

31 August 1876. Lowe came & passed the afternoon with M. I ... saw little of him.

Our newspapers are full of the Bulgarian business, partly because there is nothing else to write about, partly on party grounds ... partly because there is really a feeling of disgust, and one that is natural enough, at the useless & purposeless acts of murder that have been committed, apparently in most cases with little or no provocation.

1 September 1876. London early ... Saw Harcourt & Brincken,[71] & explained to them at length the telegram which I proposed to send. Telegraphed the substance of it to Disraeli at Hughenden, and to the Queen. Assent from both came in the evening, and I sent it, or rather the resident clerk did so, having orders to wait till the approval came from Balmoral.

2 September 1876. London again early ... ... Saw ... Harcourt, Brincken, Menabrea, Musurus, Bartholomei, & Beust: Schouvaloff was to have called, but is ill of gravel: a complaint to which he is liable,

---

[71] Franz Egon Freiherr van den Brincken (1835–1906), 1st sec. at German embassy 2 Apr. 1874–16 mar. 1881.

and which he cultivates with much claret. I explained to all the course which I had decided on taking, and found, as I had reason to expect, that there is a general wish that England should assume the initiative. All gave assurances of support: Harcourt said, 'We shall follow you blindfold': the only govt at all to disposed to hold aloof is the Austrian, and I believe that Andrassy now sees the necessity of action. When I say 'all' I exclude Musurus, to whom it is never easy to explain anything, as he is sure to mistake & misreport it: he however sees the difficulty of the situation and says he has warned his govt as to the extent to which English feeling towards Turkey has changed in the last few weeks.

The change is certainly remarkable: meetings are being held daily in the provinces ... the hope is expressed that we will have nothing more to do with the Turks, except to help in turning them out of Europe. To a considerable extent, these meetings are got up for party purposes, being generally attended by Liberal M.P.s and nonconformist preachers: but they undoubtedly represent also a large amount of genuine popular feeling. The outcry is so far inconvenient that it weakens our hands abroad, & strengthens those of Russian statesmen, but it is not unnatural, and at this time of year can do little harm.

The deposition of the new Sultan on the ground of insanity, & the setting of his brother in his place, passes almost unnoticed: it was an act of obvious necessity, and constitutional by Turkish law ... Of the real disposition of the successor we know nothing ... ... Musurus vouches for his intelligence, & for his knowing French well: & Musurus, though stupid, can be trusted in matters of fact.

3 September 1876. Disraeli writes, agreeing in my view as to the non-removal of Elliot, under present circumstances, and adds that the Bulgarian business, though it has increased our difficulties, may help towards a solution, since it gives us a reason for modifying, in regard to the Porte, a position which had become untenable even before the massacres. We may reasonably now ask securities for non-mahometans in Turkey which before the experience of the last few months would have been superfluous. ... Before receiving D.'s letter I had written in the same sense to Bourke.

5 September 1876. We are waiting for the Turkish answer to our proposition for an armistice. The Porte is still in doubt, but some hesitation is natural in such a case.

6 September 1876. London early with Sanderson ... Trouble in W. Africa, the king of Dahomey having seized & shut up all French traders within his dominions: as an act of revenge for our blockade. As we are the cause ... the French naturally complain. I sent Sir J. Pauncefote to the Admiralty to consult Sir A. Milne, & see what can be done for the relief of those people, but it requires caution, for Commodore Hewett is quite ready enough to get into a war without any prompting, & it will not do to give him an excuse.

Saw Lawson, who is anxious that I should receive a deputation on the Bulgarian business: which I have no objection to do. The excitement in regards to it is increasing ... The time of year is favourable, there is nothing else to write or talk about, the losers by Turkish bankruptcy contribute to swell the cry, Liberals naturally seize the only opportunity of damaging us which they have had for some time, and also of influencing any elections which may be pending, and a section of the high church party, represented by Liddon,[72] thinks the occasion a good one for displaying their interest in the Greek Christians. In addition to all those, there is the natural & genuine feeling of disgust produced by highly coloured narratives of massacre & brutality...

7 September 1876. Short early walk, alone: drive & walk with M. in afternoon. We discovered a picturesque little cottage...

Read Gladstone's pamphlet on the eastern question:[73] it is a fierce and violent denunciation of the Turks, the most violent, I think, that has been written: and in which religious zeal appears plainly under the guise of sympathy for the oppressed races. It contains also many attacks on the government, but these are subordinate to the main purpose of his argument. The conclusion, as in the case of his last parliamentary speech on the same subject, falls short of what might be expected from the premises. He denounces the Turks as unfit to exist, far more to rule, anywhere: but he ends by a simple recommendation of autonomy for the disturbed provinces, including Bulgaria. A tame conclusion for so vehement an invective.

Letter from Disraeli, of which the chief object seems to be to warn me against the danger of conceding anything to the agitation of the moment. This is hardly necessary, since I agree with him, but I understand his being anxious. I write in return,[74] suggesting conditions of peace as being what we may safely propose: *status quo* as regards Servia: Montenegro the same, advising, but not pressing, the grant of a port or strip of territory: the arrangements to be made for reform of administration in the provinces to be reserved for subsequent discussion.

9 September 1876. London with M. & Sanderson, by early train. Work at home till 1, when called on Disraeli at his request. I found him weak from gout, and not free from anxiety as to the political situation, but on the whole hopeful, and in good spirits. He discussed the whole

[72] H.P. Liddon (1829–90), canon of St Paul's 1870–90.
[73] *Bulgarian Horrors and the Question of the East.*
[74] Disraeli to Derby, 6 Sept. 1876, in M. and B., 53. The diaries make no reference to Disraeli's vital letter of 4 Sept. proposing to take Constantinople, and Derby's reply.

eastern affair, rationally enough, but we had corresponded and talked about it so often that there was nothing very new to be said. He is against calling a cabinet, which some of his colleagues have suggested, and altogether against the notion of an autumn session, which is being hinted at in the newspapers. Hc is confident as to the Buckinghamshire election, which is looked to with more than common anxiety just now, as being a test how far the current agitation has affected the constituencies.

Office, where saw only Brincken: he brought the same news as to the expected conditions of peace, as framed by the Turks, which I had previously received from Harcourt. They are inadmissible, & not in all probability meant to be taken seriously: people always ask for more than they mean to accept.

Returned by 4.45 train: a busy, but not disagreeable day.

10 September 1876. Occupied chiefly ... in making notes for a reply to be addressed to a deputation which calls upon me tomorrow. The public excitement does not show signs of subsiding, & making all allowance for the reasonable feeling of disgust at narratives of gross brutality, the height to which it has risen is not intelligible. Total absence of all other subjects of public interest accounts for it to some extent. I have never known in England so absolute an absence of internal agitation – I mean on any internal question. ... A more reasonable criticism is that Elliot ought to have known more of what was passing, & known it sooner, than he appears to have done: and to this there is no quite satisfactory answer.

11 September 1876. London early with Sanderson ... To office to receive two deputations on Turkish affairs. The first, headed by Mr Potter, & composed of about 60 persons, was moderate & sensible in language: the speeches were short, & to the point, and all desire to attack the government was disclaimed, as it would seem sincerely. ... I answered them at length, speaking over half an hour ... I brought out, in substance, all that I wished, but was not happy in words, & felt that it was so. The deputation were however satisfied. The second party, also numbering about 50 or 60, met in the same room: but they were very inferior. The chief speaker was a Mr Lucraft, who declaimed in a vague sort of way about war & standing armies: none of them seemed to have any clear idea of what they wanted. The first deputation, I learnt, had objected to allow them to come in jointly: I ... only answered a few of their remarks civilly but briefly.

Schouvaloff came later: he said he had been at Brussels: his substitute, last week, said he had been ill: possibly neither story is true. He made his usual protestation, that he was kept uninformed, had no instructions, knew nothing of what was doing, & so forth: as if it were likely that one of the acutest of Russian courtiers, and a personal friend of the

Czar, should be left in that condition at a critical moment. However, I had no reason for concealment, and told him what we had done about an armistice, & also what was considered by us as a reasonable basis for peace.

Returned by the 4.45 train.

12 September 1876. Telegrams ... it is now clear that the Porte will not consent to an armistice unless under extreme pressure.

The new Sultan is well spoken of ... ... some people think he is inclined to fanaticism, but of that I see no evidence. ... It is by Russians & other strangers mainly that the war is kept alive. The native Servians have never shown any enthusiasm for it, the feeling in favour of fighting being confined to Belgrade: the hospitals are full of men disabled by self-inflicted wounds, and many have been shot by their own officers for slackness in the field. Disraeli sends me an interesting letter from Lloyd-Lindsay on this subject.

13 September 1876. Saw O. Russell & specially charged him to find out if he could whether the Russians really mean war with Turkey in the event of the Servian quarrel being peacefully arranged. He confirmed my previous impression, that Bismarck has no eastern policy, cares nothing what happens at Constantinople, but is influenced only by the effect which transactions there may have on the European Powers. His object is neither to allow a quarrel between Austria & Russia, nor yet to encourage too close an alliance between them: to keep them on friendly terms, but not on terms of intimacy.

Saw Musurus, who talked wildly & foolishly ... Saw Schouvaloff, who had also heard that the armistice is refused, & said the question was what to do next? We talked, but vaguely, & I told him I could give no option on the steps now to be taken without consulting the Premier. I might have done so at once, but thought it better to gain time. From the point of view of justice the objection of the Porte to grant a suspension of hostilities is unanswerable: and so long as Russia can be restrained from moving singly, there is no cause for haste. The Turks however are making no use of their advantages in Servia, and so far they gain nothing by delay. The Servian army is now mainly Russian, so far as officers are concerned.

14 September 1876. The agitation on Turkish affairs has begun to subside ... There is curious evidence of disunion among Liberal leaders. Gladstone & Lowe rival each other in the vehemence of their abuse of everything Turkish: but one proposes to place Turkey under a sort of joint control of all the Powers, the other to leave it to be absorbed by Russia. There can hardly be a more fundamental difference of policy, & on a point as to which action in one sense or another must be taken.

15 September 1876. News by evening messenger that the Porte has agreed to grant a suspension of hostilities. ... I do not know if I have

noted here the terms of peace which we have suggested. They are, for
Servia & Montenegro status quo: for Bosnia, Bulgaria, Herzegovina
some form of local or administrative autonomy, such as may give the
population some voice in the management of their own local affairs, &
security against arbitrary acts of mismanagement.

The Porte on the other hand asks for the restoration or destruction
of the Servian fortresses, the re-investiture of P. Milan, payment of an
indemnity etc. all demands inadmissible in the actual state of affair...

16 September 1876. London by early train. Busy at home till 1, when
to office, and stayed till 4.30. Saw there Musurus ... ... I could not
but feel that much of what he said was just, and that the Porte is likely
to get less than fair play. The strong and general feeling roused in
England against Turkish administration makes it impossible for me, or
for any one who might be in my place, to support the Sultan even
against demands which in the abstract are hardly reasonable: and in
advising him, as I have done again and again most earnestly, to make
peace even on disadvantageous terms, I am doing what is best for him,
as well as inevitable in the actual state of European politics.

... Saw Schouvaloff, and pressed him ... to accept the suspension
of hostilities ... ... This he professes to agree in personally, but must
refer to Gortschakoff. ... All depends on the line taken by Russia. If
the Czar wishes for peace, it can probably be made...

17 September 1876. Long early walk in Knole park with Sanderson.
Short walk later with M.

18 September 1876. Lawson called: I told him in general terms what
has passed. At the office, Schouvaloff called: we agreed to accept the
Turkish suspension of hostilities as an armistice, expressing confidence
that it will be continued if necessary beyond the term of ten days
named at first. ... Meeting in the City today: disturbed & noisy: the
public excitement about Turkey does not seem to lessen.

19 September 1876. Many letters, one from Disraeli, who seems less
confident than he was as to the Buckinghamshire election.

Cross writes that the Queen wants to be informed as to the state of
eastern affairs. I write accordingly, giving a short, but I think intelligible
report of the situation.

... Took leave of M. who goes to Knowsley.

20 September 1876. Baring's report[75] on Bulgarian affairs has appeared
at last: he and Elliot between them have been very slow in producing
it: but it is fairly well done. It confirms a good deal of what the
newspapers have said, though disposing of many exaggerations. The
popular excitement on eastern matters is not much abated, and no

---

[75] 'Report by Mr Baring on the Bulgarian Insurrection of 1876', published as supplement
to *London Gazette*, 19 Sept. 1876.

doubt will be used largely for party purposes: Gladstone is said to be possessed with the subject ... He now threatens to return, and if ever in power again, it is expected that he will form a purely radical government.

... Wrote, or rather rewrote on a foundation supplied by Tenterden, a despatch[76] on Baring's report: the report itself having just appeared in the papers. It confirms, in substance, the popular impression as to the needless and useless cruelty with which a very feeble attempt at insurrection was put down.

21 September 1876. In the papers, a very skilful ingenious speech[77] by Disraeli ... He says much on the eastern question, but leaves us practically unpledged. The next move by the opposition will be a demand for an autumn session, lest the public mind should have time to cool down. ... If peace is made, and a satisfactory arrangement concluded as to the disturbed provinces, there will be nothing to discuss: if all ends in a deadlock, we may not be able to resist the wish for an early discussion.

... Albert Grant's new house, which with the land has cost him £200,000, is for sale, he having lost heavily, and being they say ruined.

... Saw at the office C. Wolkenstein, the Austrian, who read me telegrams and despatches at some length. He is an eccentric person: his habit is to sit as close to me as he can manage, and bawl in my ear as if addressing a large public meeting. Perhaps he thinks me deaf, and certainly he leaves me so. He came to announce that Andrassy accepts the English basis for peace, with a reserve which is to me odd and not very intelligible – that it shall be formally *constaté* that the Austrian note of last winter is to be taken as the base of the so-called local autonomy. Whether this is sheer vanity, which I rather suspect – the wish not to have it appear that his plans are superseded by any others – or whether there is a design in it, I cannot guess.

Saw also Schouvaloff, and discussed, but nothing new.

The German govt was understood to be willing to act with us, but at the last moment Bismarck reserves his opinion. Is this with a view to back up Austria in any possible difference? Anyway, it is too late to reopen discussion, and I telegraph to Elliot to propose our basis of peace.

22 September 1876. Letter from Disraeli, pleased with the success of his speech, and urging me (needlessly) not to make any concession to the popular cry. All that is not faction in it, he says, is froth.

Saw Vivian,[78] just leaving for Alexandria: we discussed Egyptian

---

[76] Derby to Elliot, 20 Sept. 1876, *Parl. P.* 1877, xc, Turkey no. 1, no. 316.

[77] At Aylesbury, 20 Sept. 1876, strongly attacking atrocities agitation.

[78] Sir H. Vivian, agent at Alexandria 1873, 1876–9.

affairs at length. I acknowledged my belief of the hopeless state of the finances, and of the impossibility of inducing the Khedive to adopt the only effectual remedy, severe retrenchment ... What is possible is to induce him to abandon his absurd notions of distant conquest & to make peace with Abyssinia: and to settle a boundary line between his territories & those of Zanzibar. As between the two, I told Vivian our interest is rather to favour the Sultan of Zanzibar, who has put himself altogether into our hands.

Musurus called, & left with me a long telegraphic despatch written in a tone quite new: in it the Sultan is made to hold decided language as to not admitting interference in the internal affairs of the empire: which after the precedents of the last 20 years, is simply absurd ... I cannot tell whether this is mere acting or a genuine display of character. Not much is known of the new Sultan: he is reported to be free from vices, economical, likely to take a serious view of his position & work: some add that he is obstinate, determined not to be governed by his ministers, and inclined to reaction...

News of the Bucks election ... The majority under 200, but it was thought likely the Liberals would win: the result proves that the existing excitement has not so far done us much harm: and is so far important, that the Liberal press was prepared to treat success as a great party victory.

23 September 1876. The Austrian & German govts both now support our proposals, so that there is for the moment entire union. Knowsley by 6 p.m. train ... Found with M. ... Mr Froude & his daughter.

25 September 1876. Left Knowsley by 4 p.m. train with Sanderson ... Letter from Disraeli enclosing one from Salisbury, with a new constitution for the Turkish empire: for it amounts to that. I keep copy of the proposal, though not believing that it will work.

26 September 1876. ... Saw Schouvaloff, who came with a startling proposition, to the effect that in the event of the Porte's refusal to accept the terms proposed, Austrian troops should march into Bosnia, Russian troops into Bulgaria, and the united fleets come up to Constantinople. I declined to answer this proposal offhand, alleging the necessity of consulting colleagues, and the improbability, as far as I could judge, of the case suggested arising. The Sultan, I said, was showing every disposition to meet the Powers halfway ... ... I treated the matter calmly, as if not surprised at the suggestion, but in truth it has an unpleasant significance. It seems to indicate that the Russians ... wish to prevent the peaceable settlement which they affect to support. It is possible however that there may be in it nothing beyond Gortschakoff's usual love of swagger.

27 September 1876. Overtures from the P. of Montenegro, who professes himself weary of the kind of protectorate which Russia has established over him, & anxious for closer relations with England. I agree, on Buchanan's advice, to send Monson[79] there.

Andrassy also does not conceal his increasing jealousy & fear of Russia: & says the Russians are detested in Servia. Russian officers, I hear elsewhere, have in several instances been shot in the field by the Servian troops whom they were commanding.

... Deputation from the City ...... They were mostly Liberals. ... The general feeling seemed to be that if nothing else would accomplish the object, we ought to go to war to drive the Turks out of Europe. I have not often seen a meeting more unanimous or determined ...... Resolutions denouncing Turkey continue to pour in, but they are now mostly from small meetings, & at least half are got up by dissenting preachers.

Saw Schouvaloff: spoke to him seriously about Russian volunteers in Servia: they are coming in without disguise, & at the rate of 2 to 300 a day. I pointed out to him that these people ... would be the great enemies of peace: and that they were not even helping Russia to acquire influence in the country, for the natives had become thoroughly alarmed, seeing the whole conduct of affairs passing into foreign hands. He admitted all this, said it was true, but he did not believe the Emperor himself could stop the movement, so strong was the popular feeling.

Telegraphed to Elliot that some modifications asked by the Sultan are sure to be rejected by the Powers, & had better therefore not be brought forward.

28 September 1876. News in the papers that Servia decides, under pressure from Tchernaieff and the Russians, to continue the war. ... If true, the consequences are impossible to foresee, and there can in that case be little doubt (I have not much as it is) that Russia is playing a double game.

29 September 1876. Saw Lawson, who is trying to induce Potter[80] and the trades union leaders to detach themselves from the agitating party ... I gather that the deputation from the City, by the noisy talk and dictatorial manner of some of its members, has done the cause harm, and that the promoters know it. Lawson says that a reaction has set in from the agitation of the last few weeks and that sensible men are growing ashamed of it. I partly believe this...

... Saw ... Schouvaloff, who professed to have no information, and asked me what was going on – the usual Russian dodge when anything specially important is in hand...

[79] Sir E.J. Monson (1834–1909), consul-gen. at Budapest, 1871; U.K. rep. at Cetinje, 1876–7.
[80] George Potter (1832–93), trade unionist; ed. *Bee-Hive*, which supported agitation until mid-Sept., then opposed it: cf. Shannon, 129.

... Wrote to the Queen, who wants to send a special mission to the Emperor of Russia ... ... Wrote to explain to her what Russian agents are doing, & how little Russian assurances can be trusted.

30 September 1876. Wrote to D. ... advising him, in the event of the Turkish answer to our proposals being a refusal, to call a cabinet without delay.

... Harcourt is sore at Schouvaloff having himself communicated the Russian propositions to the Daily News, about which he says there is no doubt, & then laying the blame on the French embassy. A truly Russian proceeding. He, Harcourt, thinks the situation serious, believing, as I do, that the Russians do not want to settle the business, but to keep it open.

3 October 1876. Gennadius read & left with me a despatch of which the purport is to recapitulate a list of grievances against Turkey, some, like the settling of Circassians on the frontier, partly real, others far-fetched, & all exaggerated. The object is plainly to lay a ground for war, or for active assistance to insurrection in the Greek provinces of Turkey. Indeed he hardly seemed to care to conceal the intention, saying with a curious simplicity that it was hard that Greece, which had taken no part in creating these disturbances, & so far deserved well of the Powers, should alone derive no advantage from them.

Schouvaloff had nothing especial to tell, but pressed upon me the Russian proposal, & seemed to hint that nothing less would be accepted, Austria & Germany being ready to give their support. This is likely enough, but we do not know it, & I cannot take it on his word.

... We hear also from Elliot that the terms of peace proposed by the Powers are rejected, though the Porte is willing to grant reforms to all the provinces. This alternative will not be accepted, nor can it well be, & what is now before us, is to consider the Russian proposals.

4 October 1876. At 1, Schouvaloff came with a new proposal from Russia, which is to insist on an armistice and follow it up by a conference. The latter was not in his telegram, but it is understood to be intended.

... Cabinet met at 2, sat till 4: all present. Much vague and general talk about eastern affairs, which Disraeli explained at length: he recapitulated accurately enough what has passed, expressed his belief that bold measures would have to be taken, and that in certain probable contingencies England ought to occupy Constantinople as a material guarantee. As this notion, which he is evidently full of and will press upon us, had no immediate reference to what is doing now, I contented myself with putting in a protest against being supposed to agree. He spoke much of the Russians having it in their power to send troops by sea to within a few miles of the capital, and so to surprise it. Our discussion was desultory, as it could hardly help being: the Russian plan of naval and military occupation was summarily and without disagreement rejected: and we concluded to adopt the alternative proposition of insisting on an armistice, to be followed by a conference.

6 October 1876. Telegrams from Loftus giving secret intelligence that unless orders to the contrary shall appear, a manifesto will be issued announcing Russian intention to occupy Bulgaria with 150,000 men – with the consent of Austria. Write on this to Disraeli: I suspect it is a secret intentionally disclosed, with the view of frightening us into consent to the plan of a naval demonstration at Constantinople. I doubt whether Russia has 150,000 men ready to move, or the means of moving them.

... Schouvaloff denied emphatically the truth of Loftus's story, which I repeated without letting him know where it came from: and indeed if it be true it is not likely that he should know of it.

8 October 1876. Decazes has been discussing matters with Lyons. He is for armistice, conference, and no military occupation: which is our view also in all respects.

Andrassy dislikes the notion of a conference, unless the basis of it be carefully defined beforehand – in which he is quite right – and appears to have made it known to the Russians that he will decline to have anything to say to an occupation of Bosnia. All very well, but will he persevere? Hitherto he has done nothing but vacillate, and the impossibility of either side relying upon him has not been one of the least of our difficulties.

10 October 1876. ... Since the Russians have shown their hand, public feeling has changed in a singular way ... A meeting last night in St James's Hall & one in Hyde Park, have attracted little attention. The agitation of the last few weeks has however done what mischief it is capable of: the Russians believe the English govt to be unsupported, & that they may do what they please. I am on the whole less sanguine of a satisfactory result than I have been since the beginning of the affair.

... Saw Schouvaloff, who argued against the admission of a representative from the Porte to the conference: saw Gennadius, who read a long despatch claiming for the Greek provinces the same kind of administrative reform ... that is given to the Sclave provinces...

11 October 1876. Telegram from Elliot ... that Porte agrees to an armistice of 5 months. One difficulty is thus removed, & we shall see if the Russian govt is sincere in its professed desire for peace.

Despatches from Belgrade, chiefly to the following effect. That Servia is becoming a Russian dependency, everything being done at the dictation of Russian officers: the Treasury is amply supplied with money, which can only have come from Russia: the late fighting has been useless as regards results, but the Russian officers say openly they will not have peace.

... Home about 5 & quiet evening ... It is odd that in what is considered to be, & really is, a diplomatic crisis, I have not personally as hard work to do as often in more quiet times I have had.

12 October 1876. Schouvaloff ... assured me ... that no communication had passed between Gen. Kaufman & the Ameer of Cabul! This is cool, for we have copies of the correspondence in our possession. I wrote to Salisbury accordingly.

... News in afternoon that the Italian govt objects to the armistice: which perplexes us.

Dined at the German embassy ... ... Münster set to work after dinner to pump me as to what we should do in the event of a Russian invasion of Turkey: seeing his intention, and feeling sure that he would communicate in some way with the Russian govt, I talked of the impossibility of our allowing Constantinople being threatened, of the ease with which it could be defended, of how the Turkish soldiers only wanted officers, whom we could supply – & more in this style: all which pledges us to nothing, and may be useful. Already in the newspapers I see that the old dread of Russia is regaining strength, and it may, a few months hence, be as inconvenient by its vehemence as it was by its absence lately.

13 October 1876. Gladstone has written a strange letter, which nobody understands: in it he deplores the influence of 'Judaic sympathies', not confined to professing Jews, on the eastern question: whether this refers to Disraeli, or to the Telegraph people, or to the Rothschilds, who refused to take part in the Buckinghamshire byelection, is left in darkness. Delane tells M. that in Gladstone's mind the principal cause of the violence that he has shown is his admiration for, & sympathy with, the Greek church.

... Münster called: I asked him to telegraph to his govt to induce Bismarck if possible to urge on the Russian cabinet acceptance of the Turkish armistice: this was in consequence of a conversation held just before with Schouvaloff, who represents the Czar, or Gortschakoff, as hesitating, and disposed to raise objections. I told both that a refusal by Russia, on pretexts evidently not serious, would be regarded in England as evidence that war with Turkey is determined on: and I added some hints, purposely vague, as to the change in public feeling which would be produced. Schouvaloff – whom I really believe to be sincere in his wish to keep peace – said he knew it, & had observed the change from the moment when the plan of Bulgarian occupation became known. Beust came, with news that Austria accedes to the Turkish proposals. France has already done so. Italy holds aloof, & raises objections: but what Italy does matters little. Germany undertakes to advise the Servians to accept, but does not seem to give the advice with much heartiness.

15 October 1876. There is as yet no official announcement of the Russian answer, but from what has been said at other courts, there can be no doubt but that it will be a refusal. I shall be curious to hear what reason is assigned for rejecting a proposal which gives all, & more than all, that Russia asked for. The explanation, or demand, was put forward in the hope that it would be refused, & so the Porte put itself in the wrong. The Austrian govt too seems inclined to back out, finding Russia hostile, & endeavours to explain that in approving the armistice, nothing was said as to its direction. But this is clearly an afterthought.

... Despatches from Athens. There seems a very sore feeling ... The intense vanity of the people is hurt ... disturbances are probable.

16 October 1876. Saw Musurus ... He talked ... in his usual strain, how the Porte was ready for a war with Russia, & did not doubt the result, unless Austria also took part.

Saw Schouvaloff who brought the official refusal of Russia to consent to an armistice for so long a period as five months. This was known beforehand ... and as to alter it is impossible, but little passed between us: I could see however that Schou. is unaffectedly vexed & alarmed at what the Emperor is doing, which he did not expect, and against which he has remonstrated as much as he dared. He has since told Ly D. that if he had been asked a week ago whether his govt really wanted peace, he would have answered without hesitation 'Yes': now, he does not know what to say.

... Wrote to Disraeli to explain the situation & suggest a cabinet: nothing will come of it, but our colleagues may reasonably expect to be consulted in a crisis such as this.

17 October 1876. Saw Münster, who came at my request: I asked him if he knew anything of the ideas of his govt, which he did not: and then requested him to suggest to Bismarck the advantage of making some proposal in the nature of a compromise, which both Russia & England could accept. He said he would, but did not conceal his opinion that it would be of no use, thinking Russia bent on a quarrel and on an occupation of Turkey. I telegraphed also to O. Russell in the same sense: rather *par acquit de conscience* than in hope of a result.

Saw Schouvaloff, who talked in a friendly way enough, but I could see plainly that he thinks very ill of the state of affairs.

... Decazes has been throwing out hints to Lyons, that Italy is open to an offer of territorial advantages, and would in that view willingly act with Russia. ... The idea prevalent in France is that Austria will be attacked as well as Turkey, and probably partitioned, Germany getting the largest share.

18 October 1876. Found Schouvaloff had called with a new proposal:

it is however from himself only, a suggestion & nothing more. He came again, & talked it over. I could give no offhand answer, & only said that a cabinet was to be held tomorrow.

... Saw Münster, who brought the German answer: it is in fact to the purport that Bismarck does not wish to take a leading part in the affair, wishes to keep the Powers united as long as possible, sees himself no objection to the Turkish proposal, but will not press it on Russia: in short, as I expected, he leaves us where we were. I observe that Münster also thinks that a Russian army invading Turkey would find very serious difficulty, as it did in 1828.

... Wellesley sends home secret information that quite within the last few days, since the 5th, large military preparations have been making. Leave to officers has been stopped ... & preparations are being carried out for immediate mobilisation.

19 October 1876. Called on Disraeli 2.30, & talk with him till cabinet met at 3.

In regard of the armistice business, the position of the powers is as follows. England accepts the Turkish proposal for six months: will not object to a modification, but will not press one on the Porte. Austria takes the same line as England. France was for six months, but would be glad of a compromise. Italy has objected from the first to an armistice of more than six weeks or two months, possibly having an understanding with Russia, & looking forward to a slice of Austrian territory as her reward. Germany professes to be neutral, does not mean to take an active part, but the German sympathy is rather with Russia. So we stand at present. If the rock on which we are now sticking were out of the way, there are others behind: Bismarck objects to a conference: so does the Porte for quite different reasons: Austria will have no conference without a settled programme, and requires the admission of the Turkish representative: Russia wishes for as little programme as possible, and insists on the exclusion of the Turk. Behind all the rest is the question of the Russian volunteers in Servia, which we have been content to ignore while the matters in dispute seemed likely to get themselves quietly settled: but which is growing more serious every day: and the general conviction in England now is that Russia wants war, and will make it on one pretext or another. The effect on popular feeling is remarkable. It is felt that the late outbreak of passion about Bulgarian matters, even where genuinely justified by what had happened, has been unlucky in leading the Russians to believe that they could march on Constantinople without resistance from us: and those who have stirred the fire are as generally blamed as they were admired a few weeks ago.

... At the cabinet today Disraeli talked much and eagerly: he seemed indifferent to the negotiations, but was full of the notion of seizing and occupying the Dardanelles in certain events. Without absolutely opposing a proposal which was not practically before us, I pointed out the bad effect on other powers, the risk of making enemies etc., but caution was not in favour. Cairns and Salisbury are both warlike, and that was the prevalent feeling. We ended only with a general understanding that enquiry should be made as to the means of fortifying both Constantinople and the Dardanelles. It is fair to add that Disraeli in what he said assumed throughout that the Porte would be a consenting party to our occupation, and that it would be done by treaty.

21 October 1876. Wrote ... Morier, who has asked me to enable him to say to the Portuguese something reassuring. They are under the fear of being some day attacked by Spain with a view to annexation, & wish to know whether we will protect them. I say in general terms that we should not 'see with indifference' any attempt of the kind.

... Schouvaloff yesterday talked as if he despaired, which I believe he does, of peace being preserved and considered the negotiations over. I believe he has been sincere in wishing to keep matters straight: and he does not disguise occasional differences between his views & those of Gortschakoff.

Monson has had an interesting conversation with the P. of Montenegro, who gives out that he should like to separate from Servia, if he can make his terms. He speaks bitterly of the Servians, & of the way in which they have allowed foreign influence to carry all before it. He means, he says, to be master in his own house: is grateful to the Emp. of Russia, but does not love the Russians in general, as they are apt to assume an air of superiority and patronage, which he resents. He wants a port, and a barren territory with about 5000 inhabitants, all non-mahometans. his people, according to Monson, are warmly attached to him, & will follow where he leads. His manner is described as cordial & pleasing.

22 October 1876. There is an offer also of an estate near the New Forest which has taken hold of my fancy, perhaps foolishly, but I have sent for particulars. It will not do to indulge my taste for estates of picturesque & ornamental kind, like Witley. They give no return, & possible involve some cost. Yet land has always kept its reputation as a good investment: and the value of money lessens so fast that one hardly knows what to trust to.

... In afternoon I had from Disraeli a letter which made me uneasy as it indicated greater alarm, and a more immediate expectation of war, than anything in our correspondence seems to warrant: he writes as though expecting the Russians to make a dash on Constantinople, which is not in the least their policy, nor do I believe that they would be able to do it if they wished. I should rather expect them to make

Servia, Roumania, and Bosnia independent, and reoccupy the strip of land in Bessarabia which was cut off from Russia twenty years ago. By these means they would gratify national vanity, and secure the real control of the petty states created by them, without seeming to add any territory to the empire. In any case, the passage of the Balkan [mountains] in winter is difficult: and on the side of Asia, snow makes all attack impossible.

23 October 1876. Saw Disraeli and Hardy: the former, to my relief, I find in a quiet frame of mind, quite different from that in which his letter of yesterday must have been written. We talked over the situation, & agreed to send out two officers to examine the possible defences of Constantinople to the landward.[81]

Saw Lawson, as I do most days.

... Schou. tells Ly D. with some uneasiness what is reported to him of Disraeli's conversation: how he announced publicly that it is more likely than not that we shall be at war with Russia, talks of seizing the Dardanelles, occupying Constantinople, and the like. I am afraid that it is likely enough that there is some truth in these reports though the story loses nothing in telling.

24 October 1876. Letter from Hunt, in which he says that Disraeli has desired him to instruct the Admiral at Besica Bay to send the fleet up to Constantinople (i.e. through the Dardanelles) in the event of a Russian vessel going through. Hunt naturally demurs, and says he must have the authority of the F.O. before giving directions of this kind. I cannot quite believe that Disraeli would have directed this to be done, without consulting me: but he is in an odd excited state, and talks carelessly about the probability of our being at war, and the steps to be taken, before people who repeat and probably exaggerate all his utterances. I foresee the probability, or at least, the chance of a breach between us: not that as yet we have differed materially in regard to anything that has been done, but that our points of view and objects are different. To the Premier the main thing is to please and surprise the public by bold strokes and unexpected moves: he would rather run serious national risks than hear his policy called feeble or commonplace: to me, the first object is to keep England out of trouble, so long as it can be done consistently with honour and good faith. We have agreed in resisting the agitation got up by Gladstone: but if war with Russia becomes popular, as it may, we are not unlikely to be on different sides.

Office ... saw Schouvaloff, long conversation with him...

25 October 1876. On the whole this was the easiest day I have had for a long while in London.

26 October 1876. The negotiations at Constantinople: these appear to

---

[81] Dwight E. Lee, *Great Britain and the Cyprus Convention Policy of 1878* (1934).

be going on better, the armistice question being apparently settled in principle. But our real difficulties remain. Is there to be a conference? Where is it to be held? What shall be the programme? Is the Turkish representative to be admitted or shut out? All these questions have to be answered, and it will not be easy, I suspect, to induce the Powers to answer them in the same sense. They might all be dealt with easily enough, if we are to suppose the Powers really anxious for a settlement: but are they? France will do what Russia wishes: Italy does not care: Austria pulled different ways by contending parties, does not know its own mind: Bismarck would probably be glad of a quarrel that would avert during some years that which he most fears – a Franco-Russian coalition against Germany: and in any case, he is not sorry to see the Russians with their hands full at home: in short, there is no union, no common purpose, & no mutual confidence.

28 October 1876. For the last few days the Premier has been pressing urgently to have a draft prepared in the sense of warning Russia that any occupation of Turkish territory by her would be regarded here as a violation of the treaty of Paris, and might lead to serious consequences. Something of the sort was suggested at the cabinet ten days or a fortnight ago, but not decided on, and since then matters have so far changed that language of the kind proposed seemed needless and inopportune. I however had a draft prepared, partly by Tenterden, partly by myself, pointing out the violation of treaty that would be involved, but without any expressions of menace. I send this to D., telling him that I had drawn it so, thinking anything of a more hostile character undesirable, and that I could not agree to alter it in that sense. I did not much see the use of it, as matters stand, but on that point I would defer to the cabinet, as in its present shape it did not commit us to any action. This was the chief business of the day.

29 October 1876. Letter from Disraeli, agreeing to my draft, and expressing doubt, whether in the altered condition of affairs, it is necessary to protest against designs of occupation at all. This having been my view from the first, I answer in the same sense, and propose a meeting tomorrow.

Letter from E. Cecil, saying that orders have been given to the War Dept. to get ready 80 heavy guns (40 to 64 pounders) for the defence of Constantinople! He says this cannot be done without attracting general attention, and wishes to know if it is ordered with the sanction of F.O. – I thank him, and write to Disraeli and Hardy to remonstrate against a step being taken which is sure to create alarm, and which has not been sanctioned by the cabinet.[82]

---

[82] Cf. *GH* 195: 'Eustace Cecil has given me trouble by most needlessly writing to Lord Derby as if he was pressed for guns when I only sent an inquiry! I have been a good deal annoyed...'

30 October 1876. Called on Disraeli, and long conversation with him.
He calm, not despondent, and altogether in a satisfactory state. He
assured me he knew nothing about the matter of the guns. He agreed
with me that either Salisbury or Lyons would be the fittest person to
send out to a conference, supposing one to take place. He was anxious
that I should consider what could be done to secure the support of
Germany: a matter which we discussed at some length. He thought
that what Bismarck really wanted was an assurance, or guarantee in
some form, that the annexed provinces should remain German: in
other words, security against a French war. So far I agreed: but pointed
out the impossibility of our giving any such pledge. Could we expect
parliament to sanction it even now? still more, could we expect it to
be acted upon twenty years hence? and if not was it reasonable to
incur responsibilities which when the time came, we might find ourselves
unable to meet? These arguments he admitted to be difficult to answer,
though, as I thought, inclined to cling to the idea of German support,
even if bought at this enormous price.

31 October 1876. Schouvaloff came twice: once, with the news that
Ignatieff had sent in to the Porte an ultimatum, threatening to break
off relations within 48 hours if the armistice was not accepted. Schou.
hinted to me that he thought this was more bluster than anything else,
intended to conciliate popular feeling in Russia which has been greatly
excited by recent Turkish successes. (The Servians have been beaten
again, & lost many Russian officers...)

1 November 1876. Saw ... Sir Drummond Hay,[83] who represented his
claims to promotion, and indeed they are good, but he is so useful in
his present post, and it is one so difficult to fill, that his very success
has stood in his way.

Saw Schouvaloff, who ill-pleased and anxious: it seems that the
ultimatum was sent from Livadia[84] when Ignatieff was on the point of
concluding an arrangement. Schou. does not altogether understand it,
but talks frankly to me of the légèreté and vanity of his chief Gortschakoff
and in conversation with M. lamented that the Emperor had no one
about him who would take the responsibility of opposing his impulses.
We hear in all directions of Russian armaments and of preparations
for immediate war. It is however always possible that these may be
demonstrations only.

... Saw Gennadius, who came with a fresh complaint about the
Circassian colonies. It was not enough that none should be established
in Epirus or Thessaly: there must be none in Europe, since the Greek

[83] Sir John Drummond-Hay (1816–93), diplomatist; served in Morocco 1845–93.
[84] Crimean resort near Yalta much favoured by Alexander II.

population would suffer by their presence. This kind of talk is evidently meant as an excuse for going to war, & I did not much conceal my opinion that it was so.

2 November 1876. News that the Porte accepts the armistice on Russian conditions, which puts an end to present difficulties, but there are plenty more behind.

... Saw Schouvaloff, whose language was to the effect that no time ought to be lost in setting the ambassadors to communicate with one another as to the arrangements to be made for Bulgaria. He said his govt attached great importance to the matter being settled without delay. I reserved my opinion, being suspicious of this haste, though I did not say so.

Saw Disraeli later, & general talk with him over the state of affairs: I thought him in good spirits, & calm. He did not start any eccentric ideas. We agreed that Salisbury will be the man to attend the conference at Constantinople, if it is to come off. As a leading member of the cabinet, he will speak with more authority than any mere diplomatist: he is able, and capable of holding his own, not liable to be easily talked over: he will be in his place in parliament ready to defend what has been settled when the matter is discussed: and he is almost the only man who can be sent without seeming to displace or to humiliate Elliot. Lyons is an equal, Salisbury is a superior, not merely by rank but by official position.

O. Russell sends Bismarck's answer to our invitation to him to declare himself. He professes desire of peace, wishes to support England, but must decline to take a leading part ... He adds more privately that he understands our interest in Constantinople, but does not see that anything else concerns us much: that Turkey cannot be kept on its legs, & is not worth disturbing the peace of Europe for: with more to the same effect: which Russell interprets as meaning that he was willing to help us when he thought we had on hand a scheme of partition (inasmuch as it would probably have led to a quarrel with Russia) but is not disappointed at discovering that we have never had any such designs.

3 November 1876. Saw Münster ... He expressed himself strongly persuaded that the Russians do not mean the affair to end peaceably, which may be true, but I cannot avoid noting that he loses no opportunity of holding this language: evidently it is by instruction, the object being (as in 1874–5) to prevent our acting with Russia, & if possible to embroil us.

Saw Schouvaloff, & explained to him that we intend formally to propose a conference, which has not yet been done, though the idea has been talked over very often: that we shall send a special representative ... We wanted fresh blood, as the English phrase is. He seemed to agree.

Saw Disraeli & talked over arrangements for the cabinet tomorrow. ... Wrote to Salisbury about his attendance at the conference.

Another & later tel. from Loftus: whom Ignatieff has told that if the Russian interpretation of 'local autonomy' is not accepted, Ignatieff has orders to withdraw & break up the conference. This is either Russian swagger, or which is equally probable, it indicates a deliberate purpose of bringing the conference to no result. It is the misfortune of the present posture of affairs, that we must act with the Russians as if supposing them to be in good faith, while we can have no certainty that all they are doing and proposing is not a trick to gain time.

4 November 1876. Letter from Salisbury, who accepts, & will attend the conference. He fears however that there 'will not be much reality' in it. He says he will 'take his part in the comedy with all due solemnity': but wishes to know before setting out what is to be the maximum of concession to Russian demands beyond which we will not go. This is a reasonable question, & must be answered, but the answer will not be easy to give.

Work at home till 2, when cabinet. There was some talk again of buying the Turkish ironclads, which some person of influence appears to be pressing on Disraeli, at least I cannot otherwise account for his bringing it again & again before the cabinet. He did not however press the matter.

We then went to the question of conference. Salisbury's appointment was well received, and the conditions of administration to be proposed were discussed in detail. We sat nearly 2 hours.

Schouvaloff called: I spoke to him seriously about the singular language of Gortschakoff, as noted above ... I propose also to telegraph to Loftus for an explanation, not in hope of getting at the truth, but to see what will be said, & to dispel the impression that we are likely to agree to anything that may be proposed.

5 November 1876. Long dispatch from Lyons on the state of France ... As regards the present moment, the French view of the situation is as follows. That the conference will fail: that Bismarck wishes Austria & Russia to go to war, in order that both may have their hands full: that of the two he will probably side with Russia, but will not be in haste to interfere. They despair, for the moment, of detaching Russia from Germany: but are hopeful that we and the Germans shall find ourselves on different sides, so that in the end a quarrel may ensue.

6 November 1876. Cabinet at 2: not much was said on foreign affairs: we discussed chiefly the bills of the coming season: Cross will bring in again his Prisons Bill, Cairns his Bankruptcy Bill, Scotch legislation is to have more attention than it had last year, the Universities Bill is to be taken up early, also the Patents Bill. In fact all our measures will be those of last year, which have stood over for want of time. We had a long talk about the Burials question, without being able to suggest anything practicable. The party will not stand giving in to the demands of the nonconformists in full: & no compromise seems available. We sat just 2 hours.

... Elliot, who dislikes the idea of a conference at Constantinople, fearing the influence of Ignatieff, says that every day matters look less like peace.

... Hobart Pasha[85] has had his fleet out for 4 months, without an accident of any kind, though all, officers & men, are Turks except himself. It is characteristic that Ignatieff, who treated his going out on a cruise as a menace, now says the same of his coming back to Constantinople.

7 November 1876. Beust brought me a satisfactory telegram from Andrassy, the purport of which was that if we would stand firm, & not allow ourselves to be driven beyond our original proposals, Austria would do the same. I gave the assurance he wanted, & asked him to sound Andrassy as to what Austria will do in the event of a Russian invasion. If Austria & England both oppose it, there is no fear of its being attempted.

8 November 1876. Cabinet at 2: Hicks Beach sat for the first time: we discussed foreign affairs in a vague & general way, & the cabinet wished to have the Russian plan of autonomy: for which accordingly I asked Schouvaloff when we met at the office.

We talked over rewards to the Arctic explorers: & also legislation for next session. Beach has an Irish Prisons bill, a bill for altering the civil courts, and one for intermediate education, to which purpose he wishes to apply part of the Irish church surplus: as to this last we demurred, not finding fault with the plan, but fearing the controversy to which the question of surplus may lead. We sat till 4.

... Sir R. Airey, who gained a sort of celebrity in the Crimean War, is just made a peer. He is old & childless, so it matters little. I asked Disraeli what he had done it for? He answered, 'It is a court job, but it gives us a vote, and it is only for a few years at the most'.

9 November 1876. Uncomfortable beforehand in expectation of the Ld Mayor's dinner, though I knew that I should have no speech of importance to make: but my dislike to these functions (which always make me ill, however cautious I may be as to food & wine) increases continually. Went to the Guildhall, & very well, indeed enthusiastically, received by a large company. So was Disraeli, and Salisbury in a less degree. ... I had a short & formal speech to make, & did it neither

---

[85] Augustus Hobart-Hampden (1822–86), Turkish admiral; commanded Black Sea fleet in Russo-Turkish war.

well nor ill. All the speeches were short, except that of the Premier,[86] who was expected to deliver himself at some length: I listened anxiously & rather nervously, as did also Salisbury, but what he said, though inexact in some details, was safe and skilful.

... Talking of Cardinal Antonelli,[87] who is just dead, Menabrea says he has left a fortune of 30,000,000 lire = £1,200,000. How was it come by? for he had not much to begin with, & his pay was about £500 a year.

10 November 1876. Working at home till 2, when cabinet. A few questions were asked as to foreign affairs, but for the most part we discussed a plan by Cross for consolidating the laws relating to burials, a new highway bill, a valuation bill, with some similar matters.

... He (R.)[88] says Nigra[89] is intriguing to establish a secret understanding between Italy & Russia, for some rectification of the Italian frontier at the expense of Austria. Q. does he know this, or is it only a plausible guess? It is not the real interest of Italy, but it is in harmony with the Italian character & with the view of politics taken by such men as Cavour.

According to Russell, Hohenlohe[90] describes Decazes as the humble servant of Russia: certainly he has of late appeared to me in no other light.

11 November 1876. From Petersburgh there is an uncomfortable telegram reporting a speech by the Emperor ... ... however construed, it is a menace, & will be understood as such in Europe.

12 November 1876. Elliot writes in a gloomy strain, as is natural: saying that Russia may not mean to go to war, but she undoubtedly does mean to weaken Turkey fatally.

13 November 1876. Saw ... Harcourt, who came to ask what is doing, & express the anxiety of Decazes to act with us in all respects: but when the time comes he is sure to side with Russia, & I said little beyond what civility required.

... Schouvaloff called to talk over the situation: neither he nor I said a word as to the Emperor's speech. ... He read me a private letter from Gortschakoff in which the idea of Russia wishing to possess Constantinople is ridiculed.

[86] Disraeli reminded the world that England did not have to ask itself if it could afford a second or third campaign.

[87] Giacomo Antonelli (1806–76), cardinal; papal sec. of state 1850–76; never ordained priest.

[88] Lord Odo Russell, amb. in Berlin.

[89] Constantino Nigra (1827–1907), Italian amb. at St Petersburg 1876–82; once sec. to Cavour; held series of major diplomatic posts.

[90] Chlodwig Karl Viktor, Prince von Hohenlohe-Schillingsfürst (1819–1901), German amb. in Paris, 1873– ; imperial chancellor 1894–1900.

... Disraeli asked to see me, & I went over to him, but nothing of much interest passed.

14 November 1876. Office at 2: saw there Schouvaloff, who was full of plans for the supervision of Turkish provincial administration by an international commission: an idea which he promised to work out more fully: I reserved my opinion, but agreed that it was a question fairly open to discussion.

... Gennadius called ... It is clear that in Greece there is now more dread and dislike of the Sclaves than of the Turks.

15 November 1876. Lawson called early to discuss the situation. The speech of the Czar is backed up by an order for mobilising a part of his army. The Queen telegraphs to know what this means. I answer that though undoubtedly war is contemplated as a possible alternative, I do not suppose it to be decided upon: but rather that the intention is by the avowed determination to carry his point, to influence and even intimidate the conference.

... Despatches from Loftus: he describes the Czar as nervous, ill, & careworn: deeply affected at the universal distrust of his intentions ... (This is the language held to Loftus, who is credulous and a courtier, & would think it a breach of good manners to doubt anything told him by a sovereign).

16 November 1876. Tenterden came at 1: I went with him and Sanderson carefully over Salisbury's proposed instructions which we altered in some respects: they are to be seen by Disraeli, & then laid before the cabinet.

... Saw Beust, convn with him as to what should be done in the event of Russia breaking off negotiations & invading Turkey. I told Beust frankly that it was impossible for an English minister to enter into engagements dependent on future contingencies, as continental statesmen might: since we were dependent on parliament, which might refuse to ratify a bargain on which it had not been consulted. I added that in my opinion we should undoubtedly fight for Constantinople, but that I did not suppose we should make the mere crossing of the Turkish frontier by Russia a *casus belli*: the question would be, at what moment we should think the danger near enough to justify interference ...

18 November 1876. Cabinet at 12: we discussed Salisbury's instructions, sat two hours, and differed more than we have done hitherto. Carnarvon and Cairns were both for modifying them in the sense of admitting military occupation by Russia as an idea which might be entertained in conference. Disraeli and I stand out against this, as being an entire reversal of our policy: for myself, I would have resigned rather than agree to it: Salisbury himself was moderate and sensible: the others took little part, except making occasional suggestions. In the end the instructions were left as they stood, with only one or two alterations of no importance. Carnarvon's opposition I expected: he is mixed up with the high church people, Liddon and that set, which for party purposes professes warm interest in the Greek church: Cairns has no such ideas, and I was less prepared for the line he took. It may be due only to calculations of what opinion here will sanction: or it may arise from general sympathy with christians as such against Turks: I have never heard him express any feeling of the kind, but it would be natural in a man who attends the preaching of Moody and Sankey.

Office at 2: saw Schouvaloff, who seemed grave and uneasy: I hear that he thinks the situation is becoming worse and worse, and indeed he has reason for the belief, since we have news today that Russia has mobilised six corps, including 160,000 men with 640 guns. He wants me to publish a despatch containing pacific assurances by the Emperor, which Gortschakoff says will influence opinion here. He, Schou., does not think so, and has expressed himself plainly as to the impolicy of this proceeding, but he has positive instructions: I deferred my answer, for which he does not press.

Beust called, and brought important news (1) that Austria is under no engagement to Russia (2) that Austria will not remain neutral if her interests are threatened. The meaning of the last phrase was ambiguous, and no doubt was meant to be so: but it implies that if assistance is forthcoming, a Russian invasion of Turkey will be resisted. I expressed satisfaction, & wrote the news to Disraeli & Salisbury.

... Left for Fairhill ... Hardy was with us: much interesting talk. ... We talked of the autumn manoeuvres: he said he meant to hold the last in the New Forest, & sent officers down to report on the fitness of the place: they reported favourably in all respects save one, but that one objection was fatal. It seems there is a kind of fly there which from the pain of its sting ... drives horses mad, and it was thought that a few of these flies getting among the artillery or cavalry horses would cause so much confusion as to be dangerous.

19 November 1876. A letter from Disraeli to the effect that Cairns and Carnarvon want a fresh discussion of the instructions which they did not understand to be finally settled: I answer that they can discuss them, and that they can if necessary be modified by telegraph, but if not sent with Salisbury he will probably arrive at Constantinople without them, which would be awkward. In fact, they are already signed. Salisbury leaves tomorrow morning ... Ly S. very noisy and violent about the arrangements: it is unlucky that she goes. She will certainly quarrel with the staff, and say and do the most imprudent things: having great cleverness, great energy, and not a particle of tact.

20 November 1876. The Russian govt is raising a special loan of Rs 90,000,000 = about £14,000,000: an internal loan ... The Russian squadron in the Mediterranean has sailed for America in order to be out of the way in case of a war: an odd, but effectual precaution.

22 November 1876. Salisbury has seen Decazes, & sums up the conversation in a letter & despatch. Decazes, as might be expected, takes a very Austrian view: says Austria is in danger, Bism. can do what he pleases etc. in other words contemplates Germany compelling Austria to keep the peace. Decazes harangued on the various kinds of military occupation ... He was clearly feeling the way for a Russian proposal, but S. appears to have been discreet ... Probably this convn is already on its way to Gortschakoff towards whom and the Czar Decazes's attitude may be described as one of habitual servility, tempered by stockjobbing.

23 November 1876. Cabinet at 3, sat till near 5. I notice that whether we have much or little business, we always sit about the same length of time. We discussed tel. from Lytton, in which fearing Russian operations in Central Asia, he asks that the usual sending home of troops whose turn for relief has come may be delayed. This was unanimously agreed to be impossible: if there is no war, it is a needless precaution: if there is a war, they will be more wanted at home. Besides, what men or money could Russia spare for a campaign against India, if engaged in an invasion of Turkey?

Hardy & Disraeli asked consideration of a proposal for stopping the export to Italy of 8 100-ton guns, ordered from Armstrong by the Italian govt. They are superior to any artillery now in existence, & no doubt in hostile hands would be a danger. But we agreed that the present state of circs did not justify the extreme measure of stopping them. It was said in the course of the convn that they cannot be made abroad, & that three years would pass before any foreign govt could get others.

Cairns called attention to a series of libels on the judges in Kenealy's notorious paper, the 'Englishman'. It seems they have complained & appealed to him. We all agreed it was better to let the matter alone.

Sclater Booth was called in: Highway & Valuation Bills were discussed, & ordered to be brought in.

A draft of supplementary instructions to Ld Salisbury was read by me & passed. It really leaves matters where they stood, but in certain cases may be useful for publication. The purport of it is that though all proposals of military occupation must be absolutely excluded from the conference, it does not follow that they may not be entertained, as subject of discussion, in the event of the conference breaking up, or of the Porte evading the fulfilment of its promises. But we again put on record our strong objections to such occupation in whatever form.

24 November 1876. Fresh reports reach us from all quarters of Russian preparations for immediate war: there is now no trouble taken to disguise them.

... Cabinet at 3: the business not interesting. Some further talk about the prosecution of the 'Englishman', raised by Richmond, who was obviously put up by Cairns: none of us supported him except Hardy, & he in a doubtful sort of way. Scotch business occupied the rest of the sitting. The new Ld Advocate[91] was called in: a shrewd precise sort of man, seems able, but not likely to be popular in H. of C.

25 November 1876. Salisbury writes from Berlin that he has seen Bismarck, who lectured him for an hour. His language was friendly, but he made it clear that he will not interfere, for two reasons: one that he considers any attempt to patch up Turkey as hopeless, the other that any interference would be considered by Russia as a threat, and he fears that it would be remembered against him when Germany is next in trouble. He took a gloomy view of the prospects of peace, saying that the Czar has gone too far to draw back: but he thinks Russian officers underrate the difficulty of the work before them. They have no money. The sea is closed against them. He doubts whether they can get to Constantinople, or even cross the Balkans. He did not, as Salisbury writes, appear to love Russia: on the contrary, he showed evident pleasure at the thought of the difficulties which he had named. He advised us not to be in haste: the enterprise might fail without our opposing it, and in any case Russia would probably be glad to accept reasonable terms after a time. He encouraged us to take Egypt, & even to occupy Constantinople. Of the Emp. of Austria he spoke bitterly, & of Andrassy with a certain contempt. He did not mention France, but in what he said of Russia it was clear that was looking forward to the time when Germany would have another French attack to meet. On the whole, Salisbury says, Bism. did not seem unwilling to help in bringing about any practical solution that might be hit on, but evidently does not believe any solution is possible: expects Turkey to fall to pieces, etc., a new map of Europe to be inevitable. The old Emp. took a more helpful, but also a more frankly Russian view of matters.

27 November 1876. By 6.30 train to Windsor: where we were only nine at dinner, the Queen and princess, Dean of Windsor and Mrs. W., elves, Ly Ely, and two lords in waiting. The Queen talked much and eagerly of foreign affairs: in fact she began before the soup was finished: her language was friendly and even zealous in support of the govt: she told Ly D. that the Turks were much better than the eastern christians: and to me she deplored the conduct of the Russian govt without saying word in favour of the eastern christians, as she has usually done. She blamed the opposition here, and more especially Gladstone. I never

[91] William Watson, Lord Watson (1827–99), lord advocate 1876–80.

knew her so unreserved, and anxious to be agreeable, and on the whole the evening was pleasant.[92]

28 November 1876. Wrote to Salisbury, dwelling chiefly on two points: the necessity of getting some sort of definition of what is meant by 'Bulgaria', a term conveniently vague, and which the Russians will interpret in a very wide sense: and secondly the danger of being drawn by Russia to cooperate in demands on the Porte, of a nature to be certainly refused, in which case our assistance will be plausibly claimed to enforce on Turkey what we have demanded.

30 November 1876. Saw Schouvaloff, who did not conceal his opinion that matters are going badly: he said that Russia & Turkey were growing more and more irritated against one another, he meant in regard to popular feeling, & he evidently expected no good to come of it...

2 December 1876. Fresh reports of Russian military preparations: 40,000 men are being brought down to the frontier of Asiatic Turkey, where there are 40,000 already.

4 December 1876. Saw Schouvaloff, who was in good spirits, saying that all his Russian news was pacific, but he gave no details. Saw Münster, who took a less sanguine view, & speaking as if from himself, but with hints that he knew well what was in Bismarck's mind, advised us to take Egypt. He said the opportunity would never return if lost: Germany would approve, Russia would not object, France would be compelled to assent: three years hence all might be different, & French opposition again formidable. I see well enough that Bism. would be glad to make us quarrel with France, or at least destroy our mutual good understanding.

5 December 1876. Letters & despatches from Salisbury: the latter contain nothing of interest, Andrassy having objected to his conversation being put into a blue book. They held two conversations, in one of which the proposed Turkish reforms were discussed, but not in much detail: it seemed to S. that his interlocutor knew & cared but little for them, & was chiefly preoccupied with the question, what should be done in the event of the conference failing? On this subject he discoursed largely & not in a very coherent manner. He did not seem to expect a favourable result. He did not like the idea of occupation, but appeared to think it not the worst of all possible solutions. He was anxious to know whether we should occupy Constantinople if Russia went into Bulgaria. S. said in answer that we should discourage all invasion of Turkey. Andrassy said distinctly that he would not make the entrance of Russian force a *casus belli*: nearly the only definite statement that

[92] Victoria had been violently anti-Turkish in Aug.–Sept. 1876, hence Derby's surprise

seems to have been got out of him. On the whole Salisbury thinks that he is in communication with, & influenced by, Bismarck: that he is not afraid of German designs on Austria: that he is afraid of Russia: & wants matters settled now if possible, believing that Russia will gain rather than lose strength as time goes on. Neither he nor Bism. in Salisbury's judgement would object to a war. They do not wish to see Russia established south of the Danube, but this result they don't expect, & they would like to see Russian strength exhausted by a war, as they believe it would be even if Turkey were the only opponent.

6 December 1876. Saw Lawson, who came to talk over the situation.

... E. Cecil told me that he had been in trouble about the information he gave me as to the guns, some weeks ago, which confirms my opinion that something was designed to which it was known the cabinet would not assent, & which therefore it was determined to do without authority (v. Oct. 29).

... Saw Schouvaloff, who continues sanguine, he does not well know why, but he thinks the peace party in Russia is gaining strength. Probably the evident desire of Bismarck that Russia should get into a war has enlightened the Russians as to his real object.

... Lyons writes, & Connolly[93] says the same, that the belief in France is universal that we are going to take Egypt, & singularly, there is no appearance of strong feeling against it.

7 December 1876. Working at home early ... Weeded out & destroyed many papers. Office at 2.30. Saw there Schouvaloff, who gave no information in detail, but expressed himself well satisfied with the general aspect of affairs.

... I went with Sanderson through the list of candidates for attaché-ships & chose two: Frere, eldest son of Sir Bartle: & Montagu, a brother of the Duke of Manchester.

... Salisbury has had his interviews with the ambassadors, & has seen Ignatieff: the meeting is so far satisfactory that the Russian has said that occupation is not a *sine qua non*: and holds moderate language, only dropping hints of the possibility of a fresh massacre, and of the necessity of an armed force of some kind to secure the Christian populations. All the other ambassadors, except perhaps the German, are against the idea of occupation.

In a letter from Rome, not otherwise important, Salisbury notes that he has found throughout Europe that the Turk has no friends. Some think his hour is come, some that it may be delayed, but no one seems to believe that the thing can be long kept on its legs. He find the Italian ministry peaceable, the court warlike, but the general sympathy of both is with Russia.

[93] Military attaché in France.

8 December 1876. Saw ... Harcourt, who came chiefly to ask about
the Dahomey blockade, as to which the French are getting uneasy and
sore. The language held among them is, I am told, that the whole
affair has been got up by the English with a view to destroy the
competition of French trade on that part of the coast.

9 December 1876. Münster repeated what the German agents say
everywhere, that Russia is bent on war. That they hold this language
by order is evident: the object is to me less clear: is it to stir up a
quarrel between us & Russia? That would seem a likely purpose for a
German politician to have in view, but warning us perpetually to be
on our guard is hardly the way to set about it.

Long tel. from Salisbury, with the provisional propositions of Ignatieff
... International commission to settle details & secure execution. They
should have sufficient force at command to preserve the peace. Ignatieff
now talks of a force of 6000 Belgians or Italians!!! The difficulty is
evidently in these last demands, which Salisbury has promised to report,
but has not encouraged.

Schouvaloff called, & I talked over some of these suggestions, but
carefully guarded myself against all expression of opinion.

... The papers today are full of a meeting held yesterday in St.
James's Hall[94] ... Many Liberals hold altogether aloof ... ... To our
own large majority we ought to be able to add a section of pro-Turkish
or anti-Russian Liberals, more than enough to balance any possible
defections.

11 December 1876. Menabrea ... brought the report that Russia is
anxious to get honourably out of the quarrel, & disposed to be moderate.
Münster, who followed him, had heard the same story. Schouvaloff
came, & read me a long tel. from Ignatieff direct to him, describing
his interviews with Salisbury, & laying stress on their general agreement
as to most points.

Then came a Mr Berkley,[95] 25 years an engineer in European Turkey:
he describes the Bulgarians as very well off, very free, having every
man his own house, his land, and cattle: they are not in general, he
says, oppressed: but from time to time the govt, knowing nothing of
what is passing in the minds of its christian subjects, takes a fit of panic,
and then there is danger of an outbreak like that of last year. He thinks
the alleged mutual dislike of the two religions does not exist: he has
had mixed gangs working continually on his railways, and was never
troubled by any objection on the part of a mahometan to serve under
a christian, or vice versa. The chief practical grievance he says is that
the tithe, or rent, paid to the state, and which is taken in kind, is often

[94] National Convention on the Eastern Question.
[95] One of a leading family of railway engineers.

not collected till after the crop has been cut for a month or six weeks: meanwhile it lies on the ground and spoils. This is sheer clumsiness and stupidity rather than tyranny.

Called on Disraeli at his request: general talk over the state of affairs abroad: his impression was the same as mine that the meeting of last Friday has been a failure. He says we shall gain a borough or two before parliament meets, open the session with numbers undiminished, and have the support of a considerable Liberal section on our foreign policy. This is possible, but I remember the tendency of D. to over-sanguine calculations, especially in 1868, when he persisted in expecting a majority up to the very time of the elections.

12 December 1876. Lawson and Greenwood both called to talk over affairs. Office ... saw there Schouvaloff, who talked with peculiar interest about Roumania, and the good disposition of the Roumanians towards Russia: which I doubt: the reason of his dwelling on this subject I have not yet found out, but no doubt it will appear.

... Tel. from Salisbury, in which he shows a leaning towards the scheme suggested by Russia that an armed force should be formed by Swiss or Belgians to keep order in Bulgaria. I do not exactly answer this, but ask sundry questions, and gently remind S. that he is only authorised to take such propositions *ad referendum*. I also warn him not to give credit to anything that Ignatieff may say he has heard from Schou as to my views, since he is sure to put something into my mouth that I never said. Cooperation with Russia is to some extent a necessity: but we cannot trust our friends, and I fear that all that is being urged upon Salisbury is only a trap: it is intended that the Porte should refuse, and that then we should be pressed to join in enforcing what we have advised, or at least to stand aloof and let Russia do as she pleases. The more I see of this whole business, the less I like it.

13 December 1876. Münster went down yesterday with his daughter to Knowsley, to shoot, F. & C. being there, & acting hosts in my place: it is probably the first time in the present century that the owner of Knowsley has passed the winter away from home. The more I have of this official life, the less it suits me, and I shall be glad though when an opportunity offers to drop it. Personal ties in politics I have none, except to Disraeli, whom I will not desert while he continues a minister.

... Saw Schouvaloff & Beust, but neither had much to say. I am obliged to be extremely cautious in communicating with Schou as matters stand, for he corresponds by telegraph direct with Ignatieff, and any remark of mine is sure to be repeated at Constantinople in a distorted shape...

14 December 1876. Fresh telegrams from Salisbury: Ignatieff who had originally proposed a single administrative arrangement for all the country which he calls Bulgaria, now consents to a division: which lessens, but does not do away with, the difficulty. The proposal that ... there should be a Belgian or Swiss gendarmerie ... is apparently well received by all the Powers, & Salisbury accepts it provisionally.

... Saw Disraeli, & talk with him over the situation: of which he takes nearly the same view as I have done.

News of the Russian loan is satisfactory: only about half of the sum required ... has been raised ... ... The sum obtained is already spent on mobilisation, & it is not easy to see where resources are to be found for a campaign.

15 December 1876. Office at 2.30: on my way there, called on Disraeli, and had a satisfactory conversation with him. He agreed that the scheme of a Belgian guard, or police force, must be accepted by us (the cabinet appear to have made up their minds about it, and I do not see how we can well reject what Salisbury has accepted, and all the powers support) and so far therefore all is plain sailing. But the question remains behind, when this plan is laid before the Porte, and is refused, as in the first instance it certainly will be, what is to be done to enforce its acceptance? As far as words go, we are pledged to use them, but words will not be enough without distinct threats of using force, and by whom is force to be applied? I said to D. that I was not prepared to concur in any plan of joint occupation or aggression – that I thought if Russia took the opportunity of going to war we might very well let her do so saving always our right to defend Constantinople: but not take part with her, though this would probably be asked and expected of us. D. agreed warmly, saying that after the attitude we had assumed, we should make ourselves ridiculous by going to war against the Porte and with Russia. I told him that I thought most of our colleagues would be of a contrary opinion – though I did not know it, but only judged by what I saw of their tendencies – and asked whether in that case he was clear enough in his convictions (as I was) to resign upon it? He said yes, certainly: he felt no doubt: we should lose self-respect, and the respect of other people, if we abandoned the position we had taken up. I said I was glad to find him so decided and we parted.

At office ... saw Schouvaloff, who expressed his hope there would be no delay in settling the Belgian scheme, since it would provide an explosion of disappointment in Russia so strong that if the Emperor were not pledged to it at once and irrevocably, its acceptance might become impossible: a reason sound enough if sincerely alleged, and very ingenious if as I suspect, it is only a device to make us feel that we have got a bargain which we ought to lose no time in securing.

Nothing more induces me to believe that the Russian govt really does not want a war just now, than the almost desperate state of Russian finance. It is doubted in the City whether money can be found to meet the January dividends: & the possibility of bankruptcy is talked of.

... Long talk with Tenterden: settled with him a plan for rearranging the consular dept in this office, so as to relieve Wylde who is overworked, having more than a capable man in his place could do properly, & he is slow & clumsy.

Read, with no great satisfaction, a C.O. proposal for treating with Dahomey: we are to make the king give up his customs, remain at peace with his neighbours, & generally behave himself as he ought. A very hopeful project, which would land us in a new W. African war.

17 December 1876. Paid Sir R. Alcock[96] £100 for a Chinese professorship at Oxford: a thing useful in its way, & which I am glad to help.

18 December 1876. Saw Lawson, and explained to him the situation. Office at 2.30: cabinet at 3, where all were agreed as to the necessity of ratifying what Salisbury has agreed to, though few of us much like it, but the powers being united, and opinion divided here, it would be unwise to break off the conference, which would be the result of a refusal. The scheme proposed for the govt of the Turkish provinces is a fairly good one and the substitution of a Belgian police force for the intended Russian occupation is clear gain so far – the substituted plan being at least harmless, if carried into practice, which from various causes it probably will not be. I put it to the cabinet that the plan (Russian in the main) is put forward with a view to its being rejected by the Porte, in which case Russia will have a good casus belli: and we shall be bound to remain, at the most, strictly neutral. I think this way of looking at the matter was generally accepted, though some, especially Cairns, dissented, thinking the Emperor of Russia a disinterested and pacific philanthropist. We sat only an hour and half: I drew a telegram conveying our conclusion to Salisbury, and sent it down to the Queen.

... My expectation was that the cabinet today would press for some kind of coercion to be exercised against Turkey, in the event of a refusal of the proposals of the conference: and on this point I was prepared for a rupture: but to my surprise the general feeling was with me, and I shall have no excuse for retiring as I had hoped.

19 December 1876. Office, where all the ambassadors came in succession to pick up news. I told them how matters stood: they had nothing new. Musurus talked sensibly and firmly: saying that the Porte expected war with Russia, and was prepared for it: that nothing would induce the Turks to accept a scheme of foreign occupation, however disguised: that they could afford to lose a province but not to surrender their

---

[96] Sir Rutherford Alcock (1809–97), min. at Pekin 1865–71; pres. of Geographical Society 1876–8.

independence: and that they would be found when the time came absolutely united. I was not surprised at his language, which is exactly what I should myself have held in the place of the Turkish ministers: and see clearly that the proposals of the conference will be rejected: as in my judgement they deserve to be. Salisbury may have had no choice, but he appears to have been hasty in accepting the Russian views – though in the actual state of feeling here, their rejection would have been difficult, and he has modified them in some not unimportant particulars. Münster ridiculed the idea of the Belgian garrison, and said that war was in his opinion inevitable. Beust was more reserved, but made it clear that he sees matters in the same light. Schou. did not speak as if hopeful. D'Harcourt said plainly 'The Turks will accept if England joins in coercing them, but not otherwise'. I have taken good care that Musurus shall understand that no coercion is to be feared from us.

20 December 1876. Saw Lawson & Greenwood on the state of affairs ... Saw Disraeli: who had been to Windsor: he reports the Queen very Turkish, saying (with some truth) that all that has happened has been a Russian conspiracy: angry with the opposition, & well disposed to support us. We discussed the state of affairs at Constantinople, & agreed to have a cabinet on Friday.

Dined at Baron Rothchild's, with M.: meeting Disraeli...

21 December 1876. Saw Disraeli, & talk over affairs.

22 December 1876. M. left for Knowsley, where all her family is assembled for the holidays. Cabinet at 3, sat till near 5: contrary to my expectation we were all pretty nearly agreed, the only difference being in the feelings which it was wished the govt should express, for in regard of action we were of one mind. We settle three questions in the event, now generally considered probable, of the conference falling through.

1. There is to be no coercion of the Porte on our part.
2. The Porte is not to expect help from us in the event of a war with Russia.
3. Salisbury will of course return, his work being done: and Elliot will also come away to report on the state of affairs (he has asked for leave on the ground of health): but relations will not be broken off, and a secretary will continue to represent the embassy.

It was suggested by Disraeli, and seemed to be agreed to by the cabinet, that Elliot shall be replaced at Constantinople: which is indeed his own wish, since the excessive work and anxiety of the last few months, which told on his health. But nothing was decided on this point.

Carnarvon showed signs of opposition, and seemed dissatisfied at our not proposing more: but on being pressed to say exactly what he would do, he did not suggest anything beyond the breaking off of relations. In this Cairns was inclined to support him. I asked him who in that case would remain to see that there was no renewal of massacres? to which the Chancellor answered oddly, that if we had no representative at Constantinople we could not be held responsible. Apart from this little discussion, there was no disagreement, and we parted, I think, relieved to find that we were less separated in opinion that we had supposed.

Dined with Disraeli alone: we had little political conversation, but much pleasant talk of old literary and political reminiscences: Bulwer, Macaulay, Forster,[97] and others.

23 December 1876. Lawson and Greenwood called for news. Delane writes to ask for news of the conference. ... Saw Schouvaloff, Harcourt, Münster, Menabrea, all wanting news. I told them in general terms the decision of the cabinet yesterday, which was not exactly new, for I had given most of them to understand what was my personal opinion, but I was now enabled to announce it as the decision of the govt.

... Menabrea ... thinks it would be a hard job for them to cross the Balkans, & one that they are scarcely prepared for. And this, he adds, is the opinion of the German strategists ... ... Münster looks at the matter in a similar light, saying that the Russian govt would be glad to back out if they could find a decent pretext, but he thinks the Turks see their advantage, & will not give them the chance.

24 December 1876. Decided on going to Fairhill with Sanderson, as we had settled. We had our reward, for the day cleared, & we got two pleasant walks.

... Buchanan writes that in his judgement Austria will support the Turks in resisting the proposals of the conference.

Elliot telegraphs that his health has given way, and he must retire. His health has no doubt suffered from overwork and anxiety, but not so as to necessitate immediate withdrawal: the evident cause is that he does not approve of, nor believe in, the views which Salisbury has been induced by Ignatieff to favour, and wishes to escape from the intolerable position of having to support officially what he personally disapproves of. I have telegraphed back to sanction his leaving as he proposes.

No doubt the Turks will be shrewd enough to see in this proceeding of Elliot's what it really implies, viz. a disagreement between the ambassadors. It has another result: that we cannot make a display of withdrawing our ambassadors in form if the conference fails (as some of the cabinet wished) for one of the ambassadors will have withdrawn himself, and the other will leave as a matter of course when his special business is ended.

[97] John Forster (1812–76), man of letters; biographer and intimate of Dickens.

... Schouvaloff came to the Square early ... ... He wants to pass two days at Paris, & we agreed to meet on Wednesday.

25 December 1876. Walk early with Sanderson ... Two messengers came: I sent back by return 5 boxes.

Letters and despatches from Salisbury, but they are all practically superseded by his telegrams, which have been frequent and full. He is more hopeful of success than I am: and seems pleased, reasonably enough, at having got all the powers to agree. He hints at doubts whether the Porte will consent to what he has proposed: but does not dwell upon them. He expresses the opinion that Ignatieff wants peace, on personal grounds: diplomatic triumph is a gain to him, Ignatieff, whereas a war can bring credit only to the generals who make it. He also thinks that the Russian govt desires peace on military and financial grounds, being ill prepared and poor: and this is very possibly true, but they are too deeply pledged to be able to back out however they may wish it. He ... says that Elliot & the English generally at Constantinople think he has been too hard on the Turks, but makes no complaint of being ill supported.

26 December 1876. Left Fairhill by 9.40 train,: London at 11 ...

... Musurus called, I tried to give him some hints, but it was no use, he would do nothing but chatter about the good intentions of the new Sultan, the ability of the new Grand Vizier, the wickedness of the Russians ... I sometimes wonder whether he talks in this way from mere foolishness, or whether there is a sort of Levantine cunning in it, for he secures himself against discussion, which might lead to his having to report disagreeable things, and these praises of his employers in which he indulges are possibly uttered in order to be written home as proofs of his zeal ... Capacity of some kind the man must have, else he could hardly have remained here for more than twenty years: but in what it lies I have hitherto failed to discover.

The Premier called, much disgusted, and acknowledging the fact, at a strange telegram of Reuter's, announcing that an ultimatum has been sent in by Salisbury – which is on the face of it impossible, since he could not have acted without the other ambassadors, and if they had joined we should have heard of it – and also at the movement of the fleet from Besica Bay. He complained moreover that Salisbury after begging us all to stay in town to be ready to give him instructions, has not sent a telegram since Friday to say what he is doing. This last grievance is reasonable, for even if there was nothing to report he ought to have said so, and I accordingly telegraphed at once to ask if he had any news for us. I endeavoured, with some success, to persuade him that the ultimatum story could only be an invention, and so far he was comforted. But he appeared unaccountably vexed at the withdrawal of the fleet, though it was a measure long ago foreseen, and known to be necessary on naval grounds, for the anchorage is unsafe in winter. He thought, in which I agreed with him, that Salisbury ought not to have asked the Admiral to remove without consulting us, and that he was taking on himself the functions of the cabinet: but beyond this, there was evidently some unexpressed cause for his annoyance. I suspect, but it is only suspicion, that he wanted an excuse of some kind for the fleet to have gone up to Constantinople, which would have realised his idea of an English occupation. I pointed out that the Turkish fleet is master of the sea, that there is therefore no danger of a Russian attack except by land, that the march to Constantinople even if unopposed is one of two months, and that the squadron at Athens is within three days reach – that accordingly it could always come back in time if wanted. All this is acknowledged, but was not satisfied, which leads me to think that since May last he has had some object in view which he did not think I should equally appreciate, and therefore has not disclosed.

We talked frankly and plainly of Salisbury's position. He is thought to be more Russian than we are ... The custom of the opposition is to praise him against us, and with the implied meaning, that he is to reverse the policy of the govt. D. dwelt on the awkwardness of allowing this last impression to prevail. I agreed, but pointed out on the other hand that the mission would almost certainly fail, that we had foreseen this from the first, and that what was of most importance was to take from Salisbury's special partisans the possibility of saying that he had failed because thwarted at home. The more certain the conference was to end in nothing, the more it behoved us to be able to prove that we had given it every chance of succeeding. He saw the force of the argument, and I added that if it appeared that our colleague, backed by all Europe, had been unable to press successfully these reforms on the Porte, it was evident that the Berlin memorandum had stood still less chance of acceptance, and therefore that the charge against us of causing the present trouble by refusing to support it must fall to the ground.

Saw Lawson: wrote to Delane.

Sanderson dined with me.

27 December 1876. Telegram from Salisbury ... the story of the ultimatum is (as I supposed) unfounded. ... Saw Lawson & Greenwood.

.. Saw ... a deputation of Jews, who came about the persecutions to which they are exposed in Servia & Roumania ... ... My answer, which was short, expressed entire agreement.

... M. returned from Knowsley, where she has had all her children round her, to their great satisfaction. She reports the place well kept, no change, & nothing gone wrong. When shall I see it again?

28 December 1876. Saw ... Solvyns:[98] the latter came to talk about the Belgian police scheme, which his govt greatly & naturally dislikes, but dares not reject by a blank refusal. The evident intention at Brussels is to get rid of it by imposing conditions & raising difficulties. But the Turks will probably save them the trouble. ... The conference is sitting while I write, & we shall know more soon, but just now we know nothing.

... Schouvaloff is at Paris: the diplomatists say, trying to patch up a silly quarrel into which his chief has got. Gortschakoff, it seems, wrote to some woman in Paris a letter in which he describes Macmahon as a blockhead ... & Decazes as a stockjobber: the lady ... let this letter become public property, & naturally the two officials – whose language & conduct have been of late almost subservient to Russia – are disgusted. The moment is not one when Russia can afford to lose friends, so Schouvaloff is sent over to make the best of it.

... Dined Baron Rothschild's meeting Disraeli ... Not much amused...

29 December 1876. Saw Lawson & Greenwood ... Called on Disraeli at his request: found him uneasy at the apparent want of a good understanding between Salisbury & Elliot, which is obvious enough, though disguised by courtesy, & restrained by sense of duty: the fact is that the two men take opposite views of the situation, as I have always felt sure that they would: I suspect that Ly S. has contributed to their disunion, but this is mere suspicion for there is no evidence of the fact. I found D. agreeing with me that a Turkish refusal is certain, & that the choice lies between war, or the acceptance of a compromise of some kind. Midhat P.[99] has had a long conversation with Elliot, & defined clearly enough what the Porte will assent to & what it will not.

The reforms proposed for the three provinces are not, in the main, objected to: differences of detail are indicated, but they are of a nature to be got over: the real trouble is with the so-called guarantees, the scheme of a so-called police, which is really a small foreign army of occupation, and of a commission of supervision.

For these Midhat would accept a police force composed of foreigners, if the Powers wish it, but subject to the condition that it must be under the authority of the Porte: & as to the supervision, he asks for a year during which the new institutions shall be tested, & will agree at the end of it to accept supervision in any form desired by the Powers, if the ambassadors report that they have not been fairly worked. It is

[98] Belgian min. in London.

[99] Midhat Pasha (1822–83), grand vizier 18 Dec. 1876–5 Feb. 1877 (dismissed and banished); under U.K. pressure, made gov.-gen. of Syria, Nov. 1878; again dismissed; strangled.

impossible to speak more frankly, or, I think, to offer fairer conditions: &
they certainly ought not to be rejected without a hearing.

Gennadius called, with a despatch: the old story: Greek against
Sclave: he told me plainly that the Greeks disliked Sclavonic supremacy
more than that of the Porte.

Schouvaloff called, & talked at length of a plan which he has laid
before his govt to meet the probable event of a Turkish refusal: it is
suspicious enough: its principal point consists in this, that peace is to
be made, on Turkish terms, if no other can be got, but Russia to
remain armed, & to declare that if there is an renewal of massacres,
she will make war. Plausible – but it looks like putting off the declaration
of hostilities for three months, by which time the roads will be fit to
travel & Russian preparations complete.

30 December 1876. Saw Lawson early, & again later at the office.

... Letter from Disraeli, in consequence of which I telegraphed at
some length to Salisbury, telling him of the conciliatory language of
the Russians, reminding him of Midhat's language to Elliot, & saying
that between the two I though the materials for an arrangement might
be found: I added that the German plan is generally considered as
unworkable, & its withdrawal would cause no dissatisfaction.

News that the armistice has been extended for two months: which
puts the Russians absurdly in the wrong, for we have now come back
to the Turkish proposal of a six months' armistice, which Russia
repudiated at the time with such a show of indignation. It is no
indication of peace, but only shows that neither side is yet prepared.

31 December 1876. A mail from Constantinople, but telegrams have
superseded it for all practical purposes. Salisbury writes ... He says
Butler-Johnstone is there doing much mischief, & is reported to give
out that he is accredited by the Premier ... Salisbury also thinks, but
does not state his reason for thinking, that Andrassy secretly wishes for
war, though affecting to adopt & support the English views.

Elliot writes that Ignatieff has been sending Midhat assurances of
friendship & good will (the two men hate each other, & always have
done so) ... ... Russian diplomacy is very clever, but sometimes
overdoes cleverness, & this is a case in point.

1877

Jan. 1877. In the course of last year, for the first time since taking the management of affairs, I have paid off no debt: which accordingly still remains at the former figure of £221,000. Of this is due to my brother £170,000, to C. Stanley £24,000, to trustees of H. Stanley £12,000, to Ly D. £15,000.

... I have bought land in 1876 as follows: Witley estate, £40,000: land in L.pool £15,000: land at Keston £10,000, and a small freehold or two in Lancashire ... In all about £70,000.

... I have ... four negotiations on hand, one with the L. & Yorkshire for enlargement of Bury station: one with the Midland: one with the 'Cheshire lines': and one with the North Western. From these I may probably expect to receive £150,000, or £200,000 in all, but not necessarily within the present year. These various sales being for the most part of land now lying waste, or covered with houses of small value, will not appreciably diminish the rental of the estates.

Acreage of Knowsley estates. From Moult ... Home estates, 27,054. L.pool & Bootle 1523. Total in south-west Lancashire 28,577. Preston, the Fylde, & north Lancashire, 13,384. Bury & east Lancashire, about 15,000 ... Cheshire estates 9,450. Kent & Surrey estates 2,250. In all, nearly 57,000 acres in Lancashire, & over 11,000 acres elsewhere, or ... an area of 166 square miles, or rather more than 21 in length by 5 in width.

1 January 1877. Busy ... till 12, when cabinet.[1] We sat 1½ hours, all apparently in good humour & no signs of division appeared. No decision was come to, nor was any required: the chief object of our meeting was to discuss the state of matters at the conference, which is anything but satisfactory. Office till 5: saw there Schouvaloff, Münster, Lawson, Tenterden, Pauncefote ...

The conference appears to have come to a deadlock. At the meeting of Saturday, the Turks declared that they had a counter-proposal to make, but did not produce it. The Russians thereupon announced that Russia had reduced her demands to the utmost & could yield no further. Discussion followed, but no definite reply was given.

On Sunday the counter-project came out, and the six representatives met (without the Turk) to discuss it. As it negatives either directly or

---

[1] As *GH*, where dated 2 Jan.: GH thought 'the hope of peace is small, Russia is clearly not ready for war...'

by implication three-fourths of what has been asked for by the Powers, there could be no question as to the decision. Ignatieff said he had formal orders not to listen to a counter-project & the representatives were unanimous in their objections. So the matter stands: the conference is sitting again today.

Salisbury writes, in a letter[2] which I have just received, that matters are looking ill. The Turks say in private that they will concede nothing: publicly they try for delay. There is, Salisbury says, a colony of Greeks & English settled at Pera, who wish for war: they think it will make their fortunes, from the quantity of English money that will be spent in Constantinople. The Turks are not easily made to believe that we are in earnest: Elliot himself is loyal, but all about him are not so, and they persuade the natives that Salisbury's mission & his language are only a feint to deceive the Powers – which is an idea so consonant to Eastern ideas as to find ready acceptance. Butler-Johnstone, a clever, but half-cracked disciple of Urquhart, is in constant communication with the Turkish authorities, & is said to have told them that he represents the views of the Prime Minister: but this is not easy to believe. If war should break out, Salisbury anticipates a general scramble – Persians, Greeks, Austrians &c. all putting in for their share.

2 January 1877. Saw Greenwood & Lawson, & told them what news I had. ... Menabrea read to me a long telegram of which the purport was that in case of failure, which now seems unavoidable, the conference had better not break up, but leave Constantinople & meet in some neutral place, such as Venice. I threw cold water on this proposal, which has many & obvious disadvantages, & no one merit that I can see. But I promised consideration, & an answer later. Harcourt threw out a suggestion that inasmuch as the Turkish measure could be considered nothing else than an insult to Europe, it ought to be resented by some measure more serious than the mere withdrawal of an ambassador – there he stopped & did not say what the next step should be. I told him that we had from the first declared that we would use no coercion, & to that declaration we meant to stick. ... It is clear that this suggestion is a feeler put forward by the Russians, who begin to think that they have before them a more difficult job than they know of, & would be glad of help.

... Salisbury's telegram of last night reporting yesterday's conference, says that the Turks refused absolutely to discuss the greater part of the scheme of the Powers: Midhat said to Salisbury, 'If it is the will of god that the empire should fall to ruin, we shall submit: but on these points no Turk will yield.'

Berlin correspondence shows that the old Emperor of Germany is

[2] Salisbury to Derby 26 Dec. 1876, in *Cecil*, 117.

much alarmed for his brother, the Czar, thinking that a Turkish war will be disastrous for Russia: in which he is probably right: & is therefore looking about eagerly to find some means of conciliation. Unluckily the newly displayed Russian fear of war is no secret to the Turks, & it partly accounts for their determination to resist.

Home about 5: quiet evening, but messenger brought 17 boxes, which obliged me to work till bedtime.

3 January 1877. Drage called, & revaccinated me, as he also did to M., smallpox being everywhere about. Malmesbury came to luncheon, better in health & spirits than last year. I was glad to see again an old friend, & my former chief in F.O. ... Office at 2.30 ... Saw ... Harcourt, who came to enquire about Menabrea's plan ... which I discouraged to the utmost of my power: but saying that if it were taken up seriously by the Powers, I must consult the cabinet. Münster came next, & told me in confidence that Bismarck disliked the scheme as much as I did...

... Home at 5 p.m. Quiet evening.

... Telegram from Elliot ... the purport of which is that the Turkish premier hints at the possibility of negotiating separately with Russia ... This has often been threatened before, & is not likely to be acted upon: but if it were, the result might be awkward, for Russia might waive the questions on which the Porte is most certain to resist, and accept, say, free passage of the Dardanelles, and the annexation of Roumania, which would be no real loss to Turkey, as Roumania is practically independent.

4 January 1877 (Thursday). Saw Menabrea, & told him plainly the objections I felt to the plan of a revived conference outside Turkey: he pressed the point, & it is clear that both Italy & France favour it for some reason of their own which will probably become clearer as time goes on.

Saw ... Schouvaloff: the latter had got news from Paris to the effect that the representatives had agreed to make large concessions to the Porte, abandoning especially the idea of a foreign police corps and that of a commission of supervision, which latter was to be modified so as to [be] merely an extension of the actual powers of the consuls. It is however noticeable that Ignatieff, in a telegram of last night to Schouvaloff, makes no mention of these changes, only saying that if the Porte agrees to a discussion, some slight concessions of detail may be made. Nor have I any telegram from Salisbury, who would certainly have sent one if anything to this effect had been settled.

5 January 1877 (Friday). ... Telegram from Salisbury, brief and not satisfactory; for he says nothing of changes reported here, but only that the Turks have given reasons for their refusals, that the matter is being argued, & that the conference meets again on Monday.

... Office ... Having telegraphed to Salisbury last night to know what truth there was in these reports of large modifications having been introduced into the proposals of the Powers, I had in the middle of the day a reply admitting the fact, but saying that it was only true under certain reservations. He does not state the precise amount of the changes ... but he says Ignatieff has not as yet been induced to give way upon them except on the impossible condition that the proposals thus softened down shall be embodied in an ultimatum ... I telegraphed back that as to secrecy, he was too late, since Decazes had made the business public ... I added that the desire for peace was universal here, & that he need not be afraid of making concessions however large that will secure that object. But in my judgment the Porte will hardly be induced to accept even this reduced demand. The Russians have allowed their reluctance to go to war to be seen: which from their point of view is a mistake. The result of their drawing back is that the Porte has assumed a new attitude: even Musurus, the meekest of mankind ... boasts of the 600,000 men that the Sultan has under arms. (The real number is about 300,000.)

6 January 1877 (Saturday). Many boxes & letters: those which relate to the conference are all in one strain. The Russians want to get out of the affair creditably, knowing that they are ill prepared for war, that bankruptcy must follow, & that the army is not in a condition to do them honour: it is said on the authority of the king of Italy, who is a soldier, & in frequent communication with Russia, that two regiments have mutinied when desired to march, & that the preparations of all kinds are utterly defective. It is probable also that the Czar does not like the idea of letting loose the revolutionary spirit. But he, or rather Gortschakov for him, has begged & blustered to such an extent that retreat is difficult. Elliot writes that the members of the Russian embassy have been saying ever since the ultimatum was accepted that their going away is only put off a little ...

... I have a telegram from Salisbury saying that there is foul play somewhere, & complaining of the proposed concessions to the Porte having become public. Gathering from this tel., that he suspects someone here, I sent him back an exact statement of the fact – viz. that Decazes told the story to the Russian ambassador at Paris who telegraphed it over here without any obligation of secrecy, so that it was in the papers yesterday, having been the talk of the clubs the day before.[3]

7 January 1877 (Sunday). Keston: walk with M. by the lakes ... Elliot writes that Ignatieff has been trying to persuade the Turks that all the proposals to which they take most objection are the work of the English

---

[3] *Cecil* makes no mention of this sub-plot.

representative, and that if they will come to a separate understanding with Russia, much easier terms can be obtained. Salisbury says that he and Midhat are 'the two biggest liars in Europe', giving a slight and doubtful preference to the Turk ... He has at last found out Ignatieff, whom in the first instance he was too much inclined to trust. In the same letter,[4] Salisbury presses me to find or make some pretext for removing Elliot: who, he says, though loyal in intention, is working against him in fact, inasmuch as his personal opinions are well known to be more favourable to the Turks than those of his colleague, and it is generally known that he does not approve the proposals of the conference as a whole. This letter I sent to Disraeli, and at the writer's request I shall circulate it to the cabinet. But it comes too late to do either good or harm. I don't think the fault is all on one side: Salisbury set out with a disposition to believe everything that was bad — though in the sense of weakness and prejudice only — of Elliot, and has ignored him in a somewhat marked manner. He has also I think made the mistake of thinking too much of the necessity of conciliating Russia and too little of that of not exasperating Turkey. But be the cause what it may, I look on success as now all but hopeless, and war as nearly certain. At the worst our position nationally will not be a bad one. We have done what could be done to preserve peace. We have held the balance as fairly as the nature of things admits, between the contending parties. We are released from obligations under the treaty of 1856, by the Turkish refusal to listen to our advice. We can always interpose to protect Constantinople if necessary: and meanwhile we are not called upon to spend a penny or to risk a man. Russia will be crippled for years to come by the war, and by the loss of financial credit which will follow her bankruptcy: and for a considerable time we have no aggression in central Asia to fear. Not the least curious feature of the situation (though I dare say I have noted it before) is the undisguised delight of the German govt at the prospect of an unsuccessful, or at least of a troublesome and costly Russian campaign. The reason is obvious: the one event really feared at Berlin is the not improbable one of a Russo-French combination against Germany. Thiers has been expressing to Lyons his alarm lest Bismarck, released from this apprehension, should take the opportunity of a fresh attack on France: which does not seem likely, but it shows that the natural feelings of fear and suspicion left by the Franco-German war are as strong as ever. Not less characteristic is the fact that the Germans are continually inviting us to profit by the occasion and seize on Egypt. Of course their idea is that the consequent resentment and jealousy of France would drive us into a close alliance with Germany.

[4] Salisbury to Derby 29 Dec. 1876, in *Cecil*, 118–9.

8 January 1877. Saw Lawson early ... cabinet[5] at 3, which sat 1½ hour.
... A telegram from Salisbury, received this morning, curiously confirms
my statement above as to Bismarck ... By Salisbury's report it appears
that while the German embassy at Constantinople is telling the Porte
that it cannot without dishonour concede what the Powers ask, Bismarck
has instructed his ambassador to object to all modifications of the
original proposals. ... I drafted by desire of the cabinet today, two
telegrams to Salisbury: one desiring him not to sign any protocol or
identical note as in the event of negocns failing it is undesirable to be
pledged to propositions which after all we accepted only as put forward
for discussion: the other saying in effect that it was too late now
to summon Elliot to England as any mischief that his presence at
Constantinople can do is done already.

Our chief business however was to discuss the scarcity (expected to
grow to a famine) in Madras & Bombay: there will be soon be over a
million of persons employed on relief works, & as the distress will not
be at its height till April, & will not cease till October, we are in for
very heavy expense. ... I do not see that we can count on an outlay
of less than £5,000,000 which as usual with all extraordinary expenses
in India, must be raised by borrowing. But if a country has an inelastic
revenue ... leaving every campaign & every scarcity to be dealt with
by loans – what can be the end except bankruptcy? Something of this
sort I said in cabinet, & the Premier agreed with me: indeed no one
dissented.

9 January 1877. It is evident from the tone of Salisbury's telegram,[6]
that he has nearly given up hope ... The Premier called, but our talk
was short.

12 January 1877. Telegrams came ... long & confused. I read them
several times over with Sanderson, & compared notes with the ambassadors: but we could not make out from them what is doing.

... Windsor: where we were summoned by a sudden message this
morning. The Queen sent for me before dinner: but then & after
dinner she was in high good humour & spirits. Only J. Manners & the
household were there, J. having been sent for by a telegram out of
Leicestershire this morning, nobody knows why, for there was no
business to do, nor any pretence of doing it.

13 January 1877. The present situation is: on Monday next, the
proposals of the conference, much modified & reduced, will be laid
before the Porte, & an answer will be asked for on Thursday: if, as
expected, this is a refusal, the plenipotentiaries will take their leave. ...

[5] As *GH*: cabinet called by Carnarvon to consider Indian famine.
[6] Salisbury to Derby, tel., 9 Jan. 1877, withdrawing request for Elliot's withdrawal, and
expecting 'further continuance of the conference will be useless' (*Cecil*, 121).

Münster however speaks of the whole affair as 'humbug' & thinks time enough has been wasted over it: he would hardly dare to talk in this way without some means of knowing that his chief took the same view.

14 January 1877. My ill health of last week has pretty well passed off, but leaves behind a singular sensation of drowsiness & objection to exertion.[7] Luckily there is but little to do just now.

15 January 1877. Message from Disraeli early, wishing to see me about the conference, but I could see nothing urgent in it, & decided not to go back till tomorrow.

16 January 1877. Salisbury telegraphs, that he has seen the Sultan, found him in appearance disposed to yield, but afraid of his ministers. He sent a message through Hobart Pasha, asking for further reductions, which Salisbury was obliged to say are impossible – as they are, for the other Powers would never consent if we did. All now rests with him personally: the G. Vizier is obstinate as ever.

... Called on Disraeli at his request: he has heard from the Rothschilds that Schouvaloff's story[8] of the intimate union of the three emperors is untrue: which I also believe. He showed me a rather excited letter from Carnarvon expressing alarm lest we should pledge ourselves against interference by force in the east: which the writer evidently thinks advisable.

Saw ... Beust. Beust laughed at the notion of a close union between Russia & Austria, which is evidently a Russian fiction, intended to help in bringing about the intimidation of the Turks.

... The Times, which up to this week has been hinting, not obscurely, that if the demands of the conference are refused we ought to help in enforcing them, now backs out, & holds the language that a failure will be unfortunate, but that we have done our part, etc., and can only stand aside.

17 January 1877. The ambassadors came only to ask for news. The conference has killed all other business and does not itself give us any business to do. Greenwood & Lawson both called. The impression today is that the Turks have made up their minds, & that there is

[7] During this lull, Derby was out of health, in his view because of revaccination (3 Jan.), smallpox being rife, and tooth extraction (5 Jan.); 'not fit for much business' (Sun. 7 Jan.) and 'woke in the night with headache and sickness ... continued all day. Did not leave my room' (Tue. 9 Jan.) Derby was at the office, Sat. 13 Jan., but at Fairhill, near Tonbridge on Sun. and Mon., with Sanderson and Lady Derby, doing 10 boxes on Mon. He saw Schouvaloff 1, 3, 4, 5, 8, 10, 11, 12, 13 (Sat.), 16, 17 Jan. 1877, but to little purpose; and 'Chinese' Gordon 'who really interested me', 11 Jan.

[8] 'Schouvaloff ... assured me as a fact within his certain knowledge that the understanding between France, Austria, & Germany, on the Turkish business is perfect, & that they will act in common. It may be so; but his eagerness to assert the reality of their union looks suspicious, & certainly neither the language of Andrassy, nor of Bismarck has been in that sense.' (D.D. 10 Jan. 1877). Cf. below, 24 Jan. 1877.

nothing more to be done. It looks as if the battle at home would be fought on the question whether we are to rest satisfied with the refusal of our demands, or not. The only alternative is war, & I do not think England is prepared for a second Navarino. Certainly neither Disraeli nor I shall assent to any step of that kind.

... The figures of last year's business are not easy to understand. ... With all the complaints of industrial depression – & they have been loud & many – it is noticeable that there has been no increase in pauperism, no falling off in the consumption of beer, tobacco, & other luxuries of workingmen, and no cries of distress. Capitalists & manufacturers talk about ruin, but the working class is profoundly quiet & apathetic. Nothing in the nature of agitation exists, in any part of the country, on any subject. Indeed but for the eastern question one does not see how the papers would be filled.

18 January 1877. Saw Schouvaloff, who read to me with evident satisfaction a draft which he is preparing to his own govt deprecating war ... ... I believe he (Schou.) is sincere in his desire for peace, but his reasoning is not of a kind to influence the Czar if an invasion is really designed.

... Letter from Rothschild asking help for the Roumanian Jews, who are being tormented in the usual way. I telegraphed to Mansfield[9] at once to do what he can for them.

News in evening that Turkish Grand Council has unanimously rejected the proposals of the Powers: which probably settles the affair.

19 January 1877. Saw Gen. Ponsonby, who was sent up by the Queen with the rather indefinite mission of finding out what the Premier & I think of the last Turkish news. I made the best of it, to avoid further fuss. Saw G. Hornby,[10] who is well pleased with his Mediterranean command: ... the only point on which he pressed me was not to order or allow the squadron to be separated if it could be helped. ... I shall bear in mind what he says, for his judgment is good & sound...

... Saw Musurus, & advised him strongly ... to warn the Porte from me of the expediency of making peace with Servia & Montenegro, if it can be managed, before the armistice expires. There will then be one pretext less for a Russian invasion.

21 January 1877. Long and serious talk with M. on a matter which is often in my thoughts. When Ld Beaconsfield retires, as from age and infirmity he is likely to do in a year or two, what is to be my course of action? If not offered the vacant post, I should not hesitate, for no one is bound to serve under a junior, and in official life both Richmond and Salisbury are my juniors. But if it should be offered, the reasons

[9] Min. to Rumania 1876–8.
[10] C.-in-c. Mediterranean 1877–80.

for and against accepting are fairly balanced. Against, is the risk of
being tied to the life of a political leader for the rest of my days, which
I do not wish, but which might not be easily avoided, if the opportunity
for escape is lost. The London life does not wholly suit me, and does
not suit M. at all, though she submits to it. I am not very fit for many
of the duties of the premier's office. To manage, flatter, and keep in
good humour the Queen is in itself an occupation (so Disraeli says,
and I quite believe him): the distribution of patronage is a kind of work
quite alien to my tastes: the filling up of ecclesiastical appointments
would please me even less: and accustomed to departmental business
only, I hesitate at the notion of advising and generally controlling that
of other departments than those of which I know something. Moreover
more speechmaking is expected from a premier than from his colleagues:
which would not especially suit me, though it could be done if necessary.
There are no personal claims upon me, for the only close political
connection which I acknowledge is with Disraeli: and I am not interested
enough in the questions which most Conservatives have at heart to
fight well upon them. All that is to be said on the other side is that to
hold the place, even for a year, would be an honour to my family: and
that having kept up a practical interest in politics for nearly 30 years,
I might feel the want of occupation if I gave them up. I say this rather
as what would be suggested to another person in like case, than because
I feel it myself. But the step once taken is irrevocable, and should
therefore be carefully considered. Ambition I have none left: indeed it
is many years since I have known the feeling: my sole regret would be
fore the loss of a kind of employment which habit has made not
uncongenial, and which if sometimes disagreeable, keeps off mere
vacancy and weariness. But on the whole I think the balance of
advantages is clearly in favour of retiring. M. would not influence my
judgment, but I could see that her opinion was the same as mine.
There is no need of speaking openly on the subject to my colleagues,
but hints may be given them as occasion offers, that they should not
be taken entirely by surprise.

22 January 1877. To Windsor, the Queen having desired to see me: I
thought the subject which interested her would be the conference and
its failure,[11] but after a few words on that matter she passed on to what
was really filling her mind; namely whether her eldest grandson,[12] the
emperor of Germany that is to be, should have the Garter or only the
Bath? She had telegraphed again and again to Disraeli to come down,

[11] Plenipotentiaries intended to depart on 22 Jan.; their last ultimatum, presented 15
Jan., withdrawing all but two demands, was rejected on 20 Jan., when Salisbury formally
declared the Conference closed (*Cecil*, 128).
[12] Wilhelm II.

but he is gouty, and could not move. He had however written to say
he saw no objection to the Garter, and I gave the same opinion, as
indeed there was no reason why I should not, for it is difficult to
suppose that anybody in England will either know or care. But the loss
of half a day, at a busy time, to give advice on such a matter
strengthened my intention noted yesterday.

Letters & despatches ... Decazes expresses confidence that Russia
will not fight, professes to be sure of peace, & is not dissatisfied at the
result of the conference. Andrassy on the other hand is anxious for an
early arrangement, or says so ... The notion of an Austrian understanding with Russia is rejected by all Magyars as impossible. ... Loftus
writes that there is a Russian circular to the Powers in preparation,
appealing to Europe, so as to avoid the appearance of isolated Russian
action. ... The state of the army is worse than supposed: the director-
general of artillery is under arrest charged with embezzling stores...

23 January 1877. Cabinet at 11: Cairns was absent, having to sit on
an appeal. Not much business done: we discussed a prisons bill, one
for consolidation of the factory acts, some Scotch & Irish legislation of
no great consequence, the state of finance etc. Northcote talked gloomily
of the revenue, & pressed reductions on Hardy & Hunt: they both said
they were willing & indeed seemed so, but that the thing was impossible.
Some talk followed as to the conference, but not much. We then
discussed a proposal by Carnarvon to send a mission to the king of
Dahomey, by way of making up our quarrel with him: but on
consideration the plan was thought too dangerous, since if he detained
our agent (the governor of S. Leone, who has volunteered for the
service) we should be in for another W. African war. Hitherto the
blockade has produced no effect, but we are not pledged to continue
it for more than a limited time. There are European prisoners in the
King's hands, but they are all French, & having stayed on after notice
that the blockade would be enforced, & that the king might take his
revenge upon them, they deserve no special consideration.

Office at 1, stayed till 5. Saw Lawson, Greenwood, Münster, Harcourt,
Schouvaloff, Menabrea, Musurus: ... I pressed strongly on the last,
and for the second time, the expediency of making peace with Servia &
Montenegro. He seemed to understand & to agree.

Received the Chinese mission:[13] the first that has ever come to
Europe: it was made up of two envoys, or as we should say a minister
and sec. of legation, but I don't know how far they are distinguished
from each other in point of rank. The elder is a shrewd-looking and
pleasant sort of person, good-humoured and very wide awake: the
younger, a heavy-featured common sort of man. They brought an

---

[13] See J.T. Frodsham ed., *The First Chinese Embassy to the West* (Oxford, 1974).

interpreter, but his English was not very clear: luckily we had one of our own. The little conversation that passed was entirely formal and complimentary. Sir T. Wade[14] was present, also Pauncefote, Sanderson, and Barrington.[15] Their dress was silk or satin, a kind of robe like a dressing gown, a fur cap, and enormously thick wooden shoes, in which they moved about, clattering as they went.

24 January 1877. Saw ... Gennadius, who had a fresh story about Circassian colonists, the truth of which I doubt: Schouvaloff, who reports the ideas of his govt to be peaceable, as far as he knows them – that is, for the moment...

... I have from O. Russell a long & interesting letter, in which he reaffirms & defends his original position, that there is between the three empires a close & intimate alliance. He thinks that they keep it in the background, remembering the offence given by the Berlin memorandum, & that they would rather have the help of England in settling eastern affairs if that should be possible. ... He adds that Andrassy tried to get up an alliance with England in 1872, but Gladstone & Ld Granville would not have it. He then turned to Germany, & supports Bismarck on condition of receiving support in return. (But this friendship is not very sincere, for both Russia & Germany, as O.R. admits, look forward to the time when Austria will be divided between them.) ... The above is the substance of O.R.'s letter: in which I believe there is a good deal of truth: but I am not disposed to believe that the friendship of the three courts is as real or as close as he seems to think it.

25 January 1877. Wrote to D. of Abercorn[16] to give him a nomination for one of his sons to the diplomatic service.

26 January 1877. Saw ... Münster who repeated his customary prediction that war is inevitable, & again, for the fiftieth time, expressed wonder that we did not use the occasion to seize on Egypt. Saw Harcourt, who was less despondent: I thought it well to give him a hint as to these repeated suggestions by the German govt, which evidently have no object except to embroil us with France. ... Saw the Persian minister, who came about the old story – to see whether something cannot be got for Persia out of the Turkish troubles. I warned him seriously of the risk his country would run if dragged into war, by which it would lose English support, & become a Russian dependency.

... Letter[17] from Salisbury, under date J. 19, gives a kind of summary of the results of his mission. He says if any good result is to be obtained,

[14] Min. at Pekin.
[15] Junior priv. sec. to Derby; 'not very sharp nor very active' (D.D. 30 Oct. 1877); hardly mentioned.
[16] Lord-lt. of Ireland 1874–Dec. 1876; leading freemason.
[17] Cecil, *Salisbury*, 124, but sense partly differing.

it will be better elsewhere than at Constantinople, where the English clique & the Turkish mob play into another's hands, & where everything is done with open doors. S. thinks that the G. Vizier would rather risk a war than the chance of assassination & the prospect of losing the Sultan's favour. ... S. argues that Russia can always be forced by Austrian opposition to withdraw, as the position of an army in Bulgaria would be too dangerous with Austria an enemy, & with no command of the sea. But he does not seem to allow for the contingency of Austria & Russia agreeing to divide the plunder between them. On the whole this letter is the strongest evidence we have yet had of the influence which Ignatieff has by some means obtained over S. It is not however a matter of much consequence, his function being ended, & the cabinet having to decide as a whole on the new questions that may arise.

27 January 1877. Letter from Lyons, he says that Decazes is much pleased at the general agreement of our views: which are in effect to wait & see how the Turkish constitution works ... He (Dec.) has heard bad reports of the Russian emperor's health, whom he evidently believes to be slowly dying.

Cross being to call on M. early this morning, I authorised her to let him know, but not as from me, that if Disraeli retires, either from age & health or from disagreement with his colleagues, I shall go with him.

... Disraeli is dissatisfied with my draft of the royal speech, & indeed I do not like it myself. He has in return sent me his, which is well-written, but rather bouncing in tone, & curiously inaccurate in point of fact. I retaliate by pointing out the mistakes, which are many.

28 January 1877. Talk with my brother about estimates, which he thinks are higher for the army than they need be, & shows where they may be cut down. This we shall have to do, for revenue prospects are not favourable, & increased taxation would be exceedingly unpopular.

29 January 1877. Cabinet at 4, which sat 1½ hours. We discussed Indian famine, for which it is now said that a loan of £10,000,000 will be required, the loan of 2 years ago not having been paid off. I cannot induce my colleagues to share the alarm I feel at the prospect of bankruptcy for India. A surplus is talked of every year, but it is made only by arbitrarily charging a certain proportion of public works (which are like the repairs on a private estate, a constant charge) to capital. The Ld Advocate was called in, & explained some Scotch bills, the chief subjects being sheriffs' courts, highways, and poor law. The cabinet agreed to his proposals, which Cross understood & Richmond knew a little about: to the rest of us they were unintelligible, or nearly so. Nothing passed in regard of foreign affairs.

30 January 1877. I have a curious letter from O. Russell, very long, of which the purport is as follows. Bismarck wishes to consult the English cabinet on two points of policy: the first being, what is to be said as to the coming Russian circular? Germany he says would be glad to back out of the Turkish question altogether, if it can be done without offence. He does not care whether Turkey is divided or not. He only wishes to withdraw from the affair & assume a 'neutral though benevolent' position if we are willing to do the same. The other question relates to France. He is again alarmed at the French armaments & at the growing intimacy with Russia. He hates Gortschakoff & ascribes the French tendencies of Russia to his 'senile vanity': wants his place taken by Schouvaloff. He dreams of a coalition against Germany, & asks 'Can Germany reckon on the benevolent neutrality & moral support of England?' in the interest of peace. He is anxious for some friendly message on this point. Russell as may be supposed, thinks the alarm unfounded, & ascribes it in part to a wish to get money for the army ... ... I send this letter to the Premier.

... Saw Schouvaloff whose views as to peace are more sanguine than before: but I don't know on what he relies. ... In fact the Russian attitude is one of somewhat sulky reserve: which may be equally intended to cover an advance or a retreat. The language of Bismarck to the Russians is violent: he says the Emperor is ... bound in honour to go on, that he cannot recede without ridicule or disgrace. Luckily the very vehemence with which his advice is given has induced suspicion: and talking over the matter with Schouvaloff, I told him plainly that the object was evident: that Bismarck wished to entangle Russia in war, to weaken her for years to come, & to prevent the possibility of a Russo-French alliance. He no doubt took the same view, but I think he was impressed by finding it thus confirmed. Talking later to Ly D., he called Bismarck a 'coquin' & expatiated on his duplicity. It is to be noticed that Bism. has never said a word to O. Russell in the sense of his advice to Russia: which shows the double game that is being played.

... Answered Russell's letter ... saying ... that in the main I agree in, & approve of, the expressed intention of the German govt to withdraw from interference: and as to his second point, I do not believe in an attack by France on Germany, but if it should be threatened, we will do what we can to preserve peace.

31 January 1877. Cabinet at 4, to discuss the Queen's Speech: we went, at least I did, expecting a good deal of controversy, but were agreeably disappointed. Disraeli at the cabinet seemed older and in worse health than I have seen him yet: but he said he had had the gout, and had taken some remedy for it (colchicum?) which had upset him.

*

2 February 1877. Cabinet at 3: sat till near 5. We read over again the Queen's Speech, making many verbal improvements: for the first draft had been done carelessly by the premier and was clumsy.

We had then a financial discussion, not at all agreeable. Northcote began it by sending round a memorandum in which he drew a very gloomy picture of the financial future: he reckons on no increase of revenue for next year, and has to meet increased civil expenditure to the extent of £500,000, almost all inevitable, besides an extra £300,000 for the debt: which condition of affairs would land us in a deficit of £800,000, but by management something may be thrown on the present year, at the end of which next month, we shall have £250,000 surplus: and the rest must be got somewhere off the naval and military estimates. There was an unanimous feeling in the cabinet that to put on new taxes in time of peace, and without special reason, would discredit and possibly destroy the govt. Reductions was therefore pressed on Hunt and Hardy, the heads of the two great spending depts, and they seemed willing enough, but explained the difficulties, which are serious. All were agreed, which is so far satisfactory. I have my suspicion that Northcote is purposely making the worst of matters and is less alarmed than he professes to be: if so he is quite right. Hardly anything was said as to eastern affairs.

3 February 1877. Letter from Lyons ...[18] It seems that Bismarck is going to raise a cry of French designs against Germany ... The semi-official press begins to snarl, the French press reply in the same tone: Decazes is alarmed and worried, and is thought to have sounded Andrassy as to what Austria would do in the event of a German attack on France.

Letter from Elliot, summing up his views on the conference. He regrets that the Turks should have thrown away their chance: believes that if the later proposals of the representatives had been made in the first instance, they would very likely have been accepted: but the first propositions created so strong a feeling of prejudice that nothing could be done. He complains, in a gentlemanlike way, but evidently under strong feeling, that he has been neither consulted nor trusted: that it has consequently not been in his power to be of any use, as his opinion was not even asked on any of the plans, until they had been settled between Salisbury and Ignatieff. He says that but for the fear of seeming to encourage the Turks in their resistance by absenting himself, & so expressing disapproval of what was being done, he would not have remained at Constantinople a day. The letter is a good one, neither angry, nor querulous, though he does not conceal his opinion that he has been ill treated: and I agree with him in that respect. It is clear

---

[18] For Lyons's views, see Lyons to Derby, 5 Feb. 1877, in Newton, *Lyons*, ii 107.

that from the first Salisbury determined to put him aside, & that in the most marked & public manner ... the decision & the result have both been unlucky.

4 February 1877. Received from Schouvaloff the Russian circular, which is not long, & generally in the sense anticipated. ... Russia invites the various cabinets to express their opinion. In other words it asks the sanction of Europe to a Russo-Turkish war.

5 February 1877. Saw ... Schouvaloff, who was anxious to suggest the language we ought to hold in order to make it easy for the emperor to demobilise his army. What he said was in substance this, 'Tell the Turks to make peace with Servia etc., to execute their reforms, or some part of them, at once, so that we may be able to say that the ends of the conference have been gained in substance...'

... Saw Currie,[19] who gave a short account of the doings of the conference. He said two things which struck me as remarkable: one that nobody knew why the Russians had suddenly lowered their terms, which he thought was a misfortune, for it had encouraged the Turks to resist everything, thinking they had the game in their own hands: the other that the dragoman of the German embassy was in close & constant communication with Midhat, and was strongly suspected of having encouraged the Porte to hold out: of course, not without orders. He thought that Bismarck had determined to break up the affair, out of jealousy of the agreement between England, France, & Russia.

Saw Disraeli, who came to talk over the session: I told him that if he retired I should go too: his more immediate object was to complain of Currie, who he says tells all the world that Salisbury has been thrown over by his colleagues: a curious statement, since we have agreed to all that he has proposed. (I have since heard from Currie, who absolutely denies that he ever said anything of the sort.)

6 February 1877. Edhem Pasha is the new grand vizier, & the change is now represented as a concession to the Powers, since Midhat was the man who advised refusal of their proposals. But the loss of an able minister, in the state in which Turkish affairs are, is serious.

7 February 1877. Cabinet early, more for form than real business: I took the opportunity of calling attention to the exact meaning & purport of the treaties of 1856, as they are sure to be referred to in debate.

... Saw Sir H. Elliot, & much friendly talk with him. I showed him the more cordiality because I do not think that in this whole transaction he has been quite fairly used: and I am on that account determined to uphold him. Spoke to Disraeli about him today, & we agreed that there is no one now in the diplomatic service by whom he could be

[19] Philip Currie, 1st Baron Currie (1834–1906), diplomatist from 1854; with Salisbury at Constantinople, 1876, and Berlin, 1878; cr. peer 1899.

advantageously replaced: it would be better that he should go back, if only as a mark of continued confidence. But possibly in his state of health he does not himself wish for this.

... Dined with Disraeli, his official dinner to the Lords. ... The party was large, over 50 peers ...

9 February 1877. Letter from Disraeli, which I did not answer, as we are sure to meet almost daily. The substance of it is as follows. The position is critical: Russia is anxious for peace: the Emperor is aware of the intrigues of Bismarck, and desires peace: but a 'golden bridge' must be built for the Russian retreat. If once war begins, he thinks it must end in the partition of Turkey: the Porte having no adequate military resources. If the Turks are beaten, England must take what is necessary for the security of the Empire! He does not think a policy of simple *laissez faire* will go down with the public. If war is to be avoided, it can only be by direct negotiation with Russia. If some local reforms were adopted by the Porte, & a term of 18 months allowed to execute them, time would be gained, & war averted. These are the Premier's ideas, & they deserve to be considered.

The issue raised ... by the opposition is now well defined. They support, & we reject, a policy of coercion as applied to Turkey. ... I do not feel confident of the steadiness of our own men. Northcote is feeble on the point, Carnarvon undoubtedly hostile, & I am not sure about Cross. On the other hand, Hardy & J. Manners are inclined to be anti-Russian, & Salisbury's Indian experience of Russian designs has neutralised his dislike of the Turk.

10 February 1877. Cabinet at 12. There was much talk about foreign affairs of a rather vague & discursive sort, & leading to no result, but I did not discourage it, as it is essential that our colleagues should not take into their heads the notion that anything is kept back from them. There was entire good humour, & no sign of probable differences: at our last cabinet on Wednesday it seemed to me as if we were watching each other with a certain distrust. The plans of the parliamentary opposition were discussed ... ... Our own men are said to be united: and if a fight comes off, we ought to win by 100.

11 February 1877. I settled a telegram for Constantinople, to press on Edhem P. the necessity of bringing into immediate operation some of the promised reforms.

Long and curious letter from O. Russell, reporting a conversation with Bismarck. He now says plainly, that he hates Gortschakoff, who humiliated him two years ago, that he fears Russia, that what he would wish for is an Anglo-German alliance, offensive and defensive, which would for ever secure Germany against French designs, and release him from the necessity of courting Russian friendship. Russell explained to him the impossibility of England entering into any such engagement as he wished for, but he is not wholly satisfied. He does not know our parliamentary system well enough to understand that it is not in the power, even if it were the wish, of an English minister to pledge his country to action in future contingencies by a secret promise, of which parliament is to know nothing: or that parliament would turn out within a month any minister who had been proved to have given such a promise. And even if this objection were not itself insuperable, I do not think Bismarck a person with whom it would be safe to enter into political partnership. We do not know his plans, and we cannot be sure of his sincerity. I shall use his overtures – as in fact I have done already – to keep alive the distrust felt by the Russian govt. of German intentions, and in this way they may be utilised in the interest of peace.

I read this letter to the cabinet yesterday, but did not ask for any expression of opinion upon it.

12 February 1877. Agreed to the Peabody report for the year: I doubt if any charitable fund in London is worked so cheaply or with so little trouble. We now lodge over 2000 families, say 10,000 persons, and make 3 per cent clear.

... Dined Travellers', but I have of late dined so little in clubs that my feeling there was that of a stranger.

14 February 1877. Saw Schouvaloff ... He either is really left without information or instructions, which is what he professes, or affects to be so, in order better to find out what is doing from me. I hear that in private he says Gortschakoff has purposely kept him ignorant of the feeling of his own govt in order to discredit him as an ambassador. It may be so, for the two men hate one another.

15 February 1877. Satisfactory talk with Hardy on the question of possible attempts to drive us into the use of coercion against Turkey: which he declares he will have nothing to do with. He & J. Manners have shown a reasonable distrust of Russia throughout, & supported me steadily: as indeed has the cabinet generally, always with the exception of Ld Carnarvon, & with some reserve on the part of Cairns.

17 February 1877. Cabinet at 1: we discussed first the debate last night. Hardy was much complimented on his speech, which he very well deserves ... the general result very favourable to us ... It is worth notice that on the question of coercion or none, the Times, steadily anti-Turkish as it is, has declared for us. The opposition have therefore not one daily paper except the News.

I hear from the diplomatists that Gladstone says he can do nothing with the present parliament, but that he can rouse the country to ask for a dissolution and will then have things his own way. Can he really have talked in this way? It is possible: he never ceases denouncing the London press and the London clubs in his private talk, & saying that neither represent the real opinion of the people.

In cabinet, we agreed to send a note of thanks to Tenterden for the help he has given us with the papers, analysing them for use in parliament &c. I explained why it was not expedient to answer the Russian circular at once, & my colleagues agreed, Salisbury alone demurring a little. Cairns asked for leave to create a new judge, which was granted: Hunt wanted to spend £16,000 in extra pay, pleading the large reductions he has made, and the necessity of the case: we told him to settle it with Northcote if he could. Much discussion followed as to course of business in parliament: & finally the Premier harangued us at some length, and with much gravity, on the discontent of the borough members. He thinks they have not been enough attended to in the distribution of patronage: at least this appears to be their chief complaint. Cross and J. Manners, with Dyke,[20] are to be a committee to hear their grievance and see whether anything can be done. But I believe that their real ground of dissatisfaction is that they have been left out in the formation of the govt: which consists almost exclusively of peers & county members:[21] not from any special preference given to the latter, but because few of the borough members have any official experience, or have shown fitness for official life. This has long been predicted as a probable result of a popular franchise. ... The best thing to do would be to pick out two or three of the best of the borough-men. Smith[22] of Westminster is quite fit to sit in cabinet.

18 February 1877. Walk early with M. Serious & rather melancholy conversation as to health & spirits: she admits hers to be now constantly low, but does not acknowledge health to be the cause: is convinced that she shall not live long, feels no interest in anything etc. I induce her to consult with Drage, & if necessary to call in some other medical men. This is not absolutely refused, but agreed to in such a manner that I am not hopeful of the result. What I fear is not exactly illness, but the growth of a fixed & chronic melancholy, such as caused the seclusion of Ly Amherst, & has at times affected other members of the family. Towards this condition there has been a growing tendency for the last two years, & I think it has increased of late.

19 February 1877. Bismarck, according to Russell, wishes nothing better than that we should send a fleet to Constantinople, as that would give him an excuse for appearing in the character of a mediator. Out of these conflicting reports it is impossible to make anything, except that no one of these conspirators in high places trusts any other, & that no reliance can be placed on anything they say.

21 February 1887. Saw ... Schouvaloff, who has had an interview with

[20] Sir W. Hart Dyke (1837–1931), Cons. chief whip 1874–80.
[21] No borough M.P.s sat in cabinet.
[22] W.H. Smith, newsagent; 1st lord of admiralty 1877–80.

Beaconsfield, & is much pleased at the language held to him ... ...
Schouvaloff's language in brief was as follows: Russia wishes to disarm,
but there must be something said to the Russian people that shall
justify or at least excuse disarmament. If the Powers abandon altogether
the cause of the Christians, Russia will have to act: & she must act
soon, for the expenses of the mobilised army are intolerable. If a war
begins, Bismarck will probably take the occasion to pick a quarrel with
France, & all Europe will be shaken. Much therefore depends on the
answer of England to the Russian circular: for what England says,
France, Italy, & Austria will also say.

... The debate of yesterday is considered as a success for the govt
... We are in effect stronger than we have been yet: with a majority
undiminished, a party undivided, and opponents who cannot agree on
any plan of common action.

22 February 1877. Dinner at the Russian embassy ... ... Pleasant
enough: Schou. very amusing, rather in the buffooning line, which is
evidently his nature: I have not laughed more for a long while.

23 February 1877. Looked over the list of Lancashire landowners as
given in the return, & find to my surprise that the number of those
possessing any large extent of land is singularly small. I am credited
with 47,000 acres, Sefton comes next with 18,000, Towneley & Sca-
risbrick each exceed 14,000, & the D. of Devonshire has 12,000: in all
only 5 with more than 10,000 acres apiece. Between 10,000 and 5,000
there are 10 more: Ld Wilton & Sir T. Hesketh over 8000, Skelmersdale & T. Parker over 7000, Ld Ellesmere & Gerard over 6000,
Messrs Ormerod, Petre, Starkie, & Ld Stamford over 5000. These are
all I can find, & I think have missed none. The return is not wholly
accurate, but probably in most cases not far from the truth.

24 February 1877. Working at home till near 12, when to cabinet. We
met at the premier's private house, he being in the gout, & in much
pain. Nothing very material was discussed: plans for a new war office, &
a new scheme for the management of London improvements, were the
chief subjects considered. I stated briefly the condition of foreign affairs.
We sat $1\frac{1}{2}$ hour. Hardy told us of the great eagerness of the D. of
Cambridge, backed by the Queen, to get away from under the same
roof as the Sec. of State: he wants to revive the Horse Guards as a
separate department, which neither the cabinet nor parliament will
sanction. He has been using the unhealthiness of the present War
Office as an excuse, & pressed strongly on Hardy the expediency of
his (the Duke's) returning to his old quarters at the H. Guards. Hardy
made no objection, but said in that case he must have a room there
also, and the same office be the headquarters for both. The Duke
dropped the scheme.

I spoke to Northcote about a gratuity, between £300 and £400, being given to the clerks in the Turkish dept, who have done double work for the last six months. He made no difficulties. We have in 1876 got up to a total of 65,000 despatches received & sent out, which is 9000 more than last year, and 5000 more than in any preceding year.

25 February 1877. Resting, and I have some need of rest, for this month has brought a greater variety & quantity of business than usual, & almost as much as I could do. But it is well over, and the long threatened attack on our foreign policy has collapsed in a manner almost ludicrous. That we should win I never doubted, but expected a series of wrangles, continually renewed from the opening day till Easter: instead of which, the debate started by Gladstone has been allowed to drop after one night, and that to the great & undisguised satisfaction of the opposition, who had no inclination for a fight: while in our house, Argyll was feebly & reluctantly supported by Kimberley & Granville & by no one else.

26 February 1877. There is no love lost between the northern powers, who are mutually jealous & suspicious, but they are kept together by their very fear of one another, each dreading what the others might do if offended or alarmed. ... What Russia wants is that a term (say of a year) shall be allowed to the Porte to make its reforms ... and that if at the end of that time, nothing, or nothing satisfactory, has been done, then Europe shall 'impose guarantees': in this last phrase lies the real difficulty, for what the Russians want is by some ambiguous phrase to pledge us to a policy of coercion, & what we want, is to avoid giving (or even seeming to give) any such pledge.

28 February 1887. The Premier still in the gout, but improving.

1 March 1877. Saw Schouvaloff: he brought strange news: that Ignatieff is coming over here on a sort of secret mission, to explain the views of his govt. This is a slap in the face to Schou. as it implies that he has not done all that might & could be done in his position: which is unjust, for he has spared no effort, & I think is as much liked, & as little distrusted, as a Russian ambassador can reasonably expect to be. It is also on public grounds a mistake, for Ignatieff is thoroughly unpopular, being thought, with truth, a liar & an intriguer: and his reception by the London world, if he comes, will be a cold one. Schou. said he had telegraphed to try & stop the mission ... I told him I could give no opinion as a minister, but as a friend I thought he had been wise.

... Sent to Disraeli draft of my proposed answer to the Russian note. It is short, & avoids controversy as far as possible.

2 March 1877. Saw Schouvaloff, who asked me to put off the answer to the circular for a few days, as further explanations are coming from his govt.

3 March 1877. Cabinet at 2, & sat till past 4. It was the least interesting we have had, and one of the least useful: being almost entirely taken up with a discussion on the question of county financial boards, raised next week by a resolution of Mr Read,[23] and even that we did not settle in any definite way. Sclater Booth was called in, & explained his ideas at some length. I noticed that nobody was disposed to resist elective boards altogether, except Carnarvon: Hardy was in favour, most of the others thought they could not be resisted, Salisbury who was strong against them two years ago, now seemed to have modified his ideas. The truth is that what with the greater powers assigned to the guardians, & what will be the increasing force of central authority, such boards as are proposed would have but little to do, whether for good or harm.

Carnarvon raised a local question of Canadian legislation on the subject of extradition, in which Cross, Cairns, & I were all against him.

... Saw Schouvaloff ... he told me that he had succeeded in stopping Ignatieff's visit, that he should go over to Paris to meet him next week, & bring back word of what he had to communicate: I said it was much better so, & congratulated him on his success.

6 March 1877. Office ... Saw there Münster, who brought a confidential telegram, stating the nature of Ignatieff's communication as disclosed at Berlin: of this I made a draft (secret) for the embassies & the cabinet. ... H. of Lds, where showed Disraeli Münster's news: he was impressed as I am with the necessity of caution. We shall have Ignatieff's proposal in a more exact form shortly.

... O. Russell writes that the 'three conspirators' are well satisfied with the progress they have made. ... They will do nothing without us, & fear another blow like the rejection of the Berlin memorandum. The Russian circular, he says, was settled with Austria & Germany.

... Loftus writes that Gortschakoff's retirement is decided, but no time yet fixed. ... Schouvaloff is the favourite candidate.

8 March 1877. Selected from a long list of candidates 12 to compete for the clerkship vacant...

9 March 1877. Wrote to O. Russell to contradict a lying report which Ignatieff has put about, to the effect that the Premier & I objected to his coming to London: whereas the whole matter was settled by Schouvaloff without a word being said by me. I gave in this letter a decided opinion as to the character for truthfulness of Ignatieff, & sent it by post, that it may be seen by the Berlin officials.

10 March 1877. Cabinet at 12, sat till near 2, discussing various questions which are to be raised in H. of C. Nothing of much interest. A good deal of talk about the burials bill in the Lds, which will certainly come to nothing, being harmless & useless.

---

[23] C.S. Read (1826–1905), Cons. M.P.; sec. to local gov. board 1874–6.

11 March 1877. Letter from Lyons: Decazes is backing up Ignatieff with all his might: vouches for the pacific intentions of Russia: & Ignatieff has been playing his old tricks, putting into Lyons's mouth ideas which he never expressed. It is a good job that he did not come here.

... In the afternoon Schouvaloff came. He read me a mem. & a draft protocol, which I kept for consideration, not expressing any opinion upon them. We walked in the grounds & talked the matter over. He came at 3, and went away at 5.

The protocol, which I have read several times, is mildly & cleverly worded, contains but few phrases which can be objected to, & has been drawn up with an evident wish to disarm opposition as far as possible. The most dangerous thing about it is the vagueness of the language: which seems to pledge us to nothing, & may be construed as pledging us to a great deal. But I cannot judge of it without further consideration.

12 March 1877. Odo Russell writes again ... his view is that the partition of the Turkish empire is settled between the three Powers, & that short of fighting them all we can do nothing to avert it: but considers the whole of the present negotiation a trap, or at least a blind, & seems to imply that the result will be much the same whatever we do. He may be right, but if he is, why should the Russians disarm, as they announce their intention of doing, just at the moment when if disposed to use force, they could do so with the least opposition & the best chance of success?

13 March 1877. Cabinet at 12: we discussed the Russian draft of protocol: the Premier opening proceedings: I then explained the situation fully, & my colleagues successively gave their opinions: all were in favour of accepting the protocol in principle, & discussing it in detail with Schouvaloff: there were scarcely any divergencies of opinion, though Hicks Beach & J. Manners expressed dislike to the proceeding, but they thought there was nothing else to be done. We sat a little over an hour. Disraeli vexed me by talking in his swaggering vein about the deference paid to English opinion, & the change in that respect since the Berlin mem. – which to my mind is a mere matter of vanity, & of no real consequence: but he sees things in that way, & it cannot be helped.

15 March 1877. Saw Disraeli ... talk to him of the necessity of letting Elliot go back, unless we meant to throw him over, & give a triumph to the 'atrocitarians': he entirely agreed, & I left him to encourage Northcote, whose only fault as a leader is that he is (naturally) a little timid, & more afraid of the opposition than is necessary with a majority of 50 at his back.

Saw ... Schouvaloff, who accepts most of my amendments: that is, so far as he is personally concerned, but he must have the sanction of his govt.

Saw Münster, who evidently dislikes the prospect of an amicable arrangement, & gives underhand hints of foul play. Having been instructed to support, he cannot do more.

... News by telegraph that Ignatieff has decided after all to come here, & on the strength of some general invitation given by Salisbury, has asked himself to Hatfield for next Sunday. He is a cool hand.

16 March 1877. Saw Schouvaloff, & settled with him the draft of a protocol, but he cannot do more than take it *ad referendum.*

... Northcote called ... He, & Cross, & Salisbury all anxious to have a cabinet held today, I do not know why, for there was nothing to decide: I saw no use in it, nor did the Premier, with whom I communicated.

17 March 1877. Cabinet at 12. Discussion on the protocol, Carnarvon making a few difficulties, & Salisbury proposing one amendment, which I thought reasonable, & accepted. I cannot but see that on the part of these two, & to some extent on that of Cairns also, there is a strong feeling of disappointment at the idea of the Russian govt backing out of its engagements to the 'oppressed races': they cannot openly say that they dislike the idea of peace, & perhaps if the decision rested with them, they would not give it for war: but they hoped for a general change in the east, & have not got it.

Discussion as to Elliot's going to Constantinople, which became a little warm. I was pressed by Cairns & Salisbury to recall him, or ask him to resign, which I refused pointblank to do: saying that I thought it unjust, that I had pledged myself, and would resign rather than give way on that question. This settled the matter & I agreed at the request of Cross & Northcote that his return to his post should be postponed, as they thought the impression on the H. of C. would be unfavourable, & till the present diplomatic crisis is over, a row is not desirable. I undertook accordingly to make temporary arrangements, Elliot retaining his position and having extended leave on grounds of health. Thus the matter ended temporarily in a sort of compromise: I saw Elliot later at the office, as Disraeli also had done, & explained the situation. He took it as I expected with good humour & good sense: & expressed gratitude to me for the support I had given him.

... Schouvaloff called, bringing Ignatieff with him: they discussed the protocol, & made a few verbal amendments, none of the slightest importance, & it seemed to me that the chief object of the proceedings was to enable Ignatieff to say that he had had a hand in the negotiation.

... At 8 to F.O ... we had dinner of 43 persons, the Ignatieffs being the chief guests, though the dinner was not made for them. Party afterwards ... probably 7 or 800. ... Ignatieff went off to Hatfield by a late train.

18 March 1877. Ignatieff is being entertained at Hatfield, & most of the ambassadors are there to meet him...

19 March 1877. Münster tells me that Ignatieff had utterly puzzled him, saying overnight that war was inevitable, & in the morning that he had little doubt of peace. This is described as his usual practice...

... H. of Lds, where a question ... as to Sir H. Elliot, which I was glad of, as it enabled me to put the matter in the light most favourable to him ... ... This suits him, & me, but it will not increase the satisfaction of the pro-Russian party in the cabinet.

20 March 1877. To Windsor ... Ignatieff, whom I avoided as far as civility allowed, conversed with me in the train, pressing for our signature of the protocol, without any corresponding assurance as to Russian demobilisation: which I answered rather stiffly ... telling him in plain terms that without a promise such as could be laid on the table, we would sign no protocol.

He held, as I have since heard, exactly the same language to Tenterden, Northcote, Forster, & others: evidently under the impression that he should find more sympathy in the English public generally, & even in the cabinet, than at the F.O.

27 March 1877. Cabinet at 12: we sat about $1\frac{1}{4}$ hours, discussing the answer to the Russian alterations. The majority of the cabinet was agreed that we could not discuss them until we had a promise of demobilisation: Carnarvon dissenting vehemently, Salisbury more mildly, and Cairns inclined to doubt. ... I called on Disraeli on my way home, and explained to him what had passed; we both fear a break-up, and agree that it will be a lesser evil than farther concessions to Russian demands.

22 March 1877. Called on the Premier ... found him very weak (he has been in the gout, and taken colchicum, on which a cold has seized him, and I never saw him looking so ill) but full of life & energy: he described a conversation which he had held with Ignatieff last night, expressing the views of the govt in decided terms: & he thought he had made an impression. We agreed to hold a cabinet tomorrow.

... Schouvaloff came ... he seemed depressed & disheartened, at which I am not surprised, for Ignatieff has very effactually undone his work ... It is certain that Ignatieff's visit has not been a success. He talks fluently & cleverly, but that is all: his undoubted talent for intrigue & underhand work has not improved his reputation in English eyes: & his loquacity & intense egotism are not suited to English tastes. Personally, he is not prepossessing: a good forehead, but the face of a Tartar: & the look of mean cunning which is its chief characteristics, seems like a warning given by nature. In one word, he is not a gentleman, & I cannot understand why or how Salisbury should have taken to him.

23 March 1877. Cabinet at 12, which sat 2 hours: the Premier opened the proceedings by a speech longer & more formal than is usual among colleagues, explaining his views, recapitulating the whole history of what has passed since the conference, all accurate enough, but to say truth a little tedious. He was evidently unwell & weak, which accounted for his style being altered. He dwelt earnestly on the impossibility of carrying on business unless we were united. Discussion followed: practically all were agreed: even Carnarvon assenting, and Salisbury waiving objections, though he said in a rather marked manner that he did so in deference to the opinion of the majority. The end was that we maintain our former position: no protocol to be signed without a Russian promise of disarmament.

Saw Schou. at the office, & told him what was settled: a long convn followed as to means of evading the difficulty, but no satisfactory result could be come to. I made this into a draft for circulation among the cabinet.

... Called on Disraeli on way home, & talk with him as to the situation. He satisfied & pleased with the result of his appeal to the cabinet.

24 March 1877. Saw Beust, who ... left with me a note of Andrassy's about our blue book, which is a sore subject. It ought not to be so, for we published nothing that seemed confidential ... but I could not guess ... that while earnestly deprecating Russian occupation of the provinces in his language to us, he had been agreeing to it with Russia on conditions of his own.

... Saw Schouvaloff, grave & anxious. He suggested another plan by which Russian & Turkish disarmament might go on together. I thought it feasible though not very hopeful, & agreed to refer it to the cabinet. ... It is useless to sign any protocol (as I have said all along) till peace is concluded with Montenegro, & of that by the last reports there seems less prospect than ever.

26 March 1877. From Berlin Bismarck sends a kind of excuse for acting with Russia, saying that he should have much preferred an English alliance, but as that is not to be had, he must yield to Russian caprices, as it is indispensable that he should have an ally to neutralise possible coalitions against Germany.

28 March 1877. Working on papers till near 2, when to a cabinet which I had asked Disraeli to call. We discussed this interminable business of a protocol, and I thought I saw that some of my colleagues were so weary of the subject as to be ready to acquiesce in any solution. There was much & long discussion, but no very marked difference of opinion. We agreed in the end that it would not be necessary to wait for the conclusion of peace with Montenegro – it being in fact doubtful whether, or when, that will come off: that Schouvaloff's last plan for bringing about disarmament (which his govt has sanctioned) might be accepted: but that our signature, if given, should be accompanied by a declaration that the protocol is null & void if peace & disarmament do not follow. This last condition, if the Russians will take it, neutralises whatever risk – and it is little enough anyway – there might seem to be in the document itself. The question of wording was left for me to settle with Schouvaloff. I am not disinclined to disagree in this conclusion: my reason is for it, but I cannot avoid a feeling of suspicion, & dislike to the whole business. We are signing a paper which is a sham, on the assurance that Russia wants it as an excuse for disarming. The best that can be said is that guarded as we propose, it can do no harm: & that if we had refused, as possibly it is wished that we should – the whole blame of war breaking out would be thrown on us. Not the least disagreeable feature of these discussions is the disadvantage at which a peer is placed, when members of the H. of C. declare that this or that is expected by parliament to be done. One cannot dispute the fact, though one may believe that the wish of the individual speaker is more concerned than that of the House. On the whole, my resolution to quit office whenever the present cabinet breaks up by Disraeli's retirement, is confirmed. I proposed Layard to fill Elliot's place for the time: contrary to my expectation, the choice was not opposed. ... Keston again by 5 p.m. train. ... I think that going in & out by rail does not agree with me: the necessity of having finished by a certain time is disturbing, keeping up as it does a constant feeling of having to work under pressure.

29 March 1877. Schouvaloff came, as agreed yesterday: we settled finally the draft protocol & the annexed declarations. At night I received from him a telegram that his govt consents to the reservation that if peace & disarmament did not follow, the protocol is to be null & void. With this security, we are safe I think against criticism at home, except that people may say with truth that the document is unmeaning: but that matters little, we did not propose it, we have accepted it only for the sake of peace, & [if] it does no good it can do no harm. I am satisfied that what we have done is right, but I have no pleasure or enjoyment in the thing, though out of doors it will probably be considered a diplomatic success.

30 March 1877. A long ramble in Holwood with M. Much talk as to official life, its effect on health, etc. She has lately consulted a doctor (Richardson), he gave tonics, which for a time did good, but the effect has not lasted, and the condition of morbid depression and melancholy has returned. It comes without reason, and seems impossible to cure. I seriously consider whether this being so I can go on with office business.

The London life, with its excitement and fatigue, is the worst possible for complaints of a nervous kind: and in the office I hold, it is a necessity not only that I should be in London, but that my wife should also take her share. I had pretty well made up my mind to go whenever Disraeli retires, but it is now a question whether I can wait till then. If only to relieve my mind, I will speak to him. To me, resignation is no sacrifice, nor on the other hand have I the weariness and disgust of official business which often came over my father: it is a respectable useful way of filling up one's time, but I should on the whole be happier as a free man. The *parti prêtre* would exult at getting rid of me, the Conservatives as a body would probably regret my withdrawal, but I have read and seen enough to know that no politician is long missed, and that there is more vanity than patriotism in thinking one's services indispensable.

31 March 1877. Musurus called, eager to know the real nature of the protocol, which I explained to him, & I think I sent him away comforted. He has of late put his govt to a good deal of needless expense ... something I told him a week or ten days ago excited his alarm (I cannot conceive why or what it was) and he telegraphed in a style that caused the Turkish cabinet to make immediate preparations for calling out their last reserves. Jocelyn telegraphed from Constantinople to ask what the news really was, & I authorised him to contradict the statement that I had said anything which could justify a panic.

At 3 came all the ambassadors, & we signed. Schouvaloff & I each reading our declaration before signing, & Menabrea adding one of his own. There was some talk of a procès-verbal to be made, & of the manner of communicating the document to the Porte: in the end we came to the rational conclusion that the simplest way was the best, & it was agreed that I should give a copy to Musurus.

1 April 1877. Fairhill: easy in mind & free from business ... Walk ... with M., who has recovered her spirits & partly her strength, after a week in the country. ... The chief business today was to settle drafts relating to the negotiations with Dahomey: which now look well, Carnarvon having been persuaded to abandon his unwise scheme of annexing part of the coast.

2 April 1877. The financial year is finished, & has given Northcote £150,000 more than he had estimated for ... He will just, but only just, be able to do without new taxes. It is certainly singular how conservative administrations have of late coincided in point of time with periods of commercial depression.

4 April 1877. The crisis in Germany continues: the Emperor will not receive Bismarck's resignation, Bismarck will not withdraw it, & all still remains unsettled.

Jocelyn[24] has communicated the protocol to the G. Vizier, who defers giving an official reply, but does not conceal his personal dislike of it.

6 April 1877. Drive with M., Mary, and Sanderson, to Tunbridge Wells, where walked about for two hours, over the common ... I never see it without pleasure. When a child (1828–1836) my time was chiefly passed in London, owing to my father's political duties: we seldom saw Knowsley, and Knowsley was far less attractive than the improvements of the last forty years have made it. Tunbridge Wells was the favourite place of rest, and hence I have more early recollections connected with it than with any other spot in England. The same also happens to be the case with M., from the nearness of Buckhurst.

... Rambled out before dark, to settle plans for planting, though the growth of young trees here is not encouraging.

8 April 1877. The papers have in general been favourable to the protocol, which was laid on the table on Thursday, & appeared in full on Friday, with a very small amount of correspondence: I thought it better to suppress the despatches which would have shown all the process of bargaining on both sides.

9 April 1877. Letter from O. Russell. He says Bismarck is really nervous & in want of rest ... ... But it is not clear from what Russell writes, & possibly it is not clear to Bismarck himself, whether he is really wanting to go or not: whether his resignation is simply a strike for more power, or the result of genuine weariness & satiety. Probably both feelings are so much mixed that he would not be able to say which is the stronger.

... Musurus talked in a strange [vaporing?] way about the protocol, saying the Porte could not accept it – that it involved a sacrifice of all that Turkey had fought for: better war at once, & in case of defeat the loss of a province or two: at worst they could only be driven back into Asia, & would be independent there. However he did add that he had advised his govt to consent to send an envoy to Petersburgh to treat of peace: but he did not know whether they would do it.

10 April 1877. M. went today to a new oculist ... who gives her satisfaction, saying that her lessened power of sight is mostly due to general weakness ... ... Saw Schouvaloff, who had no farther news, & seemed uneasy. ... Dined The Club ... well pleased with both company & talk, I did not feel in the mood to enjoy either much: I think the constant worry of this office tells upon me.

11 April 1877. Saw Greenwood, & later Lawson. Cabinet at 2:

---

[24] Lord William Nassau Jocelyn (1832–92), sec. of legation at Constantinople 1874–8; diplomatist at German courts, 1878–92; d.s.p.; 3rd s. of 3rd E. of Roden.

subjects were Scotch education, as to which we decide to continue
the present Board for a year: in opposition to the Duke, who
wanted to abolish it at once: but there is no doubt as to Scotch
feeling on the subject, & Richmond is a little too much in the
hands of the permanent officials at Whitehall, who want the
patronage kept in London. Next came cattle plague, as to which it
was settled to bring in a bill: then talk about a bill of Carnarvon's,
taking power to confederate the S. African colonies if they consent.
We assent to it, the scheme being permissive only, & pledging us
to nothing if there is local opposition.

12 April 1877. Saw ... Musurus, who left with me the Turkish
answer to the proposals of the Powers. It is long, not ill written,
but in a tone rather of defiance than of conciliation: evidently
showing that war is thought inevitable at Constantinople, for there
is no suggestion of farther negotiations, nor opening left for them.
... [Musurus] added that the only way out of the affair was that
the Powers should consent to annul the protocol! A hopeful
suggestion. But I suspect that he has been told to hold firm &
decided language, & like weak men in general who have to play a
part not natural to them, he overdoes it. I had the despatch, & one
reporting our conversation, put into print for the cabinet. Saw
Layard, & gave some last instructions before his departure.

13 April 1877. Saw ... Schouvaloff, who considers all chance of
maintaining peace at an end: & I agree with him: Beust, who had a
plan for setting everything straight, but did not seem much to believe
in it himself...
... Northcote brought out his budget last night: a very simple one,
as the nature of the case required: he puts on no taxes, & takes none
off. ... So much had been said of the certainty of a deficit, & of the
necessity of new taxes to fill it, that the announcement disappointed
our opponents, & pleased the House generally. But the anticipation of
war has killed the interest usually felt in a budget.

14 April 1877. To cabinet. Nothing was said on foreign affairs beyond
a few words of enquiry: there being in reality nothing to settle. We
discussed chiefly the course to be taken towards certain Irish M.P.s,
who have adopted a new policy of obstruction: they speak at great
length, & often divide ... ... The nuisance has become serious, & the
Speaker is seriously considering whether some attempt should not be
made to check it: but this is not easy to do ... ... It has even been
suggested that a resolution may be passed directed against these
gentlemen personally: for which it seems there are precedents: but these
precedents are 200 years old, the proceeding would be practically a
new one ... On the whole it was thought best that if the inconvenience
continued, Northcote should first try the effect of an appeal to the

House. The disturbers are only three – Biggar,[25] Parnell, & Callan:[26] though at times reinforced by others. The Home Rule party as a body disclaim their tactics: but if these tactics succeed, I doubt whether they will continue to reject them. Fifty members bent on a policy of systematic obstruction of all business would throw the whole parliamentary machine into confusion.

Debate last night on foreign affairs in H. of C. which ended to the great advantage of government. ... The feeling of the House, I am told, was strongly anti-Russian.

16 April 1877. Saw Münster, who tried not very successfully to disguise his satisfaction at the turn which events have taken: can it be that Bismarck's retirement just now is a pretence to disarm suspicion, & that he has lighted a mine which will explode presently? I half suspect it, but without proof. Saw Schouvaloff: his language is that nothing can now be done by diplomacy to avert war, that the Turkish reply is regarded as a challenge, that hostilities must begin, & that our object should be to localise the war as much as possible, & to stop it at the earliest possible moment.

17 April 1877. Saw Lawson & Greenwood: both well pleased with the state of feeling about Russia.

... Saw Disraeli, & convn with him as to possible occupation by England of the Dardanelles: no result arrived at, but I promised consideration.

... A Tichborne demonstration having been announced, over 1000 police were brought out & stationed about the approaches to Westminster, to prevent a petition being brought up to the H. of C. by a mob, which is contrary to law: all passed off quietly, though about 6000 people met in Hyde Park. It is strange how strong a hold the Tichborne imposture has taken on the popular mind: at this moment, a larger crowd can be collected in support of the 'unfortunate nobleman' than would muster about the eastern question, or about any question whatever of public policy.

The Stationery office having been resigned by Greg,[27] Disraeli asked me if Talbot[28] would accept it: I consulted him accordingly, but found as I had expected that he is not disposed to give up £1200 a year with only nominal duty for £1500 with a good deal of labour & responsibility.

---

[25] J.G. Biggar (1828–90), M.P. Cavan 1874–90; bigamist.
[26] Philip Callan, M.P. 1868–85; for tortuous career of, see A.B. Cooke and J. Vincent (ed.) *Lord Carlingford's Journal*, 141n.
[27] W.R. Greg (1809–81), millowner and essayist; comptroller of stationery office 1864–77.
[28] Col. the Hon. Sir W.P.M. Talbot (1817–98), Derby's bro.-in-law; sergeant-at-arms, H. of Lds 1858; Derby gave £2000 p.a. to Talbot's wife, for 10 yrs, for the benefit of their children 'in compliance with my mother's expressed wish' (D.D. 2 July 1876). When the post was filled, Disraeli was wrongly accused of a job.

18 April 1877. Bourke has had, since the beginning of the session, to answer, as he says, more than 100 questions, of which 40 related to eastern affairs. Since I have known parliament, attention has never been so fixed on foreign policy: which is in part owing to the interest felt in the east, partly also to the total, & very singular, absence of agitation at home. The nonconformists are working the burials question, & the teetotallers go on with their so-called permissive bills: but both these movements are sectional only, & the debates on internal questions are neither attended nor reported. Is this a gain? I doubt: the public craves for sensation, & will have it in some form. But after the incessant turmoil of change which with few intervals has continued since I entered public life, it is felt as a relief. No sign of a reaction in the radical sense has yet appeared: in fact the cabinet is quite as strong as when we took office, & the opposition not more united.

Richmond spoke to me yesterday about Carnarvon, whose manner in cabinet & towards his colleagues is peculiar. He seldom speaks to any one except Salisbury, and looks miserable: whether from failing health & overwork, of which he complains, or from absence of sympathy on the Turkish business. I cannot call it disagreement, for he has generally acquiesced with little difficulty in what was settled. But he is much mixed up with Liddon & the high church party, to whom a Russian war on Turkey is a crusade.

Dined with the Galloways, meeting Schouvaloff, the Northcotes, & a party. Pleasant enough.

20 April 1877. Not very well, weary & harassed with incessant business.

21 April 1877. Lyons writes that the alarm and perplexity of the French increases. There is apparently a suspicion that Italy is inclined to turn against them ... But he writes vaguely, and gives no details.

Saw Drage, who tells me that I am overworked, and want rest: which is not news, but he does not tell me how it is to be got.

Cabinet at 12: which sat two hours: the most interesting we have yet held, since the question before us was, what ought to be done in the event of war being declared? Disraeli pressed strongly for action, arguing that according to the best military reports, a Russian army might advance on Constantinople, or what would be worse, on Gallipoli, within four months, possibly in little more than three months: that to send out troops would for us be a matter of two months at least: that Egypt and the Suez Canal might be threatened: that a Russian entry into Constantinople would not be tolerated by England: that we should be turned out in disgrace for having done nothing to prevent it: that we ought to act, and that there was no time to lose. He did not specify the plan of action which he would suggest, but I knew, as did most of us, that it consisted in the occupation of the Dardanelles by a land force, backed by the fleet: for which about 20,000 men would be required.

The Premier's views as to the rapidity of the Russian advance were in part disputed by Hardy and myself: we argued on the difficulty of transport over a roadless country. It was thought on all sides that the Turks can make no serious resistance, and such is the opinion of our military authorities: they ought to be right, yet predictions of the same kind have been uttered and falsified before: I remember in the Crimean war it was said that Turkish troops never begin to defend a place till European military engineers would have given it up as untenable: but then they fought desperately.

As to interference by England, J. Manners supported the defence of Constantinople by us, which nobody seconded: Cairns leaned rather to the Premier's view, that action would be expected of us: Salisbury and Carnarvon spoke strongly against helping Turkey in any way: I pointed out, and Hardy confirmed what I said, that an occupation of Turkish territory by an English force was necessarily inconsistent with neutrality: it involved us in war one way or the other: if we went with the sanction of the Porte, meaning to hold the territory so occupied against Russia, we became allies of Turkey and were at war with Russia: if on the other hand we seized and held a position on Turkish soil without leave asked, we were either making war on the Porte, or committing an act of mere buccaneering: in either case, we were giving the signal for a general scramble: which is not our policy. I disputed the idea that an attack was likely to be made on Egypt, pointing out that Russia could have no motive for such a proceeding, which would bring her into collision with both England & France: & also that the Russian fleet could not keep the sea against that of Turkey. I expressed my strong conviction that Russia would not risk a quarrel with us, or with Austria, by going on to Constantinople: that we ought to act by diplomatic means, not by expeditions; say even, if necessary, that an attack on Constantinople would be a *casus belli*: that we might at any time make a naval demonstration, which was an easy matter, costing next to nothing: but that I was altogether against a land expedition: finally that in the event of war, the first thing to do was to ascertain the views of the other Powers. My opinion seemed to be on the whole that of the cabinet, as well as I could judge, but no decision was taken. It will be singular if the course of events puts me on the side of Salisbury & Co. against Disraeli. Hitherto I have always tried to keep the balance, & shall do so still, if possible. The feeling in the H. of C. and out-of-doors is described as growing more & more anti-Russian & I believe this is true.

Schouvaloff called: I talked plainly, though in a guarded way, to him about the dangers of an advance: of which I found him thoroughly aware.

22 April 1877. Layard last night telegraphed for leave to try a last plan of pacification – the Porte to appeal to the mediation of the Powers – and I do not object, but it is done solely that we may not be responsible for leaving any means untried to preserve peace. I have no hope of any result.

The chief event of the week in home affairs is the Salford election: which was won by the Conservative Candidate after a close fight ...[29] ... The Liberals confidently expected victory ... it was thought that Gladstone's agitation, though failing in London, had influenced the provincial towns...

23 April 1877. Letter from O. Russell ... ... I note that he writes as if with a strong Russian, or at least anti-Turkish bias.

Saw at the office Schouvaloff, Harcourt, Musurus, Beust, Münster: all of whom came chiefly to ask the news, but all seemed alike possessed with the conviction that nothing more is to be done, & that we can only now watch events.

Sir W. Hewett[30] also called, & gave some interesting details about Dahomey affairs: the king keeps up the custom of his ancestors, & has lately, it seems, made a sacrifice of some hundred victims ... ... The admiral is evidently 'spoiling for a fight' but we have had enough to do with Ashantee not to want more West African war.

In the Lds, I read to the House two telegrams just received: one announcing the passing over into Roumania of Russian officers & men, which is virtually war, though no shot has been fired: the other contained an announcement from Layard that the Russian *chargé d'affaires* is to leave Constantinople at once, & that relations will be suspended.

24 April 1877. Saw Schouvaloff, & received from him the Czar's declaration ... ... We did not discuss it. ... Tel. announcing that 17,000 Russians have crossed the frontier ... ... it is singular that no notice of any kind has been given by the Russian officials to P. Charles[31] of Roumania: though he is by way of being friendly to their cause.

From Layard's telegrams it looks as if the Porte were now willing to appeal to the mediation of the Powers: a month back such a step might have been useful: now it is too late.

25 April 1877. Cabinet at 2: we sat two hours, discussing points connected with the war. Disraeli opened the discussion, more eager and animated than I have ever seen him of late: urgent that something should be done and at once: he spoke of Egypt, of the danger to English interests there, of the probability of a Russian blockade of the coast, and the consequent stoppage of the Suez canal: this, he said

[29] Won with virtually unchanged Cons. majority, 19 Apr. 1877.
[30] Sir W.N.W. Hewett (1834–88), naval c.-in-c., W. Africa.
[31] Prince Charles (Carol) of Rumania (1839–1914), prince 1866–81, king 1881–1914.

would enable Russian to revenge herself at once on her two Crimean opponents. I objected to this view of the case, as not borne out by facts: the Russians were not masters of the sea, nor in a position to blockade anybody: nor did it seem likely that they would, even if able, undertake an operation which would be of no use to them against Turkey, and could only serve to alienate two neutral powers. Much talk followed, and I thought the cabinet inclined generally to my view. But I made no objection to a proposal that one or more ships should appear in Egyptian waters, by way of showing that we are alive and watching.

Then the question was raised of asking the Porte to invite our fleet to come up to Constantinople: which J. Manners supported and the Premier inclined to, all the rest against: and it was agreed that it would be at least premature. I telegraphed to Layard, who had suggested the idea, in this sense. We agreed without difference of opinion that Hobart Pasha, who now commands the Turkish fleet, must be called upon to renounce his position in the English service, if he keeps his present post: as it would not be consistent with an attitude of neutrality that one of the belligerent fleets should be commanded by an English admiral.[32] This also was telegraphed to Layard. Some minor matters were settled. Nothing passed about the formerly proposed expedition to Gallipoli, of which I think the Premier now sees the risk and difficulty. But his state of mind makes me uneasy: he evidently thinks that for England to look on at a war, without interfering even for a limited time, is a humiliating position: and of the injury to finance and industry which would be caused by taking an active part, he either does not care to think, or considers that such sacrifices are a less evil than the playing of a secondary part. In this view of things he has the Court with him, the army and navy of course, and a section of the public: but that section, though noisy, is small, and I am satisfied that the country would not allow us to go to war if we wished it. The new phase into which we have passed has the odd effect of placing me in a sort of antagonism to the Premier, with whom I have hitherto acted in the closest union: and of putting me on the same side with Salisbury and Carnarvon, whose relations with me have been of late cool, though not unfriendly.

26 April 1877. Not altogether well in early morning, & no walk: cabinet at 12, we sat only $1\frac{1}{2}$ hours: no differences of opinion, and the Premier talked in a quieter and easier tone, not bouncing, nor excited, as he was yesterday. It was agreed that the Russian circular ought to be answered, and I undertook to prepare an answer. It was also agreed that Sir A. Kemball[33] should be sent to the seat of war in Asia. We decided to put into shape a declaration of neutrality.

---

[32] Reinstated in R.N. as vice-admiral 1885; ensured Turkish mastery at sea 1877–8.

[33] Gen. Sir Arnold Kemball (1820–1908), consul-gen. Baghdad 1859–68; commissioner on Turco-Persian boundary 1875; mil. attaché at Constantinople; kt 1866, gen. 1880.

... Gennadius came to ask, in a sort of roundabout way, that Greece might not be forgotten: might have our moral support, & so forth. I pressed him as to what this meant, & it came out, as I supposed, that his govt wants a slice of the Turkish territory: but he looked rather foolish when I pointed out to him in plain terms what he was asking for.

27 April 1877. Moult dropped in ... bringing the accounts ... for the year ending 30 June 1876. They are satisfactory as regards receipt, not as regards outlay. The total receipts are £183,653, as against £181,227 last year, an increase of £2400, due solely to natural growth, & in a bad time. The expenditure is classed as follows:

Compulsory deductions	£30,498	against £33,581	in 1874–5
Estate	£67,908	against £55,489	" "
Household	£25,000	against £28,676	" "
Miscellaneous	£21,993	against £21,538	" "
Total this year	£145,397	against £139,184	" "

The margin left is only £38,256, or less than when the receipts were less by nearly £20,000. The excess is in estate expenses, as to which it seems impossible to induce Hale to practice economy: he has never been used to it, & it is too late for him to learn. The other items I do not complain of, but the whole charge of the estate ought not to have exceeded £50,000 at the outside, which would have kept the outgoings as they should be, under £130,000. On the whole I am only fairly satisfied, for I cannot believe that all this expenditure is necessary, & I am sure it does not go on to the same extent on other estates.

Great efforts made during the last week in H. of C. to get up a vote of censure, Gladstone most eager in it: Childers and Harcourt said to be also favourable: Lowe against: Hartington and the Whigs will have nothing to say to the affair. Gladstone is said to have given notice this evening on his own account: and Adam,[34] the Liberal whip, came to ours with the expression of a hope on the part of the Whig front bench that he (Gladstone), would not have a day given him.

Rather unsatisfactory talk with Cairns, who is hot, and almost violent, on the necessity of seizing the Dardanelles: if he backs up the Premier there is not much chance of successful resistance.

28 April 1877. ... Cabinet at 12: sat nearly two hours: we settled the declaration of neutrality which must be issued now that war has begun, and I read my draft reply to Gortschakoff's circular, which was accepted. Then followed a long, rather desultory and resultless discussion on the plan of sending out an expedition to the Dardanelles: in which I noted that Disraeli took very little part: Cairns having come round to his ideas he left it to the latter to urge them, which he did with energy

[34] W.P. Adam (1823–91), lib. whip 1874–80.

and even vehemence. J. Manners was eager to do something: Salisbury and I opposed: the rest discussed the question in a neutral style, not having made up their minds. We agreed to call in Sir L. Simmons[35] at our next meeting, to explain the military aspects of the question. The argument for going is mainly this: that nothing else can be attempted which will make it useless for Russia to hold or to seize Constantinople – that the occupation of territory near Gallipoli, as a temporary guarantee, involves us in no quarrel with either Russia or Turkey, while it gives England a commanding position: and if properly explained it ought not to cause offence in Europe.

... It is well to say to Europe that you don't mean to keep possession of what you have taken, after the war: but will Europe believe you? Will there not be a general league against England, lest we should set up a second Gibraltar? Again, there is the question of cash: 20,000 soldiers are necessary to hold the position: and apart from the money expense, it is not easy to find the men. Further, is there sufficient reason? Will not a mere warning to Russia that we should fight rather than let her hold Constantinople be enough? Is any English interest involved sufficient to justify what, if not necessary, is a wasteful, foolish, and dangerous procedure? We shall hear a good deal more on this business.

Saw ... Musurus, who came with a variety of foolish requests, as that we would lend the Porte money ... that we would supply torpedoes etc. It is a real misfortune to the Turks to have a man here who understands England so little, after 25 years passed in London.

30 April 1877. Much talk in the political world about Gladstone's notice ...[36] ... The Whigs are disgusted ... ... The Radicals ... are doubly satisfied: first because his action is a condemnation of the moderate Whig policy: next, because his new position of independence marks him out as their future leader: so at least they think. He is ill in health and painfully excited.

1 May 1877. Working hard on papers till 11, when cabinet: we sat $2\frac{1}{2}$ hours...

In cabinet, we began by a discussion on the strength of the Russian fleet: which Disraeli either really believes, or affects to suppose, to be very strong: but all our information shows that they have few ships, and those defective. He pressed very eagerly for the strengthening of our own navy. Much gen. convn. followed as to Egypt and the Suez

---

[35] Sir J.L.A. Simmons (1821–1903), soldier; served with Turks in Crimea; insp.-gen. of fortifications, war office, 1875–80; mil. delegate at Berlin congress, 1878.

[36] *H*, ccxxxiv, 101 (Mon. 30 Apr.). Gladstone gave notice of 5 resolutions, which he read, condemning Turkey and urging home rule for its disturbed provinces; it was agreed that the resolutions be discussed the following Monday.

Canal. Carnarvon talked about the ease with which Egypt can be
defended if once taken: in a way that led me to think he is inclined to
annexation. Cairns raised a discussion, which we agreed to continue
tomorrow, as to the possibility of negotiating with Russia and with
other powers in order to secure certain points in which English interests
are concerned: the three most important being: that Constantinople
shall not be occupied: that Egypt and the Suez Canal shall not be
interfered with: that the navigation of the Hellespont shall continue on
its present footing. Salisbury was inclined to add to these, the proviso
that Bassrah and the Persian Gulf shall not be meddled with. I
supported in principle Cairns' idea: whether we can make anything of
it or not, it is a more sensible one than the defence of Constantinople
or the occupation of Gallipoli: and may serve to draw off attention
from the more dangerous, if more popular, plan of armed interference.
Sir L. Simmons was then called in, and gave many interesting details
of the Russian advance on Constantinople. As to Gallipoli he said it
might be held for a time with 5000 men, but would require 10,000 to
make it safe: to hold both sides of the straits at least 20,000 would be
necessary. The command of the sea is taken for granted. The line of
works to be defended is about three miles long on the European side:
on the Asiatic side there are none. The works might be made fit for
defence in a week. The lines of defence in front of Constantinople
would require 50,000 men, and six weeks to prepare them. On the
whole it seemed clear from his evidence that any expedition intended
to land troops and hold a position would be a serious business, involving
much preparation & expense.

   2 May 1877. Saw Schouvaloff: talk of his intended visit to Russia: he
engages to bring back assurances of the Emperor's intentions, which
he thinks will be satisfactory. I could not in good manners say that
after all that has passed they would not be much regarded in England.
He tells me that he last night met Gladstone at dinner, and found him
more Russian than any Russian he has met: his language, Schou. said,
would have been thought exaggerated except at a meeting of the
Sclavonic societies, and there he would not have been welcome, for he
thought as much of the Greeks as of the Sclaves. He told Schou. that
he should rouse the country and that the feeling against Turkey would
be as strong as it had been in the autumn.

   ... Cabinet, which sat $2\frac{1}{2}$ hours: very discursive, so much so that it
was scarcely possible to keep to the point: for the moment no differences
appeared. We agreed that a sort of appeal should be addressed to
Russia, warning the Czar that there were certain points in which
English interests were involved: Egypt and the Suez canal being one:
Constantinople another: the navigation of the straits a third: and that
we expected none of these to be meddled with. Not much was said of

Gallipoli, but I can see that both Disraeli and Cairns cling to the idea.

4 May 1877. Summoned ... by a pressing message from Disraeli, whom I found in the gout, rather weak & low, but not in much pain: he seemed quiet and easy in mind. He was to see the Queen before night, & wished to talk over the situation with me. I feared some wild or hasty project, but he discussed matters very calmly & temperately, & seemed inclined to believe, which he was not when we discussed the question in cabinet, that the Russian demands are likely to be moderate in the event of their obtaining an early success.

... I had a useful, though brief, talk with Schou. as to the 'English interests' involved in the issues of this war.

Home, quiet dinner and evening, though not very cheerful: for to Lady Derby and me a month's separation is a new experience in our married life.

It is exactly seven years this day, counting by days of the week, that my marriage was announced; nearly half the time has been passed in office.

5 May 1877. Cabinet at 12, occupied with foreign affairs only. I read a draft letter to Schouvaloff, embodying the ideas of the cabinet as expressed at our last meeting, and it was adopted with a few slight verbal changes. Nothing was said about an English expedition, or the occupation of any foreign territory, so that I think that project is at least put off. It does not seem to find favour in cabinet, and would certainly not be approved outside.

Much talk among ourselves about Gladstone's resolutions, which stand for Monday. They have brought about a more complete disruption of the Liberal party than existed before: the radical section has now found a leader and a cause, and the Whigs have broken with it. There is no reason why this quarrel should not be made up, as so many others have been: but while it lasts there can be no organised or effective organisation. The anti-Turkish feeling of the autumn, though not dead, has been absorbed in a stronger anti-Russian feeling: and this, I am told, prevails especially among the artisan class. Pender, who has kept up his connections with Manchester, tells me that at the late Salford election one of the managers on the Liberal side said, that either candidate might have made sure of being returned, if he had only declared openly for war with Russia. Luckily, neither was disposed to buy popularity at that price.

... Sat till 5.30 with M., when we parted for a month. To the Academy dinner, where I went unwillingly enough, but it was her wish that I should show myself there, instead of accompanying her to Dover as I meant. She, Ly Sefton, & Margaret, travel together through Paris, Bordeaux, &c. to the Pyrenees.

8 May 1877. Saw Schouvaloff, who talked of the possible terms which

Russia might require: he had no doubt as to our views being in accordance with those of his govt except possibly as to the opening of the Dardanelles: an important exception, but it is one on which as at present advised I am not sure that we have right on our side.

... Many and interesting despatches from Layard ... The declaration of war creates no stir in Constantinople: the Christians are quiet, and opposed to Russia. Layard warns us against believing reports of atrocities, they are regularly made up for the European market, which is supposed to want them: no one is more active in that respect than the correspondent of *The Times*, an Italian, Gallenga:[37] it seems that dead Bulgarians are every day coming to life: having escaped and hidden themselves during the massacres, and returned to their villages now that all is quiet again.

9 May 1877. Beust went into the question of what Austria would or would not do to check Russian advances, but his language was vague, & he declared that he had no instructions. He dwelt on the dislike of his govt to an enlarged Servia or to Bulgarian autonomy, & appeared to think that the Russians would take as payment for their trouble, after a successful war (1) Batoum (2) the ceded strip of Bessarabia (3) the Turkish fleet (4) some sort of protectorate over the Christians. I made a note of what he said for the cabinet.

10 May 1877. Saw Schouvaloff, & took leave of him: his last words were the expression of a hope that no decisive step would be taken before he came back: I asked what he meant by a decisive step? He said, such as putting the army on a war footing, or sending the fleet up to Constantinople. I would give no promise, which indeed he did not ask, but said I thought either of the contingencies which he had suggested extremely improbable.

Saw Disraeli at his house: he still in the gout, pale & looking ill, but keeps up his spirits: we talk over the situation generally: he confident of a majority of 100 in the pending debate. I who am less sanguine look to 80...

... The great foreign debate continued again this evening ... ... Gladstone's peculiar tactics, in withdrawing the only really important & significant part of his resolutions, but speaking upon them as though they had not been withdrawn, are variously commented upon. Some people think them 'dodgy' ... ... The Radicals think he has been weak, & blame his concessions which take away their chance of organising themselves into a separate party with him for a leader. ... In a national point of view, the discussion will have been useful: it has cleared the air: removed many unfounded fears, & relieved that restless

---

[37] Antonio Gallenga (1810–95), man of letters; *Times* correspondent at Constantinople 1875–7.

desire in the public mind to do something, they hardly knew what, which is apt to show itself in times of excitement, & is often dangerous.

12 May 1877. Cabinet at 3: which began with some discussion on the Burials Bill. It appears that the bishops are half inclined to give way to the demands of non-conformists, provided they can get for the clergy something which the latter may consider as an equivalent, or at least as a satisfaction to their feelings. What they want is that each parson shall have a right to modify the burial service, omitting parts of it in the case of individuals of whom he does not think well. The Abp. of Cant. said as much to Disraeli, who repeated it to us. The feeling of the cabinet was unanimous, that no concession of such a right of posthumous censorship would ever be endured by parliament. On the whole we thought it best to go on, though with no idea that Richmond's bill can pass. Then ensured a discussion on the expediency of making preparations for the possible necessity of sending out an expedition. Hunt raised the question, both he and Hardy saying with truth that the necessary requirements cannot be supplied in a day: that they cannot be provided without money: and that if not provided till actually wanted, the opportunity of sending out a force to advantage may be lost. Hardy talked very moderately and sensibly, saying that he did not wish to press any particular policy on the cabinet, but only to cover his own responsibility by explaining in advance what his department could or could not do: Hunt was more vehement, and produced on me the impression of being pushed on by others. They wanted £500,000, saying the whole cost of sending out an army corps (40,000 men) would be £3,500,000, but the half-million would be wanted at once. This money could be got by a vote of credit for the amount. I took the lead in opposing the demand, both on grounds of home politics and on account of the effect which would be produced abroad. Cairns inclined to support it, dwelling much on the necessity of occupying Gallipoli. Disraeli said little, but enough to show he was on the same side. Northcote supported me, with some reserves: Salisbury also. Manners and Hicks Beach were on the side of pugnacity. In the end the matter dropped, all parties being apparently satisfied that to ask for money at the present moment from parliament would be unwise. But I foresee future trouble from this question.

15 May 1877. Cross called to talk over the division of last night, which is more favourable to government than anybody expected. We had counted on 80 or 90, & hoped for 100: the numbers were 131. Both the debate & division have strengthened our position: nearly all the world is in favour of peace, & after what has been said on our part we cannot be accused of plotting a war: while as to past transactions, the attacks made upon us have not been violent, nor made in such a way as to seem as if the speakers were in earnest. Points of detail have been fastened upon, but except by a few hotter than the rest, the policy of coercing Turkey has been disavowed. And this policy is the only alternative to ours. The opposition moreover have been damaged by the vacillation they have shown: Gladstone's compromise has dissatisfied his real followers, & been reluctantly accepted by the Whigs, who took it only to avert the greater evil of entire disunion.

... Decazes either feels or professes great alarm as to German intentions ... ... he, Decazes, is sure that as soon as England is committed in this way in the East, a German army will march into France. He contends that Germany has three objects — to crush France — to annex Holland — and to absorb Bohemia. The latter cannot be done conveniently at the present moment: the other two plans are ripe. ... The story about Holland I believe to be pure invention ... His real sympathies are probably in the main with Russia: he undoubtedly helped the Russian loan ... ... What would suit him would be a real, effective alliance with Russia: but in the present state of relations with Germany he dares not offer one: and is content to play off English & Russian jealousies, holding himself ready to side with either party as may suit his convenience.

16 May 1877. To cabinet: we sat nearly two hours: foreign affairs almost exclusively discussed. We agreed well enough: Disraeli and Cairns agreed to waive for the present the scheme of an expedition to Gallipoli though not convinced of its impolicy, but seeing that their colleagues did not go with them: the feeling appeared universal, that Russia must not be allowed to go to Constantinople: and in the end it was settled that a more definite communication should be made to Austria, to see how far Andrassy would go in joining with us to prevent such a case. Disraeli said much as to the inefficiency of Buchanan, which I could not dissent from: and wanted to send Lyons on to Vienna, specially, from Paris: to this I objected, first as it would make delay, next as it would give exceptional publicity to the business, which is not desirable whether it succeeds or fails. He made no difficulty, and it was agreed to make the communication through Beust. I sketched a rough draft of what should be said while the discussion went on: and read it.

17 May 1877. News ... of Macmahon having dismissed his prime minister, Jules Simon ...[38] In the actual state of the world, this fresh complication is a misfortune.

Dictated for the cabinet a note to Beust, suggesting common action to prevent an attack on Constantinople.

... Spoke to Beust to prepare him for an offer of alliance, in case Constantinople is threatened: but only in general terms...

---

[38] Jules Simon (1814–96), premier Dec. 1876–May 1877.

20 May 1877. It is announced that Gladstone is about to hold a great meeting at Birmingham: which will in effect place him at the head of the extreme party. He holds in all companies the language that the present H. of C. does not represent the country, & that his ideas will be those of the majority at the next general election. He has written various letters expressing his opinion that the question of the county franchise, & that of the redistribution of seats is ripe for settlement: & on that issue he will probably fight.

22 May 1877. Lawson called early and talked about the war: he said he thought we ought to fight to keep our prestige from being lessened: which is a conclusion I cannot accept.

23 May 1877. Saw Beust, who said he could give me no answer to our overture of last week: he said he had telegraphed the substance of my note to Andrassy, but had heard nothing in reply. I do not expect much from this proceeding, though it was necessary to satisfy the cabinet, and perhaps to satisfy public opinion hereafter: the truth is, that England and Austria have different interests: Austria would readily give the Russians unlimited freedom in Asia, if only no great changes are made on the Danube: whereas to us what happens in Bosnia, Servia, and on the Danube is of secondary importance.

... Reached Knowsley at 10.40.

... I forgot to note that this morning I received from Disraeli a letter[39] written in a most desponding mood. He says that something else (i.e. the cabinet) will fall before the Turkish empire: that we shall either be turned out in the present parliament, or be obliged to dissolve at an unfavourable moment: inasmuch as when the Russians begin to threaten Constantinople there will be an outburst of popular indignation, and we shall be blamed for having allowed matters to come to this pass. – I cannot see the matter as Disraeli does: but knowing his sagacity I should be alarmed at the view he takes, were it not for two reasons. In the first place, he has got the gout again rather badly, and that depresses the spirits: in the next, he has been personally very eager to send out an expedition to the Dardanelles, and the reluctance of the cabinet is a real mortification to him.

24 May 1877. Knowsley. ... Wrote to Disraeli, but briefly, not wishing to dissent from, or being able to agree to, what he says.

25 May 1877. There has been another demonstration by the Softas at Constantinople, compelling the establishment of a state of siege. It is hardly credible, but Layard reports the story as if believing it, that the instigator of the movement is – Butler Johnstone! who lives among the Turks, spends money freely, & is bent on achieving a position as the regenerator of Turkey.

---

[39] Disraeli to Derby, 23 May 1877, in M. and B., 140.

26 May 1877. A letter[40] from Disraeli written in a desponding tone, like his last, and predicting a break-up after the next cabinet. He quotes from a letter addressed to him by Cairns, which in effect repeats and reflects his own ideas: the substance is that we have pledged ourselves to defend certain British interests if attacked, and that if those interests are endangered, and we cannot show that we have taken any steps in their defence, we shall be driven from office with ignominy.

... Talk to Hale about undue expenses on the estate, but more gently than I ought. The fact is, we are old friends, & he is my senior, & on both accounts I do not speak as plainly as I should when things are done by him as agent which I do not like.

... Despatches from Rome ... ... Paget does not believe in Italian designs on Nice & Savoy, nor in any secret alliance with Germany. He thinks that Italy requires peace, & will remain neutral...

27 May 1877. The train being slow, we were not in St J. Square till near 10 p.m. Read on the way Schopenhauer's life...

28 May 1877. Letter from Loftus: who writes in much apprehension: says he has lost all faith in Russian promises: (why had he ever any?) thinks the Russian advance ought to be checked, without seeing exactly how: that time must not be lost, etc. etc. In short he is in a fuss, and after pressing us all last year to act with Russia and trust the Emperor, he has now gone sharp round, and would make or threaten a war. He is probably only a type, and thousands of equally weak persons will shift about just as he has. There is indeed another explanation: his term is nearly expired, he does not wish to be retired, and Ly Ely[41] no doubt has warned him that the Court is violently anti-Russian.

... Disraeli is worse with the gout, & cannot move from Hughenden. Long letter from Northcote, who is at Paris; he seems like many others anxious to do something, but does not clearly see what.

29 May 1877. Long & interesting despatch from O. Russell, reporting ... the convn he has had with Bismarck. He, Bismarck, is ill, nervously irritable, & strangely haunted by constant apprehensions of an alliance of the Catholic Powers against Germany: as also with the idea of a Franco-Russian coalition. Russell evidently believes this preoccupation on Bismarck's part to be real & sincere...

30 May 1877. There is between Disraeli and me a daily exchange of notes, but nothing important has passed. He is less gouty, and therefore less despondent: but his eagerness to take some early action continues, and with it the fear that unless something be done, the ministry will lose public confidence. I do not know whether time and the course of events will have brought about any change in the feelings of the cabinet,

---

[40] Disraeli to Derby, 25 May 1877, in M. and B., 141.
[41] Jane, Lady Ely (1821–90), widow of 3rd M. (d. 1857); lady of bedchamber 1851–89.

but if not, and if neither side is disposed to give way, a disruption seems not impossible. And the inconvenience is the greater, as in the actual state of politics, no cabinet except ours can be formed. The secession of Disraeli and Cairns on the one hand, or of Salisbury and Carnarvon on the other, would almost cripple us: yet we should not be set free from responsibility, for where are our successors? In the event of any modification of the cabinet as it stands Smith of Westminster would be capable and deserving of a place in it: but I really know of no one else who would give it strength: of the younger men E. Stanhope and my brother are probably the best: but they have neither of them come forward enough to be entitled to early and rapid promotion.

31 May 1877. ... Long & excellent letter from Northcote, which I sent on to the Premier. He (N.) appears to have passed his holidays in Paris, seeing & hearing all the notabilities whom he could come across: interesting enough, perhaps, but hardly my notion of rest.

... Walk about 3 hours, & more weary than I ought to be from so little: but at least the keeping up a habit of exercise, though imperfectly, has saved me from the family complaint. At my age (50–51) my father was constantly laid up with gouty attacks, which hitherto I have escaped altogether. But I have scarcely enough of bodily strength for the excitement & exhaustion of political life, as politics are now.

1 June 1877. Saw Beust, who brought me the Austrian answer to our overtures: it is vague, though clever...

2 June 1877. Read over the Austrian answer again, it being now printed for the cabinet: but I cannot make much of it. The wording is artful, and may bear various meanings: what it seems to imply is that Austria has her own reservations to make, which are not in all cases identical with ours, & that if we want to get help we must be ready to give it in return. This would be fair enough, if one could be sure the offer was sincere.

Bismarck has been expressing to O. Russell his earnest wish that we should seize the Dardanelles ... & says that Schou. has been talking to him of a first attempt at peace to be made as soon as the Russian army has crossed the Danube: which failing, he would try again after they have crossed the Balkans, & before they reach Adrianople.

... The Sultan, according to Layard, is really doing all he can in the way of reform.

Cabinet at 3, sat till 4.40. We discussed chiefly the Austrian answer, which my colleagues seem to think more explicit than I do. I was glad of the opinion, & did not dispute it, as the prospect of help in that quarter lessens the chance of an expedition being pressed upon us. We agreed to thank Andrassy, to express a general concurrence in his programme, & to invite further communications. Nothing was said about military preparations, or going to the Dardanelles: there was entire agreement on all points discussed.

It was agreed, that something shall be said to Russell about the advance of Russian troops towards Merv:[42] as to which Lytton & his council are obviously alarmed.

It was settled to drop the Burials Bill quietly as from the state of business it cannot be carried in H. of C. even if acceptable there, which I doubt it would not be.

Talk of a mutiny on board the *Alexandra*, Hornby's flagship, which has been greatly exaggerated by the papers, but something of the sort has happened, & it is an awkward sign.

The premier was in good health & spirits, & said not a word in the sense of his late letters: I do not think, however, that his feelings are altered: his secretary, M. Corry, who imitates & exaggerates the ways of his chief, talks in great disgust of the state of foreign affairs, & predicts a failure for the govt – which is evidently Disraeli at secondhand.

Saw Beust after the cabinet, & conveyed to him the feeling of the govt caused by Andrassy's answer. ... To F.O. again for the birthday dinner & party. There were at the dinner 43: the number that came to the party was about 1200.

3 June 1877. Dined with my brother ... Talk ... about Lytton, who I fear is not a success in India. His odd unceremonious ways, and fits of absence, are an offence in the eyes of a class such as the Indian civil and military servants, strongly possessed with a sense of their own dignity, & standing much on punctilio. Lytton is clever, a good talker, & in private life very capable of making himself liked: but there is a dash of Bohemianism about him: a free & easy manner, & habitual indulgence in the whims of the moment, which with him are many. No qualities could be less suited to the requirements of his present post. E.g. he lately gave deep offence by interrupting a levee, in order that he might go away & smoke: & when a native prince ... a boy of some eight or nine years, was presented to him in form, he kissed the child: a mere kindly impulse, but to a high-caste Indian youth the touch of a European is pollution: & his intended kindness was an offence which required much explanation. – With all his oddities, Lytton would make a good ambassador, but is out of his element at Calcutta.

Heard ... with real regret of the death of the Queen of Holland.[43] ... I have known no woman of greater natural ability and she added to it a wide experience of life, having friends in many countries, & keeping up with them a constant correspondence. Her mental & bodily

[42] Taken by Russia Feb. 1884.
[43] Sophie, queen of the Netherlands (1818–3 June 1877).

energy were unusual: rest, even when out of health, she neither wanted nor liked. Except in regard of intellectual activity, her life was unhappy: the king her husband, a coarse & vulgar debauchee, disliked her, & showed it very openly: her eldest son lives constantly in Paris, in the least reputable society, & her younger son, on whom the hopes of the family rested, seems likely to be an invalid for life. The history of her singular and romantic affection for Ld Clarendon – when the latter was long past sixty, & she past fifty – will never be told, nor ought to be.

5 June 1877. Walk early with Sanderson to see Lear's collection of Indian & other drawings. Bought about a dozen. ... Lawson and Greenwood both called to talk over affairs.

... Saw Midhat Pasha, whom I received with more than usual civility, lest he should think himself slighted after his fall: he is about the ablest & most honest minister the Turks have had, or are likely to have. ... Nothing passed between us that is worth recording...

... To the Lords ... went with Cairns, Richmond, & the Premier, to the Chancellor's room, where we discussed the Burials Bill: as it now stands: on the whole, we thought that to drop the bill simply, without other reason than the little chance of its getting through the House of Commons this year, would be weak, and might even expose us to defeat, since an opposition bill might not impossibly be run through both Houses. On the other hand, it clearly cannot pass as it stands. We agreed that a cabinet should be called, & arrangements made to modify the bill nearly if not quite in the sense of Ld Harrowby's amendment, Cairns laying much stress on some changes which he wants to introduce, & which he thinks will conciliate much support.

Walk home with Disraeli, who invited me to walk in St James's gardens: we did so for an hour, he talking, not on business, but very amusingly on men and things of the day. I have seldom seen him in a happier or more cheerful mood, though the gout is not out of his hand.

6 June 1877. With Sanderson to walk over the Witley estate, & to examine two adjoining properties which are likely to be sold.

7 June 1877. To Charing Cross, to meet Ly D. & Margaret ... ... Home, where dined quietly, with much content, after a separation of 33 days.

... I gather that the cabinet of yesterday was unable to agree on the Burials question: the members of H. of C. being afraid that concession would be unpopular among the party, & tend to produce disunion. The question was left open...

8 June 1877. Saw ... Schouvaloff, who brought the answer to my note of a month ago: he read it, then gave it to me [to] read, & I had it put into print at once. It is well written, with a peculiar assumption of frankness, does not promise too much, & on the whole is likely to produce a favourable impression in England.

Egypt is to be left alone: Constantinople is not to be annexed: (nothing is said as to the chances of a temporary occupation): English interests are to be respected in the Persian gulf, & elsewhere: & the question of the Dardanelles is to be settled by European agreement, not by isolated action. A long & rather declamatory conclusion, on the wrongs of the subject races, & the duty of Russia towards them, is evidently meant for the English philanthropists. Together with this answer, intended for publicity, Schouvaloff left another paper, which contains the terms on which Russia will make peace before crossing the Balkans. This is entirely confidential, & will require much consideration.

... The Russian conditions of peace are (1) Batoum (2) a slice of Roumania extending to, but not including, the mouths of the Danube, being the greater part of what was lost after the Crimean War (3) Bulgaria to be a vassal state so far down as the Balkans (4) some provision for the security of the Christian subjects of the Porte – very vaguely stated (5) Servia & Montenegro to have an extension (6) Austria to regulate the affairs of Bosnia as she pleases: this is expressed in general terms, but can have no other meaning. (7) Some fresh arrangement in relation to the Dardanelles. The paper is in the form of a simple memorandum, as though recording what had been verbally stated.

9 June 1877. Saw ... Schouvaloff, who explained & enlarged upon his mem. of yesterday. Münster & Harcourt were appointed to see me, but Schou. stayed so long, that they had to go away.

Cabinet at 3: which was chiefly occupied by conversation on the Russian mem. which I read: there was abundance of vague talk, but the only thing definitely settled was that we should try & get a clearer understanding with Austria.

It was settled to set free two Fenian prisoners, who have served for 10 years: leaving none in prison except those who were accessory to a murder.

Much talk about a Burials Bill, which ended in a decision to let things to go on & take the chance of being beaten, as that gives less offence to our supporters in the H. of C. than any voluntary surrender. All however agreed that the question is practically settled in favour of the non-conformist demands. Salisbury & Carnarvon are much mortified – Hardy also, in a less degree – at the line taken by the Archbishops, & at the comparative indifference of the H. of Lds.

10 June 1877. A vast mass of papers from Constantinople. Layard is indefatigable as a writer: but though voluminous, his despatches are generally interesting. ... The only favourable circumstance is that the Greek patriarch has denounced the war in a circular addressed to the Christian population: & he has done this without pressure of any kind being put upon him. ... Layard has been speaking to the Sultan with great plainness & frankness ... Layard has evidently acquired considerable influence over his mind. He (L.) wants to know whether he may hold out hopes of mediation on the part of England, should the Sultan be disposed to entertain the idea. This is a question which I must answer before long.

11 June 1877. Saw Schouvaloff, who talked at considerable length ... the most important point was his assurance that Russia & Austria had a complete understanding on all points: which is absolutely incompatible with the language held by Andrassy. One of the two is lying: possibly both. I related this convn to Disraeli at the H. of Lds with the intention of showing him the impossibility of relying on Austrian assurances.

12 June 1877. Dined at The Club ... ... Pleasant enough, but I experienced again what I have often done of late, that my hearing is too imperfect to allow of much pleasure in mixed conversation. I miss much of what is said, & hear the rest only by an effort which impairs the sense of enjoyment.

13 June 1877. Saw ... Beust, with whom I had a long conversation ... the purport of it was to ask him whether in the event of the Russians showing an intention of marching on Constantinople, Austria would interfere to prevent them occupying it. I wrote my question down, that there might be no mistake, & gave it him to be telegraphed to Andrassy.

14 June 1877. Added a codicil to my will ... ... Legacies now stand thus: Ly D £20,000: my sister, £20,000, if not paid in lifetime: Mary & Margaret, £5000 each: Sanderson £5000: C. Stanley £2000. E. Wilbraham, F. Hopwood, Hale, W. Hornby, Statter, Arthur C. Lionel C. & Sackville C. £1000 each. In all £65,000. I leave also £50,000 to my brother to be invested in land & settled as a part of the family estates. To Ly D. the option of Keston or Fairhill for life. All the rest, with some trifling exceptions, to my brother.

... Wrote ... to Layard ... ... A telegram of his received today, declares that the Russian terms, the substance of which I had telegraphed to him, would not be accepted by the Porte except in the last extremity. This very much confirms my own opinion.

Schouvaloff having affirmed that the terms in question had been secretly communicated to Andrassy, I directed Buchanan to speak about them: it appears that he had never heard of them, & that Schou.'s statement is absolutely untrue. It was probably made by way of leaving on my mind the impression that Austria & Russia were in close & confidential intercourse.

... Schouvaloff came, in evident annoyance, to say that his govt had changed its mind, & would now not be content with less than the whole of Bulgaria, south of the Balkan as well as north. This makes it more than ever impossible that the conditions should be accepted, which I think they were not meant to be.

15 June 1877. Saw Drage, being a little overdone with work. He gives some quieting medicine.

... Saw Schouvaloff ... ... He is out of spirits & disgusted at the turn which matters have taken: I said in convn that I regretted the Emp. having gone to the army, where he would be under exclusively military influences: he smiled & said 'There are thousands of Russians who think as you do in that respect.'

16 June 1877. Cabinet at 3: we discussed first the Burials Bill, as to which it is agreed that the feeling in the party is so strong that we must go on, though certain to be beaten: I did not dissent, for the matter is not worth a split among ourselves. Then came Irish Sunday drinking, as to which we agreed to give a day to discussing it, but it will most likely be talked out by its own friends.[44] These matters settled, we proceeded to foreign affairs: the discussion was long, very friendly in tone, no sign of annoyance or ill-humour visible: but the differences between us seem wider the nearer the time of action comes. The question raised was, shall we do nothing, or something, to prepare for the possibility of having to act in the event of the Russians marching into Constantinople? It is clear that the Turks cannot stop them, though sickness & want of transport may: it is equally clear that though they have undertaken not to stay there permanently they enter into no engagement as to the length of their occupation: nor as to the conditions on which they could retire: which may be such as to leave very little of the Turkish empire in existence. It is also certain that the conditions of peace which they put forward are such as the Porte cannot accept: & are probably not meant to be sincerely discussed. Are we then to give up Constantinople altogether, & if we do, what will the country say? It is not now a question of deciding on any expedition, but of putting ourselves into a position in which we could make one, or threaten one, if required. Disraeli pressed it strongly: Hardy, Hunt, Beach, & Cairns, all supported him: J. Manners is at Balmoral, but we know his opinion to be in the same sense: Cross & Northcote did not altogether dissent, but qualified their opinions in a way which I did not clearly understand: Richmond said little, but as usual, supported Cairns: Salisbury and Carnarvon argued against. I reserved myself as much as possible, but said plainly that the Russians would be at Constantinople if nothing were done, & that once in it would not be easy to get them out. It was agreed to think the matter over, & adjourn the discussion. Northcote had a scheme, which he rather hinted at than explained, for buying

---

[44] In 1876 Richard Smyth, a private member, defeated the govt by 57, on a resolution in favour of Irish Sunday closing. In 1877 the bill was talked out.

up the Egyptian tribute from the Porte, paying off the 1854 and 1855 bondholders, and thus establishing a kind of control over the finances of Egypt. Salisbury said two things which are more decided than any former utterances of his: that Russia at Constantinople would do us no harm: and that we ought to seize Egypt.[45] Against this last idea I protested.

17 June 1877. Letter from Disraeli, very nervous about the situation, prepared for Salisbury's resignation, and appealing to me to stand by him. I answer briefly, saying that we will talk together: doubting whether we have yet reached the point at which resignations are probable, since all that is being discussed at the moment is the making of preparations in case action should become necessary: the real difficulty, to my mind, will be later when we have to consider whether these preparations will be used or not.

18 June 1877. Saw ... Salisbury, who came to speak about the proposed vote of credit: he had not a thought of resigning, disliked the whole affair (as indeed I do) but was ready to admit that the state of public feeling might make it necessary, & that it did not in any manner commit us to war: the argument that weighed most with him was the impossibility of getting Austria to act with us, unless we showed some signs of being in earnest: we agreed that to get into a war with Russia without an ally would be unwise: and if Austria joins, our objects can be accomplished by peaceable means: and farther, we thought that it would be advisable to give a pledge to parliament that no action should be taken without their being consulted. Salisbury appeared to me moderate & inclined to yield up to a certain point rather than make a split. He had seen Disraeli, & talked to him in the same sense.

Saw Schouvaloff, who was so very eager to assure me of the absolute agreement between Austrian & Russian ideas as to make me suspect the contrary more strongly than I have done yet. I told him in plain terms my personal opinion that the programme of peace put forward by him seemed to me one which the Turks neither would nor ought to accept.

... H. of Lds at 5. Debate on Burials Bill short, as we had had it all before, but House fuller than it has been this year since the opening. Ld Harrowby carried his amendment, as it was foreseen that he would, the numbers being 127 to 111. I do not think that the result was greatly regretted, at least on our bench, as it was solely the wish not to give offence in the Commons that led to a division being taken.

19 June 1877. Saw ... Gennadius, who came to ask what share Greece

---

[45] Cf. Salisbury to Lytton, 15 June 1877 (*Cecil*, 145–6): 'I would have devoted my whole efforts to securing the waterway to India – by the acquisition of Egypt or of Crete, and would in no way have discouraged the obliteration of Turkey'.

is to have in the spoil? for that is what his question came to, apart from diplomatic disguises. I gave a purposely vague answer.

... Saw Beust: long & interesting talk ... ... I pressed him with the danger to Austria if the Russian scheme for a free Bulgaria were to take effect: remarking that it would leave the road to Constantinople absolutely open to a Russian army. I pointed out that if Austria, which is most interested, chose to do nothing: neither the English govt nor parliament were likely to be in favour of a second Crimean war without an ally. Their inaction would justify ours: & they would be the chief sufferers. He seemed to agree in all this, & promised to report it.

20 June 1877. Cabinet at 12. We sat nearly two hours, & agreed without difference of opinion on the part of any one, that a vote of credit shall be taken in H. of C. for two millions – not necessarily to be spent in preparation, but to be available if wanted. It was clearly understood that this vote pledged us to nothing farther, & especially not to anything in the nature of an expedition. Disraeli pressed it, speaking with earnestness and moderation, & relying much on the precedent of the Franco-German war. I gave a qualified support, chiefly on the ground that without some such evidence that we really meant action if necessary, it was hopeless to induce the Austrians to join us. I argued further that if Austria continues to hold aloof, being more interested than we are, it would be folly to undertake a new Crimean war without an ally (exactly what I said to Beust yesterday): on the other hand if Austria joins cordially with us, we shall secure our objects without fighting...

21 June 1877. Saw Holmes,[46] our consul in Bosnia, who has done better than any one throughout all these troubles. I complimented him accordingly. He is in weak health, & I fear not likely to be able to go back.

22 June 1877. Dined at the U.S. legation to meet Gen. Grant ... ... I sat between the host & Schouvaloff, & was well enough amused. ... Mention of Bismarck, whom Schou. knows well: and whom he described as in no way superior or remarkable by intelligence: on the contrary, he thinks him in many respects intellectually weak: but his force is in 'caractère' – will or determination. This alone, Schou. says, has made him what he is, notwithstanding conspicuous weaknesses, the chief being his excessive credulity. Anybody may impose upon him with a story of a Jesuit plot: & he is equally ready to swallow any fiction about French designs on Germany.

... Cabinet summoned suddenly at 6 p.m. – why it was so, the usual

---

[46] (Sir) William Richard Holmes (1821–82); consular service 1841–77: kt 1 Aug. 1877; onsul in Bosnia 1860–77; retd 1 Sept. 1877; s. of Ulsterman; seen by Seton-Watson as ulpably Turcophil.

day being Saturday, & why in such haste, I do not know: the Premier had been at Windsor: found the Queen very warlike, as all the Court are: the P. of W. most of any, & he talks loudly & foolishly in all companies. The object of calling us together was to talk over the situation, as it is understood that we are likely to be questioned on Monday about the proposed vote of credit. It was agreed to go on as usual with the estimates, & not to bring in the vote until they are passed: for which there is the more reason, as the situation varies from day to day. I thought Ld B. more anxious & agitated than the business we had to do seemed to explain, & suspect that there is some undercurrent of intrigue of which we know nothing. All passed in perfect good humour, indeed there was nothing to differ upon. London is full of the wildest reports: how the cabinet is broken up, Salisbury, Carnarvon, & Northcote are resigned, war is to be declared, &c. &c.

25 June 1877. A long & foolish letter from Loftus, who is as violent against Russia as last year he was willing to believe whatever Gortschakoff told him. He is eager for an expedition, & a display of British force . . .

26 June 1877. To Windsor. The party was for Gen. Grant . . . . . . He is certainly the roughest specimen we have yet had from the west. Any one who had seen him today would have said that his manners & intelligence were about on a par with those of a bulldog. . . . Ly D. tried him also, but got little out of him except his age, which he volunteered to tell, & the fact that he weighed 45 lbs. more than when first made president.

28 June 1877. Meeting of Northcote, Smith, Tenterden, Bourke, and self, to talk over Egyptian tribute question. Northcote is anxious to take over the whole tribute and pay the bondholders out of it, the latter agreeing to a reduction of interest as compensation to the Porte for the sacrifice so made: Tenterden and I dissent on the ground that there is no security for the continued payment by Egypt, and also that the consent of the Porte is not likely to be given. The fact is that Northcote has set his mind on getting hold of Egypt, which I object to, holding that we have land enough: that the acquisition would be to us a source of weakness and not of strength: that India hardly pays its way: that Egypt is an estate already mortgaged to the utmost of what it can bear.

H. of Lords . . . Disraeli was present, which was not expected as he has been laid up with bronchitis since an open-air meeting which he attended on Saturday. But he looks very ill, and his appearance suggest the prospect of an early change of hands. I have begun to make it understood among my colleagues that if he retires I shall go too: which is really my wish and intention: and if from the state of foreign affair I am not able to execute it, the knowledge that I am prepared to retire on the smallest pretext given would enable me to make my own terms

I have no confidence in the party represented by Salisbury and Carnarvon: and altogether conservative politics are assuming too much of a clerical complexion for my taste. Moreover, I do not believe the present cabinet can hold together for a week if the present Premier retired.

29 June 1877. Lawson called: talk with him over the situation, freely and confidentially enough, for he can be trusted, though his ideas are more warlike than mine. He tells me that the *Telegraph* is now selling 240,000 copies a day, which is more than any newspaper has yet done.

30 June 1877. Saw Lawson: he thoroughly friendly, will do all he can to help us.

Made up accounts for the half-year ... Cabinet at Disraeli's private house at 12: we sat till 1.30. The chief business was foreign: on which D. addressed us at length. We were startled by his appearance: it was that of a dying man: pale & ghastly: for the first few minutes he spoke feebly, often putting one word for another & repeating himself a good deal. But as he went on his strength increased: & at the end of our discussion his voice, manner, and whole demeanour were changed: he seemed another person: the excitement of business had worked a cure. He spoke of the state of affairs as grave: the Russian advance seemed unlikely to be seriously opposed: he referred to Andrassy's despatch: did not believe that there is an absolute engagement between Austria & Russia: thought Austria would take a decided line if we did. He dwelt on the great importance of having a decided policy, & not merely drifting, whether into war or peace. Here he threw in a remark which struck me as significant, but imprudent, since it avowed an ulterior object. He said the upper classes & the working classes were united against Russia. The middle classes would always be against a war: but fortunately the middle classes did not now govern. The conclusion to which he led up was less warlike than the exordium appeared to indicate. He recommended three things. 1. that we should induce the Austrian govt to put its understanding with us, now pretty well arrived at, into the form of a protocol 2. that we should send the fleet back to Besica bay 3. that we should take some steps to strengthen the Mediterranean fleet. Much convn followed, with entire agreement as to moving the fleet, & as to the protocol: on the third point, strengthening the naval forces, I reserved my opinion, the more so as we have no details of any sort before us. In the course of a rather desultory discussion, J. Manners said that if Russia were once allowed to go to Constantinople, all was over, both with the govt & the country. The Premier quoted Loftus as a high authority, which led me to fall foul of the said Loftus, & to point out that he had completely changed his opinions within a few weeks: I expressed my belief that very little importance attached to them if they were honest, but also my doubt whether they had not been prompted by a knowledge of the feeling of the court, & wish to make interest there. I have since heard that Ly Ely is supposed to have been the prompter, under the influence of Disraeli himself: but this I did not know at the time. Salisbury believes that Lytton, who is now violently anti-Russian, has been 'got at' in the same way. No objection was taken by anyone to the return of the fleet to Besica – which rather surprised me, but for myself I see no harm in it.

Saw Beust, & proposed the plan of a protocol, as to which he said he would telegraph.

1 July 1877. Letter from old Ld Wilton, saying that he hears the cabinet much blamed for their too pacific attitude towards Russia. I answer it frankly, saying that London society does not represent the views of the constituencies: that those who never really feel the pressure of war taxes are not the best judges of the burdens which a war imposes: that I remember many instances in which the majority of our class wished to interfere in European quarrels but no instance in which the nation agreed with them: & that I do not believe the majority of the public want war with Russia, so long as it is honourably possible to keep out of one.

... News that the Huntingdonshire election[47] is saved, which was hardly thought probable: the numbers were 1468 to 1418...

2 July 1877. Received from Lumley an odd letter, full of reports & rumours as his mostly are: he represents Decazes as in extreme alarm about German projects, & mentions the idea that a German invasion of France & Holland simultaneously is fixed for the autumn.

3 July 1877. Saw Lawson, who says the report about London is, that the sending of the fleet to Besika Bay was the result of a compromise, come to after a stormy discussion, in which the idea of a land expedition also was proposed & abandoned. Anything more unlike the truth can hardly be imagined...

... Disraeli came down, looking very ill, but excited, he said in a significant tone, that we should see great events before long: what he meant was not explained, nor did I choose to ask, but it seemed as if he had hopes of getting us into a war.

4 July 1877. Saw Baron Brincken,[48] & told him (to see how he would take it) that we should certainly keep out of the war. His face lengthened visibly.

... Cabinet at 3, sat till 4.30. All smooth & pleasant, no signs of any difference. The Premier better in health, & less feeble. The subject

---

[47] Lib. vote sharply up; Cons. majority down.
[48] German first secretary.

chiefly discussed was the navy: it was agreed without dispute to reinforce the Mediterranean squadron by 4 ships, which will bring it up to the strength of last year: this force to be drawn from the Channel fleet: the question of making good the deficiency in the latter was deferred. Not a word said as to an expedition: but I feel sure that Disraeli & the Queen have got some plan between them, & shall watch. Cairns is very full of the expediency of establishing a coaling station on a small island called Stampalia. We talk over the matter, but settle nothing. Discussion as to the management of public business in H. of C. which is becoming a troublesome question. The Irish members have succeeded beyond expectation in their obstructive policy, & will be encouraged to carry it farther. We agreed that to pass any resolution limiting the freedom of debate is now impossible: it would only increase the mischief: for the discussion upon it would be carried on for weeks: but there is not the same objection to the appointment of a committee, & this we resolve on.

5 July 1877. My wedding day, & we determine to keep it by going down to Keston, as peace is impossible in London. Rather painfully impressed by the contrast between the calm and happiness of this time seven years ago, & the turmoil of anxiety & excitement in which we live now. But the fault is not with us: there was no fair pretext for refusing office when offered, & probably it will not now last long. As to health, I do not think that mine has suffered: but I feel the mental effect of the life I lead: destroying the power of enjoyment, & reducing existence to a routine of monotonous labour varied only by more distinctly disagreeable sensations. What is worst, much as I dislike it, I am not sure that it will not have unfitted me for a more placid and peaceable way of living: at least for some time.

6 July 1877. Northcote called, to talk over the answer which he is to give as to the fleet going to Besica bay: we settled it between us, & then having leisure talked over other matters. I find he agrees with me that Smith is the fittest successor to Hunt: & he suggested farther, which I was glad of, that F. would be the best man to take Smith's place at the Treasury. He praises E. Stanhope, says he ought to be at the B. of T. in Adderley's place, but Adderley shows jealousy of him & does not like his being employed.

7 July 1877. Cabinet, sat from 3 to 4.30, but chiefly on home affairs: bills to be abandoned, question of when the vote of credit shall be taken (which it was agreed to put off for the present): committee of the Admiralty appointed to sit on the question of the *Inflexible* which has been declared unsafe by Samuda, Reed, & others. Some other affairs, but none of importance. I had no foreign news to give, though much questioned.

8 July 1877. Telegram from Buchanan, not very clear, but the purport of it is that Andrassy will not sign a protocol ... ... Another telegram mentions disturbances being got up on the Dalmatian frontier, which are rather encouraged than checked by the authorities on the Austrian side. All this looks like slippery dealing, to say the least.

9 July 1877. Saw Beust, & received from him an answer to our proposal of a protocol: it is vague, & difficult to understand ... ... He is not exactly unfriendly, but evidently thinks that our plan is to put Austria forward, & screen ourselves behind her: which naturally does not suit him.

... Northcote ... entirely agreed with me as to Smith being the fittest man for the Admiralty. ... I find however a feeling that the Premier would be unlikely to agree to give high promotion to a man like Smith, who is one of the middle-classes, & in business: he has an odd dislike of middle-class men, though they are the strength of our party, & the only reasonable fault that I have heard found with us is that we have not done enough for the borough-members.

We are equally divided in cabinet as between peers & commoners, six of each: one heir to a peerage (J. Manners) & two baronets, making up half the commoners. It does not seem too much to add one to the non-titled class, especially as he replaces Hunt, who is only a small squire, of no great local importance.

As regards property, we are divided into three classes. *Large land-owners* – four – Richmond, Salisbury, Carnarvon, & D. *Middle-sized* (11,000 to 5000 acres) three, Hicks Beach, Northcote, Hardy. *Small or no estates in land*: five. Hunt, Disraeli, Cairns, Cross, & J. Manners. Or, if J. Manners be taken as representing the Rutland estates, which must be his if he lives, we should have, over 10,000 acres, 6 members; over 5000, 2 more; and 4 small.

I hear through the Dean of Windsor, & am sorry to hear, that the Queen refuses to do her confidential business through Ponsonby, to whom she has taken a dislike in consequence of his allowing it to be seen that he does not agree with her in wishing for a war. Her correspondence with the Premier is all kept from him – who keeps it, or who copies the Queen's letters, is not known. I asked Disraeli indirectly if this story was true: he said it was, & that he regretted it, for Ponsonby, though not with us in politics, was a gentleman and could be trusted.

The Dean, who is more intimate than almost anyone with the Queen personally, confirms the reports of Brown being in more extraordinary favour than ever. He is with her alone for two hours nearly every day: he insists on the princes treating him like a gentleman, & shaking hands with him: & when she travels in Germany, his room must always be next hers. Hence the report generally spread abroad that they are secretly married – though on her part it is mere simplicity.

10 July 1877. Wrote ... to pay the Lpool Charity Organisation Socy a donation of £25. Wrote also to invest another £200 in the Improved Industrial Dwellings Co.

... News from the war ... ... The Turkish success in Asia is greater than was at first believed: the Russians falling back almost to the frontier. On the other hand their action on the Danube, or rather inaction, is almost incomprehensible...

11 July 1877. Cabinet at 11 ... Disraeli opened with a rather long, but clear explanation of the position: he reminded us that we had all agreed in principle to a vote of credit, but to that step the parliamentary objections are grave. The vote could be carried but the obstruction & delay that it would produce would lengthen out the session immoderately, & put a stop to all other business. The result desired might be obtained in other ways: by strengthening the garrisons of Malta and Gibraltar, & so having there a force in readiness, near enough to Constantinople or Gallipoli to be used in case of need. He wished to take 5000 men from home to add to them, which he thought would be enough, & this would require no vote at present, since it could be done with the money already voted, though it would probably involve the necessity of a supplementary estimate next year. He referred with high praise to a mem. by F.A. S.[tanley] which not being yet in print, he asked Cairns to read. From this it appears that we have (in round numbers) 104,000 men at home, 60,000 in India, and 25,000 in the colonies: in all 189,000: the largest force, I suppose, that has ever been kept up in time of peace. Disraeli disclaimed any special plan, or intention, as to the use to be made of this force about to be sent off: but only said that we ought to be prepared to meet all emergencies. He also referred to the expectation of Gladstone & Co. that a vote would be asked for, which would give them an opportunity of raising fresh agitation. They would wait for it, & would be disappointed. The entire cabinet agreed without exception, or hesitation, to the new proposal: which I think was felt by many as a relief, for they did not much like the vote of credit, though accepting it as necessary. Much general talk followed on the situation. Hicks Beach and J. Manners were both very warlike, saying that it would be intolerable if the Russians got to Constantinople, & that our position with the country would be fatally compromised. But it was remarked that it is now too late to go to Gallipoli, & if the Turks are beaten, it is not easy to see what is to stop the Russian advance. – Some discussion on cattle plague, which ended our business.

12 July 1877. Lawson called: he tells me that stories are flying about to the effect that the Premier is on the point of resigning, that he has already sent his resignation to the Queen, etc. All fictions, & I said so.

Office ... Saw there Beust, who brings a telegram from Andrassy, not satisfactory, & the less so as it would seem that Buchanan has been talking out of his own head (which is not his habit) without instructions, and in a sense which alarms Andrassy, not unreasonably, lest we should be intending to make the Austrian negotiations public.

... Went over to see Disraeli (who had offered to call on me, but that I would not allow): found him better in health, but uneasy and excited: he said matters were critical: the Russians were advancing in Europe, and there was nothing to stop them. If they got to Constantinople, there would be an outbreak of popular feeling against us, the bulk of the Conservatives would desert us, the Whigs would join, & Gladstone & his friends would say 'if our advice had been taken, all this might have been averted.' The ministry would be upset, & that with ignominy. He dilated on this point with much force and earnestness. The upshot was, he wanted the cabinet to declare that the entrance of the Russian army into Constant. would be a *casus belli*. I asked if he thought the cabinet would agree to this? He thought they would, except Salisbury and Carnarvon: & we could get on without them. I enquired where he would find men, as that was one of our difficulties even now? He answered vaguely but praised the ability of J. Manners (!!) & said that Salisbury is not popular with the party, which I believe is true. We talked on the relative strength of the feeling for & against war: I found him possessed with the idea that a violent anti-Russian agitation is about to break out, & to carry all before it. He said he had good intelligence from agents in various parts. I thought, but did not remind him, that he had been equally certain in 1868, & quite mistaken. The end was, I left him saying that I would go any length in the way of warning Schou. (as indeed I had done already) of the danger of an approach to Constant. – & if such a warning came from the cabinet, it would have more effect than from me personally – but I could not go the length of pledging the country to a war in such an event, & I thought he underrated the strength of the party of peace, who were quiet and silent till seriously alarmed, but had influence if roused, & a secession from the cabinet would rouse them effectually. We talked in a thoroughly friendly style, but did not come to an agreement. Later, I went to the Lds ... Meeting Cairns there, I had a long talk with him ... He went over the same ground as Disraeli, but was more open to reasoning, & to him it was possible to speak, as I did, of a strong conscientious objection to war, whether popular or not, unless its absolute necessity were proved.

13 July 1877. Keston. ... Drove with M ...... Walk in afternoon. ... In the Lds, a division was taken on the retention of clerical fellowships at Oxford: I did not choose to take part in it, & remained here on purpose.

14 July 1877. Beust brought the news, satisfactory as far as it goes, that Andrassy will not admit the idea of an autonomous Bulgaria extending beyond the Balkans. I suggested that as he wishes for a declaration which shall place on record the identity of our ideas on certain points, he should draw up one such as he is prepared to sign: we could then see if the form suited us both. He agreed to telegraph this.

Saw Bourke, & long talk with him: he is less afraid than the Premier & Cairns of an outbreak of anti-Russian feeling, thinking as I do that opinion is divided: & as he is by nature nervous, inclined to be afraid of the H. of C., I am not apt to think he underestimates possible danger.

Home ... ... Found M. who had come up to see Mme Schouvaloff, just arrived in England ...

... In cabinet, we had the best conducted & most orderly discussion that I remember for a long while. Disraeli began by saying that J. Manners had requested that the cabinet should be summoned, & J.M. accordingly opened it. He dwelt on the danger of the situation, ending by saying that if we allowed the Russians to get to Constantinople, we should have betrayed our trust, & humiliated our country. It was evident to me that he was put up by Disraeli as his mouthpiece, for the ideas & almost the words were identical with what I had heard from the latter. Nobody agreed with J.M. – Cairns especially answered him at length, using the arguments which I had employed in talking to him the day before, so that it was clear they had made an impression. He dwelt especially on the Austrian assurance that if Russia got to Constant. she would not be allowed to stay there: & asked with much force if we ought to go to war without an ally for the sake of interfering a little sooner, when by waiting we should have the assistance of the very power most useful to us. Hardy, Northcote, & all who spoke, held language to the same general effect: I followed in the same strain as Cairns. In the end we seemed all of one mind, except Disraeli, who while accepting the suggestion that we should give a friendly warning to Russia, intimated his disappointment that we were not prepared to do more. (I have not noted that J.M. besides wishing to make the occupation of Constant. a casus belli, & to say so publicly, proposed that the fleet should be sent up at once.) We agreed to give the warning, avoiding all threats, & to rest there for the present. So all immediate risk of disunion is averted, but the prospect is not pleasant. I thought the Premier better in health, with more bodily energy than when we met last, but uncomfortable & not in his happiest mind. He has never before been exposed to the annoyance of having to waive or modify his ideas to meet those of his colleagues: in my father's time he settled all with him, & what the two agreed on, the cabinet always accepted. I am afraid also he thinks my attitude ungrateful & unfriendly – though he has never said so. I owe him much, & have backed him to the best of my power, but questions of peace or war must override all merely personal considerations. In the course of our discussion, Salisbury threw out a remark to the effect that Wellesley[49] ought to be removed, not only as being unpopular with the Russian officers, but also, as lying under strong suspicions of corruption. This was new to me, and equally so to the cabinet, all who spoke expressed disbelief: but I have written to Salisbury to know the grounds of his accusation.

16 July 1877. Saw ... Beust, who brought a satisfactory assurance, if one could believe it, to the effect that no understanding or engagement of any kind exists between Austria & Russia. (Schou. on the other hand affirms that there is one, saying that he speaks from his own knowledge, that it is in writing, & that he has seen the text.)

... Obtained for Holmes, later our consul in Bosnia, the honour of knighthood. He is nearly the best man we have: I meant him for the new appointment in Bulgaria: but ill health has obliged him to retire from the service.

Disraeli ... says the Queen is in her most excited state, accuses her ministers of having deceived her, wishes us to threaten Russia with immediate war, &c. In fact he said she talked so wildly that he was obliged to remind her that it might not be possible for her to find advisers who would be responsible for the things she wished done. She sent three messengers after him to Buckhurst on Sunday, besides telegrams. She complained to him that anxiety was breaking down her health. In short, she is in her most difficult mood to deal with.

17 July 1877. Cabinet at 11. Long discussion on strengthening Mediterranean garrisons but the notion was dropped, or at least so far as that nothing was decided upon it, & I do not think anything will be. Our idea had been that men sent forward to Malta or Gibraltar would be more easily available for service at Constantinople if required than if they remained in England: the W.O. however does not take that view, arguing that they cannot be moved on without transport, that ships for the purpose can only be chartered in England, & that to keep them waiting in the Mediterranean would be enormously costly, besides attracting attention, & giving needless publicity to the whole affair. They say too that for men, & still more for horses, Malta & Gibraltar in summer are the worst possible quarters: & on the whole they are all against it. So matters will end in our doing nothing: which is probably the wisest conclusion. My draft warning Russia of the danger of an occupation of Constantinople was read, & altered in some respects. Some small home affairs were talked over: we sat two hours. All in perfect good humour, except that J. Manners is dissatisfied that we

[49] Mil. attaché in Russia.

don't go further. Disraeli seemed quite recovered, well in health and cheerful.

Saw ... Schou. to whom I read the paper settled in cabinet, and left it with him. We had afterwards a long and friendly talk: in the course of which I tried to persuade him that the Premier does not in reality wish for a war: in that he agreed, but thought that Ld B. was anxious for the glory of a spirited policy, and wished to take the credit of having prevented Russia from doing many things which she never meant to do. This ingenious criticism had so much truth in it that I hardly knew what to answer: but dwelt on Ld B.'s age & health, on his ambition being satisfied, & asked what possible reason he could have for running risks & following an adventurous line of conduct? I also explained to him how if capital were to be made out of a cry against Russia, the opposition would take it up: however little consistent with their former professions. This was new, & produced an effect. I dwelt on the strength of the war-feeling in England: how our most popular ministers, Pitt, Palmerston, &c. were those who had most gratified this sentiment. I could not undertake to explain the matter, peace being our strongest interest: but so it was. This also I thought was understood. On the whole, the interview passed off as little unpleasantly as could be expected.

... Talk ... with Disraeli, who just returned from Windsor: he thinks he has quieted the royal mind, but with great trouble, & 'if the volcano breaks out again, he does not know what he shall do.'

...We were beaten last night in H. of C. by 156 to 152, on a question of patronage. The head of the stationery office, a Mr Pigott, just appointed, is a clerk in the War Office, & son of the parson of Hughenden. This last circumstance probably led to the selection being considered a job ... ... I believe that the vote would not have been carried, but for the unpleasant impression caused by the appointments of Ld Hampton[50] & Sir S. Fitzgerald:[51] the first being too old for new work, & the latter suspected of corruption. These selections did harm at the time, & have not been forgotten.

19 July 1877. To H. of Lds, where the Premier made a statement relative to the appointment of Mr Pigott. He was ill, & nervous when he began, so much so that he told me afterwards that when he rose the whole of what he meant to say had passed out of his mind: but he rallied & made an excellent defence. ... I had not thought well of it, & was relieved at the completeness of the defence. ... Why Northcote did not state the facts I cannot conceive: possibly he did not know them: they would undoubtedly have turned the division.

[50] Formerly Sir John Pakington; chief civil service commr (£2000 p.a.) 1875–80.
[51] Charity commr.

20 July 1877. M. drove over to see Darwin at his house at Downe, & came back much entertained ... ... The quiet, rest, & comfort of Keston are to me a pleasure beyond any other, in the turmoil of office life: I could not get through the work without some such place of retirement.

21 July 1877. Letters & papers till 11, when to cabinet. We sat exactly 2 hours. Saw ... Beust, who had as yet nothing from Andrassy: (is all this delay intentional? I suspect it.) ...

... The Irish got up another scene ... ... I do not remember, in 30 years of political life, a time when the reputation of the H. of C. was as low as it is now. The debates have almost ceased to be reported, the public not caring to read them, & they are not the talk of society as they used to be. It is an unlucky change.

... Telegrams are full of details, real or alleged, of Russian 'atrocities' part no doubt invented or improved upon by the Turks ... but there is some truth at the bottom of it, and it is amusing to see the journals which in 1876 screamed the loudest, now discovering that all such reports, in time of war, must be received with caution, and so forth.

... The cabinet of today was interesting as well as long. We began with an Indian scheme, for separating the Trans-Indus provinces from the rest. I did not much like the idea of creating a province 1200 miles long, and scarcely 40 miles in average width: nor have I much confidence in the judgement of Lytton, who is author of the scheme: I therefore pressed Salisbury to have the opinions of the Council taken before acting, so that if they are over-ruled, they may at least have been heard. Northcote joined me,& the scheme stands over. Another plan for arranging some method of deciding fairly what expenses should be charged to India, & what to England, was talked over, but nothing settled. It is very necessary, for all is now in confusion. – I had the consent of the cabinet to the appointment of a commission on the extradition question, which is drifting into an awkward condition. – We then went back to the old subject, the strengthening of the Mediterranean garrisons, which was agreed to, the number of men not exceeding 3000. A very general and free discussion ensued on the whole question: in which opinions were expressed with less reserve than they have yet been. J. Manners is thoroughly dissatisfied & inclined to resign: he says that the approach of the Russians to Constant. ought to be a casus belli. In this view he stands alone: next to him the most warlike among us is the Premier, who says that if they cannot be got out otherwise, he would be prepared to go to war without an ally. On the other side, Cross & Salisbury both said plainly that we are pledged not to allow them to stay: & Salisbury, to my surprise, added that he would be ready to send the fleet up, if the Porte invited us, and that Russia could not be allowed to fortify the position. Carnarvon dissented, looking intensely miserable. Cairns, Hardy, and I argued that it was impossible now to prevent a Russian advance to the capital, if our warnings did not have that effect: we could not interfere by force till too late. We thought that a temporary occupn could not create a casus belli: but that the apparent intention to hold the place would do so. Salisbury's plan of sending up the fleet now was opposed by Hardy and myself on the ground of danger, if Gallipoli should be occupied and its retreat cut off.

Eastern affairs being exhausted, we considered a memorial to the Queen from 40,000 persons, clergy and laity, against the Public Worship Act. The memorialists demand that the Act shall not be put in force, and that the whole question shall be left to Convocation. It was agreed, without difference, that the Queen should be advised not to receive this document, as it calls upon her to do what is beyond her legal power.

24 July 1877. By rail to Witley...met Hale at the station, with him to Haslemere, & thence a long drive, through wild picturesque country, up to the new estate of 90 acres bought in the spring. A strangely remote spot it is out of the way of everything & everybody. ... The peasantry of western Surrey are better looking & better mannered than those I meet with elsewhere: they talk with no accent, & there is a marked absence of the loutish vulgarity so common in England. ... Home by 6...

26 July 1877. Cabinet at 11, mainly on the parliamentary trouble of yesterday. Salisbury was at Osborne ... ... After an hour and a half of discussion, in which some proposals of the Speaker were considered & rejected, we came to two resolutions, which it was agreed should be at once communicated to Hartington & his friends, that they may act with us, which they wish to do. They will mitigate the evil, but not cure it, & indeed I do not see how that is to be done. As the Irish tactics have succeeded, they will be repeated next year on a larger scale ... ... Nothing will be a check upon them except the continental plan of '*la clôture*' ... & that is a power which may be used very oppressively to the minority. But it may be the lesser of two evils.

... Salisbury just returned from Osborne, is unpleasantly impressed with the state of the Queen. She talked to him very eagerly & excitedly, & as he says using much gesticulation, which is quite contrary to her habits. I can see that he thinks her excitement may go further.

28 July 1877. Cabinet at 11: we sat full two hours: the meeting was the least orderly of any I remember in this govt: everybody talking at once: the Premier not in the best of humours: a great determination that for the sake of appearances something must be done, nobody knowing what nor seeming much to care, so long as we avoid the blame of inactivity. In the end we agreed to telegraph to Layard that he may sound the Sultan as to the terms on which he will make peace: that he is also to ascertain what batteries there are at or near Gallipoli, and whether care will be taken to disarm them, to remove or destroy the guns, lest they should fall into the hands of the Russians, in which case they will be equally dangerous to the English fleet, if it should go up to Constantinople, and to the Turkish. A hint was added that we might be willing to take possession of them for a consideration, or to help in their removal. We also agreed on a memorandum, or note, to be given to Schouvaloff, thanking the Emperor for his friendly assurances, lately sent through Wellesley, expressing our wish for peace, & adding that if disorder or disturbance at Constant. should induce us to send up the fleet, it was not to be considered as a demonstration against Russia. While assenting to this in cabinet, I added a warning that I decline to pledge myself to agree to this step, though not denying that under some possible circumstances it might become necessary: Disraeli, Cairns, & Hicks Beach made no secret of their wish and intention that the fleet should go up if any reason could be found for its going. Hardy laid before us a plan of the W.O. for occupying a point on the Asiatic side called Chanak, I think: the old idea of the expedition revived in a new form.

I left this cabinet with more uneasy and unpleasant sensations than I have yet experienced in these transactions: the war fever is clearly getting hold of my colleagues, and they have the excuse that it prevails strongly in the party generally, and in H. of C. – Even Salisbury seems in part gained over. It would be strange, after all that has passed, if I were the sole seceder on a question of war or peace. – I ought to have noted that Layard telegraphs as to the risk of disorder and massacre in Constantinople, which might be a reason, & certainly could be used as a pretext, for sending the fleet up. But Layard is eager for armed intervention by England: and I think that with this object he magnifies the danger.

In the afternoon I received a very wild telegram from the Queen, urging the immediate seizure of Gallipoli, and clearly showing an excited state of mind. The Premier goes down to Osborne, which will not tend to quiet her.

29 July 1877. Selected 12 names to compete for the vacant clerkship in F.O. Made some rearrangements & promotions in the consular service.

30 July 1877. Saw Lawson, who as before is anxious that we should occupy Gallipoli. He could not give me any definite reason, except that we should be able, holding it, to speak with more authority.

... Cabinet at 3, where a discussion on eastern affairs, the least satisfactory that we have yet had. Hardy proposed a scheme for occupying a point on the Asiatic side of the Dardanelles, but not for immediate acceptance. I was much pressed to send Layard a telegram desiring him to invite the British fleet at once to Constantinople. Cairns drew it, very artfully, so that to the Sultan it should seem to suggest the probability of assistance, while to England it would be represented as merely a step taken for the prevention of disorder and massacre. I objected, being alone, except for some partial support from Carnarvon. My reasons were, that there was nothing in the state of Constantinople to justify such a step: that it ought not to be taken except in case of clear necessity: that it would alarm Europe without necessity, that it would create expectations which we did not intend to realise, excite the jealousy of other Powers, & risk a quarrel with Russia. In point of fact, the thing is proposed only to lay the ground for a subsequent seizure of the Dardanelles, on the plea that they will be necessary for the safety of the fleet: partly also to have an appearance of activity, & so satisfy the public. After much debate, but all friendly in tone, I asked for time to consider, & another cabinet tomorrow: which was agreed to.

I had a long conversation with Carnarvon afterwards, satisfactory as showing that we are not much apart in ideas. He undertook to speak to Salisbury who of late has turned round, & is now rather inclined to war measures. Of all the cabinet, Hicks Beach & J. Manners are the most pugnacious: the Premier does not greatly differ from them: Carnarvon & I are now the most peaceable: Northcote & Cross rather on the same side, but less decidedly: of Salisbury I have written above: Cairns is restlessly eager for something popular to be done, & Richmond follows him with a blind devotion, which is perhaps not unreasonable, for Cairns has ability for both, & the Duke's concurrence gives him additional weight. On the whole the attitude of the cabinet is more pugnacious than it was a few weeks ago: it is just however to note that feeling out-of-doors has changed in the same direction, & my colleagues are rather following than leading the popular impulse.

News this morning of Ward Hunt's[52] death: he will be regretted by both political friends & opponents: a kindly, frank, good-humoured, and sensible country gentleman: a fair administrator: as a speaker he was unequal, sometimes effective from his very simplicity & directness of mind, capable of being roused into an energetic defence, but wanting tact and skill to handle a delicate question safely. We were prepared for his loss politically, but scarcely for his death. He was only 52, but enormous in size and bulk, and a great eater: a man for whom outdoor life was almost necessary: I believe office killed him.

31 July 1877. Carnarvon called early, & we discussed the line to be taken in cabinet. We agreed that to object to any telegram being sent

[52] First Lord of the Admiralty, d. 30 July.

would be peremptory & abrupt, & would place us in a false position if the matter ended in resignation: since Layard has described the state of Constantinople as dangerous, & circumstances might make it really desirable that the fleet should go up. At the same time we were determined not to put the question in such a position as to give countenance to the plan of the Premier & the Chancellor: which obviously is (indeed they do not deny it) to get the fleet past the Dardanelles on a pretext of humanity & the defence of order, & then to seize the batteries that command the strait lest a Russian force should get hold of them. I drafted a telegram accordingly, asking Layard to sound the Sultan as to his willingness to invite the fleet up in the event of imminent danger to the European population, and on the clear understanding that an attitude of neutrality is maintained. These two provisos arc a sufficient safeguard: the first reserves the question whether the fleet shall go up, for later discussion: the second makes it improbable in the highest degree that the necessary invitation will be given.

At 2 the cabinet met and sat till nearly 4. I proposed to substitute my draft for that which I had been nearly alone in resisting at our meeting yesterday: and after the sharpest struggle I ever had on any political question, succeeded in carrying my point. Carnarvon backed me up steadily: one or two others were shaken, but in the main I had all the fighting to do. J. Manners & Hicks Beach were violent for action. Northcote gave a hesitating opinion which I could not well understand. Disraeli said little, & the little he said was in perfectly good temper. I did not in so many words threaten to resign if beaten, thinking menaces of that kind to be in bad taste, but I let it be seen clearly that I did not mean to be overruled in my own department. In the end my draft was taken, with a slight alteration by Cairns, which I accepted as being harmless, in order to take off the appearance of excessive stiffness.

Salisbury, whose objection is not so much to fighting without necessity, as to fighting in favour of the Turk, surprised the cabinet both today and yesterday by a strong expression of opinion that we ought to go up without asking leave of the Porte – which in other words is to make war without declaring it. This view however was not taken by anyone else. On the whole, I count this day as a victory, but the scheme defeated in one form is sure to turn up again in another, and I move, as it were, with my resignation in my hands.

1 August 1877. Saw Drage, he thinks me well though I do not feel as if I were so.

... News, which first appeared in the papers, but subsequently confirmed by a telegram from Bucharest, of a serious defeat of the

Russians near Plevna. Mansfield calls it 'crushing' and other accounts say that three divisions were destroyed. ... Letter from Wellesley ... ... The conduct of the Bulgarians has been such that the Turkish villages ask for a guard of Cossacks to protect them. The Russian soldiers have the lowest opinion of the Bulgarians, & express it freely.

2 August 1877. Saw Lawson, & told him what news I had. Letter from Reeve, with an interesting enclosure from Thiers, in which the latter deprecates our taking Egypt, which he has heard we intend. ... In all this I entirely agree, & have told Reeve so.

Wellesley telegraphs that it is likely the Russians will have to retire north of the Balkans, in consequence of their defeat, which will render a second campaign inevitable. He, Wellesley, is coming home with a secret communication from the Emperor, the nature of which I do not know.

Layard telegraphs that there is no present danger of disturbance at Constantinople and that he thinks it therefore better to say nothing about the fleet going up.

... Cabinet at 2: we sat only about an hour, and with little result: the Premier in high spirits, perhaps at the Turkish success, but I suspect he has some new scheme in his head. He is anxious for a debate, and to speak: in which case something imprudent and dangerous is sure to be said. His fear is lest England would seem not to be playing so conspicuous a part in this affair as some other states: lest our position should be secondary: and I am bound to say that I see this feeling strong in many other people. To me it is not a very intelligible one: as long as our own interests are not touched, why should not foreigners settle their own affairs in their own way?

4 August 1877. The Russian defeat does not lose in importance when details are known ... ... The Russians are now in the position of the American federals after Bull's Run: unexpectedly beaten, & furious accordingly. In the one case as in the other, it is only a question of time: the superior force must win in the long run.

Despatches from Paget, interesting enough, showing what the Italian game really is. The ministry are alarmed & excited at the notion of Austria annexing Bosnian territory: not that they want it for themselves, but that this annexation if accomplished connects the long Dalmatian seaboard with the rest of the empire, & thus destroys whatever hope of securing it the cabinet of Rome may have entertained. They threaten agitation about the Trentino, are buying up horses, & preparing to arm.

It is worth notice that the German ambassador at Rome has been pressing on Paget in the strongest manner the expediency of seizing Egypt. Evidently this language, which is held by German representatives at every European court, is held by order of Bismarck, whose plans would be materially helped by such a proceeding on our part. In the first place, it would stop our mouths as to annexations elsewhere, & make us accomplices with Russia: in the next place, it would lock up an English force sufficient to weaken us as a military power: thirdly, & most important for his purpose, it would prevent the existence of a good understanding between England & France for the next dozen years. His eagerness on the subject has been useful, for it puts us on our guard: though for my part, I never thought Egypt, encumbered as it now is, a possession worth having.

5 August 1877. Much speculation in the papers as to the vacant Admiralty: the three candidates chiefly named are J. Manners, whom nobody approves of, but who is thought likely to find favour in the eyes of the Premier: Smith, whom I think the best choice, but there may be jealousy in some quarters of so great promotion: & Hicks Beach, of whom personally I have not a high opinion as regards judgment, but he has managed Irish affairs well, & is not incapable. He is besides in favour with Disraeli (& I suppose with the Queen also) as one of the most eager supporters of a war-policy.

Gladstone has written me a singular letter, intended for the cabinet, and suggesting that somebody should be sent out to examine into the truth of the alleged Russian 'atrocities'. I refer this to my colleagues, but I do not see that it is especially the business of the English govt to verify or disprove these stories.

Bad news of the expected famine in southern India ... millions will starve. ... The financial difficulties of India have long been foreseen by those who watched the course of events: they are beginning sooner than most people expected: & who will see the end?

6 August 1877. Saw ... Schouvaloff. ... He saw M. also, & to her expressed alarm as to the Emperor's state of mind. His religious & humanitarian feelings have been strongly appealed to, & he is now according to the Ambassador, in a very excited & *exalté* condition, talking of his divine mission, & so forth.

Saw Lyons, & opened upon him at once as to Egypt: (I know that he half persuaded Northcote that we ought to take it): I argued against the acquisition. He did not much dissent from what I said, but observed that we should be in a foolish situation if there were a partition, and England got nothing. I thought this a very diplomatic view: it comes to saying, 'It is better to acquire by questionable means, a property which you don't want, and which will be a loss to you, than to have it said that you have been outwitted.' Ld L. himself saw it so, and said 'This is the point of view from which we learn to look at things!'

Saw Wellesley, but his communication from the Emperor is only what we knew before. He will accept the terms of peace which Schou. brought over on his return from Russia. I suspect that the Emperor, or the people about him, wanted to get rid of Wellesley civilly while the present operations are in progress, and that this negotiation is only a pretext. Else it is unintelligible.

... Disraeli tells me that he has suggested Smith to the Queen, who does not like the choice, but will probably give way.

7 August 1877. Office ... ... The chief subject discussed was the alleged intention of sending the fleet up to Constantinople, which though abandoned, or rather never adopted by the cabinet, has got into the newspapers as a report both here & at Constantinople. I contradicted it, as I could with truth, while not caring to deny that the possibility of such a step being necessary in certain emergencies had been discussed. The French govt. as I gathered, was especially sore at the idea of their not having been consulted. But as they tell the Russians whatever they happen to hear, they can scarcely expect to be in our counsels also.

... Some talk with the Premier. He has carried his point as to Smith, & tells me that the place vacated by Smith must be offered, as he thinks, either to Massey Lopez[53] or to F.[54] – He is anxious & nervous about a debate which Lds Feversham[55] & Strathnairn want to bring on, raising the whole eastern question ... ... He thinks Opposition will take it up. I console him by saying that all the peers are gone, except about a dozen, & there will be nobody either to attack or defend us.

8 August 1877. Cabinet at 11 sat till 12.30. The appointment of Smith was announced & gave general satisfaction. We talked rather at random, about Austria, Greece, & the east generally: Disraeli rather inclined to press a defensive alliance with Austria, & Cairns backed him: but neither seemed to see, or were willing to admit, what such an alliance implies. It would bind us to help in defending Austria against Germany & Russia: in other words France, England, & Austria would be on one side, Russia, Germany, & Italy on the other. It is not worth while for any advantage we can get out of Austrian support to compromise our independence of action in a transaction of this kind. It would be in fact, though not so intended, a Catholic alliance which England would join. I put this to the cabinet & thought it seemed to make an impression.

We agreed to appeal to Ld Feversham to give up his speech, & if he refuses, we shall decline discussion, & say as little as possible. He is a weak harmless man with a good voice & a love for rhetorical display, put up in the present instance by old Strathnairn. Having received a

[53] Sir L. Massey Lopes (1818–1908), Cons. M.P.; civil lord of admiralty 1874–80; advocated reducing burdens on agriculture.
[54] Diarist's bro.
[55] William Duncombe, 3rd Baron Feversham (1829–1915), cr. earl July 1868.

message from Ld Granville asking what is intended (he is at Walmer & does not want to come up) I wrote to him to say what we had done.

Cairns talked of the necessity of new judges: which he regrets, but there is no help: they are not enough for the work. No one dissented, Cross & I approved, for there are great complaints in Lancashire.

Office ... ... Saw Wellesley, & arranged for his going back: drafted a mem. which he is to take with him, & sent it to the Premier. ... Heard on coming home that Ld Feversham withdraws his notice.

10 August 1877. Cabinet at 11, sat till near 1, setting the speech, which was done without any material disagreement. I had supplied the F.O. paragraphs which D. adopted nearly as drafted by me, & they were as free from controversial matter as they well could be.

Read my instructions for Wellesley, which were agreed to. ... Saw ... Bourke, whom I complimented on having got through the session: & indeed he has been more catechised than any under-secretary in my recollection. He has got through his questions well (to be sure they have always been answered for him in the office, the answers drawn out on paper, & sent to me for approval): as a speaker he has not absolutely failed, but in the department I have not found him of much use. He is however willing enough, & popular in parliament.

Very weary...the pressure of business has not been excessive, but I have been all day nervously exhausted and depressed.

11 August 1877. Heard of my brother's appointment to the vacant post at the Treasury, which I am glad of for his sake and that of his family, since it shows that Disraeli & Northcote really think well of him as an administrator. There is too much work in that place, & work of a kind which cannot be neglected or mismanaged without immediate inconvenience, for the appointment to be a job. He has now got a fair start, & if his health lasts, will probably be a secretary of state before he dies.

... The session is now virtually over, & the cabinet may think itself lucky. We have passed through four sessions, without one serious check or defeat, without open discontent in the party ... & on the whole in as strong and safe a position as any ministry can expect. For one section of the public we have not been Russian enough: for another, not sufficiently combative: but both these sections are small ... & we have the support of so large a body of the opposition as to make any concerted attack upon us impossible. We have been more Turkish than Russian in our diplomacy, but not much of either ... In all these respects we have, I believe, represented the feeling of the great majority of those who interest themselves at all in public affairs: though if a general election were to take place, I would not answer for the possible strength of a war-cry among the masses. As to home politics there have simply been none. Nobody has talked, written, or thought about anything except the war. In the Lords Disraeli has spoken very seldom, but with all his former ability. His defence of himself in the Pigott business was masterly ... He has been, I think, restrained from speaking on foreign affairs by a doubt how far his colleagues were prepared to go with him, and his reserve in that respect has done more good than harm.

... Within the cabinet, nothing is altered, except the loss of poor Hunt, and the succession of Smith to his place: an experiment which I advised, & think the best that could have been made, but an experiment nevertheless.

Disraeli varies in health, but there seems no reason why he should retire. He is not personally hard-worked, for he leaves the departments to do their own work in their own way: he likes society, & is liked by it: with the people in general he is rather popular than the reserve, as far as one can judge: and certainly he manages the Queen better than anyone else could do it.

12 August 1877. Reading for cabinet tomorrow a minute by Ld Lytton, as to policy on the N.W. frontier: very wild & dangerous as it seems to me.

13 August 1877. Free and open talk with Gennadius, as to prospects of Greece, & drove him to admit that what the cabinet of Athens really wants is an extension of territory. That is a question which involves the partition of the Turkish empire & which I am not prepared to discuss.

... Cabinet at 5.30, sat till near 7. We discussed chiefly Lytton's singular minute as to foreign policy, which involves intrigues with the Turcoman tribes, subsidies to Persia, & probably the occupation of Afghanistan. The feeling against embarking on adventures of this kind was unanimous, & we had no trouble as to the answer. Smith sat in cabinet for the first time.

14 August 1877. Cabinet at 3, sat till 4.30. No special business dealt with, but much general talk over the situation. The Premier (who seems very ill, & complains that he cannot sleep) held language that alarmed me, especially as it seemed to be intended as a reassertion of all the opinions which he seemed to have waived in deference to his colleagues. We should be disgraced, he said, if we did not interfere effectually to prevent a second campaign. England would not keep her position in Europe, if she did not take a leading part in the settlement. There was more to the same effect, not calling for reply or instant action, but enough to lead me to say that I thought the Turkish empire would survive the cabinet. The fact is that we differ not about means, but ends. The Premier sincerely and really believes that it will be better for us to risk a great war, & to spend £100,000,000 upon it, than not to appear to have had a large share in the decision come to when peace is made. Most continental statesmen would agree with him, & a considerable section of the English public. I do not think *prestige* worth buying so dear, & I feel sure that the majority are on that side.

My draft answer to Andrassy's last despatch was read by Northcote (I had no voice to read with) and agreed to: the cabinet evidently believing as I do that the Austrian policy is not sincere, & that the understanding between Vienna and Petersburgh is closer than we are allowed to know. It was settled that we should meet early & often during the holidays. Left London by 5.40 train ... weary enough, & not well with cold in the head & general weakness.[56]

15 August 1877. Very weak & indisposed to exertion, the result partly of a heavy cold, disturbing sleep &c. partly of the work & worry of the last few weeks. Messengers came, bringing 15 or 16 boxes...

16 August 1877. Sleep sound, & woke feeling comparatively well, though still weak and indisposed to active exertion. ... Wrote to Gladstone ... ... He proposed that Baring should be sent out again to report on 'atrocities' in Bulgaria & elsewhere. This we had agreed to decline, & I explained briefly the reasons why we did so.

Wrote also a minute on proposed extensions of the colony of S. Leone, which may become inevitable, but which I shall resist while the matter is in doubt. The object is, to put an end to smuggling. The expenses of the colony have grown of late years. Duties have been raised, & traders have left the settlement to establish themselves in the rivers beyond it, preferring insecurity & freedom to British protection & high duties. It is now sought to extend the jurisdiction of the colony – & the duties – to these rivers: which is in reality more like blockading the coast than opening it to trade: just what we complain of the Portuguese for doing. But it is contended on the other hand that the system which I objected to has been in force for 50 years, & that what is now suggested is only carrying it a little further.

17 August 1877. Unwell all morning with pain in stomach, as if from violent indigestion, but there is no cause for it that I know. Better by noon, but still very weak.

... Wrote to Carnarvon about the new Spanish tariff, which is so framed as to exclude England...

18 August 1877. I am vexed to find how little in my present state of mind & body I can enjoy the beauty and quiet of this place, which always hitherto has been a constant source of pleasure. ... Fatigue, anxiety, & worry have made me feel quite indifferent to and incapable

[56] Derby was at Fairhill, the remoter of his two Kentish properties, 14 Aug.–3 Sept., apart from going to London and office, 22, 27, 29 Aug. He returned to London, 3–4 Sept., working at office, leaving late on 4 Sept. to Knowsley with Sanderson. He saw Schouvaloff on 14, 22, 29 Aug. and 4 Sept. He had no guests, and was not a guest elsewhere, in this period, his only visitors in the country being Morier, and Lord Arthur Russell, a Kentish neighbour.

of enjoyment. .... Messenger brought, I think, 11 boxes...

... An excursion party of 1400 workingmen came to see Hawarden, and ... would not be satisfied unless they saw the master of the house also, Instead of either refusing civilly as most people would have done or saying a few civil words to them from his hall door...he announced to them that he was going with his son to cut down a tree, and that they might come and see him if they liked. This they chose to do, and crowded round him, sometimes singing, sometimes indulging in a little friendly chaff at the expense of their host, while the former prime minister was exhibiting himself in the character of an amateur workman. From Gladstone's oddity and his want of knowledge of what is called the world, one may doubt whether he quite saw the construction which was sure to be put on his proceedings: to the ordinary English mind they appear like a singularly vulgar and undignified bid for popularity: and accordingly I notice that the journals most in his interest say least about the matter.

19 August 1877. Still not very well ...... This is the quietest and idlest day that I have passed for many months – I think, since the last parliamentary session began.

... The distinctively socialistic idea that it is the business of the State to provide employment for the labourer, has for the first time shown itself in action in the States.[57] ... All over the world, the masses will ask 'What is the good of having votes, if we are not to use them for the advantage of our class?' & it is on the cards that we may see a social war of strikes & lockouts such as England has not yet witnessed.

21 August 1877. Morier came to see Ly D. & passed the afternoon here. – I had but little conversation with him, & that exclusively on African affairs. As his manner is, he has taken up vehemently the Portuguese side of the Congo controversy: which opinion being known at Lisbon, will make his position there comfortable. But I listen carefully to what he says, for though an intriguer, he is shrewd & able.

Gladstone has made two more speeches to large parties of excursionists who have come to visit him at Hawarden: a kind of canvassing which is new in this country. He said nothing especially significant, but it is evident that he is throwing himself on the workingmen, having given up Whigs & country gentlemen as not likely to accept his way of thinking.

Disposed today of 22 boxes, some very heavy.

26 August 1877. Much speculation as to the possibility of securing Holwood, but we shall know nothing, probably, for a long while, the owner not being in the habit of making up his mind quickly. Personally, I am content as things are: Keston gives us the benefit of Holwood

[57] Comment evoked by U.S. railway strikes.

park, & our home here is comfortable: but there is the chance that if not secured Holwood may be cut up for villas: it is a possession which will always retain its value, & probably increase it: few places so near London have equal attraction: a certain historical interest attaches to it as the residence of Pitt: and to Ly D. & myself it has associations which cannot be transferred to any other spot.[58]

27 *August 1877.* Saw[59]... Musurus, who asked about the Greek preparations for the war: I promised to say what we could to dissuade the cabinet of Athens from war, but it will be of no avail; I also warned him against Servian designs: it is nearly certain that a new war is intended in that quarter.

Saw the new minister from Hawaii, who is come about a commercial treaty with England; his govt has been overpersuaded into making one with the U.S. which establishes that country as a kind of protector of the islands: we object, and the object of the mission is to reconcile us as far as may be to the exclusive advantages which the Americans have acquired.

28 *August 1877.* Working quietly on West African & other papers. There is a controversy between the Col. Office, Treasury & F.O. as to the manner of dealing with the colony of S. Leone. It is nearly bankrupt, having a comparatively large yearly deficit. Increased expenses have been met by raising customs duties, till the trade has been driven away into the adjoining rivers, outside British territory: & the remedy suggested by the colonial authorities is to annex these for customs purposes, by treaty with the native chiefs. To this plan I object, thinking...the true remedy lies in another direction: lowering duties again, making up the deficit by a vote in aid, & so drawing trade to the settlement as has been done at Hongkong & Singapore. My view was already expressed in a minute (Aug. 15): & is confirmed by Lingen[60] of the Treasury: Northcote & F.S.[61] both agreeing. I send the papers on to Carnarvon.

[58] Purchase of Holwood on reversion agreed, 20 Oct., and contract signed, 26 Nov. 1877. Negotiations for this purchase preoccupied Derby during the August vacation.

[59] Diplomatic routine did not stop entirely during the August vacation. On 22 Aug., Derby saw at the F.O. Lawson, Menabrea, Musurus, Harcourt, Münster, the Austrian chargé d'affaires ('I forget his name') who 'came only for news and brought none'; and Schouvaloff, calmly confident that Russia superiority would eventually tell. The U.K. consul-gen. at Hawaii called to discuss the Hawaiian commercial treaty with the U.S.; and the new Liberian minister (who sought an invitation to Balmoral) was formally received. Derby also worked routinely at Fairhill: on 23 Aug. 12 boxes were sent off, the same number on the 24th. On the 25th, 13 boxes came: 'nothing of any interest in any of them'. On the 26th, Derby sent off 8 boxes, on the 28th 15, on the 30th 15 boxes ('a quiet easy day'), on the 31st 18 boxes, on 1 Sept. 15 boxes, on 2 Sept. (Sunday) 4 boxes ('no important news of any kind').

[60] R. Lingen, 1st Baron Lingen (1818–1905), perm. sec. to treasury 1869–85).

[61] F. Stanley, fin. sec. to treasury 1877–8.

Russell writes that Bismarck is exultant at the scrape into which the Russians have got themselves, & does not by any means incline to help them out of it.

29 August 1877. Saw ... Schouvaloff ... ... He did not conceal his dissatisfaction at the turn which affairs have taken, which will give a revolutionary character to the war.

... Talk with the Austrian about Servia. – Andrassy is shuffling as usual in this business. One word from him would stop the Servians from joining in the fight, but he does not choose to speak it, & professes not to believe in their warlike intentions, though that is a matter on which nobody else in Europe has a doubt.

30 August 1877. Fell in with a hop-picker ... who said he was 79 ... ... He did not beg, but accepted half-a-crown with thanks, & wished that 'I might never be in want of a shilling'. In these days of revolution, who knows?

31 August 1877. Woke with exactly the same sensations as a fortnight ago, as if poisoned, but I know no reason for it ... Great weakness, and incapacity for exertion of mind or body. ... Disposed, somehow, of eighteen boxes, but I have little recollection of what was in them.

1 September 1877. Nearly well again: but I shall require to live carefully for some time to come. ... The prestige of the Russian army is greatly affected. They may and probably will win by force of numbers; but they have shown themselves weaker and less efficient than anybody supposed. No wonder that Bismarck is satisfied.

2 September 1877. Another long speech from Gladstone, addressed to a party of excursionists, as appears to be his custom. ... Began to make notes for a speech ... as to which I feel needlessly & foolishly uncomfortable, for there is nothing specifically alarming in the occasion ... ... But disturbed health makes weak nerves,& just now there is nothing else to distract attention.

3 September 1877. London ... ... I leave Fairhill with regret, which is natural, for only there & at Keston is complete freedom from disturbance possible to me: & also with a feeling of vague despondency, which I can less explain or account for: unless health is the cause. ... Arranged with Sanderson for some changes in the consular service ...

4 September 1877. ... Office at 1.30, stayed till 3. Saw there Lister and Pauncefote, also Schouvaloff by appointment. Left at 3; early dinner at the club: home: and by 5 p.m. train from Euston to Knowsley, arriving about 10.30. Sanderson travelled with me.

5 September 1877. Knowsley: where I should much enjoy being, but for the discomfort of speeches tomorrow, which have got on my nerves more than I can explain or justify to myself.

... Receive from Moult an accurate statement of the acreage of these estates, which is (as I always thought) considerably more than the printed return makes it: 66,500 acres nearly...

... Mr Lee or Mr Nightingale ... called with a reporter, & I dictated to them such parts of my speeches of tomorrow as are likely to interest the London papers.

6 September 1877. Short walk with F. ... Set off with him & Sanderson to L.pool. ... Luncheon there with the Mayor ... Thence to the open space by St George's Hall: F. & Sanderson in my carriage ...: the crowd greater & thicker than ever I saw, it seemed as if the whole population was out in the streets: most of them of the poorest class, many ragged, but in the highest good humour, cheering, shouting, & laughing. There was no disorder, & I did not see one drunken man, nor did others to whom I put the question. The ceremony of presenting addresses to the Mayor, & declaring the new gallery open,[62] is described in the papers. ... From the high platform where we stood, the sight of the enormous crowd below was very striking. We next visited the gallery itself: a handsome sensible building, & well suited for its purpose. The pictures I thought for the most part poor ... ... In St George's hall for the dinner: but we did not sit down till 6.30. There were said to be between 400 & 500 present ... I was chairman, very well received, & said what I intended to say ... Home about midnight, weary but well satisfied: for the popular feeling towards me personally was more cordial than I could have imagined, & the whole affair went off well.

In my speeches the only points of importance were two. I declared strongly against any present attempt at mediation, as being useless: and dwelt on the importance of dealing with the Indian famine, adding some hints, cautiously worded, as to the extreme financial difficulties which may be feared in the future, in a country where population constantly increases...

9 September 1877. Church: walk afterwards with Ly D. to look at places where new clumps should be put in ... Walk with Sanderson later.

10 September 1877. Shooting on the Huyton side ... East wind, bringing smoke, fog, & some smell ... it is dull & gloomy beyond what can be imagined. The quantity of smoke certainly increases perceptibly...

... Gave Ly D £200, & Sanderson £150, for October. I advanced the date, thinking from something that Sanderson said, that the family are in fresh difficulty.

11 September 1877. Post brings 9 boxes, which I dispose of in the course of the morning ... East wind continues, & the air is full of smoke. Münster came. Wrote to Buchanan,[63] telling him that he is to have a baronetcy, & that he had better retire by the end of the year.

[62] For Derby's opening of the Walker Art Gallery, Liverpool, see *T*, 7 Sept. 1877, 8a.
[63] Amb. at Vienna.

12 September 1877. My sister left us, with her boys. She tells me that the late Ld Shrewsbury[64] has cleared off all debt from the family estate, & that the present peer at his majority will come into a rental of £50,000 unencumbered: which I am glad of, considering the position of the family & their connection with us.[65]

Münster went out after partridges: Sanderson & I walked with him as far as the Parsonage ... Ride alone, the first I have had this year. Walk later.

Settled with Sanderson to fill up the vacancy[66] at the Hague by moving Stuart from Athens, & to send L. West there, unless in future changes I can do better for him.

13 September 1877. To Preston ... the number of magistrates present was more than usually large, over 100 ... ... I was re-elected chairman for the year ... ... Got home by 4.30. Found 11 boxes, most of them heavy.

14 September 1877. Post brought 13 boxes: cleared off all in the day. ... Letter from Carnarvon, he agrees in the view which Northcote & I take as to W. African matters (v. Aug. 16): but suggests a committee by way of removing objections: which I consent to.

Letter from the Premier, to whom I had written about Buchanan and Harris: he answers by a most amusing denunciation of all our diplomatists, especially O. Russell, who just now is his favourite aversion.

After consideration I have settled to move Stuart to the Hague, & replace him at Athens by L. West from B. Ayres: Elliot to succeed Buchanan, & Layard to be confirmed at Constantinople. This leaves two vacancies, Madrid & B. Ayres: the first I think of offering to Thornton, who has been for 9 years in the bad climate & worse society of Washington.

15 September 1877. Ride early, about the park. ... Count Münster left us.

16 September 1877 Sunday. Church: walk there & back. Walk with Ly D. in afternoon.

... All public interest during the last week has been concentrated on the operations round Plevna: of which as yet we have no accurate detail. ... Diplomacy has been quiet. The Italian govt appears disposed to side against Turkey, one does not clearly see why, or what they have to gain: but Italian politicians have been so accustomed to intrigue that

[64] D. 11 May 1877.
[65] Through diarist's bro.-in-law.
[66] Sir E. Harris (1808–88), Malmesbury's bro.; min. at The Hague 1867–77, when retired from diplomacy. 'He has long suffered from ill-health, and is no loss to the service: a kindly goodnatured sort of man, who made no enemies; got into no scrapes, & did no more than he could help. The vacancy was much wanted, & will remove some discontents.' (*D.D.*, 11 Sept. 1877.)

they practice it even without an object. Corti, the Italian ambassador at Constantinople, tells Layard that he has received several instructions of such a nature that he can only suppose his govt wishes to quarrel with the Porte: he has remonstrated, he says, but only got snubbed for his pains.

Greek preparations for war continue ... The Servians have evidently made their bargain with Russia, & are going into the war again. But their army is worthless, the war is unpopular, & the Turks seem to entertain hopes, whether reasonably or not, that they may upset Prince Milan by supporting his rival, Karageorgewitch, who is believed to have a strong following in the country.

... Layard has been dining with the Sultan, Mrs Layard also: a thing entirely new. He speaks well of his host: says he has gained confidence in his own judgment & decision: is sincerely anxious to do what is right, & govern well: is less governed than at first by people about him: is grateful to us for what we have done, though it is little enough, in the matter of Greece & Servia: & talks of appealing to Europe, if the campaign ends without decided success on either side, asking for mediation, & offering to grant of his own accord all that was asked for in the protocol of London.

Some of the Turks, Layard says, are very sanguine ... ... Mansfield writes from Bucharest that the state of the Russian army is so bad that a second campaign is thought impossible ...

17 September 1877. The Russians badly beaten, though details are not clear ... Drove into L.pool with Ly D. to the new Art Gallery, which I wished that she should see, as a visit from her will be popular, & also I thought it well to make a few purchases. I bought three paintings for about £110. ... There came Mr & Mrs Pierrepont ...[67]

19 September 1877. Mr & Mrs Pierrepont left. They are better than Americans in general: she quiet & ladylike: he with a painfully strong nasal accent, but shrewd & sensible in talk.

Schouvaloff came, on his way through L.pool to the south.

20 September 1877. Sent Schou. out shooting, with Lionel: he did not do much, but seemed to enjoy himself. Some talk with him in his room before dinner ... Schou. left us in the evening ...

My conversation with Schou. was rather formal than real: I thought it right not to let him go without ascertaining his ideas as to the possibility of mediation, though for my own part I never thought it a feasible scheme. He said exactly what I expected, that it would be useless & hopeless to interfere now, but that a second campaign would be necessary if the war went on, that the present operations could not be continued for more than six weeks longer, & that during the enforced

[67] U.S. minister.

repose of winter diplomacy would have a chance of settling the affair. He suggested a congress – as to which I reserved my opinion, only pointing out that he had himself talked to me of the complete union of Germany & Austria with Russia: & if the fact were so, France & Italy being notoriously neutral, his govt would come into the congress with a majority assured.

Letter from Sir A. Buchanan, much discontented with the offer of a baronetcy, & evidently implying that he expected a peerage. He even hints that he shall refuse the minor honour. I answer civilly, but not too sympathetically...

21 September 1877. This was a day without events.

22 September 1877. Report of a Turkish victory, but no details.

23 September 1877. Church: walk there & back with Sanderson and Lionel: walk in afternoon with Sanderson. Talk of diplomatic changes, & also of the political combinations of the future, about which I am not quite easy. If Disraeli's temper is to be judged by his letters, he is in an excited state, ready for active intervention, & impatient of continued neutrality. In this mood, backed up as he is by the Queen, he may very possibly break up the cabinet. There is also the possibility of his dying or being disabled, which would be a trouble to all concerned. I should have before me the three usual courses: to stay where I am, to claim the premiership, or to retire. The last is difficult while foreign affairs are in their present confused state – it might look like running away from responsibility: the second is opposed to all my wishes & tastes: the third is disagreeable, since I should have to serve under a political junior, & there are none of my colleagues in whom my confidence is unlimited.

24 September 1877. The Turkish victory of Saturday is apparently a delusion...

25 September 1877. Received from Buchanan a second letter of complaint at not having got a peerage. The grievance, I think, is imaginary. No diplomatic peerage has been conferred to my recollection since that of Lord Stratford in 1852. Lord Napier & Ld Bloomfield[68] were both promoted to a peerage of U.K. but they had their titles before – Ld Cowley was made an earl, but he was already a baron. I do not think that the mere discharge with average ability & success of the ordinary duty of a diplomatist constitutes a claim to the highest reward which a minister has to give, & Buchanan's best friends would not claim for him higher credit than that of having made few & slight mistakes, & given little trouble. Of talent whether in writing or action he has never shown any. Wrote in this sense to Disraeli...

---

[68] Sir F. Napier (1819–98), 9th Baron Napier in the Scottish peerage, cr. Baron Ettrick 1872; John Bloomfield, 2nd Baron Bloomfield (1802–79) as Irish peer, cr. U.K. peer 1871.

Some talk with Ld Lyons about his visit to the Premier: he says he found Ld B. very full of the idea of preventing a second campaign, which he seemed to think might be done by holding determined language: but, Ld Lyons said, language of that kind means war if you do not carry your point: a mere game of brag never succeeds. I agree with him, and do not believe that the country would care to go into war. He added that he thought the Premier greatly overrated the military force of the country, talking about our being able to send out 100,000 men to the east. I note these reports, which tally exactly with what Disraeli writes to me.

27 September 1877. Answer from the Premier, treating with ridicule Buchanan's claim to a peerage: and I think not unreasonably.

... Drive with Hale to Bickerstaffe, & walk with him over great part of that estate, settling boundaries of farms, new plantations, etc. ... I cannot say that the impression left on my mind was agreeable. Smoke has increased: the buildings, though substantial, are ugly: the old hedgerows are gone: and just enough of trees remain, to produce in their half-dead condition an impression more dismal than that of utter bareness. A more cheerless gloomy place I have seldom seen. ... I am unfortunate in an almost morbid dislike to the absence of natural beauty: which in South Lancashire is not to be expected, & for which I have abundant compensations in other respects. But the feeling is not to be reasoned with, & it grows rather than diminishes.

29 September 1877. Letter from Ld Beaconsfield, who has summoned a cabinet for next Friday, & writes, full of a scheme for intervention which he wants me to propose. It is characteristic of him that he should do this, knowing that the scheme is utterly opposed to my ideas. I have written him a friendly answer, approving the summons to the cabinet, but throwing cold water on the project – very briefly however.

30 September 1877. No event of importance, in this week, either military or political. The Turks have held their positions, without serious loss or gain, and as the season for military operations is drawing to an end, it looks as if no decisive result was likely to be come to. ... I see not the least prospect of conditions being arrived at under present circs which both parties would accept.

... At home, complete repose: no vestige of an agitation in any question: Gladstone has made another speech, chiefly about the eastern Christians, but being a mere repetition of what he has often said before: it has fallen flat, attracting absolutely no attention.

2 October 1877. Rather anxious & uncomfortable as to the coming cabinet, or cabinets, for there may be more than one. I am satisfied from all I hear that the absence of agitation, or alarm, in the public mind is due to the conviction that we do not meditate intervention of a kind likely to engage us in war. If things were otherwise, the while middle class would be up in arms. It is known that the Premier is eager to do something, & suspected that the Queen is of the same way of thinking: but the country believes that as a government, we are not in favour of a policy of adventures. It is certain that we shall have some rather sharp discussions, & not impossible that disruption will follow. My position is so far peculiar, that I can probably stop whatever I disapprove of. The difficulty of replacing me at F.O. would be great just now, & the alarm caused by the resignation of the minister whose department is principally concerned would injure my colleagues more than the abandonment of any scheme. But to use such a position as I have requires not only determination – which where the interests of peace are concerned I am not afraid of failing in – but patience & coolness in discussion & perpetual watchfulness.

3 October 1877. Letter from Elliot, accepting Vienna gratefully, which I am glad of, feeling as I do that his transfer thither from Constantinople was a concession to popular prejudice. But he has not suffered by it in any way: his present post is equally important & more agreeable. His rival, Ignatieff, who appeared to have succeeded in all his plans, is ill & in disgrace: & the absurd clamour of last year has died out...

I hear unexpectedly that Sir T. Wade would like to be transferred to Athens. It might be as well that he left Pekin, for his excessive slowness & prolixity amount to a disease: he can finish nothing. But I have offered Athens to West, & doubt his being willing to exchange for China. Wade is fairly entitled to rest, & to an easy post in Europe.

4 October 1877. London ... walk in from Euston with Sanderson ... Met ... G. Hamilton, talk with him, & glad to find that he does not think as badly of Indian prospects as most people do. He is confident of increasing revenue & of the railways ceasing to be a burden on the state.

Letter from Wellesley: he has seen Gortschakoff who was in very low spirits: saying that nothing could be done except to wait, but that peace was impossible until some great victory had been gained ... Jomini[69] also talked to Wellesley in a still more gloomy strain ... thought the Emperor could not go back to Russia without having had a success: it would not be safe: there would be a popular rising. He, Jomini, thought the war would lead to a constitution...

5 October 1877. Saw Schouvaloff, but he had nothing special to tell. He would not admit that the Russian prospects were as bad as they are generally thought, & as he was not elated by the appearance of success in the first instance, I think he may be right now.

[69] Aleksandr Henrikhovich, Baron Jomini (1817–88), senior counsellor in Russian foreign office and sometime deputy for. minister, 1856–88.

Cabinet at 2, sat till 4.30: all present. The Premier addressed us at length, in a carefully arranged speech, & with an air of solemnity which he sometimes puts on. He dwelt on the danger of allowing a second campaign, on the unwillingness of other Powers to interfere, Germany having no motive to do so, & Austria having every reason for wishing Russia to be farther weakened by war. He spoke of the war as one of extermination, directed equally against a religion & a race. He thought our position as a govt was difficult. Only good luck had extricated us from a position which was last year embarrassing, & might have become humiliating. In a second campaign Russia would probably succeed. She had failed this year because she did not expect serious resistance. Her first successes had been gained by bribery of Turkish officers. (This is a favourite theory with Disraeli: I know no evidence in favour of it.) Next year things would be different. They would march to Constantinople, & stay there. Could we allow that? Ought we not to take the lead in preventing it? He proposed that we should ascertain what terms the Porte would accept, propose those terms to Russia, and say that we would join in the defence of Constantinople if Russia refused them. *Cairns* supported the proposition, which evidently was not new to him. *Carnarvon* objected strongly. *Hardy* approved in the main. *Salisbury* objected. *Richmond* (of course) agreed with Cairns. *Northcote* gave a hesitating opinion, neither for nor against, wishing that we saw our way to act with other Powers. *D*[erby] objected to promising help to the Porte, approved of mediation, but thought the time not opportune. *J. Manners* and *Beach* supported the Premier without hesitation. *Cross* thought the real question was what terms the Porte would accept, did not like the notion of the Russians getting to Constantinople, & believed our existence as a cabinet would be ended if that happened. *Smith* in the main backed Ld Beaconsfield, but thought the time for action not come. – No decision was asked for. On the whole I class my colleagues as follows. *For war*: Ld Beaconsfield, J. Manners, Beach, Cairns, & Richmond. *Against*: Salisbury, Carnarvon, & in general D[erby]. *Undecided*: Northcote, Hardy, Cross, & Smith. I see no reason why we should not come to an understanding in the end, but the differences are wide at present.[70]

6 October 1877. Up early: cleared off the little there was to do: made up accounts &c. Sent books to be bound: Sanderson came early. With him to Euston for the 12 o'clock train. Knowsley between 5 & 6: no visitors...

7 October 1877. I have forgotten to note a singular proceeding of Lytton, which I heard of at the cabinet on Friday. It seems that

[70] Derby asked Hardy 'whether the Cabinet or the Turkish Empire would last the longer' (*GH*, 6 Oct., which classes Cross and Smith as with Disraeli).

somebody has told him, or he has dreamed, that the reason why the cabinet objects to make war on Russia is that we contemplate an alliance, with Russia and France to form a coalition against Germany! This absurd fiction Lytton appears to have received without a doubt &, not taking the trouble to ask whether there is any foundation for it, he writes a letter which takes up 50 or 60 pages of print, denouncing our policy, or what he supposes to be such: and he is so proud of this production that he circulates it widely among his friends. There could not be a greater breach of official propriety: nor a greater waste of time ... Salisbury could give no explanation except that he is a little mad: & I begin to think so. With a mother insane, & father eccentric, he has every right to be in that way: & he used, like his father, to use opium. But as far as I can learn, he has managed the famine business well enough.

9 October 1877. Salisbury sends me the printed text of Lytton's letter, which is quite as extraordinary as he describes it. The motive must be either insanity or intrigue. It is, as I wrote back to Salisbury, a good election manifesto against the policy of the cabinet, ending with a sort of appeal to the Queen and to the Protestant feeling of the nation not to allow us to drag England into a quarrel with Germany. I shall call the Premier's attention to the matter, for it will probably get into the newspapers.

Mansfield writes from Bucharest that the war has come to a deadlock. ... From Berlin the news is that German sympathy for Russia is shown more & more openly ... Arms & ammunition are supplied to Russia from government stores at a nominal price ... The agitation in Poland troubles Bismarck, who as usual ascribes it all to the priests, & accuses the empress of being the head of the catholic party at court. He (Bismarck) is back again at Berlin, & working as hard as ever: no more talk about retirement!

Buchanan writes that Andrassy is not disposed to negotiate at once for peace, thinking that the Russians will fail in a second campaign as they have done in the first. (This is the ostensible reason, but very evidently not the real one.)

10 October 1877. Ride early: walk with Sanderson later. Ld & Ly Cowley & Beust came in the afternoon.

Settled with Broomfield about a new clump near the Ormskirk Lodge, & the taking down of a few trees.

Talk with Nathan about the deer: there are 250 fallow, & 180 red ... I tell him he may let the red deer increase gradually up to 200, when we shall have 450 in all: which with cattle fed in the park, I think enough.

11 October 1877. Beust left us at 3 p.m. having had with me the conversation for which he came. It was long, and in parts interesting:

I made rough notes as he went on, & expanded them afterwards into a mem. for the Premier & some other of my colleagues.

He began by saying that Andrassy was opposed to any mediation, even if it were asked for by one or other of the parties: he put aside as improbable the supposition of its being asked for by both. The reason given is that Russia ought not to be able to say in future that she was prevented from accomplishing her 'historical mission' in the east by the interference of any foreign power: that in Andrassy's opinion, she will fail in a second campaign as she has failed in the first, & it is better she should see that, with the field open to her, it is beyond her power to settle the eastern question in a purely Sclavonic sense. – I observed that this was very well in the event of Turkey continuing to win, but if there were a change of circumstances? supposing the Turks to be soundly beaten, what then? ... What would Austria do then? – Beust could not answer, said he would take the question ad referendum, but supposed that the answer would be that in that case Austria held herself bound by the understanding with Russia which I knew. He said that at the time of the Sumarakoff mission Andrassy, or the Emperor, had given fair warning to the Russians that if they went into Turkey they could not be allowed to stay there, & that their remaining would be opposed, even by force. He then dwelt on the intimate understanding between Andrassy & Bismarck. I asked what he supposed Bismarck's feelings to be towards Russia? He answered, very friendly, so much so that if Andrassy had not dissuaded him he, Bismarck, was ready to have sent German troops into Poland in case of any disturbance there: partly as thinking that the Polish agitation was a part of the Catholic anti-German movement: partly from his wish to keep well with Russia as a neighbour. It was inevitable on this that I should comment on the singularity of a policy which was adopted apparently by Austria with a view to humiliate the Russians, & by Germany with a view to their success. Beust no doubt saw the inconsistency for he did not attempt to defend it.

He then talked of Italy: said that at Vienna there was great distrust of the Italians: which I agreed with him was not unnatural under the circumstances, & told him what M. Crispi had said to me. If it came to a war, Beust said, Austria would not claim or seize an acre of Italian soil: (as to the result of the campaign, there could be in his mind no doubt): but they would follow the German example, & insist on a heavy indemnity in money.

... At some point in our conversation Beust observed that Bismarck appeared to be possessed with the idea that sooner or later all Europe would coalesce against Germany. I asked why? what was doing ... to create a suspicion of that kind, which I believed to be utterly unfounded? Beust said, laughing, 'It is his own bad conscience.' But it is singular that this notion should be so widely spread. It influences, apparently, the language of Bismarck, & it has reached Lytton at Calcutta. Through what agency?

12 October 1877. In the papers, a speech[71] by Salisbury on the eastern business, able, & in general very fair & sound, though a certain Russian bias may be detected in places. But he repudiates decidedly the policy of coercion, which is the only point on which any difference between us could in practice have arisen. He tells the public that he sees no present prospect of mediation being successful, in which he is right: it is odd that a few days ago Northcote should have spoken more hopefully, but his language was vague, & did not commit us.

13 October 1877. Received from Layard a singular telegram. It is to the effect that Zichy has been sounding him, & also the Porte, as to the willingness of the Turks to accept Austrian mediation: they seem well disposed to listen to the proposal, but consult us in the first instance. Zichy talks of Bismarck & German policy with a certain contempt, & takes pains to affirm that Austria is not under German influence. He also declares that he is authorised by Andrassy to make these overtures. The report of his language reaches me two days after I have received a message direct from Andrassy, through Beust, in a sense directly opposite. Either there is some device in this, or it is a curious case of blundering. I telegraphed back to Layard to say that Andrassy was holding very different language from that of Zichy.

The Porte has been so far encouraged by the overture that it has given to Layard a list of conditions of peace such as it would accept. They are extravagant, & even absurd. Belgrade to be restored – the principalities to be divided – Turkish fortresses to be allowed on the Pruth – the Armenian frontier to be rectified in a Turkish sense – these are the modest demands of the Turks … One would imagine that an Ottoman army was marching on Moscow.

14 October 1877. Letters … from Athens … The king, asked by Stuart[72] if he means to make war, answers frankly 'Not yet.' But preparations for war continue … … It is repeated on every occasion, that the necessity for arming has arisen solely from the neglect of the conference last winter to provide for Greek interests.

15 October 1877. Letter from Tenterden, detailing his interview with the Premier, whose language as reported by T. is moderate & sensible enough. He wishes me not to discourage the idea of mediation nor to discuss details, but to wait & see what will come of it.

---

[71] For Salisbury's Bradford speech on the Eastern Question, see *T*, 12 Oct. 1877, 10a.

[72] U.K. minister at Athens from *c.* summer 1876; 'disappointed at not getting Lisbon, and talks of resigning. I write to encourage him … it would be a loss to the service if he retired' (*D.D.*, 17 Feb. 1876); moved to The Hague, autumn 1877 (*D.D.*, 12 Sept. 1877).

Papers announce the reprieve of the 4 prisoners sentenced to death for a murder at Penge. ... I think the commutation of sentence quite right, & have written to Cross to say so. I spoke to him on the subject after our cabinet of the 5th.

Left Knowsley early for Manchester: for the meeting of the Convalescent Hospital fund...

16 October 1877. London with Sanderson: Ly D. & Margaret with us as far as Bletchley, where they turned off to go to Woburn.

... Saw Tenterden, who has been to Brighton at the Premier's request, & reports well of his state both in mind & body. Working all the evening. Sanderson dined with me.

18 October 1877. Saw ... Beust, who came to tell me with authority that Zichy had no instructions to offer mediation, or even to sound the Porte on the subject. This I telegraphed at once to Layard...

Saw Musurus, & tried to get him to talk rationally about Greece, but it was of no use. He could do nothing but gabble about the bad faith of the Greeks ... It is impossible to do business with him.

Saw the Premier, who seemed infirm, but quiet & in good spirits. He had nothing special to ask or tell: we talked over the situation...

20 October 1877. Heard to my satisfaction that Mr Alexander accepts the offer of £60,000 for the reversion of Holwood ... ... I have done a wise thing in buying.

21 October 1877. Ly D. had much conversation with Disraeli at Woburn. He appears to have given an amusing description of the divisions of the cabinet, in which he says there are six parties. The party of war at any price: Hardy, J. Manners, Hicks Beach. The party who are for declaring war if Russia reaches Constantinople: Cross, Smith, & Cairns. The party who are for letting the Russians go to Constantinople, but not stay there: Lord Salisbury. The party who are for having Christian service in St Sophia: Lord Carnarvon. The party for peace at any price – Lord Derby. The party who are for reconciling all these parties, and standing by our international engagements: the Queen and himself. – In this ingenious summary he has left out Richmond, who may be classed as a follower of the Chancellor wherever it pleases the latter to take him: and Northcote, I suppose, as undecided. – The Premier said, what is more serious, that he has two resignations in his pocket already: that of the Chancellor and of J. Manners: to be used, I presume, in the event of the decision of the cabinet being adverse to their policy. – That J. Manners should resign is natural: he was brought up in the strange traditions of the old French war, which the farmers believed contributed to their prosperity, & no reasoning will ever make him understand that the temporary stimulus given by vast expenditure entails sacrifice and suffering afterwards. He thinks fighting the natural occupation of Englishmen, and considers a war as the unnecessary corrective of the relaxation of energy caused by long peace. – The motives of the Chancellor are less easy to understand. I suspect that he has in view the place of First Lord of the Treasury, knowing that I do not cover it, & not being prepared to act under Salisbury. In his view it is essential to him to cultivate good relations with the Queen: & she is just now passionately warlike. She returned to me the draft of my report of conversation with Beust ... with a pencil note against one passage where I had spoken of a second campaign, to the effect that a second campaign ought not to be even alluded to as possible: it was our business to prevent its taking place.

... The war-news of last week is more unfavourable to the Turks than any yet received. They have lost in their Asiatic defeat at least 10,000 men ... In Europe, all remains as it was: two great armies dying in face of one another from sickness, exposure, & want.

23 October 1877. Working on papers about Zanzibar: I am much pressed to do something for the Sultan, who has alienated most of his subjects, & half ruined himself, in putting down slave trade at our request, & as yet we have given him nothing but good words in return. He wants arms: a steamer: European officers: & help in other ways. Some of these things I think we may, & should, do for him.

Mansfield sends the worst report I have seen yet of the Russian army before Plevna: the Russians have there 20,000 sick & wounded: they acknowledge a loss of 50,000 men in Europe, & with all this they have not penetrated 50 miles south of the Danube. ... Mansfield declares that if sickness continues at its present rate, the army will have melted away before the end of winter.

24 October 1877. Saw Thornton,[73] to whom I had offered Madrid, hearing that he wished for the place: he admitted that he had made overtures for the place, but on second thoughts declines, preferring to wait for an embassy.

Münster called on his return from Germany: the only remark he made that struck me was about Bismarck: the Prince, he said, was like two different men, even in the course of one conversation: moderate & reasonable in treating of foreign affairs, violent, despotic, & impulsive in home affairs. He could not explain the reason, but had noticed this often.

25 October 1877. Letter from Cross, in which he speaks sensibly of the neglect of business in the H. of C. last year, & the consequent failure to pass our bills. I answer him, advising that he, & other members of the cabinet in the H. of Commons, should bring their affairs before us in good time, so that they may be really considered. We are far too

[73] Sir Edward Thornton (1817–1906), min. at Washington 1867–81; amb. at St Petersburg 1881–4.

apt to put them aside, and waste time in mere gossip about what is passing abroad: which is a little everybody's fault, but chiefly, I think, that of the Premier. He dislikes details, detests the class of business which he is apt to call parochial, & takes peculiar pleasure in turning over & discussing all sorts of foreign questions, on which action is not necessary, & often not possible.

26 October 1877. Mansfield writes that it is difficult to know what is doing in Bulgaria. Most of the newspaper correspondents are expelled, & the rest kept at headquarters, where they learn nothing. ... Mansfield warns us against the 'Times' correspondents, who are openly Russian in sympathy: especially Sir H. Havelock, who has gone out in that capacity, & is making all the mischief he can by representing the sympathies of all classes in England to be with Russia, & against their own govt. But Sir H. is more than half-mad: lately I had such complaints of his conduct from Wellesley that I wrote to Delane on the subject.[74]

27 October 1877. Interesting letter from Morier about a fisheries dispute...between Spain & Portugal. It has been amicably settled ... but while it lasted, both king & ministers talked as if on the verge of a national catastrophe. They believe, to a man, that Spain intends to pick a quarrel with them, intending sooner or later to realise the great idea of an united Iberian state: and at every dispute that occurs, however trifling, this apprehension comes uppermost. ... I am not sure that the alarm is groundless. Vain, restless, with an exorbitant opinion of their own greatness, which they have yet sense to know is not shared by the rest of the world – haunted by the recollection of a great history, & stung by their present comparative insignificance – with generals wanting employment, & sure to conspire if they don't get it – & with financial embarrassments so hopeless that they need not care about increasing them – the Spaniards have every motive to induce them to attempt the annexation of Portugal...

28 October 1877. Disraeli is still, I believe, at Brighton, quiet & not excited. Gladstone is making an Irish tour, in the course of which he has declared that he will make no speeches: his movements are constantly reported: he has varied his experiences by choosing to travel third class, so as to see & talk familiarly with the peasantry. This may only be a freak, or the natural curiosity of a tourist: but it is sure to be thought, & perhaps it is, a piece of popularity-hunting, like the felling of a tree at Hawarden, amidst a crowd of admiring excursionists.

Telegram from Layard, to the effect that Zichy has again spoken to him about mediation, persisting that he is authorised, which Layard believes, thinking he would not otherwise dare to commit himself so far. Either Andrassy is purposely playing a double game, which is likely

[74] Cf. *GH*, 22 Oct. 1877.

enough, or he distrusts & is jealous of Beust, & is purposely keeping him in the dark.

The Turks, according to Layard, are quite ready for mediation – that is, in the abstract – when terms come to be talked of, I suspect we shall find the two parties as wide apart as ever.

30 October 1877. Sanderson returns to the office, after a week's holiday at Torquay. I am never quite easy while he is away, for Barrington[75] is neither very sharp nor very active.

31 October 1877. Reports of intended mediation have got about, & every one of my visitors questioned me about them. I denied them absolutely, which I could do with truth … though probably there is some sort of intrigue going on.

Called on Ld Beaconsfield, & found him in a satisfactory frame of mind, quiet & composed. He professes anxiety as to the chances of keeping the cabinet together, & not without reason, but talked about it with more confidence than on some former occasions. His present idea is, that we should promise to Russia continued neutrality on condition that she gives us a pledge that she will not occupy Constantinople. This is moderate & reasonable enough in principle, & I expressed my general agreement: it will however have to be borne in mind that if we make this the condition of neutrality we, by implication, allow the Russians to occupy Gallipoli, which would not suit us: & also that we have an understanding with Austria which we cannot altogether ignore, however little we may think it likely to be observed on the other side.

3 November 1877. The chief fault of Cairns as an administrator is a certain intellectual arrogance & contempt of other men's opinions, not perhaps extraordinary in the case of one who has been so able & so successful. He has formed a low opinion of the judges generally, & is not sorry to show it by passing them over in favour of a junior of whom he thinks well.

4 November 1877. The extraordinary calm of the present autumn in England is worth notice. Not one speech of any note or moment has been made, that I can remember: those that have been made are fewer than usual, & have been but slightly reported. The only movement to which any interest attaches is the continued struggle of the artisans for higher wages. The London builders have at last been driven to resist, & foreign labour is being imported: on a small scale, no doubt, but it is a beginning. Americans, Canadians, Germans, & Italians have come over … things look as if the chronic dispute of capital & labour were

[75] Probably Bernard E.E. Barrington (1847–1918), priv. sec. to Salisbury when in office 1878–1900.

entering a new phase. Shall we come to the importation of Chinese?
More impossible things have happened.

5 November 1877. Office ... till 2, when cabinet. We sat 2 hours, or
nearly so. ... Our cabinet was satisfactory: real work done: no differences, & a general feeling, as it seemed to me, that matters should not
be left to take their own course for another year as they did last session.
We talked briefly over foreign affairs, & agreed without difference to
the proposal of the Premier about a fresh communication to the Russian
govt. It is so harmless that no one can object: and so useless, that one
does not see why he prefers it. Probably he is pushed on by the Queen
to do something: and in her eager impulsive way she cares (or rather
thinks) little about the chance of success, so long as the semblance of
action is maintained. I am to prepare the draft, & I shall take my own
time about it.

We discussed plans for the session: agreeing not to bring in any fresh
bill on the burials question, as it is quite clear that no solution of that
is possible except one which we cannot propose or agree to without a
little gentle pressure. We talked over a vast variety of subjects: 1) new
public offices 2) increase of judges 3) accidents to workmen 4) factory
legislation 5) local govt 6) Scotch education 7) corrupt practices act 8)
Irish Sunday closing 9) valuation bill 10) conduct of business in H. of
C. There were other subjects, which I forget. We talked over all in a
preliminary way, but settled nothing.

6 November 1877. Cabinet at 3, sat till 5, discussing a plan for reform
of local govt by Sclater Booth, which to me appears a most confused &
clumsy production, & I cannot conceive that the House will take it.
Nor do my colleagues seem greatly to care whether it passes or not.

... Layard sends us terms of peace which he is informed the Sultan
would accept, if we proposed them to Russia. I printed them at once
for the cabinet, but refused to discuss them when we met, on the
ground of not having had time for consideration: I knew that if once
we got to foreign affairs, all our time would be spent in gossiping about
them.

7 November 1877. Saw Münster ... he told me, what is curious, that
Bismarck has been so much affected by the loss of a favourite dog that
for two or three days he was hardly fit for business, or willing to do it.

... Cabinet: sat from 3 to 4.30. Our chief business was Scotch: the
Lord Advocate[76] was called in: and after discussion with him, we agreed
to go on with three Scotch bills in the order in which I name: 1) roads,
2) secondary education (which is mainly a question of endowments), 3)
poor law amendment. It is not likely that we shall reach this third
question. Talk when the L.A. was gone of assisting him by the

---

[76] William Watson, lord advocate.

appointment of an under-secretary[77] for Scotland: Cross raised this question, I cordially supported: it is absurd that the whole business of Scotland should be in the hands of a working lawyer, who keeps on his private practice, who probably took no part in politics before he was appointed, and who looks on his term of office as a short & disagreeable passage which is to bring him into the harbour of a judgeship. We did not settle the point, Cross gave notice that he would raise it again. – I appealed to the cabinet to sanction some help in the way of arms and assistance to discipline his troops, he having quarrelled with most of his subjects by putting down slave trade, & in effect thrown himself upon British protection. This was sanctioned in principle. We had some talk as to the manner of trying election petitions: the present system, it seems, is not thought satisfactory, & must be revised, the act expiring. I foresee trouble in that question. Not a word was said about foreign affairs, except that Salisbury attacked me about appointing an Indian officer ... at Teheran, which is an old subject of dispute.

Speech[78] delivered by Hartington in Scotland ... He is clear & strong about reducing the county franchise, which is evidently going to be the next question seriously raised.

8 November 1877. Lawrence called ... He tells me that land is selling well, notwithstanding the stagnation of trade. Also that Smith, our new First Lord, has just bought an estate of 5000 acres in Suffolk, so that he may be added to the number of big squires in the cabinet.

... Long speech[79] at Dublin by Gladstone, on the whole not violent in tone, & he seems to have tried to avoid controversial topics as far as he could. He dwelt a good deal on the Land Bill of 1870, & wished the clauses which give power to help the tenants to buy their holdings extended in their operation: he declared in favour of a change in the land-laws in England, but disclaimed the notion that English land would ever be held largely by small proprietors, owing to the economic conditions of the country...

9 November 1877. Left for the Guildhall: all the cabinet dined with the Lord Mayor except Hicks Beach ... Ld Beaconsfield spoke with great caution and tact, avoiding as far as possible subjects of controversy: I have never heard him better in that respect: not an expression fell from him which could be taken hold of for any purpose of mischief. His speech was more remarkable for what it did not contain than for what he did: but he pleased & satisfied his audience. The effort was a great

[77] The first under-sec. for Scotland at the home office was Lord Rosebery, Aug. 1881. See H.J. Hanham, 'The Creation of the Scottish Office, 1881–87', *The Juridical Review*, (1965), 205–44.
[78] For Hartington's speech on receiving the freedom of the city of Glasgow, see *T*, 6 Nov. 1877, 4a.
[79] For Gladstone's speech on receiving the freedom of Dublin, see *T*, 8 Nov. 1877, 7c.

one: suffering from gout, feeble, & knowing that every word used by
him would be twisted if possible ... he had every inducement to plead
his state of health ... But ill or well his pluck never fails, & he had his
reward in an enthusiastic audience.

10 November 1877. Cabinet at 12.30. The Premier looking pale & ill,
but in good spirits, pleased with his reception & success last night, as
well he may be. We discussed the telegram to be sent to Layard, &
settled it: we approve the Sultan's desire for peace, but do not think
the moment opportune for mediation. I sent this off in the afternoon.

Long discussion on Local Govt Bill, in which we are not entirely
agreed: Salisbury & Carnarvon dislike the whole affair, & Richmond
takes the same view more mildly. They want to cut the bill down till it
is little more than a sham. But the H. of C. will not take that, & if we
had meant to do nothing we ought not to have pledged ourselves to
Reed's resolution affirming the principle of elective boards. Sclater-
Booth was called in to explain points in his bill, which he did in a
clumsy uncouth sort of way, not promising well for the success of the
measure in parliament, unless Northcote takes it personally in hand.
We sat 2 hours.

11 November 1877. Enquired of Lawrence about an estate in Argyllshire,
25,000 acres, the description of which rather takes my fancy.

In Europe, the situation is unaltered. Plevna is expected to fall, but
nothing has yet happened.

... Tricoupi is again talking big about what Greece is to do. 'One
would think' Wyndham writes 'that he had 100,000 men at his back.'
His great anxiety appears to be that Greece shall be admitted to the
conference which must follow on the conclusion of the war: and he
evidently takes as his model the conduct of Sardinia in 1854–56. The
Greek govt. with characteristic self-assertion, appears to have addressed
to Germany & Italy the modest request that in the event of war with
Turkey, the Greek coasts shall be protected. ... No encouragement
seems to have been given to these pretensions.

12 November 1877. Read to Ly D. Gladstone's article in answer to
Lowe, on the extension of household suffrage to the counties. It is a
very singular one ... ... He regrets the facilities which the rotten
boroughs gave for bringing able young men early into the House:
saying, as is the fact, that they now go to the newspapers instead: which
he considers as a substitution of the worst training for the best. He
denounces the growth of the money power, which in his eyes appears
to be the embodiment of all evil ... Though not in any degree
sympathising with the movement, I cannot resist the belief that sooner
or later, & probably in a few years, the franchises must be made
identical: but the really difficult problem will still remain for solution –
the redistribution of seats.

13 November 1877. Wellesley has had a most interesting convn with Jomini, the purport of which is that in his (J.'s) opinion the military party in Russia is greatly calmed down, & now sees the difficulties which it made light of when the war began: he thinks his govt would be glad to escape the risk of a second campaign by making peace on moderate terms. The question of the Dardanelles, he thinks, can be settled. If Kars were taken, it might be given back in exchange for Batoum. The surrender & destruction of the fortresses on the Danube he considers might be accepted as guarantee enough for the good treatment of Bulgaria in the future: (this, if true, is of extreme importance, since it removes the chief difficulty in the way of making peace): & in this way the matter might be settled without the necessity of a second campaign. The officers according to Wellesley say everywhere that they have been deceived as to the state of the Bulgarians, & that they are no longer fighting for them, but for military honour.

14 November 1877. Went over to see Ld Beaconsfield at his request: found him ill, suffering from asthma: he sleeps in Downing St for the convenience of being on one floor. He talked calmly & cheerfully of the state of things: had received an anxious excited letter from the Queen, the subject being our slowness to give effect to the decision of the cabinet of some weeks ago, when we determined to tell Russia that our neutrality was conditional on the army not going to Constantinople. I explained that to say this at the present moment would be to proclaim that the Russians might impose on Turkey any conditions of peace, no matter how onerous, without fear of interference from us, so long as they did not go to the capital: which would be wantonly throwing away our chance of influencing the negotiations. Disraeli said the matter had struck him in the same light, & agreed. We talked long about terms of peace etc. To my surprise,but also to my satisfaction, he seemed to care little about Batoum,[80] & to think that the question of the Dardanelles may be settled without injury to our interests.

15 November 1877. Talk with Harcourt, who very low & desponding as to the state of France: he can see nothing in what is passing except the approaching triumph of the Commune: will not admit that the priests had anything to do with the proceeding of May last − surely an astounding assertion. He is a worthy honourable man, & I suppose believes what he says: but where can he have lived?

Despatches from Athens ... The Greek govt has asked Russia, in the event of its joining in the war, first for a subsidy, & next for an extension of frontier to the Balkans: a modest request which has been

[80] Batoum or Batum, a Turkish port in Lazistan, in S.-E. of Black Sea; repulsed Russian attack in 1877–8, but ceded to Russia at congress of Berlin, July 1878, despite vociferous protests from much U.K. opinion.

refused. ... The king is personally very warlike. Sabouroff, whom he dislikes, is with him every day...

From Layard I have a vast heap of despatches: he is of all of our diplomatists the most active & the most voluminous: since May his despatches have exceeded 1300 in number. He writes a little too much, but it is a fault on the right side, especially in the place where he now is. According to him the Sultan & the Grand Vizier are both anxious for peace: they dislike the idea of concessions to Montenegro, but would be ready to give up Batoum, & declare the independence of Roumania...

16 November 1877. Saw Schouvaloff, who talked about conditions of peace vaguely, but not in a satisfactory way as to Bulgarian autonomy. It is here, I think, that the difficulty will be.

18 November 1877. A wild story has been going the round of the papers, which originated with the Pall Mall: to the effect that some kind of overtures are being made by Bismarck to Belgium, with the view ultimately to establish some sort of protectorate: according to this tale, Belgium is to be rewarded for helping Germany in the next war, by receiving a slice of French territory: the first step is to be the adoption of universal military service on the German system. Manning & the priests, for some inscrutable reason of their own, have been busy in spreading this fiction ... The Belgian govt ... treat the whole tale as a romance ... Nevertheless, the French minister at Brussels persists that there is some truth in the story.

19 November 1877. Fall of Kars, which is announced in all the papers ... Letter from Ld B. who wants something drafted to satisfy the cabinet, though the moment is obviously an impossible one to address Russia. I answered him, & am concocting something with Sanderson.

Not a single diplomatist called, & the boxes were very few. ... I had time on my hands – a rare event.

20 November 1877. Office at 1, stayed till 5, but found comparatively little to do. ... Saw Schouvaloff, who talked in a strain new to him, a little swaggering: did not see who or what was to stop the Russian armies: thought all serious resistance would very soon be at an end: the fall of Plevna was a question of days ... with more in the same strain. He seemed to me to be playing a part, & to play it ill. The object obviously was to convince me of the necessity of advising Turkey to submit to the Russian terms, rather than risk a second campaign: and his professed confidence that a continuance of fighting was imposs-ible scarcely disguised an apprehension that the fact might be quite otherwise. As our conversation was unofficial, I made no draft out of it, but put the substance into a letter to Ponsonby, for the Queen: with the double purpose of placing it on record, & of keeping her quiet, as she always thinks she is not sufficiently informed of what is going on.

... Letter from Disraeli, enclosing one from Cairns, who now thinks the despatch proposed at the last cabinet inappropriate (in which I quite agree) & suggests another plan of proceeding. I arrange to see him tomorrow.

21 November 1877. Saw Drage, rather because he called than from necessity: he reports well of me.

... Called on Disraeli at his request, & discussed the situation with him: he had just returned from the D. of Norfolk's wedding,[81] at which he passed the morning, having been on a visit to Gorhambury[82] for two days: which does not look as if he were overdriven with work. He was in good spirits, & apparently recovered of his asthma. He said he had great trouble with the Queen: she had written in the most violent & unreasonable way, and he had been obliged to write her 'a very stiff letter' in reply: but she had taken it well, & acquiesced. He agreed with me that there is at the present moment no chance of successful mediation, but was disposed to think that something, he hardly knew what, ought to be said or written by way of keeping our colleagues quiet. Cairns especially is growing restless & impatient, fearing lest we should be blamed for doing nothing, which as matters stand, I do not think a reasonable fear.

22 November 1877. Saw ... Lawson, who presses for decisive action against Russia if necessary ... ... Passed a singularly idle day: such as frequently comes in the midst of, or just before, a crisis.

... No telegram has been received from Layard since the news of Kars: which leads us to think at the office that the telegrams have been stopped or delayed at Constantinople, to prevent the transmission of bad news: a childish policy, but it is common there.

... There dined with us ... Madame Schou., a strange person, dogmatic and peremptory in her way of talking, extremely *dévote*, and by most persons thought disagreeable: a character which from the little I saw of her I should think well earned. Her husband is evidently subdued and uncomfortable in her presence, as not feeling sure what she may say or do next. She has taken him to hear all the best known preachers both in Brighton and London: the only kind of society which she cares for. She goes (happily) back to Russia. The couple are in fact separated, and her coming over here at all is supposed to be a mark of deference to English ideas of respectability.

23 November 1877. Office ... No diplomatist called. Another easy day.

... It is curious that we have even now no clear account of the taking of Kars ... It was not expected by either side so soon.

---

[81] At Brompton Oratory, 21 Nov. 1877, the 20th D. (1847–1917) m. Countess of Loudoun.

[82] Lord Verulam's house in Herts.

Layard writes under date of the 14th, that Turkish affairs are looking very black ... & unless help comes from some quarter, they must be crushed.

24 November 1877. Wrote to Disraeli about an alteration which he suggests in the draft ... to Schouvaloff. As the cabinet settled it, the agreement was that I should write promising on the part of England a conditional continuance of neutrality, the condition being that Russian forces should not go to Constantinople. D. now proposes to strike out all about neutrality, leaving the document a simple warning, or menace, to Russia not to go on. This is quite different from what the cabinet sanctioned, and in fact a new policy. Whether from advancing age, from the pressure put upon him by various persons in different directions, or from the complexity of the question at issue, I find the Premier constantly shifting his ground, & abandoning today the line which he seemed to have definitively adopted overnight. On the other hand it is impossible to find any one more pleasant to deal with, or more willing to listen to and consider objections to what he proposes. In that, as in many other respects, no cabinet ever had a better chief.

... News from France ... The new foreign minister is a M. Banneville, unknown to me & to most persons...

25 November 1877. Altogether Layard describes the state of affairs as 'most critical' & there can be no doubt that he is right.

26 November 1877. Signed the contract for Holwood.

... F. dined with us, despondent as he sometimes is, thinking the country will not be satisfied if we remain at peace, though he does not personally press for a war.

Letter from Disraeli, friendly enough in tone, but maintaining his point: he has in fact converted an amicable though warning message into an ultimatum. To avoid controversy, I propose to see him tomorrow. He has shifted again, & is all for action: last week he seemed quiet & moderate. Whether it is health, the pressure upon him of individual influences, or merely sensitiveness to the supposed public opinion of the moment, I cannot say: but he shifts about strangely. – There is an article in the M. Post today, violent beyond anything that has yet appeared against Russia, & announcing authoritatively that we shall make war. The Post has little circulation, & what it says is therefore not important: but in this case the article is drawn up in the form of a state paper, & with the evident intention of making it appear that it has official sanction. Now M. Corry, Disraeli's private secretary, is in constant communication with Borthwick.[83] Has there not been some hint given that this style of writing would find favour in the eyes of the cabinet? I suspect it. – Bourke too has written me a letter in favour of

[83] Algernon Borthwick, 1st Baron Glenesk (1830–1908), prop. of *Morning Post* from 1876.

war. He is a moderate man, not given to obtrude his opinion, & I cannot but believe that it is really a move of the Premier. I have no doubt, but that apart from intrigues & personal influences, there really is a stronger party in favour of war than at any former time: the notion that Armenia is in some way or other the highroad to India has got hold of many people, & though they would be puzzled to explain why they think so, their conviction is not the less real. In 'society' I have the certainty that war would be popular, as also, naturally in the army: probably the feeling would be the same among the mob: the middle class is almost to a man on the other side, but unfortunately the Premier neither understands nor likes the middle-class. The prospect of our being able to hold together seems to be worse now that it has been yet: but there is this to be said on the other hand, that neither the war-party nor the peace-party in the present cabinet are strong enough to stand alone: & they have therefore the strongest possible interest in keeping together, especially as with the present H. of C. no ministry could be formed from the opposition benches.

27 November 1877 (Tuesday). Lawson called, hot for war, and using the old arguments, how a nation that does not fight from time to time becomes enervated, loses self-respect and the respect of its neighbours, etc.

... Called on Disraeli, & long talk, amicable enough in tone, but yet with a consciousness on both sides that we are not agreed, & may be more widely divided before long. In truth, I begin to have great doubts whether we can get through the winter together. We ended in a sort of compromise: I pressed for having nothing done without a cabinet, which he did not much like, but agreed to, & fixed it for Monday. On the other hand I promised to try & sketch out something which might hit the mean between our two proposals as to what should be said: but would send nothing till it had been discussed by our colleagues. His language in general was moderate, affecting to deprecate a war, but not very heartily: in truth I do not suppose he wants one, for what minister at 72 would willingly undertake such a responsibility: but he would run great risk of getting into one rather than take up an unpopular line in parliament. He said one thing which had an unpleasant sound: I had told him that if we wrote to Russia in the sense he had suggested, we should certainly get a refusal: he answered, all the better, since then we should be free of our own engagement to remain neutral. But thinking perhaps that he had spoken too plainly, he made haste to add, 'I don't mean that we should not remain neutral, but that we should be free to act as we thought fit.' On the whole this convn did not impress me greatly.

28 November 1877. Saw ... Schouvaloff, who talked big, as on the last occasion, about the little opposition the Russian troops would meet with. It is clear that he does this under orders, & for a purpose: but for what purpose is less evident. Saw Beust, & put to him the question 'What will Austria do, if the Russian army approaches & threatens to occupy Constantinople?' He promised to report my question, & get an answer.

Received a deputation headed by Stratheden ... I answered, guarding myself as carefully as I could, & I think with success so far, but feeling all the while that the ground was dangerous. ... I corrected the Times report of this little speech.

... Layard sends a telegram to the effect that he has secret information that the Porte has decided to reject all compromise, & fight on to the last. The Russian attempt to raise a loan of £15,000,000 has failed, some say that £3,000,000 has been obtained, others put it at £5,000,000, but in any case it has been necessary to create a vast amount of paper money.

29 November 1877. Saw Gennadius, who talked about the new courts in Egypt: wanting Greek judges appointed on the court of appeal. I could not tell him the real objection, which is their notorious corruption.

... Saw Cross, & talk with him on the state of the cabinet & affairs in general. He is confident that we shall keep together, less uneasy than I am as to what the Premier may be mediating, strong as to not letting the Russians go to Constantinople, but not otherwise disposed to interfere.

My answer to the deputation yesterday appears to have produced a good deal of effect: there being much anxiety as to our intentions. In the City it is well received: but has naturally disappointed & disgusted the war-party. Unluckily the Premier has allowed his personal inclinations towards that party to become public: & a singular speech which he lately made to Schouvaloff, to the effect that England could put 300,000 men under arms, is going about the world. The result is that people out of doors think the cabinet more divided than for practical purposes we are.

3 December 1877. Menabrea talked a good deal about the Black Sea blockade, the validity of which he questioned on various technical grounds, not, I think, very sound: but it is evident that the Italian govt is more than half disposed to pick a quarrel with Turkey.

... Schouvaloff talked vaguely about terms of peace, professing, as he always does, to have no instructions: his object seemed to be to persuade me that an arrangement may be made by which the Bulgarians shall have full rights of self-government, yet without prejudice to the authority of the Sultan. The thing is possible, yet with the experience of Servia before them, I shall be surprised if the Turks are willing to try.

... Telegram from Athens, to the effect that Tricoupi expects an insurrection in Crete, & pretends to be anxious to prevent it: which is so gross a fiction that I wonder he thinks it worth telling.

... Odo Russell writes that Bismarck (through Bulow) repeats the old story of his wish to cooperate with England: but how, or with what end in view, he will not say. He does not wish or intend to mediate just now: had rather the parties fought it out...

I have received Andrassy's answer to my question of last week in two forms – through Buchanan & through Beust: Andrassy says he has already given explicit assurances as to what Austria will do in the event of a Russian advance on Constantinople. (This is not the case, for his statements have been of the vaguest character.) He strongly objects to a Russian occupation of Constantinople, though he will not interfere in the operations of the war: (in other words, he will not try to prevent a merely military occupation): but in the event of the Russians going there, he will insist on their not remaining, & he feels confident that they will not expose themselves to a demand that they should retire, which could be backed at need by a million of men.

How much of all this can we trust?

4 December 1887. Cabinet at 12, sat about 1½ hour. Foreign affairs exclusively were discussed. There was no substantial difference of opinion among us, & the Premier, who interfered little, talked moderately & reasonably, in what he did say. The end was that we ask from the Russian govt no assurances as to not going to Constantinople, it being certain that the request would be refused, & would only lead to unpleasantness, but that we give them a warning on the subject, in language as strong as we can use without pledging ourselves to make the proceeding on their part a casus belli. This warning to be in the form of a mem. to be given to Schouvaloff, & the mem. to be read to the cabinet at its next meeting. Much anxiety was shown to have something said or done in the sense of mediation – all the H. of C. men alarmed lest we should not seem to have done enough when parliament met. – I warn them that there is not the slightest chance of bringing Russians and Turks to agree on terms, as matters now stand, but they answer that that does not matter, what they look to is the appearance of the thing. I declined absolutely to undertake what I know must fail, but consented to put into the mem. a paragraph expressing our willingness to mediate, when an opportunity offers: which is only what we have said before, & if it does no good can do no harm.

5 December 1877. Saw ... Schouvaloff, who had heard something of our intended note or mem. (how? or whence? there must be a leak in the cabinet): I did not think it worth while to affect ignorance, but told him I was not yet authorised to make any communication: he seemed to understand the probable effect on English opinion, if the Russian

armies went to Constantinople. My other visitors were Carnarvon, who
wished to discuss the situation: I showed him my draft prepared for
the Saturday cabinet: and to my surprise, his brother Auberon Herbert:
a wild, half-mad, but rather clever personage, who ... has attacked me
personally with rather exceptional violence. However, he asked to see
me, saying that he had a secret of great public importance to communicate. ... He has been in Paris, & talked with a woman (respectable,
he says) who is intimate with Gambetta.[84] She told him that Bismarck
has been making overtures to Gambetta through Crispi ... the purport
... is, that Germany is to seize on Belgium, or at least the Belgian
coast: in return for being allowed to do which, she will restore to
France the lately ceded provinces. ... In addition Bismarck appears to
have announced to Gambetta, for no very obvious reason, an intention
of seizing Trieste & other parts of Austria, letting Italy have the Tyrol
as its share of the plunder. ... It is a wild tale, but there must be some
foundation for it, absolute invention is not to be thought of in such a
case ... ... The same game was played by the same person with the
Emperor Napoleon: and it succeeded.

6 December 1877. Letter from Disraeli, as unsatisfactory in tone as
his language in cabinet was the reverse. He says that he expects an
audience at Windsor which will not be agreeable: & in that I have
no doubt he is right: the Queen is furious for war, & makes no
secret of her sentiments ... He 'hopes our tone will be firm':
mentions a possible casus belli: & ends by a very exaggerated
estimate of the value of Turkey as an ally, saying that the Porte
has 400,000 men in the field admirably armed: which is at least
double the reality. I shall answer vaguely, but not in a way to invite
controversial discussion. There is nothing definite to object to in
what he says: but it is evident that he is looking forward to war as
not only a probable event, but one in a party point of view rather
desirable than the reverse. I think he is wrong there, even if there
were no other issues involved.

... Schou. tells Ly D. that whatever the Russian papers may say,
there is in Russia the strongest possible feeling of apprehension lest
England should join in the war: which I quite believe, though the
confession may not have been prudent.

... Went across to No. 10 & saw the Premier, not liking to answer
his letter lest we should get into controversy: found him quiet &
peaceably enough disposed, so that I think I must have construed his
phrases too seriously. He seemed nervous about his interview with the
Queen tomorrow, & feeble in body. He suffers much at times from
asthma, as well as bronchitis, but says he can go on a little longer. I

[84] Léon Gambetta (1838–82), French republican; premier 1881–2.

never differ from him without regret, for we are very old friends, & he is about the only man in public life for whom I have a personal feeling of friendship.

... I went today over the departmental estimates: what we cost to the public is in round numbers, Diplomacy 201: Consuls 248: Office 73: S.S. & Slave trade, 23: embassy & mission houses, 47: non-effective (pensions) 76. Total, 668 (in thousands of pounds). There is a set-off of 86, from fees, Indian repayments, etc. making net cost £582,000. With the increase of business everywhere, it is to me strange that we keep the estimates so well down: but no diplomatist can live on his pay, & half the consuls are in debt.

7 December 1877. Office 2 to 5. Saw there Musurus, Schouvaloff, Lawson: I think no one else. Easy day.

8 December 1877. Cabinet at 12, sat till 1.30: all friendly, no difference on any subject. I began by warning my colleagues that our secrets leak out in a manner not to be explained: of which several instances have occurred lately. On Monday last I found that the ambassadors knew exactly what we were going to discuss at the next day's cabinet: & on Wednesday they had heard, though not quite accurately, what had passed.

We then read the mem. to Schouvaloff, as drawn by me, which was agreed to. All the copies except one were destroyed.

I took the opinion of my colleagues on two points – the refusal of any protectorate of Samoa, & the new scheme of Zanzibar admin-istration: they were unanimous, none, except Salisbury & Carnarvon, having heard of either question before.

We then discussed a plan of the Council Office, for giving effectual protection against cattle-plague, by compelling the slaughter at the point of debarcation of all imported animals, except those brought in for breed-ing purposes: it seems this decided measure has been recommended by a committee of H. of C. almost without disagreement: the farmers naturally press us to take it up, & we are bound to do something. Salisbury, Rich-mond, Hicks Beach, & J. Manners were eager for it, seeing no difficulties – Cross & I, without absolutely dissenting, warned our colleagues of the formidable opposition they would have to face, & of the danger of setting town against country. In the end it was agreed to draw a bill, & discuss it again. Some convn on the question of tramways, which is likely also to give trouble in a small way.

Saw Schou. but did not give him the mem. as it has gone to the Queen. ... Keston by 5.15 train.

9 December 1877. Keston. Walk early alone, later with M. in Holwood & on the common. ... Despatches from Layard in great quantities: since he went out early in the year he has sent us nearly 1500: a number quite without precedent.

10 December 1877. Ride early ... Walk later, briskly, for exercise.

11 December 1877. Messenger who came early took away 14 boxes: later, I sent off 17 more. ... Walk early with M.: later for exercise...

News by tel. ... that Osman P. ... has surrendered with his whole force. It was expected that he would have to do so, but most people thought it would take a little longer. It will now be seen whether mediation can be attempted or not.

12 December 1877. Left Keston early ... Windsor for a council: Richmond, Cross, & myself: Disraeli met us there, having come across from Hughenden. Some talk with him, & not quite easy: he seems to want to call parliament together at once, which for purposes of negotiation is wholly unnecessary, & would create general alarm. While we were in the Palace, a telegram came, saying that the Porte intends to appeal to the Powers: but that Layard would be able to prevent this being done if we desired it: after consulting with Ld B. I decided to telegraph to him not to interfere with the Turkish plan, but to let the appeal go on. To have sent a different answer would have been a direct invitation to the Turks to negotiate with Russia exclusively.

... Saw Beust, who left with me a long telegram stating how Andrassy has remonstrated with Russia for allowing the Servians to prepare for war: satisfactory, if sincere, but one cannot be sure that it is not part of a preconcerted arrangement.

13 December 1877. Saw ... Schouvaloff, & gave him the note decided at the cabinet of last week. Some talk followed, on his part merely personal: that is, he had no instructions from his govt. It was rambling & discursive, perhaps intentionally so, but the general object appeared to be to hint at the probability of a separate peace being concluded between Turkey & Russia.

... Saw Münster: he told me, what is confirmed by a secret telegram from O. Russell, that the emperor of Germany will not mediate: O.R. adds, but Münster did not say, that the German cabinet see no prospect of an early peace, Russia being determined to carry on war beyond the Balkans.

14 December 1877. Layard sends over a request from the Sultan that we will endeavour to obtain for him an armistice of three months, during which terms of peace may be arranged. I am afraid it is a hopeless request, but it comes just in time for the cabinet.

The cabinet met at 12.30, & sat nearly two hours. Ld B. opened it by proposing that parliament should be called together as soon as conveniently possible, say in the first week of January: (I think he named the 7th): that a large sum, say £5,000,000, should be asked for on account of armaments: that we should at once proceed to increase our forces: & while doing this, offer mediation to the belligerents. He took pains to show that the arming was not to be connected with the mediation, but to be solely in defence of British interests. J. Manners supported the proposal warmly, saying that if we took up a bold position, we might escape war, but if not, we should be driven or kicked into war: Cross, Smith, Northcote, Hardy, Cairns, & Richmond more or less agreed in this view, though not expressing it so strongly: Salisbury and Carnarvon objected. I reserved my opinion as long as I could, but agreed finally with the objectors. My reasons were that to summon parlt at a time when no one expected it, & at unusually short notice, is a proceeding sure to create alarm & to be misunderstood both in England and Europe: that no need for haste had been shown or appeared on the face of matters: that we had just defined our interests, reaffirmed our position of conditional neutrality & should be unable to give any reason why we thought those interests threatened: that in short, we had nothing to arm for, & that to couple our armaments with an offer of mediation was in reality a menace. Did we mean to act upon it, or not? If we did, that was a new policy, which I had not sanctioned, & did not agree in: if not, we should only create false expectations abroad, & make ourselves ridiculous at home. I added that we could not be expected to decide on this proposal without consideration, and that we ought to meet again. This was agreed to, & we separated, after the least harmonious meeting we have yet had. But no one lost his temper, nor was anything unpleasant said, though I thought the Premier showed more annoyance than usual with him when matters go wrong.

Received this morning a Turkish appeal, or protest, asking the Powers collectively for mediation. It is well-written as Turkish state-papers always are: & not unreasonable in substance: but collective mediation is hopeless as matters stand.

... Home late, tired, and not well pleased, for the situation is more critical than it has been yet. Salisbury and Carnarvon both called at the office, late, to talk it over.

15 December 1877. Saw Schouvaloff, who made one communication of importance. He said that though without positive instructions, he knew that his govt would not listen to any proposal of mediation: they would insist on the preliminaries of peace being settled direct between Russia & Turkey. He authorised me to say this to my colleagues. I made a draft of it for the Premier & others.

Northcote called at my request, & we discussed at some length the proposal made in cabinet yesterday. He agreed with me that the sudden summons of parlt would look like a coup de théâtre ('of which we have had too many already'): that it was not desired, not expected, & would not be understood: that if we called the legislature together we must have some definite & decisive action to submit to it: & I found him inclined to think as I do that the secret meaning of the proposal is to force us into some such course, as it will then be strongly pressed upon us that we are bound to propose something. I said that if the question was only of meeting a fortnight earlier than usual, say, after the 20th or 25th of Jan. I should not oppose it: though doubting the advantage: but that the three measures put before us (1) immediate summons of parlt: (2) vote of credit (3) declared purpose of mediation singly: would be held by every one capable of judging events as constituting collectively a plan of armed intervention. I thought Northcote's views were much altered since yesterday: indeed he complained of having been taken by surprise.

In the actual state of politics, we did not like to leave town: quiet dinner & evening.

16 December 1877. Letter from Northcote, in which he accepts my opns as to the time of meeting, promises support in cabinet, & says others will support also.

In the day there came in a vast number of telegrams from various capitals, which taken together show a more general disposition to mediate than we had supposed to exist.

17 December 1877. Cabinet at 2, sat till 4.30: the most anxious and difficult discussion we have had yet, and ending without result. Ld B. opened it in a sort of speech, which was excellent in taste and judgment. He argued that if the Powers were sincere in wishing for peace, our action would strengthen their hands: if not, there was the more reason why we should act. There was a golden opportunity of asserting the position of England, an opportunity which if lost would never return. If we remained inactive, he foresaw discredit to the govt, and disaster to the country. We should end as the ministry of Ld Aberdeen ended. For himself, his ambition was satisfied. He remained in his present post only because he thought the party wished it. He had led a great party longer than any one in English history: he thought he knew public feeling: & he did not wish again in his life to undergo the pain of parliamentary condemnation. He had never tried to impose his opns on his colleagues, but to conduct affairs with them on the principle of liberty, equality, & fraternity. He had done his best to smooth away such little differences as had arisen: but he shrunk from the result of continuing in our present position. It was not satisfactory & he must again press for 1) an immediate summons of parlt 2) a vote for men and money 3) peace negotiations to be actively pursued. *Hardy* agreed with him. *Northcote* spoke at length, agreeing in the main to two of the three proposals, but objecting to the sudden summons. It would cause sensation, alarm, & surprise: it would tie our hands by compelling us to give pledges: it would lead to a dangerous & protracted opposn: England would be weakened by the spectacle of our divisions: & we

should not get the money we want any sooner, for every kind of delay
would be interposed. He appealed to me.

I followed in the same sense, speaking warmly of our personal feeling
for the Premier, which I did with great sincerity and truth: said we all
wanted to agree if we could: but repeated the objection which I had
already taken. *Salisbury* agreed with me, saying that to meet at once
would be to pledge ourselves to take military measures: that it would
be regarded as a definitive declaration in favour of the war party: that
it would pledge us to do now what we repudiated in May last. He
ended, as I had done, by saying that he would not object to a meeting
earlier than usual, towards the end of Jan. *Cairns* argued for the absolute
necessity of preparation: saying that we are not prepared to defend the
interests to the defence of which we are pledged. It would be enough
to tell parlt that we must be ready. *Richmond* agreed with Cairns. *Cross*
spoke in a balanced sort of way, thinking preparation necessary but
disliking the early meeting. *Carnarvon* hesitated & was scarcely intelligible.
J. Manners saw no objn to the Premier's proposal. *Hicks Beach* wished
parlt were sitting now, and thought the 7th too late. *Smith* raised the
question of whether we should go to Constant. or not: he would be
ready to turn out the Russians if they occupied the place, but not to
anticipate their going by an expedition. This gave a new turn to the
discussion. *Ld B.* threw away all disguise, said the present negotiations
were illusory, the object was to keep Russia from going to Constant.
For that purpose we must arm, & have a large increase of forces, so as
to be ready to send out an expedn. He wished the Porte to put its case
into our hands, that we should arrange the terms of peace, & press
them on Russia. That would be a decided policy. If we were to let the
Russians do what they liked, it would be better to have a Liberal govt
in power. *Northcote* spoke again, feared differences among ourselves
when we opened the session – were we to defend Constant.? Were we
to send out troops before Russia went there? We ought to know what
we wanted, else we should only lose time. Much general convn followed:
I pointed out that what was now spoken of was a complete reversal of
the policy of May last, & objected. The Premier hinted broadly at his
wish to resign, but thought we might like to discuss the matter again,
which was agreed to.

18 December 1877 (Tuesday). Letter from Cross, suggesting compromise,
but vaguely.

Called on the Premier at his request, & talk with him for half an
hour. Our relations were friendly & frank, but we did not conceal from
one another that disagreement existed. He sees things in a way that is
not intelligible to me: holding that the mere fact of Russia and Turkey
coming to a mutual understanding as to terms of peace will be
disgraceful to us, even if the terms themselves are unobjectionable. This

is the foreign view, which treats prestige as the one thing needful in politics. He assured me that he did not want a war, nor an expedition: he only wished that England should be in a posn to have some voice in the coming settlement. I cannot say that I place absolute faith in these assurances, though I do not impute to the Premier that he makes them falsely, but I think they will be forgotten if temptation comes his way. I could quite believe him, on the other hand, when he spoke of the constant pressure put upon him by the Queen, who has been in favour of war from the first, and of his resistance. We spoke also of our mutual relations, & as to these we were both sincere: for neither intellectual differences nor diversity of character can annul a political & personal friendship of nearly thirty years standing.

Cabinet sat from 12 to 2.30. The Premier opened it, saying that his object was peace, that he had nothing to say to the war-party, but wished to be able to mediate with effect. Cairns, evidently by agreement, proposed that the meeting should be on the 17th instead [of] on the 7th: and this was agreed to after discussion by Salisbury & myself. The date is earlier than I should have chosen, but it gives four weeks notice, the proceeding is not now a surprise, & on the whole there is no serious objection. As to armaments, it was agreed generally that some increase shall take place, but no details were gone into. I expressed doubt, but would not absolutely negative the proceeding. Cairns then proposed a scheme of mediation, founded on the Russian terms of peace sketched out in June last: I agreed that something shall be drafted in his sense for the cabinet, but without liking the prospect, which seems to me impracticable.

We then went into the Irish business, which Hicks Beach explained, not in the clearest way: on the question of intermediate education he seemed to me to lean too much towards the ideas of the priests. He says, & I am afraid it is true, that they are absolute masters as far as the Catholic popn is concerned: there is no independent thought or action as against them. We settled nothing: Cairns & I were the chief dissentients from his ideas.

... The crisis is over, & it is possible that the narrowness of our escape from a break-up may induce caution on all sides: but at bottom we are far from agreement. There is a restless desire for action in any sense, rather than for keeping quiet, which is not confined to Disraeli & Cairns, though chiefly shown by them.

19 December 1877. Walk early with Ly D. in thick white fog. She left for Knowsley in the afternoon.

Cabinet 12.30, sat till 2.30. My draft as agreed upon yesterday was read and passed: but I will not send it without consulting at Vienna, to which place I telegraphed. The rest of the cabinet was taken up with the local govt bill, which we seem neither to understand nor to agree upon, & I think it will come to grief in the Commons.

... Saw Schouvaloff, & explained to him, seeing his curiosity, how the prevailing excitement about the war had led us to open parliament earlier than usual – how agitation would be checked, mistaken ideas of the intentions of govt dispelled, & the public mind be set at ease as soon as parliamentary discussion became possible. This I developed at some length, & he knows England well enough to understand it. I hinted in vague terms at the responsibility which a cabinet would have to incur if action became necessary in the recess, but thought it better to say nothing definite on that head, & absolutely to avoid all mention of a possible increase of armaments. He was evidently uneasy, which I was not sorry to see & expressed fear lest the Turks should be encouraged to resist. But he is mistaken in believing, if he does believe it, that they ever meant anything else. Their appeal to the mediation of the Powers, based on their constitution, can hardly be meant to be taken seriously.

Sanderson dined with me.

20 December 1877 (Thursday). ... Lawson called to ask for news. Greenwood called, & told me in talking of French affairs that Gambetta has heart disease, and is not expected to live long[85]: a loss to French public life, if true, for he is at bottom moderate enough, though with the external appearance of violence, such as belongs to his occupation as a demagogue.

Office ... no visitors of any kind. Sanderson dined with me. Very quiet day.

21 December 1877 (Friday). ... Office as usual, stayed till near 6. Some diplomatists called, but I forget who, except Schouvaloff. He told me nothing.

Long telegram from Buchanan. Andrassy, to whom our plan of mediation has been shown, objects to it on various grounds: & as we had relied on his assistance, it is clear that a change must now be made. I went across to Disraeli, & talked the matter over with him: he agreed with me that the plan would not now work, and wanted to adopt an alternative at once: but I refused to act in such critical circs without the sanction of the cabinet, which must meet some day next week. The objections taken by Andrassy appear to be very nearly those which I had myself dwelt upon in cabinet: but I yielded to the prevailing anxiety that some step should be taken, to the conviction that no particular harm could come of it, & to the impossibility of making my colleagues understand where the difficulty lay. As matters stand, considering the chances of disagreement among ourselves, and the necessity of vindicating before parliament all that we do, it is absolutely

[85] D. 1882.

necessary that nothing material should be done, except with cabinet sanction: but there is a certain practical inconvenience in being guided by the decision of men who are too much occupied elsewhere to have given very close attention to the matter in hand, and whose knowledge or recollection of what has passed before is imperfect.

22 December 1877 (Friday). Windsor by special train, arriving about 1: left the castle at 2.30 ... The party consisted of the Premier, Richmond, J. Manners, the outgoing U.S. minister, Pierrepont, and his successor Welsh.[86] The Queen was in excellent humour, talked of various things, but not one word of eastern affairs: this I am told is her habit whenever she suspects that anyone disagrees with her. Ponsonby tells me that having let it appear that he did not share in her warlike feelings some months ago, she has never mentioned the east to him since: though before that she was in the habit of talking about it freely enough. Is this the mere dislike of anything like difference, or is it the result of a notion that royal dignity suffers by the slightest approach to discussion? Pierrepont took leave, gracefully & simply: the new minister showed to less advantage: his address 'I hope, marm, I see you well, marm', delivered in a quaint voice, nearly upset the Queen's gravity. He is, I think, a sensible sort of man at bottom, but rather pompous & uncouth, with less intellectual cultivation than Pierrepont, & no humour, of which P. has a good deal. We held a council...

Beust called upon me in St J. Square, & read a long telegram from Andrassy, for which I was prepared by one from Buchanan yesterday. The purport of it is that he objects entirely to take the Russian conditions of June last as a basis for peace, thinking them impracticable & too favourable to Turkey. This view he expands at considerable length & with much ingenuity. But oddly enough he has forgotten that it was he himself who when I made observations in the same sense in June last, answered that the terms would not do as they stood, but ought not to be rejected altogether, inasmuch as they might serve as a point of departure for negociations. It is therefore his own plan which he is criticising, and that, as I told Beust, after we had adopted it chiefly from the wish to act in harmony with Austria. He agreed, & laughed at his chief's forgetfulness, or change of mind. There is no love lost between the pair: which is amusing to see, but not always convenient. Andrassy announces a new scheme, which Beust is to communicate tomorrow. I made our conversation into a draft, & kept the telegram to be copied.

Sanderson dined with me.

23 December 1877 (Sunday). Beust called at 12, but had not got his telegram decyphered, so that I had to ask him to call again at 3. He did so, & read it, but after all there is an important mistake, which he

[86] John Welsh (1805–86), U.S. minister 22 Dec. 1877–14 Aug. 1878.

had to correct by telegraph afterwards! It is not clear what Andrassy wants or expects us to do: but I telegraphed to Layard to know if the Porte will sanction our applying to Russia to know what conditions of peace Russia will ask. The Porte is sure to agree: and our request to know the terms will at any rate simplify the situation. If Russia refuses mediation altogether, we have fair warning that she will push her advantages to the utmost: if not, we have an opening for negotiation. I told Beust that in deference to C. Andrassy's opinion, which indeed is my own also, I would in any communication to be eventually made to Russia, drop all mention of the Russian proposals of June.

Wrote to Salisbury a warning letter urging him to look out for future danger: I feared an agitation for war: a warlike speech from the throne: an excessive demand for military preparations: and generally that we should find ourselves drawn on, step by step, into a position which we did not contemplate, and would not have accepted beforehand. I mentioned my old and sincere friendship for the Premier, & said that I should always be willing to make personal sacrifices in order to support him: but I feared his love of prestige: which he would quite honestly think it worth while to make war to support, and I knew the pressure which was being put upon him by the Queen.

Early dinner at Travellers': with Sanderson to Knowsley by 5 p.m. train. Arrived about 11: found there the Galloways, Margaret, Arthur, and Lionel, and P. Hope,[87] eldest son of Beresford Hope, a strange being, who some years ago nearly drank himself to death, but is now reformed and sober. He is a friend of the lads, which accounts for his being here.

24 December 1877 (Monday). Violent storm ... Walk with Ly D. Walk later with Sanderson.

... Offered Lumley[88] the vacancy at Madrid, through Sanderson, but in such a way that he may be encouraged to refuse it if as we believe, he prefers to remain at Brussels. I suspect it is his doing that the King has asked to keep him. If I could secure an embassy for Thornton, Lumley would be fit to replace him at Washington, & would go willingly, the political importance of the place compensating for other disadvantages. The early meeting of parliament continues to be discussed in the papers, but the first feeling of surprise having worn off, people begin to see there is no reason for alarm. In fact, if anything were meditated by the cabinet which could compromise the country,

---

[87] Philip Beresford-Hope, e.s. of A.J. Beresford-Hope, politician, by Mildred, dau. of James, 2nd M. of Salisbury. B. 1851, he m. (1883) the 4th dau. of a U.S. general.

[88] John Savile (Savile-Lumley to 1887), 1st Baron Savile of Rufford (1818–d. unm. 1896); illegit. s. of 8th E. of Scarborough (who d. unm. 1856); entered F.O. 1841; envoy to Saxony 1866–7, to Switzerland 1867–8, to Brussels Oct. 1868–83; amb. to Italy, 1883–7; cr. peer 1888; art collector.

our interest would rather be to delay than to hasten the date when all that we do must be laid open for criticism.

War operations are suspended by heavy falls of snow & nothing is being done. But in Mansfield's opinion the Russian advance may & probably will be continued in winter, though slowly & with great suffering to the troops. The feeling in Petersburgh is all in favour of a continuance of the war, & against mediation or interference in any form. ... Of the Emperor's own state of mind I know nothing: he is essentially a weak man, influenced by the last speaker, & probably is just now full of the ideas which he has brought back from the camp ... At Berlin, according to O. Russell, there is a determination to have nothing to do with any projects of mediation, & to observe strict neutrality, but with a friendly leaning towards Russia. Bismarck keeps away from Berlin purposely to avoid having to give an opinion. The German ambassador at Const. presses the Porte to make peace direct with Russia: (this we know from Layard): & the same language is held to the Turkish ambassador at Berlin. There is however no expectation that the Turks will take the advice so given. Russell repeats his belief that the three Emperors have agreed on the ultimate, though not immediate partition of Turkey. The general belief at Berlin is that we are going to take part, not in order to save the Porte, but to claim our share of the spoils. Münster is triumphant, he has always said that England would be dragged into the quarrel sooner or later, & declares that now parliament will verify his predictions.

25 December 1877 (Tuesday). Cold, snow falling heavily: I did not stir out in the morning, but worked on office papers, of which I have a vast heap. I do not regret the occupation: my spirits were never quite equal to a noisy Christmas party, & the anxieties of the last two years have made them less so than before. So I am best in my room, where indeed I have enough to do: & I am content that my guests should enjoy themselves.

... Saw Hale,[89] & long talk with him on estate affairs. ... I ask Hale to consider how to reduce the cost & quantity of the shooting, which is more than we care for or can get through.

26 December 1877. Saw Hale again, & more talk on estate matters...

... Sir W. Thomson[90] shows us the new invented instrument, the telephone, a wire being carried from the house to the stables ... I could not hear very distinctly as a rule, but others could.

... Left at 3 p.m. with Sanderson for London. St J. Square before 11: we supped together.

[89] Head agent at Knowsley.

[90] Sir William Thomson, 1st Baron Kelvin (1824–1907), prof. of natural philosophy at Glasgow; involved, like Derby's friend Pender, in laying of transatlantic cable.

*On 27 December Sanderson, in London, met Monty Corry, Disraeli's secretary, in
the street. 'He told me that he knew positively from abroad that Schouvaloff had
been able to give the Emperor an account of the division of feeling in the cabinet
and of what had passed at the beginning of this month and that in consequence the
Emperor's views as regards peace negotiations have been materially altered. So I
said I was sure he had not heard it from Lord D. and there the matter ended. ...
Please do not make any allusion to Schou to what Mr. Corry told me. ... I hope
you will consider that you have received no letter from me, as I cannot ask Lord D.
what to tell you, and have not seen any of the documents', Sanderson wrote to Lady
Derby at Knowsley on the 27th. Derby, in his diary, made no reference to Corry's
imputations and never at any time hinted in his diary at any awareness that he or
his wife were suspected of leaking cabinet secrets. On the morning of 28 December
Sanderson again met Corry and 'had a satisfactory conversation with him. He was
moderate and sensible. He disclaimed any ideas of leakage here.' Corry added
significantly that if the Russians went beyond Adrianople 'we shall certainly
eventually be landed in a war either under the present govt or under another brought
in to make it'.*[91]

27 December 1877 (Thursday). Busy all morning: short walk: office at
1.30: stayed in Downing St till past 6.

Cabinet at 3, sat till about 4. The only business done was discussing
the request to be made to Russia to say whether she will state the
conditions of peace. We talked about this for an hour, in a vague
desultory way which was not very business-like: but in the end the draft
I had prepared was agreed to with some modification. Cairns took a
specially active part, Richmond backing up all he said with a persistent
fidelity which was almost comic. The tone of the Premier was calm &
studiously moderate: he seemed as if aware that his ministry had
narrowly escaped running on the rocks, & might be in danger again. I
had no private discourse with him.

O. Russell telegraphs that both Bismarck and Andrassy will do their
utmost to put obstacles in the way of any proposal of mediation, wishing
the Porte to be compelled to appeal to the Emperor direct. That this
is true as regards Bismarck I have little doubt, but in the case of
Andrassy it is less certain. He is either vacillating or playing a double
game: but there is no obvious reason why he should go out of his way
to oppose England while affecting to be anxious to consult our wishes
and to act with us.

No diplomatist called. Sanderson dined with me.[92]

28 December 1877 (Friday). Sent off 16 boxes ... No news of importance.

[91] Derby MSS, uncatalogued.
[92] The following day Sanderson wrote to Lady Derby, apparently in reply to some
warning about talking to Schouvaloff from Mary Galloway. Sanderson said that Derby

... Lumley refuses Madrid. I have hesitated about this choice, lest it should be thought a job:[93] but really I know of no one who from service & general reputation has equally high claims: & West ought not to suffer from the accident of being my brother-in-law.

... Harcourt[94] had recovered his spirits, & is better pleased with the new ministry, now that he is satisfied they do not intend to recall him. He talked about Newfoundland, & the difficulty of dealing with that question, which I did not dispute. I took the opportunity, knowing from Lyons that there is great uneasiness as to our intentions about Egypt, of assuring Harcourt in the most formal & positive manner, that we wanted nothing in that quarter, neither annexation, protectorate, nor paramount & exclusive influence, but only free passage, and the absence of any foreign influence dominating ours. I explained why: dwelling chiefly on two reasons: that by a different policy we should put an end to the *entente cordiale* with France, which was worth more to us than Egypt could be: and that having already a vast Asiatic territory, the addition of more subject races would be to us a source of weakness & not of strength. I did not do more than allude to the financial side of the question, though it is important: for Egypt is mortgaged beyond its value, & we hardly make India pay, though it came unburdened into our hands.

With Beust I had an interesting conversation, of which I have made a despatch. I pressed him, or rather Andrassy through him, to declare openly the policy which he has adopted. I pointed out that the belief was universal throughout Europe that whatever was decided at Berlin & Petersburgh would be sanctioned at Vienna: that the Russians were undoubtedly under this impression: that while it lasted we could not hope materially to influence Russian decisions: that it would be imposs-ible for any English minister even to allude to the prospect of Austrian support without being discredited – so strong was the conviction that such support could not be looked for: lastly, that the Russians themselves were entitled in justice to be told how the case really stood & not to be misled by hopes of assistance which they would not receive. All this I charged C. Beust to convey in such manner as he might think most prudent, & with due apologies for unasked advice.

could not have divulged the draft agreed in cabinet on the 27th 'as the exact terms were not settled. There was a running to and fro of Tenterden to the Prime Minister's, etc. etc. The telegram went off last night to Loftus.

I am afraid my intelligence yesterday [i.e. on 27th] was somewhat meagre but presume you heard all from Lord Derby. He scarcely told me anything except that the cabinet had gone off well, and without any difference of opinion.' (Derby MSS, uncatalogued.)

[93] Lady Derby's bro., Lionel Sackville-West, 2nd Baron Sackville (1827–1908), min. to Argentina 1872–8, became min. to Spain 1878–81, then to Washington 1881–8.

[94] French amb.

My reason for making this communication was to test Andrassy's sincerity, and brings matters to a definite issue. He is evidently tricking either the Russians or us: and that is not a satisfactory state of things. We must be able to judge whether he is to be trusted or not: and there is no harm in his seeing that we want some guarantees of good faith before agreeing to act in concert with him.

Quiet evening: Sanderson dined with me.

29 December 1877 (Saturday). Did not go to the office ... ... Knowsley by 5 p.m. train with Sanderson: found in the house, Schouvaloff, who had come down on Friday to shoot, & was just about to leave: Münster, with his daughters: the Galloways: A. and L. Cecil, P. Hope, Mrs W.S. West and daughters, and Margaret.

Long talk with Schou. before going to bed: he had stayed on purposely to see me: in the midst of our convn the answer from Loftus arrived: it is as we expected, a civil refusal to negotiate with any Power except the Porte in the first instance. Schou. was evidently uneasy, as he has been ever since the news of parliament being called together: & I do not discourage his apprehensions, as they may have a wholesome effect at Petersburgh. He presses me strongly not to treat the answer (which I read to him) as a refusal to negotiate, but simply as indicating the way in which the Emperor prefers that negotiations should be carried on. But the matter requires consideration, & I gave none but the vaguest replies to his suggestions.

Schou.[95] tells Ly D. that he finds the Rothschilds acquainted with everything that goes on: even more so than the ministers: he is convinced that they are in daily communication with the Premier, hear all that passes, & use it for their own purposes. From other sources I am certain that the leakage of cabinet secrets, of which we have so often complained, is mainly in that quarter: for when Ld B. goes out of town there is generally but little gossip of that kind. I suspect Corry, & also some of the Premier's female friends: but the Rothschilds no doubt get their news direct from himself.

30 December 1877 (Sunday). Knowsley. ... Long & curious talk with Ly D. who has heard direct from the palace, & on authority which she thinks indisputable but with so strict an obligation of secrecy as to the

---

[95] Schouvaloff's movements are of some interest. On Thursday evening at 6.30 Lady Derby heard from him that he would be in Liverpool at 6 a.m. on Friday morning and at Knowsley at 9 a.m. He then spent Friday and most of Saturday at Knowsley, in Derby's absence, presumably leaving on Sunday morning. Lady Derby had at this time just received 'very stringent advice' from Dean Wellesley, acting for the Queen, about her familiarity with Schouvaloff. She replied to Wellesley's letter on 29 December, presumably after discussion with Schou., whose own comments reflect this. Schou.'s sudden arrival at Knowsley may have been in response to the Queen's letter. (Cf. Blake, *Disraeli*, 635).

author that I would not press her to disclose the name, some details which may be very important. They are to the effect that the Queen is more than ever in the hands of J.B.[96] – that he sleeps in a room adjoining her bedroom, contrary to all etiquette & even decency – that the belief in a private marriage is general among the household, though they are ashamed or afraid to talk of it – that she insists on the princes shaking hands with him & treating him on the footing of a gentleman, which they object to, but can hardly refuse (this I had heard before): that he, & consequently she also, takes note of the civilities paid to him, & anyone who ignores him is badly looked upon at court. That the Q. divides her ministers into two classes, those who will accept Brown as an acquaintance & talk familiarly with him, & those who will not. I farther understand that these things were said to Ly D. with a view of my ingratiating myself with the said J. B. – that I am supposed to be out of favour (which is likely enough to be true, not only on that account, but because of the war, & my resistance to our taking part in it) & that it is necessary on public grounds that I should use all legitimate means to strengthen my position. – I don't see myself doing it, at any rate in that way.

31 December 1877 (Monday). Shooting … with C. Münster, Galloway, Hope, & A. Cecil … We killed 262 head, chiefly hares … I enjoyed this quiet end to a disturbed & anxious year.

… Dinner to the village children, presents distributed, etc.

… Much talk with Sanderson as to the vacant posts: Petre,[97] Corbett,[98] and Rumbold[99] have all fairly equal claims: Rumbold is the youngest of the three, and by far the ablest in point of intellect, but with an unfortunate infirmity of temper that makes him dangerous in any place where patience is requisite: Petre is senior, but though fairly competent, rather heavy and slow: Corbett has done well in S. America, and I moved him two or three years ago to Berne. – On the whole I decide that he shall go to Athens: and write to the Queen to propose him. Rumbold must then have the choice of B. Ayres or Berne: he will resent the offer as an affront: but that I cannot help: Petre shall have next choice, & if they both refuse, there can be no scruple about promoting juniors over their heads.[100]

[96] John Brown (1826–83), manservant.

[97] Sir G.G. Petre (1822–1905), diplomatist 1846–93; envoy at Stuttgart 1872–81, at Lisbon 1884–93.

[98] Edwin Corbett (1819–88), diplomatist 1847–1888; like Derby, educ. Rugby and Trin. Coll. Cambridge; min. to Guatemala 1872, and to four other Central American states, 1873; transferred to Berne, May 1874; min. to Greece Jan. 1878, to Brazil 1881, to Sweden 1884–death.

[99] (Sir) Horace Rumbold (1829–1913), diplomatist 1849–1900; min. in Chile 1872–8, in Switzerland 1878–9; finally amb. to Austria 1896–1900; succ. bro. as bt 1877.

[100] For this reshuffle, see also above, 12 Sept. 1877 *et seq.*

1878

1 January 1878 (Tuesday). In the house Count Münster and his daughters: Mary Galloway (Galloway left us yesterday): P. Hope, L. and A. Cecil, Margaret, and Sanderson.

All except Sanderson and myself went out shooting on the Moss beat. There came from the office ten boxes, mostly heavy.

Short walk with Ly Derby. Much pleased with the appearance of the outside: there is a look of neatness and order about the place which used to be conspicuously absent.

Left at 3, and 4 p.m. train to London. Found a vast heap of letters and papers, and busy till late.

The year just ended has been one of greater anxiety and labour than I have yet gone through. In regard of foreign affairs it has been one long crisis, and though the cabinet has so far gone on without loss of strength, and with the support of parliament, the effort to keep it together, and to prevent follies being committed, has been incessant and exhausting. The Queen wants a war, and presses it continually: I ✓ am out of favour as being known to oppose it. On the other hand, she does all in her power to mark her sense of the premier's greater docility in that respect. The visit paid him at Hughenden[1] was meant to be a demonstration of confidence, and she justly calculates that by these public displays of sympathy, she increases his difficulty in opposing her wishes. He, I think, does not desire a war, but he fears above all things the reproach of weak or commonplace policy: he lives among people not of the wisest sort, who lead him to believe the public feeling much more warlike than it really is: and the idea of compromising the future of the country by reckless finance, or indeed of distant results of any kind, is one which his mind is not fitted to entertain: in all matters, foreign and domestic, he has shown the same peculiarity: great acuteness to see what is most convenient for the moment, combined with apparent indifference to what is to come of it in the long run. The state of things is therefore unpleasant and dangerous: for we have a divided cabinet, no continental ally, and a public which expects it does not know what, and wishes to have the results of victory without the sacrifices of war.

[1] The Queen lunched at Hughenden, 15 Dec. 1877 (the anniversary of Mrs Disraeli's death). Beaconsfield dined and slept at Windsor on 18 Dec., making further visits on 22 and 27 Dec. On 20 Jan. the Queen offered him the Garter, which he declined.

For the first time in many years, our finance is bad: trade has fallen off, business is slack, the revenue has fallen below even the very safe and moderate estimates of last April: there is distress in many districts, especially those where the coal and iron trade prevail: under ordinary circumstances this condition of financial depression would be an unmixed evil, but in our actual state it is a partial safeguard against the agitation for war.

Home politics have been practically unnoticed: not a sign of any agitation is visible: the Whig leaders have adopted (Lowe and Goschen dissenting) the policy of equalising the county and borough franchises:[2] and the thing will no doubt be done some day: but no real interest is felt in it, and if taken up as the Liberal cry at the next election it will be only for want of anything else to put forward. Two circumstances tend to destroy the enthusiasm which might otherwise be felt or affected for a large change in the direction of popular government: one, that the result is utterly uncertain: many people think that it would make the representation more conservative than it is now: the other, that it must be combined with a considerable redistribution of seats, which nobody wants, and which the H. of C. itself always objects to. The Irish obstructives will give trouble: and it is doubted whether Northcote is quite strong enough for his place ... As far as one can see, popular feeling is unaltered.

In private affairs the year has been uneventful to me. In point of health, I have not much to complain of: labour and anxiety have not told on that: but I feel the effect of incessant worry in nerves and spirits, and will not answer for being able to go on much longer. My resolution is more and more confirmed, if it can be done without sacrifice of public duty, to retire from a position which many persons desire, which many would fill equally well, and which gives me no pleasure. Eight years passed in Downing St are a sufficient discharge of one's debt to the state.

Except £5000 to Ly D. I have paid off no debt in 1877: but the sums due from railway companies will clear the estates, except as regards my brother's fortune, which under the circs need not be taken into account. I have secured Holwood to the family, and increased my estate at Witley.[3] In Lancashire there has been no change of importance, a few fields here and there bought, and a few sold ... The sales to railways, though large in value, do not perceptibly affect the area of the estates, which including those in the south, are a little under 70,000 acres.

---

[2] See above, 7 Nov. 1877. See also John P. Rossi, 'The Transformation of the British Liberal Party, 1874–1880' (*Transactions of the American Philosophical Society*, 1978), 21.

[3] Derby's recently purchased estate, 3m. from Godalming, Surrey.

On the whole I have nothing to complain of except the too great strain of office, and if my life has not always been pleasant during the last twelve months, it has been free from all serious calamity or trouble.

2 January 1878 (Wednesday). Made up private accounts for the year: I have spent £3876, of which £2532 is for works of art, £715 for books and binding. Charities and benefactions of all kinds are excluded, being in a separate account...

... Cabinet met at 3, sat till nearly 5 p.m. Before it met I had called on the premier at his request, and found him peaceably enough disposed, but in an odd paradoxical mood: he discoursed at length on the distinction between an armistice and a truce,[4] saying that Gortschakoff had ignored it (which I don't see, and it is not of the slightest consequence if he did): then talked of Germany, and said that Bismarck would be willing enough to help us to make peace, it was the old emperor who was the real obstacle: as to this he hinted that the Queen was his informant. Altogether I could not make him out, and have hardly ever heard him talk in so unpractical a strain. However, we agreed pretty well as to the kind of answer to be given, and after a great deal of discussion, most of it not much to the purpose, the cabinet agreed also.[5] The substance is, that we agree to the Russian suggestion that an armistice should be the first step in negotiation: but we propose a modification[6] in the manner of bringing it about. In this last part of the answer I see no especial use, but also no harm, and so accepted it. I drafted a long telegram in the sense agreed to.[7]

Sanderson dined with me.

3 January 1878 (Thursday). Cabinet at 12: at which a singular scene occurred. Carnarvon had, it seems, made a speech[8] to a deputation yesterday, before the cabinet, in which he expressed strong feelings in favour of peace, condemned a repetition of the Crimean War as an act of insanity, and generally made it clear that he would do nothing to oppose Russia. The speech was certainly imprudent and inopportune,

[4] 'Military men decide on truces, not armistices', argued Beaconsfield to the Queen, 2 Jan. 1878 (M. and B., 212).
[5] All were present and 'all at one' in their reply to Russia (*GH*, 346).
[6] Britain's proposal, ignored by Russia, was that the armistice terms should be settled by governments, not by field commanders.
[7] 'Some domestic affairs occupied us afterwards' (*GH*, ibid.).
[8] For Carnarvon's speech of 31 Dec. 1877 to S. African colonists, stating there is 'nobody insane enough to desire a repetition' of the Crimean War, see *T*, 3 Jan. 1878; in Hardy's view 'a Cabinet declaration of peace at any price or nearly so', with 'Salisbury ... warm in his defence' and Derby 'favourable to what was said to be its tenor' (*GH* 347). The Carnarvon incident may be linked to Beaconsfield's attempt to separate Derby from Salisbury (*Cecil* 169–70), and to his renewed efforts to blacken Derby's name by using Col. Wellesley's report on the leakage of cabinet secrets to Russia. See Hardinge, *Carnarvon*, iii 368–70.

for with parliament about to meet in a fortnight nothing need have been said, and it was not desirable to tell the Russians in such plain terms that they have nothing to fear from us in any event. But we were not prepared for a long and formal censure of the performance by the premier, which he delivered with considerable energy, and it appeared to most of us, in unusually peremptory terms. Carnarvon, taken by surprise, defended himself as best he could, and plainly said that the expressions of the premier were such as could not be overlooked, and that he must consider his course: which plainly meant resignation. Cairns, Hardy, and J. Manners, while all civil to Ld C. joined in the censure: J.M. going so far as to say that it was absolutely necessary that some statement should be issued by the cabinet: which raised a laugh. Salisbury and I tried to mediate: the former diverging rather needlessly into a violent attack on the *D. Telegraph*: I had not happened to see the speech, and could therefore say nothing about it, which was perhaps as well, but deprecate C.'s idea of resigning, on the ground that there was no question of policy before us on which to ground a resignation, and that by leaving the cabinet he would only weaken the influence of those who thought with him. To those public arguments I added in private another: suppose that the object of the premier's remonstrance were to drive him out of the ministry, in order to put a partisan of war in his place, was not that the very reason why he should stay where he was? Cross and Salisbury, with whom I talked later, were as much puzzled as I was by the Premier's tone, which may have been due only to temper, though that is very unusual with him: but I suspect a design in it. The rest of our business was to read and approve the draft agreed on in principle yesterday: and to discuss the corrupt practices [at] elections bill, which being temporary must be renewed and will be opposed in the commons.

Office from 2 till near 6: saw there Menabrea,[9] who came with various questions to ask, which he put clearly and briefly, as his manner is: Beust,[10] who read me a long telegram, explaining Andrassy's[11] position in regard to Russia, which is fairly satisfactory: what he says is in substance, that Austria and Russia have an understanding: that Russia has nothing to fear from Austria: but that that is the case only because the Russian govt clearly understands what are the reserves made by Austria, and what are the results of the war which Austria will not accept. Musurus called also, vague and incoherent in talk: and Schou. who came to know the purport of our answer to Gortschakoff's communication. I told him this, and told it confidentially, to all the

---

[9] Italian amb.
[10] Austrian amb.
[11] Austrian premier.

other three. Lawson[12] and Hamber[13] also came for news. Quiet evening.
Sanderson dined. A great mass of papers to dispose of.

4 January 1878 (Friday). Called at the dentists to have a tooth taken
out, which was done under gas, without the least pain or discomfort,
then or afterwards. ... Working at home till 2.30, when to office.

... Office at 2.30. Saw there Carnarvon, who is just returned from
Osborne. He reports the Queen more excited and violent about war
than he has ever known her: she first sent word to C. that she would
not speak to him on eastern affairs: then changed her mind, and talked
of nothing else: she said the people were lethargic, that they must be
roused, that she was determined to use all means in her power to rouse
them, that we must fight, we should be disgraced if we did not, and
more to the same effect. C. objected that we should have no allies: the
Q. answered, in heat, that that was a cowardly argument. ... He then
discoursed at length on his personal grievance of yesterday, reverting
to the idea of resignation, which I combated by the same arguments
as before. I have little sympathy with the man, for he is weak, vain,
and fussy in his personal relations, though a good administrator: but
in the present case he really has something to complain of, and it is
essential that he should not be driven out at this moment.

... Quiet evening. Sanderson dined. Business not very heavy.

5 January 1878 (Saturday). Office about 2, and stayed till 5. Saw Schou.
who evidently thinks better of the situation, I do not know why: but
he tells me that many people are busy here spreading reports as to the
offence given by the Russian reply, and the likelihood of a quarrel:
evidently with a set purpose of making mischief. Saw Beust, who had
heard of these same reports, and came to know the truth, which I told
him. I could see that both of these diplomatists believe the origin of
the stories referred to to be in Downing St. In other words they take
for granted that the premier wants the negotiations to fail, in order
that he may have a pretext for a quarrel.

Musurus called, and left me with a tel. in which the Porte announces
that it accepts the armistice in principle, and would be glad if a
suspension of hostilities can be obtained, until a regular armistice can
be concluded.

Sanderson dined with me. At ten o'clock Mylady[14] came from
Knowsley.

Layard[15] sends a mass of correspondence: he dwells especially on the

[12] Ed. *Daily Telegraph.*
[13] Capt. Thomas Hamber, Cons. journalist; former ed. of *Standard*; ed. *Morning Advertiser*, 1877–; once close to Disraeli and Salisbury, but d. in obscurity.
[14] Lady Derby.
[15] U.K. amb. to Turkey.

bitterness against England of the German ambassador Prince Reuss:[16] who he says wants to establish a kind of Monroe doctrine in regard of the eastern question, excluding from the discussion of it all powers except the three empires. Singularly it chances that within a few hours of receiving this communication, I got a telegram from Lyons[17] to the effect that in the opinion of the French F.O., Russia would be willing to make peace if let alone, but that Bismarck for objects of his own is doing what he can to prolong the war. He is certainly also doing what he can to embroil us in it: the only intelligible reason is that he wishes to be left free to deal with France as he pleases.

6 January 1878 (Sunday). In afternoon called on Ld B in Downing St but failed to find him. Met in D. St F. Wellesley,[18] who just returned from Bucharest. He reports the Emperor as warlike in his language, much influenced by the company he has kept and the success of his army. The army on the other hand he considers as much demoralised by its campaign, the officers bad, the vacancies in the ranks hastily filled up, and all classes weary of the war. According to him the Bulgarians are disgusted with their liberators, and do not scruple to say that they much prefer the Turks. The Russians on the other hand declare that they have been duped as to the state of the populations whom they came to rescue. He thinks the Russian troops will still find much difficulty in getting to Adrianople:[19] chiefly owing to the want of transport and difficulty of subsistence.

Telegram from Loftus[20] giving Gortschakoff's[21] answer to our suggestion: he adheres to his proposal of an armistice to be negotiated between the generals, but adding they have instructions as to the terms, which alters the position.

The premier came to speak to me about the reply to be sent to Russia. To my agreeable surprise we did not differ on the terms. He was less satisfactory about Carnarvon, of whom he spoke with a good deal of bitterness, saying that he ought to explain etc whereas Carnarvon expects the same from him. I think however we shall make the quarrel up. He talked ominously about its being still possible to keep out of war: to which I replied by suggesting that it might not be easy to get into it. The convn was friendly, but the feeling of underlying difference caused it to be reserved.

7 January 1878 (Monday). Met Disraeli, and walk half an hour with

---

[16] Heinrich VII, Prince von Reuss (1825–1906), German amb. to Turkey 1877–8.
[17] U.K. amb to France.
[18] Col. The Hon. F.A. Wellesley (1844–1931), military attaché in Russia 1871 – April 1878.
[19] Adrianople fell 20 Jan. 1878 (*Cecil*, 190).
[20] U.K. amb. to Russia.
[21] Russian chancellor.

him: all pleasant, no trace of annoyance: indeed we understand each other's difficulties. He speaks of the trouble he has had with the Queen, who complains of being deceived and betrayed by her ministers, and threatens to abdicate if her policy – which is war – does not find support. She writes to him every day, and often more than once a day, always in the same excited condition. He doubts whether there is not in all this a beginning of insanity.

Cabinet at 2: sat till about 3.30. Carnarvon, who had written to me overnight to say that he should not resign, read a mem. in his own justification which was simple and sensible enough. Ld B. paid him a few compliments, rather formally, but enough to serve as an *amende* for his rough speech of the other day, and the matter ended.

We discussed the vote of credit, the difficulty of getting which I think Northcote underrates, and said so: but the question is one entirely for the H. of C. and if our friends there are satisfied I can do no more. It is at best an unsatisfactory throwing away of public money, but I suppose we can manage so that all need not be spent. We settled the answer to Gortschakoff, which is an acceptance of the Russian proposals. I told this to Musurus and Schou. who both called after the cabinet.

8 January 1878 (Tuesday). Received from Ld B. draft of the Queen's speech, which is clever, remarkably well written, but misleading and quite inconsistent in tone with the attitude of neutrality which we have hitherto observed.

F. came to dine: despondent about the prospects of the session: which is rather his habit but this time there is a reason. He showed me a mem. which he has drawn up for Northcote, proving that there is absolutely no precedent for a vote of credit at the beginning of a session, and that if the idea of a large increase of military expenditure is persisted in, it must be in the shape of a supplementary estimate. I have no doubt but that he is right, and indeed his view is exactly that which I have been trying for some time past to press on the cabinet, hitherto without result. Whether from pressure of business or any other cause, there seems a strange reluctance in my colleagues to anticipate difficulties till they occur: which leads to confusion, and sudden changes at the last moment.

9 January 1878 (Wednesday). Reading again the draft speech prepared by the premier, and liking it if possible even less than before, I wrote to Carnarvon, saw him, communicated to him my objections, and induced him to speak to Salisbury. This he did, and on going down at 12 to the cabinet I found that Northcote, Cross, and others were of the same mind. We discussed it for upwards of two hours, with a good deal of animation and earnestness, but all in perfect temper. I was obliged as Foreign Secretary, to begin the discussion, which I did unwillingly, not liking to express a marked dissent from the premier's views, connected as we are and long have been. But I had no choice. Salisbury agreed with me entirely, Cairns in part: (which latter I did not expect): and as the convn went on it became evident that no one of us, except J. Manners and Richmond, approved of the document as it stood. Hicks Beach was in Ireland, else he would no doubt have swelled the minority. The premier defended some of his positions, abandoned others, but endured our criticism with a great deal more patience than I should have shown in the like case, and in the end the speech was completely transformed by the omission of all passages (there were several) which had a warlike or menacing tendency. I have seldom been more anxious on any question, indeed my sleep last night was disturbed in consequence, which rarely happens: my mind was made up to have resigned in the event of failure, not out of pique, but because it would have been impossible for me to defend in parlt ideas which are contrary to mine. Happily all went well.[22]

Office at 2.30, stayed till 4.30 ... Keston by 5.15 train.

Whether from nervous disturbance, sudden cold, or any other cause, I was taken unwell with shivering fits, diarrhoea, and sickness: a sharp bilious attack,[23] of which luckily no one will know anything, since visitors do not often find their way to Keston.

News ... of the unexpected death of the K. of Italy ...[24] Notwithstanding unpleasant manners, gross private vices, and a total want of ability, he kept and deserved the confidence of the Italian people ... The secret lay in his perfect truthfulness and honesty, rare in his class and in his country ...

10 January 1878 (Thursday). Lay in bed till past ten, feeling still unwell and weak. In the afternoon the disagreeable sensations nearly passed off, but I have not much energy, either of mind or body.

11 January 1878 (Friday). Came up early to town, feeling ill: saw Drage:[25] stayed at home, but did business as usual. (I was unable to make notes for the next three days, and have entirely forgotten what passed).

12 January 1878 (Saturday). Cabinet at 12, which sat till 2.30. Anxious and protracted discussion, the subject being whether an expedition should be sent out to occupy Turkish territory at Gallipoli, and hold it on our own account, as a material guarantee for the security of the

[22] The Speech was agreed 'not without signs of a difference which may spring up with danger at any critical moment' (*GH* 347).
[23] Perhaps gastric flu. On 14 Jan. Carnarvon had been 'very ill during the last week, in bed much of the time, and now, though better, sometimes scarcely able to crawl from one room to another' (Hardinge, *Carnarvon* ii 373). On 18 Jan. the robust Hardy was 'in perpetual fear of sickness' (*GH*, 349).
[24] Victor Emmanuel II (1820–78), king of Italy 1861–78.
[25] Doctor.

Dardanelles. The whole cabinet, except Carnarvon and I, were either in favour of this being done, or at very least not opposed to it. We protested without hope of success, and for nearly an hour I thought I had ceased to be a minister: but in the end several came round, it was determined not to risk a disruption, and Salisbury[26] suggested as a compromise that we should ascertain from the Porte whether an application to allow our fleet to go up into the Dardanelles would be favourably received. This was agreed to without difference, though under the reserve on my part and that of some others, that we do not imply consent to send the fleet up under present circs. It was agreed also to invite the Russians to give us an assurance that they would not occupy Gallipoli: these two telegrams I sent off. A third was decided on, telling the Porte that we intended to have a voice in the final settlement.

I came away well satisfied, for this is the second time that in the last few days that I have succeeded in carrying my point against a large majority of my colleagues: but the excitement and fatigue of the struggle increased a feeling of illness with which I had begun the day, and instead of dining at the Austrian embassy, where we were to dine, I let M. go without me, and went to bed instead.

13 January 1878 (Sunday). In bed nearly all day, with much discomfort and some sickness of the stomach, but no severe pain till afternoon, when cramp fastened upon me, seizing the loins, ribs, hips, and thighs down to the knee. Drage says it is a common result of any violent internal disturbance.

14 January 1878 (Monday). Got up for part of the day, but did not dress: pain in limbs from cramp severe and increasing. It was relieved towards night by a hot bath, rubbings, and opiate draught: but I passed part of the night in an armchair, being unable to go to bed lest lying down should bring on fresh and sharper attacks. I do not think that I have ever suffered so severely, as far as mere bodily pain is concerned: though aware that it was temporary, and that there was nothing to be uneasy about. At last the opiate did its work, and I got some rest.

Saw Sanderson, and settled some necessary business with him. Also Carnarvon, who is vehement against the idea of sending ships up to the Dardanelles, and talks of resigning. I do not like it either, but advise him not to leap till we come to the fence.

15 January 1878 (Tuesday). Woke free from pain, and though it returned slightly once or twice, passed the day in comparative comfort. Dressed,

[26] At this cabinet 'Lord Salisbury said then, that, if Lord Derby retired, he must retire too' (Beaconsfield to the Queen, 12 Jan. 1878, M. and B. 219). Hardy noted 'at one moment I thought there was a break up for Derby and Carnarvon could not be moved but Salisbury averted the disruption by a proposal wh. though dangerous and inefficient was something in the way of the majority' (*GH* 348).

and did a good deal of business. Wrote to Ld B. telling him that for a week or so I shall not be fit to appear in the Lords. Worked with Sanderson, and saw Carnarvon. The latter comes much excited from a cabinet,[27] which he declares has decided on sending up the fleet: and he has in consequence resigned: it does not however appear that the thing is finally settled, and the cabinet meets again tomorrow. In the evening we get telegrams to the effect that the Sultan is not willing to admit our fleets on the terms of neutrals (which I fully expected, and framed the telegram to elicit that answer): and to convey the assurance of the Russian govt that their army shall not go to Gallipoli unless the Turkish movements compel them, in the interest of their military operations. We could not ask or expect them to say more. We have also satisfactory evidence that the Austrians are more in earnest than we had been inclined to believe, and are exerting their influence seriously to keep Russia within the bounds previously laid down. Everything is therefore satisfactory, and there is less need than ever for any hasty or hazardous step.

16 January 1878 (Wednesday). Rather better in health, and less weak, but did not leave my room. Began to write this diary again, which had been neglected since Thursday last.

Dictated to Sanderson a mem. on the inexpediency of sending the fleet into the Dardanelles: which it appears is again to be discussed in cabinet today. Sent it to Ld B. and had the satisfaction of hearing that in the actual state of the case, the Turks objecting to our going there, he entirely agrees with me. I may therefore assume that the project will drop.

F. whom I had not seen lately: I was glad to find that we are entirely of one mind as to the attitude to be maintained: the more so because in earlier stages of the affair he was rather disposed to action.

Carnarvon came in a fidget about his resignation: but all that is superseded now.

Ballard the dentist called to supply me with new teeth.

... Heard in afternoon that the project of sending up the fleet is dropped, little or nothing having been said about it in the cabinet of today, though it was apparently all but decided yesterday: an odd way of doing business, but all is well that ends well. The fact is that a committee of eleven men, all occupied, and some overworked, in their own departments, is not and cannot be a suitable body for the transaction of diplomatic business. Half the members do not recollect what was done and said last, and their attention is distracted by the multiplicity of telegrams, correcting and contradicting one another.

---

[27] Derby missed the cabinets of 14, 15, and 16 Jan., communication being maintained by means of Tenterden.

Hence confusion, and decisions come to which when they have to be acted upon turn out to be impossible to execute, or adapted to a different state of affairs.

17 January 1878 (Thursday). Sleep fairly sound: woke feeling stronger and better, but after half an hour or so of business I am obliged to leave off and rest.

Saw Northcote, and some talk with him as to language to be held at the opening. He thinks as I do that there will be great confusion and diversity of opinions, but no settled attack upon us.

... Began to receive papers again regularly from the office: they have been disposed of, except a very few, by Tenterden and Sanderson, during the last four days.

Carnarvon calls on Ly D., excited and uneasy: wanting to leave the cabinet, though the particular step to which he objected has not been taken, and though he has no public ground for doing so: but he is deeply hurt by what he thinks the injustice of the premier, and the want of sympathy of his colleagues. It seems something passed yesterday, and either they laughed at him, or he thought they did. He is hardworking, capable, and though sometimes rash, not on the whole wanting in judgment where public affairs are concerned: but in his personal relations he is vain, touchy, and egotistical: defects which were always visible in his character, and which power and responsibility have brought into prominence. He seems occupied exclusively with the effect of what is done on his personal position and makes this feeling too evident. He might leave us without injury at any other moment, but just now it will not do.

18 January 1878 (Friday). Dressed and went downstairs for the first time this week: should have gone out for a short walk or drive, but fog prevented. Saw in the day Tenterden, Carnarvon, Disraeli, and F. Declined visits from ambassadors: it is impossible to let in one without seeing all in turn, for which I have not strength.

Ballard the dentist came to supply new teeth.

Cautioned by Drage not to go back to work too soon, but give time for health to be quite restored: and I think he is right.

Carnarvon expatiated at length, as he did yesterday, on his personal grievances: which by his own showing are of a very shadowy description, since the proceedings to which he objected are not to go forward. I heard him patiently, in the interest of the party, but gave little sympathy and no encouragement.

Disraeli came, with an entirely new set of ideas: he admits it is too late to send out an expedition, sees the risk of sending up ships to Constantinople or even into the straits: is full of the negotiations with Austria, from which he hopes for important results, and dwells on the notion that Austria might be induced to mobilise her army by a promise from us to guarantee the necessary loan. He was well pleased with the result of last night in both houses, though thinking that Northcote has gone too far in the line of concession.

Occupied with reading the report of the opening debates, which have been satisfactory and favourable to the govt. In the Lords, Disraeli was thoroughly successful: he answered Granville in a very happy style, a little declamatory here and there, but in substance moderate and sensible. He seems to have pleased both the war and peace parties, if I may judge by the newspapers. Argyll[28] denounced the Turkish empire exactly as he did last year: and was answered by Salisbury, whose speech was doubly satisfactory as giving proof that the cabinet is not divided, and on its own merits. I was glad while reading it that I had been away, since if present I must have spoken, and then there would not have been time for Salisbury, whose cordial defence of our policy is under the circs very important.

19 January 1878 (Saturday). Drove out with Ly D. Called at Ballard's: walk in botanic gardens, for about half an hour. Feeling well, but curiously weak, so much so as to be obliged to lie down and rest after half an hour of writing or talking. Drage however is satisfied with the progress made.

Saw in afternoon Beust and Schouvaloff, but neither of them for more than a few minutes. Beust left me with a telegram containing Andrassy's views: and I have one from Buchanan in the same sense, but containing fuller details. The object of the Austrian govt appears to be to induce us to make a naval demonstration, by way of showing the Russians that we are in earnest. But they neither take, nor propose to take, any similar step on their side: alleging two excuses: one, that mobilisation is expensive: the other that situated as they are they cannot take a step without coming into actual collision with Russia. I declined to give Beust an official answer, which indeed he did not ask for: but explained to him the awkwardness and danger of sending the fleet up to Constantinople while Gallipoli is practically in the power of the Russians, who might cut off its retreat. This he saw clearly and I did not dwell upon it. Andrassy may be sincere, and I think he is, for Austrian interests are really far more concerned than ours: but there is something suspicious in the way in which he urges us to come to the front, while doing nothing himself.

Panic is great in Constantinople: talk of the Sultan retiring to Broussa: wild projects of all sorts discussed: Adrianople abandoned as not defensible.

The Roumanians are in alarm lest they should lose the slip of Bessarabia which was taken away from Russia twenty years ago, and

[28] 8th Duke (1823–1900), Indian sec. 1868–74.

which notoriously Gortschakoff wishes to see regained. They do not consider a slice of the Dobrudja any equivalent, and are appealing to everybody to save them from spoliation by their allies.[29]

In convn with Ly D. Schou. did not conceal his surprise at what he called the Turkish character of the speech and debates. (What would he have said if he could have seen the original draft?) He was most perplexed by Salisbury's speech: which shows how he and his govt have been encouraged to believe that anything done or attempted by Russia would be accepted by the peace party in the cabinet. I have reason to believe that he is in constant intercourse with the leaders of opposition, who tell him how far he may go with the certainty of their support. On the other hand the Court is busier than ever in beating up for recruits against a Russian policy – and this has become so far known as to lead to a good many veiled and respectful, but still very intelligible, allusions in the daily papers. Altogether a strange state of affairs, and new in our recent history. The P. of W. is if possible more violent than his mother, in the same sense: but in his case this is due mainly to old-standing jealousy of his brother,[30] who naturally takes the Russian side.

20 January 1878 (Sunday). Sat at home till 11: paid £10 to a charity through Sanderson. Made up arrears of private business. Feeling well, but still weak and wanting frequent rest.

Walk in Green Park with Ly D. Called in Curzon St after luncheon. Hear of the uneasiness of the Villiers family, at their not being able to get back the late Lord Clarendon's letters to the Queen of Holland.[31] They extend over many years, are written with the utmost unreserve, and contain gossip and scandal enough to set all London by the ears. But as they are not likely to be published, one does not see what is the ground of alarm. Hear much of social scandals, which were never more abundant, but not worth setting down. Marlborough House contributes its full share: which is nothing new.

F.[32] calls: tells me that as soon as his back is turned on the W.O. the estimates have been raised by three-quarters of a million: he asks, are they to be peace estimates or not, for according to the answer he will deal with them at the Treasury. I say, 'peace estimates certainly.' Says D. of Cambridge is angry at the vote of credit being put off, as now it will never, probably, be taken. The Horse Guards had evidently reckoned on three or four extra millions to spend – not knowing the H. of C.

[29] Both changes were made at the Treaty of Berlin.
[30] Alfred, D. of Edinburgh (1844–1900) who m. Grand Duchess Marie of Russia, 1874.
[31] Sophie, Queen of the Netherlands (b. 1817).
[32] F. Stanley, diarist's bro.

From various quarters I gather that the opening has been a success: the extreme peace party, and the extreme war party, are both dissatisfied, but the mass of moderate men seem content. The Russophiles now take up fresh ground, and profess alarm lest Russia should be in too great haste to make peace without having effectually destroyed the Turkish power (*v.* the *Spectator*). But this is an eccentricity not widely spread. The Queen's passionate eagerness for war appears generally known: which indeed is not wonderful, for she has taken every means to make it so.

More telegrams – six, I think, from Layard alone – on the war. Adrianople is either taken or on the point of being so: great panic among the population: in various districts massacres by Circassians and others: in short a state of anarchy prevails. The Sultan talks of abdicating and retiring on board a British ship in case the Russians advance to Constantinople. – More explanations from Andrassy, but they are vague and confused, and tell us nothing except that he wishes us to take some decided step, but is afraid of seeming to advise it.

21 January 1878 (Monday). Walk early, the first I have taken: slight fatigue, but not excessive, and I feel that my strength is returning.

Beust called to read me a telegram from Andrassy, which I kept for the cabinet, but the object of it is not clear.

The condns of peace were expected, but they have not come.

Cabinet at 2, sat till near 4: one of the least satisfactory we have had yet. Disraeli was full of his new scheme of an Austrian alliance: proposed a treaty for mutual defence, an urgent request to the Austrian govt to mobilise, and the promise of an English guarantee for the loan which would be necessary. These propositions I opposed, especially that of the guarantee, which I do not believe that parliament would sanction: the scheme of an alliance I said might be discussed at leisure, but the objection to it is that we can never be sure of being able to keep any promises of that kind which we may make. I agreed, not very willingly, to enquire at Vienna whether C. Andrassy would be willing to join with us in an identic note addressed to Russia laying down certain conditions which we both considered as inadmissible without our previous sanction. I do not think he will do this, and if the question of a loan, or subsidy, to bribe him into compliance is raised again, I must seriously consider whether we can agree. Disraeli was rather excited, and talked in his grandiose style, which he seldom does in cabinet: he broke out into occasional sarcasms directed at my excessive prudence, but all in tolerable good humour. He had the whole cabinet with him, except Carnarvon: Salisbury is quite gone round, and is hot for Austrian alliance, of which last summer he used to talk with marked contempt. We ended without agreement, but the enquiry sent to Vienna will at least keep us quiet till the answer comes: which is so much time gained, and if the conditions arrive we shall be started in a new track. But I never had such unsatisfactory work to do before, and personally shall be very glad when it is over. Attended at the office, worked there till about 5.30, when home, rather exhausted.

22 January 1878 (Tuesday). Carnarvon called early, but he had nothing new to say.

Cabinet at 2, sat till 3.30: the answer from Vienna not being received, nor the conditions of peace in our hands, we could do not real business, and for the most part only wasted time. Hicks Beach and J. Manners both pressed that the fleet should be sent up to Constantinople, though without any special reason for sending it: but their opinions were not accepted by the cabinet, and I had no occasion to oppose them. We settled answers to some questions in the H. of C. but did little else.

Office, where saw Musurus, Münster, Beust, Schou., Sir H. Elliot, and Bourke. Elliott[33] leaves for Vienna tomorrow. None of my visitors had much that was interesting, they came chiefly to find out what is doing.

H. of Lds at 5.15, but no business, and home before 6. Great civility shown me at the House in the way of enquiries etc.

This is the first day since Wednesday 9th that I have been in full working order, and I feel in no way the worse.

23 January 1878 (Wednesday). Received a tel. containing the answer from Vienna. Andrassy declines to have anything to say to an identic note, considering it unnecessary and that it would only weaken the position of the two govts, besides that if we say nothing about an occupation of Bulgaria we should seem, in his view, to be sanctioning that measure (this objection I don't understand for it is one of the things that we proposed to protest against, possibly Buchanan has misunderstood him): he lays stress on being prepared to back up his opinions, and says that Russia knows it: he does not understand our not having asked for a vote of credit, nor sent up the fleet to Constantinople: he, he says, would be ready to mobilise at once if he thought it necessary, without waiting for a vote of the legislature. He says something which is true enough though he seems to mean it ironically, as to the dependence of an English ministry on the votes of the H. of C. – He repudiates the idea of a subsidy to Austria, which I never hinted at either to Beust or Buchanan: this is significant, as it shows that negotiations have been going on behind my back, though it may have been while I was ill, and if so there is nothing to be said against it. The sum of the whole is that he hesitates and shuffles, wants us to take the first step, and commit ourselves to a policy of armed

[33] Appointed amb. to Austria *vice* Buchanan, 31 Dec. 1877; on leave of absence since late Feb. 1877, though nominally still amb. to Turkey.

intervention, but will not pledge himself even in that case. – I am not greatly surprised: and his distrust of the possible tendencies of parlt may be sincere. But we do not seem likely to get much help out of him. He is anxious for Elliot to come, seeming to dislike or distrust Buchanan. I do not know why.

A cabinet was summoned, at short notice, for 3, and sat nearly two hours. The premier addressed us at length, earnestly and in strong language, but without any sign of irritation or excitement, as on Monday. He dwelt on the Austrian communication, on the value of the Austrian alliance, on the impossibility of obtaining it without making some effort on our own side, and in all this, though his tone was more warlike than I could approve, there was some reason and truth. But he then went on to describe the state of things at home, represented the feeling of the supporters of govt as one of indignation and disgust, said that if we did not act at once we should ruin our reputations, and the interests of the country, with much to the same effect: and concluded by declaring for the instant sending of the fleet to Constantinople, with or without the Sultan's consent, and for immediate notice of a large vote of credit or supplementary estimate – ten millions[34] he said it ought to be. None of the rest were so strong or peremptory in their language, with the exception of Hicks Beach: but all agreed except Carnarvon and I. Salisbury was very warlike, his natural tendency to pugnacity is thoroughly roused, and considering the Turk as now destroyed, his religious zeal does not interfere with his hostility to Russia.

Carnarvon expressed his dissent regretfully and in a rather lachrymose strain, entreating his colleagues to believe in his good will etc. I argued the question shortly, abstained from any sentiment, but made it clear that my resignation must follow. The decision to give orders to the fleet was then taken:[35] it was agreed that absolute secrecy should be maintained.

I went back to the office at 5, and stayed till 7. Saw there d'Harcourt, Beust, Menabrea, Schouvaloff, Musurus – I think these were all. They came to talk over the situation generally.

Wrote my letter of resignation to Disraeli, but kept it till the morning, so that nothing may be done in haste.

24 January 1878 (Thursday). I sent my letter, worded in the most friendly style, and in this I was entirely sincere: for though Disraeli's ways are not in all respects mine, and certainly not just now, a personal

---

[34] This became £6m. of which £3m. was spent, according to Northcote's budget speech.

[35] '... & then ten spoke with absolute unanimity of our duty imposed by good faith & honour' (*GH* 350).

friendship of thirty years makes separation painful. He has answered it vaguely, deprecating premature explanations in public, which I never meant to give, and hinting at a further reply, and altogether seeming to consider the matter as not yet settled.

Walk with Ly D. in the Green park: talk of affairs. My reason tells me I am right in retiring, and the strongest feeling in my mind is relief at being free from anxiety and responsibility, but I regret the change on Sanderson's account, and to some extent on account of my brother. I know also that Disraeli and I shall never be on the same terms again: his way of looking at politics is always a personal one, and it is not easy for him to understand objections founded solely on public considerations.

Saw Beust, who had a long telegram from Andrassy, not intelligible in all respects, and seemingly the result of a misunderstanding with Beust, who did not know what it meant more than I did.

Saw Schou. who gave some hints as to the conditions of peace, but they are superseded by fuller information received through Layard. They seem at first sight not excessive, all circs considered, and Layard believes that they are, or will be, accepted by the Sultan. In that case, all this trouble of the last few days has been taken for nothing. But the important passage relating to the Dardanelles is not clear.

Late in the afternoon I heard that the orders given to the fleet had been countermanded, in consequence of news coming that the Sultan accepts the terms of peace: so that the greater part of our trouble has [been] thrown away. But the vote of credit has been revived, and stands for Monday, which is a fresh obstacle in the way of re-union.

25 January 1878 (Friday). Carnarvon called early, agitated and uneasy: determined on making his explanation at once. I advised putting it off till Monday, so as to leave an opening for negotiation: but he was feverishly anxious to get the matter settled, whether distrusting his own resolution, or simply eager to get it over.

Not having any reply to my offer of resignation, I sent Sanderson across with a paper, as a pretext for any communication which the premier might wish to make. He saw him, talked with him, but as it would seem vaguely: in the end he said [*sic*] a message begging me to say nothing in public till Monday: which I readily agreed to. He is probably perplexed, wishing me to remain, and the Queen no doubt wishes the contrary.

Tenterden came over, friendly and mournful: hoping all would be made up, and so forth: but that cannot be, unless the vote is dropped or postponed.

In the afternoon F. came, sent by somebody, I suppose by Northcote: he brought a strange overture, to the effect that I might take some other office, and stay in the cabinet: he put it on the ground of health, need of rest, and the continual strain of F.O. This was a suggestion with which I had no difficulty in dealing: I had not resigned, I said, on grounds of health: I certainly should not in any case accept a sinecure such as the Privy Seal or the Duchy: and there would be no rest or ease in changing my present post for India or the Colonies,[36] where I should have the work of a new department to learn. My retirement, if it took effect, was on public grounds: I should be just as much responsible for what was done in foreign affairs whatever post I held, and with less control over them than I have. There was no choice: if I went back it must be to the place I had left: but it was not for me to make overtures of that kind: I had offered to retire, and any proposal to me to withdraw the offer must come from the other side.

I hear that a private meeting of the cabinet was held this morning:[37] but the result is not known to me.

Schouvaloff brought a correct copy of the terms of peace: they are in the main what we expected, but vague about the awkward question of the Dardanelles. I sent them on to Ld B. and through the day I continued to dispose of the routine business of the office.

26 January 1878 (Saturday). Read in the papers Carnarvon's explanation, which was rather too long, and he unwisely brought into it his quarrel with Ld B. three weeks ago, which betrayed personal feeling. Otherwise there was nothing to find fault with. The Premier spoke briefly in reply, but refused to answer the question whether I had resigned or not. Northcote gave notice of his vote for Monday – six millions.

Telegrams came late last night from Buchanan: both Andrassy and the Emperor appear alarmed and angry at the Russian terms of peace: the Emperor openly accuses his brother of Russia of bad faith: Andrassy especially objects to Servia becoming a kingdom and to the scheme for Bulgaria which the Russian govt proposes. It is not clear to me as yet whether we have got the terms in an authentic form: the versions sent by Layard and Schouvaloff differ in some respects.

Short walk in the park with M.

Saw in the course of the day Cross, Bourke, Tenterden, Northcote, my brother, Lawson, and I think one or two more.

Northcote called twice, the second time at my request: he came as representing the P. Minister, with a request that I should withdraw my resignation, on the assurance that nothing more should be done as to sending the fleet into Turkish waters. The order given in haste after

---

[36] Derby was offered India, Colonies, Privy Seal, or Lord Presidency, according to Beaconsfield to the Queen, 27 Jan. 1878 (M. and B. 237); *GH* and *Cecil* do not allude to the offer.

[37] To discuss the Russian peace terms just received.

the cabinet of Wednesday was countermanded within 24 hours, and the folly of it is now generally recognised. The vote for a supplementary estimate must be gone on with, notice having been given: to withdraw it would create a mutiny in the party and produce an appearance of vacillation nothing less than ridiculous. But Northcote declares that it will not be spent, except to the amount of about a million, and that in the event of negotiations proceeding it will probably be dropped – wholly or in part. The matter was discussed at length, the arguments for and against resigning being very evenly balanced. – If I resign, I lose the control which I have hitherto exercised over foreign affairs, my place is filled up by some one who will do whatever the Queen and Disraeli wish, and as matters stand, the country might be involved in war before parliament could effectually interfere. If my retirement destroyed the ministerial majority, as is possible, a dissolution would follow, and either a radical govt, which I do not desire, or in the opposite event, a parliament elected on a war cry. Meanwhile we should lose all voice and influence in European affairs. As matters are, I am a check on the Prime Minister, and though I do not put much faith in them, I have the assurances of several of my colleagues that they will support me in resisting a war-policy. The immediate cause of my resignation can no longer be pleaded, since the subject of dispute is at an end. By retiring now, in the very crisis of negotiations, I should weaken both my party and my country without obvious reason for doing so. – On the other hand, my personal position would gain by withdrawal: and the friends of peace would be put on their guard. This however they are already: and the personal part of the question is not worth discussing. – On the whole, the arguments in favour of remaining in the cabinet prevailed, and I may at least take credit for acting from a sense of public duty, since the conclusion to which I came is opposed to all my personal wishes and feelings. I sent my decision to Northcote in a letter which though civil is purposely stiff and unconciliatory: expressing extreme uneasiness and distrust, hinting at the probability that I may not remain long, and making it clear that I remain rather in the hope of preventing mischief as long as I can than from sympathy with the views of my colleagues.

We shall not have a pleasant time in cabinet, but that can't be helped.

27 January 1878 (Sunday). Slept little and ill, agitated by the decision of yesterday and its consequences: though I do not doubt that on the whole I have been right. But it is one of those cases where the balance between conflicting reasons is nicely poised, and those which have not been acted on are always apt to seem stronger when the decision is taken. I have a gushing letter from Northcote, in answer to mine which was dry enough: and one from Ld B., characteristically talking of the

'rumours' of my intended resignation, which he has probably contradicted everywhere. Neither fortunately requires an answer.

Walk early, and sharply, for exercise.

Beust called with the text of the Russian conditions, which are an
unpleasant surprise at Vienna. Andrassy, he says, is now convinced of
the falsity of the assurances given by Russia. I have a tel. in the same
sense from Buchanan.

Cabinet at 5: a sudden summons: and I suspect it to be a device of
the Premier in order that my name may appear among the rest on
Monday, and so anticipate comments.[38]

We sat a little over an hour: the professed object was to hear and
criticise the statement which Northcote is to make tomorrow in the
House. All was friendly,[39] indeed there was nothing to differ about, for
the thing being settled, the reasons for it admit of little difference, and
Northcote is judicious in his way of putting a case.

Dined with F. and C. Pleasant evening.

28 January 1878 (Monday). Walk early for exercise, though day very
wet: but I wanted air. Bought some china. Office from 2 to 5: saw
there Musurus, Beust, Münster, Menabrea, and Schouvaloff. Nothing
material passed. Andrassy now wants us to say decidedly whether we
are prepared to fight rather than allow the Russian proposals as to
Bulgaria, Servia, etc. to take effect.[40] I defer an official answer but
explain to Beust, who knows this country, the impossibility of taking
an engagement to that effect. The first point to secure, is to get the
whole matter discussed in a conference or congress, where all the
Powers will have a voice.

H. of Lds at 5 ... explained my retirement and return to office in a
few words, which were well taken by the House: spoke in all about 20
minutes. Home by 7.30 and quiet evening.

Northcote made his demand for six millions, speaking as he was sure
to do, temperately and well: the taking of the vote is put off till
Thursday, which could not be refused, but is so far unlucky in that it
gives time to organise a party agitation. The unspent balance, at end
of the financial year, is to be repaid into the Exchequer: which seems
odd: for we can't spend one million, not to say six, between now and
April 1st, and it will have if wanted to be voted over again. The whole
business was hastily gone into, and seems foolish: but I could not help

[38] Seen in just that light by Beaconsfield (M. and B. 236).

[39] 'D[erby] was sullen which he showed by going to Carnarvon's old seat instead of
that reserved for him as usual next the Chief' (*GH* 352).

[40] Where Hardy saw Austria as 'troubled but hesitating & not to be depended on' (28
Jan. 1878, *GH* 352), Beaconsfield envisaged (16 Feb. 1878) an alliance which could put
'300,000 men into the field' if his private negotiations reached 'a formal conclusion' (M.
and B. 248–9).

agreeing with Northcote that the notice having been given it was too late to draw back.

29 January 1878 (Tuesday). Disposed pretty early of all business: drive to Kensington, the day being fine and sunny, and in the gardens walked for an hour with M. with much content.

Office at 2, stayed till 5. Saw Menabrea, Harcourt, Schouvaloff, Beust: I think these were all. No news as yet of the armistice or of the bases of peace being signed, though the Porte agreed to them a week ago. There is on Schou's part an affectation of surprise, but it is clear that the delay is intentional, and that the object is to enable the Russian army to advance as near as possible to Constantinople. This is bad policy, for it confirms the popular idea of Russian trickery and deceit,[41] just at the moment when the good opn of Europe, and the neutrality of England, are most important. I did not note that yesterday Schou. brought me the assurance that the Dardanelles question is not to be settled without the consent of Europe.

H. of Lds, where Ld Emly[42] had given notice of a question as to when papers relating to Greece should be produced: on the strength of this he delivered a long speech on Greek affairs in general, for which I was not prepared: I however answered him as best as I could, and to my own satisfaction, speaking about a quarter of an hour. Home, and quiet evening.

30 January 1878 (Wednesday). Walk early, just after breakfast, having no work left from last night. Home at 11, busy till 12, when to cabinet.

In cabinet much discussion as to chances of the Russians occupying Constantinople: as to the Austrian policy: the inexplicable delay in signing the armistice, though it is eight days since the Porte accepted the bases of peace. We agree at last to suggest to Andrassy an identic note protesting against an occupation of the capital: and to ask what further steps they propose that we should take in case of our joint representation failing. On this we were all united: and I drew a mem. for Schouvaloff earnestly warning him of the danger of an armed entry into Constantinople. Not seeing him at the office, I sent it with a note. The rest of our business was talk about, and preparation for, the H. of C. debate.

Convn with Ld B. afterwards at his request about the manner in which Carnarvon's place shall be filled. It cannot long be left vacant, as matters stand in Africa.[43] He had made an overture to the D. of

[41] Cf. *Cecil* 195-6 for the effect on U.K. opinion of the continuing Russian advance near Constantinople, it not then being known that this was sanctioned by the terms of the armistice.
[42] William Monsell, 1st Baron Emly (1812-94), Irish Lib. M.P. and postmaster-gen.; cr. peer 1874.
[43] Carnarvon had announced the despatch of extra troops to S. Africa to meet the Zulu threat, 31 Dec. 1877 (Hardinge, *Carnarvon* ii 368).

Somerset,[44] on what ground I do not know, for the Duke is a stiff though not extreme Whig, and has practically withdrawn from affairs. The offer was declined, in a friendly but decided letter, which I saw. The Premier had several ideas. One was to remove the D. of Richmond from the Council to the Colonies, filling up his place either with the D. of Northumberland,[45] or with J. Manners, who should be called up to the H. of Lds for that purpose: the first plan I think impracticable, the D. of N. not being a likely person to take office, especially as his wife is now always ill: the second is inconvenient as J.M. has no means of his own, and cannot be certain of his brother's dukedom,[46] though he will probably have it. – I suggested leaving the Lords alone, as we are strong enough with five peers in the cabinet: and seeing whether we could not promote Hicks Beach,[47] and fill up his place with Plunket,[48] whom everybody speaks well of. This is a disinterested suggestion on my part, for I do not think Beach a pleasant colleague: his manner is peremptory and sometimes almost offensive: but he speaks well, and is able. Ld B. seemed to like the notion. He said in this convn that he should have liked to promote J. Manners, to whose abilities he thinks the world does not do justice: but he recognises the strength of the general feeling that he is unfit for a difficult post. The newspapers have been full of Sandon's[49] name as the new Sec. of State: he has never been thought of, nor desires it. We talked of Beauchamp[50] as a possible minister: he is cultivated and has some capacity, but is a prig, and generally disliked.

Office, but saw there only Musurus and Lawson. Quiet evening. Wrote to O. Russell.

31 January 1878 (Thursday). Lawrence called with deeds to sign. Sent off 12 boxes early to the office. Walk with M. to the Marble Arch, thence by myself round Regent's Park. Office at 2, or soon after. Saw there Schouvaloff, Beust, Musurus, and I think one or two more. No

---

[44] 13th Duke (1810–91), anti-Gladstone whig; offered cabinet office, 1874.

[45] 6th Duke (1810–99), succ. Aug. 1867; lord privy seal 1878–80); anti-Disraeli and a Salisbury supporter; offered Ireland, 1874 (*Cecil*, 51); previously had only brief experience of minor office.

[46] His elder bro. the 6th Duke (1815–88) d. unm.

[47] Irish sec.

[48] David Robert Plunket, 1st Baron Rathmore (1838–1919), M.P. Dublin Univ. 1870–95, when cr. peer; solicitor-gen. (Ireland) 1875–Mar. 1877, paymaster-gen. Mar. 1880, 1st commr for works 1885–6, 1886–92.

[49] 3rd E. of Harrowby (1831–1900), styled Lord Harrowby until 1892.

[50] Frederick, 6th E. Beauchamp (1830–91), lord steward 1874–80, paymaster-gen. 1886–7; from 1874 represented Home Office in Lords; old friend of Disraeli, to whom he lent his London house, Apr. 1880; described by Disraeli as 'disagreeable' and 'quarrelsome' but considered for Ireland *vice* Abercorn, 1876; in early 1878, Queen sought his removal for annoying her servants; see Blake, *Disraeli*, 690.

news as yet of the armistice being signed. Long convn with Northcote and Tenterden on the language to be held in parlt, and the general course of debate.

H. of Lords at 5, where answered a question by Stratheden,[51] and another by Stanhope. ... Argyll, who had given no notice, took the opportunity to deliver a carefully prepared harangue against the Turkish govt ... I answered Argyll in a general way, speaking about half an hour, with ease and satisfaction to myself, and well listened to, though in a thin House ... Home rather late to dinner, and weary, but satisfied.

1 February 1878 (Friday). Office at 2, and stayed until 5. Saw Menabrea, who is going away: Münster, who had nothing to tell: Beust, who in his own defence brought the tel. he had sent to Andrassy, reporting my conversation, which is fairly accurate, but Andrassy has put an extraordinary construction upon it. He is evidently a man of loose inaccurate habits of business, though able: and distrusting Beust, he is always inclined to pick holes in his reports. Saw also Schou, who had no news of the armistice, and seemed in trouble to explain what his govt is about. Musurus came, with news that his govt has heard from the plenipotentiaries, and that the bases were to be signed yesterday: but he has not heard, nor has Layard, that they are actually signed. The unexplained delay causes great suspicion and irritation here, it being thought that the Russians are playing their usual tricks, and that time is being wasted in order to allow of an occupation of Constantinople. Schou. explains it by the difficulty of communication, there being only a field telegraph across the Balkans, which is easily put out of order. But that would not account for our hearing nothing from the Porte. Saw Lawson, who predicts a majority of 100 to 120 for the vote. – Received an odd letter from Ld B. in which he says that he no longer directs the policy of the cabinet: suggests that Schou. is tricking us, which is probable enough, and that his passports should be sent him – which would be absurd, and a direct challenge to Russia. – I think that with increasing age Ld B. has grown more impulsive: he takes up ideas and drops them in a way that is new with him.

Talk with him at the Lds about new arrangements: Hicks Beach is to have the Colonies, which is right: to my surprise, he tells me that the D. of Northumberland accepts the Privy Seal. He will not be a useful colleague, and certainly not a pleasant one: but respectable, and as his place is a sinecure, he can do no harm.

2 February 1878 (Saturday). By the parks to D. St. where cabinet at 12.

[51] W.F. Campbell, 2nd Baron Stratheden and 2nd Baron Campbell (1824–93), s. of whig lord chancellor; succ. to titles 1860 and 1861; not prominent, and d. unm.; by his bro's marriage to Salisbury's niece, on fringe of Cecil connexion.

I went with no pleasant expectations, from the Premier's letter of yesterday, but he was quiet again, and though repeating his conviction that Schou. is tricking us – which is likely, but we can't prove it – agreed that there was nothing to be done in that matter. We talked a good deal, not always to the purpose, but amicably, in fact there was no substantial difference of opinion. Two points were agreed on: (1) To telegraph to Vienna, suggesting that Andrassy should propose a conference to be held there, which we would support, and reiterating our adhesion to the understanding of last summer: (2) To ask the Italians, who are very uneasy at the prospect of a Russian occupation of Constantinople, whether in that event they would be willing to join with us in sending up our fleets, together with the French, if they will join. As to this last proposal I had no hesitation in approving it, for supposing the war to be over, it cannot be misconstrued: the more so if we act along with other Powers, and not singly. I do not think, however, that the thing will have to be done.

The Austrian dissent from Russian plans is now becoming known in Europe, and has caused huge disgust at Petersburg. Italy is apparently plucking up courage to join: France keeps in the background: Bismarck will do nothing except push both sides into a war if he can. It is understood that Russia accepts the principle of a conference: and once there, we shall have half Europe with us. On the whole the position is more satisfactory than I have thought it yet.

Saw Mr French,[52] the new consular judge at Shanghai...

Saw the Greek minister, who came with a long tel. to report that the Greek govt has decided to send troops into Thessaly and Epirus:[53] this step has been taken notoriously in consequence of the state of public feeling at Athens, which insists on a war: there have been riots, and the danger of a revolution has driven the King and his advisers into war as the less formidable alternative. Very likely they are right in their own interest: but this cannot be avowed as the motive, and they have been driven to the absurdity of alleging that the act is not one of war, and that the troops are only sent to keep order and save life. I received M. Gennadius civilly, took the freedom of laughing a little at the transparent disguise which his chief has put on, but liked him better when he said plainly that Greece was in the position of a child that is told first that it must not ask for anything, and then that as it has asked for nothing it can want nothing. This is not altogether untrue, and it is fair to the Greeks to remember that they have kept out of the affair

---

[52] George French (d. 1881), judge of supreme court for China Dec. 1877–1881.
[53] The Greek army was ordered to invade Turkey late on 1 Feb. It crossed the border on 2 Feb. with 8000 men, meeting no resistance. The Powers were assured (2 Feb.) that the action was temporary and defensive. See E. Kofos, *Greece and the Eastern Crisis, 1875–1878* (Thessaloniki 1975), 158–60.

for a long while: though fear of the Turkish fleet had much to do with that determination. – Saw d'Harcourt, who came to present his new secretary...

... One day this week ... the Persian minister called ... the Shah is coming in May next: meaning to stay some time, to live quietly, and study manners and customs. – I said what was civil, and wrote to the Queen. But his coming will be a trouble to us, and no use to himself.

Wrote to Lyons, and other letters. Keston by 5.15 train: quiet evening.

3 February 1878 (Sunday). Letters from Elliot,[54] and despatches: mostly anticipated by telegrams: the general purport of them is that Andrassy is well disposed to act with us, but distrustful, not certain whether we mean to throw him over: (he is so far right, that we depend on parliament, which no foreigner understands): he hates Beust, whom he accuses, quite unjustly, of misleading him. Our last telegrams will have reassured him a little.

News that the bases of armistice and peace are signed: which is so far satisfactory: but the Emperor has delivered an ominous speech to his troops, telling them that their work is not yet done: a threat evidently addressed to Austria: and new levies are being raised in haste, notwithstanding the ruined state of the finances.

4 February 1878 (Monday). London by 10 a.m. train ... Office at 2, stayed till 5. Saw there Münster, d'Harcourt, Beust, Schouvaloff: I think these were all. Beust brought the formal proposal for a conference to be held at Vienna, which I accepted in the name of the govt. This is a step gained: the next question is who shall represent us there? Salisbury will not do again with Elliot and Ignatieff:[55] besides, we want him at home. I should not manage the thing well myself, nor can I well be spared: Tenterden is able, but uncouth, and would not be in his place. On the whole I think Lyons the fittest person, if he can be induced to go: and mentioning this to Ld B. I found that he agreed.

To the Lords ... The house was nearly empty, half the peers having gone to hear Gladstone.

Home, found a mass of papers, worked on them after dinner till late.

The Italians express desire for a full understanding with England: and Depretis[56] throws out a hint, which is much to the purpose,[57] that if the Turks are finished the Greek should be set up as the rival of the Sclave.

Bismarck is pressing moderation on Russia: evidently uneasy: but

[54] Now amb. at Vienna.
[55] Both colleagues of Salisbury at 1876 Constantinople conference.
[56] Agostino Depretis (1813–87), Italian premier March 1876–8, Dec. 1878–9, 1881–7.
[57] See below, 9 Feb.

does not like the notion of England and Austria acting together. The language held at Berlin, but probably not believed there, is to the effect that Andrassy is only coquetting with us to extort better terms from Russia.

From a heap of despatches from Loftus I extract only two ideas: that the idea of marching on Constant. is given up: and that the Russian object is not to drive out the Sultan, or materially alter his apparent position, but to keep him under a kind of protectorate and so utilise him for Russian purposes.

In the Commons, a fine speech by Gladstone, quite unexpectedly moderate in tone, and suggesting a compromise: which might have succeeded earlier, but it is now too late. Hardy answered him, in his best style, hot, vehement, rather personal, but in a party debate such as this is all the more effective on that account. Great confidence is felt of a larger majority than even the expected 100.

5 February 1878 (Tuesday). Long early walk for exercise. Office at 2, stayed till 6. Saw there Schouvaloff, with whom I had an interesting convn. He is apparently quite aware of the Austrian opposn he shall have to deal with, and admits that there has been on the part of his govt something not very unlike a breach of faith. But he believes, or professes to believe, that all may be settled by large mutual concessions. He argues forcibly that to cut the new Bulgaria in half, and give one part advantages which are refused to the other, is the surest way to produce a new war: better treat all alike, even if you give less to all. I could not deny the truth of this. It is strange to note that he should now say to me that he has been aware all along of the Austrian difficulty: which he repeated more than once: when he has never ceased to express up to the last few days his conviction that the alliance was as firm as ever. But after all, it is not much more than the Premier denying the existence of any differences in his cabinet, at the opening of the session.

Saw Gennadius, who told me that the Greek govt are very anxious to retrace their foolish step of invading Turkey, the Turkish fleet being on its way to Athens, and the whole coast undefended.[58] Saw also Musurus on the same subject, and a Greek deputation, headed by Mr Freshfield,[59] of the City, who came to me with a letter from Northcote. Among the depn was a Mavrocordato and a Ralli. They were about

[58] On 3 Feb. Greece learned that the armistice and preliminaries of peace had been signed at Adrianople on 31 Jan., leaving them to face Turkey alone. Like the Powers, they wrongly feared a Turkish naval attack, which Turkey rejected (5 Feb.). In panic, Greek forces were ordered to halt (5 Feb.), to withdraw (6 Feb.), and were back on Greek soil by 9 Feb. (Kofos, op. cit., 160–72).

[59] Probably Charles K. Freshfield (1812–91), jt solicitor to Bank of England 1840–69; M.P. Dover 1865–8, 1874–8.

20 in number, brought no reporter, and in consequence I was doubly
cautious as to what I said to them, lest a distorted report should appear
in the papers, taken from memory. I spoke to them civilly, and with
expressions of sympathy for Greece, but made it clear that I could not
accept a breach of what is a breach of good faith and international
law. Telegraphed to Athens, as also did the French govt, to advise
withdrawal of the troops, and a peaceable settlement.

... H. of Lds at 5 ... Answered a question ... home by 6. Quiet
dinner and evening, after a busy and weary day. Much beset with
telegrams from the Queen, and letters written by her order: she is
evidently excited, and eager for something to be done: she does not
well know what, or why, but such is the nature of nervous people.

By way of a quiet ending to the day, I found 16 boxes, many of
them heavy. Sat up late, and worked off nearly all.

6 February 1878 (Wednesday). Finished what there was to do. Walk
early with M. in the Green park: thence to cabinet at 12, which sat
only an hour. I go to these meetings with the constant expectation of
having some wild scheme to resist: but today the Premier was quiet,
and all passed pleasantly. We agreed to ask for an official copy of the
bases of peace, so that it may be laid before parlt: I wrote accordingly
both to Musurus and Schou. We settled that Lyons is the best man to
represent us in conference: I wrote to sound him accordingly.[60] We
agreed to help the Greek govt out of their trouble, they withdrawing
their troops, we promising to dissuade the Porte from reprisals, and to
do what we can in their interest. I wrote to Gennadius in this sense,
and telegraphed to Athens.[61] Much vague talk about the conference,
where it should be held, what instructions shall be given, etc.

Office from 1 to 5.30: saw there Buchanan, just returned from
Vienna, Beust, Münster, d'Harcourt, Gennadius, Martino,[62] Lawson: I
think these were all. The sum of what they tell me is that the conference
is agreed on in principle: the place of meeting fixed by Andrassy, and
agreed to by all except Russia, is Vienna: but to this choice the Russians
object, whether from political reasons, or as some think from the
personal vanity of Gortschakoff, who has set his heart on presiding at
the conference, which he cannot do if it is held at the capital of a great
Power other than Russia.

Telegraph in afternoon from Layard reporting Russian advance, and
cutting of direct telegraphic communication: from the numbers it

[60] Derby to Lyons, 6 Feb., and Lyons to Derby, 8 Feb., accepting, in Lord Newton,
Lord Lyons (1913), ii 125–6.

[61] In support of an idealistic French peace initiative of 5 Feb. by Waddington, Derby's
fellow-Rugbeian.

[62] R. de Martino, counsellor at Italian legation; 'that talkative Italian' (D.D. 14 Jan.
1876).

appears that several of his telegrams are missing. This is uncomfortable news, as it will stir up the war-feeling here, and the more so as nothing has been told to the Porte as to the terms on which an armistice is to be settled: nor is the armistice itself signed. The appearance of these things taken together is as though some treachery were meditated, or at least some design which it is not yet convenient to admit. Left the office before 6 ... quiet evening.

Bourke[63] consults me as to being a candidate for the place of Common Serjeant, which is in the gift of the Common Council, and worth £3000 a year. It can be held with his seat in parlt. He thinks he has good chances of being chosen. – I encourage him to try.

Talk everywhere of F.'s speech of Tuesday night as having been excellent, and having raised his posn in the House: Northcote went so far as to say that it was the best delivered in the debate, and in point of clear argument, well and temperately put, I think it was. I was overwhelmed with compliments in cabinet. The family is holding its own!

7 February 1878 (Thursday). Considerable excitement caused last night and this morning by reports of Russian advance: it was believed that they were in Constantinople, but this is not true, though they are near it. Layard sends various telegrams, rather of a sensational kind.

Cabinet at 11, all present except D. of Northumberland, who was at Albury: sat only an hour. Agreed to take steps for restoring the telegraph (which is cut, and our communications with Constantinople are by Bombay): to ask the Russian govt for explanations: and to ask the French if they will join in sending up ships to Constantinople, for the protection of life and property in case of disorder. This is a step which now that the war is over, the armistice concluded, and a conference agreed upon, cannot well be misinterpreted, and the public is prepared for it. We settled also – in view of the prevailing excitement – that Northcote and I should each make a short statement of the circs. To office at 12, drew up the statement, and had it copied for Northcote. Sent off telegrams to Lyons and others. – Saw Beust, Schou. and d'Harcourt, also Musurus: none of them had any recent news. H. of Lds at 5, where in answer to a question from Granville, which I had invited, I related the substance of the telegrams: but I had hardly sat down when Schou. came into the library, pressed to see me, and when I came out put into my hands a telegram from Gortschakoff contradicting in vague terms the reports that are current. This I took an opportunity of reading to the House, and sent a copy to Northcote. ... On my way to the Lords I was surrounded and cheered by a crowd evidently assembled for the purpose, and who had before given a similar reception to the Premier. There has been something like a panic in the City, and wild stories going about. The Queen has sent me give or six telegrams in the last 36 hours – mostly incoherent and excited.

8 February 1878 (Friday). The French answer arrived: they will ask for leave to send up ships, but will not do it until more fully acquainted with the state of matters. I sent this at once to Ld B. who called a cabinet for 2 p.m. We sat till 3.30: not much disagreement. All were of opinion that there is now no risk in sending a part of the fleet to Constantinople, the war being over, and it being possible that disturbances may take place there. The only question argued was whether the whole fleet should go, or only a part? The former course would be a military demonstration, menacing if not hostile, since a dozen ironclads could not be wanted for police purposes: the latter admits of being represented as a mere measure for the security of British subjects. Cross, Salisbury, J. Manners, Hicks Beach, were strongest for the more decided course. Northcote and I took the other view: joined by Cairns, who has swayed round again. In the end we decided on 4 large ships and 2 small ones. Smith came across with me to F.O. to settle details. We telegraphed to all the neutral Powers to tell them what we had done, and invite them to join.

All the ambassadors came as usual for news, but I could see none. At 5 to the Lords with Sanderson, where ... I made my statement: very short, and carefully worded; feeling the risk of a careless phrase, I had written it out: the effect, I think, was good...

... I continue to hear high praise of F.'s speech, which has entirely altered his position in the House. Hitherto he has had the reputation only of a useful subordinate and good man of business: now he is ranked on our list – not too long – of effective debaters. I am mistaken however if he speaks oftener than he can help.

9 February 1878 (Saturday). Early walk: business as usual: levee at 2, which ends about 3: so I to office, and work there till 4, when cabinet. It was a complete contrast to those we have had lately, the subjects discussed being only the parliamentary questions of next week. They were of little interest, except that Northcote explained how he means to get the money he wants: 1d extra in the income tax and an addition to the tobacco duty. Back to the office, finished up what was to be done, and left for Keston by the 6.35 train. Quiet evening there.

At office, saw Gennadius, who came partly to thank for what we done [*sic*] in mediating between Greece and Turkey, partly to see what I thought of the Russian plans. On the latter point I was more frank and expansive with him than is my custom: pointing out that a sclavonic province, extending nearly from the Danube to the Aegean would cut off the Greeks from Constantinople, isolate Thessaly and Epirus, and destroy the hopes of the Greek race. He saw it all clearly, was overjoyed that I took that view, and promised that his countrymen would do what they could. I told him that they ought to agitate vehemently[64] against the scheme of an extended Bulgaria going south of the Balkans, and plead for the Hellenes in that district, who are in a minority, but by far the most intelligent part of the population: that they may not be swallowed up by the Sclave majority. It seems to me possible that on this platform we may induce Italians, Austrians, and Greeks to take their stands with us.

The week has been eventful and agitated. The feeling of panic and anger which prevailed on Thursday, under the impression that the Russians were either in Constantinople or on the point of going in, was not to the full extent justified by anything in Layard's telegrams: but it is explained by the foolish concealment of the conditions of the armistice, by a reasonable distrust of Russian intentions, and in part by the state of our home politics. The opposition has gained by it more than any one else: they were pledged to oppose the grant of six millions, they knew that they should be beaten, probably by 120 or 130, and the news came just in time to save them from the necessity of dividing as a party. ... On the other hand, the opposition are so far weaker than before, that they have shown, as in 1877, that they cannot unite on a question of foreign policy. They have in fact done nothing, and attempted nothing, except criticise details, and cry out against a war which we had never any intention of making.

The cabinet has gained in various ways. It has got its vote of confidence practically unopposed: it has shown clearly that no other combination of men can manage affairs at the present crisis: it is supported by public feeling as it has never been before: and so far from being accused of stirring up the war feeling, moderate critics admit that but for the conciliatory and pacific tone we have maintained war would probably have been made. In fact the popular dislike of Russia which has long been growing, has risen to a dangerous height. Every day open air meetings are held urging the govt to take decided steps. Many of the Conservative provincial journals are violent for immediate action: I have not often read language of stronger censure than that (for instance) which the *Liverpool Courier* uses against our alleged cowardice and timidity. Every hour brings me letters signed and unsigned in the same sense: in which my correspondents tell me that I am a disgrace to my family and my country: that I am humiliating and ruining England: that if I have neither courage nor sense of honour I ought to take myself away, and make room for a better man: some go on to insinuate that I am a traitor, and ought to be dealt with as such.

---

[64] Despite U.K. pledges, Greece was not admitted as full member to the Congress of Berlin (Kofos, op. cit., 231–3).

It is just such a cry as was got up in the Bulgarian time, only in an opposite direction.

I am afraid from what I hear that the Queen is as violent as any one. I know she wrote lately to Disraeli to say that her ministers had deceived and misled her, and that they ought to resign. He tells me that he answered that they could not do that, having a majority in both houses, but that it was her constitutional right to dismiss us if she thought fit. It is significant that at the most vehement war meetings her name is introduced with marked intention, and enthusiastically applauded: so that her feelings are evidently known.

10 February 1878 (Sunday). Walk alone early, later with M. Quiet and pleasant day: but in the evening came unsatisfactory news, that the Porte, being in abject fear of Russia, objects to British ships passing the Dardanelles. Hornby[65] has therefore anchored below the forts, and there waits for orders.

11 February 1878 (Monday). London by 10 a.m. train ... a cabinet summoned at 2. Letter from Hale ... he tells me there is a farm in Burscough of 36 acres which will shortly be sold, and which is wholly surrounded by my land.

Saw Tenterden and Sanderson: talk with them of the situation. Called on the Premier at his request: found him excited and inclined to swagger, saying war was unavoidable: it would last three years: it would be a glorious and successful war for England: with more in the same style. I dissented, but said little: being in truth disgusted with his reckless way of talking, and evident enjoyment of an exciting episode of history, with which his name was to be joined.

In cabinet, we had little difference of opinion as to the actual step to be taken: it was felt that after saying that we should send up the fleet, reasons of public safety being assigned, we could not let it go back to Besica. It was decided to tell Hornby to pass through the Dardanelles opposed or not, but to allow time for a message being sent to Layard telling him of our intention, and requesting him to urge the Porte to offer no resistance. He has already said that the Porte would do nothing more than protest, so that I hope there is no risk. The Sultan is in fact not hostile to our passing, as he has no reason to be: but is naturally afraid of the responsibility of granting the firman, at a moment when his capital is almost in Russian hands. The step is a serious one, but it involves no collision with Russia, and probably none with anybody. Ld B. talked high, as he had done to me in private: spoke of the insults offered to us by Russia: (he did not say what they are): of a war being at least probable: and I am sorry to remember that the cabinet in general seemed to sympathise. – I drew a telegram

[65] Adm. Sir G. Hornby (1825–95), c.-in-c. Med. 1877–80.

to Layard, which was accepted. Office at 3.30. Saw Musurus, and told him confidentially what has passed: pressing him to telegraph in the same sense as I had done to Layard. Saw Beust, for a few minutes only. Saw Schou. who is uneasy at our moving of the ships: his govt has sent to all the European capitals a telegram saying that Russia is considering the necessity or expediency of a military occupation of Constantinople. (Later in the evening I received a telegram from Loftus saying that this step was resolved upon.)

H. of Lds, where answered a question ... Quiet evening, but a large heap of routine business, which I got through.

12 February 1878 (Tuesday). The change in popular feeling during the last few days is remarkable. The Liberal papers have ceased to scream, and say as little as they can about the situation: the war party is vehement and noisy. It includes journals on both sides, the *Pall Mall* and *Post* being the most extravagant. We never needed coolness more, and there is not much of it in the cabinet.

... Cabinet at 11, sat till 12.30. It did not lead to much, but was so far satisfactory that there was no serious difference of opinion. Smith[66] expressed some uneasiness at the position of the fleet if Russian troops should occupy Gallipoli: fearing lest they should be in a trap: I pointed out that all this was known and discussed before, and that the cabinet determined to overrule the objection: Cairns had suggested warning off the Russians from Gallipoli, but dropped the idea, I think wisely: if they mean mischief they will not care about the warning, if not there is no use in it. We talked over a suggestion which has been made by Andrassy direct to the Premier, through Beust: which is to the effect that Austria might be ready to mobilise if we would guarantee a loan to meet the expense. It was agreed not to reject this in principle, but to consider it farther, and invite more definite explanations: on which all may depend. I did not object, feeling that if the present complications continue and increase, Austrian help may be a necessity, and in any case Austrian support in the conference is worth paying for.

Peabody [housing trust] meeting at 3, sat till 3.40 ... Our funds have grown to £680,000 nearly, and we lodge about 10,000 persons. – Office again, saw Schouvaloff, very low and miserable foreseeing increased difficulties in the future, and regretting our sending up of the fleet. He does not know what is the feeling here, and how impossible it was to avoid taking some action: while we could have taken none more harmless. I retaliated by throwing the blame on the concealment of the terms of peace, and the long delay, which has roused suspicion to the utmost. He did not, I think, disagree. Saw also Münster and d'Harcourt.

13 February 1878 (Wednesday). Telegram received through Schou. saying

---

[66] W.H. Smith (1825–91), 1st ld of admiralty 1877–80 *vice* Hunt.

that the Russians intend to enter Constantinople temporarily with a part of their army, for the same purpose as that for which the British fleet is sent up.

... A telegram from Layard, saying that he was asked to advise the Porte whether or no it should endeavour to oppose a Russian entry: there could be little doubt as to the answer, but for safety I called on Ld B. who agreed entirely, and we framed a telegram together. Saw at the office Beust, who said nothing about any intended loan or mobilisation: Gennadius, who is eager that Greece should do all that is possible against the Sclaves: and Schou. with whom I had much talk. He laid stress in conv on the vanity and precipitancy of the Russian character – the childish eagerness, which they show (as he put it) about points of mere display: and was very earnest as to the military entry signifying nothing politically, but being a gratification only to the feelings of the army. I warned him seriously of the danger of a Russian approach to Gallipoli, which would threaten, or seem to threaten, the communications of our fleet: and made what I said into a draft. He fully understood the danger.

Received a small deputation, consisting of Ld Petre,[67] Ld Denbigh,[68] Ripon,[69] and another, to plead for the Catholics in the Turkish provinces, whom the Turks have always tolerated, but they fear that Sclaves and Greeks will not.

... Dined D. of Richmond's, on the annual occasion of pricking for sheriffs. Met there most of the cabinet.

14 February 1878 (Thursday). Telegrams received that fleet is safe through Dardanelles, which I did not doubt it would be, but the certainty is satisfactory.

Cabinet at 2.30, sat a little over an hour: the meeting as little satisfactory as any we have yet held: wild excited talk, all kinds of strange proposals put forward, such as seizing on an island (nobody seemed much to care where) by way of material guarantee. Others wanted a military occupn by the neutral Powers of the Dardanelles and Bosphorus: a matter in which none of the neutral Powers have shown the smallest inclination to take part. Northcote more rationally hinted at an understanding with Russia not to impede the waterway into the Black Sea: the difficulty of which is only that it might not be easily obtained, and if obtained could not well be relied on. The Premier swaggered, J. Manners talked extravagantly, I resisted the various schemes suggested to the best of my power, but without effect.

[67] William Petre, 12th Baron Petre (1817–84), succ. 1850; not prominent in public life.
[68] Rudolph Feilding, 8th E. of Denbigh (1823–92), succ. 1865; R.C. convert (1850) and lobbyist.
[69] Converted Sept. 1874.

One thing of importance we settled, which as it is obviously within our right, and as in the present state of matters precautionary measures are reasonable, I agreed to. We decided to buy three or four of the Turkish ironclads, if the Porte will sell, as to which I doubt.

I went back to the office ill-pleased and despondent: and was not much relieved by a visit from Schou. who evidently thinks the state of things as bad as it can be. It is a strange instance of modern manners, that on two or three occasions, and especially at a ball last week, he has been treated with marked incivility, in fact all but insulted, by the P. of Wales and others of his set. The Duchess of Manchester[70] is said to have made herself especially conspicuous by violence of language.

In the Lds, I answered a question put by Granville, explaining the posn of matters as regards the fleet. A large attendance, and the interest was evidently intense. But no discussion followed ... I went back to the office, and worked there till late, talking over affairs with Tenterden.

Dinner at home, quiet evening, but working again on routine business.

15 February 1878 (Friday). Sleep disturbed, anxious and troubled about public affairs: drove to Kensington gardens, and walk there with M. for an hour. Cabinet at 12.30, sat till nearly 2.30: there was less wild talk than yesterday, indeed none: the principal question discussed was as to the orders to be given to the fleet: we agreed to draft a minute, which I gave to Schou., warning the Russians against marching on Gallipoli, and also to send ships to the back of the peninsula, to watch movements of troops there. There is in all these proceedings a certain risk of collision, which it is impossible not to feel, and which may at any moment lead to war: but there is equal risk in taking no precautions for the safety of the fleet, and probably on the whole it is safer that the Russians should be warned off formally from ground which they can have no object in occupying, unless it is to force a quarrel upon us. In our discussions, Cairns has come round and is inclined to be more cautious than most. Northcote is always moderate and sensible personally, but a little too much afraid of people who may be otherwise, especially in the H. of C. – Hardy has not taken much part. Cross, though not extreme, is rather warlike: Smith is prudent, but his prudence just now takes the form of thinking more about the immediate safety of his ships than the political consequences that may follow on an action: Richmond follows Cairns, but is pugnacious when he is allowed to have any opn of his own: Salisbury talks recklessly, and is all for fighting: J. Manners and Hicks Beach seem, and I believe really are, delighted at the prospect of a war: D. of Northumberland is new, and as yet takes little part: the Premier varies a good deal, sometimes

---

[70] Louise, Duchess of Manchester (d. 1911), Hartington's mistress.

quiet, at other times disposed to talk big. My chief business is criticism, and I do it conscientiously, insisting on nothing being decided in haste, and raising every objection that occurs to me: a necessary office in these excited times.

Office, where with Northcote and Tenterden settled a draft, or rather the substance of it, for consideration tomorrow. Saw Schou, and gave him the minute, or paper, agreed on in cabinet. I thought him a little more hopeful than yesterday, and I think also that society is less excited, on the whole, than before the fleet was sent up. Saw Beust, and raised with him the question of the guaranteed loan about which he had talked with the Premier: but he seemed to have no instructions, and I suspect that Andrassy has found more difficulties in his way than he thought poss. and does not relish the criticisms and questions of the H. of C. which are inevitable before any sanction would be given.

... Saw 'Prince' Ion Ghika,[71] who told me that Roumania is in great trouble: ruined by the war, which has stopped trade at sea, and virtually by land also, since the railways are monopolised for military use: heavy losses sustained, and expenses incurred: and now the ally for whom they have made these sacrifices wants to take away a slice of their territory, and their access to the Danube, giving them instead the pestilential desert of the Dobrutska [sic]. There is universal discontent, and he came to complain. I could hold out little hope of being able to help his countrymen.

16 February 1878 (Saturday). Papers were laid last night explaining the situation, which to judge by the language of the press, seem to have produced a favourable impression. *The Times* supports us. The *D. News* does not find much fault. The *Telegraph* approves, though it would wish more to be done. The *Post*, the organ of the ultras, continues to grumble, and cries out for war. But on the whole there is no great discontent, and less excitement than last week.

Walk early with M. in Green Park, a fine day, & all pleasant, but our pleasure was spoilt by the prospect of a cabinet, and the possible questions that may be started there. It met at 12, and sat till half past 2, which is longer than usual. We were on the whole pretty fairly agreed. A long time was spent in discussing a plan for buying the Turkish fleet, to be delivered at Malta, or elsewhere outside Turkish waters. I pointed out to my colleagues the great improbability of the ships being sold by the Porte, while absolutely under Russian control: however, and partly for that reason, I did not oppose the proposition in principle: but before we could settle anything, a telegram came from Layard that it would be useless to offer for the 4 ships of which we had sanctioned the purchase on Thursday: which ended the matter. An

[71] Jon Ghika (1817–97), Rumanian premier 1866–7, 1870–1; min. in London 1881–90.

answer was given to a sort of appeal from the Sultan for help, friendly, but vague: there was a good deal of talk about the possible defence of Constant. against a Russian entry, which we all were of opinion should not be encouraged, J. Manners only excepted. Hardy was questioned as to fitness of officers for employment in case of an army corps having to be sent out. Sir L. Simmons[72] was called in to give his opn on some military points: but the only practical question which we decided was to entertain farther the Austrian request for a guarantee to their loan, by which they are to be helped to mobilise. Beust appears to have told the Premier that to mobilise on a small scale was useless, they must put their whole 1,100,000 men into the field, which would cost £12,000,000: half of this sum Andrassy wants as a subsidy, the other half as a loan. The subsidy scheme Ld B. rejected at once, on his own responsibility and rightly: the proposal to guarantee a loan he put before us, and we agreed to go on with the negotiation. A telegram for Elliot was drafted accordingly.

This is the part of my colleague's policy in which I can most readily agree. With Austria as an ally, the risk of war appears to me almost none: while we secure a strong position in the conference, and are not obliged to concede all that Russia wishes: a result which in the present excited temper of the people is worth securing. The war-fever is upon them, and some risks must be run to avoid greater.

Office at 3: saw there Schou. Beust, Musurus, and Gennadius ... Keston by 6.35 train, where rest and quiet.

17 February 1878 (Sunday). A mild sunny day, very pleasant, some flowers out, & a general appearance of spring having begun. I have seldom more completely enjoyed the change from labour and excitement. Messengers brought 21 boxes, but none heavy or very important. Long early walk with M. in Holwood, sat by the lakes, etc. Walk by myself for exercise about the common. Passed altogether nearly half the day in country air and sun, to my great relief.

18 February 1878 (Monday). Woke nervous and anxious, as to what the day may bring. Walk in to the station: St J. Square by 10.45. Saw Drage, but he ordered nothing. Telegrams, a great heap: the most important is from O. Russell: he has seen Bismarck, whose language is that Germany will observe a strict neutrality, that he believes Andrassy may be willing to help us, but greatly doubts whether the Emp. will allow him – the three Emperors being much in the habit of settling matters behind the backs of their ministers. He does not think Austria prepared for war, and expects her to lose by it Galicia and the Trentino. He thinks in Russia a war with England would be popular. Evidently

---

[72] Sir J.L.A. Simmons (1821–1903), inspector-gen. of military fortifications at war office 1875–80; military delegate to Berlin Congress 1878.

he, Bismarck, is well pleased at the prospect, and will do nothing to keep the peace.

Saw Musurus early at his urgent request: he brought a message from the Sultan, praying us to do one of three things: to prevent the Russians going into Constantinople: to withdraw our fleet: or to become his ally. None of these are possible, but I promised to refer to the cabinet.

Cabinet at 1, sat only till 2, and did little, but it was satisfactory that the general tone was pacific. We agreed to say and do nothing about Gallipoli, not having the Russian answer before us, though its general contents are satisfactory. There was a good deal of talk about the position of Austria, and the Premier appears to think that Andrassy has either not the will or the power to interfere: in short, he takes Bismarck's view. He doubted whether a conference would be held, saying with truth that Russia had got all she wanted, and had no motive for holding one. He thought if the Russians persisted in their entry into Constantinople, we ought to withdraw our ambassador. But this point was not discussed.

Office, where stayed till 5. Saw Musurus again, and gave him his answer, which did not please, but I had no choice. Saw Beust, who had heard absolutely nothing on the subject of the proposed guarantee: which he tried to persuade me was a good sign, since it showed at least that the offer was not rejected. Saw d'Harcourt, and Münster, neither of whom had any news, but seemed to take a gloomy view of the situation: and indeed it would be strange if they took any other. Saw Schou. who brought the Russian answer about Gallipoli: satisfactory enough, as I thought: Russia agrees not to go into the Bulair[73] lines, provided we don't land troops: a fair offer, as matters stand. ... Home at 6, and quiet evening, the day ending less unpleasantly than it began.

19 February 1878 (Tuesday). Telegrams from Elliot. Andrassy wants the conference to be held early in March: agreeing to Baden as the place. He will not ask England to guarantee a loan, not having as yet authority from his two parliaments to raise one: is sanguine as to the success of the congress: and Elliot thinks will take no step to mobilise unless or until it fails. – On the whole, matters do not look as if he meant business.

Cabinet at 11. We sat only an hour, all in good humour. The Russian answer about Gallipoli was discussed: and we agreed to accept it, with a slight reservation, or rather addition, suggested by Cairns, to which I see no objection. An answer was drafted accordingly. – Talk of the Austrian communication, which all agree (perhaps a little prematurely) means that Andrassy will do nothing. At any rate it puts an end to any idea of present action by Austria. Talk over the conference – are there

---

[73] The isthmus joining Gallipoli to Turkey.

to be any bases? and what kind of instruction shall be given? Nothing settled on these points, but the convn was rational and showed general union. I pressed strongly the absolute impossibility of my going, even though the other Foreign Ministers should: Andrassy or Gortschakoff may take his orders from his emperor, and execute them as best he can: he has no one else to consult: but an English sec. of state who passes a month at Baden in attendance on a congress simply abdicates his place as a member of a cabinet. He cannot settle European questions on his own account: he must be guided by the decisions of the collective ministry: and being absent, he can take no part in framing those decisions. My colleagues all agreed in this view.

Walk with Sanderson for exercise. Office from 2 to 5 ... Gave Schou. our answer, which he thought would be satisfactory. It was less agreeable to find that he was accurately informed as to our intention of buying the Turkish ships: though I was able to put him out a little, by denying that any offer had been made: which is the truth. But it is clear that Server Pasha[74] or whoever on the Turkish side was sounded on the subject, went and told the Russians all that had passed. He had also heard, but more vaguely, of the idea of occupying Chanak if the Russians went to Gallipoli. I told this to Cairns and Disraeli, as it may be useful that the cabinet should know the impossibility of negotiating secretly with the Porte. ... Talk with Ld B. who had been to Windsor, and reports the Queen less excited, and better pleased with the state of affairs. Quiet evening.

20 February 1878 (Wednesday). The subject of the day is a speech just delivered by Bismarck in his customary tone of cynical frankness, which he carries almost to brutality. (E.g. he says of Andrassy, 'we are now very good friends, and I trust him, but there was a time when I did not believe a word he said'). He declares for an absolute neutrality, declines to mediate between the Powers, sees no German object to fight for, and hints that there need be no fighting. The speech is considered as pro-Russian by everybody except Münster, who thinks, or at least affirms, that the Russians expected more active support, and will be disappointed. It is evidently intended to deprecate Austrian action, and probably Andrassy will take the hint, together with a piece of Bosnia.

Called on Disraeli. Found him convinced that the Austrian game is up, and inclined to be pacific. We talked over the Russian entry into Constantinople, which according to the last telegrams there is some chance of averting. Also about negotiating for the non-seizure of the Turkish fleet, either by force or by way of indemnity: we undertaking

---

[74] Turkish foreign minister.

not to buy it: he liked the idea. Schou. had thrown out a hint of this yesterday.

Wrote to the Queen on the state of affairs, and also suggesting Lyons as our representative at the conference, if it meets. But Gortschakoff is now asking for delay.

At night, received the uncomfortable news that a demand is made by Russia for the cession of the whole of the Turkish fleet: and that it is proposed to send 30,000 Russia troops to occupy Constantinople. No two things could have been suggested more calculated to cause ill-feeling here.

21 February 1878 (Thursday). Early walk with M. in Green park, not very happy in mind, for the news of last night increases our difficulties, which are great enough already: but the present state of tension cannot last for ever. Cabinet at 12: sat till near 2: the first question discussed was as to the Turkish fleet: we decided not to allow Layard and Hornby to do what they were and are disposed for – resist the transfer by force, as this would be an act of war. Even Ld B. said, 'If we are to go to war, let us do it in a regular way, and not begin by a scramble in Constantinople, for which we may not be prepared': and Cairns, who has now taken the pacific side, spoke strongly in the same sense. While we were talking, news came that the Turks have determined to sink their fleet rather than give it over (but will they?) which was received with satisfaction.

It was determined that as Russia has promised not to enter the Bulair lines, and as there could be no motive for doing so except to cut off the retreat of our fleet, we should be ready to help in defending these lines if attacked.

In the event of a Russian entry into Constantinople by force, we decide to withdraw our ambassador, and decline to go into conference while the occupation lasts. This is in some respects the most decided step we have yet taken: but it is less hazardous than it seems, for 1) we neither make war nor threaten it: 2) our warning applies solely to the case of an entry to which the Sultan does not consent, while it is probable that his consent will be obtained by pressure: 3) it seems admitted on all hands that the conference would be a mockery with a Russian garrison in Constantinople.

We were on the whole fairly well agreed, and all was discussed in good humour. But all felt the gravity of the situation.

Office, where saw Martino, Beust, Münster, and Schou. I gave the last our decision of today in form of a mem. to be telegraphed. I received from him an assurance as to Gallipoli, which is fairly satisfactory.

H. of Lds where a large attendance. In answer to Granville, I explain matters as to the fleet, the conference, and Gallipoli: my statement seemed to give relief. Ld B. moved the six millions bill, in a short and very temperate speech: we had expected a debate: but Granville declined to raise one, and all ended in less than an hour.

22 February 1878 (Friday). Telegram from Elliot, to effect that Andrassy wants money at once, and would like us to advance it, on the security of a loan which he is to control.

Telegram from Layard: he and Hornby seem prepared to take on themselves the responsibility of resisting the transfer of the Turkish fleet: but the telegram has been delayed, it dates from the 20th, and they will have their orders, which is fortunate, else a collision would be inevitable.

Saw Northcote about Andrassy's request: he agrees with me that it would not be listened to in parliament: if Austria were at war, with England as an ally, or preparing for a war which seemed inevitable, in concert with England, financial assistance might be given: though even so, it is not a helpful state of things when a belligerent power cannot even put its army into the field without foreign help. But to lend money to Austria, or rather to Andrassy, without even knowing whether his own parliaments will back him up, is an impossible proposal, and one which looks as if it had been made only to be refused. – Northcote and I talked over affairs in a general way, and with entire agreement: I always find him moderate and sensible, though a little too yielding to others who are otherwise.

... Saw Beust, who I found has been kept entirely in the dark as to Andrassy's financial proposals. Saw Schou. who in reference to our decision of yesterday observed shrewdly that the conference was not proposed by Russia, nor desired by her: that our objection to go into it if they occupied Constantinople was therefore no menace to them: on the contrary, Gortschakoff would not be ill pleased to see it knocked on the head, and to be able to make England responsible. There is some truth in this.

23 February 1878 (Saturday). Drive with M. to Kensington, and walk in the gardens there, with much content: only some anxiety for news from Layard as to what is doing at Constantinople.

Cabinet at 12.30, sat a little over an hour: we all agreed without difference of opinion to refuse Andrassy's request for an immediate loan, which our M.P.s held that parliament was sure to reject. Telegram drafted accordingly. The rest of our time was wasted in vague talk: the notion of seizing an island somewhere was reverted to, and Mitylene was talked of for the purpose. I could not well make out what the island is wanted for, or what the possession of it is to do for us: still less what right we are supposed to have there. But beyond indicating doubt, I said little in the way of objection: partly as wishing to reserve myself till something definite was proposed: partly because the idea of the island seemed likely to draw off attention from more immediately dangerous questions.

... Nothing all day from Layard, and I suspect interruption of the communications: in the afternoon there came a Reuter's telegram saying that the Russian demand for the fleet is abandoned, on the understanding that no part of it is ceded to England: a fair enough compromise if the thing is true.

Keston by 6.30 train, and quiet evening.

Ld B. tells me that he either has offered, or means to offer, the Gov. Gen.ship of Canada to Carnarvon:[75] I doubt his acceptance, though the post is a very great one, but the selection is wise, and illustrates strongly one of the Premier's great merits: the entire absence of vindictiveness. He works with Salisbury as cordially as though they had never quarrelled: the only person of whom I have ever heard him speak with bitterness was Gladstone, and even there, there was more derision than anger.

24 February 1878 (Sunday). ... no news from Layard. I suspect the wire is cut: but for the Reuter news of yesterday I should be very anxious, lest some collision should occur, and as it is I am not satisfied. ... As yet there seems no prospect of an early end to these troubles.

Late in afternoon came a telegram: saying that the G. Duke has advanced with 1500 men to San Stefano, near to Constantinople, but outside it, and that peace is to be signed there.[76] The demand for surrender of the fleet is withdrawn, apparently, but from the words used I cannot be sure: the Porte refuses that, but concedes all the rest. If Layard is accurate it would seem as though the two questions which have given us most trouble during the last week were settled: but I do not yet feel sure that it is so.

News in the papers on the other hand that Austria is getting ready to mobilise: 50,000,000 florins to be asked for at once, which looks like business: but it may be only brag.

The gossiping newspapers have made a speech for Disraeli, which he certainly never uttered, but which represents him in his excited moods, so accurately that it is worth noting. He is alleged to have said, 'I have Queen, Commons, and people all with me: if I were only ten years younger, I would change the map of Europe.' How far he really wishes for war: how much he leads the Queen, or is led by her: or to what extent his policy is guided by the mere fear of seeming weak, and so of growing unpopular, I cannot decide. Of late he has professed to leave the initiative in cabinet to others, especially to Cairns: but I do not believe that the latter ever speaks without having consulted him in the first place.

---

[75] Carnarvon declined.
[76] Peace signed, 3 Mar. 1878.

25 February 1878 (Monday). London by early train ... St James's Square by 11. Found comparatively little to do: only a few letters, and no summons to a cabinet. News in the papers of a sort of riot[77] in Hyde park: a meeting was held there in the interest of peace, got up by Bradlaugh[78] and Auberon Herbert:[79] a counter-meeting in the anti-Russian sense was thereupon arranged for the same time and place: a scramble followed, in which the war party had the advantage. No great harm was done, but the folly of such meetings on either side was shown, for speaking was impossible, and the two demonstrations neutralised one another. Some roughs broke Gladstone's windows,[80] which is an excellent way of discrediting their own side.

Working at home till 2, when to office. Saw there Beust, who tells me that Andrassy has protested against any Russian occupation of Constantinople: Schouvaloff, who foolishly went to look at the Hyde park meeting, forgetting that if recognised he would probably have been insulted, and the state of affairs not improved thereby: Münster,[81] who came only to gossip: Lawson: I forget if any others.

H. of Lds at 5 with Sanderson ... Home soon after 8, quiet evening: but a vast heap of boxes, 18 in all I think there were.

26 February 1878 (Tuesday). Office at 2, stayed till 5. Saw there Münster, who talked about the Franconia case: d'Harcourt who was chiefly interested as to Egyptian finance: Musurus, who having no information as to what is doing came to ask news: Schou. who said he had been alarmed at the aspect of affairs last week, but thought them looking better now. He did not explain but I gather that the intention to enter Constantinople is given up, and that he expects peace to be signed at once. He made it clear to me that he had heard of the talk of last week about taking possession of an island (I don't know how it happens, but whatever passes in our cabinets gets known to the public somehow): and sensibly deprecated any such violent proceeding, at least before the meeting of the conference. I disclaimed any intention of the kind, which I could do with truth, for nothing was decided when we met last but it was evident that he had information, and was not talking at random. Saw Martino, who with the usual zeal of a young diplomatist left in charge, calls every day: he wanted to compare notes as to the alleged terms of peace: his version nearly agreed with mine.

H. of Lds, where answered a question ... At the House, Ld B. told me that after consulting with the naval authorities, he had satisfied himself that an island would be of no use as a station, Malta being

[77] See R. Millman, *Britain and the Eastern Question 1875-1878* (1979), 587 n.45.
[78] Charles Bradlaugh (1833-91), radical and freethinker.
[79] Auberon Herbert (1838-1906), idealist; Carnarvon's bro.
[80] In Harley St.
[81] German amb.

near enough: so there is one wild project exploded, but not till it has caused a good deal of wasted time.

In letters, despatches, and two telegrams received today, O. Russell tells us that Bismarck is exerting his influence with France and Italy to induce these states to acquiesce in the advantages which Russia has gained. He is said to think that Austria may take Bosnia, and even Servia, and having so protected herself may accept the new Bulgarian kingdom. He tells O.R. that the rule of the Sultan in Europe is over, and that partition would be better than propping up the existing state of things. He says that England if she does not wish for a Russian protectorate of Turkey, must go to war: that no other Power will interpose. He doubts whether Andrassy will be allowed by his emperor to go to war: and if he does, whether Austria will not lose Galicia. He hints that Russia wishes to delay the conference on one plea or another. He has made it plain to O.R. that while preserving a neutral attitude, he will favour Russia both in and out of the conference.

27 February 1878 (Wednesday). Cabinet early at 11. Short walk before it with M. in the parks. The Premier as usual harangued us on the gravity of the situation: saying that the position of England was not what it ought to be: he ended with the very harmless proposition that we should ask both Russia and Turkey to let us know the terms of peace being concluded between them. In subsequent discussion it appeared that he wanted a refusal, as that would give a fair reason for calling out the militia and reserves. Salisbury improving on this hoped that we should not pledge ourselves to do nothing if the answer was satisfactory: and at some length argued that it was not a question of what the details of peace might be, that the war had affected the balance of power in south-east Europe, and that we must secure some position to give us back the influence which we had. He afterwards explained that he wanted to seize an island somewhere. Cairns thought a mere refusal to let us know the terms would not be enough to justify proclaiming an emergency. Much talk followed as to military matters. Hardy explained the difficulty of calling out reserves, unless for actual war: the men being in private employments, which they will lose. They would come fast enough, he said, for a war. Six weeks was mentioned as the time that would be required to get ready an expedition – the necessity for delay being with the Admiralty. Mytilene was talked about again, with no result. The naval men don't care about it, the soldiers do. It was settled that Ld Napier[82] and Sir G. Wolseley[83] should be

[82] R.C. Napier, 1st Baron Napier of Magdala (1810–90), conqueror of Abyssinia 1868, c.-in-c. India 1870–6; cr. peer 1868.
[83] Conqueror of Ashanti, 1874. Napier was at once summoned from Gibraltar; preliminary consultations were held with Wolseley (M. and B. 251).

commander and chief of the staff respectively if an expedition were sent out. We settled to ask the two govts concerned as to the terms of peace: but I specially reserved for consideration the question of any future step to be taken.

In *The Times* is a letter from V. Harcourt,[84] in which he refers to the attacks made on me personally by the press of the war party (*Post* and *Pall Mall*) and the hostility felt towards me in society as a friend of peace. I suppose the fact is so, since I hear it said, but living quietly as I do, it hardly becomes known to me. The court and its surroundings are said to be especially violent: the D. of Cambridge[85] is reported to have declared at a ball (but after supper) that I ought to be hanged or impeached. There is however at the present moment no difference of opinion, so far as present action is concerned, between my colleagues and myself. Salisbury, the most warlike of all, is not unfrequently associated with me: which is a singular confusion of our real relations. He is, in fact, impulsive and impetuous: and has passed from vehement dislike of the Turk to equally vehement aversion to Russia.

Office: saw Beust, who had no news. Saw Schouvaloff, and gave him message of the cabinet, which he had in fact anticipated. Saw Menabrea, just returned from Rome. Also Gennadius, eloquent as usual on the destinies of the Greek race.

Received a deputation from the Chambers of Commerce, on foreign tariffs, but they had in reality nothing new to tell or ask. I heard them patiently, and answered them at length. They were about 60 in number.

Dined Stanhopes ... Pleasant evening.

1 March 1878 (Friday). Made up accounts for the month. I have spent only £310 so far in the year, being too busy to buy prints or books.

Telegram from Layard, which is satisfactory, announcing that peace will probably be signed on the 2nd, and that the demand for the cession of the Turkish ironclads is abandoned.

2 March 1878 (Saturday). Cabinet at 12.30, sat till 2: the project of an expedition to seize some position or island somewhere is revived, and discussed with general approval. I express my dissent from it in principle, which is based on the following grounds (i) It is an absolute violation of international law and right, to occupy the territory of a friendly state without its consent, and with the intention of ultimately taking possession of such territory. The only justification of such a proceeding would be self-defence: but it is not easy to show that we are in a position to make it necessary for that purpose. The matter is made worse by the consideration that we thus become accomplices in the spoliation of

---

[84] Old Trinity friend, and fellow-member of Cambridge Apostles.
[85] C.in-c. Army.

Turkey, which we have always professed to defend: and that we thus turn to our own advantage the action of Russia, which we have always condemned. (ii) It is not clear that we want a station in the Mediterranean other than Malta: the naval authorities are divided on the point, and as far as I can learn, are mostly opposed to the acquisition. Military men so far as they have been consulted seem to desire it, but only as they would desire any new station anywhere, giving occasion for another garrison and more professional employment.

(iii) The risk is imminent of inducing other states to follow our example, each snatching what it wants: the result of which may be to bring about a state of things less favourable to our interests than if we had done nothing.

(iv) The Russians will as a matter of course hold themselves free from their engagements to us in regard of Constantinople and Gallipoli: which may bring about complications in connection with the fleet, and create increased irritation here, if they march into the city. (In my private thoughts I believe this is with Lord B. one chief inducement to take the step, that he thinks it will bring about a collision in such a way that most of the blame will be thrown on Russia.)

(v) The conference will certainly be knocked on the head: Russia is not very eager for it now: and will be only too glad to take the excuse of getting out of it. We shall, by our sole act, have made a peaceable settlement, by the voice of all Europe, impossible. All today passed with good humour, and details were discussed freely. But the island scheme is to be worked out in detail[86] and I have laid the ground for resignation[87] if it is acted upon. – while I am still free to waive my opinion at last if I think fit.

3 March 1878 (Sunday). In open air early and late, walking chiefly with M. Flowers are out, and butterflies in the air. Enjoyed the rest, quiet, and sunshine thoroughly. Messengers brought (I think) 11 boxes and some letters, but no pressing or troublesome business. The day would have been entirely pleasant, but that it is impossible to shake off altogether the thought of public danger.

4 March 1878 (Monday). Walk in to station early, taking the road by Hayes, which is farther round, but pleasanter: fine bright day, and enjoyed it, though anxious as to what may happen. At station met M. and got news from the papers that peace is signed: which though expected was a relief.

... Loftus writes that the irritation against England is extreme, that

[86] By a committee. In addition, Cairns proposed a Mediterranean League at this cabinet (Northcote to Queen, 2 Mar. 1878, M. and B. 253).
[87] 'Lord Beaconsfield feels convinced that Lord Derby will retire, perhaps not immediately, but in a week's time or so' (to the Queen, 2 Mar. 1878, M. and B. 253).

it pervades all classes, that the emperor shares it, and is prepared to accept war with England if driven to it. The army is intoxicated with success: and the same feeling extends through society. Gortschakoff is on the side of peace and moderation, but is losing influence, which Ignatieff and the Grand Duke – i.e. the military party – are gaining. ... On the whole Loftus thinks the situation dangerous, and feels as if he were sitting on a powder-magazine. (Note that the evidence of Loftus is to be taken with suspicion, owing to his connection with Ly Ely[88] and the court: but in the present instance I see no reason to doubt his accuracy.)

From Berlin the news is that the policy of the govt will be entirely Russian: Bismarck wishes to find Russia employment in the east, especially if he can bring about a war with England: his only object being that she shall not be able to trouble Germany. He would like us to leave Turkey where it is, and take Egypt by way of compensation. Odo Russell thinks that Andrassy is sincere, but doubts whether opinion will support a war policy in Austria: since an unsuccessful war will break up the empire more rapidly than it has that of Turkey.

... From Vienna, I have nothing: but I believe Andrassy maintains the same attitude, either undecided as to his course or determined to keep it secret.

Office at 2, where news of peace being signed is officially confirmed: some details being added, such as the reduction of the indemnity from £40,000,000 to £12,000,000: the abandonment of the demand for cession of the Turkish fleet: the Egyptian tribute not to be touched etc. Münster called and entirely failed to disguise his disappointment and annoyance. He had hoped that the conditions would be such as to excite pubic feeling here still farther against the peace, whereas they will tend to calm it.

Schou. came and gave some additional details. Menabrea and Beust both called, but only to talk over things, in general. Saw Northcote, and satisfactory conversation with him. He agrees entirely with me as to the unreasonableness and folly of seizing on some point to occupy before or during the conference: the question what ought to be done in the event of its breaking up is a separate matter. I asked him why thinking as he did he had not backed me up in cabinet? to which he made no definite answer. But he declares he will do so when the question is raised again.

5 March 1878 (Tuesday). Office, where saw Schou., Harcourt, Beust, Musurus, Lawson, and I forget if any one else: Lawson talked sensibly,

---

[88] Jane, Lady Ely (1821–90), widow of 3rd M., who d. 1857; lady of bedchamber 1851–89; Loftus, her husband's bro., was amb. to Russia; 'dearest Jane' in Disraeli's intimate letters.

saying we had now to choose between a singlehanded war against Russia, in which we should win, but which might last for three years, and be a very big business: or accepting the Russian peace with such modifications as we might be able to make in conference. I thought I saw in his talk the indication of a wish to let down the public mind from its present excited state by putting before the world the full extent of the sacrifices necessary if anything is to be done. The organs in the press of the war-at-any-price party (*Pall Mall* and *Post*) are screaming less loudly than they did last week, and on the whole the news of the terms of peace, as far as we know them, appears to have had a quieting effect.

To the Lords ... Stayed till near 8, when to dine with The Club:[89] met there Reeve, Froude, Maine, Prescott Hewett, Leighton, & Abp. of Canterbury. Pleasant evening.

... No news from the east except that Gortschakoff has obtained the consent of Bismarck and Andrassy to have the conference held at Berlin instead of Baden: which is thought to show that Andrassy has made his terms with Russia, and will take Bosnia for the Austrian share.

6 March 1878 (Wednesday). Very busy till 11 with boxes, of which I sent off 14: then Ld Lyons called: I had sent for him to come over at the request of the cabinet. Walk with him to Downing Street, after a little discussion among ourselves he was sent for, and questioned as to state of feeling in France, especially about Egypt. His opinion is that the French will meddle as little as possible in the eastern affair: that they do not wish for the conference to be held, and will observe the utmost reserve when in it: partly as fearing Germany, and not wishing to alienate Russia: partly from a feeling that they cannot now as formerly influence events. Gambetta has some relations with Bismarck, and has avowed the policy of neutrality: he has the country at his back: and on the other hand the conservatives, or rather clericals, are bitter against England for disapproving the change of last May, which was their last hope of success. The French however will act with us in Egypt readily enough: partly in the interest of their bondholders, partly also for fear lest we should take to acting on our own account: the latter motive being probably the more powerful. – We discussed Egypt exclusively: and agreed that more active steps shall be taken to press the Khedive to consent to a real enquiry into the financial state of his country: which is going from bad to worse: nobody is paid: the taxes yield only half what they ought: and it is strongly suspected that the Khedive is cheating his creditors by collecting them through secret

[89] Diarist's favourite dining club, at which he was an almost constant attendant (*Speeches*, xliv).

agents, for his own use. Northcote has been frequently calling my attention to this subject of late.

After the cabinet, Lord B. asked me to speak to him, and proposed a new scheme, or rather a modification of the old one. It is to the effect that inasmuch as the Sultan wishes to get rid of the British fleet in the Sea of Marmora, we should agree to withdraw it, on the understanding that he consents to our occupying Mytilene, or some other island, as a naval station, to be held till the conference has finished its work. – This is obviously better than the notion of seizing the island by force: but it is still open to various objections – in the first place the Porte will probably not consent, but will inform the Russians, who will then anticipate us by occupying a station on the Bosporus: in the next place we shall alarm and alienate the other naval powers, who will each begin to play the same game on their own account: we shall have given Russia an excuse for breaking off the conference, which is exactly what she wants: and all this, so far as I can see, for no object, since we are the strongest of all powers at sea, we can take an island if forced to it, after the conference just as well as before, and the naval authorities are either indifferent or opposed to the project. The sole real inducement is the wish to do something that shall please the public here.

Saw at the office Schou., Münster, Harcourt, Beust, and the Chinese minister ... Lawson also called, I tried the effect of the island scheme on him, saying that it was suggested by outsiders: I found he disliked it as much as I did.

Home very weary, after a busy day. Sanderson dined with me.

7 March 1878 (Thursday). Long early walk with Sanderson, talking over the question of the island. Cabinet at 2, which sat till 4: all passed in good humour, but after much discussion, sometimes on principles, sometimes on details, the decision seemed to be taken to occupy Mytilene. I say 'seemed' for at the last moment Northcote and Hardy both wavered, and showed a disposition to revoke their opinion. Of all present Salisbury by far the most eager for action: he talked of our sliding into a position of contempt: of our being humiliated etc. etc. It appears to me that he was thinking more of what would be thought about the matter at home, than of the international questions involved. But both he and Disraeli laid stress on the argument that unless we do something decided, we shall not be treated with respect, or believed to be in earnest when the conference meets: which may be so. But I cannot follow the reasoning. I maintained my objection but nothing more was necessary, for we agreed to discuss the question again today.

8 March 1878 (Friday). Busy till 12, and no walk. – In view of the state of affairs, I wrote to Sanderson to tell him that if I left office, his personal allowance should be continued for three years certain from the beginning of 1878, after which we would see as to the future.

Beust called early, with a formal invitation from the Austrian govt to attend the conference at Berlin. He has also a telegram, in which he is told to inform that Andrassy maintains his objections to the Russian proposals, and is asking for a vote to enable him to mobilise.

I went to the cabinet thinking from the all but unanimous opinion of yesterday that the Mytilene project was decided on, and that I should have nothing to do except to send in my resignation. However to my surprise my colleagues having thought the matter over changed their minds, some convinced by the arguments which had weight with me, others, like J. Manners and Beach, not thinking the demonstration strong enough to be of any use. − It is fair to J.M. to note also that he objected on the ground of right. Salisbury treated scruples of this kind with marked contempt, saying, truly enough, that if our ancestors had cared for the rights of other people, the British empire would not have been made. He was more vehement than any one for going on. In the end the project was dropped, for the present: Salisbury proposed a resolution pledging us to take by force a naval station in the Levantine waters if things did not go at the conference as we wished them. This was modified by Cairns, who drew one out to much the same effect: though in less stringent terms. I dissented from both, but the latter was agreed to without other opposition than mine. As it only binds us to action in the events of certain things happening which may never happen and as probably twenty other plans will have been taken up and dropped in the interval, I do not see that I can do more than record my dissent as I have. Resignation on such a ground is impossible, especially as I have carried my point alone, against the whole of my colleagues. Yet so much more do we feel failure than success, that when I left the cabinet it seemed to me as if I had been defeated. − Salisbury's tone and language to me though not actually hostile, indicate marked personal difference, and I do not doubt the truth of what reaches me from all quarters, that he wishes to be in my place. − He is very welcome, and it might be that the sense of more immediate responsibility would steady him. But the risk of war would be considerably increased.

At the office, saw Münster, Beust, Harcourt, Menabrea, and Schou. ... In the Lds. I repeated what I had said before to Beust, that we must have before us the whole treaty made between Russia and Turkey and not merely a part of it. This seemed to be approved.

9 March 1878 (Saturday). Woke with headache, which continued all day. ... Cabinet at 12, to which I went reluctantly, considering the trouble of the last two days, and expecting fresh disputes. But I was agreeably disappointed. We discussed first the admission of Greece to the congress, as to the expediency of which there was no difference of opinion, though it was left an unsettled question whether the Greek representative should come in on the same footing as those of the Powers. – I telegraphed to all the capitals the decision we had come to, and wrote it to Gennadius.

The next subject considered was what Disraeli in rather pompous terms called 'a Mediterranean League' which practically resolved itself into sounding the Italian govt as to whether they are willing to act with us in the question of the Straits. Cairns had drawn up a mem. embodying the ideas of the cabinet on this point, which was accepted and all ended without difference. But when I came to put this mem. into the form of a draft, assisted by Tenterden, we found the words so general that they seemed to invite Italy to deal with all questions affecting the Suez Canal, and even with the English position at Gibraltar, if they cared to bring that in. Such clearly not being our intention, I sent Tenterden over to Lord B. to explain the difficulty, and the matter is hung up. At office, saw Münster, Beust, Harcourt, Schou. – I forget if any others. Keston by 6.35 train: where quiet evening.

10 March 1878 (Sunday). Quiet and pleasant day: passed mostly in walking with M. in the Holwood grounds, and later alone over the commons: day fine and spring flowers abundant. Messenger brought a few boxes, nothing important.

During the last week the war fever appears to have abated, I have not heard of any more meetings being held, letters of abuse or of encouragement (for both sorts reach me) are fewer: and the excitement in London clubs, and on the backbenches of parliament, is obviously less. This change is mainly due to the signature of peace, and to the expectation of a conference: though it may also be in part owing to the very violence of the feeling while it lasted, causing it to die out sooner. Our mutual relations in cabinet have not been agreeable: though nothing like a quarrel has occurred. If it were possible to know the Premier's real mind, matters would be simpler: but I cannot even conjecture with any probability whether he wishes for a war, whether he talks in a warlike strain, and makes ostentatious preparations, with a view to avert the necessity of action: or whether he is merely ready to adopt any course which seems most likely to be popular. The last is on the whole the more probable explanation of the three. Possibly he himself does not really know what he wants, and is satisfied to have done so far what the public seemed to expect. If I were to ask him the question pointblank, he would answer in a friendly and unreserved manner: but I could feel no confidence of hearing his true thoughts, or that opposite assurances were not being given to some other person.

11 March 1878 (Monday). Letter from Lord B. in which he says we ought to invite the opinion of the powers as to the treaty being submitted as a whole to the conference (this I see no objection to): and ends with a swagger as to accepting no compromise. Berlin and Vienna letters, but nothing new. Elliot cannot make out what Andrassy means, and suspects that he does not know it himself.

... Walked part of the way back [from the House of Lords] with Granville, who told me of the foolish way in which the P. of W. has been talking at Paris, telling everybody that England must seize upon Egypt: Bismarck has put this idea into his head, and it may be so far useful that it has driven out that of going to war with Russia. But Paris is not the place where it should have been uttered. I found Granville quite aware of the Queen's violence about Russia, and of her desire for a war.

12 March 1878 (Tuesday). Sent off this morning 23 boxes, almost the largest number I ever disposed of in one evening and early morning. ... Office at 2, stayed till 5: saw Beust, Schou. Münster, Harcourt, but they had no news. On the whole, this day has passed without any event.

... We expected some answer from Russia to our demand that the treaty as a whole should be laid before us: but none has yet arrived. It is still as before impossible to make out what Andrassy means. He remains invisible to diplomatists during the short parliamentary session: alleging business, but in truth I suppose he does not want to be questioned till he has got his vote. It is convenient to him to be able to hint to one set of questioners that he wants it in order to annex Bosnia, and to another that it is to be used against Russia.

Italy too is paralysed by a change of ministry: we are told that no difference will be made as to the conduct of foreign affairs, but a govt in the act of changing its skin cannot negotiate.

The French are friendly, but not the least disposed to act: it seems as if every state in Europe was waiting for some other to move first.

13 March 1878 (Wednesday). Cabinet at 12: sat 1 hour: the chief business was talking over the form in which our declaration should be worded as to not going into a congress without having the whole treaty before us: my colleagues thought the statement already made was not plain enough, and though not myself of that mind, I raised no objection to its being repeated in other words. The only difference that arose was on the question whether the original declaration did or did not convey accurately the meaning of the cabinet: two or three of us did not, and said so: now it chanced that the words had been read by me twice over at our last meeting: of this fact I reminded the dissentients, observing that under all circumstances I thought it a necessary pre-caution: there was silence, and no farther difficulties were made. The rest of the business done consisted chiefly of settling answers to questions in H. of C. and arranging the course of business. Northcote wants a long holiday at Easter, three weeks at least: probably the Lords will take more.

Office till 6: saw all the ambassadors except Schou. and Musurus: also Gennadius the Greek: nothing new of importance.

14 March 1878 (Thursday). Office about 2, as usual. – I find it more convenient to do most of the paperwork of the office at home, either before 11, or at night: reserving the hours between 2.30 and 5 for interviews mainly: and in truth visitors are always with me during these hours.

Saw Musurus, whom I observe to talk more rationally and sensibly in this catastrophe of his country than he has ever done before: possibly from not being hampered by instructions compelling him to maintain positions and assert claims which he knows to be untenable. He is moreover divided between duty to the government which employs him, and sympathy with his own nationality as a Greek.

... Saw Schou. and talk with him. He shows me a tel. from Gortschakoff assuring us that the whole treaty will be laid before the powers without reserve: but he says nothing as to the congress being invited or allowed to discuss it.

Saw Count Doehm, Beust's substitute, who read a long telegram from Andrassy, vague and unsatisfactory as it seemed to me.

15 March 1878 (Friday). Working longer than usual in morning, to make up last night's defeat. Sent off ten boxes, but not very heavy. Walk for exercise.

Office at 2, stayed till 5. Saw Münster: who came with a new proposal from Bismarck for a preliminary conference of ambassadors to settle how the business of the congress should be conducted: as to this I could give no opinion but referred it to the cabinet.

Saw Schou. and Beust and fairly puzzled by contradictions as to the facts. It is now admitted that the treaty between Russia and Turkey will be laid before us in its entirety: but according to Andrassy Gortschakoff has farther promised that the Congress shall be empowered to discuss any part of it: according to Schou. that is exactly the pledge which he has hitherto declined to give. I am disposed to think that Schou. is right, and that Andrassy, who is inaccurate in matters of detail, and loose in his way of talking, has taken some verbal promise, or half-promise, as meaning more than it really does. Menabrea called, to discuss things in general: Byland,[90] on the sugar question: I think these were all.

H. of Lords, where sat till near 7 ... The D. of Bedford[91] put a question about army recruiting, which I notice only because to the best

---

[90] Dutch amb.
[91] Francis, 9th Duke (1819–91), succ. 1872.

of my belief he has never spoken before. – The Duke has a theory on which he has always acted, that a man's first duty is to his family: and that [as] family life and political life are irreconcilable, one must be sacrificed to the other. He may possibly be right on the latter point, though there are many instances to the contrary, but his principle is fatal to the existence of a governing class. I suspect however that it is commonly held, and likely to be more so: as the increasingly democratic spirit infused into English politics make our public life rougher and more disagreeable, and at the same time relieves men from the feeling of obligation to enter it, when they see half a dozen candidates for every vacant post. And something no doubt is to be said for the opinion that a great English peer, the head of local society in his own county, doing unpaid work of many kinds which he is peculiarly fit to deal with, is more in his place than as a member of a cabinet which sits nearly all the year in London.

16 March 1878 (Saturday). Cabinet at 12, sat till half past one, with very little do to. It was decided to adhere to our decision as to the conditions of going or not into congress and in this view I entirely agreed. Then followed a good deal of talk about naval and military preparations, vague and not to much propose. I carefully abstained from taking part in it, lest I should seem to sanction the idea of an occupation, which at present I see no reason for. Some conversation on the parliamentary business of next week filled up our time.

Office, where saw Schou. & agreed that I should write to him for an answer about the congress, as there seems a muddle: we don't know whether to expect an answer from Petersburgh or Vienna, and we get neither. Saw also Beust, who is as much puzzled as I am by the language of Andrassy: Musurus, who talked more sensibly than I ever heard him do, admitting that we are right in taking up the cause of Greek against Sclave, but only warning us not to forget that in any future conflict the Turk may still be a useful ally.

Keston by 6.35 train, & quiet evening.

The week has been quiet in parliament: I have had no speech to make, & only one or two questions of a simple kind to answer.

17 March 1878 (Sunday). Keston. Day cold and dark ... Walk early with M., later alone. Two messengers came down, but nothing new. A sudden summons for a cabinet tomorrow disturbed us a little, not knowing the reason.

18 March 1878 (Monday). Cabinet at 12, where talk for an hour about reports (they are really nothing more) of an advance of the Russians towards some point on the Bosporus. It was agreed in the end, without dissent, that a warning should be given as to not occupying or fortifying any point there, which being only what we have said before, I have no objection to repeat, so as it is done in a friendly manner, and not as a

challenge. On the whole, the language held was moderate, and pugnacious tendencies were not very manifest. Salisbury inclined to be
violent, Cairns, who has gone through all phases, being first very
Russian, then strongly anti-Russian, has now subsided into caution. No
great good was done by this discussion, but at least there is no mischief.

Office, where stayed till 5. Saw Beust, Münster, Schou., Gennadius,
Baron Tauchnitz,[92] Lawson, Bourke, etc. Menabrea and Harcourt I
was obliged to ask to call again. Schou. gave me an answer about the
congress, so ambiguous that I could make nothing of it, and he is to
come again tomorrow. The rest came rather to hear what is doing
than to tell me anything...

19 March 1878 (Tuesday). In the *Telegraph* of this morning I see a notice
announcing as if from Constantinople the decision to which the cabinet
came yesterday, although it was specially agreed, and indeed insisted
on by me as a condition of consent, that the matter should be kept
absolutely secret. Wrote on this to Ld. Beaconsfield, calling his attention
to it, and expressing my opinion that the disclosure is not the result of
accident or of indiscretion, but that it has been made with an object.
In truth I have the strongest possible suspicion that the Premier
himself is the person concerned either directly or through some of his
subordinates: but as this cannot be proved, and may possibly not be
the case I have avoided any expression pointing to him, or to any other
individual. We shall see how he answers.

He did answer, but slightly, and as if evading the subject: I think
however my warning will have had some effect.

Walk early, round Regent's Park, for exercise: sharply, and perspired
a good deal: observed, as I have often done before, the instant mental
relief given: I had been annoyed by the incident above noted, and by
the general course of affairs, which is not satisfactory: but the muscular
exercise drove away all such discomfort.

Answer received from Schou. It is exactly what he said yesterday he
would send me: too ambiguous to be received either as a concession
or as a refusal: it plays only too well the game of those who want to
prevent an understanding being come to.

Dined at The Club...

20 March 1878 (Wednesday). Long early walk for exercise: the thorns
and horse-chestnuts at Kensington beginning to come out: pleasant,
though it is impossible to exclude the thought of our public difficulties
and dangers.

Wrote a few letters, and did such work as I had to do: easy morning
on the whole: office at 2.30. Saw there Harcourt, Beust, Münster,

---

[92] Baron C.B. von Tauchnitz (1816–95), publisher; U.K. vice-consul at Leipzig 1873–
95.

Schou., Lawson, and others: all talk of the congress: I had again and again to explain the situation which is not clearly understood, and indeed the Russian language is so confused that it would be strange if it were.

Cabinet at a quarter before six: an unusual hour, selected in order that the Prime Minister might attend the marriage of Ld Rosebery to Miss Rothschild this morning: however it was not inconvenient in the result, for time being short and most of us weary with the day's work, business was got through more quickly than usual.

I called attention to the disclosure of our secrets on Monday, about which I had written to the Premier: of course no result followed except a general disclaimer, nor did I expect any. But the warning may be useful. We discussed Schou.'s answer, which I was prepared to find treated as a refusal of our request, as indeed it is: but Cairns proposed that before dealing with it in this way, we should ascertain the meaning more exactly, and this being a safe course in any event, I willingly concurred in it. We framed a letter in this sense, with little or no difference as to the wording.

I was able to announce that the Russian project of embarking troops from the Bosporus, which led to our intended warning of Monday, is given up. Had I agreed to send it off at once, a fresh cause of irritation would have been created, and quite needlessly.

At The Club yesterday, Houghton[93] talked much of the Dilettante Society, and the service it had rendered to art, which I note that I may enquire about it. He also mentioned to me the remarkable letters of G. Smythe,[94] published in a recent memoir of the family: and on my asking about the writer (whom I knew, but not intimately, in early life) described him as 'the most perfectly vicious man he had ever known'. I was aware that he had drunk himself to death, having many years ago helped him home from a party in a helpless condition. He had something like genius, but failed both in public and private life, having broken down in his first speech and got into a disreputable scrape with a girl of good family. Yet oddly enough he was the friend of J. Manners and the late Ld Lyttelton,[95] both of whom to the last admired and respected him.

21 March 1878 (Thursday). H. of Lords at 5 ... Argyll talked sense for the Russian point of view: I gave some explanations about the hitch as to going into congress. All was over by 7.30. Home, and peace.

... Wrote ... to take shares in a London building company (Queen

---

[93] Richard Monckton Milnes, 1st Baron Houghton (1809–85).

[94] George Smythe, 7th Vt Strangford (1818–57), member of Young England.

[95] 4th Baron (1817–76), succ. 1837; high churchman and public figure prominent in educational matters.

Anne's Mansions, in Birdcage Walk) to the value of £500, but not all to be paid up at once. The speculation amuses me, and if it fails there is not much lost.

22 March 1878 (Friday). Walk for exercise: office at 2, or soon after: stayed there till 6: saw Schou. and long talk with him as to difficulties made about going into congress: saw Münster, who thinks us entirely right in our objections, but doubts whether the Russians will yield: saw also Menabrea and explained the matter to him ... Nothing material passed in any of these interviews, except that I dissuaded the German govt, through Münster, from ceding the presidency of the congress to Gortschakoff.

23 March 1878 (Saturday). Working on papers left from last night: short walk with M. in the parks: she tired with the party, though it ended at 11. We clearly are not made for the life of fashionable society.

Cabinet at 12, sat till 1.30. No disputes nor unpleasantness, but as the answer is not come about the congress, we could not well settle anything, and only discussed the terms of peace, in a general way. It was settled to appoint a committee of cabinet to consider draft instructions to be given to our representatives: Cairns, Salisbury, and Hardy, were chosen to sit with me. On the whole, no mischief is done, and though my distrust of the intentions of the Premier is undiminished, and I do not greatly care to conceal it, no farther step has been taken either to bring about a quarrel among ourselves, or to get up a war with Russia.

Office till near 6. Saw Schou. who professed to have nothing from Gortschakoff about the congress: this was not strictly the fact, for I know that he had an answer in his pocket, but was not well satisfied with it, and I suppose is trying to get it altered.

Saw Gennadius, who came with the usual stories – half true, half made up – about Turkish outrages in Thessaly. Saw Beust, who talked at some length, but as he often does, in so discursive a fashion that it was impossible to make out the drift of what he said.

24 March 1878 (Sunday). Reviewing the week, I hardly know what to think of the situation. The chances of getting into congress are less than they were: but there remains the chance of other Powers interfering to prevent its being broken up. If it fails, we shall have a pressure put upon us by Lord B. and Salisbury to make a demonstration somewhere, and occupy some point (Mytilene or Lemnos, most likely): in that event there will be a crisis at home, and my resignation may be the end: I heartily desire on personal grounds that it may, for I can have no confidence in the intentions of my colleagues: indeed they change them from day to day; and nothing except their dropping, on second thoughts, plans which they had treated as decided upon already has enabled me to stay till now. By an odd, but natural, process my very indifference to the result has enabled me to influence it more than otherwise would have been possible: for all concerned know that I would rather leave them than not, and that the giving way will not be on my side.

What the Premier wants or means is a mystery. I believe that he is really indifferent to war or peace, will take either as it may come, but that the one thing which interests him is not to forfeit popular favour. The Queen seems to have been quieter of late: or it may only be that I have heard less of her proceedings.

25 March 1878 (Monday). Left Keston by an earlier train than usual, 9.35 from the Bromley station: St. J. Square by 10.10.

Committee of Cabinet at 11, Cairns, Hardy, Salisbury, and self: we called in Lyons and Tenterden to help: the Bulgarian and Greek questions were discussed, and a sort of conclusion came to.

Office at 1, stayed there till 5: saw Harcourt, Münster, Beust, Menabrea, and Schou. The last brought me a verbal answer from his govt. about the congress, unsatisfactory enough: but I asked to have it in writing, partly for greater certainty and accuracy, partly because that is correct in form, and partly also because with the irritation that now prevails in both countries it is better to gain a day's delay, giving time to cool down on both sides.

Schou. tells me that the language of the P. of Wales in Paris was excessively violent against Russia, so much so as to create in the minds of the Russian govt. to whom it was reported, the conviction that we are bent on a war: he has in vain tried to explain the position of the P. of Wales, and the little importance that attaches to his words: but that is not easily understood in Petersburgh. He fears that the feeling is growing among his people that we are bent on a quarrel, and therefore that it does not matter what they say or do, as it will be forced upon them in the end.

26 March 1878 (Tuesday). Cleared off all papers etc. by 11: and set out for Windsor ... My business was to present the new Colombian minister ... The Queen did not speak to me privately, nor did I ask it, having nothing to say. Talk in the gallery with Ponsonby,[96] who describes her as being as much excited as ever: and in better spirits, since she thinks she sees more chance of a war.

Walk back from Paddington: office at 4: saw there Schou. who is in the same mood as yesterday: and Harcourt, who tells me of the great irritation felt at Berlin in consequence of our request for explanation about the congress. It is clear that Bismarck has entirely made common cause with Gortschakoff, and between them they are trying to gain over Austria.

H. of Lords, where Houghton raised a debate on the Bishops' Bill, but did not divide. Taking no interest in the subject, I went back to

[96] Queen's priv. sec.

the office, and worked there till near 7. Home, and quiet evening.

27 March 1878 (Wednesday). Short walk in the park. Committee of cabinet at 11. Sat till near 12: settled the general plan of instructions for a congress, if ever one comes off: and in any case it is well that the whole matter should be systematically examined, with a view to future discussion, whether in despatches or in parliament.

Cabinet at 12: sat only till 1: but the business done was important both nationally and to me in particular. Lord B. addressed us in a set speech, to the effect that we must now decide our policy, that our objects have been the maintenance of the empire, and of peace: that peace is not to be secured by 'drifting': that our attempts to be moderate and neutral have only lessened our influence, and caused our power not to be believed in. He dwelt on the weakness of Russia, with finances ruined, and armies suffering from disease. An emergency had arisen: every state must now look to its own resources: the balance of power in the Mediterranean was destroyed. He proposed to issue a proclamation declaring emergency, to put a force in the field and simultaneously to send an expedition from India[97] to occupy Cyprus[98] and Scanderoon.[99] Thus the effects of the Armenian conquest would be neutralised, the influence of England in the Persian Gulf would be maintained, and we should hold ports which are the keys of Asia. – Cairns and Salisbury both supported the Premier, showing clearly by their language, that they were aware of the plan now proposed, and had discussed it with him in detail:[100] others supported more vaguely: I declared my dissent in a brief speech, referring to what I had said before and agreeing with an expression that fell from Salisbury, that we must now decide, and that no compromise was possible. We had come, I said, to the point where two roads diverge, and must choose one or the other. I intimated that I could not agree, and it was understood that my resignation was to follow.[101] – Northcote came over to speak to me at F.O. soon afterwards, and I begged him to act as the medium of communication between the Premier and me, so as to save the awkwardness of writing. This he agreed to do, and notes passed between us, in which I asked him to arrange with Disraeli when my retirement was to be made known to the H. of Lords and when I

[97] The Indian expedition went no further than Malta.

[98] First mention by Derby of an occupation of Cyprus.

[99] Otherwise Alexandretta; insalubrious minor port in N. Syria; never occupied (M. and B. 273).

[100] The previous day the premier had written that he would propose to this cabinet 'immediately calling out the Reserves ... and at the same time will direct the Indian Government to send out a considerable force, thro' the Suez Canal, and occupy two important posts in the Levant' (M. and B. 262).

[101] For a full assessment of the controversy about what occurred at this cabinet, see M. and B. 262–77.

should go to Windsor to give up the seals. – Saw Beust, who continues to press for the congress: Andrassy reiterates his firm attention of standing by the agreement with England, but wishes to do it in congress rather than by separate negotiation.

I gave Schou. in confidence a hint as to what is going on: he says he expects that my retirement will be treated in Russia as the definitive triumph of the war-party, and that on their side preparations will be made. He adds that he does not expect to be allowed to stay three weeks longer in England.

Home early, before 5: dined before our usual hour and at 10 to F.O. for a party. There were asked about 2600 ... But in those vast rooms the crowd was never too great. Not the slightest suspicion existed of trouble in the Cabinet, and I took care to talk much to both Cross and Northcote, so that nothing should be remarked.

28 March 1878 (Thursday). Walk early in Green Park, but not long, M. being weary with the party of last night, and I not liking to be far away, lest Northcote should want to see me. Much and pleasant talk as to our recovered freedom, and the use we shall put it to: many plans discussed which may never be executed, but in any case the relief after four years of servitude and anxiety is great.

... Office at 2, to receive a deputation ... Several ambassadors called, but I would not see them, it being useless as matters stand. ... At 5 to the Lords with Sanderson ... I spoke only about ten minutes, very nervous, and a good deal affected when I had to mention my old connection with Disraeli: but I said what I intended and it seemed well taken. He followed me, in a short speech which were I not the subject of it, I should describe as having been in perfect taste: the tone thoroughly cordial, and style dignified. Cardwell apologised for Granville's absence, on the ground that he had expected nothing of this kind: which in truth nobody did. Never was a secret better kept: I do not think that either last night, at the F.O. party, or today in clubs and drawing rooms, was there the least suspicion of the state of the case. ... Home: quiet and very happy evening.

29 March 1878 (Friday). Boxes came from the office as usual but not many of them. Busy in a private way, with little details, & enjoying more than I can describe the relief from anxiety. ... Schou. and Münster called, and I had with both long and friendly conversations: Münster thinks there is an end of all chance of a Congress, and indeed as it is not desired here, nor much in France or Germany, I do not see how it is to meet. ... To Schou. I spoke freely and unreservedly, more so that I could do when in office: I pressed him to do what he could to prevent his govt. from taking any hasty determination: the danger is lest they should, like the Turks last year, jump to the conclusion that war is inevitable, and take some decision that will make it so. I spoke of the Premier: of his thirty years of party leadership, which make him look at things almost exclusively in a parliamentary and party point of view: of his age, satisfied ambition, indifference to military affairs: as indicating that he does not want a war: that he only desires the credit at home of a spirited policy: and this I am sure is the case. I did not conceal the danger of such a way of dealing with foreign relations, but thought it was essential not to have it supposed at Petersburgh that a rupture is decided upon. Schou. said his difficulty was to know what England wanted. The objections of Austria to the treaty were understood, but not ours. I answered that the difficulty was, that we did not know them ourselves: the feeling of the country was strong against the loss of prestige and influence in the east consequent on Russian successes: it was felt that Russia had substituted her influence for ours, and we did not like it: but the complaint was one not easy to formulate in words. He seemed to understand this.

I may here note that the other night at the party, Schou. talked about the Emperor in a way that surprised me: saying that if he, the Emperor, saw three of his ministers on the same day, representing three different lines of policy, he would be swayed by them all in turn: so that his decision of the evening would be the opposite of that come to in the morning. A pleasant state of things for a government in which the master's will is the only law!

30 March 1878 (Saturday). Busy most of the morning destroying letters and papers which have accumulated while I was too busy to attend to them. I am chiefly embarrassed by the minutes, habitually taken, of what has passed in Cabinet, which I know not whether I ought to keep, and yet hardly like to destroy.[102]

... Saw Schouvaloff, who has been talking with two of my late colleagues (I think Cross and Hardy must have been meant). He was astonished at their change of tune, and the peaceable language they hold. He reminded me that I had yesterday predicted something of the kind: both because the Cabinet will naturally feel anxious to guard themselves against the imputation of being too warlike, the representative of the pace party having left them: and because the withdrawal of opposition in the Cabinet itself has often a tendency to make the successful party more moderate. Antagonism stimulates where it does not control: and Salisbury is more likely to adopt my ideas, when I am not there to press them.

31 March 1878 (Sunday). Passed this day quietly at Keston, happier than we have been for a long time past, & making plans for the future.

---

[102] For Derby's destruction (in general) of his cabinet minutes, see M. and B. 264.

INDEX